CHINA

WOODEN STATUE OF A BODHISATTVA, SUNG DYNASTY

CHINA

A SHORT CULTURAL HISTORY

By C. P. FITZGERALD

THIRD EDITION

FREDERICK A. PRAEGER, *Publishers*
NEW YORK · WASHINGTON

BOOKS THAT MATTER

Third edition published in the United States of America in 1961
by Frederick A. Praeger, Inc., Publishers
111 Fourth Avenue, New York 3, N. Y.

Second printing, 1965

The original edition of this book was published in Great Britain
in 1935 by The Cresset Press; the second edition was published
by The Cresset Press in Great Britain in 1950 and by Frederick A.
Praeger, Inc. in the United States of America in 1954.

Library of Congress Catalog Card Number: 54–6804

Printed in Great Britain

PREFACE

A WORD of explanation, if not of apology, may seem to be required when offering a new short history of China to the English public. A fully detailed account of China's three thousand years of recorded history would need a work of many volumes, which it is to be feared would find few readers in the West. Faced with the enormous store of Chinese historical material on the one hand, and the knowledge that the public has only a restricted interest in this unfamiliar subject on the other, the European historian of China is confronted with the urgent question, what to leave out.

The problem has sometimes been solved in summary fashion by omitting all but a bare mention of the history of China prior to the 19th century, and concentrating attention upon the declining years of the Manchu dynasty and its conflicts with European nations. Undue emphasis upon this unhappy period of decline has given rise to the widespread belief that the history of China is a monotonous record of three thousand years of stagnation ending in a disorderly collapse. In the hope of correcting this fallacious opinion I have attempted to observe a juster proportion, and accordingly relegated the 19th century to its proper place in the story, which is the end. The history of China, as of every other country, is a record of change and development, the transformation of a loose federation of agricultural tribes into a highly centralised autocratic empire, the growth of a once primitive culture enriched and modified by contact with alien peoples.

Political history is given only in outline, so that, by avoiding a plethora of unfamiliar names, the significance of truly formative periods may be more easily grasped and retained. Cultural conditions, the development of religion, literature and art, are treated in greater detail, and I have used Chinese sources wherever possible to indicate something of the economic background which, in part at least, determines the pattern of a culture. A neglected aspect of Chinese history, the record of early contacts with the Roman Orient and the Middle East, is rather fully treated in view of the special interest which these records have for European readers.

For plates and illustrations, and much valuable advice, I am indebted to the kindness of many private collectors and directors of museums. Especially do I desire to thank Mr. George Eumorfopoulos and Sir Percival David, Bart. Also Mr. Oscar Raphael, Mr. and Mrs. Walter Sedgwick, Mr. H. Oppenheim, Mrs. M. Holmes, Professor Perceval Yetts, Dr. Gustav Ecke, Dr. Otto Samson, and Professor R. D. Jameson of Tsing Hua University, Peiping. For permission to reproduce some of the treasures of their museums my thanks are due to Professor J. G. Andersson, Director of the Museum of Far Eastern Antiquities, Stockholm; Dr. C. T. Currelly, Director of the Royal Ontario Museum, Toronto, and Bishop W. C. White, Curator of its Far Eastern Section. To these must be added the Director of the National Palace Museum, Peking, and the Trustees of the British and the Victoria and Albert Museums.

My thanks are also due to Professor Jiro Harada for permission to reproduce from Japanese official publications, to Father D. J. Finn, S.J., and the Editor of the *Hong Kong Magazine* for objects found at Lamma Island in Hong Kong Colony; as well as to Dr. Florence Ayscough and her publishers (Messrs. Jonathan Cape) for permission to reproduce her version of the poem from *Tu Fu* (printed on page 347). I must also acknowledge the skill and fidelity with which Mr. C. O. Waterhouse and Mrs. D. Cohen prepared the sketches for the text figures. To Professor C. G. Seligman, the general editor of the series of which this book is a part, I owe a debt not easily expressed in words, for his constant help and thoughtful guidance throughout. Mr. A. Waley, Mr. R. L. Hobson and Sir George Sansom have given me valuable assistance and suggestions. My sister, Mrs. Elspeth Graham, has read the manuscript in typescript.

NOTE ON THE PRONUNCIATION OF CHINESE WORDS AND NAMES

THE romanisation of Chinese words and names used in this book follows the Wade system employed by Dr. H. Giles in his Chinese English Dictionary. This system has only one advantage, that of general acceptance and use. In many respects it is inconsistent and misleading, and anyone not acquainted with its peculiar conventions will find it an unreliable guide to Chinese pronunciation. A list is appended in which the Wade spellings which are not in accordance with ordinary English usage are given with equivalent sounds. These equivalents are, of course, only approximate, as some Chinese pronunciations cannot be rendered exactly by the Roman alphabet.

In the case of certain well-known place names, such as the Anglicisms "Canton" and "Peking," and the names of the modern provinces, the popular spelling as found on maps has been retained. I have also judged it better to use "Sianfu," "Hankow," "Soochow" and "Ningpo" rather than the less familiar "Hsi An Fu," "Han K'ou," "Su Chou" and "Ning P'o."

In Chinese the surname is written first, personal name or names following, i.e. in "Chao Kuang-yin" Chao is the surname, Kuang-yin a two character personal name. There are also many instances of single character personal names, i.e. Li Po, and a lesser number of double character surnames, such as Ssǔ-ma and Ou-yang. In these cases the personal name is usually a single one, i.e. Ssǔ-ma Ch'ien. In place names the words "fu," "chou" and "hsien" are not strictly part of the name but indicate the administrative status of the place, prefecture, district and sub-prefecture respectively. Place names have been frequently changed at the accession of new dynasties, and a large scale revision of names was carried out by the Republic. These new names, as well as the more ancient ones, are even less familiar to western readers than those in use under the Manchu dynasty and still found on most European maps. It has seemed best, therefore, to use the latter to avoid confusion. Hyphens are placed between the words composing a place name by many western translators, i.e. T'ai-Yüan-Fu, but there is some risk of causing confusion between personal and place names if this practice is followed. In Chinese each of the characters stands for a separate word, as in such western place names as New York, or South Shields. There seems to be no reason why Chinese names should not be written in the same way.

Pronunciations in the appended list are those of the "mandarin" or Peking dialect, the educated speech of North China, and with slight differences, of the Yangtze valley and West China.

October 1935   C. P. F.

POSTSCRIPT

SINCE this preface was written in 1935 many of those to whom I was most indebted for assistance and for permission to photograph objects from their collections have died. In some cases the collections have now been left to the public and are exhibited in the national museums.

June 1953   C. P. F.

CONTENTS

PERIODS OF CHINESE HISTORY

	Shang or Yin Kingdom.	*circa* 1500-1100 B.C.
CHOU DYNASTY (Feudal Age)	Early Chou Period.	*circa* 1100- 722 ,,
	Ch'un Ch'iu Period.	722- 481 ,,
	Period of the Warring States.	481- 221 ,,
FIRST EMPIRE	Ch'in Dynasty.	221- 206 ,,
	Han Dynasty.	206 B.C.-A.D. 221
FIRST PARTITION	Three Kingdoms (San Kuo).	A.D. 221- 265
	Tsin Dynasty.	265- 316
	Northern and Southern Empires (Nan Pei Chao).	316- 589
SECOND EMPIRE	Sui Dynasty.	589- 618
	T'ang Dynasty.	618- 907
	Five Dynasty Period (Wu Tai).	907- 960
	Sung Dynasty.	960-1127
SECOND PARTITION	Kin and Southern Sung Dynasties.	1127-1280
	Yüan (Mongol) Dynasty.	1280-1368
	Ming Dynasty.	1368-1644
	Ch'ing (Manchu) Dynasty.	1644-1911
	Republic.	1911

LIST OF PLATES

(Plates I–XX are grouped between pages 272 and 273)

LIST OF ILLUSTRATIONS

LIST OF MAPS

CONVENTIONAL SPELLINGS OF THE WADE SYSTEM
AND APPROXIMATE EQUIVALENTS

ai	=	"y" as in "why."
ao	=	"ow" as in "how."
an	=	long "a."
ang	=	very long "a," "ong" in many words.
ch	=	initial "j" as in "jam."
ch'	=	an emphatic initial "ch" as in "church."
ê, ên, êng	=	nearly "er" or short "u" as in "flung."
en	=	as in "ten."
ei	=	"ey" as in Weybridge.
eh	=	French "é."
i	=	"ee" as in "see."
ih	=	no English equivalent, the vowel sound in the first syllable of "cheroot" is a close approximation.
o	=	nearly "or."
ou	=	"ŏ" as in "Joseph."
u	=	"oo" as in "too."
ü	=	French "u."
ung	=	"oong."
hs	=	emphatic initial "sh." ("s" in the South).
hua, huo	=	"hwa," 'hwo."
hui	=	"whey."
j	=	nearly an initial "r" ("z" in the West).
k	=	initial "g."
k'	=	emphatic initial "k" aspirated.
p	=	initial "b."
p'	=	emphatic initial "p."
sh	=	as in English.
ssŭ	=	"sir" with hissing "s."
t	=	initial "d."
t'	=	emphatic initial "t."
s	=	"ds."
ts'	=	emphatic "ts."
tz	=	"dz."
tz'	=	emphatic "tz."

The two very common words "tzŭ" and "wang" are pronounced "dzer" and "wong" respectively.

THE LAND AND THE PEOPLE

THE history of every country is, to a great extent, determined by its geography. Before considering the origin of the Chinese civilisation it is necessary to refer briefly to the nature of the land in which this self-contained culture took its rise, and the geographical background which governed its expansion and development. Until, in very modern times, the Chinese culture took permanent root in the plains of Manchuria, the northern limit of historical China was the mountain range which forms the southern boundary of the grass steppes of Mongolia, the range along which the Chinese built the Great Wall. The southern boundary of China has never had a precise and definite limit. The Chinese frontier has moved ever southward with the slow expansion of the Chinese cultural area. For, although the country called China is clearly defined on modern maps, it has never been a static geographical entity. At times Turkestan and Annam have been incorporated in the Chinese Empire, but these countries have never been truly part of China.

The frontiers of the political state have fluctuated through the centuries, but the area of Chinese civilisation has steadily increased. No territory once fully subjected to this civilisation has ever been wholly lost, and no territory permanently incorporated in the Chinese area has withstood the penetration of Chinese culture. The process of absorption has sometimes been slow, but always complete and final. This fluidity of frontiers is explained by the fact that the Chinese are less a nation than a fusion of peoples united by a common culture, and the history of China is the record of an expanding culture, more than that of a conquering empire.

Geographically China falls into three main divisions, excluding Manchuria, and the newly colonised lands north of the Great Wall. The "Eighteen Provinces" south of the Wall divide naturally into three groups of six. The northern group watered by the Yellow River and its tributaries, the central, drained by the Yangtze basin, and the six southern provinces, of which

four form the basin of the West River, which reaches the sea at
Canton, and two, Fukien and Chekiang, lie on the coast outside
the drainage system of the three great rivers. Other lines of
cleavage exist, and this geographical division is not always in
accordance with cultural factors.

The three river basins differ profoundly in climate. The plain
of the lower Yellow River and the mountainous regions of its
upper course have a dry climate, with an inadequate rainfall
confined to the summer months, and a hard, very cold winter.
The Yangtze basin has a soft wet climate, hot and humid in the
summer, rather cold and wet in winter. Snow is not uncommon
in the lower Yangtze provinces in winter, and thin ice will form
on still stretches of the river itself in exceptional years. The valley
of the West River has a sub-tropical climate intensely hot and
damp in the summer months, warm and sunny in the winter.

In one respect all three rivers are alike. All rise in the high
ranges of the Tibetan border, descend to the lowlands through
rocky gorges and mountainous defiles, and reach the sea after
traversing wide alluvial plains. The vast majority of the Chinese
race live on these eastern plains, the western mountain provinces
being thinly peopled and inaccessible.

On the west China is shut off from the rest of Asia by the great
ranges of eastern Tibet and the Kokonor region. These mountains,
among the highest in the world, extend spurs far to the east, so
that the western provinces of China are a mountainous region of
high plateaux divided by steep forest-clad ranges running east
and west. The descent to the plain is everywhere abrupt and
precipitous, the passes narrow and winding, the rivers obstructed
by rapids which make navigation dangerous or impossible. Thus,
there is a mountain barrier dividing China from north to south,
separating the western plateau provinces from the eastern
coastal plains.

Culturally this division is as important as the climatic zones of
the three river basins. The mountaineers of Kueichou and
Yunnan, provinces which are geographically in the drainage
system of the West River, have very little in common with the
Cantonese of the coastal delta of the same river. They speak a
northern dialect, their customs and architecture are northern, and

they themselves entered these provinces not by the sea coast and the West River Valley, but across the difficult passes from the north-western provinces and the Yangtze Valley. Moreover, the climate of the western plateaux is unlike that of the coastal plain. Yunnan, though within the tropics, is cooler than regions further north, for the land is high, much of it over 6,000 feet, and the vegetation of a Mediterranean type. Szechuan, the western province on the upper course of the Yangtze, differs markedly from the other parts of the same river basin. Although no further south, this country, locked in by great mountain ranges, has a sub-tropical climate, moist and warm, never experiencing the winter frosts which are common further down the river.

Compared with the well-marked division between western plateaux and eastern plains, the divisions between the three river basins are not clear cut. The Yellow River plain is not divided from the Yangtze delta by any range of mountains or even hills. The two regions merge imperceptibly near the sea in a marshy district extending along the coast. Further west the water-shed is more definite, but the easy transition from north to south in eastern China is a geographical factor which has played a vital rôle in history. Nevertheless, though the border is ill-defined, the character of the two basins is sharply differentiated. The Yellow River basin is dry and cold in winter, consequently unsuitable for rice cultivation and poorly afforested. This is the loess country, a soil composed of wind-blown dust from the Mongolian desert, which in countless ages has covered the entire surface of North China with a deep layer of friable yellow soil, fertile when irrigated, but arid and sandy if the rainfall fails. Heavy forest can never have grown on a loess soil, and to-day, after centuries of cultivation, there are no woods and few trees on the North China plain. The mountain ranges in the north-west and in the isolated hill country of the Shantung peninsula were once heavily wooded; now the natural forest is restricted to the most inaccessible valleys and to the vicinity of Buddhist temples, where alone it has been preserved from the woodcutter. North China lives on millet and wheat with subsidiary crops such as beans and roots. It is naturally a park-like country suitable for an equestrian people, and the use of wheeled vehicles. The basin of the Yangtze is wholly different.

The hills are covered with scrub, even where the original forest has been cut down. The valleys, which must once have been impenetrable moist jungles, are now carefully levelled for the cultivation of rice, while the hillsides are terraced for tea and mulberry groves. Except along the lowest course of the great river itself there are no wide plains, and the valleys of the tributary rivers are steep and narrow. Horses are not bred or widely used in the Yangtze basin, the draught animal is the water buffalo, and the means of transport, until the recent construction of motor roads, was the sedan chair, the porter and the river boat. The natural character of this region is in itself a barrier to the invasions of mounted peoples, a factor which has great historical significance.

The climate and character of the West River basin, the most southerly of the three great rivers, resembles that of the Yangtze in most respects. It is hotter and moister, and since it was civilised centuries later than the north and central parts of China, there are still considerable forest tracts in the mountains. The West River valley is, however, cut off from the Yangtze basin to the north by a high chain of mountains crossing the country from west to east till it reaches the sea, where curving north-ward it shuts off the two coast provinces of Fukien and Chekiang from the interior. This range has always been an obstacle to communication between south and central China. Railway communications across it between Canton and the Yangtze valley were not established until 1950, and Fukien acquired its first rail link with the rest of China only in 1957. Formerly it was easier and quicker to travel from Canton to Shanghai by sea; Fukien communicated with other parts of the country almost entirely by sea.

Geographically then China is not a unity, nor are the different regions easily accessible to each other. It is therefore not surprising that these different regions should be inhabited by peoples, who, although now bound together in a strong cultural union, are ethnically distinct. The vexed question of the origin of the Chinese people—in itself a misleading phrase—is discussed in another chapter. Suffice to say here that the inhabitants of the northern provinces are now, and probably always have been, to some degree mixed with peoples from the Mongolian steppes. To-day language is uniform over a large part of China, especially the northern provinces, and the same dialect, with slight local variations, is spoken from the coast to the Tibetan border, and reaches down through the south-western hill provinces to the Burmese border. Chinese culture and language have completely obliterated the distinction between the peoples of the Yangtze valley and the northern plains, although this distinction was very marked two thousand years ago. Differences of temperament however still exist. The northerner is slow, well-balanced, shrewd, but not quick witted. The Yangtze people are nervous and excitable, their minds are agile, but their tempers are short. They are eloquent, adaptable, but perhaps less reliable than the sturdy northern people.

Further south, along the coast, differences of character are defined by varying dialects. The dialect belt, which does not extend to the inland provinces, begins at the estuary of the Yangtze, and includes the whole south coast down to Annam. There are four main dialects, and innumerable local variations. The grammatical structure of these languages is very close to northern Chinese—the differences are not important—but the pronunciation of the words is widely different. In Fukienese, the most peculiar of these dialects, the language probably retains many words which are traces of the ancient speech of the non-Chinese Yüeh people who inhabited this province in early times. The Fukienese themselves, darker and shorter than other Chinese, are certainly a separate stock only slightly mixed with immigrants from the north and Yangtze Valley. A distinct people who are not regarded as "Chinese" by the other inhabitants of the province are still found in the mountains.

The dialect of Canton is not so much an alien language as an old form of Chinese, still using a pronunciation which has disappeared in the north and central provinces. An ideographic script, being divorced from the sound of the spoken word, does not "fix" the pronunciation of the language, which consequently changes far more rapidly and completely than in countries where an alphabetic form of writing is used. Canton and its hinterland became part of the empire in the 2nd century B.C., but the colonisation was not thorough until the 7th century A.D. It is the pronunciation of this period which is largely preserved in the Canton dialect.

In the upper part of the West River basin, *i.e.* the provinces of Kuangsi, Kueichou and Yunnan, which were the last to come within the cultural union of the Chinese Empire, there are still many non-Chinese peoples, now known as National Minority Peoples. It is probable that these peoples formerly occupied the whole of China south of the Yangtze, but are now found as distinct ethnic groups only in the more mountainous districts. The policy of the present government of China is to give these groups local autonomy, and they are now known by their own names in place of the variety of nicknames, mostly contemptuous, by which they were formerly called. Chinese statistics give a grand total of thirty-five million for the National Minorities, but this figure also includes the Mongols, Tibetans and Central Asian peoples who do not live within the boundaries of the old eighteen provinces. It also includes about seven million Muhammadans who are scattered throughout all provinces. The minority peoples of the south-west are perhaps not less than twenty million, divided among eight groups and a much larger number of small tribes.

One may suspect that the apparent disappearance or retreat of these peoples before the Chinese immigration is an illusion. Only those who were unwilling to become Chinese subjects and adopt Chinese customs fled to the hills. A large proportion of the population of the south calling itself "Chinese," is in fact descended from one or other of the aboriginal races. In the city of Wu Ch'ang, on the Yangtze, which for centuries has been a centre of Chinese government and civilisation, there were, as late as 1926, some families who wrote the character of their surname upside down. The explanation of this oddity is said to be that these families are descended from Miao stock, and when they adopted Chinese customs and surnames, were forced to write their new names in this unusual way to distinguish them from Chinese clans of the same name.

The Nosu, who used to be better known by their Chinese nickname, Lolo, are found in Kueichou and also in western Szechuan. In the latter district they were, until the establishment of the People's Republic, independent of the local Chinese authority. In Kueichou the Nosu formed a wealthy class of feudal landowners living in mountain castles and ruling considerable estates worked by serfs of Miao race. Under the present regime their feudal privileges have been abolished and the area redivided into autonomous districts. Members of the former aristocracy are now trained in Peking at the Institute of National Minorities and sent back to their districts as district secretaries and administrators. It is said that this system works well, and that Party officials drawn from these former ruling classes are more acceptable to the minority peoples.

The main non-Chinese minority peoples of the south-west are the Chuang, nearly seven million, who inhabit western Kuangsi. The Miao, who are found in all the three provinces of Yunnan, Kueichou and Kuangsi, are split up into a very large number of sub-tribes, geographically separated, each with its distinctive costume and usually with a peculiar dialect of the Miao language, unintelligible to other Miao. The Tung of Kueichou seem to be a branch of the Tai race who are also found along the China-Burma border, being the same people as the Shans on the Burmese side. Many smaller and more primitive peoples are found in this region, including the Chin, Wa and Lisu. The Institute of National Minorities has undertaken the study of the languages spoken by these groups, hitherto wholly neglected, and publishes school books printed in them, using the alphabetic Roman script.

The Nosu of Szechuan have, or rather had, an ideographic script derived from Chinese characters with modifications to suit the Nosu tongue. It has now fallen into disuse, unable to compete with the pervasive influence of Chinese literature, which has imposed itself on all the aboriginal peoples who aspired to civilisation. It is in this district, along the borders of Szechuan and Tibet, that the aboriginal tribes are still least affected by Chinese culture or government. Many of them are nomadic, and until very recent times, were under the rule of "kings" who admitted the suzerainty of the Chinese Emperor, but took care to avoid any closer contact with the dominant power.

The Tibetan border tribes are to some extent Buddhist, following the Lamaist religion of Tibet, but this slight touch of a higher culture seems to have little effect either upon their Shamanist beliefs or their customs and morality. In Kueichou and Yunnan the aborigines who remain in the tribes are pagans, having no knowledge of Buddhism. Their religion appears to be akin to the early form of nature worship practised by the Chinese in antiquity. Those members of the race who have left the tribe and received a Chinese education adopt the Chinese religions. Assimilated members of the minority peoples have always been accepted by the Chinese on a footing of equality; there are many examples of such persons rising to high office both in imperial and later times. The test was formerly the ability to speak Chinese and to be literate in that language. It is not clear whether under the new system a member of a national minority can opt for Chinese "Han" nationality or whether, however well educated, he must still count as a member of the minority people.

In the western part of Yunnan there are two non-Chinese peoples, the Min Chia, now known by their own name as the Pai, and the Na Khi, who have retained possession of the rich rice lands. The Pai of the Ta Li region have always been treated as the equals of their Chinese neighbours. Yet they continue to speak their own non-Chinese language and to practise many customs which are quite at variance with Chinese culture. Essentially a people of rice farmers the Pai have, it would seem, occupied the basin of the Erh Hai lake and adjoining valleys for many centuries, submitting without loss of their lands to a Shan conquest in the time of the Nan Chao kingdom (7th century A.D.), to a Mongol invasion under Kublai Khan, and subsequently to the Chinese conquest by the Mings, and the Manchu conquest in the 17th century.

The Na Khi, who live around the city of Li Chiang in northwest Yunnan, are a distinct people who still use for ritual purposes a script which is neither of Chinese nor Sanskrit origin. Though not of Tibetan stock their culture is much influenced by the Lamaist form of Buddhism, and they retain many customs which conflict with Chinese conceptions of morality.

In some parts of China there are communities descended from immigrants. The Muhammadans of Yunnan are the posterity of mercenary soldiers from western Asia introduced into the province by the Mongol Emperors in the 13th century. Although these soldiers must from the first have intermarried with the women of the country, whether Chinese or aborigine, the Yunnan Muhammadans have still a very distinct physical type, recalling the Arabs of Syria. Speaking Chinese, and wearing the national costume, they are only distinguished from the rest of the population by their religion and their features. The Muhammadans of the north-west, Kansu and Shensi, are descended from Central Asiatic immigrants who have probably infiltrated since the T'ang period A.D. 618-907. The smaller Muhammadan communities of the northern provinces are Chinese in everything but their religion, but in the west there is a distinct armenoid type proving a much closer alien ancestry. The Muhammadans do not intermarry with the Buddhist Chinese, though, as they used to make a practice of buying up female children in famine years, they are now a mixed type in which the Chinese blood is becoming predominant. Muhammadans are now classed as a national minority under the name Hui. It is claimed that there are in all ten million Moslems in the People's Republic, this figure including about four million Uighurs and Kazaks from Sinkiang.

Until recent years there was a settlement of Jews at K'ai Fêng Fu, the capital of Honan province in the Yellow River Valley. It is believed that they came to this city when it was the capital of China under the Sung dynasty, in the 10th and 11th centuries. Up to the middle of the 19th century the K'ai Fêng Jews, though poor and diminishing, had kept their religion, and had a synagogue with a resident Rabbi who could read Hebrew. After the death of this old man the community disintegrated, the synagogue became a ruin, and the Jews of K'ai Fêng Fu merged in the Chinese population. They have lost their identity and no longer form a separate community.

In Kuangtung, the province of which Canton is the capital, there is a large community called the Hakka (mandarin *K'ô Chia*) or "guest families." They speak a peculiar dialect, do not marry Cantonese—by whom they are despised—but are in other respects not differentiated from the ordinary Chinese population. According to tradition these people are the descendants of northern Chinese who migrated in great numbers to Kuangtung to escape the terror of the Mongol invasions in the 13th century. Their dialect is indeed akin to that now spoken in the northern provinces, and may represent the pronunciation which prevailed in that part of China seven hundred years ago. The origin of the Hakkas remains a mystery; some evidence exists tending to show that the Hakkas in some districts are an admixture of true Hakkas and the minority people called Yao. It is believed that Hakka immigrants, unable to obtain lands in the valleys inhabited by Cantonese, moved into the Yao districts in the mountains, and there mingled with the natives, who adopted the Hakka dialect. The term "guest families" is also applied to the Chinese settlers in Yunnan who came to that country during and after the Ming dynasty (*i.e.* since the 14th century). The older Chinese inhabitants, who arrived in the 3rd century and subsequently, are known as Lao Han Jên, or "Old Chinese." In Yunnan they were an exclusive aristocracy, who would not intermarry with the "guest families." In Kueichou, on the contrary, they were poor and despised by the later arrivals.

In spite of the existence of peculiar communities, and aboriginal tribes, more particularly in the southern and south-western provinces, China to-day presents an impressive cultural unity, which to the western traveller seems more complete than is in fact the case. The non-Chinese peoples themselves, Shans and Miao, are a kindred stock, all being members of the Tibeto-Burmese branch of the Mongolian race which is not distinguished from the Chinese branch by any very noticeable characteristics of feature or pigmentation. The traveller will see little difference between a Chinese and a Miao, and still less between a northern Chinese and a southerner. The apparent identity of type, and the real identity of culture over an area so vast and so definitely divided in climate and configuration, is the outstanding achievement of the Chinese civilisation. The eighteen provinces of China within the Wall, and the three Manchurian provinces beyond it, are each as large, and often more populous than the major states of Europe, excluding Russia. This immense population, exceeding 600,000,000, has a common culture expressed in a common written language which transcends the relatively unimportant and local difference in spoken dialects.

PART ONE—FEUDAL CHINA

Chapter I

PREHISTORY

THE traditional and orthodox histories of China present a comparatively clear and consistent account of the origin and early development of the Chinese civilisation. This is no longer accepted by modern scholarship as history. Any study of the early Chinese culture to-day is based rather on the evidence of archæological research than on these traditional literary sources. Legend and myth are important elements in the cultural background of a people, and particularly so in China, where the moral code was attributed to the teaching of the wise rulers of the earliest age. Before considering the archæological evidence it is as well to give a brief account of the orthodox tradition.

After Heaven and Earth were separated and the world came into being, the universe was ruled first by the twelve Emperors of Heaven, who each reigned for 18,000 years ; they were succeeded by the eleven Emperors of the Earth, who also each reigned for 18,000 years. They in turn gave place to the Emperors of Mankind, nine in number, who reigned altogether for 45,600 years. These were followed by sixteen sovereigns about whom nothing is mentioned except their names, and then the Three Sovereigns, Fu Hsi, Shên Nung and Huang Ti. Not all the legends agree in accounting Huang Ti as one of the Three Sovereigns, by some he is reckoned as the first of the Five Emperors. Fu Hsi and his two successors are the inventors of all the arts and crafts. They dwelt in the modern province of Honan, south of the Yellow River. Shên Nung (the Divine Cultivator) was the first to till the soil. Huang Ti, the Yellow Emperor, is the earliest ruler recognised by the historian Ssǔ-ma Ch'ien, who wrote, or rather compiled, the first general history of China in the 1st century B.C. In his time it is plain that the period of the Three Sovereigns was not considered to be historical. Ssǔ-ma Ch'ien makes the Yellow Emperor, from whom all the subsequent kings and princes of ancient China claimed descent, the founder-hero of the Chinese civilisation. Whereas the previous Three Sovereigns are not men, but divinities with the bodies of serpents and human heads,

Huang Ti is a human ruler. Under him and his four successors, Chuan Hsiu, K'u, Yao, and Shun, the people, who had hitherto been savages, were taught the crafts and manners of civilisation. These five sages established not only the forms of government, but also the sacrifices which should be made to the gods, to the mountains, and to the streams, and the rules of morality and right conduct. This was the golden age when the government of the world was perfect. The Five Emperors did not found a dynasty; indeed, their sons were unworthy of their august sires, and had to be excluded from the throne. Chuan Hsiu was the grandson of Huang Ti, K'u his great-grandson, but not the son of Chuan Hsiu. Yao also was chosen instead of the son of K'u who was not worthy. Yao in turn transmitted the empire to Shun, rejecting his own son as unsuitable. Shun chose as his successor, Yü, who was also of the posterity of Huang Ti, being the grandson of Chuan Hsiu.

Yü merited this choice by his great work as regulator of the floods which had covered the whole empire, almost to the tops of the highest hills. At this task he had laboured for thirteen years, so assiduously that he did not once enter his own house until all was finished, although in the course of his labours he thrice passed the door and heard the cries of his children. His devotion to duty has remained the classic example. Yü's labours extended to all parts of China, and there are few rivers whose course he did not alter or enlarge in his work of draining the country.

Yü is the founder of the first dynasty, the Hsia, for on his death the people insisted on recognising his son as their sovereign, and rejected his minister, I, to whom Yü had transmitted his power. The orthodox traditions assign the reign of Yü to the year 2205 B.C., but another chronology, that of the Bamboo Books, places his reign in 1989 B.C.*

The Hsia dynasty, founded by Yü, endured till 1557 B.C. (1766 B.C.) under seventeen sovereigns. Apart from the legends

*The chronology of the Bamboo Books is to be preferred to the orthodox. After the year 827 B.C. the two systems are identical. For earlier dates the version of the Bamboo Books will be given first, with the orthodox date in parentheses. The Bamboo Books in their present form are spurious. No chronology before 827 B.C. can be regarded as authentic.

clustering round Yü himself, the history of this dynasty is little more than a pedigree occasionally adorned by an anecdote. It is not until the reign of the last Hsia ruler that history enters into more detail to describe his fall. The capital of the Hsia rulers is traditionally supposed to have been in the south-west corner of the modern province of Shansi, in the angle of the Yellow River bend.

Chieh, the last ruler of the Hsia, was a tyrant whose cruelty disgusted the people and outraged the nobles. One of these, T'ang, raised a rebellion, defeated and dethroned the tyrant, and founded a new dynasty, the Shang (sometimes called Yin). This event occurred in 1557 B.C. (1766 B.C.). T'ang was descended from the Yellow Emperor (Huang Ti). His ancestors had received the fief of Shang, identified with the district of Shang Chou in the eastern part of Shensi province. He was thus traditionally a man of the western plateau region, where his family had lived for thirteen generations. His successors reigned over China until they were dethroned by the Chou dynasty in 1050 B.C. (1122 B.C.).

After the death of T'ang, the history of the Shang dynasty is almost as bare a record of deaths and successions as that of Hsia. Apart from the fact that the capital was changed five times, little is recorded until the reign of the last Shang King, Chou Hsin, who was a ruler even more barbarous and tyrannical than Chieh, last of the Hsia. More is recounted of Chou Hsin than of his predecessor. He was a man of enormous strength, very keen sight, and most acute hearing. He was eloquent and clever, but he was vicious. To please his consort, the infamous Ta Chi, he made a lake of wine, hung up quarters of meat on a forest of trees, and held a great banquet during which naked youths and women were made to pursue each other among the meat-laden trees. His cruelty was unbridled. When his uncle, the Prince Pi Kan, remonstrated with him for his bad government, he exclaimed: "Men say you are a sage, and I have always heard that a sage has seven openings to his heart." Thereupon he slew Pi Kan and tore out his heart to see if this was in fact the case. He had imprisoned the Chief of the West, known to history as Wên, the father of the founder of the Chou dynasty. But the people of Chou ransomed their chief by sending Chou Hsin a beautiful girl, a fine horse and four chariots.

When Wên returned to his own people he prepared for war and endeavoured to win over the subjects and nobles of Shang. His successor, Wu, carried out his plans and defeated Chou Hsin on the plain of Mu, near Wei Hui Fu in northern Honan. Chou Hsin fled to his capital (which was near the modern Chi Hsien, Wei Hui Fu, Honan) and there committed suicide by throwing himself into the flames of his burning palace. Then Wu of the Chou dynasty entered the Shang capital, shot three arrows at the body of Chou Hsin, and pierced it with his sword. He decapitated the bodies of Ta Chi and the other wife of Chou Hsin, who had strangled themselves. Thus ended the Shang dynasty, and Wu was recognised as founder of the new dynasty of Chou.

Ch'i, the first ancestor of the Chou family, was surnamed " ruler of the Millet," and was the miraculously conceived son of the Emperor K'u, third in succession from Huang Ti. He was given a fief in Shensi, where his descendants lived for many generations. In the course of time, when they had become poor and unimportant, they adopted the customs of the barbarous Jung and Ti, tribes who inhabited the western part of Shensi. It was not until the chieftainship descended to the father of Wên, that the Chou "renounced the customs of the Jung and Ti," and migrated eastward to the neighbourhood of Sianfu (Ch'ang An), the capital of Shensi. There the chief built a walled town and settled down in a fixed place, having, it would appear, lived as a nomad before this time. Nevertheless his successor, Wên, was one of the three "Dukes of the Palace" at the court of Chou Hsin and was regarded as a subject of the Shang ruler.

The reigns of the early Chou Kings are not accurately dated, but tradition has recorded the more important happenings of their times. Wu himself set up a feudal system of government, parcelling out the empire into fiefs which he distributed to his brothers and relatives, though the Shang were left a small territory as an appanage by which "their sacrifices might be continued."* After the death of Wu, nine rulers succeeded each other until the period called the Kung Ho regency. Of these nine

---

*Cf. Chapter II. It was essential to the rites of ancestor worship that the descendants of a princely house should possess some territory of their own, however small.

rulers tradition has retained certain records. Mu, the fourth, made a great expedition into the west against the barbarous Ch'üan Jung (the "Dog" Jung), but he returned with very little booty, though legend has grown thickly round this famous journey.

Li, the last of these nine rulers, was miserly, cruel, and arrogant. His subjects murmured against his exactions, but the King enacted such severe laws against all who criticised his government, that no man dared to speak to another in the street. The King was well content with this state of affairs, and said to his minister, the Duke of Shao : " I have suppressed all criticism, for people no longer dare to speak." The Duke replied: "You have made a barrier. But to close the mouths of the people is more difficult than to dam up the waters. When the course of water is stopped up, it overflows elsewhere, and the victims of the flood are many. It is the same for the mouths of the people." The warning was not heeded, until in the year 841 B.C. the oppressed people rose in revolt and drove the King from his capital. Then began the Kung Ho regency, and with this date authentic chronology starts, the period of prehistory is past. The regency, according to one account, was exercised by the two dukes of the collateral branches of the Chou house, Shao and Chou, and the name Kung Ho must be interpreted as the style given to this era, "Public Harmony," but according to another account, given in the Bamboo Books, it was a regency by a certain Ho, Count of Kung. Apart from this uncertainty there is no question that the Kung Ho regency is a fully historical event, and from this period onwards the leading events of Chinese history are clearly dated and established.

It is now time to examine the question, how much of this traditional history, prior to the year 841 B.C., can be accepted as fact, and what evidence archæology brings to support or deny the literary account. When modern scholarship first approached the question of Chinese origins the orthodox history was treated with the scantiest respect. Not only the creation myths and the Five Emperors were dismissed as obvious fables, but the Hsia and Shang dynasties were denied any existence, and the Chou were treated as immigrants from the west, who had brought with them from some ancient home in Chaldea or Turkestan the first elements of the Chinese culture. A further examination of the ancient sources and the evidence of archæology coming tardily into the field have shown that this judgment is too hasty.

Archæology as a science is as yet in its infancy in China, and consequently, although recent discoveries have shown how rich a field awaits the spade of the excavator, they have not yet yielded sufficient data to justify positive assertions about the earliest Chinese cultures. The discovery of "Peking Man" in cave deposits at Chou K'ou Tien has at least demonstrated the fact that North China was inhabited at a very remote period, but it is not possible to link up this discovery with later cultural sequences. Palæolithic implements have been found in the north of Shensi and in Inner Mongolia, but as yet nothing has been ascertained concerning the people who used and made them.

Recent discoveries have yielded fuller information about neolithic China. Neolithic implements had indeed been found in almost every province of China, including the most southerly, during the latter part of the 19th century, but it was not until Dr. J. G. Andersson's discoveries in Honan and Kansu that a true neolithic site was scientifically explored. Dr. Andersson's discoveries were made at Yang Shao village in the district of Mien Chih Hsien, in north-western Honan province, a region on the eastern edge of the western plateau zone. Together with stone and bone implements of neolithic type quantities of painted pottery were unearthed at Yang Shao, and subsequently ware of the Yang Shao type has been found at Ho Yin Hsien, Honan, Sha Kuo T'un in South Manchuria, Hsia Hsien in south-west Shansi, and at Ning Ting and T'ao Ho in Kansu province. "Yang Shao" sites are thus confined to the plateau country north and west of the great eastern plain.

The celebrated Yang Shao painted pottery (Fig. 1) is a beautifully potted ware, some vessels showing clear evidence of having been turned on the potter's wheel. The finest examples, which may have been exclusively funerary in purpose, are ornamented with patterns in black, red and white, the surface generally burnished. The designs are often of amazing vigour, especially some of the large multiple confluent spirals. Naturalistic designs scarcely occur; it is, however, certain that cowries are represented. Such pottery is obviously the work of people far advanced in their craft.

FIG. I. *Painted Pottery vessel from Yang Shao.*

So far as decoration is concerned, the painting on this ware has a family likeness to that of Tripolje in south-west Russia, as well as with the pottery of Susa and with finds made at Anau in western Turkestan and in Baluchistan. If a direct relationship with Tripolje is recognized, then the Yang Shao pottery would presumably date somewhat younger than Tripolje (*c.* 2000 B.C.). Probably this date is not far from that of Yang Shao, but it does not necessarily follow, as has been frequently suggested, that Yang Shao is genetically related to Tripolje; both may well owe their origin to some as yet undiscovered ancestral Asiatic site.

In any case the presence of the *li* (hollow-legged tripod) is evidence that the Yang Shao culture had some continuity with later specifically Chinese civilisation. With regard to physical characters the skeletons of the Yang Shao burials scarcely differ from those of the modern northern Chinese. The Yang Shao culture was a transitional Chalcolithic (stone to metal) culture :

no trace of inscription has been discovered. The dog and pig were known, but bones of the horse, ox and sheep have not been found. In the Kansu sites a few copper objects occur, but this does not prove that the Kansu burials are of later date. Thus the Yang Shao sites do not elucidate the problem of the oldest Chinese traditional history, and apart from the *li* do not indicate any direct cultural connection. Present indications suggest that the Yang Shao culture was confined to the north-western plateau region (Map 1).

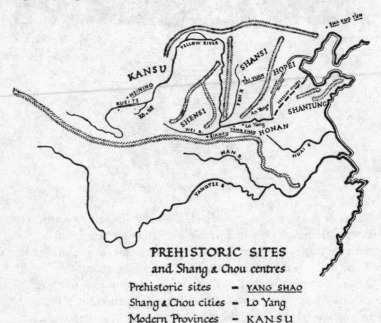

PREHISTORIC SITES
and Shang & Chou centres

Prehistoric sites — YANG SHAO
Shang & Chou cities — Lo Yang
Modern Provinces — KANSU

MAP 1. *Prehistoric Sites and Shang and Chou centres.*

Discoveries at another site in Honan province, near the city of An Yang Hsien (so called since the Republic, but still marked on most European maps as Chang Tê Fu, the name it bore under the Manchu dynasty) have thrown a flood of light on the vexed question of the historical reality of the Shang dynasty. Towards the end of the 19th century a great number of inscribed bones and some pieces of inscribed tortoise shell began to appear in the curio markets, and at once attracted the attention of Chinese scholars, since these archaic inscriptions seemed to mention the names of traditional kings of the Shang dynasty, whose existence was then disputed by modern scholarship. In the past thirty years enormous quantities of such bones have been discovered, amounting to at least 100,000 fragments The inscriptions deciphered and commented upon by Chinese scholars, especially by the late Mr. Wang Kuo-wei and Professor Lo Chên-yu, relate to the art of divination as practised by the method of scorching tortoise shell and bone, and interpreting the answer by means of the shapes of the cracks so produced. This process is frequently mentioned in Chinese classical literature, and the inscriptions are for the most part the questions put to the royal ancestral spirits, and sometimes the answers received are written on the same bone, as on the tortoise shell from the An Yang site (reproduced as Fig. 2), on which are numerous inscriptions of this kind.

The ingenuity of forgers greatly complicated the question of the authenticity of these fragments. Some bones were found without inscriptions, and the forgers would then work an inscription on the ancient bone. Owing to the troubles of the early period of the Republic no expedition was made to discover the site from which these bones came, though it was generally accepted that their provenance was the village of Hsiao Tun, a few miles from An Yang Hsien, a city in north Honan on the Peking-Hankow railway. The place had been known as an ancient site for many centuries. It is mentioned as Yin Hsü, "the waste of Yin", at least as early as the 2nd century A.D., and in the Sung dynasty it was reputed as a spot where ancient bronzes were found; but in the absence of scientific excavation scholars were unwilling to assert that the finds from An Yang were really the relics of the Yin or Shang dynasty.*

In 1928 the Academia Sinica launched the first Chinese archæological expedition to excavate Yin Hsü, under the leadership of Professors Li Chi and Tung Tso-pin. The excavations carried out then and in subsequent years up to the Japanese

* The dynasty bore two names, Shang and Yin, the latter name traditionally being adopted by the nineteenth King, P'an Kêng.

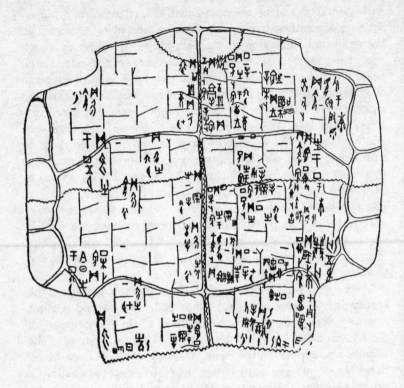

FIG. 2. *Carapace of Tortoise from An Yang inscribed with questions put to the oracle.*

invasion of 1937 have already provided material which has cleared up many doubtful points of ancient Chinese history. It has been established beyond dispute that Yin Hsü is the spot from which the oracle bones came, and that they formed the archives of what may be described as the divination department of the Shang royal house. Yin Hsü was moreover the capital of the Shang-Yin dynasty until it was destroyed by a flood from the Yellow River (which in those days passed far to north of its present bed, not far from Yin Hsü), probably under the twenty-ninth Shang-Yin King. The date at which Yin Hsü became the capital is disputed. According to one view the nineteenth King moved to this spot, while others hold that it was not until the twenty-seventh King that Yin Hsü was made the capital.

The oracle bones have been found in very great numbers, some piled in a confused mass as deposited by flood waters, others undisturbed as buried by the Shang people.* From these bones twenty-five of the traditional names of the Shang-Yin Kings have been recovered, while five other royal names, not yet equated with the traditional forms, have been found. Some of the traditional names are now found to have been miswritten, probably due to a copyist's error in antiquity. The absence of the names of the last two kings of the dynasty is explained by the probability that Yin Hsü was destroyed during the reign of the twenty-ninth King.

Although the oracle bones are the most important of the An Yang discoveries from the point of view of the historian, they are not the only discoveries shedding light on the culture of the Shang period. Clear proof has been found that the Shang not only were a bronze using people, but that they made and cast bronze at Yin Hsü itself. Although the floors of houses have been unearthed, no brick or tile has been found, which makes it probable that Shang architecture had not progressed beyond the use of mud brick and wood, much as these are still used in the construction of the peasant's cottage in North China.

Bronze implements and also stone implements have been found in large quantities, also three kinds of pottery, differing from the Yang Shao type. One of these vessels exhibits a belt of surface glaze which has been thought to have been applied deliberately which, if it is the case, would put back the commonly accepted date for the use of glaze in China by more than a thousand years. Carved ivories and antlers provide some criterion for appraising Shang art. A magnificent inscribed specimen of carved antler with an early rendering of the cicada, a typically Chinese *motif*, *lei wên* (thunder pattern) and other geometrical designs is reproduced in Fig. 3. Sea shells, cowries, and the bones of a whale prove that Yin Hsü was in communication with the sea coast. The

---

*As records of communication with the divine royal ancestors the oracle bones were regarded as very sacred. When the whole surface of the tortoise shell or bone had been used for divination the bone was buried, no doubt so that no profane hands should defile it.

presence of many bones not used for oracular purposes have shown that the pig, dog, sheep, ox, and goat were domesticated by the Shang.* Bones of elephants, bears and tigers also occur.

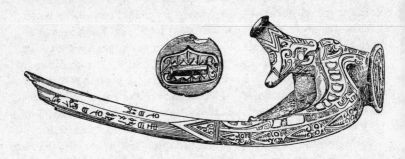

FIG. 3. *Carved Antler with incised inscription. From An Yang.*

Further excavations† at Hsiao T'un, near An Yang, revealed sites which had been successively occupied by men of the Yang Shao stone age, settlers of the "Lung Shan" culture intermediate between Yang Shao and Shang, and finally Shang cultural levels. There is thus a strong presumption that these three cultures were successive developments of the earliest Chinese civilisation. Near this site were also found royal tombs of the Shang period, richly garnished with magnificent bronzes, jades, and animal sculptures in stone. These tombs showed clear evidence of human sacrifice, for skeletons of attendants were found disposed in pits near the main tomb. There were also horses and chariots buried near the king. It is known from historical records that this custom endured in some parts of China up to the Ch'in Dynasty (221–206 B.C.).

The An Yang discoveries have thus completely substantiated the claims of the Shang dynasty to a real and historical existence. On the other hands, the nature of the inscriptions is such that little more is added to the traditional knowledge of the history

*"Preliminary Reports of Excavations at An Yang," Parts I, II and III. *Academica Sinica*, Peiping, 1929 and 1931. In Chinese.

Also: "The Shang-Yin Dynasty and the An Yang Finds." Professor W. P. Yetts. *Journal of the Royal Asiatic Society.* July, 1933.

†China Archaeological Report No. 2. *Academia Sinica*, Nanking, 1947. In Chinese.

of the Shang. As Yin Hsü was destroyed before the end of the dynasty, it was not to be expected that any mention of the circumstances in which the Chou invaders conquered the Shang would be found. However one bone appears to have a reference to the Marquis of Chou (Chou Hou) and the name Chou occurs on other fragments. If the Marquis of Chou is the correct reading (which Professor Yetts doubts) it would be a reference to one of the immediate forbears of the Chou Kings Wên and Wu, who founded the dynasty. The oracle bones which mention the names of kings also give their relationship to their predecessors, a matter of importance in the ritual of ancestor worship. It has therefore been found that the twenty-five kings identified covered sixteen generations starting with T'ang the founder, as related in the historical tradition. The disparity between the number of reigns and generations is explained by the fact that the Shang practised fraternal succession, a fact surmised from the historical tradition and now confirmed by the oracle bone inscriptions.

The An Yang finds have thus a further peculiar significance for the historian. They have confirmed the list of kings and names given in the oldest Chinese historical works, which in their present form are as they were compiled in the 5th century B.C., and reconstructed by the Han restorers after the proscription and burning of the books in 213 B.C. The site of Yin Hsü was destroyed by a flood about 1100 B.C.* and from that time for three thousand years the oracle bones lay buried in the silt. It is plain, therefore, that the historical records incorporated in the Book of History, and which tally so closely with the record of the oracle bones, were derived from another source, since Yin Hsü had been in ruins for more than 500 years. The An Yang finds provide the first archæological test of the reliability of the historical tradition, and that tradition has received from An Yang a striking testimony to its veracity. It must therefore be treated with more respect than scholars were wont to accord it.

One further deduction is permissible. The inscriptions on the oracle bones, though written in a very archaic type of character, are none the less written in Chinese characters, not in an unknown or extinct script. This therefore stamps the Shang culture of Yin

* Adopting the chronology of the Bamboo Books.

Hsü as a characteristically Chinese culture. The Chinese script used on the oracle bones is already a long way from the primitive picture writing from which it must be assumed to have grown. Such an evolution could not have occurred in a short time. The Shang script must already have been in use for some centuries, and must have developed from a far older picture writing. As there has never been any evidence to suggest that the Chinese script was in use in any country other than China, it is reasonable to assume that this long evolution of the written character had taken place in China, and that therefore the Shang culture, though it may have derived bronze from the west, had already a long history in China. Whether that history is the period which the Chinese traditionally ascribe to the Hsia dynasty, is a question which further archæological discovery has yet to solve.

The An Yang discoveries have thus proved three important points. Firstly, that the Shang dynasty had a real and historical existence ; secondly, it was the direct ancestor, or rather the childhood, of the later Chinese culture ; and thirdly, that the Shang were a Bronze Age people with an advanced technique. Whether the Chou were or were not an immigrant folk from the west, it is plain that they did not bring to China the first elements of the Chinese civilisation, since their predecessors had already invented the characteristic Chinese script and were a bronze using people.

Archæology has then confirmed the existence of the Shang dynasty, but as yet it has nothing to offer concerning the Hsia. There is no object, nor any site, which can be dated as belonging to the Hsia dynasty, nor any archæological evidence that such a dynasty ever existed. There are, however, certain facts which should be weighed before dismissing the Hsia as a fabrication of a later age, designed to enhance the glory and antiquity of Chinese history. Firstly one may ask why the romancers invented only one fabulous dynasty to precede the historical Shang. The mythical age of the Emperors of Heaven, Earth and Men, have the authentic symmetry of legend. Each sovereign not only reigns for an immense stretch of time, but has exactly the same length of reign as the others. The bare pedigree of the Hsia dynasty has none of the marks of myth. Yü, the founder, was perhaps more perfect than probable, his labours are certainly a legend in which the drainage works of many generations have been assigned to one hero. His successors are mortal men with a human brevity of life.* The very aridity of the Hsia history speaks in its favour. If the Chinese of a later age invented this dynasty, they showed a singular lack of imagination. It has more the air of some ancient pedigree, handed down perhaps by oral tradition before the invention of writing.

A second consideration in favour of the Hsia dynasty is the unanimity with which it was accepted by the ancient Chinese. The oldest documents, which in their present form are those collected by Confucius and his school in the 5th century B.C., regard the Hsia dynasty as quite historical. All the princes and noble clans of the Chou period (1050-221 B.C.) claimed to be the descendants of the Five Emperors or the Hsia sovereigns; the expression "all the Hsia" was commonly used to designate the confederacy of states, and peoples of Chinese culture and race. "The Little Calendar of Hsia," a fragment of great antiquity preserved in the work of a Han scholar of the 1st century B.C. (*The Rites of the Elder Tai*), is a primitive farmer's calendar, which was supposed to be that of the Hsia dynasty. It is improbable that it is so old, but the name attests the general belief in the existence of the dynasty. On the other hand, the Odes, the collection of very old poems and songs in the *Shih Ching*, and which are the oldest Chinese text, do not mention either Yao or Shun, and though Yü is mentioned, there are no Hsia odes.

It cannot be gainsaid that in Chou times the Chinese believed that before the Shang dynasty, displaced by the Chou themselves, there had been another dynasty, or kingdom, called Hsia, and that this name was still in use to designate the whole Chinese world, or as Professor Li Chi puts it† the "We" group. The attitude of the later Chinese to the Hsia dynasty has some bearing

---

*According to the chronology of the Bamboo Books the Hsia dynasty reigned for 431 years under seventeen kings. This gives an average reign of just over 25 years each. While the dates cannot be accepted as fact, there is nothing incredible in the length of the reigns.

†Li Chi. *The Formation of the Chinese People*. Cambridge: Harvard University Press. 1928.

on the question of the origin and composition of the Chinese people. In Chou times both the Shang dynasty and the Hsia were considered to be kith and kin of the actual rulers of the Chinese world. Moreover, there is no indication that the Chou considered themselves to be a radically different people from the Shang. The state of Sung was inhabited by the Shang people and ruled by the descendants of the Shang Kings. Confucius himself came of a cadet branch of this princely house of Sung, which had migrated to Lu. The K'ung family, his descendants, still living in Shantung, are therefore lineal descendants of the Shang Kings. Thus a considerable proportion of the Chinese must certainly be the posterity of the Shang folk. A bronze vessel excavated in 1957 carries an inscription dating it to the reign of King Chêng second of the Chou sovereigns. The inscription further records rewards given to a feudal follower of the King for his part in the war against the Shang, which it is now clear, continued in eastern China, around the state of Sung, for at least a generation after the traditional conquest of Shang by King Wu. It is therefore probable that the state of Sung was held by the Shang by force of arms rather than granted as an appanage by grace of the conqueror.

On the other hand the Chou conquerors, on the evidence of the ancient texts themselves, were, if not alien, at least very loosely connected with the Shang kingdom. They had only recently "renounced the customs of the Jung and Ti." Many barbarous tribes, as well as Chinese nobles, followed Wu on his march to the plains of Mu. On the other hand, the " Chief of the West," Wên, father of Wu, was one of the dukes of the palace in the court of the Shang ruler, and received his title of Chief of the West, so that he might defend the western borders against the barbarians. It seems probable from these accounts that the Chou were a people either of mixed barbarian and Chinese descent (like the Ch'in state which occupied the same country of Shensi in the later Chou period) or a barbarian tribe which had recently come under Shang (Chinese) cultural influence. The pedigrees which derived the descent of the Chou princes from Huang Ti would be a fiction legitimising the rule of newcomers who had wholeheartedly assimilated the Shang culture.

There is nothing in the ancient texts to support the theory that
the Chou came from further west than the Kansu plateaux.
Indeed, "the Tribute of Yü," an ancient geographical survey of
the empire, which is probably of early Chou date, while giving
the course of the eastern Chinese rivers with fair accuracy,
is very vague about the west. Kansu and Shensi are described
as being bounded to the west by a river running from north
to south, which has in fact no existence. If the Chou had
come out of Turkestan it is strange that they had retained
so little memory of the lands through which they passed.

The old Chinese texts mention settlements of barbarous peoples
in the midst of the Chinese confederacy. The Jung and I occupied
places in Shansi, Hopei and particularly on the coast of the
Shantung peninsula. These peoples have been regarded as non-
Chinese aborigines, but there is no real evidence to confirm this
view. The I, at least, seem to have been a people closely akin to the
"Chinese," that is to say to the inhabitants of the civilised states.
In a passage which has always troubled the orthodox commentators Mencius states: "Shun was a man of the eastern I."
It is hard to see how the legendary sage King can have been a
man of the eastern I, if these people were non-Chinese barbarians.
It is on the contrary more likely that the I, particularly the I of the
Shantung coast, were one of the main tribes of the early Chinese,
who later founded the state of Ch'i. Moreover the foundation
legends of Ch'i fail to provide a satisfactory link between this
state and the western Chou Kings (Chapter III).

An archæological discovery in the province of Shantung has
thrown much light on the earliest culture of this region in which
the state of Ch'i later arose. In 1930 and 1931 a site was excavated
at Ch'eng Tzu Yai, near Lung Shan, about forty kilometres from
Chi Nan, capital of Shantung. Within this enclosure, which was
walled with an ancient earthwork, there were found two successive
layers of remains, the earlier dating from approximately 2000-
1200 B.C. These finds were remarkable for the quantity of well
made black pottery, from which this culture has been called the
"Black Pottery culture." This lower level was wholly a Stone Age
civilisation, but the discovery of ox bones which had been used
for divination in the same manner as the Shang used ox bones

and tortoise shell is direct evidence that the "Lung Shan" culture, as it is usually called, was an earlier development of the higher civilisation which flourished under the Shang. None of the bones found at Ch'eng Tzu Yai are inscribed, but the upper level on the same site, in which oracle bones were also found, continued to be inhabited to *circa* 200 B.C., and inscribed pottery has been found. Moreover this later city has been identified as the capital of the small state of T'an, which was destroyed by Ch'i in 684 B.C.

It can thus be said that this site affords evidence of continuity between the Lung Shan culture, which was without writing or metal, and the well developed civilisation of the Chou period. Although it is clear that the upper level at Ch'eng Tzu Yai saw the introduction of a new type of pottery and the disappearance of the old black ware, the later culture had direct links with the earlier. It is also known that the little state of T'an existed before the Chou dynasty. There has thus been found a link between the Stone Age Yang Shao culture and the Shang period. The Lung Shan period is intermediate, and has aspects which make it appear probable that it was an earlier and primitive stage of the civilisation first known to history, the Shang. There is, however, no evidence to connect Lung Shan with the traditional Hsia Dynasty, which is recorded as preceding the Shang.

In the absence of any archæological find of the importance of Yin Hsü or the Yang Shao sites in the southern provinces, the prehistory of the Yangtze Valley and everything to the south of it, remains very obscure. We may conclude that at the dawn of the historical period these regions, in so far as they were k nown to the states of North China, were inhabited by three peoples, the Ch'u in the middle Yangtze, the Wu in the delta, and the Yüeh along the sea coast. Here again it is usual to refer to these peoples as non-Chinese, but this terminology is confusing. In the first centuries of the historical age there was no such people as "the Chinese," there were several states of kindred stock and common culture loosely united in a political and religious federation. There were also other states, apparently of equal culture and certainly not of very different race, which were outside this federation. Of these Ch'u was the most civilised. There is some reason, to suppose that the tribes which coalesced to form the

state of Ch'u had formerly occupied territories as far north as
the Yellow River Valley where there are place names retaining
the memory of the tribal founder heroes. The oracle bones
contain a mention of the tribe, or clan, of Mi, and "Mi" the same
character constitutes the name of the legendary ancestor of the
Kings of Ch'u.*

The fact that there are references in classical literature, notably
Mencius, to the unintelligibility of the speech of Ch'u does not
prove that these people were a very different stock to those of
the northern states. Dialects were various in the north also, and
the dialect of Wu, now known as Soochow or Shanghai dialect,
was still spoken north of the Yangtze as late as the 7th century
A.D.† The Chinese language has many and close affinities with
the languages of the aboriginal races of the southern and south-
western provinces, Miao, Lolo, and Shan. Also with the other
languages of the Burmese-Tibetan group and the Tai language
of Indo-China. On the other hand it has no affinities with the
languages of the northern nomads. The evidence, inadequate as
it is, tends to suggest that the Chinese of later centuries were a
fusion of many kindred peoples inhabiting the whole area between
Indo-China and the borders of the northern steppes, the area
suited to an agricultural people. The most northerly branch of
this stock, in the valley of the Yellow River and the north-eastern
plain had its principal centres on the lower course of the great
river, and a secondary centre in the valley of the Wei, in Shensi.
Kindred, but less civilised, tribes dwelt in the mountains which
divide these river valleys, and in the coastal ranges of Shantung.
The northern tribes received a bronze culture probably from a
western source, since there is no evidence to show that the use of
bronze was known to the people of the Yang Shao sites, though
some copper objects have been found in the most westerly of
these.

In any case there is definite evidence of cultural connection
with the west at what in China is an early date. The bronze

---

*Fu Ssŭ-nien: Report on Excavations at An Yang. No. 2.

†Yang Chien of the Sui dynasty, who had his southern capital at Yang
Chou, could speak the language of Wu, according to the *Sui Shu* (History of
Sui Dynasty).

socketed celt, one of the characteristic implements of the late bronze age of Central and Eastern Europe, occurs in China in considerable numbers, the evidence pointing to many of these being of Chou age. Particularly interesting is the specimen in the British Museum, bearing two as yet undeciphered characters, reproduced in Fig. 4. The distribution of this implement is indeed of great interest from the point of view of early contacts of West and East. This essentially European tool is absent from Egypt,

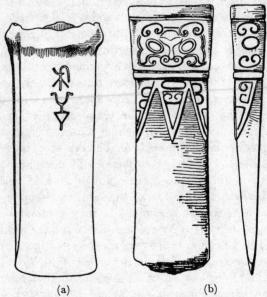

(a)   (b)

FIG. 4. *Socketed Celts of Chou Period*
(a) *with inscription.*   (b) *with t'ao t'ieh and cicada design.*

Asia Minor, Iran, and India. It occurs all over Eastern Europe, in the Siberian burial mounds (*khurgan*), in northern Burma, Cambodia, and in China, both north and south, whence it reached Indonesia. This distribution indicates that the socketed celt reached China across Siberia, not south of the Himalaya or by sea.*

Possibly as a consequence of such contacts the northern Chinese

*C. G. Seligman, "Bird Chariots & Socketed Celts in Europe & China." *Journal Royal Anthropological Institute*, Vol. L, 1920.

advanced further and faster than the southern tribes, and acquired a superior civilisation. The southern people were then treated as barbarous, and were only recognised as a kindred stock when they in turn had adopted the culture of the north. The traditional history is confirmed as far back as the Shang, who had a bronze culture. The Hsia dynasty is unknown to archæology. It may possibly be a pedigree of some earlier or contemporary line of kings ruling in some other part of North China. The Chou were a tribe from the Wei valley, who had been closely in touch with nomads, and had perhaps absorbed western nomad tribes. They conquered the Shang and adopted their culture, at least in part. The early history of the Chou period is legend adorning a pedigree which may be considered as genuine. In the early historical period there were still many backward tribes in the north, as well as in the Yangtze valley, but as time went on these were either conquered by the more advanced states or adopted their culture.

Chapter II

THE ANCIENT GODS

THE character of the earliest religious system in China is obscure
and a subject of dispute. With the exception of the inscriptions
on the oracle bones of Yin Hsü, archæology has not yet done
much to elucidate the sparse and often contradictory data found
in the oldest literature. The earliest texts were preserved and
transmitted to posterity by the scholars of the Han dynasty in the
1st and 2nd centuries B.C., who edited and republished them
after the proscription of the books enacted by the revolutionary
Ch'in dynasty (see Chapters VI and IX). Although they endeavoured to establish the original texts, they transcribed them into
the modernised characters in use under the Han dynasty, and
wrote commentaries and explanations inspired by the religious
ideas current in the 1st and 2nd centuries B.C.

The transcription of the ancient texts into modern characters
concealed the primitive meaning of the oldest forms, giving
them a specialised meaning which they had not possessed in the
dawn of civilisation. The commentaries of the Han scholars
and their successors were inspired by the ethical ideas of the
Confucian school, which had little in common with the primitive concepts of their remote ancestors of the Shang dynasty.
The Han dynasty was a civilised and sophisticated age of religious synthesis, when many diverse ancient cults were being
amalgamated in accordance with an elaborate cosmogony. This
process might have destroyed every literary evidence of the most
ancient cults, had it not been for the scholarly reverence for an
old text, which might be interpreted and commented upon in
accordance with current ideas, but was never to be altered or
corrupted. To form a just idea of the nature of the oldest cults,
the literary evidence must be approached unbiased by Han
interpretations, and assisted by the new discoveries of archæology
and palæography.

In the last chapter, it has been shown that the earliest civilisation found in China had affinities with the neolithic culture of
other parts of the old world. The oldest Chinese divinities were

fertility gods. The primitive farmer, indeed, the farmer of all ages, is peculiarly dependent upon the vagaries of the weather. In China geographical conditions made this dependence more than ordinarily pronounced. The soil of the north China plain and plateaux of the west is loess—wind-blown dust from the Gobi desert, accumulated in the course of countless centuries till it has covered the earlier formations with a deep layer of fertile, friable dusty soil. This soil is fertile on condition that the rainfall is adequate, but without water it quickly returns to its original nature, dust. The rainfall in north China is concentrated in the summer months, beginning with light spring rains in March and April, reaching its maximum in July, and ceasing altogether at the end of September. The winter, apart from one or two light falls of snow, is dry and cold, holding the country in the grip of an intense unbroken frost which terminates all agricultural work.

The farmer's crops, and even his life itself, therefore depend on the spring rains, which are variable and sometimes fail entirely. If that happens the hot sun of the sudden oncoming summer withers the young shoots, and the crop is wholly lost. Should this calamity be avoided, there is the fear of an excessive rainfall in midsummer which causes floods, washing away the unripened crops. In either case there is famine, and on the average one or other of these calamities afflicts the country or some part of it, every four or five years.

These climatic conditions have exercised a lasting influence on Chinese religious ideas, for the great forces of nature are not self-evidently beneficent. On the contrary, prosperity depends on a precarious balance of destructive powers capable, if uncontrolled, of inflicting immense catastrophes upon mankind. The earliest Chinese cults were therefore directed to maintaining, by magical forces, the harmonious balance of nature, which alone made possible man's life upon the earth. This conception was formulated as the doctrine of the Yin and the Yang, the negative and positive, female and male, dark and light, powers typified in the Earth and the Sky, the great dual forces which control the universe, represented by the symbol of the circle equally divided by a curved line. (Fig. 5.) T'ien, Heaven, the dome of the sky, was essentially Yang, and was personified as Shang Ti, the Supreme Ancestor.

Ti, Earth, was the flat surface of the world, the floor of the firma-
ment, and being innately Yin, gradually came to be a female
deity. Heaven was the arbiter of the weather, and so became in
time the supreme deity to be conciliated by sacrifices entrusted to
the highest human being, the King, the Son of Heaven.

FIG. 5. *Design symbolising the interaction of the Yin and the Yang.*

But the Chinese language has two distinct words for earth. Ti,
which means the whole world, the counterpart of T'ien, the
Heaven; and T'u which is the soil itself, the mud and clay of
which the earth is composed. This T'u, with which the farmer
is so intimately concerned, was ruled by lesser, but very important
deities. Hou T'u, "He who rules the earth" personified as the
deified hero, Kou Lung, and known as Shê, the male god of the
soil.* Equal in importance with Shê, was Hou Chi, "He who rules
the Millet," the grain god, also male, and personified as Ch'i,
son of the hero-sage, K'u. Hou Chi was only made god of the
grain by T'ang, the founder of the Shang dynasty. The ancient
god of the grain had been Chu. It is noteworthy that T'ang also
tried to change the god of the soil, Kou Lung; but "did not
succeed." The new grain god, Hou Chi, was the ancestor of the
royal house of Chou, which in later times was to displace the
posterity of T'ang. This account, preserved in the *Shu Ching*,
itself a work of the Chou period, tends to suggest that the Shang

*Hou T'u has been translated as "Prince Earth," but in Chinese a title
follows the name, and if it precedes it it becomes a verb, and must be translated as "he who rules." In later times Hou T'u was used to designate Ti, the
Earth, but this dates from a period when ancient religious ideas were being
re-shaped by the philosophers. Ti was essentially female, and Hou T'u
originally always meant a male god, Shê. The identification of these ancient
deities is the subject of much controversy. I have followed the views of Prof.
B. Karlgren. Some Fecundity Symbols in Ancient China. *Bulletin of the
Museum of Far Eastern Antiquities.* Stockholm. 1930. No. 2.

dynasty introduced new religious customs, but found that some of the indigenous gods were too firmly established to be over-thrown.* The identification of the gods of the soil and the crops with heroes of past legend was probably a later development, arising in the Chou period when the ancient religion was being rationalised.

The worship of Heaven and Earth was the prerogative of the Son of Heaven himself; the princes of the feudal states had no right to perform these sacrifices. They had their altars to the gods of the soil and crops, Hou T'u and Hou Chi, which stood on the west side of the ruler's palace, corresponding to the temple of the ancestors which stood to the east.†

The altar upon which the Son of Heaven worshipped in Chou times was perhaps an earthen mound. The modern altar of Heaven at Peking, built by the third Ming Emperor, Yung Lo, in 1420, is of white marble built in terraces: Plate I.

"Standing open to the sky in a square of dull Pompeian red walls pierced with marble gateways, this exquisite pile of white marble is built in three terraces, each encompassed by a richly carved balustrade and approached by flights of broad low steps, giving access from north, south, east and west to the third and highest platform, the middle stone of which is looked upon by the Chinese as the central point of the Universe. The entire structure is laid out with geometrical precision, being the combined work of architects, astronomers and doctors of magic. Thus, the terraces are reached by three flights of nine steps each, because the Chinese divided the heavens into nine sections and have nine points to their compass. Likewise the marble blocks of the platform are laid in nine concentric circles and everything is arranged in multiples of the same number. We may even count 360

*Shu Ching. Preface.

†The altar of Shê and Hou Chi, and the temple of the imperial ancestors can still be seen in Peking to-day. The first is now in the gardens re-named under the Republic, the Central Park (Chung yang kung yüan), and is open to the public. The T'ai Miao, the temple of the imperial ancestors, on the other side of the main entrance to the Forbidden City has not been opened to the public.

pillars in the balustrades which thus signify the days in the Chinese lunar year and the degrees in the celestial circle."*

Plate II is a photograph of the summit of the altar prepared for the sacrifice offered by the would-be Emperor Yüan Shih-k'ai in 1915, the last occasion on which these rites were performed. The surface of the altar is covered with yellow earth, and upon this stand the offerings. There is a bullock wrapped in a ritual covering from which only the head and tail project; and on a table many porcelain vessels for grain and wine offerings. A number of tall lamps flank the offerings.

In these sacrifices were centred all the most important religious functions of the prince. His rule was intimately bound up with the fate of the gods of the soil and the grain; indeed, the state or dynasty is often referred to as "the gods of the soil and grain," and the ruin of a kingdom described in the formula "the sacrifices were interrupted." Although the supreme deities, Heaven and Earth, and the fertility gods of the soil and crops were the most important and venerated deities, they were not the only divine powers worshipped by the ancient Chinese. There were also the spirits of the rivers and mountains to be invoked and propitiated by sacrifices. Other gods are occasionally mentioned, although their character and attributes remain unknown. The *Shu Ching* refers to some of these. When Shun had succeeded Yao in the government of the empire:

> "He performed the sacrifice *lei* to Shang Ti, the sacrifice *yin* to the six *tsung*, the sacrifice *wang* to the mountains and streams, and paid homage to all deities."

Shang Ti is best rendered the "Supreme Ancestor" for the term Ti was only used as an imperial title after the fall of feudalism. "Emperor on High," a translation frequently used, is therefore an anachronism at this period. The phrase, like so many other classical Chinese expressions, has been employed in later times for concepts wholly alien to the minds of the early Chinese. At the present day, for example, Shang Ti is used by Protestant

*Juliet Bredon: *Peking, A Historical and Intimate Description of its Chief Places of Interest*. Shanghai. 1922. p. 141.

Christians as the name of God. The six *tsung* are only known from this passage. The word *tsung* commonly means ancestor, but the Chinese commentators have denied it this obvious (and satisfactory) connotation in this text. Han writers interpreted it as referring to the Heavens, Earth and Four Seasons, or as meaning Cold, Heat, the Sun, Moon, Rain and Drought. No good reasons are assigned for these ascriptions, and it may be hazarded that the word carries its usual significance, i.e., ancestors.

One of the most important duties of the Son of Heaven was the ritual opening of the agricultural year, which occurred on New Year's Day according to the lunar calendar used by the Chinese. This date falls early in February, which in North China, or rather in the valley of the Yellow River, is the beginning of spring. The Son of Heaven ploughed a furrow in the precincts of the temple of Heaven, with just such a primitive hand plough as was used by the early Japanese Emperors for this purpose (Fig. 6). This ancient rite endured down to the fall of the Manchu dynasty in modern times, for it was regarded as one of the most important and significant duties of the monarch in his priestly character.

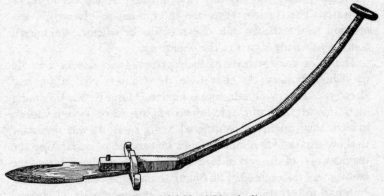

FIG. 6. *Ceremonial Hand Plough, Japan.*

Between the ruler of mankind and the powers of nature there existed a close and vital relationship. The fortunes of men depended upon the balance of forces, beneficent as long as they acted in harmony, but destructive once that balance was deranged. It was a deduction which followed naturally from observation of the climate of North China. The King, the Son of Heaven, was the instrument by which this balance was maintained. His duty was to perform the sacrifices at appropriate times and establish a relationship between Man and Heaven. In his first beginnings the King was far more priest than soldier. His terrestrial duties of government could be delegated to lesser men, his ministers. He alone could perform the magical sacrifices which assured the harmony of the divine powers. The feudal prince had only the power to sacrifice to the mountains and streams in his own domain, and to his gods of the soil and grain. The Son of Heaven alone sacrificed to Heaven and Earth.

In the early texts this idea has already been developed into the foundation of a moral code. The Son of Heaven could not properly fulfil his functions unless his moral nature was pure and his conduct above reproach. Heaven could not be served by a tyrant or a debauchee, the sacrifices of such a ruler would be of no avail, the divine harmony would be upset, prodigies and catastrophes would manifest the wrath of Heaven. This moral interpretation of the relationship between the Son of Heaven, priest-king, and the divinity was greatly developed in later centuries. The ancient texts are interpreted as giving full expression to the theory, but one may doubt whether this moral concept was truly a part of the oldest cult.

The most ancient texts in their present form do not precede the Chou dynasty. At that time the Chinese civilisation had already attained a certain sophistication. Morality was becoming more important than magic. Moreover, the Chou were invaders, indeed, they might be considered as usurpers. It was necessary to show why an alien family could be capable of performing the magical rites of the Son of Heaven, by which the harmony of the cosmos was maintained. The Shang dynasty had fallen, but their ruin had to be explained as the will of the great gods, of Heaven itself. If it could be shown that Heaven had rejected the Shang on account of their vices, and in particular of the vices of their last representative, Chou Hsin, then the fallen Shang were no longer true Sons of Heaven. The sacrifices could not be performed by these degenerates, who had lost the inherent virtue, and the new ruler could be regarded as the choice of the gods.

It is doubtful whether this doctrine of the Mandate of Heaven is older than the Chou dynasty, and it is at least possible that it arose in that age as an explanation and rationalisation of past history. The primary function of the Son of Heaven was that of a priest-king, a sacred being who had in him the power to conciliate the forces of nature and so make the sacrifices effective.

Clear evidence that the Son of Heaven was a "corn king" is found in the Book of Rites (*Li Chi*).* We may quote as an example: the following passage referring to the last month of spring :

"Its days are kia and yi. Its divine ruler is Thâi Hâo, and the attending spirit is Kâu-mang. . . .

"Its sacrifice is that at the door, and of the parts of the victim the spleen has the foremost place.

"The Elaeococca begins to flower. . . . Duckweed begins to grow.

"The Son of Heaven occupies the apartment on the right of the Khing Yang (Fane); rides in the carriage with the phœnix bells, drawn by the azure dragon-(horses), and bearing the green flag. He is dressed in the green robes, and wears the azure gems. . . . The vessels which he uses are slightly carved (to resemble) the bursting forth (of nature).

"In this month the Son of Heaven presents robes yellow as the young leaves of the mulberry tree to the ancient divine ruler (and his queen).

"Orders are given to the officer in charge of the boats . . . he reports that it is ready for the Son of Heaven, who then gets into [the boat] for the first time (this spring). He offers a snouted sturgeon (which he has caught) in the rear apartment of the ancestral temple, and also prays that the wheat may yield its produce.

"In this month the influences of life and growth are fully developed; and the warm and genial airs diffuse themselves. The crooked shoots are all put forth, and the buds are unfolded. Things do not admit of being restrained.

"The Son of Heaven spreads his goodness abroad, and

*"The Sacred Books of China," the texts of Confucianism. Trans. by James Legge. Part III, *The Li Ki*, I-X. Oxford. 1885.

carries out his kindly promptings. He gives orders to the proper officers to distribute from his granaries and vaults, giving their contents to the poor and friendless, and to relieve the needy and destitute. . . .

"The queen, after vigil and fasting, goes in person to the eastern fields to work on the mulberry trees. She orders the wives and younger women (of the palace) not to wear their ornamental dresses, and to suspend their woman's work, thus stimulating them to attend to their business with the worms. . . .

"If in this last month of spring the governmental proceedings proper to winter were observed, cold airs would constantly be prevailing; all plants and trees would decay; and in the states there would be great terrors. If those proper to summer were observed, many of the people would suffer from pestilential diseases; the seasonable rains would not fall; and no produce would be derived from the mountains and heights. If those proper to autumn were observed, the sky would be full of moisture and gloom; excessive rains would fall early ; and warlike movements would be everywhere arising."*

In extreme antiquity it is improbable that moral qualities, as the sophisticated Chou period believed, had anything to do with the magico-religious potency of the priest-king. The cult of the gods (Hou T'u, Hou Chi, and Shang Ti) established the harmony of the seasons and the fertility of the fields, but there was also in close relation with this cult, the rites by which the human race itself was nourished and continued. Ancestor worship as testified by the inscriptions on the oracle bones was already a highly developed cult in the Shang dynasty. Its object was to ensure, by appropriate sacrifices and rites, the continued existence of the ancestral spirits and to obtain the aid of these powerful beings for their living descendants. Man has two souls, the animal soul, *p'o*, which is created at the moment of conception, and the *hun*, the higher, spiritual soul which comes into existence at the moment of birth. At death the destiny of the two souls is different. The *p'o*

*Op. cit. pp. 262-267.

continues to reside in the tomb with the corpse, and draws nourishment from the offerings which are made at the tomb, but this after-life of the *p'o* is limited. When the body has decayed it gradually loses vitality and sinks down into the underworld, the Yellow Springs, where it continues a shadowy existence.

The *hun*, the higher soul, at death ascends to the palace of Shang Ti, there to dwell as a subject in his court, leading a life similar to that which the nobleman lived at his prince's court on earth. The journey is not without perils. There are evil forces to be guarded against and outwitted. The earth spirit which devours the soul; the Heavenly Wolf, who guards the palace of Shang Ti. To escape these dangers the sacrifices and prayers of the living members of the clan are necessary. Once established in Heaven the ancestral spirit becomes a mighty and beneficent deity. Participating and drawing sustenance from the sacrifices offered in the ancestral temple, the ancestor in return guides and assists his living descendants. Invoked by divination, he answers the questions addressed to him. Petitioned, his intercession with the gods is even strong enough to stay the hand of death itself. When Wu, founder of the Chou dynasty was ill and likely to die, his brother the Duke of Chou addressed a memorable prayer to the royal ancestors :

"Your chief descendant, the King Fa* is crushed with fatigue and illness, if you, oh three kings, really have need of someone to undertake the duties of a son in heaven take me, Tan, in place of the King, Fa. I, Tan, am both skilful and clever, I have many talents and qualities, I can serve the ancestral spirits and the gods. As for the King, Fa, unlike me, Tan, he has not many talents and qualities; he cannot serve the ancestral spirits and the gods. The mandate was given to him in the court of Shang Ti, so that he might show forth his virtue and come to the rescue of the four quarters of the world. That is how he has been able to maintain the security of your descendants in this world below. In all the four quarters of the world there is no one who does not respect and fear him. Do not allow this precious mandate of Heaven

*Fa was the personal name of Wu, Tan, that of Duke Chou himself.

to fail, moreover, our ancient kings will have an abiding support and refuge.* Now I am going to take your orders by means of the great tortoise [divination]. If you grant my prayer, I will return with the round and square jades and await your decision. If you do not grant my wish, I will hide the round and square jades."

The round and square jades may be a reference to the symbolic jades called *pi* and *tsung* (see Fig. 27, p. 127; and Fig. 28, p. 128; also Chapter 5, pp. 123 *seq.*).

Both souls, the *p'o* and the *hun*, depend on sacrifices for their existence. The *p'o* remains peacefully in the tomb while it is nourished by offerings, but should these cease, or be insufficient, it leaves the tomb and reappears as the *kuei*, the ghost, a famished malevolent sprite, hostile to all living men. As such it is to be dreaded, and if the *p'o* is that of a powerful man, to be propitiated. After the establishment of the Han dynasty, the *p'o* of Er Shih Huang Ti, last sovereign of the Ch'in, who had died by violence and whose posterity had been exterminated, was believed to be active and malignant. Sacrifices were instituted to appease the ghost. The *hun*, too, cannot continue its happy after-life if the ancestral sacrifices are discontinued. Should this happen, it too becomes a ghost, an evil spirit condemned to eternal misery. The ancestral sacrifices can only be performed by male descendants, and therefore the extermination of the clan could alone end them.

It is the fear of this last and irremediable catastrophe, the extermination of the clan, and the transformation of the ancestral spirits into miserable ghosts, which was, and still to the mass of the Chinese people is, the chief incentive to continue the male line, the profound cause for which male children are esteemed above all other blessings. They not only continue the living line, but, through the ancestral sacrifices which they alone can perform, they are indispensable to the continued repose and happiness of the ancestral spirits.

In ancient and feudal times ancestor worship was the cult of the noble clans. The peasantry, separated in their way of life and

*If the King lives and the dynasty is established the ancestral spirits will receive the support and refuge of the sacrifices made to them in the ancestral temple, therefore it is to their advantage to save the King.

in their marriage customs from the aristocracy, had no part in it. The peasants were not included in the clan system, had no surnames, no pedigree, and consequently could not participate in ancestor worship. Moreover, they did not possess any land of their own. They were serfs, cultivating the soil at the orders and under the direction of their masters. They dwelt in groups, in villages during the cold frost-bound winter, in huts built among the fields during the summer months when agriculture is possible. Each village of twenty-five families had its local Shê god of the soil, but this was perhaps the only point at which the peasants touched the religious system.

Their marriage customs differed profoundly from those of the nobility. Whereas the noble married, with great and elaborate rites and ceremonies, the daughter of some other noble clan, who after her marriage would be associated in the rites of her husband's ancestral temple, the peasants celebrated every spring a festival in which the youths and girls of neighbouring villages met in free association, only translated into formal marriage in the autumn if the girls were with child. The clear evidence of these customs, preserved in the Odes, later caused much embarrassment to the Confucian scholars and gave rise to many ingenious interpretations and explanations. Although unable to perform them themselves, the peasants were not excluded from the benefits of the sacrifices. The aristocracy, in fact, were as much priests as rulers and nobles. They, from the Son of Heaven down to the officers in charge of a district or of a ministry, had sacrifices to perform, not only on their own behalf, but in order to secure cosmic harmony, from which every living man benefited. It was perhaps this outlook which prevented the rise of a purely priestly class in ancient Chinese society. There was, indeed, a large class, drawn from the nobility, who were specialists in the prayers and hymns used at the sacrifices. These priests, who did not perform the sacrifice themselves but merely assisted as praying priests, were specialised into colleges, each college only concerning itself with one kind of sacrifice. The priests of the royal sacrifice to Heaven had no part in the college of those who assisted at the sacrifices to Hou T'u or Hou Chi. Their specialised knowledge of the ritual and the prayers to be offered gave them no mystic authority.

The King, or the Prince, who alone could perform the higher sacrifices, were the true priests, they alone possessed the magic qualities necessary if the sacrifice was to be effective. The prayer offering professional priest was only an assistant.

Rather more important and influential were the diviners, also specialists, passing their art down from father to son. They could interpret the cracks produced on the tortoise shell by heat, and as divination was a constant practice, their services were always required. Nevertheless neither the diviners nor the praying priests developed the cohesion and power of a true priesthood, as was found in the ancient civilisations of the Near East. They had no separate rule of life, they were not celibate, and in the course of time they merged more and more completely into the general body of the aristocracy.

There was, however, another class of priests, or strictly speaking sorcerers, the *wu*, both men and women, who had functions wholly different from the diviners and, priests of the aristocratic cult. The sorcerers were in fact mediums, persons who had, or claimed to have, psychic powers. When, after elaborate dances accompanied by music and drumming, the sorcerer, or more often sorceress, entered into a trance, the divinity, or sometimes the ancestral spirit, entered her body and spoke through her mouth. The *wu*, being confined to persons with these gifts, were necessarily of various origin, and by no means usually members of the noble clans. Indeed, partly on this account, the sorcerers lost popularity with the aristocracy in the later ages of feudalism, and tended to become the priesthood of the lower classes.

As time went on, the aristocratic cult grew more refined and sophisticated, the antics and uncouth music of the *wu* were felt to be unseemly, and the sorcerers were gradually excluded from its rites. They remained very powerful and popular with the mass of the people, and when after the establishment of Confucianism as the ethic governing the official and ancestral cults in the imperial age, sorcery was entirely excluded from these rites, the *wu* found in the rising religion of Taoism, itself a philosophy transformed into a cult, a popular field for their arts.

Ancestor worship and the cult of the gods of the soil and the grain were intimately linked together in the feudal age, but the reason for this association is not particularly clear from the ancient texts. Both were aristocratic cults, closely associated with the lordship of the soil. At the time when the first surviving books were written, the middle Chou period, the 5th century, B.C., these cults were already very old, and had undergone modifications which had almost obscured their primitive meaning. Even in the Shang period, as the Yin Hsü finds prove, ancestor worship had developed an elaborate apparatus of divination and ideas about the immortality of the soul which were the product of long development. Fortunately words of religious connotation continued to be written in the Shang period in a form more primitive than was employed for other characters. No doubt these symbols had acquired some of the sanctity attached to the things they represented, and were not lightly to be altered or improved. The study of these inscriptions tends to suggest that ancestor worship in early times was a fertility cult primarily concerned with the perpetuation of the family itself. The recent work of sinologists on the palæography of the ancient inscriptions on bronzes and oracle bones has shown that in the most ancient times the characters now found differentiated by "radicals" or parts indicating the broad sense, were written without these additions, and therefore many words now clearly differentiated were anciently written with the same character. Professor Karlgren* has shown the great importance of this fact for the comprehension of the ideas which anciently underlay ancestor worship.

He has shown that the character which now means ancestor, 祖, was written without the later radical as 且, and that this character on the oracle bones and bronzes has the form 𠙵 and, is, in fact, a plainly recognisable representation of a phallus. Other evidence exists, of a similar nature, which goes far to prove that the ancestral tablet of to-day was primitively a phallic symbol, that in fact the origin of ancestor worship was phallicism, the fertility cult widespread among primitive peoples. Moreover, evidence of a like nature shows that 社 the character representing Shê god of the soil, was written at first simply 土, without the radical, and this character also was primitively 𠙵, a phallic

* *Op. cit.*

symbol. Here, therefore, is the real and fundamental link between the cult of the god of the soil and ancestor worship, the twin cults of the feudal age which had their shrines respectively west and east of the royal palace gate. Both were offshoots of the earliest religion practised by mankind, the fertility cult which secured the progeny of the ancestor and the yield of the fields.

By the time of the Chou Kings, when the ancient legends and poetry were written down, these origins had been long forgotten. The writers of these old texts do indeed mention certain incidents which seem to have a close connection with phallicism, but they are recounted only to be condemned as the depraved practices of degenerate rulers. In the hands of the Confucian scholars these condemnations were emphasised and used as the basis of a new morality. There is plenty of evidence to show that in the early feudal period the sexual code was not at all strict, indeed it seems to have been entirely unlike the system of partial seclusion of women which later came to prevail.

The *Tso Chuan* recounts many instances of free intercourse between men and women, even of incest, which was not concealed. The minister of Ch'i, we are told, had a large harem and freely permitted his guests to enter the women's apartments. In consequence "he had one hundred sons," and does not seem to have been troubled about their parentage. Shun himself, the sage, married the two daughters of Yao, but the marriage of two sisters was regarded as a crime in the feudal period.

These are not the only evidences of a slow but profound change in the sexual morality of the ancient Chinese. The Odes, the collection of ancient poetry and sacrificial hymns, which is one of the oldest and least corrupt texts in the Chinese literature, contains many poems which are frankly licentious. Pious Confucian commentators have endeavoured to explain these songs as satires upon the evil conduct of rulers, or denunciations of the wickedness of certain districts in times of degeneracy. There can however be no doubt that such poems as this Ode from Chêng state are ancient songs, without any satirical intent :

> On the heath there is creeping grass
> Soaked in heavy dew

There was a handsome man
With clear eyes and fine brow
We met by chance
And my desire was satisfied.

On the heath there is creeping grass
Drenched in heavy dew
There was a handsome man
With clear eyes and fine forehead
We met by chance
And together we were happy.

The strange stories contained in the oldest historical text, the *Shu Ching*, have been invariably regarded as exhibitions of the vices of tyrants. But when, as already mentioned, we read of Chou Hsin, last sovereign of the Shang, holding a festival in which young women and youths pursued each other naked on the border of a pool of wine surrounded by trees hung with viands, it is not necessary to endorse the traditional condemnations of his outrageous conduct. Had Chou Hsin really invented this festival as a licentious debauch it would argue a degree of sophistication at the Shang court, more than 1000 years B.C., which is not borne out by anything found at Yin Hsü, his grandfather's capital. It is more probable that the *Shu Ching* contains here a garbled and unfriendly account of some religious festival to the fertility gods honoured by the Shang people.

It is plain that the curious legend about the foam from the mouths of dragons has its origin in the most ancient fertility beliefs. In the time of the Hsia dynasty two ancestral spirits in the form of dragons appeared in the royal palace.

"The King consulted the lots to know whether he should kill them or send them away, or keep them in his palace. No favourable reply was received. Then he asked whether he should ask the dragons for some of the foam from their mouths. The reply was favourable. Then a piece of cloth was spread before the dragons and a prayer in writing presented to them. They withdrew leaving their foam on the cloth. This object was kept hidden in a box. When the Hsia

fell, it was transmitted to the Shang, and when they fell it
passed into the possession of the Chou. During these three
dynasties no one could be found who would dare to open the
box. But at the end of the reign of King Li [of the Chou, the
tenth King], it was opened and inspected. At once the foam
spread through the palace, and no one could stop it. King
Li made his wives approach naked and utter imprecations
against it. The foam transformed itself into a black lizard
and entered into the women's apartments. There it was
found by a young girl."

The story goes on to say that this child became pregnant seven
years later and gave birth to a girl, who later became the favourite
and queen of the next King, Yu. It will be noted that the two
dragons were really ancestral spirits, and that their foam was
asked for and preserved as a precious talisman.

The belief in the transformation of ancestral spirits into dragons
(which in China are not monsters, but beneficent deities ruling
the rain and the water courses) is paralleled by the shape shifting
of inimical ghosts into the forms of animals, in order to wreak
vengeance on their enemies. Duke Hsiang of Ch'i (694 B.C.)
had a sister who was married to his neighbour, the Duke of Lu.
Before the marriage he had had incestuous relations with this
sister, and when the Duke of Lu paid him a visit at Ch'i he
renewed his relationship with the Duchess of Lu. The fact became
known, the Duke of Lu was enraged, and in order to suppress
the scandal the Duke of Ch'i and his sister plotted the death of the
inconvenient husband. At a banquet the Duke of Lu was made
drunk, and the Duke of Ch'i ordered his retainer P'êng Chêng, a
man of great strength, to put the Duke of Lu into his chariot,
using the opportunity to crush him to death in his arms. This was
done. The true facts leaked out, and to pacify the people of Lu,
Duke Hsiang had P'êng Chêng put to death. Some eight years
later the Duke, who had now many enemies who only sought an
opportunity to revolt, was out hunting.

"He saw a stag. A member of his suite said: 'It is P'êng
Chêng.' The Duke, enraged, shot an arrow at the stag. The

stag reared up like a man and groaned. The Duke, overcome with fear, fell from his chariot and injured his foot."

At the news that the Duke was injured his enemies made an attack upon the palace the same night, forced the guards and slew Duke Hsiang.

Scattered through the ancient texts there are other anecdotes which refer to forgotten religious beliefs, the meaning of which was already lost when the Chou scholars recorded them, particularly when these stories are associated with the fallen house of Shang. Wu I of this dynasty,

"Acted in an unreasonable way. He made an image in the shape of a man and called it the Spirit of Heaven. He played with it [at a kind of draughts] and ordered a man to arrange the pieces for it. The Spirit of Heaven having lost, the King insulted and abused it. He made a bag of skins and filled it with blood, he had it hung up and shot at it with arrows saying he was shooting at Heaven."

The *Shu Ching* then goes on to recount that Wu I was later struck by lightning and killed. Although this is no doubt meant to exemplify Heaven's wrath with a being so presumptuous, it is curious to observe that the tradition of this rite lingered in the royal house of Shang and was revived by the distant descendant of Wu I, Yen, last feudal prince of Sung, the appanage of the royal house of Shang after the fall of the dynasty. In 318 B.C., nearly a thousand years after the reign of Wu I, the King of Sung,

"Filled a leather bottle with blood, hung it up, and shot arrows against it, saying that he was shooting at Heaven."

Another legend, that of I, the excellent archer, appears to be connected with these forgotten rites. It is related of this hero that once, when nine suns appeared simultaneously in the sky, and the intense heat began to burn up the world, I with his bow and arrows shot down eight of them and so saved the world from conflagration.

The divinities of the streams and rivers formed a separate but important class in the ancient Chinese pantheon. They were dangerous and on the whole hostile powers who had to be propitiated if floods and catastrophes were to be avoided. The most important of these was naturally Ho Po, the Count of the Yellow River, the mighty waterway of the North China plain, the home of the earliest Chinese culture. The Count of the Yellow River, called simply the Count of the River, for the great stream is always known as *ho* "the river" *par excellence*, was the chief water deity of the Chinese, ranking above the spirits of the sea itself, for the Chinese did not in the earliest ages have much commerce with the ocean coast, on which dwelt the barbarous I of the Shantung peninsula.

Everyone who crossed the Yellow River made an offering to the deity, to secure a safe passage. This offering in the case of persons of distinction was usually a jade ring, but among the riparian people, who had most to fear from the constant vagaries and changes of bed for which the river is so famous,* the sacrifices were more elaborate and more barbarous. At Lin Tsin opposite the point where the Wei river from the Shensi plateau enters the main stream there was a famous sanctuary to Ho Po with a college of *wu* priests. Here, and at a point near the modern Lin Chang, in Honan, now far from the present course of the river, human sacrifices were offered. The sorceress chose the most beautiful girl of the district and declared that she should be the "bride of the Count" for the year. The chosen victim was then lodged in a fine tent near the bank, dressed in finery and jewels. After a preparatory fast she was placed on a marriage bed which was launched on to the stream, when before long the Count of the Yellow River claimed his bride. The barbarous custom was not suppressed until the very end of the Chou period (3rd century B.C.).†

*No river in the world is subject to such catastrophic alterations of course. Several times in the historical period the Yellow River has completely changed the course of its lower reaches, sometimes flowing far to the north of the Shantung peninsula, reaching the sea near the modern city of Tientsin, at others sweeping across the plain to find an outlet south of the peninsula, near the modern mouth of the Huai. It is as if the Rhone were on occasion to enter the Mediterranean near Marseilles, but at other times change its course and flow into the Atlantic near Bordeaux.

†When living at Hankow I observed that the idea underlying these sacrifices is still alive to-day among the boatmen of the Yangtze. They are very unwilling

The sacrifices to the Count of the Yellow River were not the only instances of human sacrifice known to the ancient religion. Kings, princes, and even great nobles were wont to have their wives and a few chosen friends accompany them in death, the victims of this honour being walled up living in the royal tomb. By the end of the Chou period the custom had been discontinued in the civilised states of eastern China, the victims being replaced by counterfeits of straw or wood. In Ch'in, the rude semi-barbarous hill country occupying the modern province of Shensi, the old custom was continued up to the reign of Shih Huang Ti, the founder of the centralised empire (d. 210 B.C.).

We see then, that the political organisation of ancient China had a religious basis, founded on the worship of ancestors and the gods of the soil and the crops, both confined to the noble clans. Though this is the established system in the earliest historical period, there are indications that both these cults were in origin fertility beliefs, and the monopoly of religious functions by the nobility was possibly a later development. In the earliest texts there are traces of customs and beliefs wholly forgotten or mis-interpreted by the scholars and scribes who wrote down the oldest traditions and legends in the Chou period. When books of ritual and divination were compiled these ancient beliefs were systematised and presented in an idealised form, which only preserves the oldest practices when these were so unintelligible to the scribes that they did not understand their meaning, and simply copied down the ancient formulæ. The religion of the Chou period from which these books date was already sophisticated, even decadent, and no true understanding of the oldest rites will be had until the Shang bone inscriptions have been more completely studied and transcribed.

---

to make any effort to rescue someone who has fallen into the river. It is believed that if they do so, the god of the river, cheated of his prey, will take the rescuer himself in revenge. A charitable society at Wu Ch'ang in Hupei, on the Yang-tze, has had to offer a high reward for such rescue work, moreover it was necessary to double the reward if the victim was drawn out living, for the boat people were more inclined to allow the river god to have his sacrifice, and then rescue the corpse for burial. Similar beliefs are entertained by other river dwellers in North China.

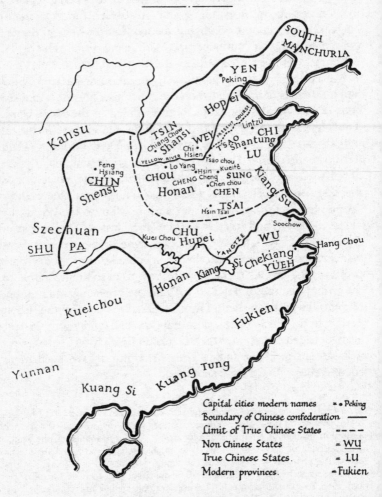

CHINA
in the
CH'UN CH'IU PERIOD
722 ~ 481 - B.C

SOUTH MANCHURIA

YEN
Peking

Hopei

Kansu

TSIN
Chiang Chow
Shansi
Chi
Hsien
YELLOW RIVER
Lo Yang

WEY
PRESENT COURSE
Lintzü
Tsao chou
TSAO
Shantung
CHI
LU

Feng Hsiang
CHIN
Shensi
CHOU
Honan
CHENG Cheng
Hsin
Kueitê
Chen chou
SUNG
CHEN

Kiang Su

TS'AI
Hsin Ts'ai

Szechuan
SHU
PA
Kuei Chou
CH'U
Hupei
YANGTZE
Kiang
Si
Chekiang
Soochow
WU
YÜEH
Hang Chou

Honan

Kueichou

Yunnan

Fukien

Kuang Si
Kuang Tung

Capital cities modern names   = • Peking
Boundary of Chinese confederation ———
Limit of True Chinese States   - - - -
Non Chinese States   = WU
True Chinese States   = LU
Modern provinces   = Fukien

MAP 2. *China in the Ch'un Ch'iu Period.*

Chapter III

THE FEUDAL AGE, 841-221 B.C.

WHEN in the 9th century B.C. authentic dated records replaced misty traditions the Chinese confederacy was organised as a strictly feudal society. The Kings of the Chou royal dynasty, if they had ever exercised the paramount authority which tradition attributed to the founders of their house, had ceased to have more than a formal primacy over the princes of the feudal states. They were in no sense emperors such as the rulers of China in later times. The term "Emperor," in Chinese *Huang Ti*, should not be applied to the sovereigns of the feudal period, for this title was only adopted by the first ruler of the dynasty that succeeded the Chou, and it was only then, when feudalism was destroyed, that the Chinese confederacy was converted into a centralised state. In the Chou period the King was known as the Son of Heaven (a title retained by the later emperors), and until the last days of feudalism none but the Chou Son of Heaven might legitimately bear the title of King (*Wang*).

In the middle of the 8th century, the Chinese feudal system, however, was already verging on decay. The authority of the Chou Kings had been shattered in 770 B.C. by a catastrophe which had transferred real power to the rulers of the larger feudal states. In that year the Ch'uan Jung, probably a nomad people from the northern steppes, had taken and sacked the royal capital, a city near the modern Sianfu, in Shensi province. The Chou Kings, forced to abandon the homeland of their house, established themselves at Lo Yang in Honan province, not far from the Yellow River. The absence of dated and detailed records of the earlier years of the dynasty is very probably due to the destruction of such records when the old capital fell.

The period following this migration, from 722-481 B.C., is known as the Ch'un Ch'iu period, from the historical work of that name, the "Spring and Autumn Annals" which was the first accurate chronological history written in China. This work is a chronicle of the feudal state of Lu, of which Confucius was a native. Chinese orthodox tradition assigns the authorship of the

Ch'un Ch'iu to Confucius himself, but this attribution cannot be substantiated and is not accepted by modern scholars. In the Ch'un Ch'iu period the lands inhabited by peoples of Chinese culture were divided between fifteen major feudal states and a large number of smaller fiefs about which very little is known (Map 2). The fifteen larger states themselves were classed in two categories, those which were truly members of the Chinese confederacy, *Chung Kuo*, "the Middle Kingdom," and those which were regarded as more or less barbarous. The fact is significant. From the earliest times it was the acceptance of Chinese culture rather than racial ties which determined whether a people were to be regarded as Chinese or barbarian. Although such analogies must not be pushed too far, the relationship between the true Chinese states and the half barbarous fringe was not unlike that which in classical times subsisted between the republics of the southern parts of Greece and the half-Greek northern lands of Epirus and Macedonia.

The truly Chinese states were confined to the basin of the Yellow River, east and south of the great southern bend which divides Shensi from Shansi. Shensi was the state of Ch'in, whose ruler claimed to be Chinese and descended from the ancient sage emperors. If this sovereign was of Chinese descent, his subjects were certainly very largely of barbarian stock, and for many centuries Ch'in was regarded in the eastern states as a barbarous country. The Yangtze valley was divided between three states, none of which were wholly Chinese. The upper province of Szechuan, forming the two kingdoms of Shu and Pa of which little is known, though they would seem to have reached a high level of culture, and in the middle Yangtze region was the kingdom of Ch'u, ruled by a family which claimed Chinese descent. The inhabitants were aborigines, though the kingdom had come under strong Chinese influence and was rapidly becoming recognised as a Chinese state. Wu, in the delta of the Yangtze, was quite certainly inhabited by a distinct people, though its kings were supposed to be descended from a collateral branch of the royal house of Chou. Whatever foundation there may have been for this legend, the ruling class in Wu were Chinese in sympathy and anxious to win recognition for their state as a member of the Middle Kingdom. The south-east coast was for a short period organised as the kingdom of Yüeh. It was regarded as barbarous by the people of the Chinese Confederacy. The modern Annamites claim the people of Yüeh as their ancestors, they were certainly one branch of the widespread aboriginal race of south China, of which remnants exist to-day in the south-west provinces (cf. Introduction).

The central group of true Chinese states, eleven in number, occupied the modern provinces of Shansi (Tsin), Hopei (Yen) Shantung, divided between Ch'i in the north and Lu in the south, and Honan. In this latter province the Chou Kings had their royal domain around Lo Yang in the west; the state of Wey,* the name of which is preserved in Wei Hui Fu, was in the part of Honan north of the Yellow River. Chêng, created out of the royal domain in 782 B.C., lay to the south of the river. Further east was Sung, the capital of which corresponds to the modern Kuei Tê Fu, Honan. Ts'ao, a smaller state, was north of Sung round the city still called Ts'ao Chou in the west part of Shantung. South of Sung was Ch'ên, corresponding to the district of Ch'ên Chou Fu, Honan. Ts'ai, also a smaller state was still further south, its capital being the modern Shang Ts'ai Hsien, prefecture of Ju Ning, Honan. The northern part of modern Kiangsu province, and the western part of Honan, on either side of these larger states, were divided between numerous small principalities, of which no detailed history has survived. In later feudal times these areas fell under the sway of the rising power of Ch'u, the southern kingdom. These small fiefs in the Ch'un Ch'iu period were very numerous, and seem to have formed enclaves in the middle of their important neighbours. The political map of China in this era must have resembled that of the Holy Roman Empire in its decadence.

*The name of this state is usually spelt Wei in European works. There were, however, two states of this name in the Chou period, and, although the Chinese characters are quite distinct, both words are spelt Wei in the Wade system of romanisation. In order to avoid a tiresome confusion I have adopted the form Wey for the name of the old state here mentioned, and used the spelling Wei only for the later state formed after the break up of the kingdom of Tsin. The accepted use of variant spellings for the two modern provinces, Shensi and Shansi, which in Chinese are both pronounced Shansi, may be cited as a precedent.

The rulers of the larger fiefs were, or claimed to be, connected with the royal house of Chou. The first dukes of Lu and Yen had been the sages Tan, Duke of Chou and the Duke of Shao, who had assisted Wu to conquer the Shang and guided the young King Chêng after the death of the founder. The states of Tsin, Wey, and Ts'ao had been allotted to other less distinguished younger brethren of Wu. The ducal house of Ch'i claimed descent from the brother-in-law of Wu. In this case, however, the traditional pedigree clearly betrays the hand of an "improver." The legends about the founder of the Ch'i house are quite contradictory. Some say he was "poor and obscure, dwelling on the shore of the eastern sea," while others make him the friend and minister of Wên, father of Wu. Both stories agree that he assisted the conqueror in his war against the Shang.

This point perhaps contains the only element of truth in the legends. It is probable that the Ch'i state, or tribe, were powerful on the sea coast in Shang times, and joined in the attack upon the Shang when the Chou advanced from the west. Whether the royal family gave the ruler of Ch'i a daughter in marriage or not, it would be consistent with the Chou feudal system for all large fief holders to claim alliance with the royal house. Ts'ai may have been founded by a Chou adventurer, much as the barbarous Wu state was supposed to have been founded by the elder brother of Wên. Chêng was a later foundation, resting on a better tradition. It had been created as an appanage for the younger brother of King Hsüan (d. 782 B.C.). Sung was ruled by the descendants of the dethroned kings of the Shang dynasty. The rulers of Ch'ên claimed to be descended from the legendary Emperor Shun. Thus all the feudal lords were members of a small group of clans traditionally descended from the sages of the golden age

It would not be possible in the short space available in a general history to enter into the detail of the varying fortunes of these states during the Ch'un Ch'iu period. The history of these centuries is an intricate and confusing record of wars and intrigue, which is chiefly of interest for the occasional light thrown on feudal customs and social conditions. Here all that will be attempted is to give a survey of the Chinese feudal age as

Confucius found it, when the old order still held intact, though fast verging on decay.

The Son of Heaven was in theory the supreme lord of the land, *t'ien hsia*, "the world under heaven." He alone bore the royal title of King (*Wang*). His vassals, the feudal lords, owed him homage and offered certain articles as tribute. When they came to his court, which they were supposed to do at frequent intervals, they were bound by a strict ceremonial which emphasised their inferior degree. The Son of Heaven was the source of all legitimate authority. He alone had the right to invest a new feudal lord with his fief, and until he gave his recognition to a newly created state, it had no legal existence. In theory he could deprive a lord of his state, and tradition recounted that the early kings had in fact exercised this power. Finally, the Son of Heaven could alone perform those sacred ceremonies and rites by which the harmony of heaven and earth was maintained and the stability and prosperity of the four seasons assured.

The greater princes, who as has been pointed out were in many cases connected with the royal house of Chou, were absolute sovereigns in their territories and entertained ceremonial relations with their fellow rulers. After the decline of the royal power had become marked, the most powerful of the princes exercised a hegemony over the whole confederacy, a usurpation of the royal authority which Confucius and his followers condemned. These overlords (Pa) were five in number, but their authority was not admitted to be part of the true feudal order, as it was an unconstitutional growth. The first hegemony was that of Ch'i (685-643 B.C.), it then passed successively to Sung (650-637 B.C.), T'sin(636-628 B.C.),Ch'in(659-621 B.C.), and Ch'u(613-591 B.C.). These dates are those of the rulers who achieved the hegemony, and do not strictly agree with the exact periods in which their authority was acknowledged. The Chou Kings were forced to accord their approval to an invasion of their own prerogatives which they were powerless to prevent.

The feudal hierarchy was organised in five grades distinguished by titles which have been translated as equivalent to the European, Duke, Marquis, Count, Viscount and Baron. In the early feudal age the title of Duke (*kung*) was restricted to the rulers of the greater states or to those connected with the royal house, Lu, Ch'ên, Chêng, Ch'i, Yen and Sung. In later years these states were not the most powerful and the upstart rulers of other states assumed such titles as they considered suited their dignity, until in 325 B.C. all the surviving rulers usurped the royal title itself.

A lesser title, held by rulers of the innumerable very small fiefs, was "lord" (*chun*), and the aristocracy in general were known as the *chun tzŭ* the "sons of the lords." *Chun tzŭ* is the word which Confucius and other philosophers use to denote the man of virtue and education, the ideal representative of their doctrines. It has been translated as "superior man" or "aristocratic man," but the true meaning in the feudal age was simply an aristocrat, a member of the limited number of hereditary noble clans to whom all power and privilege in feudal society was exclusively reserved. This very important distinction has been slurred over by the use, in later ages, of the term *chun tzŭ* to mean an educated man or scholar, without distinction of origin. Society in the feudal age, however, was organised on a basis of noble descent and clanship utterly unlike the society of later ages in which descent was in itself of no social significance. To understand the feudal age it is necessary to use the feudal terms in their true technical sense, not as interpreted in later centuries. The nobility of feudal China owed their position to descent, and not to education. They were members of a widespread clan system, which was strictly defined and sharply separated from the mass of the people, the *min* or "lesser men," *hsiao jên*, of the classics. These noble clans were not very numerous. Only twenty-two are mentioned in the *Ch'un Ch'iu*, and it is improbable that there were many others. To this nobility, founded upon ancient descent and the ownership of land, all political power was reserved. They alone filled the offices at the feudal courts. They alone commanded the armies in war. The people had no political rights; they cultivated the land on behalf of their masters, paid taxes to the prince, and served as soldiers in his armies. They could not rise from this humble status by wealth or ability. They played only a small part in the religious life of the state. The elaborate ancestor worship of which we have records was the privilege of the land-owning clans, just as the higher rites of sacrifice to the gods of the soil and crops were reserved for a prince who had absolute power over some territory, however small. Princely rank depended on such lordship, and was intimately bound up with these religious observances. The phrase by which the historians record the fall of a feudal house is "the sacrifices were discontinued"—and this catastrophe only occurred when the prince had been deprived of his last territory.

Though the aristocracy was founded on descent, education was much honoured, and almost confined to the nobility. The *chün tzǔ* were not unlettered nobles like the feudal barons of mediæval Europe. They were polished aristocrats, courtiers who served as counsellors, officers, and governors in time of peace, and as generals and warriors in war. The nobles fought in war chariots, mounted by three men, a charioteer and a "right hand man," with the chief in the centre. The mass of the popular levy fought on foot around their masters' chariots. Archery was a noble sport, strictly organised in ceremonial contests. The education of the nobles also included music, arithmetic and poetry, and most important of all, the strict fulfilment of the rites and ceremonies which governed all social relations. In the presence of his prince, of his superior officers, of the senior members of his clan and family, the *chün tzǔ's* conduct was regulated by an established and minute code of decorum, which, in turn, was related to the religious observances by which the security of the state and the harmony of Heaven and Earth was maintained. Chivalry, the necessary corollary of a feudal community, was in ancient China more than the courtesy of a polished society. It was an expression of the moral order approved by Heaven. It was not merely ungenerous, but wicked to treat a conquered foe with the last severity. Heaven disapproved of extreme measures. The virtuous man was moderate in victory, the ruthless victor incurred the displeasure of the gods and would ultimately suffer for his infraction of the moral code.

In 598 B.C. the King of Ch'u, using as pretext the fact that the minister of Ch'ên had assassinated his prince, invaded that kingdom in order, as he said, to punish the assassin. But when he found himself master of Ch'ên he annexed the conquered state to his own kingdom. One of his counsellors, however, refused to congratulate him, saying:

"O King, because Chêng Shu criminally murdered his sovereign you called the nobles to arms in the name of justice, but afterwards you seized the kingdom to profit by its wealth. How can you expect to dominate in the empire? That is why I cannot congratulate you."

The King of Ch'u, acknowledging his error, reinstated the heir of Ch'ên and left the kingdom in its former state of independence.

In 638 B.C. the Duke of Sung was at war with Ch'u. The armies met on the banks of a river. As the enemy were very strong, the counsellors of Sung urged the Duke to attack them before they had completed the passage of the river. The Duke refused. When the army of Ch'u had passed the river, the counsellors urged the Duke to attack them before their ranks were formed. Again the Duke refused. When the enemy were at last ready for battle, the Duke of Sung gave the order to attack, and was utterly defeated. His subjects were furious and remonstrated with him for his folly, but the Duke replied:

"The sage does not crush the feeble, nor give the order for attack until the enemy have formed their ranks."

Duke Wên of Tsin, who had been nineteen years in exile before he came to the throne, had received a kind welcome during his wanderings from the King of Ch'u. Unable at the time to make any return for this hospitality, he had made a vow that if ever he came to the throne, and found himself at war with Ch'u, when the armies came into contact, he would withdraw three days' journey before giving battle. Years later, when he had at last come into his heritage, Ch'u and Tsin became involved in war. When the armies met, Duke Wên, in spite of the protests of his officers, withdrew three days' journey, and then standing firm, gave battle and defeated the army of Ch'u (632 B.C.)

In 663 B.C. the Hegemon, Duke Huan of Ch'i, had assisted Yen in a war against the Jung barbarians. When returning to his state the Duke of Yen accompanied him, and crossed the Ch'i frontier. The Duke of Ch'i said:

"Except the Son of Heaven, when the princes accompany each other, they must not leave their territories. I cannot fail to fulfil the rites towards Yen."

So he marked off the land up to the point to which the Duke of Yen had arrived, and made a present of it to Yen. Had he permitted the Duke of Yen to accompany him into his own state, it would have appeared to be an infringement of the prerogative of the Son of Heaven, who alone had the right to make a prince leave his own territory.

The exclusive privileges and monopoly of political power enjoyed by the noble clans raises the question whether these rights were not founded upon an ancient conquest. It might be suggested that the clans represented the descendants of the Chou people who had conquered and imposed their rule upon the aboriginal inhabitants, whose descendants formed the mass of the people. If this was the case it is clear that the Shang people were not included in the serf population. The ruling house of Sung were descended from the kings of the Shang dynasty, and the K'ung family, that of Confucius himself, who were certainly aristocrats in Lu, were themselves descended from a cadet branch of this princely family of Sung. Whether the nobility represented the descendants of a conquering race or whether they were of native growth, in the early feudal age the states did not occupy the whole area of the Yellow River basin. They were separated from each other by uninhabited marsh lands, by mountain regions still inhabited by the barbarian tribes called Jung and I, and by sparsely peopled tracts of heath. Even in the plains there were independent settlements of Jung and I.

With the rise of the population in the Chinese states the power of the princes began to be felt in these outlying regions. Walled cities, the characteristic urban settlement of the Chinese culture, were multiplied. The rivers were embanked and the marsh lands reclaimed. The hill tribes were conquered and subdued; the barbarian settlements in the plain were subjected to Chinese rule. The states which had previously been but loosely in contact, with plenty of land available for colonisation, came into close touch with their neighbours, who had expanded in the same way. Thus began a rivalry which gradually became more intense until it destroyed the feudal system in a life and death struggle for supreme power. The contest developed slowly over centuries. At first the wars of the states were conducted with due regard to the chivalric code; campaigns were not pressed to a decisive conclusion. The conqueror retired after a raid content with the honour of victory and the movable spoils. Towards the end of the Ch'un Ch'iu period, the wars began to assume a more ruthless aspect. The small fiefs, of which little record remains, fell victims to the aggressive policy of their greater neighbours. The process is dimly recorded as it nears completion. Often the conquest of some small fief is very nearly all that is known about it, though scholars have laboured to establish the location of the capital and the clan to which its lords belonged. Up to the very end of the Ch'un Ch'iu period no one of the princely houses had "seen its sacrifices discontinued." The first major victim was Ch'ên, which was annexed by Ch'u in 479 B.C. That event, which occurred in the year that Confucius died, marks the end of the Ch'un Ch'iu period and the beginning of the agony of feudalism, the period called that of the Warring States, which endured for 260 years, and ended in the conquest of the whole empire by the state of Ch'in (221 B.C.).

The intense struggle for overlordship which developed among the states of the Chinese confederacy in the latter part of the Ch'un Ch'iu period led directly to the rise of the border kingdoms, which had hitherto been regarded as outside the true Chinese pale. It was not a coincidence that the first major Chinese state to be destroyed fell a victim to semi-barbarous Ch'u. Ch'in in the west and Ch'u in the south had profited by the quarrels of their Chinese neighbours. Both kingdoms had learned a sterner code of warfare in their struggle with the barbarians of the west and south. When these enemies had been reduced, the two border states turned their ambitions upon the states of the Middle Kingdom. The rise of Ch'in was steady and uninterrupted. Expanding westward at the expense of the barbarians, the rulers of Ch'in were for a long time content to leave the Chinese states to their quarrels. Their eastward progress was moreover for some centuries checked by the powerful Chinese state of Tsin, which occupied not only Shansi, but considerable areas on the west bank of the Yellow River, in the modern province of Shensi. It was not until internal troubles ruined and divided Tsin, that Ch'in really embarked upon her career of conquest in the east. The conquest of the non-

Chinese states of Shu and Pa in Szechuan (316 B.C.) gave the western kingdom resources far in excess of any rival among the Chinese confederacy, and turned the flank of her only serious competitor, Ch'u.

The history of Ch'u was more chequered. As early as 606 B.C., the King of Ch'u after a great raid to the north, had sent an ambassador to the Chou Court to ask questions about the size and weight of the nine tripods—a clear indication that he contemplated assuming the royal dignity.*

A few years later (597 B.C.) the King of Ch'u besieged the Count of Chêng in his capital and forced him to surrender at discretion, but, in accordance with the chivalric traditions of the time, the fallen ruler was spared and restored to his throne. Thus, the conquests of the King of Ch'u had no lasting result. His successors were checked by the rise of the barbarous kingdom of Wu, which, in 522 B.C., became very formidable under the guidance of a minister named Wu Tzŭ-hsiu, who was a refugee from Ch'u. His father and elder brother had been unjustly put to death by the King of Ch'u, and Wu Tzŭ-hsiu directed his policy of wreaking vengeance for this wrong. At last, in 506 B.C., the army of Wu captured the capital of Ch'u. Wu Tzŭ-hsiu had the corpse of the dead King of Ch'u disinterred, and flogged it with a whip to satisfy the spirits of his murdered relations. When his master, the King of Wu, ignoring the danger which menaced his kingdom from its barbarous neighbour, Yüeh (in modern Chekiang province), turned his attention to the Chinese kingdoms, Wu Tzŭ-hsiu consistently opposed these profitless campaigns. The people of Wu were a seafaring folk, and their raids on the north were made by sea and along the navigable rivers. These campaigns, however, did not add to the territory or strength of Wu, and the minister, realising that they were exhausting the state and preparing the way for a conquest by the King of Yüeh, took the precaution to send his son to Ch'i to be out of danger. The King of

*The nine bronze tripods, which legend relates had been cast by Yü the Great, founder of the Hsia dynasty, were the emblems of sovereignty. They had traditionally been transmitted to all the three dynasties, and were retained by the Chou Kings until the destruction of their dynasty. The rulers of Ch'u had in fact assumed the royal title in their own country for many years, but this dignity was not acknowledged elsewhere.

Wu, furious at this proof of lack of confidence, ordered Wu Tzŭ-hsiu to commit suicide. The minister died, saying: "Tear out my eyes and fix them on the gate of [the capital of] Wu, so that I may see the victorious entry of Yüeh." Some years later his prediction was fulfilled, and the meteoric kingdom of Wu was destroyed by its barbarous neighbour. The King of Wu, as he took his life when all hope was gone, "veiled his face so that he might not have to endure the reproachful looks of Wu Tzŭ-hsiu" in the world of shades.

Fan Li, counsellor of the ferocious King of Yüeh, and the chief instrument of his victory over Wu, was wiser than Wu Tzŭ-hsiu. As soon as Wu was conquered, he took all his possessions and fled from Yüeh to the civilised state of Ch'i. Explaining his strange flight in the hour when he was most honoured in Yüeh, he wrote to a friend in verse:

> "When the birds are slain,
> The bow is cast aside,
> When the fleet deer is caught,
> The hounds are cooked.

"The King of Yüeh is a bird with a curved beak [a bird of prey]. One may endure hardships with him, but it is not wise to share honours with such a man."

Fan Li was an exceptional character. After his flight, he settled in Ch'i and engaged in commerce, becoming the richest merchant in China. In spite of the general admiration for his sagacity, he consistently refused to take office again, and even moved into another state to avoid the importunities of the people of Ch'i. The romantic adventures of Fan Li contain a large element of folk-lore. They had probably grown into a well-known heroic tale long before history was written as a record of ascertained facts. The whole story of Wu and Yüeh is marked by this romantic quality, suggesting that it was first known as a historical romance, freely adapted from a traditional story.

The disastrous war with Wu had checked the power of Ch'u at the very time when the increasing disorder among the states of the Middle Kingdom was opening an opportunity for the other powerful border kingdom, Ch'in. In 453 B.C., Tsin, the only state which could have prevented the progress of Ch'in, was partitioned between three of its great families, the prince reduced to a figure-head, and ultimately deprived of the last shadow of power. In 403 B.C. the three usurpers succeeded in obtaining formal investiture from the Son of Heaven, and were henceforward ranked among the feudal princes. Their states took the names of the families themselves and were known as Han, Wei, and Chao, collectively called "the Three Tsin."

This event was typical of the great change in the relationship between the prince and the *chün tzǔ* which had occurred under the influence of the turbulent conditions prevailing in the period of the Warring States. Not only were ancient states falling victims to their ruthless neighbours, but the powerful aristocratic families rose up inside the states till their power overshadowed that of the prince himself. In Tsin this rise of the great families led to disastrous civil wars and ultimately to partition. In Ch'i (386 B.C.) the ancient ruling house was dethroned by an ambitious minister, assisted by his widespread family, which had long monopolised all power and authority. In Lu the prince became the plaything of rival aristocratic families whose intrigues and ambitions reduced the government to anarchy.

The old kingdoms, such as had not been destroyed by their rivals, sank into impotence. Sung, after a valiant effort to win a dominant position in the south-east was conquered by Ch'i in 286 B.C. Thenceforward the struggle for supremacy was confined to the "Six Kingdoms," Ch'in, Ch'u, Ch'i and the "Three Tsin" (Han, Wei and Chao). Yen, which continued to exist, was too remote to be involved in these wars until the conquest of "the Three Tsin" brought this northern kingdom into contact with Ch'in. (Map 3).

If the story of the period of the Warring States was merely a record of anarchy and violence it would not be worthy of detailed attention in a cultural history, but this period of military strife was also marked by a far more memorable contest, the rivalry of the philosophers. The rise of the "Hundred Schools" as they came to be called, coincided with the death struggle of the feudal age. The development was not a coincidence. The general anarchy into which the feudal world was fast dissolving stimulated

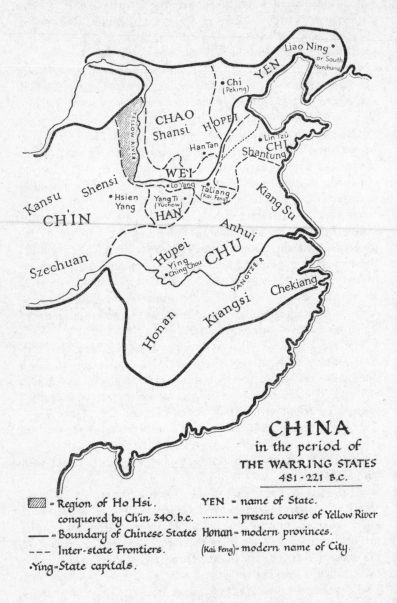

MAP 3. *China in the Period of the Warring States.*

intellectual activity, for provincial isolation was broken down, old loyalties destroyed, and established institutions overthrown. It was natural that men should begin to question the world order which had hitherto been accepted as a matter of course. While some schools* defended the past and attributed the troubles of the age to the manifest breaches of the old ethical code, others groped for a new morality on which to base the changing world. Still another school of thought turned away from the chaos of human affairs and preached a doctrine which found true enlightenment in a renunciation of all participation in the activities of mundane society.

The influence of these scholars and their disciples was as potent in shaping the new era as that of the generals who were destroying the old feudal states. A new class arose, the "wandering scholars," of which Confucius himself may be said to have been the first. When the sage resigned his office in his native state of Lu on account of the licentious character of the prince, he wandered successively through the neighbouring states of Wey, Ts'ao, Sung, Chêng, Ch'ên, Ts'ai and Ch'u, seeking a prince who would listen to his instructions and put his doctrines into practice. In later years his example was very generally followed, though not all the wandering scholars were disinterested statesmen in search of the ideal king. More often indeed, they were political adventurers drawn from the unemployed aristocracy of the lesser states, who were seeking power and advancement in the service of some warring King. The kings themselves valued such counsellors more than the true philosophers. Mencius (c. 370-334 B.C.) found that the King of Wei was only interested in schemes by which he could conquer his rivals, and did not appreciate the sage's admonitions and philosophical discourses. Although it is the writings of the true philosophers that have in part survived, there can be no doubt that it was the scheming intriguers who really moulded the policies of the time.

These wandering politicians were no longer bound by any tie of loyalty to their native princes. The destruction of many of the old states had broken down the feudal bond between prince and *chün tzŭ*. The aristocrat who found his native land ruled by some

*The views of these schools are described in Chapter IV.

alien conquering prince of Ch'u or Wei no longer felt that hereditary and life-long duty of loyalty and service which had formed the strength of the old society. He set out to travel the world in search of fortune. The border states, Ch'in and Ch'u, were at first the goal of many of these wandering scholars. A statesman from the more civilised central states was accorded a warm welcome in these countries and quickly rose to the highest posts. It is noteworthy that the most famous ministers of the princes of Ch'in all came from the eastern states.* The generals, on the contrary, were usually members of the native aristocratic clans, upon whose unswerving loyalty the prince could rely, but his council came to be largely composed of adventurers from all parts of China.

The corrosive influence of this new class upon feudal ideas and institutions was of the first importance. The wandering scholars were bound by no lasting loyalties, were attached by no sentiment of patriotism to the states they served, and were not restrained by any feelings of ancient chivalry. They proposed and carried out schemes of the blackest treachery. Frequently they secretly served two princes at once, playing off the policy of the one against the other. Moving from kingdom to kingdom, always with some eloquent and intricate scheme to propose, they forgot the particularism of the old feudal aristocracy, and envisaged plans to reduce the whole empire to the obedience of the sovereign they served. This was the bait they held out to their temporary masters, it was no longer hegemony, but empire, which had become the aim of state policy. Their lives were tortuous and their deaths, too often, terrible.†

Against this evil, and the general disrespect for the ancient moral order and chivalric code, the school of Confucius protested strongly, but in vain. The master had lived when the feudal system, though rotten to the core, still stood intact. He had preached a return to the golden age of Wu, founder of the Chou

*Kung-sun Yang, the reforming minister to whose work the success of Ch'in was largely due was a native of Wei and a scion of the ruling family of Wey. *Cf.* Chapter IV.

†Kung-sun Yang, for instance, was torn to pieces between four chariots when he fell out of favour with the Duke of Ch'in.

dynasty; he had striven to recall the princes to their forgotten duty to the Son of Heaven, and had rebuked the ambitions of "those who were doubly subjects"—the intriguing aristocrats who should have served both their princes and the Son of Heaven with a lifelong loyalty. In the new age men cared for none of these things. The Son of Heaven was now but a petty prince, the weakest of all the Warring States, saved from destruction only by a lingering respect for an ancient name. The despotic rulers of the militarised states roused no feeling of loyalty in their conquered subjects. The rulers—from 325 B.C. all had usurped the title of King—might pay lip service to the doctrines of the ancient sages, but in practice they confided in schemers who promised them victory over their rivals. The swollen kingdoms, organised solely for war and conquest, crushed the old local customs, ignored the sufferings of their subjects, and disregarded the teachings of the sages. The armies counter-marched across the northern plains, the wandering scholars travelled from court to court, busy with their leagues and plans; both trampled under foot the ancient social organisation of feudal China.

Wu Ling, King of Chao (325-299 B.C.) was one of the rulers who was least trammelled by respect for old customs. In 307 B.C. he made an innovation in his kingdom which marks a significant advance in the military methods of the ancient Chinese, the change from war chariots to the use of cavalry. The kingdom of Chao, in the northern part of Shansi province, was a border state stretching to the Mongolian steppe, then inhabited by the nomad people known to the Chinese as Hu. From experience gained in war with these barbarians the King was inspired to decree that henceforward his subjects must dress in the manner of the Hu, a costume better suited to horse riding than the flowing robes of the Chinese. This change was made to facilitate the organisation of squadrons of mounted archers, which he believed would give his armies a great advantage over the conservative methods of his rivals. The decree was strongly opposed by many of the nobility of Chao, who declared that by dressing in the costume of the Hu, the King was separating his country from the Chinese confederacy and adopting manners only suitable for barbarians. Wu Ling would not be dissuaded and enforced his innovation. Although the process is not clearly mentioned in the history of other states, it is evident that in time the example of Chao was generally followed, for the armies of the Han period were well equipped with cavalry, while the old war chariot had fallen into disuse.

No state was more heedless of the ancient code than Ch'in. Formerly it had been despised as half barbarous. Now, mighty and victorious, the rude hill men of the west pursued their calculated plan of conquest with supreme contempt for chivalrous restraints. Wholesale massacres marked their victories. In 259 B.C. the army of Chao was starved into surrender at Ch'ang P'ing in southern Shansi, and the Ch'in generals exterminated the captive host to the number of 400,000 men. Again and again the annals record the victories of Ch'in, adding "a hundred thousand heads were cut off." It is true that the Chinese have a habit of using round numbers as a superlative, and no doubt the figures given for the massacre at Ch'ang P'ing and other battles are an example of this usage. Nevertheless, it is recorded that the state of Chao was almost deprived of its able-bodied male population by the battle of Ch'ang P'ing. The Ch'in armies were certainly ruthless conquerors, and the terror they inspired magnified their atrocities.

Treachery was as profitable to Ch'in as massacre. In 299 B.C. the King of Ch'u was invited to an interview with the King of Ch'in, faithlessly seized, and kept a prisoner until his death. Year by year, as "a silkworm devours a mulberry leaf" in the graphic phrase of the Han historian Ssŭ-ma Ch'ien, Ch'in annexed the towns and territories of her neighbours. In 256 B.C., the King of the royal house of Chou, the Son of Heaven himself, was despoiled of his last possessions and "saw his sacrifices discontinued." The Chou dynasty was extinct, and ten years later, in 246 B.C., the future First Emperor (Shih Huang Ti) became King of Ch'in and rapidly completed the task at which his predecessors had so long laboured. One by one, divided and mutually antagonistic to the last, the feudal kingdoms fell. Han in 230 B.C., then Chao (228 B.C.), Ch'i (226 B.C.), Wei (225 B.C.), Ch'u in 223 B.C., and lastly, in 222 B.C., Yen, hitherto protected by its remote position. The King of Ch'in was undisputed master of the whole Middle Kingdom; feudalism was dead.

This result was profoundly antipathetic to the deepest instinct of the Chinese people of that time. The voice of protest, unheeded in the counsel of the King, rose steadily, and the school which had most openly opposed the rise of military despotism, that of Confucius, had for this very reason gained the widest popularity among the educated class. When the fall of the last feudal kingdom crowned the victorious career of Ch'in, the new universal autocrat found his ideas and his authority still obstinately disputed by a more elusive enemy, the widespread school of philosophy which relied upon the pen rather than the sword to revile and oppose the new forms of government. Military conquest was not enough; the First Emperor found it necessary to go further and root out the feudal spirit in its last literary stronghold. The conquest of the feudal states had as its sequel the burning of the books and the proscription of history.

Chapter IV

THE "HUNDRED SCHOOLS" OF PHILOSOPHY

THE period of the "Warring States" (481-221 B.C.) was a restless age of political disorder and social disintegration. It was also the most glorious age in the history of Chinese thought, a period when ethical and philosophical systems arose which have exercised a lasting influence on the culture of the Far East, similar to the influence of classical Greece on European civilisation. The parallel is indeed striking. The age of the philosophers in China was almost exactly contemporary with that of the Greek philosophers, moreover, the political circumstances which stimulated the rise of the philosophic schools were not altogether dissimilar.

It was no accident that the rise of the schools coincided with an age of political change. Though on a larger scale, the Chinese kingdoms of the feudal age represented a development akin to the Greek city states. In both countries the individual states felt themselves to be part of a larger cultural unit, Hellas, or "Chu Hsia"—"All the Hsia." And in both cases the aim of the thinkers who founded the schools of philosophy was in the first instance political, an endeavour to discover some principle of moral authority which could unite this cultural group under the harmonious sway of an ideal government. In China, as in Greece, the search for this principle led the deeper thinkers further afield, until their speculations revolved upon the great questions of the origin of the universe and the purpose of human existence. The parallel development in China and Greece ended, too, in a similar tragedy The philosophers failed to find the remedy for the evils they saw so clearly, and the cultured states of eastern China, like the cities of Greece, fell under the hard domination of a warlike people whose only contribution to civilisation was a capacity for military organisation and the ability to frame and enforce a rigid code of laws. It is noteworthy that the one school which flourished in the "Land within the Passes," military Ch'in, was the School of the Legists, in which Li Ssŭ, the man responsible for the burning of the books and the ruin of the Hundred Schools, received his training.

These points of agreement between the development of classical Greece and China, though suggestive, cannot be pushed too far. In some fundamental matters the mind of China and Greece did not meet. The conception of political liberty for the citizen class and its corollary, democratic government, never found a place in any Chinese system. Nor was there any parallel development of arts and poetry such as made the classical age in Greece supreme in every field of intellectual endeavour. In China the arts and poetry did not reach their highest perfection until many centuries after the age of the philosophers. While the Greek culture flowered suddenly and reached its highest development in every field at the same time, the Chinese civilisation grew slowly over a long course of centuries, each great dynastic period contributing a new unfolding of the national genius.

In China the form of the political organisation was never questioned. Monarchy was accepted as the natural and inevitable vehicle of sovereignty. It was rather the moral foundations on which the monarchy should be based that were the subject of the rivalry of the Hundred Schools. This preoccupation with moral principles rather than with political forms is characteristic of all Chinese thought, and is in sharp contrast to the point of view adopted by western peoples, who tend to devise political forms first and adjust moral principles to them afterwards. All Chinese thinkers held that the moral character of the ruler was the factor which determined the value of his government, none ever advanced the view that a change in the form of government would help to establish the rule of virtue and benevolence.

On the other hand, the Chinese did not invest the monarch with the attributes of divinity and deny the subject any right but that of existence, and any duty but blind obedience. Their conception of monarchy approached more nearly to that which prevailed in Mediæval Europe. Above the King, who was not a god, was T'ien, "Heaven," or Shang Ti, "The Supreme Ancestor," and the earthly sovereign was but his deputy, standing in the relation of an adopted son who had received the Mandate of Heaven (T'ien Ming), by virtue of which he ruled over the earth. This "Mandate" was not a patent of divine right, irrevocable and eternal. It was conferred upon a sage King whose virtue had entitled him to act as the deputy of Heaven. His descendants enjoyed it only so long as their virtue made them worthy representatives of the Supreme Ancestor. A tyrant who misruled his kingdom, and did not possess the virtues of justice, benevolence and sincerity was deprived of the Mandate of Heaven, and rebellion against his rule was not crime, but the just punishment of outraged Heaven acting through the medium of the rebels. Thus, Mencius, in a famous passage, when questioned about the execution of the last Shang King by Wu, founder of the Chou dynasty, denied that this act could be described as the assassination of a prince by his minister. He replied: "I have heard of the execution of the fellow Chou (last King of Shang); I have not heard that a prince was assassinated by a minister." Chou, for his tyranny and crimes, was no longer fit to be accounted a King. He had lost the Mandate of Heaven which had already been conferred upon Wu, founder of the next dynasty. Thus, he was "executed," and Wu was not a "minister" or subject, but the true King by the appointment of Heaven.

For the Greek conception of liberty, the prerogative of the citizen class, the Chinese nobility, who likewise were the sole possessors of political power, had loyalty (*chung*), the loyalty of the son to his father and clansmen, of the officer to his prince, of the prince to the Son of Heaven. This was the principle upon which the feudal system was founded, with its corollary that the ruler to deserve loyalty must govern with justice, benevolence and sincerity. The noble clans were not subject to the rule of law. Law was a system of penalties devised for, and applicable only to, the common people. The *chün tzü* were controlled by their own code of chivalry and morality, known as *li*, the rites. An offence against the *li*, if serious, could only be expiated by the suicide of the offender. Suicide was thus a noble act, the way in which the nobleman wiped out disgrace.

This system worked well when the courts of the feudal princes were still numerous, intimate and local. The pressure of public opinion—the opinion of his fellow-nobles—the honour of his clan, and the authority of the prince, forced the ambitious noble to conform to the *li*. With the conquest of the smaller states, the decay of the royal power, and the usurpation of great nobles, the whole foundation of feudalism collapsed. Loyalty became a meaningless term when every minister served the prince with an eye to his own personal ambition, and was ready to move to the court of a rival if the chances of preferment seemed better. The princes, by flouting the Son of Heaven and conquering their weak neighbours, set an example of violence and unscrupulous ambition which was soon imitated by their own great officers. Government was no longer in accordance with the moral principles upon which it was supposed to be based. In protest against this state of affairs the Hundred Schools arose. Thus, whereas in Greece the philosophers prospered as the result of the triumph of free institutions in the city states, in China the philosophers appeared at the same time as the decay of the political system and the spread of lawlessness and disorder.

The name "The Hundred Schools" must not be taken literally as meaning that there were in fact no less than a hundred competing systems of moral and political philosophy. Every sage or philosopher was attended by disciples who formed his "school," wrote down his sayings, and gradually composed the canon of his works. It was in this way that the philosophic books grew out of the schools rather than from the hand of one single teacher. The followers of Confucius, for example, not only compiled his teaching into a book, the Analects, *Lün Yü*, but also in time attributed to their founder the authorship of the ancient writings which he had held in especial veneration. The real authorship of the early books cannot be known, nor, indeed, is it at all likely that they came from the pen of any one teacher.

The philosophers can, however, be classed in a few broad categories, though when such words as Taoist or Confucian are used in the classical period they must not be understood to mean adherents of a rigid body of doctrine upholding or opposing an accepted orthodox system. The followers of Confucius himself were traditionalists, interpreting ancient texts in the light of their own views on morality and political philosophy. Confucius lived from 551 to 479 B.C., and was the earliest philosopher of whom definite record remains. The Taoists in later centuries claimed a certain Lao Tzŭ as their founder, and attributed to him the authorship of the *Tao Tê Ching*, the best known classic of this doctrine. Lao

Tzǔ however cannot be regarded as an historical figure, nor his supposed date (*circa* 590 B.C.) as anything but a fiction. The authorship of the *Tao Tê Ching* is unknown, and the date of the book is certainly not earlier than the 3rd century, about 240 B.C.*

The later schools, which arose in the 4th century B.C., were the Mohists, followers of Mo Tzǔ (500-420 B.C.) and the School of Law, of which the earliest exponent was Wei Yang (d. 338 B.C.), Lord of Shang and minister to the Duke of Ch'in. While the date of Confucius may be regarded as established, the others are based upon traditions which lack contemporary confirmation. There were also a number of philosophers, such as Yang Chu and Hsun Tzǔ who cannot be classed as either Taoist, Confucian, Mohist or followers of the School of Law. In some cases their doctrines have only been preserved in fragmentary form and they are best known by the hostile comments of rivals whose teaching has been accepted in later times as orthodox. As it is not possible in the limits of a single chapter to examine all the philosophies in great detail, an attempt will be made to summarise the teaching of the leading schools and give typical examples of their doctrine.

The Taoists represented a revolt from the trammels of a decadent society. They preached a renunciation of the world, a return to primitive simplicity. They held all teaching and active propagation of their doctrines to be useless, and indeed harmful. The sage should himself find the Tao (the Way), and then by his passive example lead men to follow him. They regarded organised society as an evil in itself, and denied the possibility and the value of any attempt to reform it. Such a doctrine was not offered to common men. Only the sage could find the Tao. It was aristocratic and necessarily exclusive.

Confucius was essentially a political philosopher. He sought the reformation of the world by a return to the virtue of a golden age, that of Yao and Shun, the sage rulers of remote antiquity, revived by the founders of the Chou dynasty. The only way to put the world right was to return to this primitive virtue. Consequently the Confucians prized the literature of the past and preserved it. They were true reactionaries in that they held

*The date suggested by Mr. Waley, *The Way and Its Power*. 1934. p. 86.

firmly to the belief that the past contained the model on which present and all future society should be patterned.

The Mohists, a school which passed into complete oblivion after the Ch'in revolution, taught doctrines which were morally the most sublime of all the ancient Chinese schools. Mo Tzŭ believed that the remedy for the ills of the world was the practice of all-embracing, universal love. Not merely the narrow love of clansmen and the loyalty of feudal society, but an equal love reaching beyond the family and the state. "The man of Ch'u is my brother." Consequently he held no brief for feudal society, condemned war as the greatest of crimes, and looked for a world-wide kingdom founded on love. This system, preached some five centuries before the birth of Christ, contained all the distinctive doctrines of Christianity, except that of immortal life for the blessed, and eternal damnation for the wicked. Mo Tzŭ promised no heaven and threatened no hell.

The school of Yang Chu has left less literature than any other, yet we know from Mencius that it was in his day one of the most widespread. The fact proves the extreme misery and despair of thinking men in the age of the Warring States, for Yang Chu erected pure selfishness into the cardinal virtue. Going beyond the Taoists, Yang Chu regarded all human activity with complete indifference. Evil and good, virtue and vice, were meaningless terms, human society and its ills were no concern of the sage, whose sole pursuit should be his own pleasure. He declared that if society could be saved, or ruined, by lifting his little finger, he would not make the effort. It was perhaps because his doctrine was so completely at variance with the ultimately triumphant Confucian teaching that Yang Chu's teaching has only survived in fragmentary form.

The school of the Legists, the last to arise, was not strictly a philosophic school at all. On the contrary, the central doctrine of this school was the futility and baneful effect of philosophic disputation. As it exercised a very profound influence on Chinese culture it is fitting that it should be discussed in relation to its opponents. Coming after the nihilistic teaching of such men as Yang Chu on the one hand, and the idealistic teaching of Confucius and Mo Tzŭ on the other, the Legists rejected all these systems and sought a new principle of authority, not in morality, but in the sovereign power of a reorganised state.

Following Hsün Tzŭ, a philosopher who had differed from Confucius and Mencius on this point, the Legists* declared that the nature of man was evil, not good, and in consequence it was useless to attempt to reform society by preaching idealistic doctrines. The history of the past, they further declared, was of little value as a pattern for present policy, for times had changed. They therefore exalted the law and the authority of the state. A perfect prince was not likely to be a frequent occurrence, so his authority must be upheld by severe and rigid laws, equally applicable to all his subjects. Then the reign of a weakling would not be the signal for intrigues and rebellions, for the law, operating irrespective of the character of the ruler, would shield him from his mistakes.

As a consequence of the triumph of the Legist school under the Ch'in dynasty the records of their opponents suffered the famous catastrophe of the burning of the books. Much of the ancient literature thus perished for ever, and of what was afterwards collected and re-edited, a great part is now regarded as spurious or corrupt. In order to give a just idea of the materials which survive, a brief mention of some of the principal ancient books will be given. The best known Taoist books which can be regarded as authentic, are the *Tao Tê Ching*, a work of the 3rd century B.C., and the book of Chuang Tzŭ, which contains the teaching of that philosopher as well as other matter which is either the work of later Taoists or interpolations.

The Confucian School, on which the Han restorers of the ancient literature lavished their labours, is naturally better represented. This literature, usually dignified by the name of the Classics, contains not only the actual teaching of Confucius, Mencius and Hsün Tzŭ, but also many ancient books which the Confucian reverence for the past saved from oblivion. Of these the most important are the *Shu Ching*, or Book of History, a collection of very old documents, speeches, orations and harangues which are the earliest literary source for Chinese history. The book suffered many vicissitudes in the Ch'in period and is now known

*Han Fei Tzŭ, a prominent Legist, is said to have been a pupil of Hsün Tzŭ.

only in part, and from two versions. The text called the "modern", because it was transcribed in the script of the Han dynasty, was obtained from Fu Shêng, a very aged scholar who remembered twenty-nine chapters by heart.* The second or "old text" was found in the wall of Confucius' own house, where it had been hidden by the head of the family, his descendant. It contained sixteen chapters not found in the "modern" text.† Other Confucian books suffered similar fates, but have come down in better preservation than the *Shu Ching*, which would seem to have been singled out for destruction with especial fury.

The Book of Poetry, *Shih Ching*, is one of these. It is a collection of very ancient poems, hymns and songs, from different states of ancient China, and the anthology was attributed by Han scholars, without evidence, to Confucius himself. As evidence of the ancient customs and beliefs the Book of Poetry is of great value, though the traditional interpretation of these poems cannot always be admitted.

The *I Ching* (Book of Changes) is a work of great antiquity which was used as a book of divination. It is in fact not one text but two, which have been run together. One part of the book is an omen text giving rhymed interpretations of ordinary country omens such as:

> "If a ram butts a hedge
> and cannot go back or in,
> your undertaking will completely fail,"‡

*According to another account he had hidden his books during the proscription, and in later years found only the fragment of twenty-nine chapters in the ruins of his old house. This text appeared in the reign of Han Wên Ti (179-157 B.C.). Ten of these chapters are known to be substitutes for lost chapters, but which the substitutes are has not been determined.

†The authenticity of the present text of the "old" *Shu Ching* has been denied. The question is highly complicated, but the truth would seem to be that it represents a number of disconnected citations pieced together from fragmentary documents, an explanation easily credible when it is remembered that in ancient China books were written on strips of bamboo tied together. When the strings had perished the order of the book was lost, and could only be retrieved with great difficulty. This question is very fully discussed by Chavannes in the preface to his translation of the Shih Chi. Chavannes: *Memoires Historiques de Se-Ma Ts'ien*. Paris. The accounts of the manner in which these texts were recovered or re-collected are no doubt largely legendary.

‡A. Waley: "The Book of Changes." *Bulletin of the Museum of Far Eastern Antiquities*. No. 5. Stockholm. 1934.

which bear a strong resemblance to the age-old peasant lore of all countries. The other part of the text is a divination manual containing formulæ such as have been deciphered on the oracle bones and tortoise-shells. Ten appendices were added to this book by followers of the Confucian School, but not by Confucius himself as the Chinese scholars of later centuries long believed. The importance of these additions is due to the fact that the Sung scholars who in the 11th and 12th centuries re-shaped Confucian doctrine, took the appendices of the *I Ching* as texts upon which to found their teaching. *Cf.* Chapter XX.

The divination text of the *I Ching* devotes much space to the interpretation of the 8 trigrams or Pa Kua. These symbols, traditionally invented by Wên, father of Wu the first Chou King, have at all times played a great part in divination, and in later times and at the present day the design is used both for decoration (as on porcelain) and for protective purposes. It is to this end that it is so often hung up in houses (Fig. 7).

The *Li Chi* (Book of Rites) and *Chou Li* are two books on ritual, which, though re-shaped and interpolated in Han times, or towards the close of the feudal era, contain a detailed account of the ritual employed at the Chou Court and in feudal society. These ceremonies, such as the "capping" of youths when they reached the status of manhood, and the rites observed at banquets, archery tournaments and funerals, no doubt represent the idealised rites which the traditionalists wished to see generally observed. As regards the royal rites followed by the Son of Heaven, they cannot be said to be based on current practices, since at the time when they were compiled, about the 3rd century B.C., the Chou Kings were reduced to the possession of the capital, Lo Yang itself, and exercised no authority over the rulers of the Warring States. The *Li Chi* which is a collection of varying date, contains the Great Learning (*Ta Hsueh*), a work which was used by the Sung philosophers in the 13th century A.D. as the source of the later Confucian philosophy.

The *Annals of Spring and Autumn*, or *Ch'un Ch'iu*, a history of the state of Lu from 722-481 B.C., which has been claimed by the Confucians of later times as the work of the master himself, is an arid, but accurately dated chronicle, such as there is reason

FIG. 7. *The Eight Trigrams, Pa Kua.*

to believe were produced in all the major feudal states. The *Tso Chuan*, a composite work, is another, much longer and more lively chronicle of feudal history, in which a very brief ritual commentary on the *Ch'un Ch'iu* is incorporated. It was written, or attributed to, a certain Tso Shih about 300 B.C. These two books have really no intimate connection at all nor is the *Ch'un Ch'iu* the work of Confucius.

The school of Mo Tzŭ is very poorly represented in surviving works. The work of Mo Tzŭ himself, in fifty-three books, some of which are known to be spurious, is the only connected exposition of his doctrine, and this book, preserved more as a curiosity than as a classic authority, has suffered much corruption at the hands of copyists. The later Mohists are only known by the fragmentary book of Kung-sun Lung and a few scattered texts included in collections. This literature, neglected for two thousand years, has recently begun to receive the attention of modern Chinese scholars, and it may be hoped that their labours will recover the sense of many corrupt and unintelligible passages.

The Legists have not left very much more than their rivals. *The Book of the Lord of Shang* (Wei Yang) and the *Han Fei Tzŭ* are the principal sources. Fragments of the works of other Legists, which are known to have been very voluminous, are represented in the collections attributed to Shên Tao and Yin Wên Tzŭ. These sparse surviving books enable us to estimate the extent of the loss and arrive at an imperfect knowledge of the systems which they expound.

The Taoists denied the value of any active participation in the affairs of mankind. Non-action was preferable to benevolent activity, which was itself a sign of the corruption of the times. With many pointed illustrations the *Tao Tê Ching* emphasised the principle of non-activity. The value of a bowl is not in the utensil itself, but in the empty space it encloses. Again, the utility of a wheel depends, not on the rim or the spokes, but on the empty space within the hub. This theory of government advocated simplicity and denied the value of instruction for the mass of the people.

"By not exalting merit the people are kept from rivalry. By not valuing what is hard to obtain the people are kept from theft, by not contemplating what is desirable the heart is kept untroubled. Therefore the government of the sage empties the hearts of the people, and fills their stomachs. He weakens their ambitions, but strengthens their bones. Always he keeps the people without knowledge and without desire, so that the crafty do not dare to act. By non-action nothing is ungoverned."

The virtues praised by the Confucians were to the author of the *Tao Tê Ching*, not virtues at all, but evidences of the lapse from primitive excellence.

"When the great Tao becomes obscured, benevolence and justice appear. When knowledge and wisdom are manifested, there is much deception. When the six relationships are not harmonious, filial piety and tenderness arise. When the states and the clans are disorderly, there is loyalty and sincerity."

The human virtues were thus not the cure for the ills of the world but a symptom of the disease itself. Elsewhere this doctrine is even more strongly expressed, and the origin of the virtues prized by the Confucians is described as the consequence of a progressive decay.

"Wherefore, when Tao is lost, virtue comes, when virtue is lost, comes benevolence; when benevolence is lost there is justice, when justice is lost there are the rules of conduct. [Li, the chivalrous code.] The [Li] rules of conduct are the range of loyalty and sincerity and the source of disorder."

Teaching and any active attempt to inculcate these virtues was worse than useless. The example of the sage was the sole way of bringing men to an understanding of the Tao. Therefore the *Tao Tê Ching* says: "Requite injury with good."

Chuang Tzŭ (3rd century B.C.) a famous Taoist philosopher, taught a more mystical doctrine, denying the power of human reason to arrive at any solution of life's problems. Referring to the disputes of the schools, he said:

"Suppose that you argue with me. If you beat me, instead of my beating you, are you necessarily right, and am I necessarily wrong? Or if I beat you and not you me, am I necessarily right and you wrong? Is one of us right and the other wrong? Or are both of us right or both of us wrong? Both of us cannot come to a mutual understanding and others are equally in the dark. Whom shall I ask to decide this dispute? I may ask someone who agrees with you; but since he agrees with you, how can he decide it? I may ask someone who agrees with me; but since he agrees with me how can he decide it? I may ask someone who differs from both you and me, but since he differs from both you and me how can he decide it? I may ask someone who agrees with both you and me, but since he agrees with both of us, how can he decide it? Therefore, you and I and all the others are incapable of understanding one another. Upon whom shall we depend for a decision?"

Chuang Tzŭ gives the answer:

> "Reconcile all in the rhythm of nature [Tao]. Take no heed of right and wrong or of time. Aspire to the realm of the Infinite and take refuge therein."

Chuang Tzŭ not only denied the value of disputation, but questioned the reality of the world of appearances. In his famous anecdote of the butterfly this view is clearly expressed:

> "Once Chuang Chou [Chou was Chuang Tzŭ's personal name] dreamed that he was a butterfly, flying about enjoying itself. It did not know that it was Chuang Chou. Suddenly he awoke, and veritably was Chuang Chou again. I do not know whether it was Chuang Chou dreaming that he was a butterfly, or whether now I am a butterfly dreaming that I am Chuang Chou."

Chuang Tzŭ had a somewhat impish sense of humour and delighted in expressing Taoist doctrines in the form of imaginary conversations with Confucius, in which the leader of the rival school was made the mouthpiece of a teaching totally at variance with Confucianism.

> "I have made some progress," said Yen Hui.
> "What do you mean?" said Confucius.
> "I forget benevolence and righteousness," said Yen Hui.
> "Very well, but that is not perfect," said Confucius.
> Another day Yen Hui again saw Confucius and said:
> "I have made some progress."
> "What do you mean?" asked Confucius.
> "I forget ceremonies and music," said Yen Hui.
> "Very well, but that is not perfect," said Confucius.
> Another day Yen Hui saw Confucius and said:
> "I have made some progress."
> "What do you mean?" asked Confucius.
> "I forget everything," said Yen Hui.
> Confucius changed countenance and said:
> "What do you mean by forgetting everything?"

"I gave up my body and discarded my knowledge. By thus getting rid of my body and mind, I became one with the infinite [with Tao]. This is what I mean by forgetting everything."

Finally, Chuang Tzŭ makes a "nameless man" thus answer a questioner who wanted to know how to put the world to rights:

"Make excursion in pure simplicity. Identify yourself with non-distinction. Follow the nature of things and admit no personal bias, then the world will be in peace."*

Taoism was thus a mystical creed, of which the appeal was necessarily limited to men of philosophical temperament free from the pressing cares of the world. The scholar or the nobleman might renounce the cares of state or family and retire to a mountain, but the mass of the Chinese people, incessantly occupied with the need to earn their livelihood, could not find much guidance in a rule of life which denied the value of any earthly activity. No state could be organised on Taoist lines, for Taoism condemned the organisation of society as a folly. Inevitably Taoism was rejected by the statesmen and the rulers who were recasting the destiny of the Chinese people.

Yet Taoism, for all its unpractical idealism, or perhaps on that account, continued to find a certain support, for its roots were in one of the outstanding qualities of the Chinese character, the capacity for patient endurance. It has always appealed to the Chinese dislike of meticulous regulation, and to the attitude of contemplative detachment with which the Chinese are wont to regard affairs which do not immediately concern them. If there is truth in the view that a nation emphasises the importance of those moral qualities which are not naturally strong in the national character, then the appeal of Taoism lies in the reaction from the Confucian insistence on virtues and qualities which are antipathetic to the genius of the race.

The desire for a system of morality which denied the value of family ties and public duties, and which emphasised contemplation

*Translations from *Chuang Tzŭ*, by Yu-lan Fung. Shanghai, 1931.

and non-participation persisted after Taoism had long ceased to be a school of philosophy and had sunk to the level of a popular religion. Buddhism owed much of its success to the fact that the doctrine of renunciation of the world was already established in China, and met an abiding need of the Chinese mind.

It is difficult to escape the feeling that Confucian doctrine is based on a shrewd appreciation of the real character of the Chinese people, and endeavours to stimulate by precept and regulation the qualities which are not naturally well developed in the national character. Like the reformers of the modern age, Confucius deplored the particularism of his countrymen, and emphasised the virtues of filial submission and loyalty, virtues, which as he himself attests, were all too rare among his contemporaries. The Confucian insistence on filial duty and the strict training of the young would seem harsh until it is realised that the Chinese, a people naturally over-kind and indulgent to children, are also averse to discipline. Confucius, essentially a practical-minded statesman, saw that unless the virtue of filial submission was stressed, youth would be corrupted by the kindly indulgence of parents. Unless loyalty and public service were made the cardinal virtues of the nobleman, the selfish interests of clan and family would prove fatal to the state. The detached indifference with which the Chinese are prone to regard the affairs of the world beyond the family circle must be corrected by a firm insistence on the value of benevolence, submission to authority, and loyal service to the prince.

Finally, in his person the superior man, the ideal nobleman, must be correct, reserved, placid and self-controlled. So well have the Confucians succeeded in preaching these last virtues that western nations have come to believe that the Chinese character is really naturally in accordance with them. Confucius attached weight to these things not because they were inherently easy to his fellow-men, but because, on the contrary, he observed that on all sides men were casting aside the restraints of morality, giving way to violent passions, and were prone to sudden phases of hysteria. He insisted on the glory and virtue of the past ages of Wu and the sages Yao and Shun, because he saw that the social order was rapidly decaying, that men, far from being naturally averse to change, were easily adapting themselves to new ideas of morality and conduct.

Thus the whole teaching of Confucius was a reaction against the loose spirit of his times, a protest against the excesses of the national character unrestrained by moral inhibitions. Filial piety was preached to an age where parricide was not uncommon. Loyalty, he taught to ambitious nobles who were only intent on grasping the authority which rightly belonged to the prince and the Son of Heaven. Ceremonies and the rites were exalted when men were neglecting the ancient sacrifices and violating the chivalrous code; rules of conduct and decorum were very necessary at a time when sexual morality was loose and even princes were not ashamed to commit incest. Such was the society in which Confucius lived, and such were evils which he sought to remedy. The starting point of his doctrine was the belief that there had been in the remote past an age of perfect virtue, brought about by the rule of sage kings. That happy era had left on record the words and deeds of the sages, the regulations they made, and the sacrifices they instituted. There was thus a standard by which the present state of society could be judged, and by which it stood condemned. The remedy lay in making known the virtues of the past as recorded in ancient books, and in bringing men to a sense of their present degeneration by awakening their consciences, or as the Confucians put it, by giving them a sense of shame.

To this purpose Confucius set about the preliminary task of "rectification of terms." When words, or terms including names, no longer meant what they had been intended to mean, they lost their value. When an usurper was called Duke, or a parricide described as a murder, then men could not distinguish the truth from falsity, their consciences were blurred, they lost their sense of shame, and they abandoned virtue and adopted vicious courses. For this reason the Confucians highly esteemed the *Ch'un Ch'iu*, the history of the State of Lu. To understand why this dry chronicle was so admired it is necessary to study the manner in which it was written. The *Ch'un Ch'iu* states nothing but bare facts. No comment is offered, no enlargement or explanation of the circumstances ekes out the cold record. That task has been left to the so-called commentaries, which by contrast make lively reading. The significance of the *Ch'un Ch'iu* lies wholly in its choice of words to record the facts. It is not the matter but the manner of the book that conveys the moral lesson. To begin with, in an age when the Son of Heaven had lost all authority and was a disregarded petty prince, the chronicle uses the calendar of the royal house of Chou, and thus conveys a first censure on the usurping feudal princes. The princes themselves are invariably referred to only by the title which the ancient kings had bestowed upon their ancestors, the high ranks they had subsequently usurped are never mentioned. The ruler of Ch'u, the most powerful sovereign in the Chinese world at that time, had been a King in his own country for many generations. In the *Ch'un Ch'iu* he is always called the Count of Ch'u for that was the only title that the Kings of Chou had conferred upon his ancestors.

If no other chronicle existed, the facts and real nature of the events which the *Ch'un Ch'iu* records would be obscure and deceptive. The *Tso Chuan*, a chronicle attributed to a certain Tso Shih of whom nothing definite is known, throws light on all these obscure events and explains the formal language of the *Ch'un Ch'iu*. Thus for the year 599 B.C. the *Ch'un Ch'iu* records:

> "11th Year of Duke Hsüan (of Lu).
> The Duke of Ch'ên slew his minister Hsieh Yeh."

The circumstances are not explained, but the word used for "slay" instead of "execute" indicates that the act was unjust. The *Tso Chuan* thus expands the story:

> "Ling, Duke of Ch'ên and two of his ministers, Kung Ning and I Huang Fu had relations with Chi, widow of Hsia [a nobleman of Ch'ên]. All three [the Duke and the two ministers] wore one of the lady's undergarments, and made a jest of it at the court. Hsieh Yeh admonished the Duke, saying: 'If the Duke and ministers make a display of their immorality the people will have no good example to follow. Also there will be scandalous stories repeated. Your Highness must put away these garments.' The Duke replied: 'I can change my conduct.' [Later] the Duke told his two ministers [of this conversation].

The two ministers requested that Hsieh Yeh should be executed. The Duke did not forbid them [to slay him]. Therefore they slew Hsieh Yeh."

Although the *Ch'un Ch'iu* expresses disapproval of this scandalous intrigue, the principle of loyalty was expressed in the same way when recording the sequel. Under the heading for the next year (598 B.C.) the record runs:—

"Hsia Chêng-shu assassinated his lord, P'ing Kuo, Duke Ling of Ch'ên."

Hsia Chêng-shu, the son of the widow Chi, was vindicating the family honour, but his act is stigmatised as " assassination," and the condemnation emphasised by adding the words " his lord" showing that he had not merely assassinated a sovereign, but his own sovereign, to whom he was bound by the special ties of loyalty existing between the prince and the noble. Nothing in the *Ch'un Ch'iu* shows that Hsia Chêng-shu really acted under great provocation, for nothing could be held to palliate or excuse the assassination of one's prince. The *Tso Chuan*, however, gives the whole story:

"Duke Ling of Ch'ên with the ministers Kung Ning and I Huang Fu were drinking wine in the house of the Hsia family [the residence of their mistress, the widow Chi]. The Duke said to I Huang Fu: 'Chêng-shu resembles you.'* I Huang Fu replied: 'He also resembles Your Highness.' Hsia Chêng-shu felt insulted. When the Duke took his departure, Hsia Chêng-shu, from the stables, drew his bow upon the Duke and slew him."

It was this use of words to convey censure which made the fame of the *Ch'un Ch'iu* so great that Mencius declared: "Confucius wrote the *Ch'un Ch'iu* and rebellious sons and disloyal ministers were overwhelmed with consternation."† To the modern, the

*Hsia Chêng-shu, the son of the house, whose mother Chi, was the mistress of the Duke and the two ministers. The remark was a joke, for Hsia Chêng-shu was too old to be the son of any of them.

†This saying is the authority for the tradition that the *Ch'un Ch'iu* was the work of Confucius. It may be an interpolation in the Mencius canon.

method appears, at least, inadequate to reform a decadent society, but it must be remembered that the book was written at a period when literature as an art was in its infancy. The use of such forms as irony and sarcasm was wholly new to the world, and made a correspondingly deep impression.

Mencius and the later Confucians held firmly to the doctrine of "rectification of terms" as instanced by Mencius' reply, quoted above (p. 76), to the question whether Wu was justified in putting Chou Hsin of Shang to death. This insistence on the correct use of terms, though only intended by Confucius to be a means to the great end of reforming morals, tended to become a pedantry which obsessed the scholars and obscured the real facts. The later Confucians, talking and acting as if the feudal world of Wu could be recreated without difficulty, lost touch with the vital forces which were shaping a new age. Up to the last they remained blind to the growing urge for unity and centralisation which was to end in the formation of a centralised empire; and when that empire was an established fact, they continued to uphold the feudal ideal, ignoring the misery and confusion which had been the rule under decadent feudalism. Although, as will be shown in a later chapter, the empire finally adopted a modified Confucianism, Confucianism itself contributed nothing to the foundation of the new political system. That was the work, first of its enemies the Legists, and later of adventurers trained in no school at all except the hard upbringing of an age of war and revolution.

Confucius (Fig. 8) himself found very little support for his teaching among the rulers of his own time. Although he was employed as minister at Lu, his native state, he resigned the post and left the country, ostensibly on account of the Duke's partiality for the dancing girls which his neighbour, the Duke of Ch'i, had sent to him. Confucians contend that the Duke of Ch'i made this gift because he was alarmed at the growing power of Lu under the ideal administration of Confucius, and cleverly devised this plan to force the sage to resign. This is a pious view of the importance of Confucius to his contemporaries. Actually the chief power in Lu, already a weak and decadent state, was held by three collateral families issued from the ducal house. In their hands

FIG. 8. *Confucius, from an engraving on a stele in the Pei Lin, Sianfu, Shensi. Manchu Period.*

the Duke was a plaything, and it is hard to believe that powerful Ch'i was really afraid of the influence of Confucius on a ruler who did not exercise the real power in the state. It is more consistent with the character of Confucius to believe that he resigned because he had come to realise that his influence was impotent when the Duke himself was under the authority of ambitious nobles. He proclaimed the dancing girls as his reason in public in order that, true to his doctrine of rectification of names, the acts of the nominal and rightful ruler should appear to be the cause of any change in the government, while the illegal power of the three families must be ignored. After the death of Confucius the school which he founded was carried on by enthusiastic and loyal disciples, though it does not seem to have found much favour with the feudal princes. To these sovereigns, who were concerned with the policies of the present, and constantly threatened by the ambitions of their neighbours, a doctrinaire teaching which emphasised values no longer current, and proclaimed the merit of a political system which had long been in ruins, must have appeared wrong-headed and pedantic. In view of the later dominance of Confucianism which has interpreted the past by its own light, it is necessary to emphasise the fact that during the feudal period itself Confucianism was only one of many competing schools, derided and ignored by the actual wielders of power. It was in no sense the "orthodox" philosophy of the Chinese world. Its literature was not accorded the reverence which it now receives, and, indeed, from other books it is certain that somewhat different traditions concerning the remote past were preserved by rival schools.

In the period of the Warring States the writings of a later Confucian, Hsün Tzǔ, had more influence on contemporary thought than the canons of the sage himself. Hsün Tzǔ differed from his master and from his contemporary, Mencius, on two important points. He held that the nature of man was not good but evil, and he regarded the Confucian golden age of Yao and Shun as too remote and idealised to be a useful and convincing pattern for the modern world. He urged instead that the later kings, those of the early Chou dynasty, about whom more historical facts were known, should be honoured as the true prototypes of the ideal monarch. These heterodox ideas of Hsün Tzǔ have not been accepted by Confucianism, but they exercised a great influence on the thought of his own times. Hsün Tzǔ said:

"The nature of man is evil; his goodness is only acquired training. The original nature of man to-day is to seek for gain, if this desire is followed, strife and rapacity results and courtesy dies. Man originally is envious and naturally hates others. If these tendencies are followed, injury and destruction follows; loyalty and faithfulness are destroyed . . . therefore the civilising influence of teachers and laws, the guidance of the Li and of justice is absolutely necessary."

Elsewhere Hsün Tzǔ amplifies this idea, and the need for a firm government:

"Man's nature is evil. Anciently the Sage Kings knew that man's nature was evil, partial, bent on evil, corrupt, rebellious, disorderly and without good government. Hence they established the authority of the prince to govern man; they set forth clearly the Li and justice to reform him; they established laws and government to rule him; they made punishments severe to warn him, and so they caused the whole country to come to a state of good government and prosperity."

Here was the germ of a doctrine which, in the hands of the Legists, developed into the theory of the supreme state based not on benevolence, but law. Hsün Tzǔ also enunciated the other doctrine which was dear to the Legists, the futility of quoting the remote age of Yao and Shun.

"Previous to the Five Emperors there is no record, not that there were no worthy men, but because of the length of time intervening. Of the Five Emperors there is no record of their government, not because they did not have a good government, but because of the length of time intervening."*

And he concludes by declaring that though some record of the

*Translations from the Works of Hsün Tzǔ. H. H. Dubs. London. 1928.

Hsia and Shang sovereigns remains, the history of the Chou Kings is preferable, because more detailed. Hsün Tzŭ, although he is classed as a Confucian, thus expressed two doctrines which proved to be the greatest weapons in the hands of the Legists, the enemies of the Confucians. Carrying these doctrines further than he did, they made them the foundation of a theory of government diametrically opposed to that of Confucius. He had taught that men are naturally good and only fall into error through lack of instruction. The sovereign had only to be perfectly virtuous and his subjects would imitate him, without constraint and of their own accord. The people were grass, and the prince was the wind; as the wind blows, the grass will bend in obedience. Hsün Tzŭ, who opposed this fundamental Confucian tenet, can scarcely be said to have been a true Confucian.

It is a singular proof of the Chinese preference for compromise and the middle course, that the two schools of philosophy which perished almost without trace, and exercised a negligible influence on the later culture, were that of Mo Tzŭ and that of Yang Chu, the morally highest and morally lowest respectively. The fact is the more interesting as we know from Mencius that in his day these two schools were the most popular. Mo Tzŭ (500-420 B.C.) founded a school which developed into something not unlike a religion and was ruled, after his death, by a succession of leaders styled "master."

It might be expected that this organisation would have preserved his teaching better than the nihilistic Taoists preserved the writings of their sages, but the reverse was the case. Little authentic Mohist literature remains, and the Mohist system fell into complete oblivion after the Ch'in revolution. Mo Tzŭ opposed both the contemplative Taoists and their extremist wing under Yang Chu, and the Confucian reactionary doctrines. He preached as the cardinal virtue, love. The remedy for all evil, the cure for all disorder, was the practice of universal love. If every man loved strangers as he loved his own parents and children, there could be no crime or wickedness in the world. He opposed the Confucians on this point for their partial and restricted view of filial piety, only applicable to the parents and family, and their narrow loyalty, which only served the prince.

"The way of universal love is to regard the country of others as one's own, the families of others as one's own, the persons of others as one's self. When feudal lords love one another there will be no more war. When heads of houses love one another there will be no more mutual usurpation. When individuals love one another there will be no more mutual injury. . . . When all the people in the world love one another, then the strong will not overpower the weak, the many will not oppress the few, the wealthy will not mock the poor, the honoured will not disdain the humble, the cunning will not deceive the simple."*

Secondly, he taught simplicity, even asceticism. Here he found himself sharply opposed to the Confucians who attached such importance to ceremonies, sacrifices and funerals. Mo Tzŭ held that this was a cause of extravagance which wasted the resources of the people and consequently led to misery and crime. He also opposed music as a waste of time. He does not, in fact, seem to have had a developed artistic nature. Confucius who was very fond of music, laid the greatest importance on the art as a civilising influence.

Mo Tzŭ also taught the belief in the active existence of the spirits of the dead, and supported his view by quoting historical instances of supernatural phenomena. Since we now know that the Shang Kings constantly sought the guidance and advice of their ancestors by means of divination, this doctrine of Mo Tzŭ was clearly in accordance with an ancient belief. Mo Tzŭ does not seem to have attached any special significance to the survival of the soul. He did not teach any doctrine which related the conduct of men on earth to their condition in the afterworld.

It was natural that believing in universal love, Mo Tzŭ condemned war as the greatest of crimes, and deplored the blindness of his contemporaries who could not see the evil in war. His pacifism sometimes has a very modern note:

"The murder of one person is called unrighteous, and incurs a death penalty. Following this argument, the murder of ten persons is ten times as unrighteous and there should be a

*Yi-Pao Mei. *The Works of Mo Tse*. London, 1929.

tenfold death penalty. The murder of one hundred persons is a hundred times as unrighteous, and there should be a hundredfold death penalty. But when it comes to the great unrighteousness of attacking states, the gentlemen of the world do not know that they should condemn it, on the contrary they applaud it, calling it righteous. Shall we say that these gentlemen know the difference between right and wrong ?"

Although the leaders of other schools contested the value of Mohist doctrine, it is significant that they frankly acknowledged the sublime idealism of the man himself; Mencius, his opponent said of him: "Mo Ti loved all men and would gladly wear out his whole being from head to heel for the benefit of mankind." Chuang Tzŭ said of him: "Mo Tzŭ was certainly a glory to the world. What he could not attain, he would never cease to seek, even though he be in privation and destitution. Ah, what a genius he was."

It is obvious that in an age such as that of the Warring States the ideals of Mohism were no more likely to be translated into action than were the doctrines of Christianity in the Dark Ages. Whereas Christianity survived as a system, admitted by all to be sublime, Mohism passed into complete oblivion. This fate was probably the consequence of the development of Mohism under the later exponents of the school, called the Neo-Mohists. Kung-sun Lung (*circa* 325 B.C.) and Hui Ssŭ (370-319 B.C.), who was minister of King Hui of Wei, were chiefly famous as dialecticians and are remembered for their paradoxes. Of these the most famous were Hui Ssŭ's:

"The sun shines obliquely at noon. A thing dies as it is born."

"The South has no limit, and has a limit."

"I go to Yüeh [in the south] to-day and arrived there yesterday."

"Love all things equally. The universe is one."

These have been explained as a monistic theory of the universe: "A metaphysical basis for the Mohist doctrine of universal altruism."*

*Hu Shih. *The Development of the Logical Method in Ancient China*. London. 1922.

The paradoxes of Kung-sun Lung were even more famous than those of Hui Ssŭ, and perhaps did more to discredit Mohism in the eyes of the multitude. It is noteworthy that some of them are equivalent to the paradoxes of Zeno:

"The shadow of a flying bird has never moved."

"A swiftly fleeting arrow has moments both of rest and motion."

"If a rod one foot in length is cut short every day by one half of its length, it will still have something left after ten thousand generations."

"A hard white stone makes two."

"A white horse is not a horse."

It will be seen from these that the Neo-Mohists had advanced far in scientific speculation, and in the study of the "meaning of meaning." Their purpose was to prove the unity of time and the universe, and justify the doctrine of universal love.

The real object of their teaching was ignored and misrepresented by their rivals. Their thought, far above the heads of ordinary men, was distorted and made to appear unreal and meaningless. Mohism thus became discredited as a visionary and fantastic creed without practical application or value. The Chinese are essentially a practical race of men of the world. A doctrine which taught men to love strangers as they loved their own parents, and condemned an everyday necessity of state such as war as the greatest of crimes was perhaps very noble, but certainly contrary to the normal instincts of men. When they further beheld the Mohists proclaiming such paradoxes as "a white horse is not a horse," they came to regard Mohism as a play of words, fit for the disputes of dialecticians, but useless as a rule of life. Mohism never recovered from the proscription of the schools and the burning of the books. In the later history of Chinese culture it played no part.

The doctrines of Yang Chu met a similar fate. In normal circumstances the Chinese are too social a people, too attached to the ties of family life, to accept a doctrine of selfish and cynical despair. Yang Chu represented the intellectual misery of the age of Warring States. "Regard the world, and let it pass, be drifted away into annihilation." Virtue he regarded as a complete waste of time, the sages had lived a life of toil and care to no purpose, whereas the wicked, at least enjoying the brief span of human life, were equally obliterated in death, and indifferent to the censure of posterity. After describing the laborious lives of the sages Shun, Yü, Duke Chou and Confucius, Yang Chu adds:

"All these four holy men failed to get a single day's enjoyment out of life. Dead, their fame will last ten thousand generations; but they will get no reality out of that. Though praised, they do not know it, though rewarded, they do not know it, any more than if they were blocks of wood or clods of clay.

"Chieh* inherited vast wealth and enjoyed the dignity of the throne. He had enough wit to enable him to hold his officers in check, and power enough to make himself feared within the empire. He gave himself over to the lusts of the ear and the eye; he carried out to the uttermost every fanciful scheme and had a glorious life until the end. Here was a divine man whose life was all pleasure and dissipation."†

These words might bring comfort to men who had no hope in a society given over to war, crime and violence, but when a more orderly age dawned the Chinese turned away from the teaching of Yang Chu to more constructive philosophies.

In contrast to the four true philosophic schools the School of Law did not seek a moral basis for human conduct and the organisation of society. They accepted Hsün Tzǔ's view that man was by nature evil. They also welcomed his distrust of the Confucian insistence on the golden age as a pattern for all time. The Legists were hard realists, statesmen rather than philosophers,

---

*Chieh, last King of the Hsia dynasty, is one of the two arch-tyrants of Chinese orthodox history. He and Chou Hsin, last King of the Shang, are invariably held up to execration in contrast to T'ang the Victorious, founder of the Shang, and Wên and Wu, founders of the Chou, who are the ideal rulers of a golden age. Yang Chu, in praising Chieh, was thus adopting the standpoint of a European who should declare that Nero was an admirable sovereign.

†The fragments of Yang Chu have been published by Professor A. Forke in an English translation. *Yang Chu's Garden of Pleasure*, Wisdom of the East Series. London.

who endeavoured to reorganise society for the express purpose of carrying on successful war, and obtaining the mastery of the Chinese world for the princes they served. As such they recognised that the *Li*, the controlling code of feudal society, was no longer adequate to impose discipline on the numerous and turbulent subjects of a greater kingdom. Moreover, the old feudal relationship was clearly dead, and as practical men they did not believe in the possibility of reviving dead customs or reverting to the primitive organisation of the heroic age.

They exalted the law as the true principle on which government should be based. The law should be equally applicable to noble and serf, the prince alone, supreme and autocratic should be the arbiter of the national destiny. With these views they naturally not only disapproved of the rival schools but considered that their very existence was a danger to the state, since their divergent views would lead to the formation of parties, intrigues and rebellions. When the Legist ministers of Ch'in had the direction of the new empire in their hands, they put these theories into practice with results fatal to the learning of ancient China. Before the Ch'in revolution such ideas had already been advanced by a Legist who was not born a subject of Ch'in, but of one of the rival kingdoms.

Kung-sun Yang, often called Wei Yang, was a descendant by a concubine of the ducal family of Wey, but was a subject of Wei. He became minister of Duke Hsiao of Ch'in (361-338 B.C.) who rewarded him with the title of *Shang Chün* or Lord of Shang, a title by which he is often known and which has given its name to the book in which Kung-sun Yang's ideas and legislation is set forth. The book is certainly not the work of Kung-sun Yang himself. It probably represents the writings of many officials trained in the Ch'in school of law, who looked back to Kung-sun Yang as the patron and founder of their school. It is certain, however, that the ideas and measures expounded in this book were developed from those which Kung-sun Yang put into practice in Ch'in, and which were the direct cause of the rise of that state to supreme power. In the *Book of the Lord of Shang* all the revolutionary measures which were enforced under the Ch'in dynasty are advocated, and there is no doubt that many of these laws had been in force in Ch'in ever since his time.

The teaching of this book is strongly opposed to the ideals of the feudal world. The nobility themselves are regarded as an anachronism which should be replaced by a hierarchy of soldiers filled by merit acquired on the battlefield. The teaching of music, history and philosophy is violently condemned as a poison which will corrupt the people and ruin the kingdom. Agriculture and war are praised as the foundations of national power. This was the doctrine which held the first place in Ch'in and which triumphed throughout China after the downfall of the cultured states of the plains:

"A country where the strength has been consolidated, is powerful, but a country that loves talking is dismembered. Therefore, it is said: 'If there are a thousand people engaged in agriculture and war, and only one in the odes and history (i.e. Confucian learning) and clever sophistry then the thousand will all be remiss in agriculture and war; if there are a hundred people engaged in agriculture and war and only one in arts and crafts, then all those hundred will be remiss in agriculture and war.'"

Kung-sun Yang, or his followers, thus pay a striking tribute to the civilising influence of art and literature, even while condemning all culture. The anti-cultural bias of the book is still more clearly expressed elsewhere:

"If in a country there are the following ten evils: rites [Li, rules of chivalrous conduct], music, poetry, history, virtue, moral culture, filial piety, brotherly duty, integrity and sophistry, the ruler cannot make the people fight and dismemberment is inevitable."

In his revolutionary ardour to destroy the feudal ideals and the virtues approved by the philosophic schools the author of the book does not hesitate to preach a kind of social revolution directed from the throne with the purpose of eliminating the power of the nobility:

"If the poor are encouraged by rewards they will become rich, and if penalties are applied to the rich, they will become poor. When in administering a country one succeeds in making the poor rich, and the rich poor, then the country will have much strength, and this being the case it will attain supremacy."

The Legists thus proposed to root out all cultural influences and substitute for moral virtues the fear of a cruel law. Penalties must be severe, even for the lighter crimes, so that great crimes would never be committed. Han Fei Tzǔ, a statesman of Han, the kingdom which was most endangered by Ch'in expansion, himself upheld the Ch'in Legist theories as the only antidote to the growing weakness of his native state. He says:

"The way of the sage is to eliminate knowledge and cleverness, if knowledge and cleverness are not eliminated it will be difficult to establish stability."

He had no use for the Mohist theory of love as a regenerating influence. His ideas on the education of the young were grim:

"The love of a mother for her son is twice as great as that of a father, but for getting orders obeyed by a son a father is worth ten mothers."

And again:

"Take a boy who is a bad character. His parents may get angry with him; he does not change. His neighbours may reprove him; it does not have any effect on him. His masters may moralise to him; he does not conform. All the excellent devices of which love of parents, conduct of neighbours, and wisdom of teachers may dispose are applied to him, but they remain totally without avail, and not a hair on his shins will change. But when the district official sends his soldiers and in the name of law searches for wicked individuals, then he becomes afraid, changes his principles, and reforms his conduct. So the love of parents is not sufficient to teach a son morality, but the severe punishments of the officials are needed. People become naturally spoiled by love, but obedient to severity."*

*J. J. L. Duyvendak. *The Book of Lord Shang*. London. 1928. And *Han Fei Tzu*. Chapters 2, 18 and 19.

The triumph of the Legist school under the Ch'in Empire was due to the fact that it alone could point to a record of successful application to state policy. Confucius had not been able to avert the ruin of his native state of Lu. The doctrines of the Mohists, Taoists, and their sub-divisions, had flourished in the states of eastern China, yet these states had one and all fallen victims to the military power of Ch'in. The Legist school had flourished in Ch'in. It was the Lord of Shang who, as minister to Duke Hsiao of Ch'in, had first formulated a code of rigid laws and reorganised the state on autocratic lines, forcing even the most privileged nobles, and the Crown Prince himself, to obey the law. The subsequent rise of Ch'in, it was believed, was the consequence of Kung-sun Yang's reforms. Thus, the rule of law had been proved to be the only doctrine which really built a strong state, and the rival schools were only capable of undermining the authority of the sovereign and ruining the kingdom. This was the conclusion which the Ch'in Legists drew from the history of the last century of feudalism, and this was the theory on which they condemned the schools to extinction and their teaching to the flames.

The Legist school failed in its chief endeavour, the permanent suppression of every rival doctrine, and in the reaction against the brutal regime of the Ch'in Empire this school suffered the fate which it had meted out to the others. Confucianism, as will be seen later, was the ultimate victor, but the Legists bequeathed one of their principal tenets to their enemies, the idea of a single orthodox doctrine which was alone deserving of government patronage and support. This idea, part of the theory of autocratic government so opposed to the feudal system of early Confucianism, was taken over by the later Confucians of the imperial age, and used to invest their doctrine with a sanctity which it had never enjoyed, or even claimed, in the feudal period. Confucius had not desired that his doctrine should receive the force of law, for he was firmly opposed to the idea of law. He did not want men to be constrained by fear of penalties, but charmed by the lustre of a brilliant virtue. Let the sovereign be truly virtuous and he will be "like the North Pole star, which keeps its position, while all the other stars turn towards it."

Confucianism, though borrowing these Legist ideas when it became the orthodox teaching upheld by the imperial authority, never developed the fury of persecuting fervour which orthodox doctrines elsewhere have assumed. It contented itself with a monopoly of official positions and identified itself with polite society. To be a scholar was to be a Confucian. The memory of the other schools faded away. Taoism became a religion for the uneducated classes, tolerantly despised by the Confucian gentry. The Confucian literature became sacred, and was the basis of all education and public instruction.

Orthodox Confucianism reverted to the teaching of Mencius, that man by nature was inherently good, and only lapsed into evil courses through lack of instruction. This conception of human nature has coloured the whole organisation of Chinese society. The state was professedly based on a moral authority, not on military force or legal sanctions. Later dynasties did not deny that their tenure of the throne was by virtue of Heaven's mandate, which would be withdrawn if their virtue failed. Since man, being naturally good, needed only instruction to be virtuous, it followed that the education of youth in the proper principles of conduct—the Confucian doctrines—was the first duty of scholars and parents. Legal penalties, the severe laws inherited from the Legist school, were only fit for the ignorant and unlearned. The scholar, inheriting the privileges which had once belonged to the aristocracy, should not be subjected to such indignities. Thus arose the curious contradiction of Chinese society ; it was a state based on the rule of moral authority, honouring learning above birth or wealth, ruling through a class of men of letters rather than by means of military power and police authority. On the other hand there was a legal system applied to the lowly and ignorant which was based on fear as the only deterrent, and was exercised through cruel and barbarous penalties. Justice and benevolence, Confucian ideas, were prominent in the theory of government, but absent in the legal tribunals. Force and severity, absent in the theory of government, were the basis of the legal system. The theory of government came from the Confucian school, the practice had retained most of the ideas of the Legists. Such was the final outcome of the disputes of the Hundred Schools.

Chapter V

SHANG AND CHOU ART

IN comparison with the extensive remains left by the early civilisations of Egypt and western Asia the ancient Chinese have left very few material traces of their culture and achievements. There is no Chinese Sphinx, and no site yet discovered has yielded finds comparable to those made at Ur or Nineveh. In spite of this paucity of archæological evidence it is certain that the Shang culture of the 2nd millennium B.C. was relatively advanced, and that it had already a long history behind it. The script on the oracle bones and some inscribed bronze vessels, although archaic, is the parent of the modern Chinese ideographic script, and is to a considerable extent intelligible to scholars. The Shang script had passed beyond the stage of picture writing. The vocabulary was still limited and the characters had not yet been differentiated and refined to express the more subtle shades of meaning, yet it is an ideographic, not a pictorial script, and can only have reached this stage through a long period of use and development.

How long this period was, where the script originated, and the course of its early development, are questions which cannot yet be answered. The An Yang site, which belongs to the very end of the Shang period, about 1100 B.C. at the earliest, is the only site so far scientifically excavated even in part. Archæology has therefore only discovered the Shang culture towards the end of its existence when it had already attained an advanced stage of development. The beginnings of this civilisation, the locality of its origin, and the intermediate stages of its growth, are still unsolved problems awaiting the discovery and excavation of earlier sites than An Yang. In 1956 construction workers developing a new residential area outside the ancient city of Cheng Chou, Honan province, unearthed a new and earlier Shang site, now preserved for future excavation as an archaeological park. Preliminary investigations indicate that the site was a capital of the Shang kingdom some two or three centuries earlier than An Yang. A number of bronze vessels recovered from the site display a simpler style of decoration and a less advanced technique than those found at An Yang. The Cheng Chou bronzes are all flat bottomed. Oracle bones were also found, but only a small number are inscribed.

The geographical features of the region in which early Chinese civilisation flourished make such discoveries largely a matter of chance. The early Chinese did not live on the margin of a desert, but in a rich alluvial plain, subject to floods, and continuously cultivated during the last three thousand years. Consequently their tombs and towns have not remained untouched or buried in the sand as in Egypt and Mesopotamia. The ancient Chinese sites have been ploughed over, flooded, ploughed again and deeply buried by the silt deposited by flood waters. Only the erosion of a river bank, a landslip, or some other accident can reveal these long forgotten sites, for the ancient Chinese did not construct great monuments of stone or brick which would serve to guide the modern excavator. Their buildings were made of wood or unbaked bricks, materials which have perished leaving no trace. Their records were written on wooden tablets, which have equally perished, and there is little hope that future discoveries will unearth any long inscriptions of an early date.

Almost the only material remains of this early period are the oracle bones (not always inscribed), carved ivories and antlers, pottery and bronze vessels, some of which have short inscriptions. The oracle bones, and also the carapaces of tortoises, were used for divination and were sometimes inscribed after use with the question put to the oracle (that is, to the ancestral spirits), and the answer received. These inscriptions indirectly serve to establish the names and sequence of the Shang kings, and afford valuable material for the study of the early forms and meanings of the ideographs. After use the bones were ritually buried, perhaps in order to "stabilise" the oracle, and it is therefore to be hoped that other rich and earlier deposits will be discovered. The oracle bones, however interesting to scholars and historians, can hardly be described as art objects, for they were not carved or decorated, being intended solely for ritual use.

The art of the Shang and Chou periods is known through the survival of pottery, bronze vessels, jades and carved objects including antlers, ivories and stone sculpture. While the provenance of these objects is often unknown and their dates subject to dispute except in the rare cases where an inscription exists, the excavation of the Shang site at An Yang has provided a great quantity of bronzes, pottery and carved objects which are indisputably Shang, and anterior to 1100 B.C. These discoveries, especially those made in excavating the Royal Tombs of the Shang kings have made it necessary to revise previous ideas concerning the dates of ancient bronzes and the styles prevailing in different periods. It is now clear that the Shang excelled in the art of casting decorated bronze vessels and that the most beautiful specimens of this art, which were hitherto thought to be late are in fact more likely to be Shang than Chou.

The bronze vessels and jade emblems, the two most important categories of surviving art objects, were certainly made for ritual use in the ceremonies of ancestor worship and its related fertility cult. They were venerated as sacred objects and preserved with the greatest care. It is therefore probable that the decorative motifs with which these precious vessels were ornamented had a religious significance, and were not merely artistic designs evolved by the

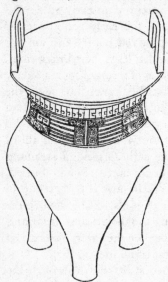

craftsmen who made them. Fortunately, this preoccupation with the ritual significance of the decoration did not prevent the ancient artists from making bronzes of great beauty delicately and yet vigorously ornamented, works of art whose æsthetic appeal to the modern connoisseur is as great as the admiration and veneration aroused in the ancients by their sacred character.

Although the introduction of bronze at some time between the Yang Shao period and that of the An Yang site (*circa* 1100 B.C.) must have been the result of contact with peoples at a higher level of civilisation, there is nothing to indicate an

FIG. 9. *Tripod Bronze Vessel, li.*

FIG. 10. *Pottery Fragments with geometrical patterns, from An Yang. Shang Period.*

alien source for the decorative designs on the early bronzes. The forms of these vessels were traditional, copies in metal of pottery ware, as is clearly proved by the pottery specimens found in the An Yang site. The skeletal remains found at Yang Shao sites prove that these people were the ancestors of the northern Chinese of later ages, and though the links between Yang Shao culture and the Shang period at present rest upon a particular form of tripod (Fig. 9), the *li*, further excavation may reveal a continuous development in which the introduction of bronze was but one important step.

The style of decoration found on the earliest bronzes is also found on pottery recovered from the An Yang site, and on various small objects of bone, stone, bronze and on carved antlers. This decoration is a combination of geometrical patterns, spirals, squares, triangles, with zoomorphic forms more or less stylised and often amalgamated with the geometrical design. In the pottery fragments (Fig. 10) the geometrical pattern of triangles is in fact a stylised representation of the cicada, which, in early summer, infests the trees and fills the air with a cheerful whistling sound. The cicada was an emblem of spring, and the leaf-like shape of the insect led, by an easy association of ideas, to a development of the pattern into a palm leaf and cicada motif, in which the original cicada, represented by a triangle, now encloses a true cicada as the centre of the design.

The animal-headed marble pieces (Fig. 11) and the bronze object which was perhaps the head of a staff (Fig. 12) are examples of this art in which the zoomorphic character is more easily detected. The ox-like head of the first piece has not developed the geometrical formalism which is dominant in the horn-shaped bronze object. Here the arrangement of the geometrical patterns as well as the horns are intended to suggest an animal head, but the character of the animal is not clearly defined. On both these pieces and on the pottery there are geometrical patterns akin to those on the richly carved piece of bone shown in Fig. 13. On this piece early forms of the two well-known bronze patterns, the *lei wên*, thunder pattern or Greek meander, and the "cloud pattern" with its up curling flourishes can be recognised. The meander, though best known to the west from Greek pottery, is found in ancient art in all parts of the world, and cannot

FIG. 11. *Animal head in Marble from An Yang.*

FIG. 13. *Bone Carving from An Yang.*

FIG. 12. *Bronze Horned Head from An Yang.*

FIG. 14. *T'ao t'ieh mask in Marble from An Yang.*

be adduced as direct evidence of communication between China and the Levant in prehistoric times. In China it is called the thunder pattern because, like the cloud pattern, with which it is often associated, it frequently forms a background for the dragon, the rain spirit.

One of the principal animal motifs of the early bronze art is the *t'ao t'ieh*, an ogre-like head with massive muzzle (the lower jaw usually missing) and vast staring eyes (Fig. 14). The frequency with which this monster is represented on bronze vessels and other antique objects is clear evidence of the important part which it played in the mythology of the early Chinese. It is difficult, in the absence of really ancient literary evidence, to say what the *t'ao t'ieh* was intended to represent. Opinions on this question are many but the view which sees the *t'ao t'ieh* as the dragon regarded under its destructive aspect seems the most satisfactory. The dragon was the rain spirit of the ancient Chinese. Unlike the western monster, the Chinese *lung* was not an evil creature malevolent to mankind, but the rain giver who gathered the clouds, brought the welcome moisture and presided over the water courses. The word dragon, though long sanctioned by use, is thus a misnomer for the *lung* of Chinese mythology. To the European the dragon is instinctively associated with evil, and the brave knight who sets out to rescue the fair maiden. To the Chinese, on the contrary, the rain-giving dragon represents a beneficent force in nature.

None the less the climate of north China with its sudden and fierce extremes, its destructive floods as well as its prolonged droughts, brought home the fact that the activities of the rain-giving dragon were sometimes catastrophic. There is the timely rain of spring, which saves the crops, and the terrific thunderstorms of midsummer, which often wash them away. The *t'ao t'ieh* may well be a representation of the dragon in this second and terrible manifestation, the storm spirit of destruction.

In the designs found on bronze vessels of the early period the dragon itself has not yet become fully developed. The body is heavier and less sinuous than in later art, and the scales and hair are absent. In the early representations of the dragon the "pearl" placed before the dragon's jaw is never present. On the other hand the dragon is sometimes shown in company with a bird, usually called the phœnix, *fêng huang*. On the early bronze however, the bird bears little resemblance to the phœnix of later art, which took the pheasant as its model. The archaic bird cannot be said to resemble a pheasant in any way; its curved beak is more reminiscent of a bird of prey.

In time the pair became associated with the dualist system of the *yang* and *yin*, the positive and negative forces which form the universe by their constant flux. The dragon was the *yang* positive, moist and male principle, the phœnix the *yin*, negative, dry, and

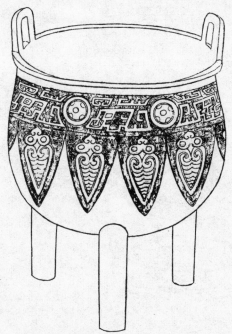

FIG. 15. *Tripod Bronze Vessel, ting.*

female principle. In later times the dragon and phœnix thus became the symbols of the Emperor and Empress respectively. The transition from the archaic bird with its curved beak into the phœnix of later art seems to be connected with this *yin* and *yang* symbolism. The phœnix is in fact a pheasant, and it is well known that the pheasant is a bird susceptible to changes in the weather.

FIG. 16. *Bronze Cups, tou.*

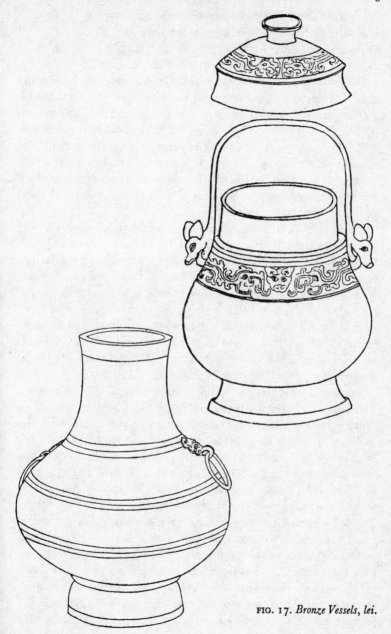

FIG. 17. *Bronze Vessels, lei.*

Its alarmed and agitated cries when thunder is heard have been commonly remarked by all peoples, and are referred to in classical Chinese texts. In western China, the kingdom of Ch'in, a pheasant deity was worshipped (see Chapter IX).

Bronze vessels of the Shang and Chou period were of many shapes. The ritual of the ancestral sacrifices, in which these vessels were employed, was complicated and involved the preparation of solid food as well as rice wine. No part of these preparations could be made with vessels of inferior value, consequently the ritual objects included every type of vessel needed to cook as well as to serve the sacrificial food. The names and uses of these vessels are known, although the exact use to which a particular vessel was put is sometimes in dispute.

The vessels used for solids were five in number. The *ting* (Fig. 15) a tripod caldron, with a rounded body. There are some *ting* with four legs, but three is the usual number. The *yin* is a globular pot resting on three legs. The upper half of the pot forms the lid. The *ho*, in shape like a three-legged kettle, was nevertheless used for the preparation of solid foods according to the accepted view, and the spout was intended not to pour out liquid, but to allow steam to escape. The *tui* and *tou* (Fig. 16) were both cups or bowls in which the cooked viands were served. The latter is a peculiarly graceful cup, on a long stem, reminiscent of a wine goblet.

Vessels for preparing or holding the sacrificial wine were more numerous. The *tsun*, a tall and ample vase with a lid was made in a great variety of shapes, and in Chou times richly decorated. The *lei* (Fig. 17) was a low, rather squat vase; the *yu* (Fig. 18) round, with a low base and a lid crowned with a knob. This vessel was sometimes made in the form of an animal or bird. The beautiful *ku* (Plate III), a tall slender vase with a wide mouth and narrow waist is the most graceful of the vessels for liquids. The *p'an*, a large flat, low-rimmed bowl, was used for ablutions, or according to some authorities, to hold fruit. The *i* and the *tsieh* were shaped something like a modern sauce boat, the latter, however, having long legs, while the *i* has short legs, or sometimes rests on a base.

Occasionally these vessels were inscribed, usually with a short statement of the maker's name and the occasion for which the presentation of a new vase was intended, followed by an invocation

FIG. 18. *Zoomorphic Bronze Vessel, yu.*

to posterity to preserve the precious vessel. This at least has been faithfully carried out by subsequent generations of Chinese scholars who have always held the ancient bronzes in the highest esteem. It is only rarely that a vase is inscribed with a date or with a reign name which can afford a clue to its age. Vases so inscribed are greatly valued by Chinese collectors on account of the evidence they afford for the development of early forms of the script.

The vase, an *i*, used for pouring wine, which is illustrated in Plate IV is a particularly interesting example, as not only the date, but the country of its origin is stated in the inscription on the base. This vessel was made in Ch'u, the southern kingdom in the Yangtze Valley, which was not a member of the Chinese confederacy, the Middle Kingdom. The indications in the inscription point to a date before 704 B.C. Perhaps on account of its origin

in Ch'u, a state less civilised, at that period, than the northern
countries of the Middle Kingdom, this *i* has not the technical
perfection of some which have been found near An Yang, the
Shang capital. The decoration is also less elaborate than that of
many pieces of northern origin. It has none the less a simplicity
and strength of form which make it a remarkable product of the
ancient bronze worker's art.

Great archæological interest attaches to this particular vase on
account of its inscription which indicates that it was made in Ch'u
for a member of the royal house of that state. As at this time
(*circa* 704 B.C.) Ch'u was not yet regarded as a truly Chinese land,
it is important to have a concrete example of the artistic achievements of a country which the northern Chinese were inclined to

FIG. 19. *Archaic Inscription on Bronze, i.*

describe as half barbarous. This bronze suggests that the terms in
which these northern Chinese referred to the southern state must
not be taken too literally. Ch'u, perhaps, was "barbarous" to
them because, as we know, the language spoken in the Yangtze
Valley at that date was incomprehensible to the northerners, and

FIG. 20. *Bronze Vase, tsun.*

also because Ch'u did not form a part of the political confederacy presided over by the Chou King, the Son of Heaven. The inscription further proves that the script used in Ch'u was substantially the same as that used in other parts of China. This inscription runs: (Fig. 19)

"On the first day of the first month, according to the imperial calendar, it being a *kêng wu* day, Hsiung [or Ying] of Ch'u caused this ewer to be cast. For a myriad years may his descendants continue to use it for sacrificial offerings."*

Hsiung was the family name of the royal house of Ch'u.

In contrast to the simplicity of this *i*, the *tsun* illustrated in Fig. 20 is a type of vessel which displays the full range of the ancient decorative style. In this rich ornamentation the geometrical patterns of the background serve to emphasise the dominant *t'ao t'ieh* masks on the lid and on the waist of the vase, though the dragon-like creatures on the base and neck are less distinct. The cicada pattern of the rim is here stylised into formal triangles which hardly retain any suggestion of the original insect.

Sacrificial vessels were not the only bronzes made in the Shang and Chou period. The metal was also used to make chariot fittings, buckles, and horse equipment. Some of these have survived the passage of centuries and have recently been unearthed in increasing numbers from the tombs near the old city of Lo Yang in Honan, a city which was the capital of the Chou Kings during the feudal period. Swords, daggers and spear-heads were made of bronze in China, as elsewhere. The Bronze Age indeed lasted late in China. The introduction of iron, towards the end of the feudal period, did not at once oust bronze from the armourer's shop. Bronze swords were still in use, side by side with iron ones, in the Han dynasty. Recent discoveries in Annam, where bronze weapons of Chinese and local makes are found in the same tomb as iron swords imported from China, show that even in the middle Han period iron was exceedingly rare in the south.

The introduction of iron-working into China, almost certainly from a western source, is a subject which is very little illuminated

*Translated by Professor W. Perceval Yetts.

by the classical texts. The immense importance that the iron smelting industry attained in the Early Han dynasty (see Chapter VII) seems to suggest that the industry was a new one, under-

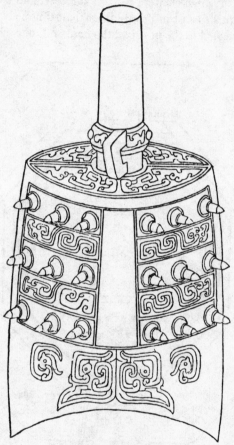

FIG. 21. *Bronze Bell.*

going rapid expansion as iron came to be preferred to bronze. We may hazard the guess that the phenomenal military successes of Ch'in, the western state which controlled the caravan routes to Central Asia, may have been due to the fact that the people of Ch'in became possessed of iron weapons in large quantities earlier than the eastern states. If, as seems certain, iron working was introduced from the west, the new metal and the technique of its manufacture into weapons would have come first to Ch'in, the border state of the north-west.

Bells (Fig. 21), which were used in the ceremonies of ancestor worship, were also cast in bronze in ancient times. Great importance was attached to the purity of the note and tone of these bells,

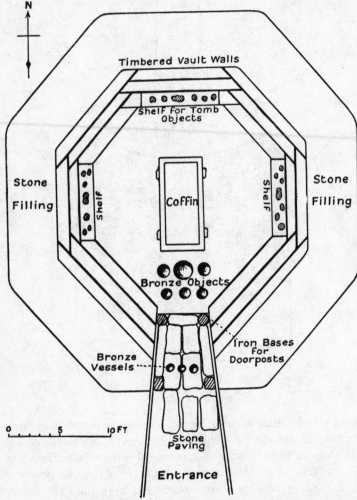

FIG. 22. *Plan of the Tomb of the Lord of Han at Lo Yang.*

and consequently the casting was undertaken with especial care. It was usual to mix the blood of a victim, a sheep or bullock, with the molten metal. Chinese bells have no tongue, the sound is made by striking the bell with a mallet, and they are of widely varying shapes. Oval and round are perhaps the most common, but square bells are also found. Like the sacrificial vessels, the bells were elaborately decorated and sometimes inscribed.

Recently the discovery of a set of inscribed bells in a tomb near Lo Yang has raised an interesting archæological problem. These bells, which were found in a richly furnished tomb with other bronzes, bear an inscription which though dated with a regnal year, omits the name of the ruler. Chinese and European scholars are divided in their interpretations of the inscription and the identification of the events and places mentioned in it. It is clear that the tomb (see plan in Fig. 22) was that of a lord or prince of the Han state (not the Han dynasty, but the feudal state, one of the "Three Tsin"); but it is uncertain whether the bells and the tomb are of the same date, or whether the bells were buried in the tomb of a later ruler. In the inscription the Lord of Han is referred to in terms which suggest that he was not at that time King of an independent state, but still only chief of a powerful fief subject to the state of Tsin. The furniture of the tomb, and the stylistic character of the objects found in it point to a later date.

The dated inscription mentions the "twenty-second year," but not the King's name. It has been suggested that this omission would only occur when the reign of the Son of Heaven was meant. If the twenty-second year of a Chou King is intended it can only be either 550 B.C., in the reign of Ling Wang, or 379 B.C. in that of An Wang. In the first case the Lord of Han was not an independent feudal prince, but in the latter period the Han state had become one of the leading kingdoms. The situation of the tomb, which is close to the Chou capital city, Lo Yang, is also perplexing, if it was that of a King of Han. It has been suggested that the tomb is that of the last King of Han, who, after the fall of his state, took refuge at the Chou capital and was interred there with such heirlooms of his family as he had been able to preserve. This would explain the presence of the bells of early date in a tomb with objects of a style which has hitherto been regarded as belonging to the very last years of the feudal period, if not to the Ch'in and early Han age.*

To the ancient Chinese jade was the most precious of stones, a sacred material containing the quintessence of virtue, and its use was confined to ritual objects. The sacred jades used by the kings

FIG. 23. *Jade Dragon, possibly a pendant.*

and princes of the Chou period were not always decorated, perhaps because the pure beauty of the stone was felt to be sufficient ornament. It is true that jade was used for purposes which do not at first sight appear to be strictly religious. Princes received jade tokens of investiture, and the nobility wore jade pendants and belt buckles attached to their girdles. The dragon illustrated in Fig. 23 is possibly one of these tokens, for it has a perforation which would suggest that it was used as a pendant. Investiture by the Son of Heaven was as much a religious as a political act, and the girdle pendants (Fig. 24) were intended to reinforce by their mysterious power the natural virtue of the wearer. This class of jades was richly decorated with motifs such as the *t'ao t'ieh* mask and cloud pattern which are found on the bronzes.

The use of the sacred stone upon weapons probably had a like

*The contents of this tomb and the question of the date to which it should be assigned are the subject of Bishop W. C. White's book, *Tombs of Old Lo Yang*. Shanghai: 1934.

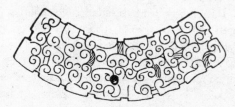

FIG. 24. *Jade Belt Buckles and Girdle Pendants.*

FIG. 25. *Sword Guard of Jade, decorated with t'ao t'ieh mask.*

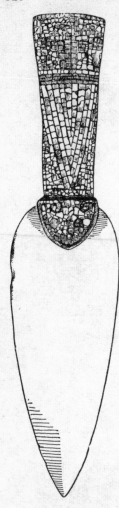

FIG. 26. *Jade Dagger with haft inlaid with turquoises.*

religious significance. Sword guards made of jade, decorated with the oft recurring *t'ao t'ieh* mask (Fig. 25), may have been believed to confer an especial protection upon the owner of the weapon. When the weapon itself is made of jade, it was no doubt intended for ceremonial or ritual use, for jade, though hard, is brittle and unsuitable for ordinary utilitarian purposes. These weapons were sometimes decorated with other precious stones, as the blade in Fig. 26, with its haft ornamented with turquoises.

It is obvious from the shapes of the jades used in the worship of the gods that these symbols had a very ancient origin. It is apparent that the sacred jades of the Chou period were conventionalised representations of primitive tools and weapons serving as tokens of power and emblems of the nature deities. The ancient Chinese did not make anthropomorphic images of their gods, their religious symbolism was governed by mathematical and abstract conceptions, consequently the jade symbols do not readily suggest to the modern mind the ideas which they were intended to represent. There were six sacred jade symbols: of the Heavens, the Earth, and the four points of the compass. The Heavens were of course also *yang*, the positive, light principle (male by later connotation) and the Earth was *yin*, negative dark, and by extension female. The four points of the compass were identified with the four seasons, the north with winter, the east with spring, perhaps because in North China the rain which ends the dry cold winter is brought by the east wind from the Pacific Ocean.

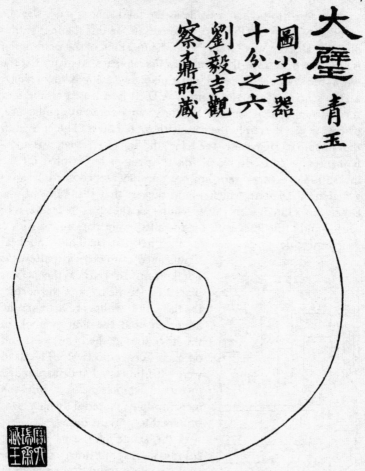

大壁 青玉

圖小于器
十分之六
劉毅吉觀
察古鼎所藏

FIG. 27. *Jade Disk, pi, symbolising Heaven.*

The south was associated with summer, which needs no explanation, but the reason which made the Chinese choose the west as the "direction" of autumn is perhaps also due to local climatic conditions. The strong dry north-west winds which sweep down on to the Chinese plain from Mongolia are the feature of autumn, and their coming regularly marks the sudden end of the hot season and the passing of summer.

The *pi*, a round disk of jade with a circular perforation, which was supposed to be half as wide as the solid ring of jade, was the emblem of Heaven (Fig. 27). The reason for this shape is rather obscure. Heaven was "round" but the meaning of the perforation is not known. It is worth noting that the explicit statement that the *pi* was the symbol of Heaven is first made by Chêng K'ang-ch'êng, a Han scholar of the 2nd century A.D. It is at least possible that this jade emblem at some earlier time had a different significance, or use, as was certainly the case with some others. The *pi* used in the worship of Heaven by the King, the Son of Heaven, was unornamented, a perfectly plain disk of green jade. *Pi* used for the investiture of princes were, however, ornamented. Sometimes with a design of dragons, which would suggest that this emblem was closely associated with sky worship—as the dragon is the rain spirit—and sometimes with the so-called grain pattern, or with a geometrical design of lozenges called net pattern. The symbolical significance of these two patterns is not known. In burials the *pi* was placed under the back of the corpse, the *tsung*, the symbol of Earth, on the abdomen, and the four symbols of the directions at the head, foot, and on each side, respectively. The dead were thus protected and surrounded by sacred symbols made of jade, the incorruptible material which was supposed to prevent decay.

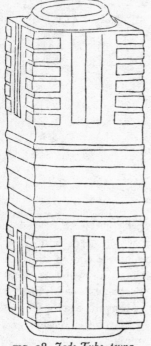

FIG. 28. *Jade Tube, tsung, symbolising Earth.*

If the shape of the *pi* does not readily suggest the idea of Heaven to the modern mind, the emblem of Earth was even more abstract. The *tsung* (Fig. 28) which served this purpose was a tube of jade circular within, but squared on the outer face. The circular part of the tube projected both above and below the squared portion, like a rim. The squared face is often grooved so that at the corners the edges are notched. It is stated in the

Chou Li that the *tsung* represented Earth because it was square on the outside, but circular inside. This explanation explains nothing, and it seems probable that the *tsung* is the conventionalised form of some very ancient instrument which became the emblem of Earth due to an association of ideas. It must be remembered that the explanations of these symbols are comparatively late, often the work of Han scholars writing at a time when schematic cosmology was the intellectual fashion. Their highly rationalised geometric ideas cannot faithfully represent the thought of the prehistoric people who first made the objects which are only known to us in their later, elaborated and refined form.

A theory concerning the original purpose of the *tsung* has been put forward by Dr. B. Karlgren* which, discarding the traditional explanation, attempts to find the real use for which the *tsung* was intended. His conclusion is that this tube, round and hollow inside, but square on the outer face, was in origin a protective cover for the ancestral tablets when, in remote antiquity, these were still made in phallic shape. The square face of the *tsung* prevented the sacred objects from rolling if accidentally over-turned. This theory, the only one which gives an acceptable reason for the curious shape of the symbol of Earth, will also explain why this object came in time to play that sacred rôle. In the same paper Karlgren has pointed out that the character for Earth, *t'u* 土 was originally written 𐌀, was in fact, a representation of the phallus. Earth being thus associated in the earliest script with the phallus (which also served to represent the word ancestor), it was not unnatural that the emblem for Earth should be the object most closely associated with the phallic ancestral tablets. These phallic tablets themselves could not of course be used to symbolise Earth as well as the ancestors, so the *tsung*, originally the cover and shield of the phallic image, became in itself the symbol of Earth.

Certain literary evidence exists to support this conclusion. The upper rim of the *tsung*, which would have enclosed the end of the phallic image, is known as the *shê*, and the same character

*"Some Fecundity Symbols in Ancient China." *Bulletin of the Museum of Far Eastern Antiquities*. Stockholm. 1930.

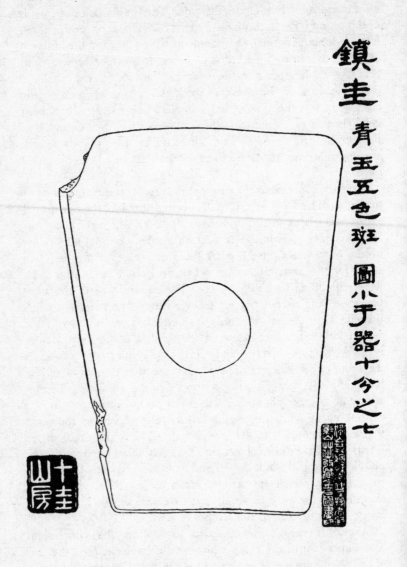

鎮圭 青玉五色斑 圖小于器十分之七

FIG. 29. *Jade Sceptre, chen kuei.*

is used to designate the pointed tip of the jade tablet called *kuei*, emblem of spring and the east, which has been recognised to be of phallic origin. The position of the *tsung* in burial rites, on the abdomen of the corpse, and the fact that the Son of Heaven presented his bride with a *tsung*, which was called the "venerable *tsung* of the inner apartments" (i.e. women's apartments) and became the emblem of the Empress, would also tend to suggest that there was an ancient, almost forgotten genital character about this emblem. The use of the *tsung* (if its origin as the protective shield of the phallic image is correct) as the emblem of Earth may have been one reason which led to the gradual identification of Earth as a female deity.

The *kuei*, a tablet of jade, is the name given to two objects which appear to be of quite different origin. The *chen kuei*, an implement with a perforation in the middle, perhaps to hold a wooden handle, was the symbol of royal power, the sceptre of the Son of Heaven. Plainly this was a ceremonial object derived from the primitive stone tool of remote antiquity. The specimen described by Wu Ta-ch'êng, a scholar and collector of the 19th century, was of dark green jade veined with other colours.* (Fig. 29.)

The more common type of *kuei*, the tablet with a pointed tapering end, was the symbol of the east and of spring (Fig. 30A). It was placed on the left side of a corpse in interments, as the body was placed head to the north and the left side was therefore the east side. The spring symbol *kuei* was made of green jade, the typical colour of the season, and its pointed end indicates that this tablet was originally phallic. It was one of the gifts made by the Son of Heaven to his consort, which bears out this assumption supported by the commentator Pan Ku of the 1st century A.D., who remarks that the pointed end represents the principle *yang* and the rectangular end the principle *yin*.

The *huang*, emblem of the winter and the north, was made of black jade. In shape it was a half *pi* or semi-circle, which is explained as symbolising the fact that only half the heavens are visible in winter. This piece was buried at the foot of the corpse.

*Wu Ta-ch'êng. *Ku yü t'u k'ao* in Chinese, from which we have taken illustrations of the *kuei*, *pi*, *chang* and *ya chang*.

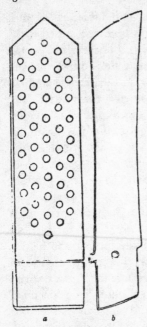

FIG. 30. *Jade Sceptres*

(a) *kuei, decorated with* "*grain pattern,*" *emblem of spring.*

(b) *ya chang, in the form of a knife.*

FIG. 32. *Jade Plaque in the form of a Stag.*

FIG. 31. *Jade Ornament in the form of a Crouching Tiger.*

The *chang*, a piece of jade shaped like the half of a *kuei*, the division being made lengthways, was the symbol of the south and summer. It was made of red jade, but no specimen of the Chou period has been identified. There were also knife-shaped tablets called *ya chang*, "teeth *chang*," manifestly derived from the antique stone knife (Fig. 30B). This emblem, appropriately enough, was the symbol of military authority over an army, the marshal's baton of the Chou period.

The *hu*, made of white jade and symbol of the west and autumn, was the only sacred jade made in the form of an animal. The *hu* was an image of a tiger, regarded by the Chinese as the king of beasts, and the west was the region over which he held sway. This fact may have been due to the situation of the Chinese settlements on the Yellow River plain, with the continuous belt of mountain country, in which tigers would be most common, to the west.* In the autumn the tiger, which litters in the spring, comes down to the plain in search of food. The tiger was therefore a natural

*This possible origin of the shape of the *hu* is suggested by the late Dr. B. Laufer in his volume *Jade*, Chicago (1912).

FIG. 33. *Jade Dragon in "Ch'in" or "Eastern Chou" transitional style.*

symbol for the west, and had no doubt been the deity of this "direction" from a very remote period.

In another class of jades the formal geometrical symbolism of the sacred emblems is enlivened by a wonderful feeling for rhythm and movement inspired by the zoomorphic character of the pieces. Objects such as the magnificent crouching tiger (Fig. 31) mounted on the head of a ceremonial object may, indeed, have been used in rites connected with the divinity of the west, but the stag (Fig. 32), a pendant as the perforation seems to suggest, was probably inspired by a bronze of the Scythian style, for it has something of the sense of movement and tension characteristic of that art (see Chapter X, Fig. 41).

With the fall of the feudal society, and the opening of wider horizons, there was a corresponding expansion of Chinese art. The formal, almost mathematical character of the Shang and Chou decoration was modified by the freer styles which the Chinese learned from contact with the nomads of the steppes and later from the civilisations of western Asia. The period at which these new influences first began to exercise a potent effect is undetermined, and only the further progress of archæological discovery can decide whether the late centuries of the feudal era, or the short-lived Ch'in Empire was really responsible for the introduction of styles which are firmly established under the Han dynasty. The transitional style, of which the jade dragon (Fig. 33) from the tombs of the lords of Han at Lo Yang is a typical example, has often been called "Ch'in," although some scholars prefer the name "Huai Valley" from the area where many objects of this type have been found. Eastern Chou has also been suggested as a comprehensive designation for the style of the later feudal period.

PART TWO—THE FIRST EMPIRE

Chapter VI

THE FORMATION OF A CENTRALISED STATE

IN the long course of Chinese history there have only been two revolutions which have radically altered the political and social structure of the state. The first was the great revolution of 221 B.C., by which the feudal system of ancient China was utterly destroyed and a centralised monarchy formed in its stead: the second, the revolution of 1911, by which that ancient monarchy was overthrown, and the Chinese people, under the impact of cultural influences from the West, attempted to readjust their political and social conditions to the new age of international contacts.

The great revolution which began after the conquest of the last feudal kingdoms by the Ch'in state in 221 B.C., ended in the consolidation of the autocratic universal monarchy under Liu Pang, founder of the Han dynasty, in 202 B.C. To later ages the full significance of this great change was not always apparent. The glory of the Han dynasty under the successors of Liu Pang obscured the humble origin of the founder, and in the new society, where men of the people rose easily to the highest posts, the memory of the ancient feudal system grew dim. Nevertheless, the Ch'in-Han revolution was the most profound and far-reaching social upheaval in all Chinese history.

Shih Huang Ti, "The First Emperor" as the King of Ch'in styled himself after the conquest of all his rivals, was himself a prince of ancient lineage, claiming descent, like all the feudal lords, from the mythical hero Huang Ti. When he began his revolutionary reign China was still a feudal society, even if it was a feudal society *in extremis*. The rulers of the surviving kingdoms were aristocrats of divine ancestry. The nobility, members of a limited number of ancient clans, were the only class which had political power, the peasantry and merchants were rigorously excluded from all privileges and posts of authority, their sole duty to the state was to provide the man-power and the money for the interminable wars under which they suffered. When the consolidation of the Han dynasty at last gave enduring peace to the ruined country this system had been swept away. The Emperor, Liu Pang, was by birth a poor peasant. The feudal aristocracy had been exterminated, the nobility ruined and dispersed, adventurers of the basest extraction had risen to the highest rank. So vast a change has had no parallel in eastern Asia until our own times.

Shih Huang Ti was more than an Emperor. He was one of the great destroyers of history. He destroyed not only the kingdoms of his rivals, the social and political system of ancient China, the literature of the past, but even the heritage of his ancestors and his own family. Such was not his intention. When he assumed the title of First Emperor, it was his hope that the empire which he had founded would be transmitted to his descendants for "ten thousand ages," and these successors would commemorate the fact by taking rank as Second, Third and Fourth Emperor, and so on, until the end of time. In point of fact his son and only successor had reigned less than four years before the mighty structure of the Ch'in Empire was utterly overthrown and the imperial family exterminated to the last man.

No hint of this dismal fate troubled the great innovator during his own lifetime. He died peacefully in 210 B.C. after thirty-seven years of rule in the kingdom of Ch'in, and eleven years as Emperor of all China. During those few years of unchallenged power he enforced his revolutionary plans with such ruthless thoroughness that the storm of reaction which broke after his death was powerless to undo his work. Shih Huang Ti has earned the detestation of all succeeding generations of Chinese scholars for his burning of the books and his contempt for the past, but their denunciations have not availed to destroy his true monument, the ideal of a unified empire, which he left as a legacy to all succeeding dynasties.

Determined to make the unity of the new empire complete and enduring, the Emperor and his minster, Li Ssŭ, paid as much attention to changing the customs of the people as to eradicating the power of the feudal aristocracy. Not only were the laws of the old states suppressed and the code of Ch'in enforced in all parts of the empire, but the varying standards of weight and measurement which had complicated commerce and hindered the collection of taxes (which were collected in kind) were abolished and the standards of Ch'in brought into universal use. Another important reform, for which the scholars might have given the Emperor a measure of praise, was the unification and standardisation of the numerous ways of writing the characters of the written language. Formerly every kingdom had its own peculiar script, which differed from those in use in other parts of China. Shih Huang Ti abolished a usage which might become a powerful obstacle to his plans, and this reform, which made the written language intelligible from one end of China to the other, has proved in later centuries to be the most enduring and effective bond of unity.

The security of the state, both from inside revolt and the attacks of barbarians, was provided for by measures conceived on the same grand scale. All weapons of war not required by the armies of Ch'in were collected, transported to the capital, and melted down. The conquered population was thus disarmed, and the danger of revolt decreased. When it is remembered that the recently conquered kingdoms had maintained large armies of war-trained men, who were now deprived of a livelihood, this precaution cannot be regarded as an act of tyranny. Nevertheless, it was one of the most unpopular of the acts of the new government, and in the bitter criticisms which this law provoked we can perhaps catch an echo of the resentment felt by the disinherited aristocracy of the old kingdoms, the *chün tzŭ*, now deprived of their hereditary right to command in war.

The building of the Great Wall, to form a barrier against the incursions of the nomads of the Mongolian steppe, was equally unpopular. Shih Huang Ti, as a matter of fact, was not the first sovereign to build such walls, and not all the present wall is due to him. The kings of Chao and Yen (Shansi and Hopei), whose states bordered the nomad country, had previously built stretches of wall to cover the passes. Shih Huang Ti linked up these earlier defences, extended the wall to the sea in the east, and westward to the remote north-west frontier of his own state of Ch'in, a distance of 1,400 miles. Upon this stupendous construction tens of thousands of exiled criminals laboured ceaselessly under ruthless task masters. If the scholars of every succeeding century have cursed the name of the First Emperor for burning the books, popular tradition has held his memory in undying hatred for building the Wall. Even to-day, after more than 2,000 years, the people repeat that a million men perished at the task, and every stone cost a human life.

Perhaps Shih Huang Ti and Li Ssŭ, fearing the hostility of a newly-conquered population long inured to war, endeavoured to occupy the energies of the nation by these gigantic public works. For while thousands laboured at the Wall, another multitude were employed on the construction of trunk roads, which, radiating from the capital, Hsien Yang in Shensi, stretched to the farthest frontiers of the empire. A curious piece of legislation, the law standardising the length of the axles of carts, must certainly be connected with the Emperor's projects to improve communications. In western and northern China, the loess country, the wheels of the carts cut deep ruts in the friable sandy soil, so that every cart is obliged to follow the existing ruts, the roads themselves being deeply sunken gullies below the general level of the plain. Carts having a different length of axle cannot use the same road, for the wheels will not fit the ruts. Consequently, it was frequently necessary to tranship goods or fit new axles to the carts. This system, typical of the particularism which marked the feudal age, was a great hindrance to the transport of merchandise, tax-grain, and the commissariat of the army. Shih Huang Ti therefore standardised the axle lengths so that changes of gauge no longer existed.*

The construction of roads was a benefit to the empire, but it proved a danger to the Ch'in dynasty. When the great revolt occurred the armies of the rebels found that the new roads served their purposes as well, or better, than those of the soldiers of Ch'in. For all the roads centred on the capital. The rebel armies were thus able to move swiftly and easily into the western hill country, hitherto so difficult of access, while the Ch'in generals, endeavouring to cope with rebellion in all parts of China, were hampered by the lack of lateral communications.

*It is curious that in one province, Shansi, this reform did not prove durable. To the present day the axles of Shansi carts are longer than those used in any other province, and consequently a Shansi cart has to have its axle changed before it can pass into the neighbouring provinces.

While the iron hand of the new universal authority was crushing local traditions and forcing the unwilling empire to conform to the revolutionary pattern of the new state, the policy of the Emperor was bitterly resented by that class which had suffered nothing but ruin and degradation from these changes. The *chün tzŭ* of the conquered kingdoms were unanimously opposed to the Ch'in Empire and the centralised state. The overthrow of the feudal courts had deprived them of their hereditary authority, their influence, and of much of their wealth. Ch'in officials, directly responsible to the throne, ruled in the former capitals of the princes. They did not require the services of the provincial aristocracy, a class which they rightly suspected of being the enemies of their master. The imperial Court was filled with revolutionary ministers and officials, who conferred their patronage on men of similar opinions Although there were not less than seventy "Scholars of Great Learning" attached to the Court, they were hardly employed, and their advice was neither sought nor followed.

The Emperor and the Court were well aware of the strength and danger of this opposition. Immediately after the conquest and pacification of the empire, he caused 120,000 families of the aristocracy, collected from all parts of China, to be transported to Shensi, thus at a blow destroying the ancient landed power of the noble clans. This vast transportation, which ruined the influence of the noble clans in their hereditary lands, was a staggering blow from which feudal society never recovered. It is noteworthy that many of the leaders of the great revolt were men of the people, and this leadership could only be the result of the absence of the local aristocracy, who were the bitterest enemies of the Ch'in Empire.

The anti-feudal attitude of the Court has been made perfectly plain by the record of the great discussion on the question of re-establishing feudal kingdoms for the profit of the Ch'in princes. Ssŭ-ma Ch'ien, the Han historian, has preserved the speeches of the protagonists, which if perhaps touched up by literary artifice, nevertheless truly represent the arguments advanced. One of the conservative ministers urged this re-establishment of feudal states:

"The kings have recently been destroyed, but the lands of Yen [Hopei] Ch'i [Shantung] and Ch'u [the Yangtze Valley] are very far away. Unless kings are set up in these countries there will be no means of assuring their fidelity and obedience. It is suggested that the sons of the Emperor be made kings in these countries."

Li Ssǔ, the most revolutionary of Shih Huang Ti's ministers, held very different views. He replied:

"The Kings Wên and Wu of the Chou dynasty [the founders] gave fiefs to their sons and brothers in great numbers. In the course of time, these close relations being dead, the branches divided and the relationship grew distant. Then the kings attacked each other as enemies and destroyed themselves in war, while the Son of Heaven could not control them. Now all within the four seas, thanks to the divine genius of Your Majesty, has been reduced in a uniform manner to prefectures and military districts. The sons of the imperial family and all meritorious subjects have been amply rewarded with titles, pensions from the taxes, and customs duties. That is quite sufficient. The empire will be easy to govern if the present arrangement is not disturbed. To establish kings would not be advantageous."

Shih Huang Ti approved Li Ssǔ's view in these words:

"If the whole empire has suffered and has been the prey of wars and rivalry which destroyed peace, it is because there were nobles and kings. Thanks to the aid of my ancestors the empire has been re-established. If new kings are set up, wars will break out again and the present tranquillity will be disturbed. Would not this be disastrous?"

The decision of the Court against any re-establishment of feudalism increased the animosity of the *chün tzǔ*. The School of Confucius, which appears to have already become the most widespread of the "Hundred Schools," furnished the bitterest critics of the imperial régime. Confucius had lived when the feudal age still stood intact. His teaching was designed for the world as he knew it. Living in an age when feudal obligations were growing lax and the old chivalry giving way to the brutal methods of a period of intense strife, the aristocrat of Lu had striven to recall his contemporaries to half-forgotten duties and the ritual obligations of the golden age of feudal society. He turned back to the past for examples of true virtue. To rebuke the growing disorder of his own day he painted, perhaps in too ideal colours, the perfect era of harmony and mutual respect which tradition alleged to have flourished under the sage rulers of the earliest time, and to have been revived by Wu, the founder of the Chou dynasty.

Since Confucius himself had never known a centralised empire, his writings did not expressly condemn such a state, but as they lauded the early feudal age as the era of true virtue and justice, his followers considered that the authority of the sage could be invoked to justify the past, and condemn the changes which Shih Huang Ti had made. Moreover, these critics, who constantly cited the literature of the past, were not slow to point out that the state of Ch'in appeared in these old books in the unfavourable light of a semi-barbarous kingdom. In the *Ch'un Ch'iu* period (722-481 B.C.) the "land within the passes" (the modern Shensi province) had hardly been considered part of the Middle Kingdom. It was impossible that changes inaugurated by these rude men from the west could be preferred to the divinely sanctioned system set up by the hero-sages of the past.

Li Ssǔ, Shih Huang Ti's minister, and the most ardent revolutionary at the imperial Court, saw the danger of this insidious propaganda. With education in the hands of the enemies of the régime, and the instruction which they imparted based on a literature wholly hostile to the new order, the forces of reaction, though beaten on the battlefield, had still a dangerous weapon with which to attack the new empire. He decided that the revolution must go a step further. It was not enough to destroy feudalism. Even the memory of the past must be rooted out, history itself must be abolished, and the enemies of the state silenced. The occasion for this step was offered by the conservatives themselves, who made one more fruitless petition for the re-establishment of feudal fiefs under the princes of the house of Ch'in. Then Li

Ssǔ proposed his famous plan to burn the books, which has earned him the undying hatred of subsequent generations of scholars. He said:

"The Five Emperors* did not copy each other, the three dynasties [Hsia, Shang and Chou] did not imitate their predecessors. Each had its particular form of government. It was not that they were opposed to the methods of their forerunners, but that times had changed. Now Your Majesty is the first to accomplish a great achievement. He has founded a glory which will endure for ten thousand ages. This is what narrow scholars cannot understand. Moreover, the matters about which Shun-yu has spoken† concern the three dynasties. Why should we take them as a model? Formerly the princes were continually at war. They esteemed the wandering scholars and sought their advice. Now the empire has been pacified. Laws and commands emanate from a single authority. The common people are engaged in industry and agriculture, the superior classes study law and the methods of administration. Nevertheless the scholar nobles [*chün tzǔ*] do not conduct themselves in the new way, but study the past in order to defame the present. They cause doubt and trouble among the black haired people [the Chinese]. The Counsellor, your subject, Li Ssǔ, not disguising from himself that he merits death‡ advises : in the past the empire was troubled and divided. No one could succeed in uniting it. Thus the princes reigned simultaneously. In their discussions the scholars speak of ancient times in order to decry the present. They use false examples to stir up confusion in the actual state of affairs, they proclaim the excellence of the doctrines they have studied to abuse what Your Majesty has established. Now that the Emperor possesses the whole land and has imposed unity, they

*The five legendary emperors who preceded the Hsia dynasty, Huang Ti, Chuan Hsiu, K'u, Yao and Shun.

†Shun-yu Yüeh, a conservative minister, had just proposed the re-establishment of feudal fiefs, basing his argument on the fact that such fiefs had always existed under the preceding dynasties.

‡A formula of respect used when offering advice, which, in theory, might be displeasing to the sovereign and so justify the death of him who offered it.

honour the past and hold private consultations. These men who oppose the new laws and commands, as soon as they hear of a new edict, discuss it in accordance with their doctrines. When they are at Court they conceal their resentment, but when they are elsewhere they debate these matters in the public streets and encourage the common people to believe calumnies. This being the case, unless we take action the authority of the sovereign will be abased, the associations of the malcontents will grow powerful. It is necessary to prevent this. Your subject proposes that the histories [of the feudal states], with the exception of that of Ch'in, shall all be burnt. With the exception of those holding the rank of 'Scholars of Great Learning,'* all men in the entire empire who possess copies of the *Shu Ching*, the *Shih Ching*, and the works of the Hundred Schools, must all take these books to the magistrates to be burnt. Those who dare to discuss and comment the *Shu Ching* and *Shih Ching* shall be put to death and their bodies exposed in the market place. Those who praise ancient institutions to decry the present régime shall be exterminated with all the members of their families. Officials who condone breaches of this law shall themselves be implicated in the crime. Thirty days after the publication of this decree, all who have not burnt their books will be branded and sent to forced labour on the Great Wall. Those books which shall be permitted are only those which treat of medicine, divination, agriculture and arboriculture. As for those who wish to study law and administration,† let them take the governing officials as their masters."

The decree, as drafted by Li Ssŭ, was "approved."

Such was the cause of the famous burning of the books, a catastrophe which has left irreparable gaps in the history of ancient China, and almost destroyed the philosophical writings of the Hundred Schools. The heroic courage of scholars who

*There were seventy of these scholars. Judging from the great difficulty later experienced in finding copies of the ancient books, these scholars do not seem to have availed themselves of their privilege, or else their libraries perished in the turmoil of the great revolt.

†In certain editions of the *Shih Chi* the two words "law and administration" (*fa ling*) are omitted.

defied the decree did indeed preserve the essential skeleton of the ancient literature. Particularly the works of the Confucian school escaped annihilation, and this fact alone goes far to prove that that school had already by far the greatest number of disciples. For a time the ancient literature entirely vanished. Much was burnt, the rest hidden in walls and tombs, often to be forgotten in the tumults of succeeding years. The decree was ruthlessly enforced during the duration of the Ch'in dynasty, and no less than 460 scholars were put to death for concealing their books.

Li Ssǔ's purpose was accomplished. The burning of the books, and the proscription of all ancient teaching and history broke the power and influence of the *chün tzǔ*, already shattered by the transportations and suppression of the fiefs. Though his legislation did not succeed in establishing the Ch'in dynasty on an enduring basis, it did destroy even the memory of the ancient institutions. When, under the Han dynasty, the ancient literature was painfully collected and reassembled from fragments and the retentive memories of aged men, it had ceased to be the expression of a living political and social system. Within less than a hundred years the historian and scholar Ssǔ-ma Ch'ien himself no longer clearly understood the difference between the names of the noble clans and the surnames of the families into which they had divided. He constantly confuses the meaning of the ancient words for clan and family.* Yet this distinction was of the first importance in feudal times, when only a limited number of noble clans had any part in the political life of the states. So completely had the aristocracy lost caste and position at the end of the revolution that a scholar and conservative no longer clearly understood the fact that their ancient privileges had been founded on noble descent and not on education.

The burning of the books ruined the last hopes of the feudal party. It also weakened the Ch'in dynasty itself. With the exception of the official class in Ch'in, the nobility of the entire empire was now united in hatred and hostility to the imperial régime. Moreover, the opposition now spread to classes which had

*This significant fact was pointed out by the great French scholar E. Chavannes in his translation of the works of Ssǔ-ma Ch'ien. Chavannes. *Les Memoires historiques de Se-Ma T'sien.* Paris, 1895, Vol. 1, page 1, note 3.

hitherto taken no interest in political questions. The ruin of the aristocracy, to whose rule they had been accustomed, exposed the peasantry to the cruel weight of the Ch'in despotism, its ruinous taxation, and its incessant forced labour. Local customs were trodden under foot. Strangers from the west ground down the provinces with merciless disregard for the sufferings of the people.

The people, though misruled in the period of the Warring States, and ready to welcome any relief, now found that they had changed King Log for King Stork. Their old princes they had known and respected with a hoary tradition of loyalty. The new rulers were military officers from Ch'in who treated the eastern provinces as a conquered land. Thus when the *chün tzǔ* preached revolt the peasantry were willing to listen. Crimes and brigandage rose like a tide. The Emperor, aloof and mysterious, confided in his revolutionary ministers and ignored all discontent.

From the moment of his accession to the position of sole and supreme autocrat Shih Huang Ti surrounded himself with a mystery and pomp, which, though intended to enhance his prestige, in reality concealed from the sovereign the consequences of his decrees. He had abandoned the ancient royal title to assume the new and imposing style of Huang Ti, which is translated as Emperor. The Chou Sons of Heaven had been content with the title of King. Only the semi-divine legendary heroes of the past had been styled Huang Ti. The new title was thus to the men of that age equivalent to a mark of divinity. The Emperor lived and worked in the most carefully guarded secrecy. When he travelled, it was a crime, instantly punished with death, to reveal his movements. In the vast palaces which he constructed at Hsien Yang he moved secretly from one apartment to another, only a handful of eunuchs knowing where he was to be found. So secret was his life, that when he died, journeying in the eastern provinces, not even the imperial cortège was aware of the fact, and the strange procession travelled across the length of China, to the capital, with the dead Emperor's body, the secret only known to five or six eunuchs and the minister Li Ssǔ. As the weather was summer, and the corpse became decomposed, it was found necessary to place a quantity of rancid salt fish on a cart which followed the imperial chariot, lest the soldiers and attendants should suspect that the sovereign was dead.

There was another reason for concealing the death of the great conqueror. The Crown Prince was known to be an opponent of the extreme measures which Li Ssŭ had taken against the scholars. He had protested against the burning of the books, and in consequence had been ordered to leave the Court, to reside with the army of the north which guarded the Great Wall against the incursions of the nomad Huns (Hsiung Nu). Li Ssŭ and the chief eunuch Chao Kao feared, with reason, that if the Prince succeeded his father, they would be dismissed and probably put to death. If the death of the Emperor became known, the Prince with the army of the north could march on Hsien Yang long before the ministers could reach the capital. Accordingly they suppressed the sealed letter by which Shih Huang Ti had declared the Crown Prince to be his successor. In its place they sent a secret forged decree ordering the Crown Prince and Mêng T'ien, general in command in the north, to commit suicide. The deception was not discovered, and the Prince and Mêng T'ien perished. This general was the most famous of the Ch'in commanders, to whom the final victory over the feudal states was largely due. Li Ssŭ and the eunuch Chao Kao then placed Shih Huang Ti's second son on the throne. He reigned, in accordance with his father's wish, as Er Shih Huang Ti, "The Second Emperor."

This palace intrigue, made possible by Shih Huang Ti's secret mode of life, was fatal to the Ch'in dynasty. The new ruler was a youth of twenty-one, without experience or capacity. He entrusted all authority to Chao Kao. The all-powerful eunuch, fearing the authority of the generals and ministers, dismissed the most capable and trusted of Shih Huang Ti's officials and substituted his own creatures. The taxation was increased, the severity of the laws enhanced, exiles and convicts multiplied. Through jealousy or fear, even the princes of the imperial house were not spared. Li Ssŭ himself fell victim to the rivalry of his eunuch colleague and perished under the torturers' hands.

The downfall of the Ch'in dynasty, which occurred before the Second Emperor had been three years on the throne, provoked a Han scholar, Chia I, to compose one of the most remarkable and penetrating political documents of the ancient world. The "Faults of Ch'in" (*Kuo Ch'in Lun*) has been preserved in the work of the Han historian Ssǔ-ma Ch'ien (145-86 B.C.), who lived some years after Chia I. The author of this dissertation was a scholar, and therefore a conservative; he regrets the feudal age, but cannot deny the chaos which preceded the Ch'in dynasty. Then he discusses the great opportunity which came to Shih Huang Ti by virtue of his conquests and the natural strength of his ancestral kingdom, for Chia I, unlike so many Chinese scholars, had an eye for strategy. Then he exposes the condition of the empire under the Ch'in rule and the causes of the great revolt. Chia I, who lived from 198 to 165 B.C., was almost a contemporary of the great revolution and certainly had talked with men who remembered the Ch'in times:

"When Ch'in faced south and ruled over the empire there was once more a Son of Heaven. Immediately the innumerable multitude of the people began to hope for the peace to which they are inclined by nature. There was not one that did not give Ch'in their allegiance and regard him with respect. In this was the true principle of security, of enduring glory and the elimination of danger. But the King of Ch'in was of a base and greedy character. He relied upon his own judgment, did not trust ministers of proved ability, and was not willing to conciliate the nobility and the people. He multiplied the tortures and made the punishments more terrible. His officers governed with the greatest severity. The rewards and penalties were unjust. The taxes and levies were unbearable. The empire was crushed under forced labour, the officials could not maintain order, the hundred families [the people] were in the last extremity of misery, and the sovereign had no pity for them and gave them no help. Then crime broke out in every place and the Emperor and his subjects deceived each other mutually. The condemned were an innumerable multitude; those who had been tortured and mutilated formed a long procession on the roads [on their way to exile]. From the princes and ministers down to the humblest people every one was terrified and in fear for their lives. No man felt secure in his office; all were easily degraded.

"So Ch'ên Shê, without needing to be a sage like T'ang or Wu [founders of the Shang and Chou dynasties], without having any high rank such as Duke or Marquis, had only to wave his arms for the whole empire to answer like an echo.

"When a man has the rank of Son of Heaven, and all the wealth of the empire as his riches, and yet cannot escape being massacred, it is because he·has failed to distinguish between the means by which power is safeguarded and the causes which lead to disaster."

Before Er Shih Huang Ti had been four years on the throne he had indeed ruined not only his father's life's work, but fatally jeopardised the heritage transmitted by all the preceding Kings of Ch'in. In the year 209 B.C., before Shih Huang Ti had been in his tomb a year, a common soldier in the country of Ch'u (Hupei) persuaded his comrades to mutiny, and started the great revolt. Ch'ên Shê, as Chia I is at pains to recall, was neither a scion of some fallen royal house nor even a member of the aristocracy. He was a man of the people, poor and entirely unknown. Yet the empire "answered him like the echo." As if at a preconcerted signal, though in reality each revolt was a spontaneous expression of the universal despair, the whole of the "land outside the passes" —eastern and southern China—rose in revolt. The leaders of the rebellions were for the most part adventurers, but at first they secured popular support by restoring the old feudal kingdoms. Obscure descendants of the old royal families were sought out in their hiding places and proclaimed Kings of Ch'u, Han, Wei, Chao and Ch'i.

Although the Ch'in generals, whose troops were well armed, succeeded in suppressing the first risings, others broke out immediately, and proved far more formidable. The rebel leaders made a convention dividing the empire between them. In the last month of 207 B.C. the future founder of the Han dynasty, Liu Pang, advanced unopposed on Hsien Yang and received the surrender of the Ch'in capital. Er Shih Huang Ti had already perished at the hands of the eunuch Chao Kao. His successor, who reigned only forty-three days, having surrendered to Liu Pang and abdicated the throne, was a few months later put to death with all his family by Hsiang Yü, the leader of the rebel confederacy.

Although the rebels had begun by restoring the old royal families, and even accorded the title of Son of Heaven to the restored King of Ch'u, all power and authority really remained with the generals, adventurers of obscure origin. The most powerful of these military leaders was Hsiang Yü, who, unlike the majority of his colleagues, was of aristocratic origin, descendant of a noble family of Ch'u who had held the hereditary rank of general in the old kingdom.

While Liu Pang had captured undefended Hsien Yang, his superior and chief rival, Hsiang Yü, had defeated the great army which was the last hope of the Ch'in dynasty. Supreme in eastern China as a result of this victory, Hsiang Yü proceeded to impose a new political system on the lands which had been freed from Ch'in tyranny. The old kingdoms were restored, but with a diminished area, for large territories had to be given to the powerful adventurers who commanded the armies. Thus, not merely the seven old kingdoms were reconstituted, but a large number of new artificial states were created at their expense. Ch'in was divided into three parts and awarded to the Ch'in generals who had surrendered to the rebels. The future founder of the Han dynasty received as his portion the country now known as Szechuan and southern Shensi, which received the name of Han from the river which waters it. Hsiang Yü himself assumed the title of Pa Wang, the Hegemon King, and distributed the territories of the east to his generals and companions.

This attempt to revive the feudal system was a failure from the very beginning. Hsiang Yü speedily got rid of the nominal Ch'u Emperor. His generals, dissatisfied with their portion of the spoils of Ch'in, attacked and despoiled the restored scions of the ancient royal families. Liu Pang dispossessed the three new Kings of Ch'in and made himself supreme in the "land within the passes." The new feudal system broke down completely, and at once; there ensued a furious and ruthless war between the former allies.

No more striking proof of the thoroughness of Shih Huang Ti's revolution can be adduced than the utter failure of his enemies when the hour of reaction gave them their chance to restore the old system. Ch'in was destroyed, divided and humbled. No better opportunity could be asked for; if the feudal system was the true solution for the troubles of the state, it had now a fresh lease of life, but it collapsed at once. The ancient royal families had lost all prestige, and they were dethroned by adventurers. The new kings were not attached to their dominions by any ties of blood or established loyalties. They attacked and despoiled each other without any regard for the sanctity of treaties and alliances. In less than a year the new settlement had been destroyed, and the struggle developed into an undisguised contest to restore the unified empire for the profit of the strongest military chieftain. This war, between Liu Pang in the west and Hsiang Yü, who controlled the eastern provinces, ended five years later in the complete triumph of the former, and the foundation of the Han dynasty.

The Chinese have delighted, in history, in romance, and in drama, to relate the story of this famous war, emphasising the strong contrasts in character which marked the rival leaders. This contrast has more than a dramatic significance. The contest was one of the new and the old, the ideal of the unified state, and the ideal of feudalism, the struggle between the peasant adventurer and the aristocrat. Liu Pang had all the qualities and defects of his class in an exceptional degree. He was shrewd and cautious, an excellent judge of men, jovial and good natured, but he was not accustomed to courtly manners and cared little for chivalrous traditions. He understood his own class, the people, and, being unhampered by an education in outworn ideas, he judged a situation in terms of reality. In the field he was neither conspicuously brave nor very successful. He was more often beaten than victorious in pitched battles, but he never lost a campaign. He was a consummate politician.

Hsiang Yü was an aristocrat as typical of his class, the ruined chün tzǔ, as Liu Pang, product of the great revolution. The Hegemon King was a man of exceptional physique, very tall and of enormous muscular strength. Educated in the traditional culture, he was a poet, a courteous and polished gentleman, a brave and intrepid fighter; the terror of his enemies. He never lost a pitched battle until the very end of his career, but he never profited by his victories. He was arrogant and cruel. His temper was uncontrollable, and led him to commit excesses for which he repented too late. He alienated his allies and generals by his pride and ambition. He had no political programme other than the restoration of a discredited feudalism, which he himself was not prepared to support when its restrictions ran counter to his ambition.

Ultimately, after five years of fluctuating fortune, Hsiang Yü found himself surrounded by his enemies, their numbers swollen by his own former followers, now won over by the political skill of his peasant adversary. The last scene of this memorable struggle is thus described by the Han historian*:

"At night Hsiang Yü heard on all sides men singing the songs of Ch'u [his own countrymen, now in his enemy's camp]. He was greatly alarmed, and exclaimed: 'Has Han gained all the people of Ch'u?' Then the King rose and spent the night drinking in his tent. He had a beautiful wife named Yu, and a superb horse named Ch'ui, which he always rode. The King sang sadly of his sorrows. He composed these verses:

> My strength uprooted the mountains,
> My force dominated the world.
> Fortune no longer favours me.
> Ch'ui can gallop no more:
> If Ch'ui can gallop no more
> What can I accomplish?
> Yu, Yu, what will be your fate?'

"The King and Queen Yu sang many stanzas together. The King wept, and his attendants could not restrain their tears. Not one of them could lift his head and look upon the King."

Hsiang Yü, after cutting his way out through the besieging army, perished by his own hand, when capture was inevitable, on the banks of the river Wu near Ho Chou in Anhui. The great revolution was at an end and Liu Pang, the peasant, was undisputed master of the whole empire.

*Ssŭ-ma Ch'ien, Shih Chi, here quoting the Ch'u Han Ch'un Ch'iu, a book composed by Lu Chia, who was a follower of Liu Pang and an eye-witness of the war. His book, now lost, is only known by the quotations in the Shih Chi.

The empire which Liu Pang founded was in many respects a restoration of the Ch'in autocracy which the whole nation had combined to destroy five or six years before. Like his predecessor, Shih Huang Ti, the new Emperor, though a native of the southeast (north Kiangsu), fixed his capital in that well defended "land within the passes," Shensi, which had been the strength of the Ch'in kingdom, and which Hsiang Yü had not had the strategical insight to keep for himself. Nor, indeed, were the scholars and gentry much in favour at the new Court in the early years of the Han dynasty. Liu Pang was himself a man of little education and obscure origin. It was not to be expected that he would favour the aristocratic party who so constantly advocated a return to the past. The new Emperor was clever enough to realise that though the policy of Ch'in Shih Huang Ti was the only one possible for the ruler of a unified empire, it was necessary to go about it more tactfully and gradually. He did not, therefore, condemn feudal institutions outright. He gave fiefs to his followers, but made a rule that no man who was not a member of his own family might be made a King. The new feudalism, or rather the façade of feudalism under which the Han Emperor concealed the hard fact of autocracy, was very different from the old. The new kings ruled over small and diminished territories. Their states formed enclaves in the midst of provinces governed by imperial officers in the Ch'in manner. They were frequently displaced, either to be given a new kingdom in some other part of the empire, or to be degraded altogether. Liu Pang with ruthless ingratitude, which was yet politically most wise, deprived his generals of the kingdoms which they had received as a reward for their services. Even Han Hsin, to whose military skill he owed the victory over Hsiang Yü, was degraded and finally put to death. With few exceptions the generals who had won the victories which founded his dynasty were degraded and executed for real or alleged conspiracies.

The successors of Liu Pang pursued his policy with success. The feudal princes, all members of the Liu imperial family, were supervised by officers who were directly responsible to the Emperor. They were frequently summoned to court, and degraded or displaced for the lightest faults. Finally, the clever policy of the

Emperor Hsiao Ching found a means to reduce them to complete unimportance. By the decree of 144 B.C. all the sons of a feudal lord were made co-heirs of their father, and his estates divided amongst them. When any branch became extinct the state was suppressed and made an imperial prefecture. Thus, when Liu Pang reigned there were 143 feudal fiefs in the empire; by the end of the Han dynasty these had been increased to 241, but they were now merely petty lordships, covering only two or three towns. This policy was not carried out without checks. Occasionally the emperors had to sacrifice a minister who had gone too fast, notably after the revolt of the seven chief kings of the eastern provinces in 154 B.C. But the power of the court grew steadily stronger, the importance of the feudal lords decreased with every generation. After the reign of the Emperor Wu, 141-87 B.C., the feudal states ceased to be of any importance and are rarely mentioned.

The disappearance of feudalism was rendered possible by the policy of the Han Emperors towards a very important and hitherto irreconcilably reactionary class, the *chün tzŭ*. The aristocracy had been virtually destroyed by the revolutionary measures of Shih Huang Ti, but they transmitted their ideals and their political outlook to a new class, the scholars and officials of the centralised empire. From this time onwards the *chün tzŭ* cease to be an hereditary nobility distinguished by membership of a limited number of clans. The revolution had destroyed the territorial and clan basis of the old aristocracy for ever. The *chün tzŭ*, including many of the old aristocratic families, became a class marked off from the mass of the people by education, and only by education. While from Han times until to-day the ancient families, such as that of Confucius himself, have received a respect rarely accorded to upstarts, the true ruling class in no way depended on noble blood. The very meaning of the old terms became obscure. *Chün tzŭ* had meant the son of a lord, member of a noble clan. Under the new régime it gradually came to mean a gentleman in much the same sense as that word is used in modern English— one who had received a polite education.

The later Han Emperors adroitly favoured the new educated class. Themselves of peasant origin, with no trace of divine or noble blood to fortify their claim to the throne, it was of vital importance to the new emperors to discover some principle of legitimacy for their power. Noble blood and divine descent they could not claim; force, upon which the Ch'in had relied, had proved to be a double-edged weapon. The master stroke of the Han Emperors was to enlist in support of the centralised state the very school which had upheld feudalism to the last. The successors of Liu Pang not only repealed the proscription of the books, but bestowed the imperial patronage on the followers of Confucius. The ancient literature was brought out from its hiding places and pieced together. The sages and heroes of the feudal age were honoured as never before. And yet all the time the Han Emperors undeviatingly pursued their policy which aimed at the eradication of the last vestiges of feudalism.

Their supreme achievement was to persuade the new scholar class, to whom the feudal age was personally unknown, that the doctrines of Confucius could be applied to the new political régime. The Sage of Lu had taught the obedience of sons to their parents, of the nobles to their lord, and of the lords to the Son of Heaven. The Han rulers expanded this last allegiance, and extended the scope of Confucius' aristocratic ethical code to include all subjects of the Emperor. Not only the hereditary nobility, but every man who served the state, should make his ideal the Confucian loyalty to the prince, and this prince must be none other than the Emperor himself.

By this clever distortion of the ancient feudal ideal the Han Emperors made the doctrine of Confucius the strongest support of that centralised autocratic monarchy which the Sage himself had never known, and which his followers had formerly opposed to the last gasp. The triumph was complete. In time the true character of the feudal age became obscure to the scholars themselves. The past was interpreted in terms of the present, and the legend of a unified empire in remote antiquity which had later degenerated into feudalism, became widely accepted. Shih Huang Ti tried to destroy the memory of the past; the Han sovereigns, more subtle than he, succeeded in distorting it.

The interpretation of the Confucian doctrine which gained currency during the Han dynasty proved one of the most enduring results of the revolution. The ideal of a centralised state became closely associated with the scholar class and the followers of the Confucian school. Henceforward fissiparous movements are always opposed by the scholars, the very class who had defended ancient feudalism. The temporary interludes between centralised dynasties when not caused by partial foreign conquests, have always resulted from the rise to inordinate power of military chiefs, and these periods of division have been unsparingly condemned by the scholars as "ages of confusion."

Chapter VII

THE SOCIAL AND ECONOMIC REVOLUTION

THE triumph of Liu Pang and the wise policy of his successors towards the fief-holding princes established the political basis of the new centralised empire on a firm and enduring foundation, but the social and economic consequences of the great revolution were as far reaching as the political changes, and raised problems which the Han Emperors found less easy to solve. Though Liu Pang and his successors pursued a consciously anti-feudal policy in their endeavour to build up the supreme power of the imperial Court, some of the results of the fall of the feudal aristocracy tended not to strengthen, but to undermine the power of the Emperor and to jeopardise the dynasty.

The ruin of the aristocracy left a gap in the social system which was too often filled by very undesirable elements. While the Han dynasty saw the beginning of a new conception of society in which education and culture rather than divine or noble descent were the marks of the ruling class, the revolution was still too recent to permit this new form of society to win general respect and recognition. Men still looked back to the feudal age, still doubted the permanence of the new empire, still secretly thought of the imperial family as upstarts. While the Han Emperors achieved the destruction of feudal traditions in the provinces, the Court, which was intended to be the central and unshakeable authority from which the whole empire took the law, was, in fact, disturbed by frequent and sanguinary palace revolutions.

These disorders were due to one of the unforeseen consequences of the revolution, the rise to great power and influence of the families allied to the Emperor by marriage. Under the feudal system this source of instability had not existed. The Chinese marriage customs, which forbade the intermarriage of members of the same clan, and therefore still more of persons with the same surname,* forced the feudal princes to seek their brides among

*This rule of exogamy was of great antiquity and formed part of the primitive organisation of the Chinese tribes in the prehistoric period. Surnames,

their social equals of another clan, and these were necessarily the princely families of other states. Thus, the family of the Queen was a foreign family, not resident in the King's state, and unable to exercise any influence on court policy. Equally the Queen herself, having no family backing in her adopted country, was negligible as a political force in internal affairs, though her influence might sometimes be exercised in foreign affairs in favour of her native country, as in 645 B.C., when the Queen of Ch'in, herself a member of the royal family of Tsin, interceded with her husband and saved the life of the captive Duke of Tsin.

Under the Han Empire a very different situation arose. There was now only one sovereign family, and as the emperors could not inter-marry with the collateral branches of the imperial family— since these all bore the same surname—they were obliged to marry the daughters of their own subjects. This custom introduced a new and dangerous factor into political life. Marriage, so far from being a means to secure a profitable alliance, as in the feudal age, now tended to raise up a rival family. The empresses were chosen either for their personal charms, or to confer favour upon a deserving minister or general. Their influence in either case was a menace to the imperial house. If they owed their rank to their beauty, they persuaded the emperors to lavish favours on their own upstart relations. If their family was already distinguished in the state service, it now acquired a potent influence in the very centre of the government.

As the mother of the heir the Empress was a person of the first importance. On the death of the Emperor, should her son (as was frequently the case) be still a child, she exercised the regency, and forthwith the whole imperial authority passed into the hands of her family. Her brothers or uncles occupied the highest posts and filled the administration with their clansmen and clients. Since their power depended on the Empress alone, they endeavoured to prolong the regency, even when the young Emperor was of an age to govern. A change of reign, or even the marriage of

which came gradually into use in the feudal period, were at first confined to the nobility, and had either a place name origin or were derived from the name of an office or rank, i.e. Ssǔ-ma, "commander of the horse," and Kung-sun "grandson of the duke." Persons of the same surname were therefore held to be members, however distant, of the same family.

the new Emperor, would spell the end of their influence, consequently they used the heyday of their power to amass vast wealth and form a party to sustain them in the evil hour to come.

In the new revolutionary society these consort-families were no longer aristocrats with an ancient tradition of loyalty and obedience, they were upstarts whose only support was the imperial favour conferred upon the Empress. Previously they had been men of no account; on the death of the Empress they would be deprived of their power, their wealth, and probably also of their lives. They were the target for every envy and jealousy. No sense of aristocratic privilege moderated their rapacity or restrained their arrogance. From the perils which menaced them at a change of reign there was but one escape, to go one step further and seize the throne itself. The fatal logic of their position impelled almost every consort-family under the Han dynasty to make the attempt and, with one exception, all failed. Their history, and that of the Han Court, repeats itself with hardly any variation. The family of the Empress is rewarded with titles and high positions. They seize all power, they aim at the throne, and upon the death or fall of their sole support, the Empress herself, they are ruthlessly exterminated to make way for the relatives of the new Empress.

The family of the first Han Empress, the Lu, were the first to set an example which so many of their successors followed, and the family of Wang, who first married into the imperial house in the reign of Han Yüan Ti, 49-33 B.C., was the only one which gained a temporary security by usurping the throne itself. Wang Mang, the usurper, enjoyed his power for only fourteen years (A.D. 9-23). The house of Han was not without support in the provinces, and after a violent civil war the throne was regained by the Emperor Kuang Wu Ti, who thereupon transferred his Court eastward to Lo Yang in Honan. This event marks the separation of the Han dynasty into two periods, which are known as the Western or Early Han dynasty (206 B.C.—A.D. 25), and the Eastern or Later Han dynasty (A.D. 25-221).

Palace intrigues and court revolutions due to the new power of women were not the only disturbing consequences of the social revolution. The rise of classes hitherto excluded from political power raised other problems, intimately associated with the economic troubles of the new empire. Under the first Han ruler the old law which forbade merchants and artisans from occupying any official post was maintained. Liu Pang, himself a peasant, favoured his own class. Accepting the teaching of the Legist School, he believed that agriculture was the foundation of the economic system and the only industry which should be patronised and protected by the government. The need for recovery was indeed obvious enough. The Han Emperor found the Chinese world in the last extremity of exhaustion and poverty. The great revolution, following upon the Ch'in despotism, and the endless wastage of the period of the Warring States, had reduced the country to a condition which has been vividly described in the work of Ssŭ-ma Ch'ien. On his accession Liu Pang could not find four horses of the same colour in all his empire to draw his chariot. The highest officials employed oxen for the same purpose; as the price of a horse was 300 pounds of gold, the fact is not surprising. Rice, the staple food of the south, and the common food of the well-to-do in all parts, had risen to the fantastic price of one pound of gold for a weight equivalent to 120 lbs. It was no doubt these conditions which inspired Liu Pang's legislation against the merchant class, which he suspected of speculating and hoarding to raise prices. Merchants were forbidden to wear silk, ride in carts or hold office. They were also subjected to a great variety of taxes.

Liu Pang hoped to restore prosperity to the peasantry and revive the agricultural economy of the feudal age, but the effects of the revolution were as inescapable in economics as in politics. Feudalism was dead, even the artificial restoration of Hsiang Yü had failed to bring it to life. Soon it became clear that the old social and economic system had perished with it. The first century of the Han Empire offers an interesting example of the efforts of a strong, and in many ways enlightened, government to cope with an economic crisis which was as unexpected as it was misunderstood.

The revolution had swept away the barriers to commerce which the wars and jealousy of the feudal princes had maintained for centuries. New territories, potentially very rich, had been incorporated in the empire. The landowning nobility were ruined and dispersed. Side by side with the sudden expansion of the empire itself there came an equally important expansion of industry and commerce, which raised up a new class of industrial magnates and millionaire merchants. The Han sovereigns had no sooner found a policy to counter the political dangers of feudalism than they were assailed by a series of economic difficulties wholly new to the experience of the Chinese world. These troubles were three, and they have a familiar ring to the statesmen of the 20th century. Currency depreciation, instability of prices, and the cost of defence measures.

Throughout the Early Han period the war with the nomads of the Mongolian steppe taxed the resources of the empire and complicated economic conditions. These nomads known to the Chinese as Hsiung Nu, *i.e.* the Huns, were of Turki stock. Their incursions into China had begun during the period of the Warring States, and had caused Ch'in Shih Huang Ti to build the Great Wall as a measure of defence. Under the Han dynasty the struggle was continued almost uninterruptedly until 51 B.C., when the southern hordes were compelled to accept Chinese sovereignty owing to their internal dissensions. The value of the Great Wall as a defence must not be underestimated. In an age when artillery was unknown, this formidable barrier, built along the crest of a precipitous range, was an obstacle to raiding cavalry not easily overcome. The Wall as a defence had one severe disadvantage. It was only effective if garrisoned, and it was immensely long, traversing a poor country which could not supply sufficient provisions for the army stationed along the frontier.

The difficulty under which the Han Emperors laboured in supplying the needs of the frontier was increased by the lack of any adequate means of transport. The northern border is ill-supplied with navigable rivers, apart from the Yellow River, and as this flows southward from the mountain plateaux to the plains, the transport barges had to make their way upstream against the current when fully laden, and only benefited by the speed of the stream when returning empty. The shortage of horses, which were mostly bred in Mongolia, and had to be purchased or captured from the nomads themselves, added to these difficulties.

The troubles of the frontier were not the sole cause of the economic crises, but they aggravated the disorders of the empire and drained away huge sums in a profitless expenditure. The Court, unable to meet the demand out of its ordinary resources, was compelled to devise exceptional measures. Official ranks were granted to those who could arrange the transport of grain to the frontier, and this system was soon amplified by the sale of titles to supply a fund for the same purpose. Under the Emperor Hsiao Ching (157-141 B.C.) the price was lowered to attract a poorer class, and criminals were allowed to obtain a reduction of their sentences in return for arranging the transport of grain to the frontier. The fall of the aristocracy had made the court hierarchy of titles, first established by the Ch'in, attractive to that large class of newly risen men who could not claim an ancient name. The Court was quick to realise that snobbery had a value which could be turned to good account, but these measures deeply offended conservative scholars.

The Han Emperors were even less successful in dealing with the purely economic difficulties which beset them. The evil of speculation and grain hoarding by rich merchants was at first attributed to a shortage of currency, which the Emperor Hsiao Wên attempted to remedy by a most unwise decree. In 175 B.C. private minting of copper coinage was permitted, and, indeed, encouraged. The results were disastrous. The Prince of Wu, a feudal lord of a collateral branch of the house of Han, found a rich copper mine in his fief (Chekiang) and exploited this until he became "richer than the Emperor himself." Têng T'ung governor of Szechuan, did the same, and soon the whole empire was flooded with "Wu" and "Têng" coins. Other capitalists on a lesser scale added their quota with the result that prices soared, money became valueless and the revenues of the government were seriously diminished. The right of private minting was then withdrawn, but the evil had been done and illicit coining continued on a vast scale.

In spite of this debasement of the currency the reigns of the Emperors Hsiao Wên and Hsiao Ching (180-157 and 157-141 B.C.) were a period of comparative prosperity for the mass of the people, and particularly for the merchant classes who had been more considerately treated after the death of Liu Pang. The early part of the reign of the Emperor Wu (141-87 B.C.) saw this improvement maintained. Ssǔ-ma Ch'ien, who had no cause to love his sovereign, has recorded the prosperity of this time, even if he has perhaps painted the picture too rosily in order to blacken the days of trouble which were to come.* No longer was there any shortage of horses. On the contrary, even in the poorest streets of Ch'ang An horses were to be seen, and it was now considered ill-bred to mount a mare; indeed, respectable people would not be seen in the company of one who did so. The treasury was piled high with strings of cash, so long accumulated that the cords had rotted with age. The granaries in which the tax grain was collected were so filled with old grain that much had become rotten, and was no longer fit to eat. Men peacefully occupied their fathers' official posts, undisturbed by jealous office hunters, so that the minor positions were tending to become hereditary and families were beginning to take their surnames from the posts they occupied. The merchants had grown rich and powerful; taking the place of the vanished aristocracy, these new magnates lorded over the countryside† and sometimes terrorised the people by means of gangs of paid retainers. Indeed, the conduct of the rich was the dark side of the picture. Extravagance and luxury marked the court nobility as much as the provincial millionaires. None had grown so wealthy as the salt boilers and ironmasters. The inland provinces of China are poorly supplied with salt, which sometimes has to be fetched great distances. The salt boilers of the coastal region had profited by this circumstance to force up the price of salt and establish a complete control of the industry. The ironmasters had also become "richer than the princes." It is probable that the working of iron was at this time greatly expanded.‡ In China the bronze age lasted very late (bronze swords and halberds were standard weapons in the early Han

*See Chapter IX in which the value of Ssǔ-ma Ch'ien's testimony for his own times is appraised.

†This was an evil result of the fall of the aristocratic monopoly of land. The peasants fell into debt and sold their land to money-lending merchants and speculators.

‡The *Book of Lord Shang* and the *Hsün Tzu* refer to the "iron-tipped lances of Ch'u" (the southern state) made from the iron of Yüan, in Honan.

period), but it is plain that now the new metal was coming into more general use, and its production had been monopolised by a few enterprising industrialists. All this wealth was so far untapped by the government, which continued to base its revenue system on the old-fashioned capitation tax and contributions of grain. Commerce and industry were only subject to various navigation taxes and market dues which were private monopolies owned by princes and fief holders.

The Emperor Wu succeeded his father when still a youth, a fact which permitted him to reign for the long space of fifty-three years, during which the civilisation of the Han period reached its apogee. The new ruler was a masterful character, well educated and fond of literature, but also ambitious, ruthless and subject to violent rages. He had, however, an unprejudiced mind, and was willing to break with tradition if policy demanded it. Under an energetic and capable autocrat the Chinese Empire, rested by the peaceful rule of the earlier Han sovereigns, was ready to embark on a career of expansion at the expense of the uncivilised peoples to the south and west. In the next Chapter the influence of these foreign conquests upon Chinese culture will be reviewed. Fortunately an account of the economic crisis which developed as a result of these wars, and which completed the social revolution begun by Ch'in Shih Huang Ti, has been preserved in the Chapter "P'ing Chun" of Ssŭ-ma Ch'ien's history.

The long war with the Hsiung Nu (Huns), which broke out again in 133 B.C., necessitated enormous expenditure for the upkeep of the army and for an extension of the Great Wall to the west. At the same time the campaigns in the south-west, by which Szechuan and the valley of the West River were made part of the empire, required the construction of a road through the mountains which was only accomplished at a stupendous cost, both of money and lives. A third drain on the treasury was the conquest and colonisation of north-west Korea, the province called Lak Lang (128 B.C.), which has in recent years yielded the most striking evidence of the high level of Han art and craftsmanship even in a remote border territory of the empire.* The Emperor's measures for the relief of famine

*See Chapter X.

imposed a further burden upon the imperial treasury, already
heavily depleted by the wars. Partly as a measure of pacification,
and partly to increase the value of the wet lands in the lower
Yangtze basin, a large part of the population of the newly-
conquered country of Yüeh (Fukien and Chekiang) were transported to the lands between the Huai and the Yangtze, and
settled at the government expense. In 120 B.C. a serious
famine afflicted Shensi, the province of the capital, and the
distress of the people being thus brought home to the sovereign,
a vast scheme of relief was inaugurated. No less than 700,000
families were moved into the recently conquered territory of Hsin
Ch'in (in the northern bend of the Yellow River, beyond the
modern province of Shensi), where they were settled on the virgin
land under the care of an army of government supervisors and
officials. As these immigrants were mostly indigent, the state
advanced money to them, but owing to the mismanagement of
the officials and the peculation of those in charge of the finances,
the government never recovered the loans and the loss to the
state was excessive.

Meanwhile the adulteration of the currency due to the still
unchecked illicit minting was constantly causing the most violent
fluctuations in prices, which added to the misery of the poor,
embarrassed the government, and enriched a class of speculators,
who were so far uncontrolled and almost untaxed by the state.
The Emperor, always ready to try a new experiment, now
attempted to grapple with this currency crisis, though his first
efforts were far from successful. In the imperial park at Ch'ang
An the Emperor had a white stag, a very rare beast, which had
no fellow in the empire. On the advice of a minister, the Emperor
had this animal killed, and made a kind of treasury note out of
its skin, which he believed could not be copied. These pieces of
skin were a foot square, and were made with a fringed border
and decorated with a pattern. Each piece was assigned the
arbitrary value of 400,000 copper coins. The princes, when they
came to pay their respects to the throne, were compelled to buy
one of these pieces of skin for cash, and present their gifts to the
Emperor upon it. This precaution ensured the circulation of the
"White Stag Notes." The skin of the white stag was, however, a

limited quantity and the time soon came when this device ceased to supply the treasury with much needed money. The Emperor had already (124 B.C.) revived and amplified the policy by which his predecessors had tried to obtain the transport of provisions to the army of the north. Merchants were now permitted to purchase titles and thus for the first time won a place in official life. Sheep were accepted instead of cash or grain, and the historian Ssŭ-ma Ch'ien (who despised all these innovations) satirically remarks: "One could obtain the rank of *lang* by giving the government sheep." The first attempt to remedy the currency crisis having produced only a limited result, the Emperor now coined new money of an alloy of silver and tin, giving his issue the arbitrary value of 3,000, 500, and 300 coppers for the three types of coin. The death penalty was enacted against coiners, but failed to check the evil.

The new white metal coinage was soon copied as abundantly as the old copper money, and, consequently, rapidly lost its value. In 114 B.C. it had to be withdrawn in favour of a fresh issue, this time of copper coins with a red border, manufactured by a process which the historian unfortunately does not reveal. However, it had no better fortune than the white metal coins, for the people soon discovered the secret, and copied it so extensively that the red border coins also lost all value. The following year, under the advice of new ministers, the Court finally settled this evil. All existing coins were declared to be without value, and minting of copper coins was centralised under the direct control of the officials of the mint at Ch'ang An. An amnesty was proclaimed for the vast multitude of coiners who had been imprisoned or sent to forced labour, and Ssŭ-ma Ch'ien alleges that a million people were set free by this act of clemency, though they had only been a fraction of the guilty. Indeed, coining would seem to have been a home industry practised throughout the country. From this time, however, the currency crisis was solved by government minting of copper coins to which no arbitrary value above their intrinsic worth was attached. Coining rapidly dwindled until only a few gangs of professional criminals remained. It had ceased to be profitable.

The currency crisis was only one aspect of the troubles. Speculation, price raising, and hoarding were more difficult to deal with. In 120 B.C. the Emperor took a bold step; fiercely condemned by conservative scholars, he turned for advice and assistance to the very class which had given proof of its business knowledge and rapacity, the newly risen commercial magnates. In that year the government declared a state monopoly over the iron and salt industries, the stronghold of the new capitalism, and entrusted the organisation of this enterprise to the leading men in the industry itself. Tung Kuo, a salt boiler millionaire from Shantung, and K'ung Chin, an ironmaster of Honan, were put in charge of the office, and they used the provincial salt and iron masters as their deputies. Not only the production, but also the manufacture of salt and iron were under their control. Government foundries and boiling pans replaced the private enterprises of the profiteers. Even old iron was only saleable to the government officials who collected it to be melted down in the state foundries.

Another new man who rose to power in this age of innovation was Sang Hung-yang, the son of a petty shopkeeper in Lo Yang. At first made financial secretary to the new salt and iron monopoly he soon became the Emperor's chief adviser on economic questions. In 119 B.C. the counsellor Yang K'o had suggested a new form of taxation, intended to reach those classes which had hitherto escaped. It was decreed that all merchants, shopkeepers and speculators should be obliged to declare the total of their fortune, not merely of their income, but of all that they possessed, and should then be taxed accordingly 10 per cent on every 2,000 coppers of their possessions. Artisans who had to collect the raw material of their industries and store up necessary stocks were only charged on every 4,000 coppers. A further tax was imposed on merchants and non-officials who used carts, and on boats more than 50 feet long. It was also decreed that those who did not declare their fortunes could be denounced by their neighbour, who would receive half the fortune, the rest being confiscated by the state, while the delinquent would be sent to forced labour on the frontier for one year. Merchants, artisans and financiers were forbidden to class themselves as agriculturists and so escape the tax.

This law was carried out with the greatest severity and before long produced the most unfortunate effects. The confiscations indeed filled the treasury and the pockets of the officials, but the merchants were faced with ruin. Since thrift might expose one to the dreaded denunciation and entire ruin, no one troubled to save money, and a general orgy of extravagance was the consequence. In 110 B.C., the Emperor, finding that his difficulties continued, turned to Sang Hung-yang, who found a remedy for the crisis in an ingenious system of state trading intended to keep prices level. This system, called *p'ing chun*, "levelling," was operated through a government department at the capital, which regulated the tribute and commerce of the entire empire. In the provinces officers were stationed who bought up the glut of produce when prices fell, and sold the government stocks when scarcity began to raise prices. At the same time the tributes in kind which formed the bulk of the provincial taxation were regulated so that each province provided the produce which was most plentiful, and which had hitherto been the subject of speculation and hoarding by the merchants. The government maintained an extensive transport system by which the tribute of one province was transferred to another district where this product was scarce, and so prevented any sharp rise in the price. In the event of a famine in any district all the neighbouring provinces were made to send grain to the distressed area.

Although himself opposed to these policies and still more to the men of obscure origin who were responsible for them, Ssŭ-ma Ch'ien admits that the system was a success. There was no further difficulty in raising the tribute grain. The public granaries were once more filled to overflowing, the speculators found their operations impossible, and prices remained steady, even when the government required large quantities of produce for the frontier garrisons. Henceforward the treasury was well filled and it was not necessary to increase taxation when the Emperor, on a tour of inspection in the north, made heavy demands for the pay of the army and for rewards to the frontier troops. The law permitting the denunciation of private fortunes acquired by commerce, which had been so unpopular with the merchant class, was repealed, for the government no longer needed the revenue derived from confiscating these estates, while the new system was designed to make the acquisition of large fortunes by speculation impossible.

Nevertheless, the system devised by Sang Hung-yang had its critics, who made persistent efforts to have the reforms abolished. In the reign of Chao Ti, the successor of the Emperor Wu, sixty scholars were permitted to place their views before the Emperor and ventilate the grievances of those who opposed Sang Hung-yang's administration. This famous debate on the question of the salt and iron monopoly and the *p'ing chun* system took place in 81 B.C., the sixth year of Chao Ti's reign, when Ssŭ-ma Ch'ien had been dead some five years. Fortunately, a record of the discussion has been preserved in the work of another scholar, Huan K'uan, who lived in the reign of Han Hsüan Ti (73-49 B.C.).*

The criticism of the scholars was based on two counts. Firstly, they denied the good effects of the reforms, alleging that salt had become so expensive that the people could not buy it, and that the iron implements issued by the state foundries were both more expensive and inferior in quality to those formerly made by private enterprise. Secondly, they denounced the reforms on the general ground that they were innovations which had no precedent in the golden era of the past—a characteristically Confucian argument. Sang Hung-yang defended his administration on the grounds of necessity. He pointed out that the defence of the frontier was a necessity of state which could not be argued away, that revenue was essential for the pay of the troops, and that experience had proved that the old system of taxation was inadequate for the needs of the new empire. When the scholars further urged that the government monopoly of minting brought hardship to the people, the minister was on surer ground, for he had only to point out the disastrous effects which private minting in the hands of great capitalists had produced under the reigns of Hsiao Wên and Hsiao Ching (180-141 B.C.). Whether the system worked as well as he claimed, or as badly as the scholars declared,

*"The discourse on Salt and Iron," or *Yen T'ieh Lun* in the Han Wei Ts'ung Shu. A translation has been made by Prof. E. M. Gale. *Discourses on Salt and Iron.* Leyden. E. J. Brill, Ltd. 1931.

must remain uncertain, but the pedantic arguments advanced by the critics tend to suggest that there were few real grounds for complaint, while the testimony of the hostile witness Ssŭ-ma Ch'ien proves that the reforms had been beneficial when first applied. When Sang Hung-yang asked the scholars how they proposed to defend the frontier if the monopolies which supported the army were abolished they replied:

"Confucius observed that 'the ruler of a kingdom or the chief of a house is not concerned about his people being few, but about lack of equitable treatment, nor is he concerned about poverty, but over the presence of discontent.' Thus, the Son of Heaven should not speak about 'much' and 'little,' the feudal lords should not talk about 'advantage' and 'detriment,' ministers about 'gain' and 'loss,' but they should cultivate benevolence and righteousness, to set an example to the people and extend wide their virtuous conduct to gain the people's confidence. Then will nearby folk flock lovingly to them and distant peoples submit joyfully to their authority. Therefore 'the master conqueror does not fight; the expert warrior needs no soldiers; the truly great commander requires not to set his troops in battle array.' Cultivate virtue in the temple and the hall, then you need only to show a bold front to the enemy and your troops will return home in victory. The Prince who practises benevolent administration should be matchless in the world; for him, what use is expenditure?"

The minister, who had to deal with the problems of real life rather than with the dream world of doctrinaire scholars, did not believe that 'benevolence and righteousness' would suffice to keep the nomads north of the Great Wall. He answered:

"The Hsiung Nu, savage and wily, boldly push through the barriers and harass the Middle Kingdom, massacring the provincial population and killing the keepers of the Northern Marches. They long deserve punishment for their unruliness and lawlessness. But Your Majesty graciously took pity on the insufficiency of the multitude and did not suffer his lords and knights to be exposed in the desert plains, yet unflinchingly

You cherish the purpose of raising strong armies and driving the Hsiung Nu before You to their original haunts in the north. I again assert that the proposal to do away with the salt and iron monopoly and equable marketing would grievously diminish our frontier supplies and impair our military plans. I cannot consider favourably a proposal so heartlessly dismissing the frontier question."

To these practical arguments the scholars could only advance the well-worn Confucian dogma that the practice of virtue by the sovereign would automatically cure the ills of the state and pacify its enemies. They declared:

"Your Majesty has but to manifest Your virtue towards them and extend Your favours to cover them, and the northern barbarians will undoubtedly come of their own accord to pay you tribute at the Wall."

It is not surprising that Sang Hung-yang impatiently declared:

"Your learned men in their arguments would either try to reach high Heaven or penetrate the Abyss. Then they would attempt, and how ineffectively, to compare the conduct of the affairs of some village or hamlet with the great business of the nation. . . . They have certainly proved unfit to take part in discussions."

Huan K'uan has amplified the discussion and used it as a text to dilate upon the Confucian view of morality and state policy, but it would seem that Sang Hung-yang got the best of the argument, for the monopolies were not repealed. Indeed, the minister had proved his point, that, however well the Confucian ideal sovereign might govern, the barbarians were not to be tamed by moral precepts. Nothing better emphasises the gulf between the new men which the revolution had thrown up and the hide-bound scholars of the old tradition than the debate on salt and iron. The question was one which the scholar officials did not understand in the least. The economic crisis was not to be cured by quoting Confucius, but by the original and ingenious reforms initiated by a member of the merchant class which had hitherto been debarred from holding any office.

Sang Hung-yang and his colleagues understood the essential economic unity of the new empire and the need for framing policies which took the whole state into consideration, not merely the restricted territory of the feudal fief. Industry and commerce, like administration and national defence, had to be adjusted to the wider horizons of the centralised empire, the feudal economic system, like the feudal political system, no longer sufficed.

Chapter VIII

HAN IMPERIALISM AND THE DISCOVERY OF THE WEST

Up to the end of the feudal period the Chinese confederacy had dwelt in isolation unbroken by any direct contact with another civilised people. Hemmed in on the north by the untamed nomads of the Mongolian steppe, and cut off from India by the wild forest clad mountains and malarial valleys of the Burmese borderlands, the civilisation of the Middle Kingdom had progressed along its own lines, developing those peculiar and imperishable characteristics which have remained the distinctive mark of the Chinese culture.

The great revolution which destroyed the social and political structure of ancient China, prepared the way for a new era of conquest, discovery and expansion, the age of Han imperialism, when China emerged as a world power dominating the eastern half of Asia. The foreign policy of the emperors now embraced a wider scene than the oft disputed territories of the Yellow River plain. The unified Chinese Empire was soon engaged in a desperate and prolonged struggle with the barbarians of the north. The details of these wars, one acute phase of the secular struggle between the desert and the sown, are not important, but one consequence of the long struggle, the Chinese discovery of the West, was of the first importance in the cultural history of eastern Asia.

It was during the reign of the Emperor Wu (141-87 B.C.) that the war with the Hsiung Nu nomads developed into a desperate contest engaging the full strength of the Chinese Empire. The Hsiung Nu, a Turki people, as some traces of their language preserved in Chinese transliterations suggest, have been identified as the same people as the Huns who invaded Europe in the 4th century A.D. In the middle of the 3rd century B.C. this people had achieved a measure of unity and organisation which rendered it formidable to the Chinese kingdoms north of the Yellow River. The nomads differed from the Chinese in customs, religion, diet—indeed, in almost every respect. Consequently the Chinese regarded them as scarcely human; creatures who had the "hearts of beasts."

Nevertheless, the Hsiung Nu were by no means so primitive a people as the forcible expressions used by Chinese historians tend to suggest. They obeyed a single chief, the Shên Yu, a title which the Chinese regarded as equivalent to Emperor. Under the Shên Yu were two kings, of the Right and Left—the west and east respectively—and this identification of right and left with west and east is still a Turkish usage. The Kings of the Right and Left had subordinate officials organised into like categories, and, lastly commanders of one thousand, of one hundred, and of ten men. Their social customs, which the Chinese regarded with horror, included the practice by which a son took into his harem all the wives of his dead father, except his own mother, and also married all the wives of his deceased brothers. Being nomads, the Hsiung Nu did not cultivate the soil, nor form fixed encampments. Their diet was mainly meat and milk, a fact which the semi-vegetarian Chinese found repulsive.*

During the early years of the Han dynasty, the emperors, inheriting an empire worn out by incessant wars and the turmoil of the revolutionary period, were content to pursue a passive policy of defence against the Hsiung Nu raids, endeavouring to secure the frontier by defending the Great Wall, and obtain peace by making the Shên Yu presents of silk and other luxuries unobtainable in the steppes. With the accession of the energetic and forceful Emperor Wu there was a change of policy. The new sovereign found the empire fully recovered, prosperous and populous. The cessation of internal wars, the diminished power of the feudal princes of the imperial family, and the increased prestige of the throne, gave opportunity for a policy of expansion and conquest which earned this Emperor his posthumous title of *Wu*, i.e. "the Warlike."

At his accession (141 B.C.) the Han Empire covered the whole of what is now North China up to the Great Wall, except the remoter western districts of Kansu province (Map 4). South of the Yangtze

---

*The Chinese have never employed cow's milk as an article of food, and to the present day regard European dairy products with aversion. In Chinese the only word for milk means mother's milk. Cow's milk has to be described as such in Chinese at the risk of causing embarrassment. Similarly, butter is known as "cow's milk oil," or simply as "yellow oil."

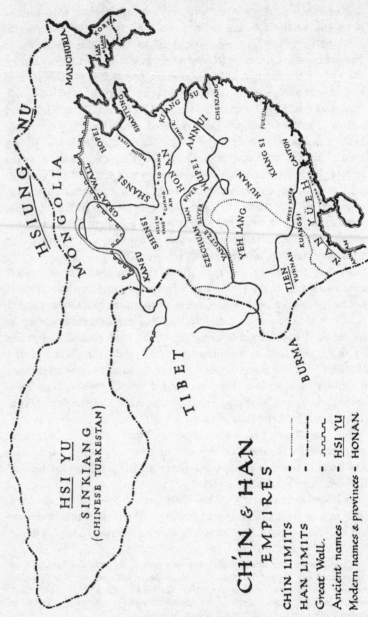

MAP 4. *The Ch'in and Han Empires*.

it only included the modern provinces of Szechuan, Hunan and Kiangsi, with the small parts of Anhui and Kiangsu which lie south of the river. To the west the mountain lands and plateaux of the south-western provinces were occupied by aboriginal tribes, few of whom had attained any measure of civilisation. An exception was the kingdom of Tien, which was situated on the shores of the Kun Yang lake with its capital near the site of modern Yunnanfu. Tien had been conquered by Wei, the King of Ch'u (339-329 B.C.), who had despatched a general to reduce the mountain lands to obedience. When the advance of Ch'in deprived the kingdom of Ch'u of its western provinces, the general, finding his communications cut, established himself in the fertile well-protected plateau of Yunnanfu and reigned as an independent King. His descendants, supported by the posterity of the Chinese who had composed the original army, were still in possession of this isolated region.

The south-east coast, from the neighbourhood of modern Hang Chou down to Tongking, was divided in the reign of the Emperor Wu between three kingdoms, Yüeh Tung Hai (Chekiang), Min Yüeh (Fukien), and the great kingdom of Nan Yüeh, which comprised both the modern provinces of Kuangtung and Kuangsi and also Tongking and northern Annam. Nan Yüeh had been conquered by Ch'in Shih Huang Ti, but upon the fall of the Ch'in Empire, the Chinese general in command made himself King of Nan Yüeh, and ceased to pay allegiance to the Chinese Emperors.

The Emperor Wu did not at first pay attention to these southern kingdoms, for in 135 B.C., acting on the advice of one of his generals, the Emperor attempted to entrap the Shên Yu and his army in an ambuscade at Ma I, "Horse Town," a frontier post on the Wall in north Shansi. The Shên Yu, by an accident fortunate for him, learned of his peril at the last moment, and escaped with his horde. This affair led to a renewal of hostilities which lasted without intermission throughout the reign of Wu and his immediate successors. The varying fortunes of the long struggle need not concern us. The Chinese, developing a new technique of warfare in which cavalry played the greatest rôle, were on the whole successful, though their victories were checkered by disasters when whole armies, surrounded by the mobile desert horsemen, were compelled to surrender. The importance of the Hsiung Nu war is that it led directly to the Chinese discovery of the West, and, indirectly, to the conquest and permanent incorporation of the southern kingdoms.

On one of these campaigns the Chinese learned from Hsiung Nu prisoners of the existence in the west of the nation called the Ta Yüeh Chi, who had been completely defeated by the Hsiung Nu in 165 B.C., and had fled westward. In 138 B.C. the Emperor decided to attempt to find the Ta Yüeh Chi and induce them to renew the war against the Hsiung Nu with Han support. For this embassy into unknown lands he chose one Chang Ch'ien, and with his usual skill in picking his officers, he selected a man eminently fitted for the hazardous task. In 138 B.C. Chang Ch'ien started from the western border of Kansu with 100 Chinese followers. Almost immediately he was captured by a roving band of Hsiung Nu, and kept prisoner for ten years. During this long captivity the envoy never forgot his trust and watched for his opportunity. At last, when the Hsiung Nu, believing him to be forgotten by his sovereign and content to pass his life as a nomad, had ceased to guard him closely, the intrepid Chinese escaped with some of his suite and his Hsiung Nu wife, whom he had married in his captivity.

Chang Ch'ien fled westward, towards the Ta Yüeh Chi, not eastward to China. He reached the Ili Valley, only to find that the Ta Yüeh Chi had been driven from that country by the Wu Sun, a nomad people believed to have been of Khirgiz stock. Chang Ch'ien, undeterred, passed on into the kingdom which the Chinese henceforth called Ta Yüan, which was situated in Ferganah near the site of Kokand, in what is now Russian Central Asia. There he learned that the Ta Yüeh Chi were still further south and west in the land between the Oxus and the Jaxartes or Syr Daria. After reaching the Ta Yüeh Chi across such vast distances and in face of so many perils, the ambassador found them entirely unwilling to return to the east. The Ta Yüeh Chi had recently invaded and partially occupied the land of Ta Hsia, driving the inhabitants south of the Oxus. Chang Ch'ien stayed among them for a year, but finding that he could never persuade them to return, he started back to China, being recaptured by the Hsiung Nu before he reached the frontier. This second captivity lasted a year, after which Chang Ch'ien, profiting by a revolution among his captors, escaped once more, and in 126 B.C., after twelve years' absence, reached Ch'ang An with his Hsiung Nu wife and one single survivor of the hundred Chinese who had started with him.

The importance of this voyage is apparent when the lands visited by Chang Ch'ien are identified by their Greek classical names.* Ta Yüan is the modern Ferghana, the Sogdiana of the Greeks, and Ta Hsia is Bactria. These countries, which had been conquered by Alexander, had later become an independent kingdom under dynasties founded by Greek adventurers. Shortly before Chang Ch'ien's journey the Euthydemid dynasty of Bactria, which had also conquered a large part of India, was itself overthrown in Bactria by Eucratides, a Greek general. In 145 B.C. his son, Heliocles, in turn invaded India which was still ruled by scions of the displaced Euthydemid dynasty. Four years later, in 141 B.C., the Parthians invaded Bactria, and at a date unknown, following upon this blow, the Bactrian Greek kingdom of Heliocles was overwhelmed by an invasion of nomads.

These nomads are called Asii or Asiani by Greek writers and have been identified as the Ta Yueh Chi whom Chang Ch'ien found in 128 B.C. as the masters of Bactria. Their conquest of the Greek kingdom therefore took place at some date between 141 and 128 B.C. The Yueh Chi were a people who had been settled on the western borders of China, and had fled westward after being defeated by the Hsiung Nu. They are also called Tochari by the Greeks, and Tukhara by the Indians. Later in India they were known as Kushans. It is probable that they were a mixed horde of which the Asii were the dominant element and the Tochari subordinate. There is some evidence that the latter were a people who had originally migrated eastward from the borders of Europe, and spoke a language with Italo-Celtic affinities.

When Chang Ch'ien reached Bactria the nomad conquest was

*For these identifications and the history of the Greek kingdoms in Central Asia and India see *The Greeks in India and Bactria*. W. W. Tarn. Cambridge University Press, 1936.

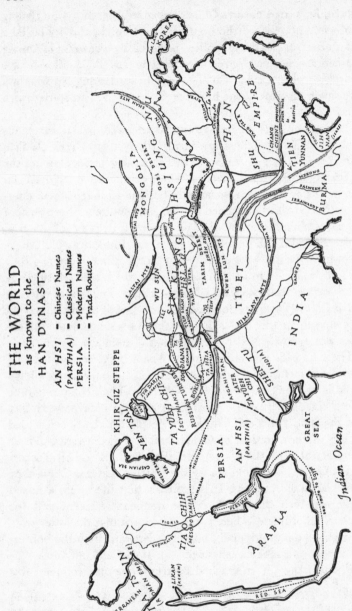

MAP 5. *The World as Known to the Han Dynasty.*

still recent, and it is probable that the inhabitants of the towns which he describes were a mixed people certainly including many Greeks, although as he communicated through the Yueh Chi he does not seem to have realised that the Greeks were a distinct people among the inhabitants of Ta Hsia. Nevertheless he had in fact reached the fringes of the Hellenistic world, and it is extremely interesting to learn what impression was made upon a Chinese Ambassador by these last outposts of Greek civilisation. His report has been preserved, apparently in his own words, in the Chinese annals.

"Ta Yüan [Kokand, Sogdiana], the people are sedentary [not nomads] and cultivate the soil. They have many superb horses, which sweat blood when they perspire. There are cities, houses and mansions as in China. To the north-east is the country of the Wu Sun [the Ili Valley], to the east is Yü T'ien [Kashgaria]. West of Yü T'ien the rivers flow westward into the Western Sea [The Caspian and Aral, Chang Ch'ien did not distinguish between the two]. From Yü T'ien eastward the rivers flow to the east into the salt swamps [the Tarim river system]. From these swamps the waters flow underground until they reappear as the source of the Yellow River. From the salt swamp to Ch'ang An, the distance is 5,000 Li.* The Right horde of Hsiung Nu live between the salt swamps and the Great Wall of Lung Hsi [Kansu]. The Wu Sun [Khirgiz], K'ang Chu, and Yen Ts'ai, who are north-west of the K'ang Chu, and Ta Yüeh Chi, are nomads with customs similar to the Hsiung Nu.† Ta Hsia [Bactria] is south-west of Ta Yüan and has similar customs. When your servant was in Ta Hsia he saw large bamboos and cloth of Shu [Szechuan]. When he asked the people of Ta Hsia how they obtained these things they told him that their merchants bought them in Shên Tu [Sind, India] which is a country several hundred li south-east of Ta Hsia, and is a sedentary nation, like Ta Hsia. Both Ta

*The Chinese Li is equivalent to one-third of a mile. Chang Ch'ien's belief that the Yellow River was really a reappearance of the Tarim is not correct.

†The K'ang Chu and Yen Ts'ai lived north of the Jaxartes or Syr Daria in the country now called the Khirgiz Steppe.

Hsia and Ta Yüan are tributary to An Hsi [Parthia*]. So far
as your servant could judge Ta Hsia is 12,000 li [4,000 miles]
from China. As it is north-east of Shên Tu, this kingdom cannot
be so far from China."

Chang Ch'ien, who had experienced to the full the dangers of
the northern route to the Greco-Bactrian kingdoms, urged his
sovereign to attempt communication by means of India, arguing
that as the people of Bactria used the bamboos and cloth of
Szechuan there must be some route by which they obtained these
goods. The Emperor followed up this suggestion and sent envoys
through Yunnan to find the road to India. The country between
Burma and Yunnan is in reality one of the most inaccessible
regions in the world, traversed by deep malarial valleys and steep
forest-clad ranges. This region, the modern prefectures of Ta Li
and Têng Yüeh, was then inhabited by savages who killed or
arrested all the Han envoys, so that not one ever got through to
India.   The manner in which the Bactrian Greeks obtained the
products of Szechuan thus remains a mystery. Perhaps the tribes
of the borderlands themselves traded these goods to their neighbours in Burma, or again Chang Ch'ien may have been mistaken,
and the big bamboos and Szechuan cloth which he saw in
Bactria may have been similar products coming from some part
of India.

For some years after Chang Ch'ien's adventurous journey, the
Chinese Court, pursuing the will-o'-the-wisp of an Indian trade
route, did not profit by the discovery of the road to the Ili Valley,
which moreover was in the hands of their enemies. Nevertheless,
the idea of finding a way through Yunnan to the new world of
Chang Ch'ien's discovery led indirectly to important results,
partly through the intelligent observations of another Chinese

*The Chinese name for Parthia, An Hsi, has been thought to be derived
from the dynasty of Arsaces but an alternative view put forward by W. W.
Tarn, *op. cit.*, seems more probable and satisfactory. The Chinese like other
ancient travellers frequently confused the names of cities and countries; Merv
was officially one of the many Antiochs under the Seleucid empire and the
Chinese took this name—Antioch—rendered it An Hsi and used it for the
whole Parthian kingdom. A close analogy to this mistake is the early European
voyagers' corruption of the name of the province of Kuangtung, which they
rendered Canton and applied to the city of Kuangchou.

envoy. In 135 B.C. a war broke out between the Kings of Nan Yüeh whose capital was Canton, and Min Yüeh, a kingdom occupying the modern province of Fukien. The King of Nan Yüeh appealed to China for help, and a Han general, who had recently subdued Tung Yüeh (Chekiang), despatched one of his officers, T'ang Mêng, to Canton as an envoy.

At Canton the Chinese ambassador was given a delicacy made from the fruit of a kind of mulberry which T'ang Mêng had reason to believe grew only in Szechuan, the land of fruits and flowers. Like Chang Ch'ien a few years later, T'ang Mêng promptly enquired how the Cantonese obtained this fruit, and was told that it came down the river system of the West River (which reaches the sea at Canton) being traded from the country called Yeh Lang. Yeh Lang was an independent state occupying the northern part of modern Kueichou, around the city of Tsun I. On his return to China T'ang Mêng enquired of the Szechuan merchants, and learned, as he suspected, that this fruit was exported by them to Yeh Lang, whence it was carried across the Kueichou mountains to some point on the Pan Chiang river, which is in fact one of the headwaters of the West River.* T'ang Mêng thus discovered the river system of the West River and the overland route from Szechuan to Canton. This route had hitherto been unknown to the northern Chinese, a fact easily explained by the extreme ruggedness of the country, which to-day is still only traversed by small paths unsuitable for wheeled traffic.

Several years passed before T'ang Mêng's discovery was used by the Chinese Court. In 111 B.C. the troubles of Nan Yüeh gave the Emperor an opportunity to intervene in the south, which he was the more anxious to do as he thereby hoped to open the long discussed trade route to India and Bactria. In that year the Queen of Nan Yüeh, herself a Chinese by birth, was regent for her son, the infant King, who had recently succeeded his father. The Queen, perhaps fearing that powerful China would soon pick a quarrel with Nan Yüeh and conquer the kingdom, decided to avert the danger by offering a voluntary submission. When the

*It would be interesting to know exactly where the Pan Chiang was navigable at this period, for at the present time it is not navigated in Kueichou, where it flows in a deep, rock-encumbered gorge.

Emperor Wu heard of her intention he sent as his ambassador a Chinese officer who had formerly been the lover of the Queen of Nan Yüeh before she had left China. On his arrival the ambassador and the Queen renewed their intimacy and together planned the submission of Nan Yüeh.

Unfortunately for them their plans became known to the chief minister, Lu Chia, who opposed them vigorously. The Queen attempted to have him assassinated, but, failing in the attempt, was herself put to death together with the King and the Chinese ambassador. Lu Chia then put another infant prince, son of a concubine of the late King, on the throne, and published a manifesto declaring that the Queen and her foreign lover were about to betray the state to the Chinese. On hearing this news the Emperor Wu, ill-disposed to tolerate the murder of his ambassador, declared war.

The campaign was swift and successful. Six Chinese armies, some of which went by sea, and one of which followed the new road revealed by T'ang Mêng's intelligent enquiries, invaded Nan Yüeh, and, after some easy conquests, took Canton. Lu Chia and the young King attempted to escape by sea, but were made prisoners, and the whole kingdom of Nan Yüeh reduced to the status of Chinese provinces. This campaign, which cost so little effort, was none the less one of the most important advances made by the Chinese in the Han period. The two provinces of Kuangtung and Kuangsi, and also Tongking, were incorporated in the empire, where, with the exception of the latter, they have ever since remained. The destruction of Nan Yüeh was followed by that of all the petty states of the south, Min Yüeh, and even Tien or Yunnanfu, which was reduced to the status of a tributary. Had Nan Yüeh remained independent it is very possible that a separate culture would have arisen in the south, and the Chinese might never have established their influence in the valley of the West River. Although the Han conquest of Yunnan and Kueichou proved imperfect and transitory, the southern coast and the rich valley of the West River was for ever made an integral part of the Chinese land.

Recently there have been discovered near Hong Kong, in territory which formed part of this kingdom, a series of finds in

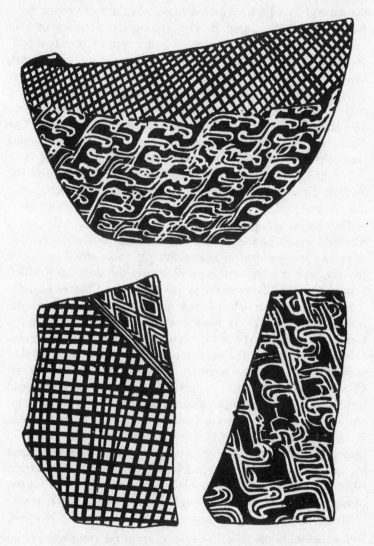

FIG. 34. *Pottery found at Lamma Island, near Hong Kong.*

pottery and bronze which may well date from the time of the conquest of Nan Yüeh, or perhaps somewhat later. The specimens, such as those illustrated in Fig. 34, consist of potsherds with designs upon them clearly derived from northern bronze motifs. With these there occur bronze weapons (Fig. 35) and implements, including halberds of Han type, the whole associated with quartz discs, rarely stone beads, ground stone knives, and perhaps ground stone axes, though on the relationship of these last to the pottery and other objects it is probably wise to suspend judgment.* The decoration on the bronze dagger (Fig. 35) is also strongly reminiscent of the decoration on numerous bronze daggers of the same type found at An Yang, and therefore Shang. The date of the finds on Lamma has not been determined, and this resemblance may be due to the survival of an old style in a remote district.

The Emperor's purpose in subduing these countries, as is expressly stated by the historian of the Early Han dynasty, was to make a chain of provinces stretching to India and Ta Hsia, or Bactria, and this fact strikingly illustrates the impression which Chang Ch'ien's discoveries had made on the Chinese Court.

As has been pointed out, the geographical obstacles to the realisation of this project were immense, indeed before long the Emperor realised that the southern route to Bactria was impassable. His interest in the remote west did not decrease on that account. Events in the north had now made the road across Chinese Turkestan more accessible, and the Emperor, still seeking an ally in the west to turn the flank of the Hsiung Nu, sent Chang Ch'ien on a second embassy, this time to the Wu Sun in the Ili Valley. Chang Ch'ien actually set out in 115 B.C., before the conquest of Nan Yüeh, and his journey was facilitated by the fact that the Chinese had just conquered the two districts of Su Chou and Liang Chou, which form the long "arm" of the province of Kansu, stretching out along the road to Turkestan.

Chang Ch'ien, though welcomed by the King of the Wu Sun,

*Investigation in this area is in active progress. For past discoveries see papers by Professor J. L. Shellshear, "Pottery Associated with Bronze Implements from Hong Kong" (*Proceedings of the First International Congress of Prehistoric and Protohistoric Sciences, London,* 1932); and D. J. Finn, S.J., "Archæological Finds on Lamma Island near Hong Kong" (*Hong Kong Naturalist,* Vols. III, IV and V, 1932-34).

hereditary enemies of the Hsiung Nu, found the tribe unwilling to enter into hostilities with their powerful foes. He did not persuade the Wu Sun to ally themselves with the Chinese, but he

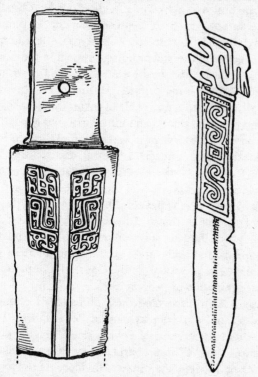

FIG. 35. *Bronze Dagger and upper part of Bronze Sword, from Hong Kong.*

did secure their goodwill and open a road through their country by which other Chinese embassies passed frequently to Ta Yüan and Ta Hsia (Bactria). The first of these new contacts were made by officers of his suite whom he despatched to An Hsi (Parthia), Shên Tu (India) and Ta Hsia (Bactria). Unfortunately no record of their travels or their success or failure has survived. However, several embassies reached Ta Yüan (Kokand) during the next few years, charged with the duty of obtaining some of the famous horses which had so much impressed Chang Ch'ien on his first voyage.

The King of Ta Yüan, however, absolutely refused to sell any of these horses to the Chinese. At last one Chinese envoy, employing in these distant countries the high-handed manners which Han prestige made possible in lands nearer home, carried off several of the best horses by force, and set out for China with his booty. The authorities of Ta Yüan sent soldiers in pursuit, who, having waylaid the Chinese envoy in a pass, slew him and his suite and recovered the stolen horses. Probably the King of Ta Yüan imagined that these positive measures would rid him of the nuisance of Chinese importunities. He doubtless considered the Chinese a distant people incapable of taking vengeance, and probably far less powerful than their ambassadors were wont to claim.

The Emperor Wu, for his part, was no more disposed to tolerate the assassination of his envoys in Central Asia than he had been in Canton. In 104 B.C. the general Li Kuang-li, brother of one of the imperial concubines, was despatched with an army to reduce Ta Yüan to obedience. The magnificent disregard of geographical obstacles and distances displayed by such an expedition, which had to cover more than 2,000 miles, largely across deserts, is a striking proof of the atmosphere of confident imperialism which prevailed at the Court of China, and also of the general ignorance of geography.

Li Kuang-li soon discovered these difficulties for himself. The Tarim basin, the vast country now called Chinese Turkestan, was then divided between thirty-six small kingdoms, each of which occupied one of the separate oases into which the cultivatable area of Chinese Turkestan is divided. As the food supply of these oases is barely sufficient for the inhabitants themselves, and the year 104 B.C. had not been a good one, the cities were quite unable to feed the large Chinese army without incurring the risk of famine. Consequently, Li Kuang-li was obliged to capture every city he came to before obtaining provisions. Worn out by famine, desert marches, and constant fighting, the Chinese army was finally completely defeated outside the city of Yü Ch'êng, a town in the kingdom of Ta Yüan, near which the Chinese envoy who had carried off the horses had been slain. Li Kuang-li then carried out a retreat to China, arriving at the frontier with hardly a tenth of his army.

Far from considering this retreat something of a feat in itself, the Emperor was so enraged that Li Kuang-li and his ragged survivors were forbidden to cross the frontier into China on pain of death. They remained encamped just outside Tun Huang, the last city of China, in the far west of Kansu province. It is indeed very likely that only Li Kuang-li's powerful influence in the Inner Palace—his sister was one of the imperial favourites—saved the general from decapitation, the usual fate of defeated Han commanders. However, the Emperor had not renounced the plan of conquering Ta Yüan, believing that if he let the murder of ambassadors go unpunished, it would be impossible in future to maintain contact with the western world. In 102 B.C. he sent Li Kuang-li a reinforcement of 60,000 men and ordered him to renew the attack. This time the general, who had no doubt learned from his previous experience, was more successful. After great suffering and the loss of half his army through the hardship and perils of the long march, Li Kuang-li with 30,000 Chinese arrived before the city of Er Shih, capital of Ta Yüan, and seat of the King,* whom the Chinese call Mu Kua.

Mu Kua has been identified as the name Maukes or Maues, the Greek version of a Saca name which occurs more than once in the Greek records of the Saca in India. The kingdom of Ta Yüan, which had been known to the Greeks as Sogdiana, and had been a province of the Greek kingdom of Bactria, was conquered by the Saca nomads about 159 B.C. It was this Saca Kingdom of Ta Yüan that Li Kuang-li invaded. After defeating the Ta Yüan army outside the walls of Er Shih, the capital, the Chinese laid siege to the city, and carried the outer town by storm. The citadel held out, although the Chinese had cut the water supply, because the Saca had obtained the services of "a man of Han," that is a Chinese, who knew how to dig wells. This Chinese was presumably either a prisoner or a deserter. Nevertheless after forty days of siege the nobles murdered their king, who had refused to negotiate, and opened peace parleys with Li Kuang-li. The Chinese general knew that the citadel had now got water

*Er Shih is, of course, the Chinese name of this city. The Greek name has not been identified, but the site is believed to correspond to Oura Tepe on the road between Khojent and Tashkent in the upper valley of the Syr Daria. (*Memoires Historiques de Se-Ma Ts'ien.* Chavannes.)

and a large stock of provisions; his own forces were short of supplies and in danger of being attacked in the rear by the K'ang Chu nomads whom Mu Kua (Maukes) had called to his aid. It is possible that the arrival of these nomads would have been no more welcome to the Saca nobles than to the Chinese, and the policy of inviting them into Ta Yüan may have been one cause of the murder of king Mu Kua.*

The Chinese general therefore wisely agreed to peace. In return for several of the best horses and 3,000 of inferior quality, together with provisions for his army, Li Kuang-li agreed not to enter the city and to withdraw to China. After his departure another revolution occurred in Ta Yüan. The usurper was killed and a relative of the late King restored to the throne. However, the new King was quite willing to maintain friendly relations with China. His son was sent to the Han Court, the Chinese regarding him as a hostage, and frequent embassies passed between China and Ta Yüan.

Half a century after Li Kuang-li's expedition to Ta Yüan the Chinese came into direct contact with the last surviving Greek Kingdom in north-west India. According to the history of the Early Han Dynasty,† in the reign of Han Yuan Ti (48-33 B.C.), who was the third successor to the Emperor Wu, Wu T'ou Lao, King of Chi Pin, killed the envoys whom Wen Chung, the Chinese commander on the Central Asian frontier, had sent to his court. When the Chinese protested, Wu T'ou Lao sent an ambassador to tender apologies. Wen Chung decided to accompany this envoy on his return to Chi Pin, perhaps because he wished to investigate the situation for himself. His suspicions were justified, for the prince of Chi Pin, Wu T'ou Lao's son, plotted to assassinate Wen Chung. The Chinese commander forestalled him, and allying himself with Yin Mo Fu, son of the King of Yung Ch'u, attacked Chi Pin, killed Wu T'ou Lao's son and installed Yin Mo Fu as king of Chi Pin under Chinese suzerainty.

This obscure frontier episode would be of little interest were it not that Professor W. W. Tarn‡ has shown that Yin Mo Fu, the

*Ch'ien Han Shu. Chap. 61.

†Ch'ien Han Shu. Chap. 96.

‡Op. cit.

son of the king of Yung Ch'u, whom Wen Chung installed as a Chinese vassal king of Chi Pin, is none other than Hermaeus, the last Greek king to rule in north-west India. Hermaeus, who reigned, as his coinage shows, between 48 and 32 B.C., was the son of Amyntas, King of Alexandria in Parapamisadae, and was probably a descendant of Eucratides, founder of the second dynasty of Greek kings in Bactria. The region which the Greeks called the Parapamisadae lay east of the Hindu Kush in what is now eastern Afghanistan and the North West Frontier province of Pakistan. Amyntas did not rule all of this region, for the district which the Greeks called Kophen, the Kabul valley, had fallen into the hands of the Saca invaders, and was ruled by a certain King Spalyris. Like other barbarian kings who had seized part of the old Greek kingdoms in India, Spalyris used Greek inscriptions on his coins (which were probably struck by Greek workmen) and it is the Greek word "Adelphou" on the coins of Spalyris that the Chinese rendered as "Wu T'ou Lao." Wu T'ou Lao is in fact Spalyris, Saca King of the Kabul valley, which is the Chinese Chi Pin, a name taken from the Greek Kophen.

The identification of Hermaeus and Yin Mo Fu is not so strange when the old pronunciation of Chinese is taken into account, for then the first syllable probably ended in "M" rather than "N." Moreover, Wen Chung and his suite certainly did not use Greek when communicating with Hermaeus. Yung Ch'u, the Chinese name for Alexandria in Parapamisadae, which was Hermaeus' hereditary kingdom, comes from "Yonaki," the Indian word for a Greek city, in turn derived from the Indian rendering of "Ionian."

The position of Hermaeus after this alliance with China had restored Greek rule in the Kabul valley, was still far from secure. For years the Greeks had been losing ground in all parts of their once extensive Indian empire, and before many years had passed Hermaeus found himself threatened by a new race of nomad invaders, the Kushans, who were the same people as the Yueh Chi who had conquered Bactria. One horde of Yueh Chi had occupied the country now called Sind, a former Greek province, and they now began to press north into the Panjab. Under this danger Hermaeus appealed to China in 30 B.C., and sent envoys to the

Han court. The reigning Han emperor was Han Ch'eng Ti
(32-7 B.C.), almost the last of the line of Early Han, and the last
to reign as an adult. The court was already preoccupied with
internal troubles, and the pretensions of the Wang family, who
were soon to usurp the throne, dominated the political scene.
Han Ch'eng Ti turned down the appeal of Hermaeus, and refused
to intervene in such distant lands. The Greek envoys returned
empty handed, and a few years later the Kushans overwhelmed
the last Greek kingdom. Thus a contact which, had it been made
a century earlier when the Greek empire in India was strong,
might have proved most fruitful and left invaluable records in
both civilisations, came too late to have any deep influence.

There remains one other very important advance made by the
Chinese in the reign of the Emperor Wu, a period which saw a
sudden expansion of the Chinese world greater than all the slow
progress of many centuries. In 108 B.C. the Emperor, attempting
to apply his outflanking strategy against the Hsiung Nu to the
east, sent an expedition, which, after some fighting and much
intrigue, conquered the kingdom of Chao Hsien, northern Korea,
which like Nan Yüeh and Tien had been founded by a Chinese
adventurer. The importance of this conquest was great. The
Chinese province of Lak Lang, founded in place of the destroyed kingdom, became rich and prosperous, diffusing the
culture of the Han Empire throughout the peninsula, whence
it passed over the sea to Japan. The wealth and high standard of
art and luxury prevailing in Lak Lang has been revealed by
archæological finds.*

After the death of the Emperor Wu (87 B.C.) his successors
maintained some contact with the western world, but did not
extend the area of new geographical discovery. The long war
with the Hsiung Nu came to an end, if only for a time, in 51 B.C.
when the nomad nation, having split into two warring sections,
the northern and southern hordes, the Shên Yü of the south paid
homage at Ch'ang An. The spur of nomad menace was now
removed. As has been mentioned, the Emperor Wu's embassies
had been despatched, not primarily with the intention of dis-

*For the influence of Lak Lang on Japan see G. B. Sansom, *Japan*, 1932.
Chap. I. p. 13 *seq.*

covering new lands, but to contract alliances with nations who could attack the Hsiung Nu on their exposed western flank. The Han Court, no longer having the Hsiung Nu war on its hands, relaxed its interest in the western lands.

Moreover, the Han Empire was soon to be shaken by an internal crisis which prevented any attention being paid to foreign affairs. The recurrent troubles at the Han Court caused by the ambitions of the consort families, the relatives of the Empress, have been referred to in the last chapter. Only the Emperor Wu devised a method, brutal and ruthless as it was, of overcoming this danger. When he finally made choice of his heir, he had the young prince's mother put to death. By this savage precaution he effectually prevented the rise to overweening power of the family of the Empress mother. His successors, more humane or less far sighted, did not perpetuate this cruel custom. The consort families rose once more to high positions, until at last the family of Wang, which had already dominated the Court for some thirty years, achieved the height of ambition and, in the person of Wang Mang, usurped the throne itself (A.D. 9). The usurper soon found that the authority which his family had acquired at the capital did not extend to the provinces, where the collateral branches of the Han house were still numerous and popular. Claimants arose who gained a large following, and a devastating civil war broke out. This long destructive war ended in A.D. 25, with the accession of the Emperor Kuang Wu Ti, founder of the later Han dynasty, who removed the capital to Lo Yang in Honan, Ch'ang An having been ruined in the turmoil. The new Emperor had several minor revolts to suppress even after this event, not the least of which was the rebellion of the Red Eyebrows, the first of those recurrent half-mystical, half-bandit secret societies which have often gained very wide popular support in times of distress.* When Kuang Wu Ti had at last restored peace, the empire was so

*Since Han times these societies have frequently reappeared, and usually with a very similar ritual and belief. In modern times the "Boxers" (whose real title was the "Society of the Harmonious Fist") were the most famous, but since then there have been the Red Spears, the Heavenly Gates and the Big Swords, all flourishing in north China, the land of the original Red Eyebrows, and their more famous imitators the Yellow Turbans at the end of the Han dynasty (see Chapter XI).

exhausted that the Emperor forbade the word "war" to be spoken in his hearing.

It was not until his son and successor, Han Ming Ti (A.D. 58-77), had been some years on the throne that the Chinese Court once more turned its attention to the affairs of Turkestan and the western world. As before, it was an outbreak of war with the Hsiung Nu which led to fresh contacts with these countries. Although the two hordes still remained hostile and divided, the confusion in China after Wang Mang's usurpation had left the border exposed to raids and forays in which the nomads delighted. In A.D. 73 the Emperor Ming Ti despatched armies into the nomad country, and, as before, the Chinese strategy was directed against the western flank of the Hsiung Nu. It was regarded as essential that the kingdoms of Turkestan be once more brought under Chinese suzerainty.

It was now more than sixty-five years since the Chinese had held any communication with the west. The generals in charge of the expedition against the Hsiung Nu were thus ill-informed as to the situation in the Tarim Valley. In A.D. 73 the commander-in-chief despatched one of his officers on an embassy to these kingdoms to contract alliances, and if possible obtain recognition of Han suzerainty. This officer was Pan Chao, the most famous Chinese administrator ever sent to Turkestan, the man who took up the task begun by Chang Ch'ien 211 years before, and this time brought it to a successful conclusion. The full story of Pan Chao's career of thirty years in the west cannot be told here, but an example of his methods and his character is afforded by the events of the first mission.

Pan Chao, accompanied by a civil colleague and only thirty-six followers, went first to Shên Shên (or Lou Lan) in the Lop Nor district. At first the Chinese were well received, but after a few days the attitude of the King of Shên Shên changed. The subordinate members of the embassy attributed this coolness to the fickle nature of the Central Asiatic peoples, but Pan Chao, who knew that during the long withdrawal of Chinese influence the Hsiung Nu had gained the ascendancy in these kingdoms, suspected that the King's changed attitude was due to the presence of an envoy of the Shên Yü. Pan Chao at once sought out the officer appointed to care for the Chinese embassy, and, assuming a menacing tone, as of one who already knew the truth, he demanded the whereabouts of the Hsiung Nu envoy. The Shên Shên official, impressed by this bluff, admitted that the Shên Yü had in fact sent an envoy, who had arrived three days before, and was now residing at a place ten miles outside the city.

Pan Chao decided to impress these petty kings once and for all by a resolute action. He imprisoned the Shên Shên official in the Chinese camp, and, taking his thirty-six followers, but not mentioning his plan to his civilian colleague, he set out after dusk to the residence of the Hsiung Nu envoy. After posting ten drummers around the house, Pan Chao set fire to the wooden buildings, while the drummers beat the attack with all their power. The Hsiung Nu, believing that they were attacked by a large force, and unable to see the number of their opponents for the darkness and smoke, rushed half-clad out of their burning house, and were promptly despatched by Pan Chao and his handful of Chinese. The Hsiung Nu envoy himself and thirty of his followers were killed. The rest, thinking escape impossible, fled back into the burning house, where most of them perished. Pan Chao, without losing a single man, returned safely to his quarters.

On hearing the news of this high-handed action his civil colleague was much annoyed, since he feared that Pan Chao would claim all the credit for himself. Pan Chao had kept his plans secret because he realised that in affairs of this sort the hesitations and caution natural to a man of letters would ruin his plan. Now he reassured his colleague, saying: "I am not the man to claim all the glory for myself, you shall be associated in our success when we report to the throne." His colleague being thus won over, Pan Chao sought an audience with the King of Shên Shên, and showed him the head of the Hsiung Nu envoy. The King, astounded at the hardihood of the Chinese, promptly concluded the alliance Pan Chao offered, and sent his son as a hostage to Lo Yang.

Following up this success Pan Chao presented himself at other Courts as far west as Kashgar (Yü T'ien) and everywhere gained his ends by his firmness and strength of character. However, these adventures were not pleasing to all the ministers of the Han Court.

A party existed who deprecated any advance into the west as useless and expensive. In A.D. 76 Pan Chao was recalled on their advice, and his first mission left no permanent result. On his departure the people of Turkestan, who had come to respect and admire the justice of the Chinese envoy, and appreciated the peace and order which Han suzerainty had introduced into the country, were filled with despair, and implored him to remain. Pan Chao, however, returned obediently to Lo Yang where a new Emperor, Han Chang Ti, was now reigning.

Four years later Pan Chao managed to reverse the policy of the Court, by proposing to the Emperor a policy by which he said it would be possible to reduce the whole of the west to the Han obedience without employing either Chinese armies or provisions drawn at great cost from China. He declared that he would be able to use the troops of the submitted states themselves against those who remained recalcitrant, and that with a few hundreds of experienced Chinese soldiers and officers, he could form an army which would easily reduce the whole country. The Emperor agreed to let him make the attempt.

For the next seventeen years Pan Chao carried out this plan with unbroken success. One by one the kings of the Turkestan oases were reduced to obedience, until the whole Tarim Valley was under the peaceful rule of the Chinese viceroy. In A.D. 97, after reducing the last contumacious prince, Pan Chao crossed the T'ien Shan Mountains and, with an army of 70,000 men, advanced unopposed to the shores of the Caspian Sea. Never before, and never since, has a Chinese army encamped almost on the frontiers of Europe. The whole stretch of country between the T'ien Shan and the Caspian submitted to the Chinese without fighting. More than fifty "kings" acknowledged Chinese over-lordship and sent their heirs as hostages to Lo Yang. Encamped on the Caspian shore, Pan Chao despatched his envoy, Kan Ying, to enquire into the nature and state of the western world.

Before recounting the embassy of Kan Ying, it is necessary to consider the state of the Near East in A.D. 97. Many changes had occurred since Chang Ch'ien had first made contact with the Hellenistic world. It is at first sight surprising that Pan Chao should have been unopposed in the countries which bordered the

Parthian Empire, and which had at times owed allegiance to the King of Kings. But Parthia was then passing through an internal crisis, of which little is known. The King Pacorus had to contend against several pretenders throughout his reign, and no doubt this weakness of Parthia contributed not a little to Pan Chao's easy successes.* West of Parthia was Rome, a power which had not emerged in western Asia in Chang Chi'en's day. The Roman Empire was then at the plenitude of its power, under the Emperor Nerva. The two world empires, the Han and the Roman, were now separated only by the Caspian Sea and the Armenian mountains.

The Han history† contains an account of the western world which is undoubtedly based on the report made by Kan Ying after his return to Pan Chao's headquarters. The identification of the countries visited by the Chinese envoy has been the subject of considerable dispute, but recent studies based upon the directions given in the Han history have established that it was not the Persian Gulf, but the Black Sea, that Kan Ying reached.

After visiting An Hsi, *i.e.* Parthia, which he describes as a populous land with many towns and villages, Kan Ying reached the coast of the "Great Sea" probably at a point near the modern Batum. His aim was to reach Ta Ts'in, that is to say, the Roman Empire. However, the seamen at this port warned him of the dangers of the voyage, saying:

"This sea is very wide. With a favourable wind one may cross it in three months, but if the winds are adverse the voyage may take two years. Moreover, there is about this sea something which gives people such a longing for their own country that many die of it. For these reasons those who embark take at least three years' provisions. If the Han ambassador is willing to forget his family and his home, he can embark."

On hearing of these perils, Kan Ying's heart failed him, and he went no further. There is little doubt that the Parthians deliberately misled the Chinese envoy, fearing that close relations

*Sir Percy Sykes. *History of Persia.* London. 1921. Vol. I. Chapter XXXIII.
†Hou Han Shu. Chap. 118.

between China and Rome would lead to an alliance of the two great empires. Pan Chao's conquests must have seemed an alarming portent, and of the hostility of the Roman Empire, there was no doubt. Nevertheless the seamen had only exaggerated, not invented the dangers of the route. From Parthia, as the Chinese learned, the sea voyage across the Black Sea led to T'iao Chih, which has now been identified as the Crimea, the Chinese name being derived from the Greek name Taurica. Thence ships coasted round to Byzantium, which the Chinese, perhaps from later information, knew as the capital of Ta Ts'in (the Roman Empire) and called An Tu. This was for long thought to be a rendering of Antioch, a confusion which led to the belief that T'iao Chih was Mesopotamia. It is now known that in the period between A.D. 196 and A.D. 330 the old Greek city of Byzantium was officially called Augusta Antonina by the Romans, and it is from the word "Antonina" in this name that "An Tu" is derived.* By various ways the Chinese in the Han period came to know much about the Roman Empire. Some of this information came from the Chinese officers whom Pan Chao sent on missions to the kingdoms of western Asia, some from merchants who came to China either by the caravan route across Central Asia, or by the sea route via India. All this information is summarised in the Hou Han Shu, or History of the Later Han Dynasty; the account of Ta Ts'in is as follows, much of it having the air of being the report made by an envoy, and his observations on the road:

"Ta Ts'in, also called Li Chien, lies west of the sea, and is known as the Land West of the Sea [*i.e.* the Black Sea and Mediterranean]. It is many thousands of *li* in extent, has more than four hundred cities, and scores of small vassal states. The walls of cities are built of stone. There are chains of courier stations, all white-washed. There are cedar trees, and all kinds of woods and plants. The people cultivate the land (*i.e.* are not

*The arguments in favour of these identifications of the place names given in the Hou Han Shu are set out in an unpublished paper, *Byzantium and the way thither*, by Prof. Yang Hsien-yi, to whom I am indebted for permission to use this information.

nomads). They grow many crops, and plant mulberry trees. Their hair is cut short and they wear embroidered clothes. They ride in chariots. Their chariots are small, and have white awnings. On leaving or approaching [a city] drums are beaten and flags and banners displayed. The circuit of the [capital] city exceeds one hundred *li*. There are five palaces in the city, each ten *li* apart. In the palaces the pillars of the halls are made of crystal, and so are the dishes on which food is served. The King goes daily to one of these palaces and transacts business. After five days he completes the round. An official is appointed who carries a bag and follows the King's chariot. Those who wish to bring up some matter of business write petitions and drop them into this bag. When the King arrives at the palace, the bag is opened and the cases are judged on their rights and wrongs. The King appoints thirty-six generals who all participate in discussions of affairs of State. There are officials for all kinds of State business. Their Kings do not rule permanently; they always appoint worthy men as Kings; if there are ill-omened portents, or the seasons are disordered, the King is deposed and another set up. The one who has been degraded takes his dismissal in good part and shows no resentment. The people are all tall and have an air comparable to those of China, and for this reason are called Big Ts'in [*i.e.* big Chinese, Ts'in being a name for China from the Ts'in dynasty]. The land produces much gold and silver. There are rare gems, including shining jade, bright pearls like the moon, and the rhinoceros hide called 'bird scaring rhinoceros hide' [apparently a magic substance], coral, amber, glass, red jade, cinnabar, and green jade. They work gold thread and have embroideries and brocades of various colours. They can gild and have asbestos. They have also a fine cloth which is called 'water sheep's down,' and is made of wild silkworm cocoons. They collect perfumes, decoct the juice and make gum. Every foreign thing, precious or strange, is produced here.

"They use gold and silver for money. Ten pieces of silver money equal one of gold. They trade with India and Parthia by the sea route, making a ten-fold profit. They are upright traders, and have fixed prices. Corn and food are always cheap; so that the country is very wealthy. When neighbouring States send embassies, on arrival at the frontier they are mounted on post horses and sent to the royal capital. When they arrive the King makes them presents of gold.

"Their King has long wished to send an embassy to China, but as the Parthians desire to obtain Chinese silks for re-sale to the people of Ta Ts'in, they block the way so that none could get through. In the reign of Huan Ti [A.D. 166] the King of Ta Ts'in, An Tun, sent an embassy which arrived at Jih Nan [Tong King] beyond the frontier. They presented ivory, rhinoceros horn, and tortoise shell. The things they offered were in no way precious or rare, and it was suspected that they had been exchanged. This was the first time contact had been made. Some say that to the west of this country there are vaporous flowing sands near to the dwelling place of Hsi Wang Mu [a legendary deity of the West] nearly at the place where the sun sets. The Han Shu [i.e. Ch'ien Han Shu, the History of the Early Han Dynasty] says that more than 200 days' journey west of T'iao Chih you come to the place where the sun sets, but this is not in accord with the present book; for in former times Han envoys all turned back at Wu I [a mountain range in Parthia], none reached T'iao Chih. Another account says that from Parthia the land route winds round north of the sea [i.e. the Black Sea] coming out to the west of the sea at Ta Ts'in. The population is thick and continuous. Every ten li there is a pavilion, every thirty li, a posting station. There is no danger of thieves or bandits; yet on the road there are many ferocious tigers and lions which are a danger to travellers. Unless travelling in companies of over a hundred carrying arms they would be devoured. It is also said that there is a very high bridge of several hundred li by which one can cross to the countries north of the sea. They produce many strange and precious gems and stones and all kinds of rarities, but many of them are not verified and are therefore not recorded."

It is not clear from this account whether the royal city with five palaces is Rome or Constantinople, or perhaps a confusion of the two. The account of the political system is clearly a garbled description of the annual Consuls of the Roman Republic. The Embassy from An Tun was probably not really an embassy, but a trading expedition by Alexandrine Greeks, who passed themselves off as ambassadors when they arrived on the confines of China. An Tun is Marcus Aurelius Antoninus. It is clear that, blocked by the Parthians, the Romans were trying to open up a sea route to the land of Serica, and it is at least possible that the visitors to Tong King carried letters of credence. The legend about the place where the sun sets, two hundred days west of the Black Sea, may possibly be a faint echo of a description of the Atlantic seaboard of Europe, the end of the world to the Greeks. The story about the bridge over the sea is probably also an echo of Xerxes' bridge of boats across the Hellespont.

After the second century A.D. intercourse between China and Rome seems to have become more difficult, perhaps because the Chinese grip on Central Asia was relaxed. Pan Chao himself returned to China in A.D. 102, after thirty years of service in the west. He reached Lo Yang, the capital, after his petition to be allowed to return had been granted at the request of his equally famous sister, Pan Ch'ao, usually considered to be the foremost woman scholar in Chinese history. One month after he reached home Pan Chao died. It would seem that even to-day he is not forgotten in Central Asia, for at Kashgar there are the "Springs of Pan Chao," said to have been miraculously discovered by the great administrator.*

*Sir Percy Sykes, *op. cit.* Vol. I, page 387.

Chapter IX

LITERATURE AND RELIGION IN THE HAN PERIOD

In 191 B.C., in the reign of Hui Ti, second sovereign of the Han dynasty, the decree proscribing the teaching of the "Hundred Schools" and the literature of the feudal period was formally repealed. Although the prohibition of ancient learning had not been effective since the fall of the Ch'in dynasty in 209 B.C., eighteen years before, the repeal of this law is a convenient starting point for a review of the great literary achievements of the Han scholars. From this date began the painful task of research and criticism which resurrected a large part of the proscribed books and preserved for posterity the ancient texts upon which almost all knowledge of the feudal period still relies.

The restoration of letters was at first the work of private scholars, and did not receive the patronage or support of the imperial Court. We have seen that the founder of the new dynasty, Liu Pang, canonised as the Emperor Kao Tsu, the "High Ancestor" was an unlettered peasant, who despised and ignored such scholars as were to be found at his Court. Most of the prominent men in his service were equally uneducated, and of those who had some pretensions to learning, very few belonged to the Confucian school. The complexion of the early Han Court was, on the contrary, more Taoist than Confucian. The Empress Tou, wife of Hsiao Wên, who exercised great influence during the reigns of her husband and son, and did not die till her grandson, the Emperor Wu, had been some years on the throne, was a convinced Taoist; and used her influence to frustrate the Emperor Wu's first attempt to confer favour on the Confucian scholars.

Although by contrast to his predecessors, the Emperor Wu has often been regarded as a patron of Confucianism; he was eclectic in his religious beliefs, conferring the highest favour on the professors of magical arts who had certainly no common ground with the scholars. Nevertheless, it was during his reign (141-87 B.C.) that the Confucian school laid the foundations of its future exclusive domination. There can be little doubt that the ultimate victory of the Confucians was due to their antiquarian labours in restoring the lost literature of the feudal age. Confucius himself had laid the greatest stress on the duty of preserving and cultivating the ancient literature. His followers in Han times devoted their researches to this purpose, and it is primarily to their work that we owe any knowledge of the ancient texts.

This interest in the past gave the Confucians a notable advantage over the rival schools. The Taoists had not the same care for ancient books, and tended in the new atmosphere of religious innovation to associate themselves with the superstitious practices of the magical cults then in favour. In consequence, as time passed scholarship became more and more identified with Confucianism, and Taoism, seeing analogies between the mystical language of its ancient philosophers and the magical receipts of the fashionable cults, was slowly modified into a popular religion, a synthesis of all the varied superstitions and local cults of the expanding empire.

Confucianism, originally the ethical and philosophic system of an aristocratic school, was itself transformed in the new atmosphere of the Han period. The search for a principle of moral authority which had occupied the philosophers of the "Hundred Schools" was no longer the dominant intellectual problem of the new empire. Authority had now no need of moral foundations. The problem to which the varying teachers of the feudal age had propounded such different answers had been solved over their heads by the rude violence of less educated men. The centralised empire was now a fact, power emanated from a single supreme source, government was vigorous and stable. Under these conditions Confucianism slowly acquired a new authoritative, religious tone, and, as the Confucian scholars were the great doctors of ancient learning, their claims were buttressed by an appeal to precedent, always powerful to the Chinese mind.

Moreover, the men of the Han age were intensely interested in past history. After the storms of the great revolution the dead world of feudalism appealed to them with all the romance of a half forgotten civilisation. The Confucian scholars had taken the chief part in the restoration of the lost literature, and they naturally tended to magnify the importance of their own school and to devote their main efforts to its literature. Consequently, the Han age saw the past through Confucian spectacles, coloured, moreover, by the ideas current in the new empire. When history came to be written, the Han scholars drew upon Confucian sources—necessarily, for the Confucians were the great preservers of ancient books—and interpreted the ancient texts in accordance with ideas peculiar to their school. The legends of the remote past were accepted without cavil. Yao and Shun were as historical as the feudal kings, and were represented as ruling an empire as united and as extensive as that of the Emperor Wu himself. This belief in the ancient unity of the empire, to which feudalism had succeeded as a period of decay, was a reflection of contemporary political ideas, which accepted the new unified empire as a restoration of the conditions prevailing under the Sage Kings. It was, besides, entirely in consonance with Chinese mental habits to represent a revolutionary innovation as a return to past precedents.

The Han scholars are thus dangerous guides to any true understanding of the feudal and prehistoric past. But they were misinterpreters, not falsifiers. They treated every ancient text with reverence, transmitted it with care, without additions or corrections. It is true that they were sometimes misled into accepting texts of doubtful authenticity, which subsequent scholarship has revealed to be corrupt or interpolated, but in general they confined their emendations and often erroneous explanations to a commentary kept strictly apart from the ancient text itself. This tradition has persisted throughout Chinese literary history. A text was regarded as sacred, not to be altered, nor to be emended, except in a definitely separated commentary.

For these reasons the ancient Chinese literature has been transmitted in a manner wholly unlike that by which the western world has received the records of the classical age. There are hardly any copies of Chinese books extant which date earlier than the Sung period (A.D. 960-1280), nor are there stone inscriptions*

---

*The well-known inscribed stone drums, now preserved in the Temple of Confucius at Peking, are monuments of the feudal period. The exact date of these drums is disputed, but the inscription refers to a hunting expedition of a King of Ch'in, and has no bearing on classical texts.

of real antiquity to confirm and check the work of the copyists. China, however, has never known a "dark age" such as that which overwhelmed the civilisation of the west. There have been great literary catastrophes, such as the Burning of the Books, but no complete break in the continuity of the literary tradition. From century to century, from the time of Confucius to the present day, the Chinese scholars have faithfully reproduced the old books, neither adding to nor paraphrasing the original text. Books have been lost, and on occasion "rediscovered" in a form which is far from authentic, composed of the odd citations found in extant literature, but the keen criticism of Chinese scholarship, a critical faculty which may be traced back to the laborious work of restoring the feudal literature in the Han period, has always been quick to detect and denounce forgery.

The absence of ancient copies on stone or brick, and the importance and reverence which Chinese scholars have paid to their ancient literature has stimulated the art of scholastic criticism in all ages. The Chinese scholars discovered and practised the higher criticism centuries before the west. On the whole they tended to be more severe on the extant books than their present successors. This hard discipline had invaluable results. It not only preserved, in all its archaic difficulty, the most ancient literature, but it trained up a school of historians who have recorded the events of two thousand years with an attention to chronology and a sober abstention from the fanciful and the heroic, which has no parallel in any other eastern literature, and has only been equalled in the west since the Renaissance. This historical tradition arose in the Han period, and was originated by the famous Ssǔ-ma Ch'ien, whose work has served as a model for all succeeding ages.

It would be impossible, in the short space of one chapter, to give a detailed account of all the Han scholars who laboured at the restoration of the classical books, nor is it always certain to whom the preservation of the most famous books is due. Mao Ch'ang, who lived under the first Han Emperors, edited the Odes, or *Shih Ching*, the anthology of ancient poems and folk songs which Confucius esteemed so highly. The *Shih Ching*, with the commentary of Mao Ch'ang, is universally recognised as one of the most pure and uncorrupted of the texts which have survived from antiquity. As the Odes are the oldest writings in the Chinese language, the importance of Mao's work cannot be over-estimated.

The preservation of the oldest historical text, the *Shu Ching*, was the work of more than one scholar. The so-called "new" text was preserved by Fu Shêng, an aged member of the Ch'in academy of Scholars of Great Learning, who, surviving till the reign of Hsiao Wên (179-157 B.C.), wrote down twenty-nine chapters, which, according to one account, he remembered by heart. It is also recorded that he found this fragment in the ruins of his old home, where he had hidden it in the time of Shih Huang Ti. These stories of books hidden in walls are common at this period, but in all probability they are merely romantic tales, seeking to prove that the book in question was an undoubted survival from the feudal age. The *Shu Ching* also exists in another form, the "old" text, which was supposed to have been found in the wall of Confucius' house, and edited by his descendant, K'ung An-kuo, in the reign of the Emperor Wu (141-87 B.C.). The authenticity of the "old" text as at present extant has been disputed by Chinese scholars, and also by European sinologists. The question is complicated, and the true history of the text will perhaps never be known. The additional books found in the "old" text, which are usually regarded as forgeries, are certainly old texts, as their style and phraseology show. It is perhaps most likely that several versions of these old stories existed in Chou times, some esteemed by one school, and others upheld by their rivals. K'ung An-kuo's "old" text was not in favour with the Han Confucians, as Ssŭ-ma Ch'ien's sparing use of it proves. It does not however follow that the texts are forgeries of the 5th century A.D.

The distinction between "new" and "old" texts was due to the change in the system of writing introduced under the Ch'in sovereigns. The archaic characters had already given place, at some date in the Chou period to the type known as "great seal" and this in turn had been modified to the style now known as "lesser seal." In the Ch'in dynasty an important advance was made. The ancient books had been written on strips of smoothed bamboo, and inscribed with a sharp stylus, but in the reign of Shih Huang Ti the brush pen was invented, traditionally by the general Mêng T'ien. The use of silk as a material combined with the brush pen as an instrument made a notable change in the style of the characters. The stiff angular forms of "lesser seal" characters were modified into the easy curves and simplified styles suited to the use of the brush. This was the "new" style, in which Fu Shêng's *Shu Ching* was written, and which has ever since, with slight modifications, been in use. The "old" style, in which K'ung An-kuo's supposed find was said to have been written, was already becoming forgotten and disused by the reign of the Emperor Wu.

Two renowned scholars of the 1st century B.C., Liu Hsiang and his son, Liu Hsin, distant connections of the imperial family, were responsible for the publication of the *Chan Kuo Tsê*, an important source for the period of the Warring States. They also worked on the *I Ching*, or Book of Changes, and popularised the *Tso Chuan*, regarded as a commentary on the *Ch'un Ch'iu*, though much of it has no relation to that work. Liu Hsin was a supporter of Wang Mang, the usurper, and has been attacked by Chinese scholars on that account, but his work is now accepted as genuine. Hsiu Hsin, a scholar of the later Han, *circa* A.D. 100, compiled the *Shuo Wên*, the first dictionary of the language to employ the system of identifying and grouping the different classes of characters by their "radicals," i.e. the part of the character which broadly indicates the sense, a system which is still in vogue. Hsiu Hsin's identifications were not in accordance with the oldest meaning of many characters, as a study of the inscriptions on oracle bones and ancient bronzes has revealed, but his work helped to classify and standardise the manner of writing the script, as well as to reveal the meaning attached to many ancient words in Han times.

In another field of study, the preservation of Taoist doctrines, the name of Liu An, King of Huai Nan, is supreme. Liu An, who is generally known as Huai Nan Tzŭ, "the philosopher of Huai Nan," was the grandson of the Emperor Han Kao Tsu (Liu Pang), and feudal sovereign of Huai Nan, a region between the rivers Huai and Yangtze. He was an ardent Taoist, and composed a book in which the doctrines of the *Tao Tê Ching* and

Chuang Tzŭ are expounded. In Huai Nan Tzŭ the transition of Taoism from a pure mystical philosophy to a religion can be observed. The allegories in which Chuang Tzŭ represented the sages who had comprehended the Tao as immune from the cares of the world, riding upon the clouds, and living without sustenance as hermits upon the mountain tops, are now beginning to be accepted as realities, possible to those who had acquired the supreme knowledge. Huai Nan Tzŭ, in tune with the spirit of his age (he was a contemporary of the Emperor Wu), was soaked in the supernatural and his book did much to transform Taoism into a religious cult.

The declining years of the Chou dynasty, the period of the Warring States, has come down in literary history as the age of philosophers; the Han dynasty, the age of the first unified empire, is equally celebrated for its historians. The Chinese world had emerged from the feudal anarchy into the comparatively calm and assured era of the united empire; a period of stability in which scholars could reflect upon the past and trace the steps by which so vast a revolution had come about. The work of restoring the proscribed literature had already roused a critical interest in the customs and traditions relating to the early Chou period and the dimly remembered dynasties which had gone before. The time was ripe for a great work of historical research which should gather up the fragmentary and contradictory records of the feudal and legendary age and present, for the first time, a connected and comprehensive history of the Chinese world. This was the task which was undertaken and completed by two scholars, father and son, in the reign of the Emperor Wu.

Their joint work, the *Shih Chi* or Historical Memoirs* was planned and begun by Ssŭ-ma T'an, the father, and completed after the death of the elder man by Ssŭ-ma Ch'ien, his son. As by far the larger part of the book was the work of the son, it is Ssŭ-ma Ch'ien who is usually regarded as the real author. The *Shih Chi*, as the model which all later historians copied, and as one of the principal sources for the history of ancient China, and also

---

*So translated by Chavannes *op. cit.* Professor Hu Shih considers that "Memoirs of a Historian" would be more correct (*Development of the Logical Method in Ancient China*).

for the early Han period, is one of the most famous and valuable works in the Chinese literature. It is therefore of importance to consider what manner of man Ssŭ-ma Ch'ien was, and why he was qualified to write this monumental book.*

Ssŭ-ma Ch'ien was born about 136 B.C. and died early in the reign of Chao Ti, successor of the Emperor Wu, about 85 B.C. Although the exact dates of his birth and death are not known, many details of his life have been preserved, partly in his own writings, and partly in the notices devoted to him by later historians. The Ssŭ-ma family were of aristocratic origin as their name—meaning "commander of horse," a military title— denotes. They descended from a general of the Ch'in state, who had conquered Shu, or Western Szechuan for that country. They were thus natives of Ch'in, the western state which had been considered half barbarous in the early Chou period. The Ssŭ-ma came from the eastern part of Ch'in, the district now called Han Ch'êng Hsien on the Shensi bank of the Yellow River. This district had formerly been part of the Tsin state, until it was conquered by Ch'in. Ssŭ-ma T'an, and after his death, Ssŭ-ma Ch'ien himself occupied, at the Han Court, the post of Duke Grand Astrologer, a position which was not so important as the high sounding title might suggest. As Ssŭ-ma Ch'ien himself says, the Grand Astrologer was not a great officer, indeed, his functions were confined to matters relating to the observation of the heavens and the calendar. It is possible that the title indicates that this position had formerly been more honourable, but at the court of the Emperor Wu it was something of a sinecure. However, the Grand Astrologer had one advantage eminently useful for an historian, he had access to the imperial library and archives in which were stored not only copies of every historical record which survived, but also the vast accumulation of official reports to the throne, decrees and ordinances.

Ssŭ-ma Ch'ien, before inheriting his father's office, had travelled widely. His youth was spent at the ancestral home in Shensi, where he was educated, and also engaged in the homely pursuits of agriculture and pasturage. At the age of twenty, he set out on a

*The *Shih Chi* contains one hundred and thirty chapters, of which ten are now lost.

long series of travels, a kind of grand tour of the empire, which it would seem was regarded as part of the education of a young man, much as the tour of Europe formed the last stage in the education of an 18th century gentleman. Ssŭ-ma Ch'ien visited the southeast of China, going as far as the modern Chekiang, then recently incorporated in the Han dominions. There, near the modern Hang Chou, he saw the alleged tomb of Yao, and the inscriptions set up by Ch'in Shih Huang Ti, which he copied and later included in his history. Travelling up the Yangtze he visited the modern provinces of Kiangsi and Hunan, the extreme southern limit of the civilised world in his time, and took care to see all the places famous in myth or history.

Returning across central China he made a devout pilgrimage to Lu and Ch'i—the modern Shantung—which had been the intellectual centres of the "Hundred Schools." At Chu Fou he saw the tomb and house of Confucius, where the carriage and other personal relics of the sage were still preserved. He made a considerable stay in these famous cities of the east, and no doubt profited by the occasion to inspect the libraries of the scholars who resided there. Returning to the court, Ch'ang An, in Shensi, he received an official post and was shortly afterwards sent on a government mission to the newly conquered countries of the south-west. He therefore visited Szechuan, including the western region of the upper Yangtze, and penetrated far into Yunnan to the district of Ta Li, then the furthest point known to the Chinese. Ssŭ-ma Ch'ien was thus more than a traveller, he was an explorer.

In later years, though he does not say on what occasion, he travelled in north-western China, the modern Kansu and the region of Inner Mongolia around the great bend of the Yellow River. There he followed the course of the Great Wall as far east as the modern province of Hopei (Chihli). He accompanied the Emperor on his religious pilgrimages to Mt. T'ai Shan in Shantung, and was present on the famous occasion (109 B.C.) when the Emperor, passing the breach where the Yellow River had broken its banks, personally supervised the work of closing the gap and set the example by carrying bundles of faggots himself, followed by the whole court. Ssŭ-ma Ch'ien had thus travelled in all parts of the Han Empire, and had been an eye-witness of many of the most important events at the Court of the Emperor Wu.

Of his official life, less is known. In 104 B.C. he was one of the scholars charged with the great reform of the calendar, a matter of religious significance to the men of his day. In 99 B.C. there occurred the tragedy which darkened his later years, but which does great honour to his character. In that year, in the course of the long wars against the Hsiung Nu, the celebrated general Li Kuang-li had invaded the enemy country in the direction of the eastern end of the T'ien Shan Mountains. Li Ling, grandson of another Han general,* had requested permission to make a diversion with 5,000 men in the direction of Hami. The Emperor had only consented to this after much persuasion, and when in the event, Li Ling, encountering unexpectedly the full force of the Hsiung Nu, was compelled to surrender after a heroic but vain retreat, the imperial wrath was unbounded.

The flatterers at Court, men whom, as Ssŭ-ma Ch'ien says, took good care not to expose themselves to the perils of a campaign, fanned the Emperor's rage by condemning Li Ling as loudly as they had formerly praised him. Only Ssŭ-ma Ch'ien, though not an intimate friend of the luckless general, had the courage to take his part. He pointed out that the disaster had occurred because Li Ling had not been supported, he recalled that the general had made a desperate stand, executed an heroic retreat, and only yielded when his men, trapped in a gorge in the mountains, had shot away all their arrows, and were reduced to fighting with their broken spear shafts. Few generals in the past, he declared, had fought so well as Li Ling, and if he had been compelled to surrender rather than perish on the field, it was doubtless because he hoped to find another occasion on which to avenge his misfortune.

Unfortunately, the Emperor did not accept this generous defence in the manner it was intended. He suspected that Ssŭ-ma Ch'ien meant to cast the blame on Li Kuang-li, who being himself in difficulties, had been unable to support Li Ling. Li Kuang-li,

*Li Kuang, from whom the imperial house of the T'ang dynasty claimed to be descended.

whose sister was the imperial favourite of the moment, was then high in favour. More enraged than ever at what he considered to be a covert criticism of his favourite, the Emperor caused Ssŭ-ma Ch'ien to be handed over to the judges on the grave charge of attempting to deceive the Throne. The judges subserviently condemned the historian to the penalty of castration. According to the laws then in force Ssŭ-ma Ch'ien could have escaped his penalty by making a heavy payment to the government, but, as his family were not wealthy and his friends, fearing the enmity of the powerful faction of Li Kuang-li, deserted him, he suffered the penalty to which he had been so unjustly sentenced.

This event embittered the last years of Ssŭ-ma Ch'ien and sharpened his hostility to the Emperor. Although in later years he was given the important post of *chung shu ling*, a secretary whose functions included the supervision of all reports to the throne and decrees issued, he harboured a lasting enmity to his sovereign, and in his chapters on the events of this reign there are many covert satires against the Emperor Wu.*

The story of Ssŭ-ma Ch'ien's disgrace is told by himself in a letter to his friend, Jên An, which was also written in tragic circumstances. Jên An, a military officer, had been compromised in the fatal intrigue towards the end of the reign of the Emperor which cost the life of the Crown Prince and many notables.† He appealed to Ssŭ-ma Ch'ien for help, and the letter is the historian's reply. The sense is concealed, but has been regarded as a refusal justified by Ssŭ-ma Ch'ien's lack of influence as a condemned and mutilated man. In recounting his own misfortunes Ssŭ-ma Ch'ien

---

*The chapter which was devoted to the reign of the Emperor Wu itself is missing, no doubt because it was too hostile to be published even in later years. In his Chapters on the sacrifices, and on economic matters (Fêng Shan and P'ing Chun), and also in the biographies of his contemporaries, Ssŭ-ma Ch'ien uses very plain language.

†The Crown Prince was accused by his enemies of having practised magical arts to shorten his father's life. They obtained leave to search his palace, and produced images (which they had previously placed there) which the Prince was accused of using in his nefarious rites. The Crown Prince attempted to flee, and on his way tried to obtain the support of Jên An, commanding part of the garrison stationed near the capital. Jên An did not aid him, but was later accused of "sitting on the fence," waiting to see what the outcome of the trouble would be.

advances as the reason why he had submitted rather than take his life, his determination to finish his history. Covertly, therefore he suggests that Jên An, who was not engaged on similar literary work, had no reason to prefer dishonour to death. Jên An, in fact, was executed.*

The *Shih Chi*, the great historical work which was composed by Ssŭ-ma Ch'ien during the course of his busy life, is in reality less his original work than a compilation of all the ancient historical material available. He reproduces integrally the texts of ancient annalists, modern writers, and Government documents. It is a method wholly unlike that which historians in the west have followed. Ssŭ-ma Ch'ien does not cite his authorities, he copies them down and includes their work in his own compilation. In the early chapters he uses the *Shu Ching*, sometimes slightly altering the archaic language to make it more intelligible. In the feudal period he quotes, or rather cites, the *Ch'un Ch'iu*, and the Annals of Ch'in (which alone wholly survived the proscription of history) and also fragments from the annals of other feudal states, which are now lost. Other works, some of which have disappeared, are used to cover the Ch'in and early Han period. Ssŭ-ma Ch'ien rarely writes himself, invariably using the existing material. It is only when he is actually dealing with contemporary matters, and the biographies of famous men, where his predecessors had not already recorded events, that he himself writes original history. This method, strange to western ideas, has merits and drawbacks. It lacks, too often, the dramatic quality found in such historians as Herodotus. There is no unity of style, for Ssŭ-ma Ch'ien has included documents of the most diverse ages, some written in terse archaic language, others in the polished periods of his own day. Furthermore, his attitude to the legends of the heroic age is uncritical. Yao and Shun are treated as historical sovereigns, and where the legends concerning them are contradictory Ssŭ-ma Ch'ien includes all the accounts without expressing any judgment upon their authenticity.

Even when dealing with an intensely dramatic situation, such as the flight of Liu Pang after sustaining a great defeat at the

*This letter is translated in full in Chavannes's translation of the *Shih Chi*. *Op. cit.*

hands of his rival, Hsiang Yü, Ssǔ-ma Ch'ien, compiling from the lost *Ch'u Han Ch'un Ch'iu*, a work by the eye-witness Lu Chia, makes no attempt to dramatise the narrative or comment upon the facts:

" . . . At P'êng Ch'êng, in the middle of the day [Hsiang Yü] inflicted a great defeat on the army of Han; all the soldiers of Han fled; they threw themselves one after another into the rivers Ku and Ssǔ; more than 100,000 of the soldiers of Han were slain. The army of Han fled southwards towards the mountains, Ch'u [Hsiang Yü] pursued them still fighting and arrived to the east of Ling Pi on the banks of the river Sui. The army of Han fell back, pressed by Ch'u; more than 100,000 of the Han soldiers perished together, drowned in the river Sui. The water of the river Sui was dammed up [by their bodies]. Hsiang Yü surrounded the King of Han [Liu Pang] with a triple ring; at this moment a great north-west wind arose, tearing up the trees, overthrowing houses, and raising clouds of sand and dust; the sky was darkened, and it was night in broad daytime.* The hurricane blew straight towards the army of Ch'u. It was thrown into confusion, and the ranks were broken and dispersed. The King of Han was then able to flee secretly with a few tens of horsemen. He planned to pass by P'ei [his native place] to rescue his family, and then escape to the west. Ch'u for his part sent men to pursue him to P'ei and to capture the family of the King of Han. The members of this family had fled and did not meet the King of Han. The King of Han found on the way Hsiao Hui and the Princess Yüan of Lu.† He took them into his chariot. As the horsemen of Ch'u

---

*This was not a miracle, but a severe north China dust storm. It is not uncommon, during the height of such storms, to find the air so thick with fine particles of dust, that it is impossible to see more than two or three yards. It is rare to experience so violent a dust storm at a place as far south as P'êng Ch'êng, which is in northern Kiangsu, but there is some historical evidence tending to prove that these storms were more violent in past times than those which occur to-day.

†Hsiao Hui and the Princess of Lu were the son and daughter of Liu Pang, at this time mere children. Ssǔ-ma Ch'ien uses the posthumous titles by which they were known in his own time, for Hsiao Hui was the successor of Han Kao Tsu (Liu Pang). His personal name was Ying.

pursued hard after them, and they were closely pressed, he threw Hsiao Hui and the Princess of Lu out of the chariot. The governor of T'êng [Hsia-hou Ying, one of his officers] dismounted, and put them back in the chariot. This scene was repeated three times. Then the governor of T'êng said: 'Although we are closely pursued, we cannot go any faster, what is the use of abandoning them?' Thus, they were able to escape."

Ssǔ-ma Ch'ien adds no word of comment upon the inhumanity of Liu Pang, prepared to abandon his children to facilitate his own escape. He proceeds tranquilly with his narrative.

Fig. 36, part of a battle scene which may represent one of the episodes of this war, occurs in the bas-reliefs of the Wu tombs in Shantung, which date from the 2nd century A.D. (see Chapter X). The combatants, who are fiercely disputing the passage of a river, are armed with the iron swords with ringed pommels which are known to have been in use in Han times. One such sword in the possession of Professor C. G. Seligman is 2 ft. 10 ins. in length from the ring to the tip, which is still protected by the bronze chape of the original scabbard.

If the *Shih Chi* thus lacks qualities which western readers are accustomed to expect in historical writing, it has certain outstanding merits, not always found in ancient western literature. Firstly, it was a work based upon a vast research. Ssǔ-ma Ch'ien tells us that he had read practically every book extant in his day, and he had used to the full his opportunities of investigating the imperial archives. He includes not only every work of antiquity which was considered genuine, but also extracts from official papers. For example, Chang Ch'ien's report on his adventurous journey to Bactria is given in the words of the traveller himself. The *Shih Chi* are thus a veritable encyclopædia of ancient literature, a touchstone by which the authenticity of other versions can be tested by the citations which the historian included in his book.

Moreover, as a consequence of Ssǔ-ma Ch'ien's own travels he had developed a keen interest in matters not strictly historical. Although, due to his method of compilation, he never uses his

FIG. 36. *Part of bas-relief representing a Battle on a Bridge. Han Dynasty.*

own geographical knowledge to elucidate the text, he wrote monographs on all the countries newly conquered or discovered. He has chapters on the Hsiung Nu, the south-western barbarians, the western kingdoms of Central Asia and Bactria, on Korea, and southern China. He tells us that it was in consequence of his experiences at the repairing of the breach in the Yellow River dyke, that he decided to write a chapter on the rivers and canals of the empire, an invaluable record of the river conservancy and irrigation schemes carried out by the Emperor Wu. He also wrote the chapter on economic policy which has been cited in Chapter VII. His position as Grand Astrologer gave him an intimate knowledge of the religious observances at the Court, and in his chapter "Fêng Shan" he has described the innovations made by the Emperor and the careers of the magicians who exercised so great an influence at Court. It is particularly interesting to see that Ssǔ-ma Ch'ien himself was by no means the dupe of their arts, and regarded their pretensions with profound scepticism. Other branches of science, as known to the Han scholars, are accorded equal treatment. There are chapters on astrology, the calendar, music and divination. His biographies of famous men cover not only the great names of the past and contemporary times, but also the famous comedians, celebrated assassins, brigands, court favourites, generals, poets, and scholars. The *Shih Chi* is a mine of information on every aspect of the Han civilisation, and it set a standard of historical writing which has been imitated throughout the course of Chinese history.

In the Later Han period the historical work of Ssǔ-ma Ch'ien was carried on by three members of a famous family, the Pan. The exploits of Pan Chao as administrator and conqueror in the remote countries of the west have been mentioned in Chapter VIII; the stay-at-home members of his family were no less famous—indeed, to the Chinese far more famous—in the field of letters. Pan Piao (A.D. 3-54) was the father of these remarkable children. Himself a scholar of repute, he, like Ssǔ-ma T'an, began to assemble the materials for the history which his children completed after his death. Pan Chao, the general, was the second son, his elder brother, Pan Ku (d. A.D. 92), is the author of the *Ch'ien Han Shu* or History of the Early Han dynasty, a work which follows the plan laid down by Ssŭ-ma Ch'ien, with the difference that as Pan Ku wrote with the knowledge and authority of the Emperor, his book stops at the fall of the Early Han dynasty, and does not deal with contemporary events. Pan Ku did not live to complete the book. Already once accused and imprisoned on the charge of falsifying history (a charge trumped up by his political opponents) he was later involved in the fall of the leading minister of his day, and died in prison. His book was completed by his sister, Pan Ch'ao, the first and the most famous woman scholar in Chinese history.*

Although the Han scholars and historians were keenly interested in the past, and devoted their labours to perpetuating the ancient literature, the Han period, a post revolutionary era, was a time of change and innovation. The sweeping political and social changes brought about by the fall of feudalism were necessarily reflected in the sphere of religion. The old cult had become corrupted and devitalised by the decay of the royal power in the later Chou epoch. New deities, hitherto worshipped only at local centres, became popular throughout the unified empire. The emperors strove to fortify their weak title to the throne by religious innovations, and the scholars sought in religious sanctions a check to control the supreme power of the sovereign.

The religious system of the Han period was a fusion of two distinct elements. On the one hand there were the local cults, now spread widely through the empire, and enjoying popular favour and imperial patronage; on the other there was the court cult, derived from the ancient religion of the Chou period, but enriched by rites and ceremonies designed to enhance the prestige of the throne. The court cult reflects the great paradox of the Han political system; the immensely increased power of the unique, autocratic monarch, and the insecurity of the imperial family's tenure of the throne. The fall of the aristocracy left the Emperor as the sole source of authority. His power was limitless, his authority reached to the confines of the known world. As against this his family had no sound title to the throne. They were

---

*Pan Ch'ao's poems have been translated and her biography traced in *Pan Chao*, by Nancy Lee Swann, New York, 1932. The Ch'ien Han Shu has been translated in part by Professor H. H. Dubs.

not of divine descent, but, as everyone knew, the posterity of a peasant adventurer. It was true that they had "received the Mandate of Heaven," but this was an uneasy title, revocable at the will of Heaven, perhaps to be bestowed on some other family equally humble in origin. In fact the Han house were constantly menaced by the ambitions of the consort families, the clansmen of the empresses, who were well placed to snatch the crown from a weak or infant Emperor.

In feudal times the situation had been exactly opposite. Then the ruler found his power limited at every turn by "those who were doubly subjects," the heads of the aristocratic clans, too powerful to be exterminated if they conspired or rebelled, always prepared to seek refuge at a rival court beyond the authority of the ruler. On the other hand, the royal and princely houses enjoyed an unmatched prestige. They were the posterity of gods and heroes. No man dreamed of displacing them, for sovereignty was the prerogative of these divine families, beyond the ambition of lesser men.* Under the empire all this was changed. There was no place of refuge for the subject who had incurred the imperial wrath, no clan sufficiently powerful to withstand his authority.

In the development of the state cult, the worship of T'ien (Heaven) played a dominant part. T'ien (Heaven) was personified as Shang Ti, the Supreme Ancestor† of the created world, the ruler of the seasons, who delegated his power on earth to the Emperor, the Son of Heaven. The Confucian scholars in the Han age were sedulous in their efforts to foster the cult of Heaven, the supreme power which could hold in awe the mighty autocrat of the empire. They interpreted the ancient legends in accordance with this conception. Ignoring, or at least not emphasising, the fact that the oldest literature mentioned other deities as co-equal with Heaven (notably Hou T'u, "He who governs the Earth,"

*It is true that two ruling houses were dethroned. That of Tsin, at the partition of the old kingdom into three states (453 B.C.), and the old house of Ch'i. But in both these cases the usurpers were also of high descent, whereas the fallen rulers were not of the highest descent—the royal house of Chou itself. The collateral branches of that house in Lu and Yen remained on the throne long after their power had wholly passed into the hands of the nobility.

†"*Ti*" in the Ch'in and subsequent dynasties was used as the imperial title, but anciently this word was reserved for deities, the highest title used by men being *wang*, king, which, in later times came to be equivalent to prince.

and Ti, the Earth itself), they developed a theology of Heaven
which exalted this supreme deity above all others.

Heaven, the presiding deity, rewarded virtue with auspicious
signs, prosperous seasons, and peace. The wrath of Heaven,
excited by evil conduct on the part of the ruler, was manifested
by warnings and catastrophes. Such were eclipses of the sun,
floods, drought, earthquakes, and plagues of locusts. The cul-
minating punishment of a ruler's ill-conduct was the withdrawal
of the "mandate of Heaven," and the fall of his dynasty to make
way for another family. This deity stood in a peculiar relation to
the Emperor, who alone had the right to perform sacrifices to
Heaven. It was his virtue which was rewarded by prosperity, his
vices which were punished by calamities. The Emperor thus bore
the heavy responsibility of securing, by his virtue, the general
well-being of the world; and equally he was to blame if by his
misconduct he called down the anger of Heaven upon society in
general. This theory was admirably suited to its purpose of
inculcating a sense of moral responsibility in an otherwise
uncontrolled autocrat.

There were other elements in the Han state cult which were of
less ancient origin and derived from a different cosmogony. The
theory of the Five Elements does not seem to be older than the
late Chou era, and is attributed to the speculations of a certain
Tsou Yen, a contemporary of King Hui of Wei (370-335 B.C.).
The Five Elements were Earth, Wood, Metal, Fire and Water,
mystic powers which had correspondences with the colours, the
cyclic characters of the calendar, the points of the compass and
the notes of the musical scale. They were a manifestation of the
power and operation of the Yang and the Yin, the alternating
forces expressive of light and darkness, birth and decay, male and
female. These powers, which in their combined operation form
the Tao, the Way, the great principle of the universe, are the
mainspring of every activity, the mechanism of constant change
and balance which maintains the harmony of the cosmos. They
are symbolised by that geometrical design devised by the Chinese,
the circle divided into two equal parts by a curved line (see
Chap. II, Fig. 5), representing equilibrium maintained by the
ceaseless flux of two balanced forces.

The Five Elements are the manifestations of the Yin and the Yang. They form a cycle which constantly renews itself. Earth is vanquished by Wood, which yields to Metal, which succumbs to Fire, which is quenched by Water, which in turn is overcome by Earth, so renewing the cycle.* From this theory was derived a system of beliefs governing the rites and ceremonies of court worship. It was held that each dynasty had reigned by virtue of one of the Elements, and had fallen when the predominance passed to the succeeding element. The Ch'in had claimed to rule by Water, hence the virtue of the Han was Earth, its colour Yellow, its direction North. In Han times this theory was further elaborated, though the innovations were not regarded as such, but attributed to ancient lore. Each of the elements was now controlled by a celestial ruler, Yellow, Green, White, Red and Black respectively. The Black Emperor seems to have been added by Kao Tsu himself. Ssŭ-ma Ch'ien recounts that in 205 B.C. Kao Tsu (Liu Pang) asked the names of the celestial Emperors to whom the Ch'in sovereigns had sacrificed.

"They answered: The four Emperors are the White, the Green, the Yellow and the Red. Kao Tsu replied: 'I have heard it said that there are five celestial Emperors, but here are only four, how is that?'

"No one knowing the explanation, Kao Tsu then said: 'I know. It is because they waited for me to make the complete number five.' Then he instituted the sacrifice to the Black Emperor, and gave to his sanctuary the name of the sacred place of the North."

Under the reign of the Emperor Wu a further addition to the pantheon was made. A certain Miu Chi, a man from the eastern provinces, where many local deities were held in honour, petitioned the Emperor to institute sacrifices to T'ai I, the Supreme Unity, who he declared was the ruler of the Five Celestial Emperors. This deity resided in the North Pole Star, regarded by the Chinese as the fixed point in the heavens. The

---

*The order of the Five Elements given above is that which prevailed under the Han. In later times it was changed, and became, Wood, Fire, Earth, Metal, Water.

Emperor instituted this cult, and a few years later T'ai I was elevated to an equal position with Heaven and Earth, the ancient supreme deities. As usual the innovation was declared to be the revival of a forgotten practice held in honour by the sages of the distant past.

A still more important development was the revival, or rather the invention, of two supreme sacrifices, the Fêng and the Shan, to Heaven and Earth respectively, which were to be the supreme ritual acts of the state cult, performed by the Emperor himself at the sacred mountain, T'ai Shan in Shantung, the highest peak in north China. These sacrifices were to symbolise the divine support of the existing dynasty, and set the seal of heavenly approval on the acts and person of the Emperor. Unfortunately, although the sacrifices were said to have been performed by the great rulers of the golden age, all memory of the rites and ceremonies employed on these occasions had been lost. This, indeed, was easily explained. Only a sage could perform these sacrifices. An unworthy ruler could never ascend the sacred T'ai Shan. Heaven would manifest its wrath, and violent storms would rage upon the mountain. Ch'in Shih Huang Ti had presumed to make the ascent, but a violent gale had arisen, forcing the tyrant to fly for shelter. The Emperor Wu was anxious to avoid such a disaster, which would have the very opposite effect to that for which he hoped.

Consequently the preparations for this sacrifice occupied a long time. The Confucian scholars, consulted upon the rites to be employed, hesitated and deliberated, but lacking authority founded upon an ancient text, they could formulate no plan. The Emperor, displeased by this attitude, turned away from them and consulted the magicians. They were not deterred by the lack of records. The ceremony to be employed, they suggested, was that formally used by the Chou kings in the sacrifice to Heaven made outside the capital. When this point was settled the Emperor still hesitated. There can be no doubt that the Emperor Wu sincerely believed in the high spiritual import of these rites and feared that he was not worthy to perform them. He first made trial at other sacred, but less august peaks, which he ascended alone. The court having declared that celestial voices had been heard on the mountain, the Emperor was encouraged to proceed, and in 110 B.C., accompanied by a great retinue, he reached T'ai Shan.

Even then, fearing the displeasure of Heaven, he first made the sacrifice at the foot of T'ai Shan. No signs of divine disapproval being manifest, and the weather auspicious, he next ascended the mountain accompanied only by Huo Shan, his charioteer, son of the famous general Huo Chu-P'ing. Of what passed when the Emperor, alone upon the highest point in his domains, sacrificed to the mighty powers of Heaven, no record could be made. Huo Shan died suddenly and mysteriously very shortly after the Emperor had descended the mountain. Ssŭ-ma Ch'ien, mentioning this fact without further comment, undoubtedly intends it to be understood that the Emperor had the sole witness of the supreme rite secretly poisoned.

The sacrifice Shan was performed on a small eminence near the foot of T'ai Shan, and was not a secret rite. The Emperor Wu revisited T'ai Shan in 106 B.C. when he once more ascended the mountain, this time quite alone. In 98 B.C. he performed the sacrifices for the third time. On all these occasions the weather was fair and clear, the omens auspicious and Heaven's approval thus made manifest.

While the imperial cult was being enriched by these additional sacrifices and deities, the popular religion of the Han period, which also received imperial patronage, was developing into a many-sided polytheism, a synthesis of all the local cults of the empire, now spread abroad and served by a numerous priesthood. The ancient gods of the soil and the crops, and the ancient worship of the ancestral spirits continued as ever high in the popular estimation, destined to outlive the strange cults from the coast country which were now in favour. These fundamental beliefs would seem to have continued their millenial existence unaffected by the tide of religious innovation which flowed so strongly in the Han period.

Fig. 37, part of a scene from the bas-reliefs of the Wu tombs, shows a number of the divinities and spirits of the Han pantheon. Nu Kua and Fu Hsi, the legendary rulers of the world in the highest antiquity, are shown holding in their hands the geometrical

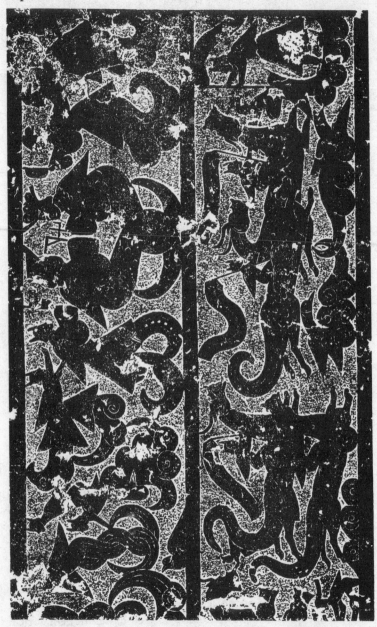

FIG. 37. *Bas-relief representing Fu Hsi and Nu Kua with attendant genii.*

instruments with which, as we may suppose, the land was delimited. Their snake-like tails are entwined. The winged figures and dragons whose bodies are partly formed of clouds are possibly spirits of the wind and rain.

Ssŭ-ma Ch'ien has accorded space in his history to these new creeds, and to the magician priests who ministered to them. He does not seem himself to have felt much faith in their potency, but he attests their popular appeal. The Precious One of Ch'ên, a god of Ch'in, had a great popular following. It would seem that the Precious One of Ch'ên was a pheasant god, which had originated in the worship of a meteorite. Ssŭ-ma Ch'ien describes the origin of this cult:

"[In 747 B.C.] the Duke Wên [of Ch'in] found on the north slope of Mt. Ch'ên Ts'ang [near Pao Chi Hsien, west Shensi] a being which resembled a stone. He sacrificed to it in that city. This god sometimes does not come during a whole year, sometimes several times in one year. When he comes it is always at night: he shines and sparkles like a shooting star; he arrives from the south-east and descends over the town where sacrifice is made to him. Then he resembles a male pheasant, his voice is powerful and the female pheasants answer him during the night. His name is the Precious One of Ch'ên."

Another deity, who received the patronage of the Court, was the Princess of the Spirits. Her origin was as follows:

"The Princess of the Spirits was a woman of Ch'ang Ling who, after dying in childbirth, appeared as a divinity to her sister-in-law, Wan Jo. Wan Jo sacrificed to her in her house and the people came in crowds to sacrifice to her there. The Princess of P'ing Yüan* having come there to sacrifice, her descendants were covered with honours and glory [her descendants included the Emperor Wu]. When the reigning Emperor came to power, he gave importance to this cult and made it one of the official sacrifices. One could hear the divinity speak, but one could not see her person."

*The Princess of P'ing Yüan was the maternal grandmother of the Emperor Wu himself. Hence the favour which this cult enjoyed at Court.

From another passage it is clear that this cult included Shamanism, for the Princess of the Spirits entered the body of a sorceress and answered questions put to her.

The magicians of the coast country, the coast of Shantung province, were the chief priests of these new gods, and rose to great honour at the Court. It is clear that this region was the home of many cults, which hitherto had not been practised in the western provinces. The worship of the eight principal gods of this country was transplanted to the capital and flourished exceedingly. These gods were the Masters of Earth, War, the Yin, the Yang, the Moon, the Sun, Heaven, and of the Four Seasons. Although it would appear that their attributes and functions overlapped those of deities already established and honoured in the other provinces of China, the Eight Masters were installed in Ch'ang An and accorded temples and sacrifices. The people of Han times were not discriminating in their allegiance to the gods.*

Among the beliefs of this sect were the legends relating to the mysterious isles of the eastern sea. These three islands, P'êng Lai, Fang Chang, and Ying Chou, were situated not far from the mainland, and anciently had been visited by men. Now, whenever a ship approached them, just as the islands appeared like clouds on the horizon, violent winds arose, and the ship was driven away. In these islands lived the Happy Immortals, who possessed the secret of eternal life, and the means of making gold. There every living thing, animal or vegetable was white. The temples, palaces and towns were made of gold and silver.

The legend of the mysterious isles obtained a strong hold on the minds of the emperors of that time. Ch'in Shih Huang Ti made several attempts to send emissaries to them, who might obtain the secret of immortality and the receipt for making gold, but he failed in his purpose. He sent a magician with a band of young boys and girls, who were supposed to be more welcome to the Happy Immortals than other envoys. The magician and his young companions never returned. It has been suggested that the

*T'ien Chu, the Master of Heaven, bears the same title in Chinese as that adopted by the Roman Catholic missionaries for the Christian God. The unfortunate fact that this title had been that of a very minor deity of the Shantung coast, escaped the attention of the early missionaries.

emissary made off with his ships to some part of Japan or the Liu Chiu islands and there founded a colony. However that may be, the fascination of this legend continued to inspire similar expeditions.

The Emperor Wu placed great confidence in the magicians who promised to obtain for him the secret of immortal life. The first of a long succession was Li Shao-chun who enjoyed great favour until his death. He had not only claimed to know the secret of immortality, but to be an immortal himself. In proof of this he had recounted to an aged scholar at the Court details of past events and happenings in the old man's boyhood, which had only been known to persons long since dead. He claimed to be able to make gold from cinnabar powder, and to have visited the magical island of P'êng Lai. When he died, Ssǔ-ma Ch'ien maliciously says that the Emperor would not believe it, but thought Li Shao-chun had disappeared on some mystic errand in the guise of a spirit.

Li Shao-chun was succeeded by Shao Wang, also a man of Ch'i (Shantung), who gained the monarch's favour by evoking the shade of one of the imperial concubines who had been much beloved by the Emperor and had recently died. The phantom appeared at night, when the Emperor, hidden behind a curtain, was able to see his beloved in the further recesses of the hall. For these arts Shao Wang received honours and titles, but his influence was of short duration. After a year he was detected in an attempt to deceive the Emperor by passing off an inscription which he had written on a piece of silk as the work of a divinity. He was then secretly put to death.

In 113 B.C. the Emperor conferred his favour upon the most famous and enterprising of all these magicians, Luan Ta. He was a eunuch, formerly in the service of one of the Han feudal princes, and had studied magic in the same school as Shao Wang. Luan Ta was an eloquent speaker and did not hesitate to make extravagant claims. He declared that he had often visited the mysterious isles of the eastern sea, but that as he was only a subject, the Immortals had despised him and would not give him their secrets. He therefore insinuated that if the Emperor wished to obtain this precious knowledge it would be necessary to send as his emissary a man of high position. The Emperor followed this advice, and as Luan Ta himself was the only man who seemed likely to be successful, he was given high official posts, the title of marquis with a territory of 2,000 households for his support, a palace, and 1,000 slaves. Still more remarkable, this eunuch of base extraction was given as a bride the Emperor's own eldest daughter, with a dowry of 10,000 pounds of gold.

The amazing fortune of Luan Ta is a most significant indication of the faith which was placed in these magical cults. Luan Ta was no longer treated as a subject or as a eunuch, so that when he arrived in the mysterious isles the Immortals would treat him with respect and reveal their secrets to him. He was the messenger who should bring the Emperor into relation with the gods, and to signify this duty he was given a seal with the title of General of the Heavenly Way. After enjoying these immense favours and a prestige, which, as Ssŭ-ma Ch'ien says, made the whole empire tremble, the magician set forth to embark for the mysterious isles. When he reached the seashore, however, he did not dare to embark, but instead sacrificed on T'ai Shan, declaring that he had met the Immortals at this place. The Emperor, who seems to have had certain doubts, had secretly sent spies to observe his proceedings. When he learned from these men that Luan Ta had not embarked, and, moreover, that they had seen nothing of the alleged appearance of the Immortals, he caused Luan Ta and his followers to be put to death.

Perhaps warned by these unfortunate examples, the next magician to the Court made more modest claims. Kung-sun Ch'ing, who, to judge by his aristocratic surname (Grandson of the duke), must have been a man of better family than his predecessors, urged the Emperor to make the Fêng sacrifice on T'ai Shan as an essential preliminary to obtaining the secret of immortality. He also represented that this consummation could only be achieved after a long life devoted to the study of the magical arts. Huang Ti, the legendary Emperor of the golden age, who had attained immortality and ascended to heaven on a dragon, had spent a hundred years in study of the arts of pleasing the spirits before he achieved his purpose. The Emperor, therefore, must not be impatient. The spirits, said Kung-sun Ch'ing, did not seek out the Emperor, it was the Emperor who had to learn how to approach them. Such was their nature that if pestered and importuned, they would refuse to hold communication with men. By these counsels of delay Kung-sun Ch'ing gained the entire confidence of the autocrat, and it was his advice and assistance which the Emperor followed in performing the Fêng and Shan sacrifices. In his later years the Emperor gradually tired of the vain search for the mysterious isles, but Kung-sun Ch'ing by his prudence avoided the fate of his predecessors.

The reign of the Emperor Wu and the revival of letters in the two Han periods left an enduring influence on the Chinese civilisation. In place of the mosaic of feudal states with their local traditions and cults, there was created a truly national culture, common to all parts of China. This culture arose as a consequence of the new political unity, but it proved stronger than the political system which had fostered it. The centralised empire fell, to be followed by long centuries of partition, but the cultural unity of China, created by the Han, survived every political catastrophe, and triumphed over the inroads of barbarian nomads. This has ever been the true unity of China, not founded on race or empire, but on the possession of a common script and the preservation of an ancient literature.

Chapter X

HAN ART

THE influence of the great revolution which substituted a central-ised universal empire for the loose feudal federation of the Chou "Middle Kingdom" was naturally reflected in the art of the Han period. The ancient ritual conventions lost their force; in the stimulating atmosphere of a new society fresh forms of art were developed reflecting changed social and religious conditions, and deeply influenced by the wider horizons opened up by the enlarged and expanding empire. It was not only in the develop-ment of new artistic forms that the Han artist found himself freer than his predecessors, his services were now required by a wider circle of patrons and for a greater range of activity. Art ceased to be purely religious and the cultivation of art ceased to be the prerogative of kings and nobles.

The surviving Chou works of art come almost without exception from the tombs of feudal rulers; the best known examples of Han art, on the contrary, were made for families of minor importance. The bas-reliefs of Hsiao T'ang Shan and the Wu family in Shan-tung were the property of provincials far from the Court, and the beautiful lacquer objects recently discovered come from the necropolis of a distant frontier colony. The fact that these examples have survived does not prove that the best Han art was confined to Shantung or the frontier, on the contrary it suggests that the appreciation and use of beautiful works of art was very wide-spread, and that what has by chance survived in the provinces is only the pale reflection of the splendours of the Court at Ch'ang An and Lo Yang. Unfortunately, the sites of the Han capitals have never been scientifically excavated, and as these cities were frequently destroyed and rebuilt in later ages it is to be feared that archæology will never reveal more than scanty traces of the Han period.

Han graves are discovered from time to time in all parts of China, but with the exception of the necropolis of Lak Lang in Korea and certain garrison points in Central Asia, no purely Han site has yet been excavated. In Shantung there exist two well preserved Han tombs, those of the Wu family (2nd century A.D.) at Chia Hsiang Hsien in the south-west of the province, and those at Hsiao T'ang Shan near Fei Ch'êng Hsien, about thirty miles south of the provincial capital, which belong to the 1st century B.C. It is from these two tombs, and from a number of other stones and memorial pillars scattered in different provinces that the characteristic Han art of bas-reliefs is known. It is at least probable that the excavation of other Han tombs will yield further examples equally well, if not better preserved.

These bas-reliefs were engraved on slabs of stone built into the wall of a mortuary chamber, but the scenes depicted have nothing of a funerary character. The Han gentlemen who were interred here were not surrounded with bas-reliefs of a religious character depicting the after-life of the spirit, but with vivid and forceful representations of everyday life, historical events, or mythological scenes. The art of the bas-reliefs, though intended for the tomb, is concerned with terrestrial life. There are hunting scenes, battle pieces, notable historical happenings such as the attempt to assassinate First Emperor, Ch'in Shih Huang Ti, when he was still only King of Ch'in, and legends such as the visit of King Mu of the Chou dynasty to the divine ruler of the far west, Hsi Wang Mu, "Royal Mother of the West."* It was with these scenes of secular life that the Han Chinese of wealth and standing wished to surround themselves in death.

The secular character of the subjects of the bas-reliefs—a priceless gift to the historian who has so few sources from which to reconstruct the life of that age—raises an interesting question. The Han Chinese, like other peoples in every part of the world, furnished their tombs with cult objects designed to assist the spirit of the deceased in the next world. Such were the clay figures

---

*The legend of Hsi Wang Mu has greatly intrigued western scholars. The early sinologists were tempted to believe that it confirmed their theory of a western origin of the Chinese people. Later research has established the fact that the story is a legend or folk tale, perhaps a romance which has been enriched from century to century. It is now believed that the name Hsi Wang Mu, "Royal Mother of the West," should not be interpreted, but really represents a Chinese rendering of the name of a barbarian tribe settled in western Kansu in Chou times. The question is fully discussed by Chavannes, *Memoirs Historiques de Se ma Ts'ien*, Vol. II.

which begin to appear in Han tombs, though this purely funerary art did not attain perfection until much later. The bas-reliefs cannot be forced into this category. The subjects chosen preclude such an idea. There are indeed scenes of mythological character in which the multifarious gods of the Han pantheon are represented. Such scenes are not the most common and are not given a peculiar prominence. It is the secular scenes which predominate.

These representations of historical events and everyday life can have had no religious meaning. A bas-relief showing the meeting of Confucius and Lao Tzŭ outside Lo Yang (an apocryphal event) or Ch'in Shih Huang Ti trying to recover the lost bronze tripod from the river Ssŭ cannot have been intended to assist the deceased in his future life. A scene which shows the funeral procession of the deceased himself, or that of a battle against the Huns (Hsiung Nu), may perhaps have referred to the special interest which the ghost would take in matters of a personal nature, for one of the members of the Wu family had been lieutenant-governor of Tun Huang, a frontier city on the Kansu border.

Nevertheless, these bas-reliefs were intended solely for the dead, for they were placed with the carved surface facing inward, a position which made it impossible to see the carvings as long as the tomb remained undisturbed. The bas-reliefs were therefore intended for the pleasure of the dead man's ghost, not merely to commemorate his achievements. It seems reasonable to believe that the bas-reliefs were intended to recall to the deceased the scenes of glory or honour in which he had participated on earth, and also to provide examples of his favourite scenes from history or myth for his pleasure in the timeless ages of death. Were these scenes the particular choice of the deceased, executed for the first time for his tomb, or were they well-known pictures copied in stone to preserve them against time and decay? Such a question cannot be answered positively for lack of evidence. The sculptor of the Wu tomb bas-reliefs is mentioned by name in the inscription which records the building of the tomb.

The inscription runs:

"In the 1st year of *Chien Ho* [A.D. 147] the cyclical year *ting hai*, in the third month which began with the day *kêng hsu* on the fourth day *kuei ch'ou* the filial sons Wu Shih-kung and his younger brothers Sui-tsung, Ching-hsing and K'ai-ming, erected these pillars, made by the sculptor Li Ti-mao, styled Mêng-fu, at a cost of 150,000 pieces of money. Sun Tsung made the lions which cost 40,000 cash."

One of the lions has disappeared, but there seems no reason to doubt that Li Ti-mao was the sculptor of the bas-reliefs which lined the mortuary chamber as well as the maker of the pillars. The Wu family were of ancient lineage, claiming descent from the Shang royal line, who were also ancestors of the K'ung family to which Confucius belonged. The apparent bad taste of mentioning the cost of their father's tomb on the inscription was not therefore the vulgar solecism of an upstart family, but is perhaps typical of the Han age in which wealth counted for as much as noble descent. Li Ti-mao must have been a man of distinction to deserve a mention in the inscription, and the price of the work shows that he was no local sculptor from the district city. Probably he and his colleague, Sun Tsung, were well-known artists living at the capital. It is possible therefore that Li Ti-mao's work at the Wu tombs was original, specially commissioned by the "filial sons" or by the dead official himself prior to his decease. It is also possible that Li Ti-mao was either reproducing in stone works which had already been executed in some other medium, less suited to a memorial, or was a recognised artist who specialised in bas-reliefs for this purpose. Further excavation may bring to light other specimens of his work in some other district.

The bas-reliefs of Hsiao T'ang Shan, which are certainly earlier than those of the Wu tombs, are not dated, and we do not know the name of the family for whom they were made, or of the artist who made them. Later inscriptions made by pilgrims or visitors show that the reliefs are older than the 2nd century A.D., and it is the opinion of Chinese scholars that they were made towards the end of the Early Han dynasty, in the 1st century B.C. These reliefs are lightly carved, in comparison with Li Ti-mao's work, but the delicacy of outline and grace of the workmanship are superior to the later series at the Wu tombs. It seems possible that the owner of this tomb had been a general, for one of the most spirited scenes shows a battle between Chinese troops and the Huns (Hsiung Nu). The King of the Huns is seated before a tent, his identity indicated by a short inscription. Mounted men gallop across the scene, the slain encumber the battlefield, and riderless horses show that some of these corpses are those of the cavaliers. On the right of the picture men are emerging from a group of conical objects which have been identified either as tents, or perhaps more probably as hills, for which this design is a convention.

Other reliefs show processions, one including a personage labelled the "Great King" (*Ta Wang*) who is riding in a chariot drawn by four horses abreast and accompanied by mounted men and other chariots. The Great King cannot be the Emperor, for the imperial title is distinct. He may perhaps be one of the Han princes who were "kings" of the much reduced feudal states which still existed under the empire in strict subjection to the imperial Court. Like the scenes in the Wu reliefs, this procession may be an historical picture relating some episode of the Chou period. Legends such as the visit of King Mu to Hsi Wang Mu are portrayed in these reliefs, for this subject seems to have been a very popular one in the Han period. The palace of the Hsi Wang Mu, no doubt showing the contemporary style of Chinese architecture, is a valuable piece of historical evidence, as no Han buildings survive. From the bas-reliefs it is clear that very little change has occurred in Chinese architectural styles in the 2,000 years that have passed since the Han period. See Chap. XXVI, Fig. 61.

The horses shown in these reliefs, and also in those of the Wu tombs are worthy of a special attention. These proud high stepping steeds are not the ordinary Chinese, or rather Mongolian pony, but the marvellous horses bred in the west, in Ta Hsia and Ta Yüan, Bactria and Sogdiana. It was these horses which so greatly attracted the Emperor Wu that he undertook the amazing attempt to conquer these countries in order to obtain them. The Han were great lovers of horses, and jade heads such as the magnificent specimen in Plate V attest the popularity of this subject in works of art. Another feature, the trees with inter-laced branches, sometimes two trees joined by one or more branches, may perhaps owe something to the Chinese contact with Iranian art, but this design also had roots in Chinese legend. The joined trees, one of the objects of good omen, seems to have originated in the legend of two lovers who were separated in their lifetime, but were buried in contiguous graves. After their death two trees sprouted from the graves, the branches intermingling and joining together. This legend of the joined trees was a popular subject in the Han period, typifying conjugal happiness and fidelity. Among the ancient Chinese motifs found in the bas-reliefs is the dragon, the rain spirit, here depicted in a form foreshadowing the familiar dragon of later Chinese art (Fig. 38).

An extremely vigorous scene on the Wu tomb bas-reliefs relates the famous attempt to assassinate Ch'in Shih Huang Ti, the future First Emperor, when he was as yet only King of Ch'in.

FIG. 38. *A Dragon. Han Dynasty bas-relief.*

In 227 B.C. the Crown Prince of Yen, the state which occupied the north-east corner of the Middle Kingdom, corresponding to the modern province of Hopei (Chihli) and South Manchuria* determined to procure the death of the tyrant who had already enslaved the majority of the feudal states.

The King of Ch'in was so well guarded that no would-be assassin, without the most convincing credentials, could have any chance of approaching the monarch's person. The Crown Prince of Yen therefore devised a most ingenious if ruthless scheme. Yen had a general of great ability, the bulwark of the kingdom. The Crown Prince believed that if he could send an assassin who carried the head of this general as token of his enmity to Yen, he would be admitted to an audience with the King of Ch'in. The general consented to sacrifice his life, and the chosen assassin, one Ching K'o, carried his head to Ch'in, pretending to be a traitor to Yen, come to claim his reward at the hands of the rival Prince.

The ruse was successful, and the assassin was admitted to an audience. The scene which followed is vividly shown on the bas-relief reproduced as Fig. 39a. Ching K'o, displaying the box containing the severed head, immediately attacks the King of Ch'in with a poisoned dagger. His thrust cuts off the King's sleeve, but the King, throwing himself behind a pillar, evades a second blow, while a courtier grapples with the assassin and calls for help. A confederate of the assassin lies on the ground, terrorised, and a soldier of the guard, armed with a sword and shield, is running up from the right. The dagger, with a silk tassel at the handle, has stuck through the wooden pillar, or perhaps has been thrown at the King. At the foot of the pillar is the box holding the severed head of the general of Yen, above which the King's sleeve cut from his gown by the blow, floats to the ground.

The panel above commemorates an episode of feudal history, the faithful charioteer of enormous strength, who, to protect his wounded lord, has wrenched off the canopy of the chariot and shelters the wounded man with it. The enemy noble, with a bow in his hand and two followers behind him, comes up in friendly courtesy to congratulate the charioteer on his courage and strength, an incident typifying the chivalry of feudal warfare.

*The capital of this state was on the site of the city of Peking.

FIG. 39. Headpiece to bas-relief shown in fig. 39a.

The lowest panel represents the two gods, Fu Hsi and Nu Kua, the founder deities of the Chinese world. They have entwined fishlike tails and are attended by winged spirits. Scenes of this character, strongly coloured by Taoist myth, are valuable evidence of the popularity of the cults which under the Emperor Wu enjoyed the full patronage of the Court. If evidence were needed to disprove the Confucian legend of the Han dynasty, which represents the literate class of that day as Confucian purists, despising and ignoring Taoist myth as "superstition," these tomb bas-reliefs, made for people of wealth and culture, amply fill the gap. The Emperor Wu was no exception among the cultured Chinese of his time. His trust in magicians and faith in the cults which flourished on the coast of Shantung was shared by the majority of his subjects. It is true that most of the bas-reliefs so far known come from Shantung and the region immediately to the south of that province, the area which according to Ssŭ-ma Ch'ien was the home of the exotic cults, and, consequently, these beliefs may well have been stronger in that district than in other parts of China.

The sudden appearance of the Han art of the bas-reliefs, which has no counterpart in earlier times, has naturally raised the question of foreign influence. There are obvious resemblances between the Chinese reliefs, and Persian or Assyrian work. The fact that the art arose in China at the very time when the Han Empire was making contact with the Greco-Bactrian

238 CHINA

FIG. 39a. *Bas-relief from the Wu Tombs, Shantung. Han Dynasty.*

kingdoms and with Parthia justifies the view that the Chinese were inspired by western models. Contact does not imply mere imitation; the subjects chosen by the Han artists were drawn from Chinese sources, and the style is characteristic of Chinese artistic traditions. Some motifs seem to have been either borrowed from or at least changed by Iranian models, but in general the Han artists continued to be inspired by traditional conventions, such as the cloud pattern, and by their observation of the actual life of their own time and country, as in the scenes showing banquets, hunts and processions. It was the idea rather than the style which the Han Chinese acquired from the west. A new medium for art, carving on stone, was suggested to them by their contacts with Parthia and the Hellenised east. They developed that idea in accordance with their own artistic tradition and the natural genius of a period rich in creative ability.

In another branch of art the Han now appear as pioneers. Up to recent years it was believed that porcelain was the discovery of a comparatively late age. The Chinese themselves attributed the perfection of ceramic ware to the Sung period, and traced the beginning of porcelain manufacture no further back than the 6th or 7th centuries A.D. Discoveries made in Han tombs in the province of Shensi early in the present century show that in late Han times, the 2nd and 3rd centuries A.D., a glazed porcellaneous ware (proto-porcelain) was being made, though as yet in limited quantities. Pieces of this ware, not to be confused with the well-known green glaze on countless Han vases, had been known to collectors in the 19th century, but were then supposed to be T'ang or even Sung work.

The late Han porcellaneous ware is not true porcelain, but it is technically the intermediate step between glazed pottery and porcelain proper. The final perfection of the potters' art was not attained until several centuries later, and is recognised as the most characteristic and widely known achievement of the Chinese culture. The initial stimulus, however, was a product of the contact with Iranian culture under the Han dynasty.*

Side by side with new forms of art the Han carried on the traditional bronze working and jade carving, but their work was

*B. Laufer. *Beginnings of Porcelain in China.* Chicago. 1917.

not a perpetuation of the classical style unchanged. A freer, less conventional and more catholic taste had arisen under the empire. Art was more secular, even when dedicated to religion, for the influence of foreign styles was pervading branches of art which in the feudal period had been governed by rigid conventions. Bronze as a metal was now slowly giving place to iron for purposes of general utility. It remained the chosen medium for sacrificial vessels and ceremonial weapons, and mirrors (Fig. 40), for which no doubt the new iron was regarded as ritually unsuitable.

The intimate contact, both in war and peace, between the Han Empire and the Huns (Hsiung Nu) introduced a new type of ornamentation for metal work, the animal or Scythian style.* This art probably originated in western Asia, whence it spread throughout the steppe regions of the Eurasian continent. The motifs most often found are those of animals in combat, or single animals represented in the act of bounding away. Very often the figures are confronted, and frequently elaborated into mixed forms, in which the limbs of one beast become the body and head of some totally different creature. The tiger, deer, ox and horse are the animals most frequently represented on the true Scythian pieces, but when the art reached China it was enriched by the addition of the mythical dragon and phœnix, and by elephant motifs which had been unknown to the northern people. When the artist has not been forced to subject his fancy to the restrictions of a conventional arrangement, the animal figures are executed with vigorous feeling and a keen sense of movement.

Of Scythian art proper the most common objects are pieces of horse equipment and rectangular plaques which may have been worn as amulets (Fig. 41). These bronzes are found throughout northern Asia as well as in China itself. It is very probable that many of them were made in China, either for sale to the nomads in the north or for the use of Chinese cavaliers, for, in riding fashions and cavalry equipment the Chinese freely adopted the customs of their neighbours. The Han artists, however, employed the Scythian style of ornamentation not only in bronze and other metal work, but also in textiles.

*Also called Scytho-Sarmatian, Sarmatian, Siberian, Scytho-Siberian and Sino-Siberian.

FIG. 40. *Bronze Mirrors of the Han Dynasty.*

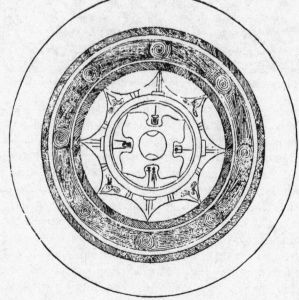

FIG. 41. *Bronze Plaques with open work designs in Scythian Animal Style.*

The axe head illustrated in Plate VI, a very beautiful ceremonial weapon, is a magnificent example of the free choice of ornament open to the Han bronze worker under the influence of the Scythian style. The confronted supporting figures between the haft and the blade, although rather lizard like, are wingless dragons. On the upper part of the blade between these dragons the head and wings of a bird with a curved beak are cut in low relief. The end of the haft has the shape of an elephant's head with up-raised trunk, but the trunk itself is furnished with an eye which transforms the tip of the trunk into a bird's head. On the end of the haft itself this design of an elephant's head and trunk is repeated in low relief, while the head and front leg of another animal, perhaps a tiger, rounds off the design on the lower side of the haft. On the flange projecting above the haft a heart shaped design, with two prominent eyes, is perhaps a degeneration of the ancient cicada motif. Other motifs from the old tradition are the *lei wen* or meander in the band round the haft and the scroll cloud pattern where blade and haft join. This specimen is a fine example of the blended animal forms of the Scythian style and Chinese geometrical patterns.

Chinese historians do not usually devote much space to accounts of those arts which were not included in the pastimes of the scholar. We hear of painting, caligraphy and poetry even when no specimen of the artist's work has survived the centuries. On the other hand contemporary Han texts do not speak of the bas-reliefs or of the lacquer and textiles which we now know from archæological discoveries. Ssŭ-ma Ch'ien in his all embracing work does indeed refer to the silk industry, but he does not give detailed information about the quality and designs which found favour with the wealthy classes of his time. From western classical sources it is known that the silk from China was a valued and extremely expensive import into the Roman Empire. This information, however important to the history of trade in the ancient world, made no contribution to the history of art. Fortunately archæology has in some measure filled the gap. The discoveries of Sir Aurel Stein at Lou Lan* and Tun Huang in Chinese Turkestan and of the Kozlov Expedition in Mongolia have brought to light, from these widely separated sites, priceless examples of Han silks, in addition to a great number of other products of Han industry.

Sir Aurel Stein's discoveries were made in 1914 at Lou Lan, a deserted ruin in the Lop Nor region of Turkestan which had been a garrison point on the Han southern route across the desert to Kashgar and Parthia. Towards the end of the Han period this southern route became impassable owing to the failure of the wells, and Lou Lan was abandoned. The dry sands have preserved

---

*Lou Lan in Central Asia must not be confused with Lo Lang in Korea. Both are sites of great importance for the art of the Han period. The latter is sometimes spelt Lak Lang in the Korean manner. To avoid confusion this spelling is adopted here.

materials which would have perished completely in any moister soil. The exact date of the Lou Lan finds would be difficult to ascertain if comparative data had not existed. Fortunately Sir Aurel Stein discovered in a ruined watch tower outside the frontier fortress of Tun Huang, in the extreme north-west of Kansu province, similar silk materials in conjunction with other finds which could be exactly dated as belonging to the 1st century B.C.

The discovery of rich silken garments and hangings in such remote and uncongenial places far from the civilised capitals of the Han Empire may seem surprising. The explanation lies in the fact that silk was used to pay the troops in Han times. Ssŭ-ma Ch'ien relates that the Emperor Wu, when he inspected the garrisons in the north along the Great Wall, distributed more than a million pieces of silk as bounty. It is by no means impossible that some of the silks found in the ruined watch tower near Tun Huang had formed part of this imperial largesse. Whether these silks were part of the pay of the army, or part of a cargo destined for export to the west, they supply a valuable criterion for judging the quality and technical achievement of the Han silk industry. If these silk stuffs were judged suitable for the pay of soldiers and for trade to barbarians, it is reasonable to believe that those reserved for imperial use, or purchased by the wealthy official class at the capital, were very much superior.

The finds at Lou Lan and Tun Huang are polychrome figured fabrics, showing refined and intricate patterns in which many motifs familiar from other branches of Han art appear. There are the dragon and phœnix, animal style ornamentation with confronted beasts and birds, equestrian figures, strongly reminiscent of those shown on the bas-reliefs, as well as geometrical designs which seem to have influenced the decorative motifs of textile art in the Byzantine Empire and Iran.

The work of the Kozlov Expedition sponsored by the Russian Academy of Sciences has provided fresh evidence of the high quality of Han silks, and the value which was attached to them by barbarian peoples. The expedition excavated the tombs of Hsiung Nu (Hun) chieftains in the valley of the Selenga River which drains northern Outer Mongolia and flows into Lake

Baikal. The evidence of the finds themselves suggests that these chieftains were contemporaries of the Han dynasty, and like the nomads of later periods, catholic collectors of luxuries from every civilised race with whom they were in contact. Han silks are found with textiles of Iranian workmanship in which Hellenistic art motifs are strong. Some of the embroidered hangings have a purely Greek design, and if not the product of some Black Sea or Asiatic Greek city, are directly copied from Greek work. The Selenga tombs therefore afford a direct proof of one important channel of diffusion between the Hellenised east and the Han Empire.

The tombs contained other products of Chinese industry as well as silk fabrics. It is possible that these are choice specimens of the booty made on some frontier raid, or perhaps part of the gifts bestowed by a Chinese embassy. The Han historians frequently mention such gifts, which at times amounted to a form of "Danegelt" paid to keep the restless nomads content and peaceful. Among the Chinese objects found in these tombs is a lacquer bowl, which, if the attribution of the tombs to the Han period is correct, confirms the recent discovery of Han lacquer—hitherto unknown—at a site in Korea.

Until the Japanese authorities in Korea undertook the scientific excavation of the necropolis of Lak Lang, a site close to the modern city of P'ing Yang (Japanese Heijo) in northern Korea, the existence of Han lacquer ware was unknown. It was generally believed that lacquer was the invention of a much later period. The Lak Lang finds therefore have a special importance for the history of Chinese art. Not only have they revealed the existence of lacquer at an early period, but as the site is purely Han, and many of the objects recovered are inscribed and dated, it is possible to use the Lak Lang discoveries as a standard by which to judge other finds or objects of which the provenance and date is unknown.

Lak Lang was a military colony founded by the Emperor Wu in 108 B.C. It remained the centre of Chinese authority in Korea until the period of nomad invasions following the fall of the Han dynasty, when the Chinese colony was absorbed by a rising native Korean kingdom. Although only a remote frontier colony it is evident that the Chinese officials of Lak Lang surrounded themselves with the products of Chinese art and industry imported from distant parts of the Han Empire. Here, as in the case of the textiles found in Turkestan, the degree of luxury enjoyed by the Chinese rulers of this remote colony offers a suggestive indication of the standards prevailing at the capital. Lak Lang no doubt imitated the fashions of the Court and the governor's mansion was furnished in modest imitation of the imperial palace.

Over two hundred pieces of lacquer ware—many polychrome—in various states of preservation, have been recovered from the Lak Lang tombs. Many are inscribed and bear dates covering the period between 85 B.C. and A.D. 52. The inscriptions show that these pieces were made in China, in the western part of Szechuan province, not far from the city of Chêng Tu (Fig. 42).

FIG. 42. *Lacquer Bowl from Lak Lang, Korea. Han Dynasty.*

Jewellery, such as the gold belt buckle illustrated in Plate VIIa, has also been found in the Lak Lang graves. This beautiful piece was recovered from a grave of the 1st century A.D. As it was found inside the wooden coffin it probably served as a fastening on the funeral clothes. The work is set with stone inlay, at first sight suggesting beads, which emphasise the lines of the intricate pattern of entwined dragons. It is rather remarkable that a personal ornament with this pattern should be found in the tomb of a provincial official. In later times the dragon is an imperial emblem, which a subject could not use. The custom apparently was not so rigid in the Han period, although it is always possible that this gem had been an imperial gift which the possessor took with him into the tomb.

PART THREE—THE AGE OF CONFUSION

Chapter XI

THE FALL OF THE EARLY EMPIRE

THE period of exactly four hundred years which divides the collapse of the first strong centralised empire, the Han, from the restoration of unity at the foundation of the Sui dynasty, is the age which in China most nearly approaches the character of the "Dark Ages" of European history. The causes were alike. The collapse of the world empire of the Han was followed, as in the west after the fall of Rome, by barbarian invasions, which, though less destructive in China, overthrew the centralised state and checked the cultural development of the eastern world. In China the consequences of the collapse and the barbarian invasions were by no means so serious as in the west. The memory of the past was never lost. The language and literature of the Han dynasty continued to be spoken and read, the continuity of Chinese civilisation was not irremediably impaired. In the southern empire, which escaped the Tartars, the traditions and culture of the Han period were kept alive, while even in the north, the Chinese proved too virile to be transformed by the Tartar conquest; on the contrary, they absorbed their conquerors and assimilated them into the body of the Chinese nation.

Nevertheless, the Tartar conquests and the wars and troubles which preceded it spread havoc. The ancient centres of Chinese civilisation were ruined and left desolate. The vast imperial library of Lo Yang was destroyed, and with it perished many ancient books which had survived the Ch'in proscription. Great numbers of people fled before the invaders to take refuge beyond the Yangtze, and their place was filled in some measure by an alien stock. This migration had a lasting effect. Up to the end of the Han dynasty the northern plain and plateaux of the north-west had been the hub of Chinese civilisation; the lands of the Yangtze valley and further south were colonial territories, inferior in culture and sparsely populated. After the Tartar invasions the centre of gravity moved south. The Yangtze valley was fully and finally incorporated into the true Chinese area, and henceforward contributes largely to the cultural life of the nation. To Ssǔ-ma

Ch'ien the modern provinces of Chekiang and Kiangsu were still strange, semi-barbarous lands, but in the T'ang dynasty, when the empire was once more united, these countries, which had been the heart of the southern empire during the partition, were as Chinese, and as cultivated, as the provinces of the Court.

The fall of the Han dynasty was the consequence of the inveterate evil which had manifested itself from the beginning of the centralised empire, the inordinate power of irresponsible elements near the throne. The Early Han had been brought to ruin by the ambitions of the consort families, ending in the usurpation of Wang Mang. When the Han were restored, the evil was in some measure abated, few of the consort families in the Later Han attempted usurpation, though several were degraded or exterminated on charges of planning treason. The restored Han line was thus able to govern in comparative peace and stability for over a century, a great period which saw not only the conquests and discoveries of Pan Chao but the literary activities of his family and their contemporaries.

It was not until the reign of Han Shun Ti (A.D. 126-144) that a new weakness in the government made headway, destined in time to bring the empire to ruin. The power of the palace eunuchs, which first became a serious political factor in this reign, was in part a consequence of the ambitions of the consort families, in part due to the secluded manner of life which court etiquette prescribed for the Emperor. He rarely left his palace, or the vast gardens attached to it. The ministers of state only saw their sovereign at formal audiences, where a rigid etiquette governed the proceedings. When he travelled the roads were guarded and cleared of the populace, who might not even gaze upon the monarch. It was never true in China that a "cat may look at a King."*

On the other hand the ladies of the palace, and the eunuchs who attended upon them, and who were the only males allowed to

*The term of address to the Emperor in Chinese, "Chieh Hsia," literally meaning "below the steps," well illustrates the aloof majesty of the occupant of the throne. The ministers at the audience might not directly address the sovereign to offer their advice or opinion. They addressed their words to the officials nearer the high raised throne, those who were "below the steps," by whom they were transmitted to the Emperor. Thus "Chieh Hsia" became the Chinese synonym for "Your Majesty."

reside in its precincts, were of necessity in constant and intimate association with the Emperor. They alone had ample opportunities for discovering the weaknesses of his character, playing upon his prejudices, and gratifying his whims. They alone were the channel by which he learned of events beyond the palace walls. The ministers might offer memorials, or write reports, but it was from the eunuchs that the Emperor heard the gossip of the outer world, and he heard only what they chose to tell him.

In the early reigns, when the sovereigns themselves had been bred outside the palace and only came to the throne as mature and middle-aged men, these influences were unimportant. When the heir to the throne, as was often the case in the 2nd century A.D., was a boy born and bred in the palace, under the care and in the company of eunuchs from his childhood, the Emperor became the plaything of these servitors, who knew his foibles, coloured all he ever learned of the outer world, and prejudiced him against those ministers who attempted to oppose their influence.

Han Shun Ti was the first to gratify his eunuch favourites with titles and official rank, but, though their power and their unpopularity with the mass of the people grew rapidly in his reign, it was offset by the great authority of the consort family of the Liang, brothers of the Empress, a family which dominated the government for twenty years, and which had numbered among its members seven princes, three empresses, six imperial concubines, and three grand generals of the forces. Three princesses had been given in marriage to this family, and no less than fifty-seven members of it had been employed as ministers of state and governors of provinces. None the less the triumph of the eunuchs was the direct consequence of the over-weening power of this family which threatened to usurp the throne itself.

Han Huan Ti (A.D. 146-167) used the eunuchs as a counterweight in the political struggle against the Liang family, who had poisoned his predecessor, though a mere child, believing him to be opposed to their pretensions. In A.D. 159 the Empress died, and the young Emperor relying on his eunuch supporters, who detested the Liang clan, carried out a palace revolution and exterminated the would-be usurpers. Once the Liang were destroyed, the Emperor, who considered that the eunuchs had proved his best friends against these formidable enemies, relied upon them in all things. Before long their power was greater than that of the consort families had even been, and it was wielded far less wisely. The single aim of eunuch policy was personal enrichment. They were recruited from the lowest strata of society, and, in consequence, they lost no opportunity of laying hands on such wealth as came their way.

Established in the centre of the governmental machine they soon obtained complete control of the civil service which they filled with their relatives and creatures. Promotions and appointments depended on eunuch goodwill, and their favour was only to be purchased with gold. Honours, rewards, titles and power were bestowed upon those whom the eunuchs praised to the Emperor, while imprisonment and the torture chamber were the fate of the upright officials who attempted to stem the tide of corruption or enlighten the Emperor as to the true state of affairs. The provincial officials, forced to purchase their appointments by heavy payments to the eunuchs, and only retaining them as long as they made further costly presents, recouped themselves by misappropriating the revenue and exploiting the populace Popular risings occurred, and were put down with severity, without the cloistered Emperor ever learning their extent or their cause.

Throughout the twenty-one years of Han Huan Ti's reign, the evil grew by leaps and bounds, but the new power of the eunuchs was not unopposed. The scholar class, who since the reign of the Emperor Wu had come to consider the civil service as their own, and scholarly learning as the only and proper qualification for official rank, were offended and outraged to find official posts distributed by eunuch favour or bought for money paid to the same quarter. Many of the scholarly families were far from rich, and these were now denied any chance of preferment, no matter what their merit. The generals, who found incompetents promoted by reason of payments made to the eunuchs and deserving officers degraded for their inability or unwillingness to do the same, were estranged and their loyalty cooled.

Among these two classes a powerful opposition to the eunuchs developed, but the lack of contact between the scholars and the military prevented any combined effort to purge the Court. The scholars in A.D. 166 founded an association which, while ostensibly a college devoted to the spread of Confucian doctrine, soon became an instrument of open opposition to eunuch power. The popular feeling was on the side of the scholars, not only because the Chinese have always felt a profound respect for education and scholarship, but also because the poor suffered from eunuch exactions as much as the official class. With the backing of the people the scholars and the officials who were not in eunuch favour obtained some success.

At the death of Han Huan Ti (A.D. 167) the association had secured the conviction of several of the more notorious eunuchs and their creatures in the provincial administration. Had the new Emperor Han Ling Ti given his support to the scholars the power of the eunuchs could easily have been checked, for it rested solely on the confidence of the Emperor himself. Unfortunately Han Ling Ti came to the throne at the age of twelve. The Empress Regent at first supported the scholars, and entrusted the administration to members of the association. The child sovereign, however, was from the first under the influence of the eunuchs who wasted no opportunity in an assiduous attempt to prejudice his mind against the scholars and their association, which they represented as a treasonable body.

Having established a dominating influence over the boy Emperor, the eunuchs lost no time in striking a death blow at their enemies. In the first year of the new Emperor's reign, A.D. 168, they brought about a palace revolution, imprisoned the Empress Regent, and, having represented the association of the scholars to the Emperor as a body aiming at his deposition, easily persuaded him to sign decrees by which all the leading officials and members of the association were arrested, condemned, and executed. The association was proscribed, its followers and subordinate members persecuted or imprisoned, and the administration cleared of all who had supported it.

The Emperor, learning nothing of these events except in the form in which the eunuchs represented them, was convinced that a dangerous sedition had been suppressed by his faithful eunuchs, and from that day they exercised supreme power, having merely to accuse any critic of supporting the association, to obtain his death sentence. The consequences of this intrigue were fatal to the empire. The eunuchs themselves, who were not allowed to leave the palace in the ordinary course of events, were ignorant of the disorder which their rapacity caused in the provinces. The administration was filled with their clients who took care not to criticise the policy of their masters. The peasantry, exploited and despairing, was ready to follow any leader who offered to alleviate their distress.

For some years the central provinces had been swept by an epidemic for which a certain Chang Chüeh, an itinerant magician, discovered a remedy. Whether Chang Chüeh had some medical skill or whether the pestilence was of a character susceptible to faith healing, the magical cure, which consisted in drinking pure water over which a formula had been pronounced, had a marvellous success. Soon the provinces were filled with devoted adherents of Chang Chüeh, who believed that they owed their lives to his art. Finding himself at the head of a numerous band of disciples, and with great popular support, Chang Chüeh determined to exploit his success by taking up arms against the unpopular and tyrannical administration of the eunuchs (A.D. 184).

Thus began the famous rebellion of the Yellow Turbans, so called from the distinguishing headdress which the followers of Chang Chüeh adopted. This rebellion, the direct cause of the fall of the Han dynasty, is the prototype of all the mystical secret society popular movements which have arisen as protests against misrule in subsequent periods. Many of the later movements, if not all, actually claimed to have inherited the secret instructions of the founder of the Yellow Turbans, who promised immortality to his followers on the battlefield after they had partaken of magical medicaments.*

To suppress the rebellion of the Yellow Turbans the Han Court

*This is a doctrine common to all these movements. It was held by the Boxers (Society of the Harmonious Fist) in 1900 and is held at the present time by the Heavenly Gates and Red Spears, who are locally known as "hard stomachs" as they claim that a bullet cannot penetrate their skin. Repeated disproof fails to shake the faith in this superstition, which is stimulated by carefully staged demonstrations.

was obliged to call into being large armies; the support of these forces drained the treasury, and the corruption of the eunuchs, who interfered with military operations and even took bribes from the rebels, prevented any effective action. In consequence the able officers were disgusted with the policy of the court, and developed a keen animosity towards the eunuchs. When Han Ling Ti died in A.D. 189, leaving no direct heir, there ensued a fierce political struggle between the army and the eunuchs. The power of the scholars had been shattered by the proscription of the association; consequently, when the new war trained army came into collision with the Court, controlled by the eunuchs, there was no mediating body to stave off disaster.

The eunuchs openly opposed the Prince who had the support of the commander-in-chief, Ho Tsin, brother of the Empress. To carry his policy, if necessary by force, Ho Tsin obtained an order from the Regent, his sister, ordering the elite of the troops to gather at the capital. He expected to overawe all opposition by this display of force. Many of the generals, reverting to the policy which the scholars had advocated, urged the general to exterminate the eunuchs to the last man. The Empress, however, was unwilling to give in to this plan, and her brother deferred to her wishes. The result was fatal to him.

Believing that with his troops in the city the eunuchs would not dare to touch him, he advised them to withdraw into private life, before other generals, less willing to spare them, arrived at the capital. The eunuchs, who perhaps failed to understand the force of the opposition and the hatred they inspired, unwisely attempted to intimidate the army by striking at its leader. Ho Tsin was summoned to the palace on a false order, and assassinated in the great court as soon as he appeared. The eunuchs then displayed his head at the gate to overawe his lieutenants. The consequences were exactly the opposite. Led by their commanders the troops forced the palace gates and massacred every eunuch they encountered. In the confusion the Emperor was abducted and fell into the hands of an army commander of notorious brutality.

From that day the Han Empire dissolved into anarchy, the capital and palace were sacked and destroyed, and the Emperor became a pawn to be captured or stolen by the rival military freebooters between whom the empire was divided. The dynasty nominally endured until A.D. 221, the year in which the last Han sovereign, who had been many years the puppet of the celebrated general Ts'ao Ts'ao, was compelled to abdicate his throne in favour of Ts'ao Ts'ao's son (Ts'ao P'i). This anarchic age is known as the period of the Three Kingdoms (San Kuo) from the kingdoms of Wei, founded by Ts'ao Ts'ao in the north, Wu founded by the Sun family in the east, with its capital at Nanking, and the Shu Han* founded by Liu Pei, a distant scion of the Han family, who reigned at Chêng Tu in Szechuan. (Map 6.)

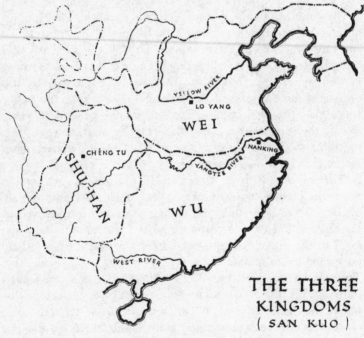

MAP 6. *The Three Kingdoms (San Kuo).*

In China this age has a curious fame, resting upon the fact that it has become celebrated in literature by the famous cycle of stories, half history, half legend, known as the *San Kuo chih yen i*,

*So called because it was established in Shu or Szechuan province.

which, though in its present form does not antedate the Ming dynasty, is based on stories far older.* Owing to the popularity of this novel and the many plays drawn from it, the San Kuo period, in reality an age of bloodshed and turmoil, has become idealised to the Chinese as the golden age of chivalry and romance, better known to the mass of the people than any other epoch in their long history. There are few Chinese who do not know Ts'ao Ts'ao's celebrated epigram, when justifying himself for murdering his host under a misapprehension, "I would rather betray the whole world than let the world betray me." Kuan Yü, one of the generals of this period is now canonised as Kuan Ti, god of war, one of the most popular deities with the common people, because he is not a Mars, but the god who prevents war. Fig. 43, showing a popular representation of Kuan Ti, mounted and armed with a long halberd, is reproduced from a stone tablet in the Confucian temple at Sianfu.

When the San Kuo period is stripped of the thick growth of romantic tales which cluster round its leading figures, it appears as a deplorable epoch of treachery and violence. In A.D. 220 Ts'ao Ts'ao's son, Ts'ao P'i, dethroned his nominal sovereign, the Emperor Han Hsien Ti, and terminated the last semblance of the Han Empire. To accomplish this purpose a ceremony was invented which henceforward passed into the constitutional practice of China. Up to this time there had been no instance of a peaceful transmission of the imperial authority to a new family. The Ch'in had been exterminated before the Han were recognised as Emperors, the Chou Kings had been deprived of their last possessions by force. Wang Mang who usurped the throne of the last Emperor of the Early Han line, had simply appropriated the seal of his infant sovereign and forced the Court to recognise him as Emperor. He had been stigmatised as a usurper, and his reign was not admitted as legitimate. Ts'ao P'i first obtained from the Court a petition asking him to ascend the throne. This he rejected, and refused all such offers until the Han Emperor, who realised what was required of him, had three times offered in writing to resign the throne, and sent the seal to Ts'ao P'i. On the fourth

*It has been translated into English, under the title San Kuo, or Romance of the Three Kingdoms. C. H. Brewitt-Taylor, Shanghai. 1925.

FIG. 43. *Kuan Ti, from a stele in the Pei Lin, Sianfu, Shensi.*

occasion the all-powerful minister yielded to these urgent requests. The renunciation of the throne was made the occasion for a public ceremony in order to emphasise its legitimacy. A huge stage was erected outside the palace, and having ascended this, in the sight of the assembled court, Ts'ao P'i received the seal of the empire from Han Hsien Ti, and then mounted the imperial throne. The new Emperor's first act was to make sacrifice to Heaven in order to obtain the divine approval. The deposed Emperor was granted an appropriate title, and Ts'ao P'i took into his harem both Hsien Ti's daughters, in imitation of Yao, who was said to have married both the daughters of Shun.

The new dynasty, known as the Wei, did not last long, nor did it ever govern more than the northern provinces. The sovereigns of the southern states, the Princes of Wu and of Shu Han assumed the imperial style also, and later historians have considered that the rulers of the latter state, as members of the Han imperial clan, were the legitimate emperors, although their territory was smaller than that of their rivals. In A.D. 265 Ssŭ-ma Yen, grand general of Wei, member of a family which had long monopolised the military authority in the northern state, treated Ts'ao P'i's descendant as that usurper had the last Han, and usurped his throne with due formality, based on the earlier ceremony. The new dynasty, the Tsin, reunited the whole empire for a brief spell by the conquest of Wu in A.D. 280, but the Ssŭ-ma family, a collateral branch of the same ancient clan to which the historian Ssŭ-ma Ch'ien had belonged, proved quite incapable of organising their conquest on a lasting basis.

The founder, Ssŭ-ma Yen, posthumously known as Tsin Wu Ti, had no less than twenty-five sons, and he made the fatal error of dividing up his dominions into numerous principalities among them. His successor was a weakling without the necessary character to control his brothers. Civil wars broke out between the princes, the government was soon reduced to anarchy. In A.D. 304 one of the princes made the mistake of calling in the Hsiung Nu tribes to his assistance. At about the same time one of his rivals invoked the help of the Hsien Pei, another nomad tribe of Turki stock.

Just as the Goths, first enlisted as Roman auxiliaries, ended by seizing the empire for themselves, so the Hsiung Nu chief, who claimed descent on his mother's side from a Han princess, did not hesitate to make war for his own advantage. The empire, distracted by the jealousies of the Tsin princes, made no effective resistance to the invaders. In A.D. 311, the Hsiung Nu, who had already founded in Shansi a kingdom which they called Han in honour of their chief's descent, captured Lo Yang and made the Tsin Emperor a prisoner. In A.D. 316 they captured his successor who had taken refuge in Ch'ang An, and from this date the whole of north China, everything north of the Yangtze watershed, was lost to the Tsin.

Although the first leader of the Hsiung Nu, Liu Yüan, had adopted a Chinese name, and was even well versed in Chinese literature, his followers were barbarians, and their progress was marked by destruction and slaughter. Lo Yang was sacked and burned, and in this catastrophe perished the imperial library of the Han dynasty. The condition of Ch'ang An, once the capital of the empire, when it had already been once sacked by the invaders is thus described:

"At this time in the city of Ch'ang An there were not more than one hundred families. Weeds and thorns grew thickly as if in a forest. Only four carts could be found in the city. The officials had neither robes of ceremony nor seals. Instead they used tablets of mulberry wood on which their names and rank were inscribed."

In A.D. 316, following the definite collapse of all resistance in the north, the Tsin Court fled to Nanking, where a new Emperor was set up. This city, which had been the capital of the Wu state, was already the chief centre of the southern provinces. It now afforded a safe refuge for the fallen Tsin Emperors, who reigned there over the southern provinces in comparative peace until A.D. 420. Meanwhile the north was delivered over to several competing nomad kings and their tribes. (Map 7.) This anarchy saved the south from a like fate. No ruler in the north was sufficiently secure to risk an invasion of the Yangtze valley, which in any case is a country highly unsuitable to cavalry, upon which arm the Hsiung Nu and other Tartar tribes principally relied. A determined

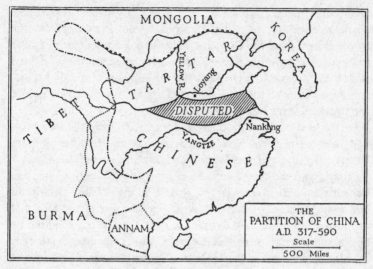

MAP 7. *The Partition of China.*

attempt to invade the southern empire was indeed made in
A.D. 387, but was disastrously repulsed in a decisive battle.

The consequences of this battle (Fei Shui) were twofold, the
south was saved, and the northern kingdoms, weakened by the
disaster, succumbed to a new nomad invasion by the Wei, or Toba
tribes, who conquered the whole north and founded a dynasty
which endured from A.D. 386 to 557. The Wei were of Tungusic
stock, and proved better rulers and organisers than the Hsiung
Nu and Hsien Pei tribesfolk. They rapidly assimilated Chinese
civilisation and intermarried with the natives of the soil. In A.D.
500 the Wei Emperor actually issued a decree prohibiting the use
of the Tartar language, costume and customs in favour of those
of China. The Wei dynasty was thus completely identified with the
Chinese culture, and did much to preserve and restore the
literature of the Han era.

The ease with which these invading nomads, who entered as
untamed barbarians, were assimilated into the Chinese civilisation
argues strongly against the supposition that the invading tribes
were very numerous. Ancient statistics are not reliable, but the
traditional figure of 50,000 for the fighting force of the first

invasion, which if multiplied by four would give 200,000 for the whole strength of the tribe, is probably not very far from the truth. When the Wei Emperor issued his decree against Tartar customs, the region of Honan, in which province the Wei held their Court, is said to have had a Tartar population of only 14,700, and even if this be taken to refer to families, it still indicates that the invaders were but a handful.

By the end of the period of partition, A.D. 589, the two races had intermarried to such an extent that few families of pure Tartar blood could be found, and all had acquired Chinese language and culture. Similarly the modern Manchus long ago lost all use of their own language and adopted Chinese customs and manners in almost every particular, in spite of the fact that up till the fall of the late dynasty in 1911 they were forbidden by law to intermarry with the Chinese. The 4th and 5th century invaders, who were certainly not more numerous than the Manchus, never enforced a prohibition against intermarriage with the Chinese, and as has been said, actively encouraged the adoption of Chinese culture and customs. By the 6th century they must have been even more completely absorbed than the Manchus of to-day.

The southern empire, in spite of long periods of border warfare and tiresome sieges of walled cities, in the defence of which the Chinese excelled, was never really menaced with destruction after the battle of Fei Shui. Although the Tsin dynasty fell in A.D. 420, to be succeeded at short intervals by four minor dynasties, these internal troubles did not open a road to northern conquerors. Under the Liang dynasty, which endured from A.D. 502 to 557, the Court of Nanking was a centre of culture and arts patronised by the fervent Buddhist Emperor Liang Wu Ti (A.D. 502-549), almost the only personality of interest to occupy the southern throne during these dynasties. When he died, aged 86, after Nanking had fallen to a rebel invader, the glory of the southern empire passed away. The Ch'ên dynasty, the last of the Nanking lines, never controlled the whole Yangtze valley, and succumbed ingloriously to the attack of the new northern power, the Sui. This dynasty was founded by a Chinese general, Yang Chien, who was himself the son-in-law of the last ruler of the

Northern Chou dynasty, which had replaced the Wei. After the fall of the Wei the north had undergone a new period of division and anarchy which was terminated by the usurpation of Yang Chien, the restoration of a Chinese imperial family, and the reunion of the empire under one sovereign in A.D. 589.

The instability of the throne, and the fall in the imperial prestige, is characteristic of all these short-lived dynasties northern or southern, Chinese or Tartar. Hardly one of the prominent personalities was born in the purple. The founders were soldiers of fortune, sometimes of base extraction, sometimes like the Hsiao family who ruled in the south as the Ch'i and Liang dynasties, of ancient and noble extraction.* Their descendants were all equally without prestige and for the most part, without ability. In consequence every successful general or powerful minister was a rival to the Emperor, a potential usurper. The sovereign himself was a usurper, or the son of a usurper, and in no position to command the loyalty and reverence offered to an ancient line. The provinces had fallen into the hands of powerful clans who could not be displaced from the governorship, which became hereditary. This was particularly the case in the south, though many instances of such feudal revivals existed in the north-western provinces also. Szechuan was for long periods an independent kingdom owing no allegiance either to Nanking or to a northern dynasty. The Han civil service based on scholarship was almost forgotten.

During this period of the Six Dynasties, or of the North and South partition as it is sometimes called, the dynasties in north and south were as follows:

SOUTH, capital at Nanking

Tsin	.. ..	A.D. 317-419	103 years	
†Sung	.. ..	A.D. 420-477	59 years	
Ch'i	.. ..	A.D. 479-501	23 years	These dynasties were both of the Hsiao family
Liang	.. ..	A.D. 502-556	55 years	
Ch'en	.. ..	A.D. 557-587	32 years	

*They descended in the twenty-fourth generation from Hsiao Ho, chief minister of Liu Pang, founder of the Han dynasty.

†This Sung dynasty should not be confused with the more famous Sung Dynasty of A.D. 960-1278. The Sung of the Six Dynasties is called Liu Sung in China to avoid this confusion. Liu was the surname of the ruling house.

NORTH, at Lo Yang, Ta T'ung, etc.

Northern Wei ..	A.D. 386-532	149 years	
Western Wei ..	A.D. 535-554	22 years	in north-west and north-east respectively
Eastern Wei ..	A.D. 534-543	16 years	
Northern Ch'i ..	A.D. 550-577	39 years	
Northern Chou	A.D. 557-581	32 years	
Sui (in north) ..	A.D. 581-587	7 years before conquering the southern Ch'en and re-uniting China	

Some of the northern dynasties did not rule all the north, but the minor regional kingdoms are not accorded the status of "dynasties" by Chinese historians.

These melancholy conditions and the apparently incurable anarchy of the times tended to encourage the progress of Buddhism, which now became the dominant religion both in the northern and southern empires. The doctrines of the new religion offered comfort to men living in a world of violence and instability. To renounce society, abandon possessions, and seek peace in a monastery among the mountains became the fashion among thoughtful men. Those who could not take the extreme step contributed to the building of temples and pagodas and their enrichment with artistic treasures.

The Court of Nanking exerted a strong cultural influence over the provinces of the southern empire, which had been backward areas in the Han period. The flight of the scholars after the fall of Lo Yang had brought civilisation into the south, and gave these provinces an importance which they had not possessed in the Han Empire, but which was to grow more and more marked in succeeding ages, until the southern provinces became the true centre of the empire.

Chapter XII

TAOISM AND BUDDHISM

(A) LATER TAOISM

THE age of confusion which followed the fall of the Han Empire was a period of great importance in the history of religion in China. The 3rd and 4th centuries A.D., an era of turmoil and war, saw the rise and development of the two religious systems which henceforward offered the only alternatives to Confucian orthodoxy. The introduction and spread of Buddhism is described in a later section; here a brief survey of the progress made by its chief rival, Taoism, will be made.

The transformation of Taoism into a religion was one result of the triumph of the Confucian school, now established as the state protected orthodox philosophy. The new Confucianism, as it emerged at the hands of the Han scholars, was entirely divorced from the ancient magical rites of the *wu* magicians. The scholars who exalted the moral virtues and placed them under the patronage of the supreme deity, T'ien, Heaven, grudged any favours shown to the heterodox deities worshipped by the *wu* priests. Taoism, with its doctrine of non-action, its mysticism, and its disregard of the rites and ceremonies esteemed by the Confucians, was equally frowned upon by the orthodox scholars. Both Taoism and the cults of the *wu* priesthood were deeply rooted in the cultural life of the Chinese. The rather arid doctrines of the Confucian scholars had little appeal for the mass of the people. It was not unnatural, therefore, that the principal heterodox philosophy, Taoism should join forces with the popular religion which Confucianism had rejected.

This alliance, from which later Taoism, a religion more than a philosophic school, was born, was stimulated by the appearance of a new rival, Buddhism. Both Buddhism and Taoist philosophy denied the value of the world of appearances, and directed their appeal to the mystical side of human nature. Since this religious instinct was neglected by Confucian orthodoxy, it was inevitable that the new creeds should awaken a widespread response.

Buddhism offered the hope of Nirvana, or eternal happiness in the Western Paradise. Taoism, which had hitherto known no doctrine of after-life, promised the achievement of immortality by alchemistic practices. Thus the cults which the magicians had popularised at the Court of the Emperor Wu were now systematised by Taoist interpretations and synthesised into a comprehensive pantheon rivalling, and often borrowing from, Buddhist legend and lore.

Traditionally the new movement is ascribed to Chang Tao-ling, a native of Chekiang province—the stronghold of the *wu* cults—who lived in the reign of Kuang Wu Ti, first Emperor of the Later Han dynasty. Chang Tao-ling is said to have been born in A.D. 34 and to have lived till A.D. 156, a space of one hundred and twenty-two years, which, to say the least, appears improbable. Most of his life was spent in retirement upon a mountain, where he studied alchemy and sought the drug of immortality. Taoist tradition regards him as the first T'ien Shih or Heavenly Teacher (a title sometimes translated as "pope") and he is said to have achieved immortality and ascended to Heaven on a dragon. There are indeed, few historical facts about Chang Tao-ling, although the present Taoist T'ien Shih claims to be his lineal descendant. Another story states that Chang Tao-ling was a descendant of Chang Liang, the general of Liu P'ang, founder of the Han dynasty, and this Chang Liang was himself a scion of an ancient family in the Han state.*

Although the stories about Chang Tao-ling are manifestly legend, it is probable that about this time the Taoist philosophy began to assimilate the practices of the *wu* cults, and the *wu* themselves became known as *Tao Shih* or Taoist Teachers. Side by side with the growing infusion of magical practices, there persisted a pure school of Taoist teaching which continued to attract scholars and poets who found Confucian doctrine unsatisfying. Early in the Tsin dynasty (A.D. 265-316), there was a famous coterie of Taoist scholars who called themselves the Seven Sages of the Bamboo Grove. Their lives and outlook are character-

---

*This Han state is not the same as the Han dynasty. The former was one of the Three Tsin, the states among which the old Tsin kingdom had been divided. The supposed pedigree of the Chang Taoist popes is a fiction designed to rival the real antiquity of the K'ung family, descended from Confucius.

istic of the Taoism of this period, expressing the revolt against the formalism of Confucianism and the turmoil of contemporary politics. The historians, who are, of course, Confucians, thus describe the activities of the Seven Sages:

"They all revered and exalted the Void and Non-Action and disregarded the rites and law. They drank wine to excess and disdained the affairs of this world."

The leader of the club, Hsi K'ang (A.D. 223-262), was put to death by Ssŭ-ma Chao, father of the first Tsin Emperor, who at that time was the all-powerful minister at the Court of Wei, the northern state of the Three Kingdoms period. Hsi K'ang was in the habit of expounding his doctrines to his disciples, and had achieved a very great reputation. Ssŭ-ma Chao came to listen to him, but Hsi K'ang made no attempt to treat the minister with ceremony; indeed, he did not appear to notice his presence. Ssŭ-ma Chao was offended, and later hearing that Hsi K'ang in a letter to his friend Shan T'ao had spoken slightingly of T'ang and Wu, the hero founders of the ancient Shang and Chou dynasties, the minister made this a pretext to execute Hsi K'ang as one who "disturbed the times and confused right doctrine." The real cause of his enmity was that as he himself was contemplating usurping the throne of his nominal sovereign, the Emperor of the Wei dynasty, he considered that Hsi K'ang's slighting reference to T'ang and Wu was a covet criticism of himself, these ancient heroes being, in the opinion of the Taoist, usurpers, not legitimate heirs to the throne.

Shan T'ao, Hsi K'ang's friend, was also one of the Seven Sages, and a native of the southern kingdom of Wu. Under the Tsin dynasty he held high office as president of the Board of Civil Service. He seems to have been less eccentric than his friends Liu Ling, another of the Seven, was a great drinker. He used to declare that to a drunken man the "affairs of the world appear as so much duckweed in a river." He rode about the capital in a small cart drawn by deer, with a servant following with a large pot of wine. Another servant carried a spade, and had orders to dig a grave and bury his master forthwith without ceremony, wherever he chanced to die. Yüan Chi and Yüan Hsien were uncle and nephew, and like Liu Ling were heavy drinkers. They were both famous musicians although soldiers by profession. Yüan Hsien had a shameless passion for a lady's serving maid. On one occasion, when he was entertaining guests, he saw the lady send the maid away. Rising without apology, he hastily borrowed one of his guest's horses and pursued the young woman, bringing her back on his crupper.

Yüan Chi, his uncle, though sincerely attached to his mother, and sick with grief at her death, scandalised the scholars by drinking heavily throughout the period of mourning. Wang Jung and Hsiang Hsiu, the other members of the Bamboo Grove, were both scholars of distinction. Wang Jung's brother, as magistrate of a town in the northern provinces, put into practice the Taoist theory of government by Non-Action, with results which were a conspicuous success. Hsiang Hsiu wrote the best known commentary on the works of Chuang Tzŭ, although, as he died before it was complete, it has generally been wrongly attributed to Kuo Hsiang, who only completed the unfinished portion.

All the Seven Sages of the Bamboo Grove cultivated these eccentricities as a deliberate protest against Confucian formality and the elaborate rites with which the scholars wished to surround every human activity. Behind the façade of drunken eccentricity they pursued the true Taoist ideals of simplicity and harmony with the rhythm of life. In their writings, which took the form of commentaries on the Taoist classics, they developed the philosophic side of the doctrines which Chuang Tzŭ had propounded. Wang Pi (A.D. 226-249), a writer who lived in the period of the Three Kingdoms, after the fall of the Han Empire, devoted himself to this branch of Taoism. His commentary on the *Tao Tê Ching* shows that the higher interpretation of the old Taoist writers was still understood in the 3rd century. Indeed the philosophic character of Taoism never entirely disappeared even when the new religious and magical type of Taoism had gained the ascendant. In the tenets of more than one of the Buddhist schools, and particularly in the Ch'an School, Taoist influence is very evident.

Only a few years after the Seven Sages of the Bamboo Grove there flourished a Taoist writer who emphasised the new magical element which was transforming the old philosophy. Ko Hung, who wrote under the pseudo name of Pao P'u Tzŭ, was a native of Kiangsu, a contemporary of Tsin Yüan Ti, the first Emperor to re-establish the capital at Nanking after the fall of Lo Yang to the invading Hsiung Nu. Ko Hung wrote a book in two sections, an "inner" treatise which deals at length with the alchemistic processes by which the drug of immortality may be made, and the transmutation of cinnabar and mercury into gold. His "outer" treatise deals with matters of philosophy and government on Taoist lines.

The inner treatise is of considerable interest as early evidence of the extent to which the theory of alchemy had been developed and associated with Taoism. After arguing at some ler,th that the long-lived animals demonstrated the possibility of man attaining immortality, since if animals could live so long, man with the aid of knowledge and power could certainly surpass mere brutes, Ko Hung gives several instances of men and women who had attained immortality in the past. One chapter of his book is devoted to methods of attaining immortality, for which he gives recipes. These drugs were not only believed to be capable of postponing death for centuries, but also rejuvenated the body. The results to be expected were that:

"White hair will become black, lost teeth will grow again, the strength of the body will be renewed. He who takes it will never grow old, an old man will become a youth once more, he will live for ever and not die."*

These drugs, and others of a similar nature, enabled the immortal to walk through fire without being burned, to walk on the surface of water without sinking, to rise into the air, to command the spirits and demons, and to revive the dead.

In conjunction with the study of drugs to procure immortality Ko Hung devotes much space to the method of making gold, which it was hoped could be produced by chemical action. He gives most definite and precise instructions about this process, though he does not actually say whether he had succeeded in

*Pao P'u Tzŭ. Nei Pien 4.

making gold himself. As an example of the chemical knowledge and methods of his time his process is instructive:

"Process for Making Gold.

"Use a large iron vessel 1 ft. 2 in. in diameter, 1 ft. 2 in. in height, and a small iron vessel, diameter 6 in. Take one catty of pounded red clay, one catty of nitre, one catty of talc, one catty of Tai iron ore*, half a catty of sulphur, and one catty of ice. Pound all together until fine and mix thoroughly. Daub the inside of the small iron vessel to a thickness of two and one-tenth inches with one catty of mercury, half a catty of cinnabar and half a catty of 'liang fei.' The method of making 'liang fei' is to heat ten catties of lead in an iron dish on a furnace; soon three ozs. of mercury will appear out of the melted lead, ladle this out with an iron spoon. It is called 'liang fei.' Stir all [the above ingredients] together until the mercury cannot be seen. Then put [the mixture] away in the little iron vessel, and cover it with talc and an iron lid to protect it. Put the iron vessels on to the furnace. The melted lead will sink into the big vessel. Take out of the small vessel the top half inch of molten matter, heat it on a fierce fire for three days and nights; it becomes what is called red powder. Next take the ten catties of lead and heat it in an iron vessel for twenty days and nights, then transfer it into a copper vessel, and add the red powder to the molten lead. Stir with a spoon one square inch in size and it immediately changes into gold."†

Ko Hung also wrote about spell magic, and gives specimens of charms (Fig. 44), which were of use to those who dwelt in

*Iron ore from Tai Chou in Shansi province. A catty is equivalent to one and a half pounds avoirdupois.

†*Pao P'u Tzŭ.* Nei pien 16. The spoon for stirring the mixture at the climax of the process was possibly one square inch in size because this measurement was

FIG. 44. *A Taoist Spell.* believed to be that of the human heart.

out-of-the-way places, mountains or forests. These he recommended should be pasted upon the door, beams and pillars of the house.

The new school of alchemistic Taoism also prospered in the northern empire under the Wei dynasty (A.D. 386-557), where it received imperial patronage. In A.D. 415 a certain K'ou Ch'ien-chih, a man of good family and younger brother of a provincial governor, who had dwelt for some years as a hermit on Mt. Sung in Honan, had a vision in which Lao Tzǔ appeared to him. From the divine founder of Taoism K'ou received a new book of doctrine in twenty rolls, and also was appointed *T'ien Shih*, or Celestial Teacher, chief of the Taoists among mortal men.* In A.D. 423 K'ou had a further vision in which the great grandson of Lao Tzǔ, himself an immortal, appeared to give further instructions and confirm K'ou's position as T'ien Shih.

In A.D. 428 K'ou Ch'ien-chih left his retreat on Mt. Sung and came to the Court of the Wei Emperor T'ai Wu (A.D. 424-452), which was then established near Ta T'ung Fu in north Shansi. The Emperor welcomed K'ou and accepted him as the chief of the Taoists. He and his disciples were lodged at the public expense, and a temple built for them outside the capital. The new cult was highly honoured, the Emperor himself paid a visit to the temple in the year A.D. 442, and received a book of charms. After this every Emperor of the Wei dynasty used to proceed to the Taoist temple at his accession and obtain a charm book.

A few years later, in A.D. 448, K'ou Ch'ien-chih died, but the death of their leader did not destroy the faith of the disciples. Indeed, it was the cause of renewed honours.

"After his death his corpse stretched and when the disciples measured it, it was found to be 8 ft. 3 in. in length, but after three days it began to shrink and when coffined was no more than 6 in. long. Then the disciples believed him to be one who had attained immortality on death, and had become transformed and disappeared as an immortal."

Taoism prospered under the Wei dynasty, and when the capital

*This incident sufficiently refutes the claim of the Chang family to have held the rank of *T'ien Shih* from father to son since the time of their supposed ancestor Chang Tao-ling.

was moved to Lo Yang in Honan, the Taoist temple was established there. Numerous other adepts appeared, though none attained the fame of K'ou Ch'ien-chih. It was to be expected that the Taoists should resent the competition of Buddhism, which, being an alien creed, offended the conservative sense of the nationally minded Chinese, nevertheless the Taoists found it wise to compromise with the intruder to some extent. K'ou Ch'ien-chih, it would appear, described Buddha as one who had found the Tao among the "western barbarians" (Indians) and become an immortal. As such he might be honoured, though not of course in a manner equal to Lao Tzŭ or other Taoist immortals of superior rank.

The rivalry of Buddhism and Taoism was the cause of persecutions which fell equally upon both religions. Taoism had escaped the persecution directed against Buddhism by the Emperor of the Wei dynasty in A.D. 444. In fact, the Taoists inspired this movement on the grounds that Buddhism was an alien creed, which had no traditional connection with the golden age so beloved by all Chinese scholars. In A.D. 555 the ruler of the northern Ch'i state, which occupied the north-eastern provinces, called a congress of Buddhists and Taoists with the idea of unifying the two rival religions. The priests of Buddha having proved victorious in the argument, the Emperor ordered all Taoist priests to shave their heads and become Buddhist monks. There was at first some opposition, but when four recalcitrant Taoists had been put to death, the others "obeyed the decree" and thenceforth there "were no Taoists in the Ch'i domain."

The persecution, however, was not of long duration, for not many years later, when the north had passed under the rule of another dynasty, the Northern Chou, the two religions seem to have been as flourishing as ever. In A.D. 574 the Emperor of that dynasty issued a decree proscribing both Taoism and Buddhism. The priests and monks were made to return to secular life, their scriptures were burnt and the images of Buddha and the Taoist divinities smashed. A few years later in A.D. 579 his successor reversed this policy and restored the temples of both cults, and it is improbable that these short lived persecutions had much effect except in the vicinity of the capital. Throughout the period

PLATE I. THE ALTAR OF HEAVEN, PEKING

PLATE II. THE ALTAR OF HEAVEN PREPARED WITH OFFERINGS FOR SACRIFICE

PLATE III. BRONZE VESSEL, KU, CHOU PERIOD

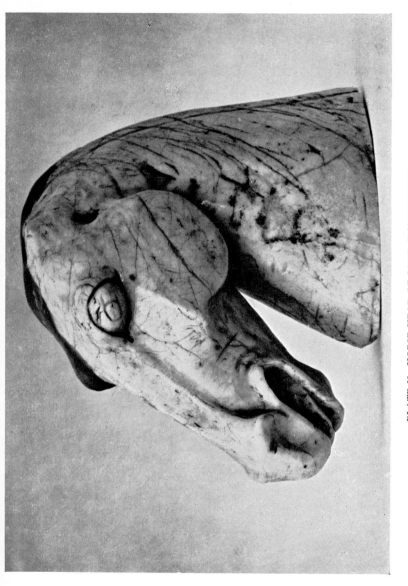

PLATE V. HORSE HEAD OF JADE, HAN DYNASTY

PLATE VII. (*a*) GOLD BUCKLE FROM LAK LANG, KOREA. HAN DYNASTY
(*b*) BRONZE FISH, CHOU PERIOD

PLATE IX.
POTTERY FIGURES,
T'ANG DYNASTY
(a) A SOUTHERN
INDIAN
(b) AN ARMENOID
TYPE

PLATE XI. BRONZE MIRRORS, T'ANG DYNASTY

PLATE XII. LANDSCAPE ATTRIBUTED TO WU TAO-TZU OF
THE T'ANG DYNASTY

枯柯帶老
松枝浮雲
年將雪時懷
向說家程一
每云憐山景
為遠之
硬本新去
尚能

李成寒林平野

PLATE XIII. LANDSCAPE BY LI CH'ÊNG. "WOODS IN WINTER."
SUNG DYNASTY

PLATE XIV. PIGEON BY THE EMPEROR HUI TSUNG. SUNG DYNASTY

PLATE XV. HORSE AND KHOTANI GROOM, BY LI LUNG-MIEN. SUNG DYNASTY

PLATE XVI. TO PAO T'A PAGODA, LIANG HSIANG HSIEN, HOPEI,
THIRTEENTH CENTURY

PLATE XVII. WU MEN, GATE OF THE FORBIDDEN CITY, PEKING. MING DYNASTY

PLATE XVIII. CITY WALL AND CORNER TOWER, T'AI KU HSIEN, SHANSI

PLATE XIX. LACQUER SCREEN, SEVENTEENTH CENTURY

PLATE XX. PHEASANTS AND FLOWERING TREES BY WANG SHIH. A.D. 1662

of division the new Taoist cult gained steadily in influence both with the mass of the people, and also in Court circles. Taoism does not seem to have suffered any persecution in the southern empire, while the influences of Taoist priests and magicians at the Court of Nanking was a factor of importance.

By the end of the 6th century Taoism was firmly established in its new form as a popular cult, the rival of Buddhism. It had also adopted the pseudo-sciences of alchemy and astrology as an integral part of the system. The object of the Taoist devotee was to achieve immortality by means of magical practices and carefully compounded drugs. If this high aim was beyond his powers, he might at least hope to gain wealth by making gold, or failing that, to prolong his life by the study of drugs less potent than that of immortality. The consequences of this new turn to Taoist speculations were far more important than has usually been admitted.

Alchemy and medicine became identified with Taoism, and Taoism was an unorthodox cult, opposed by the scholars of the Confucian school. When Taoism was favoured by the Court the Confucian hostility could be ignored, but when Taoism lost this support, the weight of the Confucian influence was against it. Taoism therefore gradually became a despised popular religion, regarded as gross superstition by the scholars and educated classes. As alchemy and medicine were the stock-in-trade of the Taoist priest, these sciences shared the contempt lavished upon Taoist teaching. Alchemy, though its hopes were too high and its methods unsound, was none the less the parent of true scientific chemistry. In China all such sciences incurred the derision which was meted out to Taoism as the superstitious cult of the "stupid people." Medicine, which was inspired by Taoist ideas about the *elixir vitæ*, shared this neglect. Educated persons left such practices to Taoists, who were more and more frequently men of low origin and little learning.

This was the cause of the divorce between learning and science which prevented the Chinese from discovering the principles of the exact sciences. Discoveries were made, but they were left to the Taoist priests. The magnetic compass was used to determine the favourable location of graves. Gunpowder had been discovered by Taoist investigators in their search for the "philosopher's stone," yet until the Mongol invaders put it to the uses of war, the Chinese had only employed explosives in fire crackers, used to scare away evil influences. Science, anything which smacked of alchemy or the drug of immortality, was treated as a charlatanism only fit for the ignorant and lowly. The scholar should concern himself with book learning, literature, history, poetry—but not with science.

(B) BUDDHISM

Prior to the contact with European civilisation in the 19th century, Buddhism was by far the most important cultural influence of foreign origin introduced into China in the historical period. The effect of Buddhism upon Chinese thought, art, and the customs of daily life is comparable to the influence of Christianity upon the nations of the west. Buddhism is the only foreign element in the Chinese culture which has penetrated every class of society, maintained its hold over long centuries, and become accepted as an essential part of the national civilisation. Politically the history of China can be broadly divided into the feudal and imperial periods, and in religious history there is a Buddhist and pre-Buddhist age.

The new creed not only altered the religious system of China; it familiarised the Chinese with the pre-Buddhist Indian philosophies and religions, and in the realm of art it served as the conduit by which Hellenistic influence flowed eastward across Central Asia. So many sided and powerful a force as Indian Buddhism could not fail to modify the Chinese civilisation profoundly, but in the end it was Buddhism, rather than Chinese culture, which underwent the greatest transformation. The merits of Indian philosophy have been much discussed in the west where they have found vigorous defenders, but to the Chinese, a people with an intensely practical side to their character, the illimitable vagueness of Indian speculation proved unpalatable. As time passed they began to interpret Buddhist doctrine in terms of moral virtues already familiar from the Chou Schools of philosophy. Chinese Buddhism reshaped under these strong native influences took a form which bears only a faint and superficial resemblance to the Indian system from which it sprang.

The Chinese artists who were called upon to illustrate episodes in the life of Buddha naturally portrayed the Indian sage in surroundings with which they were familiar, just as the Italian primitives painted the Christian saints in the costumes of renaissance Italy. The illustration reproduced in Fig. 45

FIG. 45. *Buddha at the Death-bed of his Father.*

shows Buddha attending the death-bed of his father, King Suddhodana, in a typical Chinese palace hall.*

The exact nature of the original Indian doctrine is itself very uncertain. Buddhism, when it reached China in the 1st century

*Reproduced from L. Wieger, S.J., *Bouddhisme Chinois,* 1913.

A.D., was already an old religion, with some four or five centuries of history behind it. The dates of Gautama Buddha's life are not precisely known. It has indeed been argued that no such person ever existed, or that if he did, he was not the founder of Buddhism, but a reformer who reshaped an ancient creed. This controversy must be left to Indian historians and Sanskrit scholars. Conservative opinion regards Gautama as a historical personage, who probably lived and preached in Northern India in the first half of the 5th century B.C., the date of his death being either 479 or 477 B.C. No contemporary evidence either of his life or teaching exists in any language. The monuments of King Asôka, *circa* 272-231 B.C., attest the existence and flourishing state of Buddhism in India at that time, but the evidence of these inscriptions does not always confirm the theology of the most conservative Buddhist School, the Hinayana.

At an unknown date, usually believed to be in the early part of the 1st century A.D., Buddhism split into two opposing camps, Hinayana and Mahayana, the Lesser and Greater Vehicle respectively. Needless to say, the Hinayana do not themselves accept this opprobrious epithet, applied to them by their adversaries. The Hinayana, who to-day are the Buddhists of Ceylon, Burma and Siam, hold to what they believe to be the true and simple doctrines of Gautama, and regard the Mahayana system as a tissue of inventions and accretions, having little in common with the primitive doctrine. Modern scholars have been inclined to dispute this traditionally accepted view. It is now contended that Mahayana Buddhism, though perhaps not holding closely to the teaching of Gautama, is none the less founded upon a religious system as ancient as the Buddha, if not earlier, incorporating beliefs long current in India, but which were ignored, or perhaps opposed, by the primitive Buddhists.

In the Hinayana system, Gautama is the Buddha, the sole Buddha, who now reposes for ever in Nirvana—the absence of desire and striving—having left to mankind a simple rule by which they may attain a like bliss, either at the end of their present incarnation, or at most at the end of seven reincarnations. This creed knows no prayers, invocations or offerings, for Buddha is not God, but man who has attained perfection and thrown off the *Karma* of sin, which dooms mankind to successive re-incarnations in the world of pain and sorrow.

Whether Mahayana Buddhism was reshaped under Hellenistic influences which took a less melancholy view of human existence, or whether it represented the Indian taste for cosmic speculation (which Gautama condemned as profitless) the "Greater Vehicle" framed what is in effect an entirely new religion. Gautama now becomes merely one reincarnation in a vast series of Buddhas stretching from an illimitable past into an equally infinite future. Not only in this world but in other worlds "numerous as the sands of the Ganges" Buddhas have lived and preached at intervals separated by myriads of years, from a time past human calculation. This world is but a speck in space and an instant in time ; it will pass away and Maitreya will be the Buddha of the next period.

In the later developments of Mahayana Buddhism the Buddhas past and to come gradually become gods of transcendent power, hearkening to the prayers of mankind, responding to invocations, delighting in offerings and incense. Ultimately Amida or Amid-abha Buddha, a personage unknown to the early Buddhist scriptures and conjectured to be a revival of the Indian Brahma or the Zoroastrian Ahura-Mazda, became the object of almost exclusive devotion, and his pure paradise, the "Western Heaven," the goal to which the pious may aspire. Nirvana and Gautama Buddha are almost forgotten.

It was Mahayana Buddhism which was introduced into China in the year A.D. 65 in the reign of Han Ming Ti, of the Later Han dynasty. The Hinayana system, though known to the Chinese, never gained any wide currency in the Far East, and died out there altogether in the 10th century. Both forms of Buddhism are extinct in their native India, where they succumbed under the brutal impact of Islamic invasion and the subtle opposition of the ancient Hindu religion. According to Chinese history, the Emperor Han Ming Ti dreamed that there was a powerful divinity in the west, and sent an embassy to bring his cult to China. The ambassador travelled to India and returned with Buddhist images and Sanskrit books, which were translated into Chinese at Lo Yang by two Indian monks who had accompanied the envoy. These two Indians were Kasyapa-Matanga and Dharma-aranya, listed in the index of the authors of the Chinese *Tripitaka*, or collection of Buddhist Scriptures, as the first to translate Buddhist works into Chinese. They worked at the White Horse Monastery outside Lo Yang, so called from the white horse which carried the sacred books from India to China. This monastery, Pai Ma Ssŭ, or rather one upon the same site, still exists.

It is probable that some knowledge of Buddhism had already been acquired by the Chinese envoys to Central Asia and Bactria, for that region, now purely Mohammedan, was an early and active centre of Buddhism. It is even probable that the first Buddhist mission came from one of these countries, and not from India proper. The Han Emperors, as has been mentioned in an earlier chapter, were keen religious innovators, and were always prepared to welcome a new deity. But the welcome given by the Court to Buddhism remained without any influence on the nation as a whole in the Han period. Buddhism was a curiosity of the capital, its teaching was in the hands of foreigners, and it does not appear to have exercised any notable influence either on the masses or upon the educated class, which was strongly Confucian. This early imperial patronage of foreign monks is exactly comparable to the welcome accorded to the first Catholic missionaries by the last Ming Emperors and their first successors of the Manchu dynasty. In both cases the first contact led to no visible results.

The translation of Buddhist works and the propagation of the faith in the Han period were almost entirely the work of foreigners. Only one Chinese author or translator appears in the list. The others were drawn from a variety of nations in Central Asia, Indians, Turanians, Parthians, Kushans, like the equally international recruitment of the ranks of the Christian Missionaries in modern China. The vogue of Buddhism was in fact confined to the Court, and its teaching firmly opposed by the Confucian scholar class, who formed the dominant party among the educated and had the administration of the empire in their hands. Had the centralised empire endured, relying as it did on this scholar class, it is probable that Buddhism would never have taken firm root in China, and would have withered away as Nestorian Christianity, introduced and flourishing in the T'ang dynasty (7th to 10th centuries) disappeared, leaving as its only record the famous Ch'ang An tablet.

The fall of the Han Empire, and the partitions and barbarian invasions which followed, opened the road to Buddhism, and effected a religious revolution which was the most significant development in what the historians of Confucian tradition describe as an "Age of Confusion." While Indian translators, assisted by an increasing number of Chinese colleagues, continued to work upon the vast task of rendering the Sanskrit originals into Chinese, the northern Tartar dynasts extended their favour to Buddhist monks in the conquered provinces. The Confucian scholars had for the most part fled south when Lo Yang fell. Those who remained in the north were not favoured by the invaders, who rightly suspected this class of secret loyalty to the Chinese Emperor and hostility to the conquerors. The new sovereigns, needing the assistance of a literate class, found in the Buddhists and Taoists, who had been the opponents of the orthodox Confucians, a body of scholarly men who were trustworthy and loyal.

In the 4th and 5th centuries A.D. there was an immense expansion of Buddhism in northern China. This area being in contact with the Central Asiatic trade route, by which communication with India was made, it was naturally the region to which the Indian missionaries of Buddhism paid the greatest attention. The petty kingdoms of northern China under their short-lived Tungus and Hun dynasties were distinguished in the richness and productivity of their Buddhist schools, by which alone they are remembered. At Ch'ang An in A.D. 401-412, then the capital of the small state of Later Chin, the celebrated Kumarajiva, a monk of Indian descent born in Central Asia, worked and taught, spreading the doctrines of new schools of Buddhism, hitherto unknown in China.

Nevertheless the Buddhists did not enjoy uninterrupted favour. Inspired usually by Taoist opposition, persecutions were directed against them in all the states of China, but, fortunately for Buddhism, the persecutions were not simultaneous, and did not endure for long. In A.D. 446 the ruler of Wei, the northern empire, issued an edict against the Buddhists, but as his rival in the Chinese Empire was prepared to receive them, the monks were able to escape its effects. A few years later Buddhism was at the height of its favour in Wei, and was enjoying the fruitful patronage of the great Buddhist Emperor Liang Wu Ti of the southern Chinese Empire. These persecutions never resembled those so familiar from western religious history. There were no burnings, no torture or massacre of the faithful. At most the authorities ordered the destruction of some or all of the monasteries, and forced monks and nuns to return to family life, sometimes by the expedient, repugnant to all good Buddhists, of mating the monks and nuns themselves.

These ineffective and intermittent persecutions failed to arrest the progress of the new religion. In A.D. 405 the historians confess that nine out of every ten families in the northern empire had embraced the Buddhist faith. The proportion is significant, for the non-Buddhist tenth fairly represents the educated class of Confucian scholars and Taoist sectaries who alone remained detached from the new religion. The mass of the people, finding in Buddhism a religion which offered them in the next world all that they lacked in their present existence, had adopted the practice of the foreign faith, even if the dogma and theory were but little understood.

A hundred years later, in A.D. 500, it is admitted that the whole of China, north and south alike, was Buddhist. That is to say, Buddhist rites and ceremonies were everywhere practised; temples and monasteries had arisen in every district; priests and nuns were numerous and highly respected. A few Confucian scholars refused for themselves the salvation which their own families and particularly the women, eagerly embraced. The Taoists, borrowing shamelessly from the rival religion, maintained a more effective opposition.

It would be a mistake to represent this national conversion as a complete break with the religious past, such as marked the conversion of the Roman Empire to Christianity. Strange as it may seem to westerners, the Chinese have a capacity for believing, or at least honouring, several apparently incompatible doctrines at the same time. It is the most remarkable manifestation of the national gift for compromise. At the present time the vast majority of Chinese honour Confucius, worship Amida Buddha, and use

Taoist rites without any sense of incompatibility. "Three ways to one goal" they say. It would, however, be incorrect to treat this attitude as a mere materialist desire to be on the safe side, a kind of triple insurance against calamity.

In the Far East religion has never assumed the categorical absolutism of the western religions deriving from Judaism. Neither Buddha, nor Confucius, nor the Taoist sages ever said: "Thou shalt have none other gods but me." Buddhism, in its Mahayana form, accepts, and at the same time ignores, the complicated pantheon of Hinduism. The gods exist, but the worship of them is not the best way to escape from the cycle of reincarnation and attain everlasting repose in the Western Paradise. Confucius, who undoubtedly revered the deities of his own time, refrained from proclaiming them as the only true gods, perhaps because alien systems were unknown to him. For the men of his time worship of the gods consisted in the strict fulfilment of certain ritual acts, and was not associated with ideas of personal salvation. Taoism, in becoming a religion rather than a philosophy accepted any and every deity and made them its own, with an appropriate place and function in the celestial hierarchy. Buddha himself did not escape this fate.

It is significant that this tolerant attitude was never adopted by the Chinese converts to Islam. The Mohammedan Chinese regard all their Buddhist, Confucian and Taoist compatriots as "unbelievers" with whom the Moslem will not intermarry. True to the exclusive attitude which Islam borrowed from Judaism, they remain a class apart.

Buddhism, therefore, although accepted by the Chinese people did not displace the older gods and the worship of the ancestral, spirits. The Buddhist emperors continued to worship Heaven, and the gods of the soil and grain. Taoism enriched its pantheon with Buddhist and Hindu deities of Indian origin. Nevertheless, early Chinese Buddhism retained its corporate character and regarded the native systems as opponents. The priesthood were perhaps exclusively Buddhist, venerating only the Three Precious Ones, Buddha, The Law, and the Priesthood. The present tolerance which has wholly submerged Buddhism in a tripartite system in which Confucianism and Taoism hold equal rank, had not then quenched the faith and vigour of the missionary priests.

The translation of Sanskrit books was continued by a succession of monks and laymen, both Indian and Chinese, and with the wider knowledge of Sanskrit, the literary quality of the translations, which had at first been poor, began to improve. Earnest pilgrims, not content with the partial versions known in China, undertook hazardous voyages across the breadth of Asia in search of purer sources. In A.D. 399 Fa Hsien, a Chinese monk of Ch'ang An, travelled across Central Asia to India, and has left a valuable record of his wanderings.* After passing through the region known to-day as Chinese Turkestan, where he found Buddhism in a flourishing state, the pilgrim crossed the Hindu Kush and made his way into India through Afghanistan. At that time, before the rise of Islam, the region now famous for its fanatical Mohammedanism was a centre of Buddhism, the cities adorned with pagodas and monasteries from which some of the most famous doctors of the faith had come. In India itself, Buddhism, though still an active force, was already showing signs of the decay which ultimately destroyed it. Many of the famous sites and centres of Buddhist learning were already desolate or dying.

After several years in India Fa Hsien sailed from Bengal to Ceylon, then as now, a country of Hinayana Buddhism. From Ceylon the adventurous pilgrim took ship for Java which he reached after narrowly escaping shipwreck. This country was not Buddhist at that time. At last Fa Hsien returned to China by sea, landing on the Shantung coast after a perilous voyage, in which, the captain having lost his reckoning, the travellers passed seventy days at sea without sighting land, and finally reached the Chinese coast hundreds of miles north of their proper destination, which was Canton. Fa Hsien had been fifteen years away from his native land. After his return he settled at Nanking, the capital of the southern empire, and devoted his remaining years to translating the numerous books which he had brought home through so many dangers.

*Several English translations exist. The best known is H. A. Giles' *The Travels of Fa Hsien*. Cambridge. 1923.

A hundred years later, Liang Wu Ti, the most famous Emperor of the southern Chinese realm, took Buddhism under his protection. By his orders and under his patronage the first *Tripitaka* or collection of all Buddhist scriptures was prepared and published in the year A.D. 517. Ten years later, the Emperor himself, in spite of the protests of the Court, enrolled himself as a monk and entered a monastery at the capital.* He was only persuaded with difficulty to return to the throne, and insisted on paying the monks a large sum as a ransom for leaving their order. Two years later, in A.D. 529, he once more renounced the world, and was again persuaded to leave the monastery after paying a further large ransom. Confucian historians console themselves by pointing out that this great ruler by neglecting his empire exposed it to the perils of rebellion and himself died at the age of 86, when the capital had fallen into the hands of a soldier of fortune. In the northern empire Buddhism was honoured in equal measure. In A.D. 533 Hsiao Wu, ruler of the Wei state, then dominant in the north, issued a second edition of the *Tripitaka*, shortly after the Empress Hu of this dynasty, a fervent Buddhist, had spent vast sums in building temples and monasteries.

As the knowledge of Sanskrit works translated into Chinese spread, the Chinese monks obtained a better understanding of the diverse schools of doctrine into which Indian Buddhism had long been divided. Many of these schools were introduced into China and some developed new branches on purely Chinese initiative. Of these the most distinctive was the Ch'an, a Chinese name for the Indian Dhyana. The Ch'an School claim that their system was founded by the Indian monk Boddhidarma, who was living at Lo Yang between A.D. 516 and 534. It is, however, more than doubtful whether Boddhidarma, who is described in a contemporary account as a Persian, was in reality as important a person as the Ch'an believed. His life story, as preserved in Ch'an tradition, is almost wholly legendary, although some of the details, such as his miraculous passage of the Yangtze on a reed, have become

*This monastery is traditionally supposed to be Chi Ming Ssu, the "Cock Crow Monastery" which still exists, although the present buildings are of later date. It is on a hill overlooking the Hsuan Wu Lake, above the Academia Sinica. The palace of the Six Dynasties covered the area to the south of this hill.

famous folk tales, and have inspired a long succession of artists.*

The Ch'an school laid the greatest stress upon contemplation as the only and essential road to enlightenment. The duty of man was to discover, by contemplation, the germ of Buddhahood, which lies latent in every human being. As soon as this discovery is made, the enlightened one attains the status of a Buddha in this life, without needing a reincarnation. The school cared little for theology, and avoided written tracts, relying on the personal oral teaching of master and disciple. It was vigorously opposed by all the other schools, who regarded its tenets as heretical. Nevertheless, the Ch'an school flourished both in China and, later, in Japan.

There can be little doubt that, although certain Ch'an tenets were of Buddhist origin, much of the theory and practice of the sect came from Chinese Taoism. Indeed, stripped of its Buddhist terminology, Ch'an seems to bear a very close resemblance to the Taoist teaching of Chuang Tzŭ and the *Tao Tê Ching*. Already, by the 6th century, the pervasive force of Chinese thought was colouring Indian Buddhism with a native hue, but Indian schools and sects continued to win converts and enjoy high favour at the Courts of the Buddhist Emperors of that period.

In A.D. 563 the Indian monk Paramartha introduced the only Hinayana school which flourished in China. This school, known in India as Sarvastivida, and in China as Chiu Shê Tsung, was conservative, clinging to the Hinayana doctrines which were regarded as the most authentic tradition of Gautama's teaching. Although this school made some appeal to scholars and intellectuals, it never captured the popular approval and died out in the 10th century, when the rise of what was in fact a new religion, Amidism, the worship of Amida Buddha, changed the whole character of Chinese Buddhism.

Towards the end of the period of partition Chih K'ai, a Chinese monk of the great monastery at T'ien T'ai, near Ning Po in Chekiang province, founded the purely Chinese school which is

*The question of Boddhidarma and his life has been elucidated by Prof. P. Pelliot. *T'oung Pao*. Vol. XXIII. p. 253.

Ch'an Buddhism, introduced into Japan, has played an important part in that country, where it is known as the Zen School.

usually known as T'ien T'ai, and in Japanese Tendai. The tenets of this school clearly reflect its Chinese origin. Chih K'ai tried to reconcile the diverse accounts of Buddha's teaching by a compromise which treated the texts as a series, each proper only to its context. Apparent contradictions could thus be explained by interpreting the text in accordance with the supposed occasion of its delivery and the matter with which it dealt. The teaching could be divided into an early and developed doctrine, which had gradually been expounded to the disciples as their enlightenment progressed. It further reconciled the Mahayana theory of ultimate Buddhahood for true believers by teaching that every man had in him the capacity to attain Buddhahood if he nourished this side of his nature.

The influence of Confucian ideas on the interpretation of difficult and inconvenient texts by some theory of the occasion on which they were uttered, is plain in the teaching of the T'ien T'ai school. Perhaps on account of its attitude of compromise, it made a wide appeal to the Chinese and became one of the most flourishing schools of Buddhism in the Far East. It was not until the 14th century, when Amidism had almost entirely replaced early Buddhism, that the T'ien T'ai school began to decline. Chih K'ai, its founder, an able and fluent writer, died in A.D. 597 shortly after the reunion of the empire under the Sui dynasty.

Amidism, the ultimately dominant school of Buddhism, or rather the new religion which displaced the traditional Buddhism of the early period, was introduced into China during these centuries, but did not at first meet with much favour. It was not until the monk Kumarajiva translated the work known to the Chinese as the Amida Classic* that the new cult began to spread. Further works translated a few years later helped to popularise the Amida cult, which soon captured the imagination of the people, who found the obscure and transcendental philosophies of the other schools too difficult.

Amidism substitutes for the original, authentic Gautama, Amida, or Amitabha, a personage unknown to early Buddhist dogma. He is not a man, but a deity born of a lotus, in the

*A Mi To Ching, in Sanskrit Sukhavati-vyuha.

marvellous paradise Sukhavati, which the Chinese call *Hsi T'ien*, the Western Heaven. The road to salvation is no longer the arduous life of abstention and contemplation which Gautama had preached. To escape the torments of hell and be reborn in the Western Paradise it is only necessary to invoke the name of Amida. A higher ideal was indeed offered to those who found this simple rule of life too easy. The new ideal was no longer Nirvana, the extinction of desire and the relief of all suffering, it was to become a Buddha by devoting the whole activity of terrestrial life to benevolence towards all men. Thus, Kuan Shih Yin or Kuan Yin, originally the Bodhisattva Avalokitesvara, became a goddess of mercy "who hears the cry of the world," as the Chinese name indicates. She is the compassionate Bodhisattva who, when about to enter into Buddhahood, turned back to listen to the cry of suffering which rose up from the earth, and vowed to postpone her own eternal deification until every living creature had been raised in the scale of existence to her own sublime elevation.

Three other major Bodhisattvas share the veneration paid to Kuan Yin, although their functions and characters are not very clearly differentiated from hers. Ti Tsang (Kshitigarbha) is the divinity who, renouncing Buddhahood as Kuan Yin had done, devotes his existence to alleviating the suffering of souls condemned to pass æons in hell. The Buddhist doctrine does not admit of eternal punishment, but erring souls are condemned to suffer torments in hell for very long ages to expiate the crimes they commit on earth. Ti Tsang has power over Yen Wang, the King of Hell, and can deliver or mitigate the tortures of the damned. Wên Shu (Manjusri) and P'u Hsien are associated in China with the sacred mountains Omei in Szechuan and Wu T'ai Shan in Shansi respectively. They too are Bodhisattvas who renounced Buddhahood in order to assist imperfect mankind in the long ascent to divinity. Maitreya, in Chinese Mi Lo Fo, often called the "laughing Buddha" is not strictly speaking either a Buddha or a Bodhisattva. He is the Buddha to come, who will be reborn on earth for the last time as a Bodhisattva, who like Gautama will achieve the supreme height in that existence.

Amidism, in which the cult of these Bodhisattvas plays a conspicuous part, did not gain the ascendency it now enjoys until several centuries after the period of partition, when it was first introduced into China. Constantly advancing in popular favour, it was at first disregarded in scholarly circles, and it was not until the 10th century, at the end of the T'ang dynasty, that the cult of Amida Buddha outstripped all others.

The reunion of the north and south under the Sui dynasty in A.D. 589 and the consolidation of a second unified empire by the T'ang in A.D. 618 gave Buddhism a new impetus. Although Confucian scholars attempted to enforce measures limiting the number of priests and monasteries, their efforts met with only fleeting success, and Buddhism flourishing under the patronage of the Court, became established as a national religion which continued to throw out vigorous new branches. The Sui sovereigns ordered the publication of three new editions of the *Tripitaka* in the short space of two decades. Early in the T'ang dynasty the celebrated pilgrim Yüan Chuang* set out on a voyage to India as famous as that of his predecessor Fa Hsien.

Starting from Ch'ang An, Yüan Chuang made his way across Turkestan to Samarkand. Most of these countries were still strongly Buddhist, as they had been two hundred years before in Fa Hsien's day. Yüan Chuang travelled into India by way of Afghanistan, where he found Buddhism flourishing. He visited Kashmir, and was hospitably entertained at the Court of the King. After a long stay in this country he went on to Central India, where he visited and described the Court of the great Hindu King, Harshavardhana or Siladitya, at Kanauj, not far from the modern Lucknow in the United Provinces. Siladitya had heard of the fame and glory of the great T'ang T'ai Tsung, the real founder of the T'ang dynasty, who was then on the throne. He treated Yüan Chuang with great consideration, and made many inquiries about China and its famous ruler. The pilgrim, who was a man of good family and personally acquainted with the Emperor, was able to answer these questions with many details.

*Also called Hsüan Tsang, and Hiuen Tsang in French works. Several translations of this work have been made in English and French. T. Watters, *Yüan Chuang's Travels in India*, Royal Asiatic Society, London, 1904, is the most recent.

After an absence of sixteen years Yüan Chuang returned to China by the land route, bringing with him no less than 657 Indian texts, a number of images of the saints and Buddhas made of precious material and curious workmanship, and 150 "genuine" relics of the Buddha. It is not often that one finds so well documented an account of the introduction of new artistic influences as this importation of Indian and Central Asiatic works of art. Yüan Chuang also brought back to China the teaching of a new school, the Madhyamayana, which preached a subjective idealism. The ego alone is real, the universe, being the product of thought, is imaginary. This school had a certain success in the T'ang period, but died out under the constant pressure of the all-conquering Amidism.

Yüan Chuang, who was received with great honours on his return, enjoyed the favour and friendship of the Emperor T'ai Tsung, and spent the rest of his days at the labour of translating the books he had brought from India, and in composing, at the Emperor's wish, a record of his travels. He died, nineteen years after his return to China, in A.D. 664.

The Hua Yen Tsung, another school which appealed to many Chinese by reason of its agreement with certain ideas already well known from Taoist writers, was propagated by the Chinese monk, Tu Shun, a contemporary of Yüan Chuang, though a much older man. He died at the age of 84, in A.D. 640. His school claimed to preach the higher and complete doctrine of Buddhism. It accepted the Mahayanist belief in a multitude of Buddhas, past and future, and the doctrine, taken up by Amidism, that all may become Buddha in the course of time. Its principal tenet, which agreed with Taoist philosophy, was the belief in an absolute unity transcending all divergencies, in which even contraries were seen to be but forms of the Primal One.

The speculative philosophy of these schools before long provoked a positive reaction among the practical minded Chinese. Tao Hsüan, who died A.D. 667, was also a contemporary of Yüan Chuang. He founded the Lu Tsung, a purely Chinese school which returned to the primitive Buddhist standpoint. Philosophic speculation was decried as contrary to the true teaching of Buddha. Leaving theory aside, Tao Hsüan and his disciples concentrated on the practice of benevolence. The duty of the true Buddhist they declared, was to purify the heart, then the actions, to practise charity and to arrive at the profession of universal benevolence. These ideas bear a strong Confucian impress. On that account, perhaps, the Lu Tsung has always appealed to Chinese Buddhists and succeeded in resisting the influence of Amidism and maintaining itself to the present time. Its influence on morality and public conduct has been considerable and beneficent. With the decay of other schools under the influence of Amidism this doctrine gradually gathered to itself all the more intellectual elements of Chinese Buddhism.

In the next century, the last important addition to the schools of early Buddhism was made by two Indian monks, Vajrabodhi, a Brahman by caste, who worked between A.D. 719-732 and his disciple Amogha, also a Brahman, who died in China in A.D. 774. These Indians were responsible for introducing Tantrism, the form of Buddhism which has conserved the greatest part of pre-Buddhistic Hinduism. Strongly influenced by Yogi doctrine and the cult of Siva, the sect makes use of formulæ of magic power called in Hindi, *mantra;* in Chinese, *chên yen* "true words," and of the Yogi respiratory exercises which produce self hypnotism. It recognises a kind of trinity composed of Gautama Buddha, Amida, and Vairocana, who form a single Buddha. This sect also venerates Siva and his bride Vajrapati and numerous other Indian deities and demons. It has had a considerable influence, of an unfortunate kind, on Chinese superstition, and still flourishes. In reality, Tantrism is only Buddhist in name, being a compound of Sivaism and other Hindu cults, with a flavour of Buddhism and a foundation of still more ancient animism. Amogha, who was mainly responsible for its success in China, made a voyage to Ceylon and India to obtain the books of his sect. On his return he enjoyed high favour, was given titles and the rank of minister and spent his life in translating the books which he had brought from the west.

By the end of the T'ang dynasty Buddhism, considerably modified by Chinese ideas and beliefs, had won a lasting place in Chinese culture, from which it has never been displaced. Although constantly opposed by Confucian scholars such as Han

Yü (A.D. 768-824) in the T'ang period, and a long succession of men in later ages, the mass of the people accepted Buddhism after their fashion, and gave Buddha an equal place with the national sages and deities. Although the Court favoured Buddhism, and largely endowed monasteries and temples, the Buddhist Church, perhaps on account of its own divisions and loose organisation never acquired political power and domination comparable to the Christian Churches in Europe. Even at the height of Buddhist fervour, the political power remained in the hands of laymen who were Confucian in training, even if Buddhist in sympathy and the practice of daily life.

PART FOUR—THE T'ANG EMPIRE

Chapter XIII

THE RESTORATION OF UNITY

THE consolidation of the T'ang dynasty, which succeeded the short-lived Sui, is a turning point in the history of China, marking the second foundation of a centralised empire of long duration. Chinese historians have been accustomed to divide the history of their country into dynastic periods, regarding the ruler who governed the largest domain as legitimate Emperor of all China, even when other princes had seized upon wide provinces. This treatment of Chinese history has usually been adopted, for convenience sake, by western writers, but it is apt to convey an erroneous idea of the development of the Chinese monarchy.

As was mentioned in Chapter XI, the "dynasties" of the period of division which followed the downfall of the Han Empire were tor the most part military dictatorships founded by usurpers who rarely governed more than a few provinces, and only transmitted their power to their immediate descendants. These rulers never enjoyed the authority and prestige which the Han Emperors had wielded, no enduring sentiment of loyalty to an established imperial house bound their subjects to them. They resemble rather the dictators of the South American Republics or the Tuchuns of republican China, and to compare them on an equal footing with the long-established sovereigns of the Han and T'ang dynasties is to misconceive the character of the true dynasties founded by Liu Pang of the Han and Li Shih-min of the T'ang.

The fact that every ruler of part or of all China has assumed the title of Emperor, and the regime he set up—even when it endured for little more than a decade—has been treated as a dynasty, has obscured the history of the Chinese throne and led to the mistaken idea that in all ages the functions and authority of the Emperor were identical. An historian who argued that as Alfred and George the First were both Kings of England, therefore the English monarchy had remained an immutable institution for a thousand years, would be treated with contempt in the west, but an Asiatic unacquainted with European history might be deceived. It is hardly less inaccurate to portray the Han, Liang,

T'ang and subsequent dynasties as an unchanging repetition of the same political system.

The second centralised empire founded in China, the T'ang, differed in many important respects from its predecessor, the Han. The difficulties under which the emperors of the Han dynasty laboured have been discussed in Chapters VII and XI: the compromise with a feudal system, which though dying, still had the support of influential classes; the constant struggle against the ambitions and usurpations of the consort families; the power of the palace eunuchs, which the emperors themselves fostered as a barrier to the ambitions of the consort families, but which in the end brought the dynasty to ruin. All these difficulties arose primarily from the lack of a sound moral title to the throne, which the Han dynasty, sprung from a soldier of fortune, did not enjoy. To the very end of the dynasty the imperial family were regarded as the posterity of an illiterate peasant adventurer, and as such, no better than their rivals.

The T'ang suffered from none of these disadvantages. In A.D. 617 the Sui dynasty, founded thirty-six years earlier by the Chinese general Yang Chien, who reunited the empire (A.D. 589), collapsed owing to the misgovernment of his son, Yang Ti. This second Emperor of the Sui was a megalomaniac who destroyed his father's work by excessive extravagance, unnecessary and unsuccessful wars with Korea, and tyrannous misgovernment. In the anarchy which broke out in protest against his misrule, the newly won unity of the empire disappeared, and would certainly have perished, perhaps for ever, had it not been for the genius of one man, Li Shih-min, the real founder of the T'ang. A long era of division and turmoil made the idea of reunion remote and almost unacceptable to the well-established sectional interests which had grown up under the partition.

The significance of Li Shih-min's work can be appreciated by a comparison between the course of European history and that of China after the Han Empire. In both regions the first centralised Empire which had embraced the civilised world collapsed under internal disorder and barbarian invasion. In both the fall of the empire was followed by four centuries of division and strife. In Europe Charlemagne revived, briefly, the fallen empire, and for a time it seemed that the newly restored unity would survive. In China the same task was performed by the Sui dynasty. But whereas in Europe the Holy Roman Empire withered and became an empty name, covering an ever increasing separatism, in China the T'ang dynasty completed the work which the Sui had failed to maintain and made unity the enduring pattern of the Chinese political system.

Li Shih-min, a youth of sixteen when the Sui power collapsed, was the son of a provincial governor, descended from an illustrious family of North China, which had intermarried with the Tartar aristocracy of the immigrant conquerors. Forcing his timid and hesitant father, Li Yüan, to revolt against the Sui, Li Shih-min in seven years of violent and intricate civil war destroyed his numerous competitors and reunited the whole of China, although his father exercised the titular sovereignty. After his own accession in A.D. 627 he repulsed and dispersed the Turkish hordes menacing the northern provinces, and during the twenty-two years of his reign reorganised the empire to which he had brought peace and unity. His work was so well done that he left an administration obedient to the throne and capable of withstanding many calamities.

The personality of Li Shih-min conferred upon his descendants a prestige which the Han sovereigns never acquired, and the high rank of his family contributed to give the Li a moral title to sovereignty which long outlasted the real power of the throne. The house was accepted from the first as worthy to rule, by virtue of intermarriage with two previous dynasties, the Sui and the Northern Chou,* and the importance of the official positions which members of the family had filled under the various dynasties ruling in the north. For these reasons they were acceptable to their former equals, the scholars and generals of the fallen Sui Empire.

It was the immense personal prestige of the founder, Li Shih-min, which secured to the T'ang dynasty a moral title to the

*The Li, and the imperial families of Sui and Northern Chou had all intermarried with the Tu Ku family, descended from Tartar invaders. The Li were directly descended from the sovereign Princes of West Liang, a small state founded in Kansu after the fall of the Tsin dynasty. They claimed to be the descendants of Li Kuang, a famous general of the Emperor Wu of the Han dynasty.

FIG. 46. *The Emperor T'ang T'ai Tsung. After an engraved stele formerly at Chao Lin, Shensi.*

throne which remained unchallenged for generations. He had appeared as the man of destiny, to whom no task seemed impossible, the saviour of society, the restorer of unity and peace. In China where the pen has always been held in higher honour than the sword, the merits of Li Shih-min as a scholar and administrator counted for as much as his prowess in war. The long peace which his conquests and administration secured fostered the arts and literature, for which this dynasty is famous. So dynamic was his personality that he inspired all who came into contact with him, and became a legend with posterity. He has had no equal on the throne of China.*

Li Shih-min (Fig. 46), known in history under the posthumous title T'ai Tsung, died in A.D. 649, at the early age of forty-nine, but his work had been so well done that China enjoyed internal

---

*For an account of the life and times of Li Shih-min and the foundation of the T'ang Dynasty see C. P. Fitzgerald, *Son of Heaven.* Cambridge University Press, 1932.

peace for more than a century after his death. This happy result was in part due to the singular fortune of the T'ang dynasty which was ruled in turn by two outstanding personalities, worthy to carry on the tradition of the great T'ai Tsung. The Empress Wu, and her grandson the Emperor Ming Huang successively governed China in the age which the T'ang poets have immortalised. Orthodox Chinese historians, shocked at the spectacle of a woman openly governing the empire in contravention of all the Confucian theories of sovereignty, have not done justice to the Empress Wu, and, since they cannot deny the excellence of her administration, have concentrated their criticisms on her private life, which was not beyond reproach.

The career of this famous woman well illustrates the new prestige which surrounded the imperial throne, and marks the essential difference between the character of the monarchy in the Han and T'ang eras. Wu Chao entered the palace at the age of twelve in A.D. 637 as concubine to T'ai Tsung. At the Emperor's death, in accordance with custom, she, together with all the concubines of the deceased ruler, entered a Buddhist convent, where with shaven head she was expected to pass the rest of her life. Wu Chao was too intelligent and too beautiful to accept this fate. Profiting by the visit of ceremony which the new Emperor Kao Tsung paid to the convent, she won his heart, and achieved the unprecedented fortune of escaping from this living death, and returning to the palace as concubine of Kao Tsung, to become in time his full consort and acknowledged Empress.

Kao Tsung was good-natured, but lazy and weak. He soon resigned the entire direction of affairs to his consort, who wielded undisputed power throughout his long reign (A.D. 649-683). After his death she openly assumed the sovereignty during the purely nominal reign of her son, the Emperor Chung Tsung. It was not until A.D. 705, when old and ailing, that the famous Empress was compelled to resign her power in his favour and pass the last months of her life in that retirement to which the laws would have condemned her fully fifty years earlier. She died in the same year at the great age of eighty-one.

The Han dynasty had offered only too many examples of an ambitious Empress seizing the authority of a weak Emperor, but the career of the Empress Wu is notable for the very different consequences which followed. Never, in all her long rule, did she entrust the administration to her own relatives, and, although she flirted with the idea of transmitting the throne to her own family, she found that the formidable opposition which the plan aroused made the execution of this design impossible. As consort of the Emperor, or as Empress Dowager, the official world willingly consented to her usurped authority, recognising her great qualities and the incapacity of the rightful prince, but her most devoted ministers were unalterably opposed to any attempt to transfer the throne to her own family. Considering the long duration of her undivided power this fact is a most striking testimony to the immense prestige which Li Shih-min had transmitted to his posterity.

Chung Tsung (A.D. 683-710), her son, was an incapable ruler who had passed the greater part of his life as an impotent state prisoner. Suddenly restored to the real authority he proved quite unfitted to bear his new responsibilities. During the five years that followed the death of the Empress Wu the Court was convulsed by the intrigues of the ladies of the palace and the princes of the imperial family who endeavoured in turn to dominate the Emperor. Fortunately this dangerous interval did not endure long enough to impair the administration of the provinces, which remained tranquil and obedient under the efficient officers appointed by the Empress Wu. In A.D. 710 the Emperor was poisoned by his consort, who hoped to occupy the place left vacant by the Empress Wu.

This design was frustrated by the emergence of the third great personality of the early T'ang period, Li Lung-chi, who later reigned as the Emperor Ming Huang, posthumously known as Hsüan Tsung. Li Lung-chi was the nephew of Chung Tsung, and grandson of the Empress Wu by her second son, Li Tan. Seizing the palace by a *coup d'état*, he made his father Emperor, and on his abdication two years later ascended the throne himself. His long reign (A.D. 712-756) secured the empire another forty years of peace, a celebrated half-century enriched by the lives of the greatest Chinese poets and famous artists who received the patronage of this cultivated ruler.

The reign of Ming Huang would be without question one of the most glorious in Chinese history had it not been darkened at the end by the great rebellion of the Tartar general, An Lu-shan, which ended the long internal peace of 132 years and wrecked the administrative machine of the T'ang Empire. In poetry and drama Ming Huang has been immortalised not for his long and successful rule of forty-four years, but for the romance of his love for the beautiful Yang Kuei Fei, his concubine, which was the prelude to the rebellion of An Lu-shan. This story, however, regarded in its historical as opposed to its romantic aspects, bears a somewhat different interpretation. Yang Kuei Fei may have been as beautiful as the poets would have us believe, but the Emperor himself was a man of seventy-two when he was forced to sacrifice his favourite to the fury of the soldiers. This fact, though it diminishes the romantic quality of the story, does much to explain the political catastrophe of which this infatuation was one of the causes.

The true story of the romance of Ming Huang and Yang Kuei Fei, the facts of history, are not very edifying. In A.D. 745, the Emperor, then over sixty, was attracted by the beauty of the wife of his son, Prince Shou. He forced the Prince to divorce his wife, gave him another bride in compensation, and took the famous Yang Kuei Fei into his own harem. Yang Kuei Fei soon managed to acquire a complete domination over her aged consort. It was through her influence that An Lu-shan rose to the highest favour and obtained the power to organise his terrible revolt.

An Lu-shan was a Turk of the Kitan tribe, of very obscure origin, born beyond the Wall in the country of Liao Tung (South Manchuria). At an early age he was captured or sold as a slave to a Chinese officer in a northern garrison. Showing some ability in war he was promoted in time to the rank of officer, and finally became a general. Grossly fat, with a simple ingenuous manner which concealed a shrewd cunning, he ingratiated himself by flattering the Emperor and amusing him with clumsy gaffs and clownery. His pretence of simple uncouth barbarism, and ignorance of etiquette became one of the standing jokes of the gay Court, particularly amusing to the favourite, Yang Kuei Fei. She took An Lu-shan under her protection, and even adopted him as her son. The Emperor, who regarded the Turk as a good-natured buffoon, accorded him high favours to please his mistress. An Lu-shan was allowed to visit the concubine in the inner palace, an unheard of privilege, and even took part in private dinner parties at which only the Emperor and Yang Kuei Fei were present. At gay fêtes and festivals the uncouth general submitted to ridiculous and even indecent practical jokes at the hands of the ladies of the palace. The Emperor, completely under the sway of Yang Kuei Fei, made no objection, and, indeed, was highly amused. Even the spread of scandalous rumours connecting the general and Yang Kuei Fei left him unmoved.

An Lu-shan, for his part, obtained increased honours. He was made governor of the frontier province of Liao Tung, in charge of the best troops in the empire. In A.D. 750 he was made a second-class Prince, although this title was reserved by law for members of the imperial family. Meanwhile the concubine's brother Yang Kuo-chung had become first minister of the empire, ousting his predecessor through the influence of his sister. He now became jealous of the power of An Lu-shan, and, perhaps genuinely, declared that he suspected the Turk of intending to revolt. The Emperor treated such insinuations as nonsense, and, when the minister and even the Crown Prince insisted, he summoned An Lu-shan to Court, the surest way of putting his loyalty to the test. The Turk, whose preparations were incomplete, promptly obeyed, and, with tears, protested his loyalty at the Emperor's feet, repudiating the calumnies of his enemies. The Emperor, completely convinced, restored him to his high command with fresh honours (A.D. 752). Henceforward no representations, however urgent, however well supported with proofs, could shake his faith in Yang Kuei Fei's hideous adopted son.

Three years later, when the Court was least prepared for it, An Lu-shan threw off the mask. His success was immediate. The best troops of the empire were under his command, the other garrisons far distant. Marching from his base, the site of modern Peking, the rebel crossed the Yellow River, captured Lo Yang, the second capital of the empire, and, after defeating the army which the Emperor had hastily gathered against him at Ling Pao, captured the T'ung Kuan Pass and pressed straight on to the capital. The Court, distrusting the possibility of defending the enormous city with inadequate and unwarlike troops, fled precipitately towards Szechuan. An Lu-shan entered Ch'ang An unopposed.

When the imperial party, which had escaped too hastily to take provisions for the journey, reached the small post of Ma Wei, in west Shensi, the soldiers, hungry and dispirited, broke out in sudden mutiny. The minister, Yang Kuo-chung, was the first object of their rage. Seeing him in conversation with the Tibetan ambassador, or according to another account, addressing a party of Tibetan mercenaries, they raised the cry that he was betraying the state to the foreigners. Forthwith the infuriated mob set upon the minister and murdered him. The Emperor, alarmed by the tumult, attempted to calm the soldiers, but instead they cried insistently for the head of Yang Kuei Fei, sister of the hated minister, and patron of An Lu-shan. At last, when convinced by his terrified Court that nothing else could appease the turmoil, and that any refusal would cost him his own life, Ming Huang gave the order. Yang Kuei Fei was conducted by the chief eunuch to the pagoda in the village, and there strangled. This is the "everlasting wrong," the subject made famous by the poem of Po Chu-i, and countless tales and stage plays.

The rebellion of An Lu-shan made little progress after the fall of Ch'ang An. The Emperor, a broken man, fled to Szechuan and abdicated in favour of the Crown Prince. The new Emperor, Su Tsung, rallied the people of the north-west and obtained valuable aid from the foreign nations friendly to China. With a mixed army of Central Asiatics, Chinese, Turks, and even Arabs sent by the Caliph, the imperial commander-in-chief, Kuo Tzŭ-i, a man of great ability and unfailing loyalty, gradually obtained the ascendant. The war dragged on for ten years, even after An Lu-shan and his son had both been assassinated and replaced by other pretenders. Peace was finally restored in A.D. 766, but the empire had suffered irreparable harm from the war.

The actual loss of life is certainly exaggerated in the official histories, as will be shown in the next Chapter. The real damage done by the great rebellion was not so much to the population or even to the wealth of the north, but to the integrity of the administrative machine of the T'ang Empire and the strength of the state. It is certain that after the war the imperial throne never recovered the same authority over the provincial governors as it had exercised in the first 130 years of the dynasty. A full century was to pass before the T'ang Empire entered upon its final agony, but in this second T'ang period there is a marked change in the character of the government. Thanks to the established prestige of the imperial family, An Lu-shan and his followers were finally crushed, the Emperor returned to Ch'ang An, and peace was restored. Unfortunately, this result had only been obtained by giving the generals in charge of the war the fullest powers in the rebel provinces, and, after the end of the campaign, these powers could not easily or safely be withdrawn.

During the century between A.D. 766, when peace was established, and A.D. 868, when the empire entered into a period of intense strife, the prelude to its collapse, the Court was constantly contending against two besetting evils, hitherto unknown. On the one hand the empire suffered from the raids and invasions of its western neighbours, the Tibetans, and, on the other, the Court was frequently in conflict with powerful provincial governors, who, not content with exercising an absolute sway over their provinces, strove to transmit their power to their sons.

Both these dangers were the dragon's teeth sown by An Lu-shan's rebellion, for the regular army, which that rebel had led into revolt, was now destroyed. The frontiers were exposed to the barbarians, and the provincial armies, obeying their governors rather than the Court, could not be effectively controlled by the government. It was particularly in the eastern provinces which had been the seat of the great rebellion, and which had subsequently been handed over to the generals charged with suppressing it, that the new spirit of insubordination was most prevalent. The Court was compelled, for the sake of peace, to tolerate the great power of these viceroys, but it firmly opposed their efforts to make the succession to the viceroyalty hereditary.

The conflict between the policy of the Court, ever seeking to restore the central authority which it had formerly exercised, and the separatist tendencies of the eastern viceroys led to several insurrections, one of which, from A.D. 809-822, seriously menaced the throne, though for the most part they were local in their effects and soon appeased. These revolts were all confined to the eastern provinces, Shantung, Honan, and Hopei, while the Yangtze basin and southern provinces continued to enjoy the profound peace which had not been interrupted in those regions since the foundation of the dynasty. The long peace in the south had far-reaching consequences, for it was now that on this account the centre of gravity in the Chinese Empire slowly shifted from the ancient cultural centres in the north and west, too often disturbed by wars, to the fertile southern valleys which were becoming increasingly populous. The T'ang dynasty is the last era of the greatness of the north-western provinces, the famous "land within the passes" which had been the cradle of the centralised empire. The rise of the south truly dates from this period, and it is not surprising that the Cantonese to this day use the expression *T'ang jên*, "man of T'ang," to denote the Chinese race, whereas in other parts of China the old term *Han jên*, "man of Han," is still used.

The second difficulty against which the emperors of the later T'ang period had to contend was the sustained hostility of the Tibetans, their western neighbours. It is noteworthy that during this century the northern borders, which in other ages had been subject to the raids of the nomads of the steppes, were very little troubled. The break up of the Turkish hordes which had followed the conquests of Li Shih-min had left lasting divisions among the nomads, and no formidable united power developed in the Mongolian steppes until the very end of the dynasty. The new enemies came from the west. The Tibetan tribes had coalesced into a strong kingdom in the early years of the T'ang Empire, and during the reign of Ming Huang there had been several clashes with their warlike kings. After the rebellion of An Lu-shan had weakened the frontier defence, the Tibetans invaded in great strength and actually captured and sacked Ch'ang An in A.D. 763, when the city had only recently been recaptured from the rebels.

During the second half of the 8th century and the first half of the 9th, the new western power made constant encroachments upon the Chinese border provinces until most of western Kansu, large parts of western Szechuan, and all the Central Asian territories which Li Shih-min had added to the empire, fell into their hands. The wars with these uneasy neighbours continued intermittently throughout this period, mostly to the disadvantage of the Chinese, until Tibetan expansion was brought to an end in A.D. 849 by the troubles which followed upon the extinction of their line of native kings. The Chinese were then able to recover their lost territories without much difficulty; but the long drain on the enfeebled resources of the Court was a contributing cause to the decline of the empire.

The Tibetans were not the only western enemies of the T'ang Empire. In the extreme south-west of what is now China, but was then outside the empire, the province of Yunnan, a warlike kingdom had come into being. Nan Chao, as this state was called, occupied the high plateaux of Yunnan and part of Kueichou, and throughout the last two centuries of the T'ang dynasty it opposed a powerful check to the advance of the Chinese in these provinces. The kingdom of Nan Chao in the T'ang period has the distinction of being the only example of prolonged and successful resistance organised by the aborigines of the south-west during their secular struggle with the invading Chinese.

In spite of the border wars with Tibet and Yunnan and the occasional revolts of the north-eastern viceroys, the period from A.D. 766 to A.D. 868 was one of relative peace and prosperity, particularly in the south. It was only gradually that the Court lost its power over the provinces. Had the dynasty been fortunate enough to produce a ruler of dominant character who could have reigned long enough to enforce a real reorganisation of the administration, the T'ang Empire might have recovered its strength in the later 9th century, when Tibetan aggression had ceased.

Unfortunately, although several of the later emperors were capable men, none had the fortune to reign for any length of time. Only one Emperor of the later T'ang period, Tê Tsung (A.D. 779-805), reigned for twenty years, and many of his successors were less than a decade on the throne. These frequent changes of reign prevented any ruler acquiring the experience and personal authority to dominate the great governors and reduce them to a proper obedience. A new Emperor, fearful of revolt, found it easier to confirm the existing viceroys in their positions in return for their allegiance. The great weakness of the Court was therefore due to the feeble health of the later T'ang Emperors, few of whom lived to be fifty, while many died well before reaching middle age.

In contrast to the last years of the Han dynasty, the T'ang Court was in the main free from the twin evils of eunuch domination and feminine intrigue. Not one of the later T'ang Empresses attempted to imitate the Empress Wu, or to elevate her own family at the expense of the reigning dynasty. This shows clearly the immense prestige which still attached to the royal blood of the Li clan. The eunuchs, though they gained in influence as the dynasty declined, never obtained the fatal ascendancy which had brought the Han dynasty to ruin. In the reign of Wên Tsung (A.D. 826-840) they did indeed endeavour to concentrate the power of the Court in their own hands, but the successors of Wên Tsung had the strength to oppose their plans and confine them to functions more proper to their condition.

The real reason why the eunuchs of the T'ang Court failed to acquire great power was less the opposition of the emperors than the condition of the provinces. As the 9th century wore on the viceroys became more powerful and less easily displaced by the authority of the Court. They still affected the manners of subjects, and paid respect to the Emperor, but the administration became more and more decentralised. The Court having less influence on the appointment of provincial officials, aspirants for a provincial post were not induced to flatter the eunuchs, even when they had great influence with the Emperor. The provincial officials were dependent upon the favour of the viceroys, and the eunuchs had little outside scope for the power they acquired at Court.

Up till the later years of the 9th century the T'ang Empire, though weakened by the consequences of An Lu-shan's rebellion, had preserved the unity of China and internal peace, more especially in the south, where for nearly 250 years the tranquillity established by Li Shih-min had remained undisturbed. There have been few periods in the history of the world when so large and so civilised an area has remained unafflicted by war for more than two centuries. However, the peace of the south and the stability of the T'ang Empire as a whole were both destroyed by the second great rebellion which finally shattered the power of the dynasty.

In A.D. 868 the army stationed on the Annam border to repel the incursions of the King of Nan Chao, mutinied in protest against its long sojourn in unhealthy country with little or no pay. The mutineers were northern troops, from the region of Kiangsu north of the Yangtze, for the inhabitants of the southern provinces had long lost the habit of arms. The rebel army, homesick for the north, marched back, looting all cities which refused to pay ransom. The Court, at first ignoring the danger, only sent troops to check them when the rebels had already crossed the Yangtze, and, having arrived in their homeland, found plenty of malcontents to swell their ranks.

The dilatory behaviour of the imperial generals, who were divided by jealousies, permitted the war to drag on in the eastern provinces for some years until a leader arose among the rebels, who suddenly took the offensive and swept victoriously over the country. Huang Tsao was an educated man who had failed to pass the examination for the civil service. In the ranks of rebellion he proved more successful. In A.D. 875 the rebels led by Huang Tsao invaded Honan, and moving south, over-ran Hupei, crossed the Yangtze, and penetrated through Kiangsi and Fukien to Canton, which they captured in A.D. 879. Throughout this invasion of the south they met with no effective opposition, for the Court, indifferent to a danger which appeared to be remote, retained the best troops in the north.

The climate of Kuangtung proved unhealthy for Huang Tsao's northern soldiers; decimated by disease they turned north and marched through Hunan to the Yangtze, but, after crossing the river, were severely defeated in Hupei. Had the imperial generals pursued the rebel army, Huang Tsao and his following would have been destroyed, but the indifference of the Court and the jealousies of the generals, who were more eager to obtain a rich province for themselves than to fight the enemy, prevented any concerted action, and permitted Huang Tsao to escape down the Yangtze and reorganise his forces. In A.D. 880 he passed the river again, and, moving through Anhui and Honan, approached the Court with great rapidity. The key to Shensi, T'ung Kuan, fell into his hands, and the rebel army advanced on the capital unopposed. In A.D. 881 Ch'ang An fell, and the Emperor, like Ming Huang, his predecessor, fled to Chêng Tu in Szechuan.

The fall of Ch'ang An in A.D. 881 was the real end of the T'ang Empire. Although the dynasty maintained a nominal existence for another twenty-seven years, the Emperor became the plaything of rival military leaders and provincial governors, who made war upon each other and divided up the empire between them. Huang Tsao's rebellion was put down, and the leader perished in A.D. 884; but, although the Emperor returned to ruined Ch'ang An, the wars between the viceroys continued incessantly. All the evils which had followed the rebellion of An Lu-shan were multiplied after that of Huang Tsao. Hardly any province in the empire, except Szechuan, had escaped the rebel invasion, and the generals who reconquered them ruled in their territories as masters, paying a purely nominal respect to the shadow Emperor.

In A.D. 904 Ch'ang An was totally ruined and depopulated by Chu Wên, one of these governors, who had originally been a rebel general under Huang Tsao. He carried off the Emperor to his own headquarters in Honan, where, in A.D. 907, he forced the last T'ang Emperor to sign a deed of abdication in his favour. Chu Wên's usurped sovereignty was repudiated by the other viceroys, who one and all set themselves up as full sovereigns in their provinces and mostly claimed the imperial title. With the division of China into eleven states the second centralised empire came to an end.

Chapter XIV

SOCIAL AND ECONOMIC CONDITIONS

THE T'ang period is well known as one of the great creative epochs in the history of Chinese civilisation. The poetry of this age has never been surpassed, and in the arts the work of the T'ang masters, particularly the sculptors and painters, stands on a par with anything produced before or since. T'ang art and poetry are becoming increasingly known to the West through the work of collectors and translators, but as yet little has been done to illuminate the social background against which the artists and poets passed their lives.

Fortunately the highly organised civil service of the T'ang Empire has left records, which, incorporated in the official history of the dynasty, provide valuable information on social and economic conditions in the 7th and 8th centuries, when the empire was at the height of its material prosperity. These two centuries, the greater part of which were peaceful, were also the years in which the most famous T'ang poets lived and in which new artistic influences took shape.

The empire founded and stabilised by the great T'ai Tsung was the largest and almost certainly the most populous state in the world at that date. It was governed from Ch'ang An by a civil service, which, though based on the Han model, was both more effective and more powerful than its prototype. The T'ang Emperors had no need to disguise their rule under a façade of feudalism. The empire was theirs to govern as they chose, no tributary or vassal kings rivalled their authority, no feudal lords could organise opposition in distant provinces. Until the rebellion of An Lu-shan (A.D. 755) weakened the imperial authority and diminished the prestige of the throne, the whole empire was under the direct control of the central government, administered by a hierarchy of officials chosen by public examinations.

At its greatest extent, as left by T'ai Tsung at his death, the empire measured from north to south 16,918 li, and from east to west 9,511 li.*

---

*T'ang Shu. The official history of the dynasty, published in the Sung dynasty. All data in this Chapter are from this source.

Taking the Chinese li to be equivalent to one-third of an English mile, the distance from the northern outposts beyond the Great Wall to the borders of Annam was 5,640 miles, and from the borders of Tibet to the Pacific Coast, 3,170 miles. As these figures are considerably in excess of the actual distance from the northern point of the Great Wall to the southern border of Annam, and from Tibet to the sea, they are probably intended to include all the Mongolian tribes who had acknowledged the suzerainty of China in the north, and also all the Central Asiatic kingdoms over which Ch'ang An claimed overlordship. Actually, the T'ang Empire did not include the greater part of the modern provinces of Yunnan and Kueichou, in the south-west, which were still inhabited by aboriginal tribes, usually very hostile to the Chinese. It was therefore somewhat smaller than the territory of the Republic to-day and considerably less than the area of the Manchu Empire.

Under the early central empire of the Ch'in and Han dynasties the largest administrative unit in the provinces had been a prefecture, corresponding to the *chou* or medium sized district of the Manchu dynasty. There were no provinces under the Han dynasty. The first division of China into provinces, as opposed to feudal kingdoms and states, was one of the reforms of T'ai Tsung. By his orders China was divided into ten provinces, called *tao*, or circuits, which were arranged in accordance with the natural divisions of the empire, ignoring earlier political boundaries (Map 8).

The first, Kuan Nei—a name which is a synonym for the older Kuan Chung, the "Land within the Passes"—corresponded to the modern province of Shensi. In it was situated Ch'ang An, capital of the empire. To the north-west of the metropolitan province was Lung Yu, broadly equivalent to the modern Kansu, bordered on the west by the mountain land of the Tu-yu-hun nomads, the country now called Kokonor. Through this province ran the great road to the west via the oases of Central Asia. Ho Tung, "East of the River" was the T'ang name for the present day Shansi, a plateau country clearly defined by the Yellow River on the west and south, and the T'ai Hang mountains to the east.

The great eastern plain was divided by T'ai Tsung into three provinces, Ho Pei "North of the River"—a name which the Republic has recently revived—covered the lands north of the Yellow River, the province called Chihli under the Manchu dynasty.

MAP 8. *The T'ang Empire.*

Ho Nan in T'ang times included not only the modern province of that name, but also the part of Shantung which lies south of the Yellow River. Huai Nan "South of the Huai (river)" covered all the territory between the Yangtze and Huai rivers which is now divided between the provinces of Honan, Anhui and Kiangsu. In this instance the T'ang division was both more logical and more convenient than the modern distribution, which runs across the topographical and economic boundaries of this area.

Under the T'ang dynasty the whole of southern China, including the Yangtze Valley, was divided into only four provinces. This region, equivalent to half the territory of the modern republic, is now covered by nine provinces, and the wide extent of the T'ang provinces is explained by the undeveloped and uninhabited state of much of south China in the 7th century. The four T'ang southern provinces were:

(1) Chien Nan, "South of the Gorges," comprising western Szechuan with parts of Yunnan and Kueichou up to the border of Tibet.

(2) Shan Nan, "South of the Mountains" covered the middle part of the Yangtze basin, to-day divided between eastern Szechuan, Hupei and northern Hunan.

(3) Kiang Nan, "South of the River" included all the vast region now divided between Chekiang, Kiangsi and Fukien with parts of Hunan, Kiangsu and Anhui.

(4) Finally, Ling Nan, "South of the Range" corresponded to modern Kuangtung and Kuangsi provinces with part of Annam.

For the purposes of land revenue the T'ang government conducted several censuses of the population of the empire, and these figures have fortunately been preserved. A fragment of a census return, probably relating to the census of A.D. 740*, has been found among the MSS. recovered from the cave temples at Tun Huang, Kansu province. This return concerns a family of farmers settled in the district and records the numbers and sex of all members of the household, adults and children. It is therefore evident that T'ang statistics were not compiled with only taxpayers in mind, but represent a real count of the actual popula-

* *The Census of China During the Period A.D. 2-742.* H. Bielenstein, B.M.F.E.A., No. 19. Stockholm, 1947.

CENSUSES OF THE SUI AND T'ANG DYNASTIES

Date.	Families.	Persons.	Prefectures.	Sub-Prefectures.
Sui				
A.D. 609	8,907,536	46,019,956	190	1255
T'ang				
A.D. 640	No data	No data	358	1551
A.D. 726	7,069,565	41,419,712	No data	No data
A.D. 740	8,412,871	48,143,609	328	1573
A.D. 754	9,069,154	52,880,488	321	1538 Also 16,829 villages.
After the Rebellion of An Lu-shan				
A.D. 764	2,900,000	16,900,000	No data	No data
A.D. 780	3,080,000*	No data	No data	No data
A.D. 839	4,996,752	No data	No data	No data
A.D. 845	4,955,151	No data	No data	No data

tion, reflecting a degree of organisation and efficiency in the working of the civil service never equalled elsewhere until modern times.

It will be observed from these figures that during the 150 years preceding the rebellion of An Lu-shan the taxpaying population was between eight and nine million families, which were calculated to amount to between forty and fifty million persons. The cities, or rather the number of administrative divisions, which as a rule corresponds closely to the number of walled cities, varies somewhat, perhaps on account of administrative changes rather than the destruction or building of towns. After the rebellion of An Lu-shan a catastrophic change is evident, not only do the figures show a huge decline in the population, but also the figures themselves are meagre and obviously only approximate. It has always been argued that this change reveals the damage done by the rebels, a slaughter of more than 35,000,000 people. Such an interpretation is quite incredible.

*Definitely stated to be taxpaying families only.

The rebellion of An Lu-shan has been represented as a devastating storm which swept away all the culture of the great 7th and 8th centuries, and left the T'ang dynasty a mere empty name and China depopulated. This is part of the poetic exaggeration which is permissible in the romantic stories about Ming Huang and Yang Kuei Fei, but unforgivable in history. An Lu-shan's army and that of the imperial generals opposed to him did indeed devastate the northern provinces and wreck Ch'ang An, the capital, but it is often forgotten that the rebels never penetrated the southern provinces of the Yangtze basin and the south-east coast, nor even the rich western province of Szechuan, to which Ming Huang retired at the fall of the capital.

After capturing Ch'ang An the rebels made no further progress, and the rest of the long-drawn-out war was confined to the eastern provinces of Honan, Shantung and Hopei. At this period the southern provinces, which escaped the horrors of war, were already as rich and civilised as the older centres in the north, for ever since the partition in the Tsin dynasty, when many hundreds of educated and official families fled before the Tartar invasions, these provinces had rivalled the north in wealth and culture. It is no accident that so many of the famous T'ang poets such as Li Po were natives of Szechuan or the Yangtze Valley.

The theory that China was depopulated and ruined by this war is based on the census figures of A.D. 754, the year before the revolt, and those taken in A.D. 764, the year after peace had been restored. In the first year the population of the empire is given as 52,880,488 persons and in A.D. 764 no more than 16,900,000.

If these figures are taken as an exact record of the full number of the inhabitants of the empire at these two dates it must be admitted that An Lu-shan, his successors in revolt, and the imperial generals, were responsible between them for the extermination of 35,000,000 people, and this vast slaughter was accomplished in the space of ten years, and confined to three or four provinces only. Wars in 8th century China, even when accompanied by sacks and massacres, were fought in a desultory fashion, with long intervals when the armies were in winter quarters, and their encounters were only occasional pitched battles. Yet if these figures are admitted this war accounted for a slaughter several times greater than that of the two great wars of 1914-18 and 1939-45, in which six great empires, all as populous as 8th century China, were continuously engaged with every device of scientific destruction. Such an inference is fantastic.

It is more probable that after the confusion and disorganisation of the great rebellion the census of A.D. 764 represents no more than a rough estimate of the number of persons who could be made subject to taxation. These would naturally have greatly diminished after the devastation of the provinces which, being nearest the capital, were no doubt those in which the register had been most carefully compiled. Unless this explanation is correct it is impossible to reconcile the reported enormous shrinkage in the population with the known fact that many of the most wealthy and populous provinces in the empire were left untouched by the war.

Even in north China there is little in the recorded history of the war to explain this tremendous loss of life. An Lu-shan, whose rebellion came as a surprise to the Court, advanced almost unopposed until he reached Ling Pao in Honan. There a decisive battle was fought, as a result of which the rebel captured the T'ung Kuan Pass and advanced straight upon the capital. The later phases of the war, after the rebels had been forced back to Honan and Shantung, were long drawn out and probably very destructive to commerce and wealth, but they do not seem to have been accompanied by wholesale massacres. The experiences of these same provinces in the last thirty years prove that the depopulation caused by frequent and prolonged civil wars (fought moreover with modern firearms) is easily exaggerated. A census of the wealthy taken in 1920 and repeated in 1948 would no doubt reveal an even more staggering decline. It is a matter of common observation that the actual population of this afflicted area has not sensibly declined, if it has not actually increased. There seems to be every reason to believe that the war against An Lu-shan and his followers was of a similar character.

The real cause of the decline in the figures for the censuses after the rebellion was the dispersion of the officials who had been in charge of the revenue department. The provinces freed from the rebels remained under military rule, and the working of the civil government was permanently impaired. The shrunken and admittedly approximate figures for the later years of the T'ang dynasty reflect the decline in the power and efficiency of the government rather than the ravages caused by the rebellion itself.

The social system of China under the T'ang dynasty, though no longer feudal, remained aristocratic. At the top of the social scale a large privileged class of nobles and officials, immune from taxation, provided the government with loyal servants whose interests coincided with that of the imperial family itself. Nine grades of nobility existed, but this nobility was no longer settled on the land, but supported by a charge on the taxes proportionate to the rank held (see Table). The three superior grades, Princes of the blood, second-class Princes, and first-class Dukes, were confined to members of the imperial clan, the first grade being the sons and brothers of emperors reigning or recently deceased, the second and third grades comprising the more distant descendants and collateral branches.

The T'ang Nobility

Rank.	Emolument.
1st Class Prince (*wang*)	Taxes of 10,000 families
2nd Class Prince	,, 5,000 ,,
1st Class Duke (*kung*)	,, 3,000 ,,
2nd Class Duke	,, 2,000 ,,
3rd Class Duke	,, 1,000 ,,
Marquis (*hou*)	,, 1,000 ,,
Count (*po*)	,, 700 ,,
Viscount (*tzu*)	,, 500 ,,
Baron (*nan*)	,, 300 ,,

The lesser ranks were recruited from eminent officials who had rendered conspicuous services at the foundation of the dynasty, or on subsequent occasions. Each nobleman was supported by the taxes of some thousands or hundreds of families proportionate to his rank. Hereditary titles did not in themselves confer any administrative power, but each grade of the aristocracy had a corresponding grade in the official hierarchy, which was also organised in nine degrees, each divided into a senior and junior division.

The civil service itself was confined to persons of education, chosen by a rudimentary form of the public examination system which later dynasties developed more completely. T'ai Tsung was responsible for this very important innovation, which gradually substituted a caste of scholars for the men chosen by favour or nepotism who had formed the official class under the Han and subsequent dynasties. The Imperial College at Ch'ang An, which this Emperor greatly enlarged and upon which he bestowed many favours, was the training ground for the new civil service. After T'ai Tsung had added to it, no less than 3,260 scholars were enrolled as residents, while the total attendance including those who lived elsewhere was 8,000. The education provided was entirely confined to the Confucian classics and their commentaries, which were regarded as the best possible training for those embracing an official career.

The whole body of this official class; the princes of the blood, nobility, families of imperial concubines and consorts, the superior grades of the official hierarchy, and the scholars of the imperial college, were exempt from the land revenue tax. Allowing for the laxity and corruption which would certainly exist, a very large number of people must have benefited by this coveted privilege.

Nevertheless the government machine, until it was dislocated by rebellion and military usurpations, was highly organised and reasonably efficient. The whole administration was centralised in Ch'ang An, for, although T'ai Tsung had divided the empire into ten provinces, these were only employed as convenient groupings of the lesser administrative unit, the *chou* or prefecture, which was directly answerable to the ministries in the capital. The government itself was organised on a pattern which, familiar enough in modern times, was perhaps at that time the most advanced type of centralised administration ever attempted.

The Emperor was advised by a council, called the Shang Shu Shêng, consisting of certain high Court officials and the ministers of the six departments of government. These constituted the Li Pu or Ministry of the Civil Service, in charge of the official hierarchy, supervising the administrative machine. The Hu Pu, literally "Family Ministry," which was the Finance and Revenue department, had under its care the collection of taxes, the taking of censuses and the agrarian system on which revenue was based. A most important function of this ministry was the maintenance of the grain transport to the capital, on which the government depended for all expenditure on the army and civil service. The Li Pu (written with a different character to the first mentioned) was the Ministry of Rites, in charge of the public cult and observances of the state religion. The Ping Pu was the Ministry of Defence, controlling the army and the garrisons on the frontiers. The Hsing Pu, Ministry of Punishments, was in control of the law courts administering penal law, for civil disputes were settled by custom and arbitration, not forming part of the official legal system. The judiciary was thus merely a function of the executive. The Kung Pu, Ministry of Works, was charged with the public works of the empire; dykes, roads, flood prevention and irrigation schemes.

These six ministries transmitted orders and received reports direct from the prefectures. The prefectures were in charge of a varying number of sub-prefectures (*hsien*) and the magistrate of a sub-prefecture had direct authority over the villages in his territory. His functions, and those of the government as a whole, were three ; the collection of revenue, supervision of public works, and the maintenance of the peace, including the adminis-tration of the penal laws. Five degrees of punishment were recognised by the official code, and, although T'ai Tsung had greatly modified the severity of the laws enacted by the Sui dynasty, the penal code was still very severe.

The lightest punishment was flogging, divided into two degrees, the heavier sentence not infrequently proving fatal to the victim. For more serious offences the punishment was banishment, also divided into two degrees. The lesser, for not more than three years to another part of the offenders' native province, the heavier, for life to the frontiers of the empire. These latter life exiles were employed as soldiers on the Great Wall, in the garrisons of Central Asia and on the unhealthy southern frontiers of the empire. The fifth penalty was death, in various forms proportionate to the heinousness of the crime committed. T'ai Tsung had enacted that every death sentence should be reviewed on three separate days, and that during this period the judge must abstain from meat, music and entertainments in order that the serious nature of his duty should be constantly present in his mind. As in all Chinese dynasties the laws against rebellion and conspiracy were very severe, the family of the criminal being liable to penalties varying in proportion to the degree of kinship with the chief accused. This system was a consequence of the clan organisation of society, for it was held that the individual was inseparable from his family, and in serious crimes such as rebellion and sedition the family must necessarily share the guilt of any member.

The real function of the government was not so much the administration of the laws, which were largely customary, but the collection of revenue, and the promotion of agriculture on which revenue depended. For this purpose the rural population, excluding the official class and townsmen, was divided into five categories. Infants under four years, children from four to sixteen, adolescents from sixteen to twenty-one, adults from twenty-one to sixty, and the aged, over sixty. Adults, and boys over eighteen were assigned land to cultivate as tenants of the state. The terms of their tenancy were divided into two classes, rent and services. As rent the tenant paid five *hu* of rice, a *hu* being the equivalent of 120 lbs. weight. According to the nature of the soil he also paid two rolls of fine silk and twenty feet of inferior quality, or in areas where silkworms were not reared, a proportionate quantity of hemp, cloth, or fourteen ounces of silver. He further had to serve twenty days of forced labour on public works, paying three feet of silk for every day missed. The scale of taxes and rents was posted on city gates, and in the market place of every village, in order that no one should have the excuse of ignorance of the law.

Remissions of rent and services were given in bad years, according to the loss sustained, and also to men who brought new land into cultivation. Land was allotted to landless adults, and if the population of any village or district was insufficient to cultivate the soil, the surplus was detached and incorporated in the next village, or sub-prefecture. This fact perhaps accounts for the varying number of sub-prefectures at different times.

Land was measured (as it still is) by the *mu*, a strip 240 paces by one in area, one hundred of which made a *ching*, which was the standard allotment for an adult farmer. The hundred *mu* plot was in theory intended to provide for all the farmers' dependents, forty *mu* for the aged and feeble, thirty for the widows and orphans, and the remainder for the family itself. The farmers were divided into two classes, known as "broadlands" and "narrowlands" respectively, the former having on the average double the holding of the latter. In the remissions for bad years the "narrowlands" received somewhat more favourable treatment. Merchants and artisans from the cities were not allowed to register themselves as state tenants, no doubt to avoid absentee tenancies and subletting. Merchants and townsmen were subject to a separate scale of taxation, graded in nine degrees and based on their property. The tolls and navigation taxes also fell mainly upon this class. The poor, that is to say the landless coolies of the cities, who owned no property, and also foreigners—by which nomads and Central Asiatic merchants seem to be indicated—paid no taxes at all. The coolie class, which must have been numerous in the big cities, as it is to-day, therefore does not appear in the census lists.

For one or two years the record of what the state actually received by this taxation has been preserved. Changed values and some uncertainty as to the units mentioned make it difficult to assess the total in terms of western currencies. In the year A.D. 746, on the eve of the rebellion of An Lu-shan, when the empire may be said to have been at the peak of prosperity, the revenue reaching the treasury was as follows:

In money, "more than" 2,000,000 strings of 1,000 cash per string.

In grain, "more than" 19,800,000 *hu* of 120 lbs. each.

In mixed kinds of silk, 7,400,000 rolls.

In fine silk, 1,800,000 rolls.

In cloth, 1,350,000 pieces.

A string of cash was theoretically the equivalent of one ounce of silver, which gives the value of the money received as 125,000 lbs. of silver. The grain amounted to 1,060,714 tons.

In A.D. 780, some years after the rebellion of An Lu-shan had finally been suppressed, the revenue raised was:

In money, 20,500,000 strings of cash.

In grain, 4,000,000 *hu* (214,285 tons);

and the state expenditure amounted to:

Money, 9,500,000 strings of cash.

Grain, 16,000,000 *hu* (857,140 tons).

It is evident that in this year the grain transport had not recovered from the effects of the rebellion, and that the government must have bought grain for cash.

The transport of the tax grain to Ch'ang An was a source of perennial difficulty for the government. The capital in this respect was awkwardly situated, for, although the valley of the Wei River, in which Ch'ang An stands, may have been less afflicted with drought than it is at present, it could not supply the wants of what was then the largest city in Asia, if not in the world. Figures for the actual population of the city itself are lacking, but those for the metropolitan district, including Ch'ang An itself and several small cities in the vicinity, are known for A.D. 742—at the height of its glory. There were 362,921 families, making 1,960,188 persons. In T'ang times the city of Ch'ang An was a rectangle six miles by five, an area of thirty square miles, and the population cannot have been less than a million. The modern city of Sianfu, built upon a small part of the T'ang site, is not more than two miles by three, and is not fully occupied. The population does not exceed 300,000, and is certainly much smaller than in T'ang times. (Map 9.)

The grain producing areas were all in the eastern and southern provinces, the great plain and the Yangtze Valley, regions far removed from Ch'ang An, which was, moreover, in a plateau country on the upper course of the Wei River, and above the dangerous San Men rapids on the Yellow River. These facts, which made the strength of the "land within the passes" from a military point of view, were a serious drawback from the economic aspect. The tax grain came by water, up the Huai River and Grand Canal to the Yellow River, and thence to the mouth of the Lo River east of Lo Yang. To proceed further west it was necessary to enter the defiles where the river passes through high loess hills; this was dangerous navigation, impeded by a very strong current and difficult rapids.

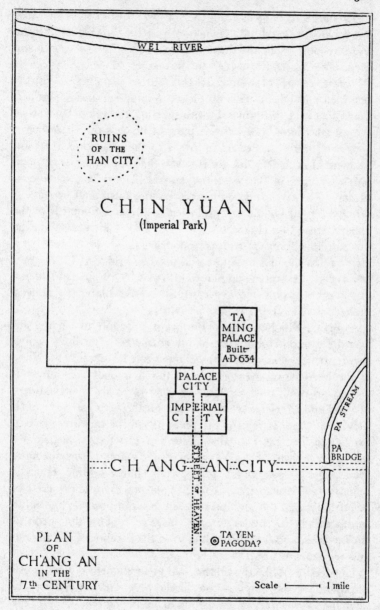

MAP 9. *Ch'ang An in the 7th Century.*

The large river boats from the south and from the east could not go further west than the mouth of the Lo, necessitating a transhipment—with all the attendant possibilities of waste and theft. The loss by shipwreck in the higher reach of the Yellow River was severe, in spite of strictly enforced penalties against the boatmen and officials responsible. At one period an attempt was made to avoid the rapids by transporting the grain by land to the mouth of the Wei. For this purpose not less than 1,800 carts were constantly in use. As the road to the west, then the most frequented in the empire, for it led to the capital, passes through narrow gorges in the loess and crosses high ridges, the inconvenience to travel and commerce and the waste and expense of using the road for the tax grain led to the abandonment of the experiment. Ming Huang tried to instil a spirit of rivalry into the boats from various provinces and districts. Honours were conferred upon the first boat to reach the Wei bridge at Ch'ang An. It was gaily decorated and played into port by a troupe of dancing girls and musicians. How successful the artist Emperor's remedy proved, is not related by the annalists.

A further disadvantage of the grain transport to Ch'ang An was the uneconomic nature of the enterprise. The boats which spent many weeks slowly travelling upstream against the force of the current, returned empty in less than half the time, but earned no profit on their journey. The large army of boatmen, officials and overseers were a charge on the very revenue which they were transporting. As the years passed the quantity of grain needed to feed the capital and its host of nobles, officials and soldiers rose year by year. In T'ai Tsung's time it was not more than 200,000 *shih*, about 10,714 tons, but by Ming Huang's reign it had risen to 160,714 tons (4,000,000 *shih*), and there can be no doubt that the cost and waste of this transport was one of the causes which led the eastern provinces to support the revolt of An Lu-shan, and free themselves from the incubus of Ch'ang An and its parasite Court.

The decline of Shensi and the final abandonment of Ch'ang An as capital of the empire—the T'ang were the last dynasty to reign there—was very probably due to a growing realisation of the inherent difficulty in transporting grain up the rapids of the

Yellow River, and the adverse currents encountered on the whole journey. Later dynasties fixed their capitals in the eastern plain, or on the Yangtze, where access was easy and water transport short and safe, but they did not avoid the danger from which Ch'ang An was immune, exposure to the raids of nomad horsemen from the steppes. In the last years of the T'ang dynasty, when the provinces under their military despots withheld the tax grain and brought the transport system to an end, Ch'ang An and even the Imperial Court suffered famine. The inhabitants fled to happier districts, a general carried off the Emperor to Lo Yang, and the city, ruined by wars and hunger, was left an empty shell.

The land revenue and tax grain, though the most important, was not the only source of revenue at the disposal of the government. Minting of money, salt, iron, and later copper, were state monopolies, and taxes were imposed on wine (rice spirit) and later, after its rise to popularity as a beverage, in the 8th century, a tax was placed on tea (A.D. 793). In the middle of the 9th century the revenue derived from these sources amounted to 9,220,000 strings of cash, but the collection cost the state 3,000,000.

Figures also exist for the annual production of the mines of the empire and the salt wells. There were eighteen salt lakes including coastal marshes, and 640 salt wells, from which an annual revenue of 400,000 strings of cash was obtained. The mines of the empire produced in one year:

Silver	25,000	ounces (*liang*)		
Copper	655,000	catties (*chin*)	= 390	tons
Lead	144,000	,,	= 85	,,
Tin	17,000	,,	= 15	,,
Iron	532,000	,,	= 317	,,

The minting of copper coinage was a government monopoly, but it was not centralised at one mint. There were not less than 99 mints scattered over the empire, but mostly in the province of Shansi and in the lower Yangtze Valley, near the sources of the metal. The annual output of each mint was supposed to be 3,300 strings (of 1,000 cash each) which would give a total of 399,300 strings, but, in fact, it is stated that the total output was rather less, 327,000 strings, suggesting that not all the mints were worked at full capacity.

The government was constantly beset with the difficulty of counteracting illegal coining, which as in the Han dynasty, seems to have been practised on the largest scale. In A.D. 722 the Emperor was obliged to declare a government monopoly of the manufacture of copper utensils, in order to prevent coiners from acquiring the raw material for their industry. This measure does not appear to have had very much effect on the evil, no doubt because the coiners were able to utilise existing stocks or evade the prohibition.

Chapter XV

FRESH CONTACTS WITH THE WEST

UNTIL modern times there has been no period in Chinese history when the country was so open to foreign influences as in the T'ang dynasty. The Mongol conquest did indeed see a greater immigration of foreign settlers and mercenaries, but these were followers of the Mongol conquerors, hated and feared by the Chinese. Their influence, which was resisted by the nation at large, was short and transitory. On the other hand the T'ang Court welcomed foreigners, took a keen interest in alien customs and religions, and extended a friendly welcome to priests and travellers from western regions. Consequently the art and thought of the T'ang period was strongly influenced by the nations with which China was in contact. The charge of "Chinese exclusiveness" cannot be substantiated in this period.

Secure in their isolation and confident of their power to repel invasions, the T'ang Emperors did not fear foreign intercourse as a menace to the state, while the spirit of intellectual curiosity and tolerance which marked this age encouraged a sympathetic attitude to religious and artistic ideas of foreign origin. Until the close of the dynasty the Court was in constant diplomatic relations with the major powers of western Asia, and the merchants and priests of these countries found easy access to all parts of the T'ang Empire (Map 10).

The T'ang world, if not larger, was far better known and more easily travelled than the world of the Han period. Regions which had only been known to the Han by hearsay, or by infrequent and hazardous voyages of exploration, were now perfectly familiar to the Chinese. The streets of Ch'ang An—as the grave figures, apart from literary evidence, amply attest—were frequented by men of the most diverse races, from Siberian tribesmen to the jungle peoples of southern India, Greeks, Arabs, Persians and Japanese. Japan, indeed, was then almost a new land, hardly known in the Han period, but now sending embassies to China, and enthusiastically borrowing the culture and political organisation of the T'ang Empire.

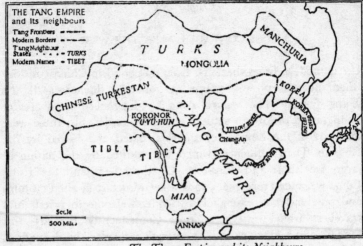

MAP 10. *The T'ang Empire and its Neighbours.*

To the south, the countries of Cochin China, the islands of the East Indies, Ceylon and India, lands little frequented in the Han period, were visited by Chinese merchants and Buddhist pilgrims in search of relics and Sanskrit books. India, indeed, the sacred land of the Buddhists, was probably better known to the Chinese at that date than it has been at any subsequent period until modern times. Ch'ang An was in regular diplomatic contact with the more important states of Northern India, and even interfered in Indian politics on more than one occasion.

Almost coincident with the rise of the T'ang dynasty in China, a great revolution had transformed the map of western Asia. In A.D. 642 the battle of Nehavend decided the fate of Persia, which fell before the Moslem arms. Persia had long been familiar to the Chinese. The Sassanian Empire and the northern Chinese Wei dynasty had been in close contact. This great empire, Rome's only successful rival, was destroyed to make way for the warlike Omayyad Caliphate, under which the Moslem faith was carried into the heart of Central Asia. These events touched the Chinese closely, for their own empire reached westward to the fringes of the fallen Persian state.

The western limit of the Chinese world was the "kingdom of Fu Lin"—the Byzantine Empire. The Chinese knew this country very well, better perhaps than China was known to the Greeks. The T'ang histories have recorded four embassies from Byzantium to China, all between A.D. 643 and A.D. 719, the period when Byzantium was hard pressed by the first onrush of the Arab armies of the Caliphs. There seems to be little doubt that the purpose of these embassies was to enlist Chinese assistance in the war against Islam. To what extent the Chinese interested themselves in this question is obscure. Certainly no T'ang armies were despatched to oppose the Moslems, but it is possible that the Greeks who came to China on these missions brought back with them some new knowledge of a technical nature, for at that time China was technically more advanced than the western world.*

In A.D. 643, when T'ai Tsung was on the throne, an embassy from "P'o To Li, king of Fu Lin" came to Ch'ang An and offered red glass and gold dust. The reigning Eastern Roman Emperor at that time was Constans II, who was a child. "P'o To Li" is clearly not a rendering of his name, and has often been supposed to be a version of "Patriarch," the suggestion being that the mission was really a religious one. The Chinese histories, however, plainly state that it was the embassy of a king. At the time the government of the Byzantine Empire was largely in the hands of the chief military commanders, who bore the title of "Patrician." It is far more probable that it was one of these generals who sent the embassy to China and that "P'o To Li" represents the word "Patrice."

Fu Lin, the Chinese name for the Byzantine Empire, has been shown to be derived from the name Byzantium, for in the pronunciation of the 7th century, Fu Lin would be sounded "But Zan." The T'ang histories have a section devoted to Fu Lin, which while incorporating some of the Han account of Ta Ts'in (the Roman Empire) obviously contains further and contemporary information, perhaps gathered from these embassies, or from other travellers. There is nothing in the T'ang histories to show that any Chinese embassy reached Constantinople.† Extracts

*Yang Hsien-yi, *Byzantine Embassies to China in the 7th and 8th Centuries.* Unpublished.

†Yang Hsien-yi, *op. cit.* and Chiu T'ang Shu, Chap. 198. Hsin T'ang Shu, Chap. 221.

from these T'ang accounts give the impression of observations made in the streets of Constantinople, rather than of the reports of ambassadors.

"Fu Lin is the ancient Ta Tsin. It is situated on the Western Sea. To the south-east it borders Persia, to the north-east is the territory of the Western Turks. The land is very populous, and there are many towns. The walls of the capital are of dressed stone, and more than 100,000 families reside in the city. There is a gate 200 feet high, entirely covered with bronze [the Golden Gate]. In the imperial palace there is a human figure of gold which marks the hours by striking bells. The buildings are decorated with glass and crystal, gold, ivory and rare woods. The roofs are made of cement, and are flat. In the heat of summer machines worked by water power carry up water to the roof, which is used to refresh the air by falling in showers in front of the windows.

"Twelve ministers assist the King in the government. When the King leaves his palace he is attended by a man carrying a bag, into which any person is free to drop petitions. The men wear their hair cut short and are clothed in embroidered robes which leave the right arm bare. The women wear their hair in the form of a crown. The people of Fu Lin esteem wealth, and they are fond of wine and sweetmeats. On every seventh day [the Christian Sunday] no work is done.

"From this country come byssus, coral, asbestos, and many other curious products. They have very skilful conjurers who can spit fire from their mouths, pour water out of their hands, and drop pearls from their feet. Also they have skilful physicians who cure certain diseases by extracting worms from the head."

This account, which so clearly bears the character of a traveller's observations in the streets of Constantinople, is unfortunately the only detailed description of a European people which appears in T'ang records. It is curious that no direct reference is made to the religion of the Greeks, although, as will be shown presently, the Chinese knew a great deal about Christianity at that time. The traveller to Constantinople, whoever he was, does not seem to have known the reason why the inhabitants "did no work every seventh day."

The first news of the rise of Islam was brought to China by an embassy from Yesdegerd, last Sassanian King of Persia, which reached Ch'ang An in A.D. 638. The Persian monarch, then desperately defending the last corner of his kingdom at Merv, appealed to China for assistance against the conquering Arabs. T'ai Tsung did not grant this request, no doubt feeling that his own empire, so recently delivered from civil war and Turkish attacks, was in need of peace, and Persia too far for military expeditions. The Persians, although they did not get Chinese assistance, were welcomed as refugees. Firuz, Yesdegerd's son, whom the Chinese still called King of Persia, came to Ch'ang An in 674, when the Arab conquest of his hereditary possessions was complete. He was kindly welcomed and made a general of the Imperial Guard. He died in Ch'ang An some years later. His son, only known by the Chinese form of his name, Ni-Ni-Shih, also lived in Ch'ang An, and is mentioned in the history of the time. The Persian refugees were allowed to build temples and practise the Zoroastrian faith, which flourished among this refugee community for many years.

From these fugitives, and perhaps from Chinese travellers, the Court soon learned the origin of Islam and much about the country of its adherents, the Arabs. Arabia was known as Ta Shih, from the Persian word Tarzi, meaning an Arab.

"Ta Shih," says the *T'ang Shu*,* "was formerly part of Persia. The men have large noses and black beards. They carry silver mounted swords on a silver girdle. They drink no wine and have no music. The women are white and veil the face when they leave the house. There are large halls for worship which can hold several hundreds of persons. Five times daily they worship the god of Heaven. Every seventh day [Friday] their King [the Caliph] seated on high, addresses his subjects, saying: 'Those who die in battle will be reborn in Paradise. Those who fight bravely will obtain happiness.' Therefore their men are very valiant soldiers. The land is poor and cannot grow cereals,

*Hsin T'ang Shu. Chap. 221, part 2.

they hunt and live on meat, and collect honey among the rocks. Their dwellings are formed like the hoods of a cart [tents]. They have grapes which sometimes are as big as a hen's egg. In the Sui period Ta Yeh [605-616] a man of the western peoples (*hu*), a Persian subject, was guarding flocks in the mountains near Medina. A Lion-man [The Archangel Gabriel] said to him: 'To the west of this mountain, in a cave there is a sword and a black stone [the black stone of the Ka'ba] with white lettering. Who ever obtains these two objects will reign over mankind.' The man went to the place and found every thing as he had been told. The letters upon the stone meant, 'Arise.' He took the stone and proclaimed himself King. His countrymen tried to oppose him, but he defeated them all. Afterwards the Ta Shih became very powerful. They destroyed Persia, defeated the King of Fu Lin, invaded northern India, attacked Samarkand and Tashkent. From the south-western sea their empire reached to the western borders of our territory."

This information was soon to be supplemented by direct contact with the new power. Between A.D. 707 and 713 Kutaiba, the general of the Caliph Walid, began the conquest of Central Asia, and the region now forming Afghanistan, which, as Yüan Chuang's pilgrimage proves, was then a strongly Buddhist country. The kingdoms of Samarkand, Bokhara and the confederacy of the western Turks, finding themselves hard pressed by this formidable enemy, appealed to China. The Central Asiatic states had recognised the vague suzerainty of Ch'ang An, or rather they hastened to do so when the Moslem invasion appeared imminent. The T'ang Court had hardly recovered from the perturbations which followed upon the death of the Empress Wu, consequently, the new Emperor, Hsüan Tsung (Ming Huang) was more prepared to listen to an Arab embassy proposing peace, than to the appeals of his neighbours.

In A.D. 713 the ambassadors of the Caliph arrived at the Court, and were courteously received. The fact is interesting, for these proud strangers refused to perform the ceremonial prostration, *k'o t'ou*, which Chinese etiquette demanded of all who appeared in the imperial presence. The Moslems declared that they prostrated themselves to no living man, but only to their god, and only bowed in the presence of kings. Tolerantly deciding that "Court etiquette is not the same in all countries," the Chinese Emperor waived the custom, and the Arabs were received. More than a thousand years later the Manchu Court refused a similar concession to the English ambassador, Lord Amherst, and brought the mission to an end. The purpose of the Arabs was to prevent China assisting the Central Asiatic states, and whether as Arab historians say, the Chinese were too impressed to oppose the Moslems, or whether the Court regarded the quarrel as too distant to merit interference, the T'ang Emperors did nothing at that time to hinder the Arab advance.

In 751, however, the Chinese Empire did clash with the new Abbasid Caliphate, known to the Chinese as the Black Cloth Arabs, from the black flags of the Abbasids. A Korean officer in Chinese service, commanding the troops stationed in Turkestan, was sent by the Court to settle the differences between two small states in the upper Indus Valley. The Chinese army, after crossing into this region and settling the questions at issue, returned and entered the kingdom of Tashkent, operations which had not been sanctioned by the distant Court. The general in command perhaps thought that at such a distance he was free to do as he pleased. In Tashkent he behaved most treacherously, seizing the King of that country after a treaty of friendship had been concluded.

This conduct outraged all the Central Asiatic states, which were perhaps tiring of a Chinese suzerainty which did nothing to protect them from the Moslems. The small states formed an alliance against the Chinese and called in the Arabs to assist them. The combined armies totally defeated the Chinese at a point in the Ili Valley, and this event, soon to be followed by the revolt of An Lu-shan, was fatal to the Chinese rule in Turkestan. The western states were swallowed up by the Moslem invasions, while the eastern part of the country fell into the hands of the Tibetans. This war, in which the Arab army was commanded by the general Ziyad, serving the Caliph Abul Abbas, was the only occasion on which Chinese and Arabs actually engaged in formal hostilities.

Friendly relations with the Caliph were indeed soon restored, for a few years later Arab mercenaries sent by the Caliph Abu Jafar al Mansur in A.D. 756 helped the T'ang Emperor to defeat An Lu-shan and drive him from the capital. These Arab mercenaries are of some importance in Chinese history as being the probable founders of the Muhammadan community in China, which to-day is variously estimated to number from five to ten million people, the higher figure being the more probable.

After the war against An Lu-shan was at an end the Arab troops did not return to their own country, either because having married Chinese women, they were unwilling to return, or,

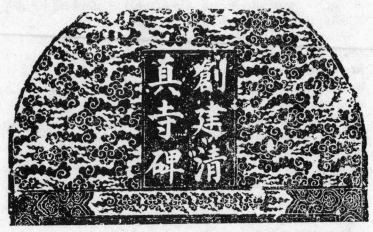

FIG. 47. *Head-piece of the Muhammadan Tablet in a mosque at Sianfu. A forgery of the Ming Period.*

according to Arab accounts, because having lived so long in a pork-eating country they were regarded as defiled by their stay-at-home compatriots. For whatever the reasons, the mercenaries settled in China, intermarried with the Chinese, but kept their faith. Unfortunately, no numbers are given for this settlement in contemporary accounts, though later sources say on the one hand that there were 4,000 men, and on the other, that there were as many as 100,000, which is very unlikely.

Curiously enough, although the introduction of Buddhism, Nestorianism, and Manicheism are noted in Chinese history, even though some of these religions did not take permanent root, the coming of Islam, which still flourishes, is nowhere recorded. The subject is one of the most obscure points in later Chinese history. To-day the Moslems are very numerous, if not the majority, in Kansu province, and form a large proportion of the inhabitants of Shensi and Yunnan. There is no province without a Moslem community, though with the exception of Yunnan, the provinces south of the Yangtze have not more than a few thousand Muhammadans each. But of the origin and growth of this community very little is known.

The Muhammadan tablet (Fig. 47) in the principal mosque at Ch'ang An bears a T'ang date, but, unfortunately, this monument is a forgery of the Ming period, in imitation of the genuine Nestorian tablet. Muhammadan tradition is manifestly unreliable, for it claims that Islam was introduced into China in the Sui dynasty, which came to an end some years before the Hegira. It is unquestionable that, although the Muhammadans now speak Chinese, dress as Chinese, and are in every way except their religion naturalised, they are of alien origin. Yunnan Muhammadans are most un-Chinese in appearance, and in the Muhammadan quarter of Ch'ang An Armenoid types predominate. The camel men of Shansi and Peking—who are all Moslems—frequently have well-grown beards and aquiline features, quite unlike the smooth-faced Chinese.

The Muhammadan settlers are believed to have greatly increased under the Mongols, when men of all the races of Asia followed the conquerors into China. They have also expanded through the practice of buying up Chinese children in famine times, who are then brought up in the faith. This custom has considerably diluted the blood of the Moslem community, so that a Moslem is not always to be recognised by his looks. The Chinese of adult age do not seem to have been converted to Islam in appreciable numbers, and certainly not in the early centuries. An Arab traveller who visited China at the end of the T'ang dynasty reports that he never heard of a single native who had embraced Islam, although he found flourishing communities of foreign Moslems in several cities.

Islam escaped the persecution which at the end of the T'ang

dynasty dealt a mortal blow to other alien creeds. It is not known why this leniency was shown, for the religion is never mentioned in the records of the time. Perhaps the Caliph was too powerful a neighbour to permit liberties to be taken with true believers, or perhaps the Muhammadans were all foreigners and were therefore left in peace. The faith slowly increased its hold and numbers during subsequent centuries, and, in spite of the massacres which followed the Yunnan and Kansu Moslem risings in the 19th century, Islam is to-day in a flourishing state in China, more actively in touch with Muhammadan centres in western Asia than it has been for centuries.

The rebellion of An Lu-shan, the conquest of eastern Turkestan by the Tibetans, and the disturbed state of the country further west during the Moslem conquest, combined to turn trade away from the ancient land route in favour of the sea route which then terminated at Canton. The fact is important as one of the influences which led to the rise of the southern provinces and the coincident decay of Shensi and the north-west. In Han times the sea route seems to have been very little used by the Chinese, though Egyptian Greeks made their way to Tonking by this route. In the period of partition, no doubt on account of the lawless condition of the north-west, the sea route became more important. Fa Hsien and other Buddhist pilgrims used this way to travel to or from India and Ceylon. In T'ang times Canton became a great centre of sea-borne trade, largely in Arab hands. The Arab and other foreign communities resident in the port were very large. The Moslems had a Kadi elected by themselves, and were subject to Koranic Law, administered by him, an early precedent for the extraterritorial system. Abu Zaid, an Arab traveller who was in China towards the end of the T'ang period, relates that when Canton was taken by storm by the rebel Huang Tsao in A.D. 879, 120,000 foreigners, Arabs, Jews, Zoroastrians and Christians, were massacred, as well as the native population of the city.

Abu Zaid may be exaggerating his figures, but the mere fact that such a number can have been regarded as possible proves that Canton had a very large foreign community, far larger than it has to-day. The mention of Jews is important. Jews are not mentioned by the T'ang history, and if Abu Zaid is correct this is the first record of Jews in Chinese history. The sack and massacre of Canton by Huang Tsao marks the end of an epoch in Chinese intercourse with the west. For many years the sea traffic did not recover from this blow and when, in the Sung dynasty, internal peace was restored, it was Kanpu, the port of Hang Chou, which held the first place as a resort of foreigners. Although the Muhammadan states were the most important and nearest foreign power with which China had intercourse in the T'ang dynasty, other influences played a prominent part. The Persian refugees introduced their own religion, Zoroastrianism, which though permitted, does not seem to have gained converts among the Chinese themselves. There were Zoroastrian temples in Ch'ang An, and probably in Canton also, where Abu Zaid records the presence of "fire worshippers." A more important and wide-spread Persian creed was Manicheism, which flourished for some centuries.

This creed, which borrowed both from Christianity and Zoroastrianism, was founded by Mani, a Persian, who was put to death in A.D. 274. It spread both east and west after his death, westward as far as France where the Albigenses were heretics of Manichean faith, and eastward to China, where it is first mentioned in A.D. 694. In A.D. 732 the Buddhists initiated a persecution, which was not encouraged by the government, on the ground that this religion was that of the western "Hu," the Central Asiatics, whom the Court was anxious to conciliate. The fact that the Buddhists opposed the new religion argues a certain progress as it was evidently looked upon as a rival. The attitude of the Court was decided by the fact that the Uigurs, the Turkish tribe now dominant among the nomads, were almost entirely Manichean. During the war against An Lu-shan the Uigurs lent the Emperor valuable assistance, providing the cavalry, and they were rewarded by fresh favours to their co-religionists resident in the empire.

Archæological finds in Central Asia have shown that Manicheism was strong in Turfan and other places, and it was clearly not confined to foreigners resident in China. In 768 and 771 special edicts permitting the building of new Manichean temples were promulgated, and the second specifically names the four cities of Ching Chou in Hupei, Yang Chou near Nanking, Nanking itself, and Shao Hsing in Chekiang as places where temples might be built. These places are all in the Yangtze basin, not an area where many foreigners or nomad Uigurs were likely to reside. The communities they served must have included a large number of Chinese converts. Manicheism endured as long as the Uigurs, its protectors, remained powerful, but as will be related presently, when that support failed, the religion was speedily assailed and extirpated.

Somewhat earlier than the first mention of the Manicheans in China, another religion of western origin had been warmly welcomed at Ch'ang An. The Nestorian tablet relates the history of the introduction and subsequent fortune of that Christian sect during the first two centuries of the T'ang dynasty, and the substance of the story is confirmed by other Chinese documents. In A.D. 635 a Nestorian monk called O Lo Pen in Chinese— Father Weiger suggests Ruben—arrived at the Court of T'ai Tsung. O Lo Pen was received by the Emperor in person, and orders were given that his books should be translated into Chinese. Somewhat later the monk was granted an audience in which he expounded his religion to the Emperor. A favourable impression of Christianity was the result of this audience, for in A.D. 635, T'ai Tsung issued an edict couched in the following terms:

"The Way* has more than one name. There is more than one Sage. Doctrines vary in different lands, their benefits reach all mankind. O Lo Pen, a man of great virtue from Ta Ts'in (the Roman Empire) has brought his images and books from afar to present them in our capital. After examining his doctrines we find them profound and pacific. After studying his principles we find that they stress what is good and important. His teaching is not diffuse and his reasoning is sound. This religion does good to all men. Let it be preached freely in Our Empire."

Lest it be thought that this eulogy suggests that the Emperor was converted to Christianity, it must be remembered that T'ai Tsung also received and honoured the Buddhist pilgrim, Yüan Chuang, approved of Taosim, favoured the Confucians, and permitted

*Tao, the way of truth, religion in general.

Zoroastrianism. The great T'ai Tsung was in this respect typical of his age and nation.

Nevertheless Nestorian Christianity had a considerable following in China, and, unlike the other alien creeds, it was supported by very influential people. The tablet states that under T'ai Tsung's son and successor, Kao Tsung, churches were built in every prefectural city, which, if it is true, would mean that Christianity had a greater success in the 7th century than it has achieved in modern times. In A.D. 698 under the Empress Wu, who was a fervent Buddhist, Nestorianism was persecuted to some degree, and as the Buddhists were responsible for this change of attitude it is probable that Christianity was felt to be a dangerous rival. The disfavour did not last, for at the succession of Hsüan Tsung (Ming Huang) Nestorians were once more befriended by the Emperor, who sent his brothers to attend the restoration of the altar at the principal church in Ch'ang An. Later emperors continued the favour first shown by T'ai Tsung, even attending Nestorian religious services on more than one occasion.

When the tablet was erected, in A.D. 781, some years after the suppression of An Lu-shan's rebellion, the Nestorian Church was in a very flourishing condition, counting among its protectors and benefactors the celebrated Kuo Tzǔ-i, grand general of the forces and chief minister of the empire, the man to whom the T'ang Emperors owed the restoration of their throne. Kuo Tzǔ-i is one of the paragons of loyalty and good faith most famous in Chinese history; if, as the tablet seems to suggest, this great man was a Nestorian, the Christians had the most powerful and upright man in China as their patron. It is recorded of him that he spent large sums in restoring and enlarging churches, giving alms to monks and priests and also held conferences with the Nestorian hierarchy. If Kuo Tzǔ-i was not a baptised Nestorian, he must have been very near to the Christian faith.

With such powerful protectors, the first personages of the Court —for Kuo Tzǔ-i's daughter was Empress, and his son married an imperial Princess—it seems strange that Christianity should have totally disappeared within a century or so of the erection of the tablet. Catholic writers explain the fact by pointing out that Nestorianism is a heresy, not orthodox Christian doctrine, but this argument (which in any case would not appeal to Protestant apologists) ignores the fact that Buddhism, which is not even a Christian heresy, survived the persecution it suffered in common with Christianity and the other alien creeds, but which proved fatal to the latter.

The great persecution, marking the end of the T'ang tolerance of foreign creeds, occurred in A.D. 843, when it was first directed against the Manicheans. This religion had only been tolerated because it was that of the powerful Uigurs. The Uigurs, however, were destroyed by their enemies the Khirgiz in A.D. 840, and the Emperor Wu Tsung, an ardent Taoist, immediately suppressed the Manichean faith by force. Seventy Manichean nuns were put to death in Ch'ang An, their temples were pulled down, their lands confiscated to the state, and their priests forced to abandon their distinctive dress and wear the costume of Chinese laymen. Manicheism in China never recovered from the blow. Although stray references to the religion occur as late as the Mongol period, and isolated communities in the mountains seem to have practised the rites of the faith for some centuries, the Manicheans dwindled swiftly, and ultimately disappeared entirely from the Far East.

Two years later, in A.D. 845, the Emperor struck at all the alien creeds, including Buddhism. This religion, no doubt because it was the most widespread, was permitted under severe restrictions. Only one temple was allowed in each city, and not more than thirty monks were permitted to reside in each temple. All other Buddhist priests were secularised, all other temples and monasteries seized and destroyed by the state.

The Christian and Zoroastrian churches and temples were suppressed without exception, the priests forbidden to preach their religion, and the monks secularised; 4,600 temples of these three religions were destroyed, and 260,500 priests and nuns forced to return to the world. Of this number only 2,000 are said to have been Christian, and 1,000 Zoroastrian; the rest must have been Buddhists. The number of priests is not perhaps an accurate guide to the number of Christians, for the Buddhist priests, or more correctly monks, form a much higher percentage of the faithful than the ratio of Christian priests to their flocks.

The persecution, though severe, was short. Wu Tsung died in

the following year, and his successor reversed the treatment of the Buddhists, whom he favoured. Buddhism at once recovered its former strength. Christianity and Zoroastrianism collapsed. In A.D. 987, a hundred years later, Abu Faraj, an Arab writer, records that when in Bagdad he met a Nestorian monk who had recently returned from China, where he had been sent by the Patriarch to inquire into the condition of the faith under the newly-founded Sung dynasty. The monk had found the churches ruined and deserted, the Christian community extinct, and, as there were no co-religionists for him to minister to, he had returned to Bagdad.

Christianity, however, seems to have left some impression on the Chinese Court, as is evidenced by the wide knowledge of foreign religions shown by the Emperor I Tsung, who in 872, thirty years after the persecution, gave an audience to the Arab traveller Ibn Wahab of Basra, who related his experiences to Abu Zaid after his return to Iraq:

"When I was received by the Emperor," Ibn Wahab relates, "he told the interpreter to ask me, 'can you recognise your Master, if you see him?' The Emperor referred to Mahomet, upon whom be God's Blessing. I replied: 'How can I see him, since he is in Heaven with the Most High God?' 'I am talking of his likeness,' said the Emperor. 'I would know that,' I replied. Then the Emperor called for a box containing rolls which he put in front of him, and passed them to his interpreter, saying: 'Let him see his Master.' I recognised the portraits of the Prophets, and I said a blessing. 'Why are you moving your lips?' asked the Emperor. 'Because I am blessing the Prophets,' I answered. 'How did you know them?' he asked. 'By their attributes; for instance, here is Noah with his Ark, which saved him and his family when at the command of God all the earth was drowned in the Food.' At these words the Emperor laughed, and said, 'You have certainly recognised Noah. As for the Flood, we do not believe it. The Flood did not submerge the whole world. It did not reach China or India.' 'That is Moses with his staff,' I said. 'Yes," said the Emperor, 'but he was not important and his people were few.' 'There,' I said, 'is Jesus on his ass, surrounded by his apostles.' 'Yes,'' said the Emperor: 'He lived only a short time. His mission lasted only thirty months.' Then I saw the Prophet on a camel, and his companions, also on camels, around him. I wept, being much moved. 'Why do you weep?' asked the Emperor. 'Because I see our Prophet, my ancestor.' [Ibn Wahab was of the Koreish.] 'Yes, it is he,' said the Emperor. 'He and his people founded a glorious empire. He did not see it completed, but his successors have.' Above each picture was an inscription [in Chinese] which I supposed to contain an account of their history. I saw also other pictures, which I did not recognise. The interpreter told me that they were the prophets of China and India.''

From this fascinating story it can be seen that the Chinese Court had a library containing much information about the western religions, and, moreover, that the Emperor was perfectly familiar with the leading events and characters of western religious lore. This audience, in A.D. 872, took place a very few years before the rebellion of Huang Tsao reduced the T''ang Empire to chaos and partition. During those violent years foreign intercourse naturally diminished, and was not fully restored till China had recovered internal peace under the Sung dynasty, nearly a century later.

Chapter XVI

THE GOLDEN AGE OF POETRY

BEFORE the T'ang period poetry had lagged behind the other branches of literature in China. The classical period nevertheless had the very ancient anthology of songs, poems and ritual hymns, which together make up the *Shih Ching* (The Odes). In the eyes of a Confucian scholar these would always rank higher than the poetry of later times, but that is because they were valued not so much for their poetic qualities as for the moral instruction they were supposed to contain, and, because tradition attributed the compilation to Confucius himself. In the late feudal age, the 3rd century B.C., there was one very famous poet, Ch'u Yüan, a minister at the Court of the King of Ch'u. Ch'u Yüan's elegies were a new form of poetry which seems to have been confined to the south, and, though imitated by less inspired poets after the master's death, did not exercise a lasting influence on poetry in other parts of China. The most famous of his poems is the *Li Sao*, "Encountering Sorrow," a love allegory which alludes to the poet's fall from favour with the King of Ch'u. Ch'u Yüan drowned himself in the Mi Lo River in Hunan, and the celebrated Dragon Boat Festival is said to have been instituted to commemorate the search for the poet's body.

The Han period was not a great age of poetry. There were indeed poets who are still admired, but, compared to the prose works of this dynasty, the poetry is insignificant. The period of partition which followed the fall of the Han dynasty was dominated by the powerful influence of new religions, Buddhism and the new forms of Taoism. The poetry of this period is not rated very highly by the Chinese, although it was then that an important development originated. Shên Yo (A.D. 441-513) was the first poet to use tone values, inventing the kind of verse called *lu shih*.

The Chinese language, being monosyllabic, is very rich in homophones, i.e. words distinguished only by the use of differing tones. In *lu shih* verse tone values are developed in accordance with certain rules, as the name *lu shih*, "regulated poetry," implies. Before the time of Shên Yo tone had been ignored. This old poetry (*ku shih*) was not entirely superseded by the tone poems; it continued to be written, not only in the T'ang period, but down to modern times. It was not until a hundred years after the death of Shên Yo that the T'ang poets, taking up his idea, raised poetry to a height which it had never before attained, and which has hardly ever been equalled in later centuries.

The three centuries of the T'ang period were beyond dispute the golden age of poetry in China. There was, indeed, hardly any branch of art in which the astonishing genius of that age did not excel. In the first half of the 8th century the greatest painters, poets and sculptors gathered at the Court of Ming Huang the well-named "brilliant Emperor" who made Ch'ang An the most civilised capital in the world, the admiration and despair of succeeding dynasties. In literature, however, it was poetry which suited the genius of the T'ang age more than any other branch. The quantity produced in that dynasty is enormous, and the long list of T'ang poets amounts to nearly 3,000 names. Obviously, not all T'ang verse is first-rate, and perhaps some T'ang poets would not be highly esteemed if they had written under later dynasties, yet almost all the most famous poets of China lived in that period, and many of them were contemporaries. There was some quality in the culture of the T'ang epoch which was peculiarly favourable to poetry and less in tune with the classical tradition which inspired the philosophers of an earlier, and again of a later dynasty.

The T'ang period was the romantic age in China. The long reigns of the Empress Wu and Ming Huang, covering the second half of the 7th and first half of the 8th centuries, favoured the development of refined culture, and were at the same time a period of innovation and experiment. Confucian traditionalism was in temporary eclipse. There has never been an age since it became the established and orthodox doctrine when the influence of classical scholarship was weaker. The Empress Wu was a fervent Buddhist, and Ming Huang himself was more inclined of Taoism than to the traditional doctrines. With the exception to T'ai Tsung, who was orthodox, but completely tolerant, hardly one of the T'ang Emperors wholeheartedly favoured the

Confucian ethics. This negative attitude did not imply an open repudiation of the orthodox doctrine upon which the whole educational system reposed, and upon which the moral authority of the government was supposed to be founded. Even the poets themselves, with the possible exception of the greatest, Li Po, were Confucian in outlook, though Taoist in inspiration.

In the T'ang period, an age at once more refined than the preceding Han Empire and less sophisticated than the Sung dynasty which followed, Chinese civilisation attained a harmonious balance between Confucian objectivity and Taoist introspection which was an ideal atmosphere for the cultivation of the arts. The society of Ch'ang An was not wholly frivolous nor was the Court entirely occupied in ministering to the extravagant caprices of ladies such as Yang Kuei Fei. The century of the artists and poets was also the century of the fervent Buddhist pilgrims and preachers and of the vigorous imperialism of the frontier generals. It was a many sided age, less hide-bound by conventions and more receptive to new influences than other periods of Chinese history.

It is a truism to repeat that poetry of all the arts is the most national and the hardest to appreciate for those unacquainted with the language of the originals. Translation may capture the spirit, but it must inevitably lose the form of the poem itself, and when as in the case of translations from Chinese into English, the structure and sound of the two languages differ profoundly, the task of the translator is immeasurably increased. In this field scholars well equipped to render the Chinese into English with poetic form have published a wide selection of the most famous Chinese poems,* which since they convey the spirit of Chinese poetry, are infinitely preferable to halting prose renderings.

The European reader will find certain differences between Chinese and western poetry which are independent of questions of language and technique. Love, which plays so large a part in European poetry, is a rare theme. Metaphor is hardly employed

*Arthur Waley. *A Hundred and Seventy Chinese Poems.*
H. Giles. *Chinese Poetry in English Verse.*
F. Ayscough and A. Lowell. *Fir Flower Tablets.*
F. Ayscough. *Tu Fu.*

and simile is restricted. Such a line as "Vaulting ambition which o'erleaps itself" cannot be found in Chinese poetry. Classical allusions, obscure to anyone who has not been brought up on the Confucian classics, are frequent. This, indeed, became the vice of later Chinese poetry, ultimately reducing it to an elegant but lifeless artificiality. In the T'ang period the disease was in its infancy, and had not produced the petrifying effects which makes so much Ming and Manchu poetry arid and conventional.

The absence of love poetry in Chinese literature is a consequence of the social system which admitted no courtship or free choice in marriage. A man married a girl chosen by his parents without his consent or opinion being asked. He never saw his bride until the marriage ceremony was ended, and should a chance meeting have occurred, this in itself was looked upon as a reason for cancelling the betrothal. Love therefore came after marriage, if at all. Illicit love, later the theme of the novelists, was not a subject which could decently be treated in a scholarly art such as poetry.

One result of these marriage customs was to enhance the emotional value of male companionship, making friendship the most intimate and binding relation outside the ties of family life. In Chinese society friendship plays a part and imposes obligations which would seem excessive in the west. Even the most ardent supporter of his "old school" in England would flinch at the prospect of having to support his former schoolmates in his home for an indefinite period, merely because they had no relations of their own in that part of the country. In China this would be regarded as a matter of course. The ties of friendship, and the evil corollaries of nepotism and cabal, permeate Chinese social and political life, and are a dominant theme in literature.

In poetry friendship fills the place which love occupies in European poems, and, as the emotional crisis of friendship is the moment of separation, parting from a friend inspires many of the best poems in China. The circumstances of the poets' lives in China made such separations frequent and prolonged. Poets were necessarily members of the educated class of scholars from whom the ranks of the officials were filled. Unlettered poets could hardly exist in a country using an ideographic script which requires several years of study before the student can read or write. Moreover, since poetry was written in the literary style which used an idiom not employed in every-day speech, only the sons of the rich, or those who were sent to school at the expense of the wealthy members of the clan, could acquire the necessary education.

The great poets of China, therefore, were one and all members of the scholar class, though not all of them were employed in the public service. Whether serving the state or living in retirement they were constantly parted from their friends, who might at any time be appointed to a distant post, or banished from the capital as a result of some political change. The immense distances of the Chinese Empire, the dangers of travel, and the inadequate means of communication made these partings a very real and often final separation of two friends, who might not meet again, at best, for many years. The fact explains and illuminates the frequent theme of leave-taking in Chinese poetry.

Friendship and parting take the place of love and frustration, and war, too, is treated from a different standpoint. There were no soldier-poets in China—scholars were not warriors—and when a Chinese poet writes of war or battles it is to paint the horrors and desolation of warfare rather than the glory and joy of battle. For the same reason the patriotic aspect of military life is ignored by Chinese poets. Deeply penetrated by the Confucian doctrines which formed the basis of their education, the Chinese scholar looked upon war as a calamity, whether the imperial arms were successful or the reverse. The very necessity of war was proof of inferior virtue in the Son of Heaven, for Confucians had always contended that a truly virtuous prince would have no enemies. The force of his moral qualities would in itself suffice to keep the peace within the empire and pacify the barbarous peoples beyond the frontiers. Rebellion was an indication of bad government, and foreign wars a confession of inferior virtue.

Taoism, at least in the T'ang period, was as strong an influence on poetry as Confucian morality. From this source the poets learned the doctrines which sent them to nature for inspiration. Taoism rejected the world and its honours, teaching that truth could only be found in the secluded hermitages of the high mountains and wild forests, the haunts of the immortals who had obtained the secret of long life and a true understanding of the Tao. The influence of Taoism, so apparent in Chinese painting, is equally strong in poetry, though Confucian writers, unwilling to admit the fact, have tried to make light of the obvious Taoist inspiration which dominates the works of Li Po.

The career of Li Po, who is generally recognised as the greatest of Chinese poets, is typical of the life of a scholar poet in the T'ang period, and illustrates the opposing influences of Confucian duty and the Taoist ideal of retreat. Although Li Po claimed descent from Li Kao, Prince of West Liang in the 4th century, who was the ancestor of the imperial house of the T'ang dynasty, this distant connection, if acknowledged by the Emperor, does not seem to have conferred any remarkable privileges on the poet's family. Li Po was born in Szechuan, most probably in the year A.D. 701, but his family were not very well to do or influential.

He is said to have been a precocious child, mastering the classics at an early age. Perhaps this intensive education in Confucianism produced a reaction, for, when still a youth Li Po went to a secluded retreat on Mount Min, where he studied Taoism with a hermit. He does not appear to have made any attempt to qualify for the public service, for, when he left Mount Min he did not visit the capital, but set out on extensive travels in all parts of China. In A.D. 724 he was in Shantung, where he made one of a literary coterie known as the "Six Idlers of the Bamboo Grove," a name clearly intended to recall the famous Taoist "Seven Sages of the Bamboo Grove" of the Tsin dynasty (see Chapter XII).

During further travels in Honan and Shansi he had occasion to befriend a poor soldier who was one day to repay the service by saving Li Po's life. This obscure soldier was none other than Kuo Tzŭ-i, who, after the revolt of An Lu-shan, became the commander-in-chief of the imperial armies, chief minister of the empire, and the patron of the Nestorian Church in China. In A.D. 738, in Shantung, Li Po met his great contemporary, Tu Fu, a poet who ranks as his equal, and in the eyes of many Chinese critics, his superior. Li Po and Tu Fu became lifelong friends, and their intimacy is mentioned in many poems by both writers.

It was not until A.D. 742 that Li Po went for the first time to the capital, where he was introduced to Court circles by a Taoist scholar whom he had met on his travels in Chekiang. The Court was then dominated by the famous Yang Kuei Fei, the beautiful concubine who reigned supreme in the affections of the ageing Emperor, Ming Huang. Li Po was already famous as a poet, indeed, he was introduced to the Emperor as a "banished immortal"—a divine genius in mortal form—and Ming Huang immediately gave him a sinecure post with the duty of writing poems to commemorate Court festivities.

This does not seem to have been a very exacting task, for Li Po had plenty of leisure to indulge his weakness for wine, and enjoy the society of a group of friends of similar tastes who called themselves the "Eight Immortals of the Wine Cup." Tu Fu has written a celebrated poem about the Eight Immortals, who were all men of distinction and culture:

> Chih-chang, astride a horse, seems on board a boat;
> Giddy, eyes dim, he drops into a well and sleeps under water.
>
> Prince Ju-yang drinks three measures, then starts for an
> audience before Heaven;
> On the road he meets a cart of barm: from his mouth trickles
> the saliva;
> He feels annoyed that he is not transferred to govern beside
> the Wine Springs.
>
> High Adviser of the Left day after day wastes ten thousand
> pieces;
> He drinks like a long whale, sucking in the one hundred
> streams;
> When holding a wine-cup to his lips, he says: "I rejoice in
> clear wine of Enlightened Men; I fly moreover from thick
> draughts of Virtuous Worthies."
>
> Tsung-chih in beauty of his early years is distinguished and
> exceedingly refined;
> Grasping wine goblet, he turns up his bright eyes towards
> blue empyrean;
> His skin is white as tree of jade which bends before the wind.
> Su Chin sits for ages in abstraction before Maitreya Buddha;

When in his cups, gone, gone, is this desire; he flies from
meditation.

Li Po after one measure produces one hundred poems;
He sleeps in a wine shop at Ch'ang An market-place;
The Son of Heaven summons him to the Presence; he does
not board the boat;
He styles himself "Official who is an Immortal of Wine."

Chang Hsü, after three cups, writes inspired characters;
Throws off his cap, appears bare-headed before the Prince
and high officials;
Strokes of his long-haired writing brush drop on the paper
like clouds or driving mist.

At five measures, Chiao Sui becomes extremely eloquent,
Talks learnedly, argues vigorously, startles all who sit on the
four sides of the feast.*

Li Shih-chi had been a minister of the government until he
resigned to avoid the jealousy of rivals; Chin, Prince of Ju-yang,
was a member of the imperial family; Tsui Tsung-chih, a close
friend of Li Po, was a historian; and Chang Hsü a celebrated
calligrapher; Su Chin was a Buddhist, although he did not allow
his religion to interfere with his love of wine; and Ho Chih-chang
was the friend who had first brought Li Po to the Emperor's
notice.

Li Po enjoyed the society of these friends and the favour of
Ming Huang for three years, until he was forced to leave Ch'ang
An for ever as a result of a Court intrigue. The causes of his disgrace are variously attributed to the jealousy of rivals and to the
enmity of the powerful chief eunuch, Kao Li-shih. It is said that
on one occasion Li Po, when drunk at a Court banquet, made the
eunuch pull off his shoes, an insult which Kao Li-shih would not
forgive. Li Po had written a poem to commemorate a spring
festival in the peony gardens of the palace, and Kao Li-shih told
the favourite, Yang Kuei Fei, that in this poem Li Po, while
seeming to praise her beauty, had compared her to Lady Flying
Swallow (Fei Yen), a Han dynasty beauty. This was a back-

*Florence Ayscough. *Tu Fu, the Autobiography of a Chinese Poet.* 1929. pp. 83-5.

handed compliment, for Lady Flying Swallow had deceived the Emperor, and fallen into disgrace. Yang Kuei Fei resented the comparison and obtained the poet's dismissal. Whether this story is true or not it is quite in character.

After leaving Ch'ang An, which was soon to experience the fury of An Lu-shan's rebel soldiery, Li Po went to Shantung, where he studied Taoism at the residence of the T'ien Shih, the spiritual head of the Taoist religion.* Later, the poet wandered south again to Nanking, where he found his friend Tsui Tsung-chi also in exile. The rebellion of An Lu-shan found Li Po at Lo Yang, from which city he escaped just before the rebels captured it. He took refuge in the south once more, and joined the staff of Li Ling, Prince of Yung, who was organising resistance to An Lu-shan in the Yangtze Valley. Li Ling, however, attempted to profit by the confusion following the abdication of Ming Huang to make himself Emperor. His plans fell through, and he was disgraced, Li Po being put into prison as an accomplice. In this extremity, for he was under sentence of death, Li Po was saved by the intercession of Kuo Tzǔ-i, then commander-in-chief and chief support of the tottering throne, who remembered the poet's kindness to him thirty years before.

Li Po was reprieved, but sentenced to banishment to the frontier district of Yeh Lang, in what is now the modern province of Kueichou. He travelled slowly up the Yangtze, making many and long stays with friends on the way. After three years he still had got no further than Wu Shan, above the gorge of the same name in Szechuan, when a general amnesty relieved him of the necessity of proceeding further. He was now an old man, and the glory of Ming Huang's Empire had departed. Li Po travelled slowly back to T'ai P'ing in Anhui, where a relative held office, and there, in A.D. 761, he died.†

Li Po was not the only famous poet of Ming Huang's age and

*The modern T'ien Shih lived on Lung Hu Shan (Dragon and Tiger mountain) in Kiangsi until, in 1928, he was driven away by the Communist armies.

†Traditionally by drowning in the waters of the Yangtze when trying to embrace the reflection of the moon in the water. A temple on the bluffs at Ts'ai Shih Chi, about fifteen miles from Nanking, marks the site.

Court. His friends, Tu Fu (A.D. 713-768) and Mêng Hao-jan (A.D. 689-740), are two of the greatest poets of the T'ang or any other period. Tu Fu was a more scholarly writer than Li Po, paying strict attention to the rules of the *lu shih* form of poetry, which Li Po sometimes contravenes or ignores. Tu Fu, for this reason, is sometimes considered to be the scholar's poet, while his friend's work makes a wider appeal to the less literate class. Chinese critics as a whole prefer Tu Fu, but the universal appeal of Li Po's poetry can be better appreciated in translations. Tu Fu, like his friend, never rose to any great eminence in the public service. He failed to qualify in the civil service examinations, on account, it is said, of the jealousy of the examiners. Later, this unjust disqualification was reversed, and he held small posts at the capital and elsewhere before the rebellion of An Lu-shan.

During the chaos following the fall of the capital he suffered every kind of misfortune and privation. He was captured by bandits, and, even after he had escaped and joined the fugitive Emperor Su Tsung, Ming Huang's son and successor, he was in such poverty that some of his children died of undernourishment. The last years of his life were spent in happier circumstances in Szechuan, a fortunate province which escaped the ravages of the war. Tu Fu died in A.D. 768 as the result of privations experienced on a journey in the mountains of eastern Szechuan.

Mêng Hao-jan and Wang Wei (A.D. 699-759) were slightly older men than their more famous contemporaries. The former, indeed, died some years before the fatal rebellion broke out. Li Po's poem, "Taking leave of Mêng Hao-jan at the Yellow Crane Tower" must have been written on some occasion before Li Po went to Ch'ang An, for by then the elder poet was already dead. Mêng Hao-jan holds a high place in the estimation of the Chinese, but his poetry has as yet been very little translated into English. Wang Wei, who is equally famous as a painter, was an ardent Buddhist, and occupied important government posts under Ming Huang. When the capital fell into rebel hands An Lu-shan carried him off captive to Lo Yang, where the rebel had his headquarters, and Wang Wei was forced into his service. He managed to send a secret letter to the T'ang Emperor, Su Tsung, protesting his fidelity, and when he escaped from the rebel country this precaution saved his life. Although pardoned and re-employed, he could not forget the disgrace of having preferred life in rebel service to the Confucian ideal of a "loyal death," and he soon retired. In the mountain retreat, where he spent his last years he pursued his Buddhist studies, and when he died left this property to the church to be converted into a monastery.

Po Chu-i, one of the greatest names in Chinese poetry, who is usually ranked with Li Po and Tu Fu, belonged to a later generation, the period of comparative quiet and recovery which followed the suppression of the rebellion by Kuo Tzǔ-i. He was born in A.D. 772, and like Wang Wei, was a native of the northern province of Shansi. Unlike Li Po and Tu Fu, who never had a regular official career, Po Chu-i spent a long life almost entirely in government service, in which he rose to very high rank. His career, as was so often the case with Chinese officials, was checkered with the usual ups and downs of favour, banishment, promotion and disgrace, but at the end of his life he obtained the governorship of Honan with his residence at Lo Yang, the alternative capital of the T'ang dynasty.

Much of his life before this long-awaited promotion had been spent at minor posts in the south, Szechuan, the Yangtze Valley and Chekiang, where he was governor of Hang Chou, and he was very little at Court. Even when, in A.D. 831, he finally retired, he chose the secluded village of Lung Mên, the Buddhist shrine near Lo Yang as his retreat, in which to pass the last fourteen years of his life. It was during the leisure hours of this long official career that Po Chu-i wrote the great volume of poetry which won him, even in his own lifetime, recognition as one of the greatest of Chinese poets, although the poems which gained the popular approval were not those which the poet himself valued the most.

Po Chu-i was orthodox and Confucian in his outlook and the poetry which expressed this doctrine did not make the appeal which he expected. It was his romantic poems, and in particular the long poem called the "Everlasting Wrong," which aroused the enthusiasm of contemporaries, and it is for this poetry that he is remembered. "The Everlasting Wrong," one of the longest poems in the Chinese language, is a romantic account of the tragic love of Yang Kuei Fei and Ming Huang, interwoven with the rich thread of Taoist legend. When Ming Huang, old and broken in spirit, returns to the ruined capital from which the rebels have recently been expelled, he endeavours by magic arts to find the soul of his beloved. At last a Taoist discovers her, neither in Heaven nor the underworld, but in the spell-bound isle of P'êng Lai in the Eastern Sea, on which no ordinary mortal can ever land. There Yang Kuei Fei is able to give the imperial messenger a word of hope. One day, in some future existence they will be re-united, but time cannot efface the "everlasting wrong" which Ming Huang committed in sacrificing his beloved to the mutinous soldiery.

At a time when the story was still recent history it is easy to understand how this poem became so well known that even dancing girls could recite it by heart. Po Chu-i, who did not regard it as his best work, could never make his moral poems prevail against the romantic tendencies of the age, tendencies to which he yielded in such poems as "The Everlasting Wrong," with its very un-Confucian moral.

Although the T'ang dynasty is especially renowned for poetry other branches of literature were not neglected. Among the contemporaries of the famous poets there were Buddhist theologians, Confucian scholars and historians, as well as the first writers to explore the hitherto untouched fields of drama and fiction. Every literary development of later Chinese history, Sung philosophy alone excepted, can be traced back to those great centuries. The drama which is the only intellectual glory of the Mongol Yüan dynasty, originated at Ming Huang's Court, and that Emperor is still venerated by actors as their patron. The novels of the Ming and Manchu dynasties developed from the short stories which were first written in the T'ang period.

The most famous prose writer of the T'ang dynasty is without question Han Yü (768-824), who is reckoned as one of the greatest Confucian scholars of Chinese history, not only on account of his resolute orthodoxy in a lax age, but also for the vigour and purity of his style. Apart from the literary qualities of Han Yü's writings, he is an important figure as the link between the Han Confucian scholars and the Sung philosophers. He represents, superbly, the basic practical and anti-mystical outlook which characterises the Chinese mind. He typifies the unchanging realism of the Confucian tradition which opposed and defeated the Buddhist evangel.

Han Yü, however, was not a blind conservative reiterating moral maxims in a scholarly detachment from practical issues. He proved in action that the Confucian theory of government by moral authority was not a vain ideal. He had the moral and physical courage not only to oppose the fervent Buddhism of the Court in outspoken essays, but also to go unarmed into a rebel camp and preach Confucian loyalty to a contumacious governor. His anti-Buddhist memorials and essays brought him disgrace and exile to a remote region of Kuangtung province, then an uncivilised district on the frontier of the empire. Han Yü, however, rose superior to his misfortune. In his exile he applied his principles to the government of the district, and had the triumph of leaving it happy and prosperous when he was recalled to the capital.

In his time, the generation following the rebellion of An Lu-shan, the Emperor no longer wielded undisputed authority over the distant governors. The viceroys of the eastern provinces far from the Court could not be coerced without plunging the empire into civil war, and, consequently, they tended to grow more and more independent, transmitting their authority to their sons and grandsons. In A.D. 822 the governor of a district in Hopei refused obedience and attacked his neighbour in the hope of adding more territory to his fief. The imperial armies, ill paid and without provisions, were unable to reduce him to submission. In this emergency the Emperor sent Han Yü to try the effect of persuasion where force had failed. Attended only by a few bodyguards Han Yü made his way to the rebel's camp and demanded an interview with their leader. His arguments made some impression upon the rebel governor, and still more upon his officers, who had less to gain and more to lose by opposing the Court. Probably fearing that defiance would be followed by a mutiny in his army, the rebel chief agreed to terms, and Han Yü returned to Ch'ang An, having triumphantly vindicated the authority of the Emperor and the Confucian theory of government.

In A.D. 819, the Emperor Hsien Tsung, who was a fervent

Buddhist, proposed to bring a celebrated relic, the finger bone of Buddha himself, from the monastery of Fa Mên Ssŭ at Fêng Hsiang Fu to Ch'ang An, where it was to be lodged in the imperial palace for three days and then exhibited in the various temples of the capital. This was the occasion on which Han Yü penned his famous memorial to the throne against Buddhism. The piece is too long to cite in full, but the condensed version included in the official history sufficiently indicates its character:

"Buddha is a god of the western countries, and if Your Majesty honours and worships him it is only in the hope of obtaining a long life and a peaceful and happy reign. In antiquity, however, Huang Ti, Yü, T'ang the victorious, and the kings Wên and Wu all enjoyed long lives and their subjects dwelt in unbroken peace, although in those days there was no Buddha. It was only under the Emperor Ming of the Han dynasty that this doctrine was introduced into the empire, and since that time wars and disorders have followed in quick succession, causing great evils and the ruin of imperial dynasties. It was not until the period of the Six Dynasties that the sect of Buddha began to spread, and that age is not far distant from our own.

"Of all the sovereigns of these dynasties only one, Liang Wu Ti, occupied the throne for forty-eight years, and what had he not done to obtain happiness and peace from Buddha? Three times he sold himself to become a slave in a monastery*, and what reward did he receive for this?

"Only a miserable death from hunger when besieged by Hou Ching. Yet he always used to say that he only did these things so little suited to an Emperor in the hope of obtaining happiness from Buddha, but all it brought him was greater misfortune. For Buddha was only a barbarian from the western kingdoms who recognised neither the loyalty which binds a subject to

---

*This refers to the fact that Liang Wu Ti renounced the world three times and became a Buddhist monk. On each occasion he was only persuaded to return to the throne when the monastery had been compensated by payment of a large ransom. Hou Ching was the rebel who captured Nanking and brought the Liang dynasty to an end.

his prince, nor the obedience which a son owes to his father.*
If he was living now and came to your Court, Your Majesty
might accord him one audience in the Hsüan Chêng Hall,
invite him to a banquet at the Li Pin office,† bestow gifts upon
him, and escort him to the frontiers of the empire, without
permitting him to have any contact with the people.

"This man, Buddha, however, has long been dead and
decomposed, and now a dried bone, which is said to be his
finger, is offered to Your Majesty and is to be admitted into
the imperial palace. I dare to ask Your Majesty rather to hand
this bone over to the magistrates so that it may be destroyed
by fire or water and this pernicious cult exterminated. If
Buddha is what he is claimed to be and has the power to make
men happy or unfortunate, then I pray that all the evils which
may arise from this act shall fall on me alone, for I am confident
that he has no such power."

It was for this memorial that Han Yü was banished to far-off
Kuangtung. When he returned to Court and high office under the
next Emperor, Mu Tsung, his protest was still fresh in the public
memory. Han Yü was appointed assessor of the ministry of war,
a post which gave him authority over the discipline of the army.
There was at once a marked improvement in the conduct of the
soldiers, and the men were heard to say that one who was prepared
to burn the finger of the Lord Buddha himself would think
nothing of executing common soldiers.

*Gautama renounced the kingdom to which he was heir and fled secretly
from his father's palace. In the Confucian view he thus contravened two of the
cardinal duties of man.

†The office for entertaining guests and embassies from foreign and tributary
states. In T'ang China there was no ministry for Foreign Affairs.

Chapter XVII

T'ANG ART

In the Chou and Han periods the foreign influence in Chinese art is never dominant and rarely direct. Native motifs, more or less modified by contact with alien cultures, are in the ascendant; foreign motifs are subordinate and have been transformed by Chinese traditions. The introduction of Buddhism at the end of the Han dynasty, however, brought a new and very powerful foreign influence which not only permeated the religious conceptions of the Chinese, but also imported a great artistic tradition inspired by ideals alien to Chinese thought. As its chosen medium this Buddhist inspiration sought expression in plastic forms, a branch of art which in China had hitherto remained restricted to tomb sculpture.

Buddhist art, when it reached China in the 4th and 5th centuries A.D., had already an ancient history in India and Central Asia, where it had been moulded by the Hellenistic influences radiating from the empire of Alexander, his Seleucid successors, and the Roman orient. At Gandhara and Mathura in north-west India Hellenised sculptors, perhaps actually Greek settlers, worked for Buddhist patrons, clothing the Buddha and the Bodhisattvas in the familiar forms of their own classical Mediterranean deities. They were not inspired artists, these Greco-Indian sculptors; but they were competent craftsmen perpetuating a long established tradition, the copying of copies, which reached back to Pergamum and Greece itself. They transferred to the Indian religion all the poses and traditional attitudes of Hellenistic art. The motifs, such as garlands, and the attributes of the pagan deities of the west, including the trident of Poseidon, appear in the unfamiliar surroundings of Buddhist legend and in the inappropriate hands of the disciples of the Indian teacher.

It was from these Indian centres of Hellenised Buddhism that the religion, and the art, spread eastward across Central Asia until it penetrated China, and later crossed to Japan. The Hellenistic influence, strong and dominant in Gandhara, weakened as it passed eastward, absorbed many purely Indian characteristics; and, after it had become acclimatised in China, underwent a further profound modification at the hands of artists who had never known the Gandhara and Mathura originals, still less the classical art of the Mediterranean.

FIG. 48. *Ewer showing Hellenistic motif.*

The Hellenistic spirit was felt, more or less strongly, in all branches of T'ang art, and in the period of the Six Dynasties which preceded the T'ang, but, although many interesting examples of this influence on T'ang pottery exist, such as the ewer, with its classical figure shown in Fig. 48, it was the sacred art of Buddhism which transmitted and maintained the new ideas in their purest form. The characteristic medium of this Buddhist art in China during the ages of its ascendency was sculpture. Painting, pressed into the service of religion, always retained a close connection with secular, or rather non-Buddhist, sources of inspiration, Confucian on the one side and Taoist on the other. Sculpture was the peculiarly Buddhist art, and when pictures came to be preferred to statues in the shrines and monasteries, the force of Buddhism was already in decline.

This fact, the close connection between Buddhism and sculpture, emphasises the alien character of this art in China. It was almost always at the service of the Indian faith, and when it derived its inspiration from other sources, such as in the monumental figures, human and animal, which decorated the approach to imperial tombs, it was with certain very rare exceptions, formal, stylised and massive. This indigenous sculpture, now only represented by the figures placed near imperial tombs, can be traced in literary notices at least as far back as the end of the Feudal period. Discussed later in this Chapter, this Tomb sculpture* is here only mentioned to distinguish it from Buddhist sculpture, which alone inherited the Hellenistic tradition.

Although Buddhist sculpture was under Hellenistic influence, and declined when that influence and the faith which transmitted it lost vigour, yet the western observer, familiar with Greek and Pergamene work, will find the masterpieces of Chinese Buddhist sculpture unsatisfying and inferior. Hardly any Chinese sculpture is executed as a plastic group; it is intended to be seen from the front alone. Physical organic features are not well developed, individual character is hardly ever visible in the treatment of the face. The influence of Hellenistic art appears more in minor ways and in details of motif. Chinese Buddhist sculpture has something of the Greek manner but nothing of its spirit. It has, however, another inspiration, not Greek, but Asiatic, and it can be appreciated only in the understanding of this spirit, and not for degenerate traces of Greek style.

The ideals of the Greek and Buddhist sculptor were completely different. The great artists of the classical age in the west expressed more perfectly than any other people the ideal of humanity. To them man was the centre of the universe, their gods were heroic human beings, gods like men. They were concerned to express individual character, and human beauty. The Buddhist sculptors of India and China were not interested in these conceptions.

---

*This name seems appropriate in view of the character of all surviving examples, exclusively associated with tombs. No connection is intended with the clay grave figures which were placed inside the grave.

They tried to portray not a god in the form of a perfect human being, but the Buddha; and the essential character of the Buddha, the sign of his Buddhahood itself, was that he had transcended humanity and become entirely detached from all human emotion, and earthly desire.

The sculptors who worked at Lung Mên and for the many monasteries of other parts of China, inspired by an ardent faith, succeeded superbly in conveying this ideal of immaculate inhumanity. Their Buddhas are not human, and therefore the physical organism is not stressed. They are not individual, for Buddha is universal, ageless, and beyond desire. He sits in the posture of meditation, calm, aloof; the face subtly illuminated by the smile of all-embracing, divine knowledge. Emotionless and sublime, the discarnate Buddha has no contact with the human race. He has left this earth for ever; he dwells in Nirvana, the absence of striving.

The Indian ideal of renunciation could not for long satisfy the temperate Chinese mind. The violent contrast between asceticism and sensuality which seems to possess Indian art, found no echo in China. After Buddhist art became established in China, and when native artists became the sculptors, the traditional balance and harmony of Chinese taste began to modify the ascetic tradition of India. The Buddhas and Bodhisattvas became less ascetic, more human, and less aloof. The Chinese no longer made gods who had passed beyond the reach of human desires, but tranquil, reposeful figures who have not so much transcended all human cravings as reconciled and conciliated the clash of desire in a peaceful, harmonious compromise. This expresses an essentially Chinese philosophy, but it is neither Indian nor Buddhist.

The break away from Indian tradition did not lead the Chinese nearer to the western ideals of individuality and humanity in the Greek sense. The Chinese never conceived the supernatural powers in human shape. In the earliest religion the representations of the deities were abstract, almost geometrical, symbols of jade. The Chinese outlook in religion was intellectual, and not emotional. The Han Confucianists, when they began to exalt the worship of Heaven above that of the other natural powers, never personified the ruler of the universe, and never made an image of their deity.

Buddhism, under the influence of Indo-Hellenistic artistic traditions came to China with the convention of sacred images well established. To the Chinese it remained something rather alien, reflecting an outlook which was not their own, and with which they never felt at home. Under the inspiration of foreign models, and with the ardour of converts, they adopted the new art and for a time raised it to a high level. It never, however, achieved the perfection attained by other arts, more native to the genius of the race, and the best of the Buddhist sculptors fell far short of the contemporary painting and ceramic art. Under the first impulse this sculpture of the Wei period, neglecting physical form, achieved an abstract but intense realisation of the spiritual meaning of Buddhism. When later, under the T'ang, greater interest in technical accomplishment made the Buddhas more human, more graceful and more refined, they lost the spiritual force which makes the earlier sculpture, in spite of its limitations, a great art. Tao Hsüan, a scholarly Buddhist monk of the second half of the 7th century, already detected the development which within fifty years was to devitalise Buddhist sculpture. He said of the sculptors of his day that their religious images looked like dancing girls, so that every Court lady came to imagine she resembled a Bodhisattva.

Buddhist sculpture seems to have been almost confined to north China; and, although there are a few pieces which are known to have been made in the Chinese Empires south of the Yangtze,* the material is too scanty to establish a comparison between the styles. It has been suggested that this southern style, transported to Korea by sea, lived on in that country and reappeared in the earliest Japanese Buddhist work.† North China, on the other hand, has considerable material from an early date, although neglect and the vandalism of curio seekers has greatly depleted

---

*At Ch'i Hsia Shan, near Nanking, where there are Sui period rock hewn figures and a marble pagoda decorated with bas reliefs. There is also a similar pagoda, of Six Dynasties date, at Ling Yin Ssu, a celebrated monastery near Hang Chou in Chekiang.

†*Chinese Sculpture*. O. Sirén. 1925. Vol. I. p. 34.

the cave temples which held most of the surviving sculpture. Yun Kang, the earliest of these cave shrines, is situated in the north of Shansi province, not far from the city of Ta T'ung Fu, which in the 5th century was the capital of the Wei dynasty, the non-Chinese Tobas, of Tungusic stock.

The frequent presence of Indian, Iranian and Hellenistic motifs in these sculptures, the corresponding absence of characteristically Chinese motifs, and the almost total lack of contemporary inscriptions in Chinese, are strong indications that the artists who worked at Yun Kang were not Chinese, but foreigners, most probably Central Asiatics from Khotan and other cities of Turkestan, which were at that time strong Buddhist centres. Tne Yun Kang sculptures are indeed of more interest as clear evidence of the Buddhist diffusion of Hellenistic influence, than as works of art in themselves. The stone is soft, and has in consequence weathered badly, but the artists were of indifferent quality,

FIG. 49. *Hellenistic figure with trident of Poseidon. Buddhist Sculpture at Yun Kang, Shansi. After Sirén, Chinese Sculpture.*

copying, without any clear understanding of their purpose, the Hellenistic motifs derived from Gandhara, as for example the divinity bearing the trident of Poseidon (Fig. 49). It is the minor figures at Yun Kang, which, by their affinity to Han art in the treatment of the draperies, suggest the presence of Chinese artists, and forecast the rich development which followed when imperial patronage was transferred to a centre where native artistic traditions were strong.

At the end of the 5th century the Wei Emperors moved their capital from the frontier city of Ta T'ung Fu to Lo Yang, the old Han capital in the valley of the Yellow River. At Lung Mên, near the new capital, the Wei Emperors, ardent Buddhists, began to construct a new cave shrine, patterned upon the existing grottoes at Yun Kang. Here, however, the artists were Chinese, and Chinese cultural traditions were deep rooted in the cradle of her civilisation. The Lung Mên sculptures executed under the Wei, Sui, and T'ang Emperors up the end of the 7th century mark the highest achievement of this art in China ; the culmination of the period being the short Sui dynasty (A.D. 580-617), particularly the reign of the fervently Buddhist Emperor Sui Wên Ti (A.D. 580-604). The heads of the Sui Buddhas rank with the finest religious sculpture, the supreme expression of the inspiration of the Buddhist faith. The colossal statues shown in Plate VIII are typical of the more vigorous school of sculpture decorating the Lung Mên caves.

With the T'ang dynasty, especially during the ascendency of the Empress Wu (A.D. 650-700) began the period of refinement and humanisation. Already the Sui figures are less abstract, more plastic, with less emphasis on line and drapery, than those of the Wei dynasty. In the T'ang sculptures these features are still more pronounced. Pilgrims who had visited India and Central Asia brought back and popularised the cult of Amida Buddha, less austere and unworldly than the earlier forms of the faith. In response to this tendency in worship art became more human. The feminisation of the treatment of the Bodhisattvas, commented upon by Tao Hsüan, introduced a new, less religious quality into sculpture. The gradual transformation of the Bodhisattva Avalokitesvara, the Chinese Kuan Yin, into female form, though not complete until the Sung period, can be traced from the 7th century. Kuan Yin, the giver of sons, a Madonna-like figure often holding a child, is indeed a later development, but the process which ended in the conception of a divinity so little in accord with primitive Buddhist ideals began with the change of style in sculpture which robbed the Buddhas of their divine detachment from earthly desires.

Religious sculpture had always been an art fostered and sustained by imperial patronage, and when, after the death of the Empress Wu, the Court became more interested in painting and poetry than in sculpture, the decline was swift. The Lung Mên sculptors ceased to work, for the Emperor Ming Huang, artist though he was, cared more for Taoism than Buddhism, and more for painting, poetry and music than for sculpture. Other influences less direct than a change of religious fashion at Court assisted the decline. The Muhammadan invasions of Persia and Central Asia had made the road to India unsafe for Buddhist pilgrims, and had already begun the extermination of the once great centres of the faith situated in what are now the essentially Islamic countries of Turkestan and North-West India. In the 9th century (A.D. 845), the great persecution of foreign faiths, which destroyed Manicheism and Nestorian Christianity in China,* dealt a graver blow to Buddhist art than to the faith itself. Though the monks were secularised and not butchered, the temples and images were destroyed. Buddhism swiftly recovered from this calamity but Buddhist art did not.

Henceforward in the Sung and later dynasties, sculpture sank to the level of a secondary art, devoted to the adornment of temples as before, but lacking the spiritual force which inspired the Wei, Sui and T'ang sculptors to greatness. Sung sculptors preferred to work in wood, and, although their work is often charming and sophisticated, it is not the chosen medium of the great artists of the period. This indeed was already the case by the 8th century, for it is recorded of a rival of the great painter, Wu Tao-tzǔ, that, realising his inability to equal the work of that master, he gave up painting and became a sculptor.

The technique of the Han bas-reliefs was also used by the

*See Chapter XVI.

FIG. 50. *Part of a relief representing the dedication of a Buddhist temple.*
Wei period. Dated A.D. 525.

Buddhist sculptors of the Wei period, although the style was modified to suit religious subjects. The relief illustrated in Fig. 50, which is of particular interest since the associated inscription dates it to 525, is characteristic of the Wei style. The scene represents the dedication of an altar by an official accompanied by two attendants and umbrella bearers. A groom, wearing the typical Wei hose, leads the official's horse, which is protected on the neck and shoulders by an elaborately decorated harness of what may well be moulded leather to judge from pottery specimens in the Eumorfopoulos collection.

The fact that there existed a native, non-Buddhist sculpture in China has already been mentioned. This art was older than the Indo-Hellenistic tradition which informed Buddhist work, but though colossal figures in bronze and stone are mentioned in Han literature very little survives from this age. All existing non-Buddhist sculpture is found at tombs, usually at those of Emperors or princes. Although some pieces found at An Yang attest the antiquity of this art, it would seem, from the few surviving works of Han date, that a marked change in style occurred at the end of the Feudal Period. The Shang pieces are conventional and decorated in the manner of the Shang bronzes. The Han and later figures are massive works executed in the round, representing animals or standing human figures, such ornament as there is being a naturalistic rendering of harness or armour. The art was continued up to modern times, indeed is still alive, the latest examples being the lions adorning the approaches to the Mausoleum of Sun Yat Sen at Nanking. Though never lacking a certain heavy dignity, the later examples are formal and rigid.

The figures which guard the tombs of the emperors were both human, representing civil and military officials, and animal, very often lions, but also fabulous beasts, griffins and winged monsters. The treatment of the human figures is inferior to that of the animals, and this in itself suggests that tomb sculpture derived inspiration from an Iranian source and owed nothing to the Indo-Hellenistic current.

Tomb sculpture as a whole is monumental, heavy, and lacking in vitality. The principal piece dating from the Han period, a horse trampling the figure of a Hsiung Nu (Hun), which adorns

FIG. 51. *Winged Lion from Liang Tombs, Nanking.*

the tomb of the Emperor Wu's cavalry general, Ho Ch'u-p'ing, is more important as a historical monument connected with this well-known personage than as a work of art. It has, indeed a certain massive brutality which is not inappropriate in a memorial to a general of those ferocious wars. Compared to this group the winged lions which guard the sepulchres of the Liang princes, near Nanking, mark a great advance (Fig. 51). These monuments, which were no doubt erected at or shortly after the death of these princes (A.D. 518-522), are not intended to be faithful representations of real lions. The lion is not native to China, and the living animal was only occasionally presented as a gift by embassies from western Asiatic states.

Chinese lions were heraldic beasts on which the artist could freely exercise his imagination. The Liang lions, winged, with slender bodies and huge sunken heads, gaping jaws and lolling tongues, are embodiments of tense energy, inspired by that vigorous sense of line which distinguishes the animal style in Scythian art. It is probably from this source that all the best tomb sculpture drew its strength. There is a certain corre-

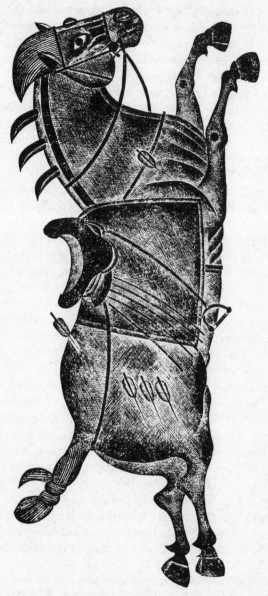

FIG. 52. *One of T'ang T'ai Tsung's six chargers. Drawing from the bas-relief Sianfu, Shensi.*

spondence between the Chinese guardian beasts and the winged
monsters of Persian and Assyrian art, and it is very probable that
the custom of making such monuments, and in particular the
frequent use of the non-Chinese lion, was a consequence of contact
with Parthia in the Han period.

Guardian figures of this kind may have been made for the
tombs of the emperors who followed the Liang dynasty at Nanking,
and perhaps in the north also, but if they ever existed they have
disappeared. The T'ang dynasty, revived, or continued the
custom. It was for the tomb of the second Emperor of this house,
the great T'ai Tsung, that the finest surviving works of Chinese
tomb sculpture were made. The bas-reliefs of the Emperor's six
chargers stand in a class apart. According to tradition they were
executed from the designs of the celebrated painter, Yen Li-pên,
who had perhaps painted the living horses themselves. It is easy
to believe that they were in fact the work of a great artist, and the
use of bas-reliefs, unusual in Tomb sculpture, suggests that the
sculptor was working from the drawings of an artist who was not
at home in the plastic arts. Unlike the heavy figures found at
other imperial tombs the six chargers are spirited and vital
portraits of horses of the short, stocky, Mongolian breed (Fig. 52),
such as are still in common use all over North China.*

T'ai Tsung was a great lover of horses, and it is likely that he
had commissioned Yen Li-pên to design his monument before
he died. The unusual nature and high quality of the work is not
found in the later T'ang tombs, or in those of the Sung Emperors.
The figures which surround their sepulchres are in every way
inferior, apparently the work of stonemasons rather than
sculptors. The two bas-reliefs of ostriches at the tomb of the third
T'ang Emperor, Kao Tsung, alone deserve mention, both
because they are competent works of art, and also because of the
unusual subject. These reliefs, perhaps designed from living
birds presented by a Persian embassy, are faithful representations
of the ostrich, unlike later Chinese pictures of the bird, which bear

---

*The six reliefs have now been saved from the ruin of the Emperor's tomb
at Li Ch'uan in Shensi. Four of them are preserved in the Shensi Provincial
Museum at Sianfu (Ch'ang An), the other two are in the University Museum
at Philadelphia. Casts of this pair are in the British Museum.

little resemblance to reality, and were evidently made by artists who had never seen an ostrich.

The low level of all T'ang and Sung tomb sculpture, the six chargers of T'ai Tsung excepted, is the more remarkable when it is remembered that these periods excelled in other arts, painting, ceramics, and metal working. There was something alien to the Chinese genius in sculpture in stone. Great works of art in this medium were produced only under the stimulus of an alien tradition, like the Hellenistic influence in Buddhist sculpture, or under the borrowed inspiration of an artist who was primarily a painter, as in the reliefs of the six chargers. Ordinarily the best artists did not become sculptors, perhaps because, being trained from childhood in the use of the brush for calligraphy, they turned naturally to the kindred art of painting, and felt that the hammer and chisel were not appropriate tools for a man of culture.

Stone sculpture was entirely at the service of Buddhism and the Court, by which this art was encouraged and sustained. Buddhism, however, even in the centuries of its vigour, never displaced the ancient and enduring native religion of China, ancestor worship, or more properly the cult of the dead. For this popular cult another plastic art, that of the pottery figures, was perfected, until in the T'ang period it far surpassed the sculptures of Lung Mên or the imperial tombs. This art, and the religion which it served, needed no imperial patronage, and received no recognition in literary records. It was popular, universal, taken for granted by the men of that age, and therefore testifies better than any other product of the T'ang period to the innate artistic sensibility of the Chinese people.

The high æsthetic quality of many of the grave figures produced in such quantities during the T'ang era is now well known to the west through the many examples which have been excavated in recent times and exported to Europe and America. Probably the modern world is better able to judge their quality than any other age, for it is a strange fact that these beautiful and graceful figures, executed with so much feeling and care for detail, were never intended for the pleasure of living men. They were made only for the service of the dead, and were sealed, as their creators hoped, for ever, in the darkness of the tomb. The grave figures were made and used in all parts of the empire. Those from tombs in Szechuan or from the lower Yangtze are as fine as the figures recovered from graves near the capital. So far as is known they were not the work of artists of great reputation, indeed their names are unrecorded, yet at their best their work far excels any other plastic art produced in China.*

The grave figures possess all the qualities which Buddhist and tomb stone sculpture lack. They are conceived in the round, not only to be seen from the front, they are full of life and movement, graceful, intimate, human and individual. It is obvious that the craftsmen who made them were seeking ends very different from the Buddhist sculptor, even if it be admitted that they worked in a more tractable medium. To appreciate the significance of the grave figures it is necessary to consider what was the inspiration and motive which guided their makers. The Buddhist sculptor, endeavouring to make an abstract image of a divinity, minimised rather than accentuated the humanity of his figures; the maker of clay figures, on the contrary, set himself the opposite task.

He was not consciously making a work of art to be admired by living men, and he was not making an image of a divinity. His clay figures were objects of magical significance, intended for the use of the deceased in the after life. In the tomb these figures would become transformed into animated, spiritual counterparts, serving the dead man as the living models upon which they were based had served him on earth. The wealthy Chinese of the Wei and T'ang periods were surrounded in death with dancing girls, servants, guards, grooms, actors and concubines. Horses and camels, with their foreign grooms and drivers provided for his long journeying in the spirit world. Models of houses and inanimate objects of all kinds assured him of the same degree of comfort in death as he had enjoyed on the earth. Nothing could be omitted, for unless a model was placed in the tomb, the spiritual counterpart would not exist in the after life.

The figurine of a soldier with a long body shield is of the slatey

*The magnificent life-size pottery figure of a Lo Han in the British Museum is, of course, Buddhist. It is, however, akin in feeling to the grave figures rather than to Buddhist stone sculpture.

coloured (Fig. 53) clay regarded as typical of grave figures of the Wei period. Another common type wears scale armour and often a quiver. Both types exhibit the typical Wei hose bound below the knee.

The aim of the maker of clay figures was therefore to give his work life and realism. The more perfect his image the more serviceable it would be to the spirit of the deceased in the after world. Consequently, the skilful artist tried to inspire his work with the very qualities that the Buddhist sculptor tended to ignore. He was not concerned to portray spiritual feeling, abstract wisdom and divine detachment. Tao Hsüan's comment illuminates the attitude of Buddhists towards sculpture. Realism and humanity were a defect. The maker of clay figures, however, was trying to copy the human original as nearly as he could.

In this task the artist succeeded admirably. The grave figures reveal, more perfectly than any literature, the social life of that time. The fashions in dress, the type of feminine beauty then admired, the armour of soldiers and the style of dancing, all are shown with faithful attention to detail, and astonishing vitality. Even more interesting is the great variety of racial types represented. Nothing could prove more conclusively the international character of the T'ang age, and the intimate contact which then existed between China and distant countries. It was evidently a commonplace for the wealthy Chinese to employ Central Asiatics as grooms and camel drivers, Indians as jugglers, Syrians and perhaps even Greeks as singers and actors. We may add that the frescoes at Bazaklik in Chinese Turkestan show Buddhist monks with brown hair, European features and blue or green eyes.*

FIG. 53. *Pottery figure of a Wei warrior.*

*A. v. Le Coq. *Chotscho.* Berlin. 1913. Plates 17 and 21.

These foreigners are portrayed with such accurate attention to the facial types and style of dress as to make their identification beyond question. The armenoid faces of the camel drivers, the high boots and fur-lined coats of the Mongolian grooms, the curly hair and toga-like garments of the Syrian singers and musicians, are all faithfully rendered. Dwarfs were evidently popular as entertainers, and examples are not lacking of slaves imported from the primitive peoples of southern India. The figure in Plate IXA is possibly a pre-Dravidian tribesman from one of the jungle peoples of the south, or he may be a *mahout* brought back by one of the T'ang ambassadors to an Indian king.

Figure B of Plate IX is that of a man of marked armenoid type, perhaps a Central Asiatic. He is wearing a Phrygian cap and riding boots, and is apparently training a small bird. His heavy beard, whiskers and moustache, and the very prominent nose are probably slightly exaggerated, as these features always strike the hairless Chinese as strange or comic, as can be seen to-day in the illustrated Chinese press. Some of these figures, of which this is a good example, seem to be actual portraits modelled from life.

It is quite possible that wealthy men had their favourite singers and dancers copied in clay from the life, so that when they came to die they should still enjoy the entertainments which had pleased them on this earth. It is obvious that the T'ang Chinese were keenly interested in foreign peoples and closely observed their national peculiarities of feature and dress, and foreigners must have been numerous in the households of the wealthy.

All this observation, skill and artistic feeling, were spent upon an art which was never intended for the living, which remained almost forgotten until modern times, and which is ignored by the literature of the period. The Chinese from the 5th to 10th centuries developed a plastic art of the highest quality, and buried it in their graves. The fact perhaps provides the key to the neglect of the plastic arts in secular life. Sculpture was abstract and Buddhist, the clay figures, realist and human, were designed for the tomb, and this association made them improper and ill-omened as a decorative art. Representations of the human figure in clay were too closely connected with ideas of death and burial to be appreciated on artistic grounds, and when centuries later a change of custom, probably brought about by economic causes, replaced the clay grave figures by paper images which are burned at the funeral, the artistic tradition of the workers in clay died out.

The frequent representation of foreign types among the clay figures confirms the fact, known from historical records, that there were large colonies of foreigners resident in China during the T'ang period. There were Persians, Indians, Turks and Central Asiatics at Ch'ang An, the capital, and also a considerable settlement of Arabs, Jews and Indians in the chief ports of the south-east coast. Probably, with the exception of the short-lived Mongol dynasty, there has been no period until modern times when China was in such intimate contact with so many alien peoples. Unlike the Mongol period, however, when the foreigner was in the service of an enemy conqueror, the strangers who came to China in the T'ang dynasty were merchants, mercenary soldiers or religious missionaries; in fact, very much the same type of traveller as the foreigners resident in China at the present day.

It would be strange if this peaceful invasion had not left traces of foreign culture in the art of the period, and as many T'ang works prove, there was, in fact, a strong foreign element in the motifs employed in the decorative arts. The marble bowl illustrated in Plate X which may be attributed to the T'ang period, although it was found at K'ai Fêng Fu, a Sung city, is a striking testimony to the force of this foreign influence. The design of children with vine boughs and bunches of grapes which encircles the side of the bowl is, of course, so familiar as to be hackneyed in the classical and renaissance art of the west. It has no relation to Chinese tradition or culture; the grape, though well known as a fruit, is not commonly employed to make wine in China, and the whole train of Dionysian associations is therefore lacking. This bowl was nevertheless made in China, as the Mongolian features of the children prove, and is not either an importation from the west or a very accurate Chinese copy. The Chinese of that period were attracted by the foreign motif, but they modified the human type to accord with their ideas of beauty, just as, some centuries later, Europe adopted the "willow pattern"—said to be originally derived from Chinese pictures of the West Lake at Hang Chou—and westernised that famous landscape into an 18th century water garden.

In bronze work the T'ang artists were carrying on an old traditional art in which completely exotic motifs might have seemed unsuitable. Nevertheless, there is a new importance accorded to floral themes, side by side with the antique dragon and phœnix. The use of flower patterns in bronze work, as on one of the mirrors shown in Plate XI, marks a change from the geometrical and symbolical motifs of the Han period. The dragon and phœnix themselves are treated with a new freedom, particularly in the graceful lines of the bird's wings and tail feathers, well shown in the descending phœnix illustrated in Fig. 54, a bronze masterpiece of the T'ang period.

FIG. 54. *A phœnix in flight. Bronze. T'ang Period.*

PART FIVE—THE SUNG DYNASTY

Chapter XVIII

THE SUNG MONARCHY

Fifty-three years of partition and anarchy followed the final extinction of the T'ang dynasty in A.D. 907. This period is known in Chinese history as that of the "Five Dynasties," so called from the ephemeral military dictatorships which controlled the provinces of North China. The five dynasties were the

Later Liang, A.D. 907-923, seventeen years,
Later T'ang, A.D. 923-936, fourteen years,
Later Tsin, A.D. 936-947, twelve years,
Later Han, A.D. 947-951, four years,
and Later Chou, A.D. 951-960, ten years.

The "emperors" of these short-lived lines were military adventurers mostly of barbarian stock who had risen to high commands in the chaos following the rebellion of Huang Tsao (Chapter XIII, p. 306). Short though the duration of these dynasties was, the government was in reality more chaotic than would appear from this list, for these brief periods were distracted by civil wars, the succession to the throne was determined only by force, and was usurped by distant relatives of the deceased Emperor, if they had more armed support than closer heirs. Thus, the so-called Later Liang house really covers the reign of four rulers who belonged to three different families, only loosely connected by adoption. Similar conditions prevailed in the other periods, which are only described as "dynasties," because Chinese political terminology lacked an expression for what was really an interregnum of successive dictatorships.

These governments were only acknowledged by a few of the northern provinces of the eastern plain; south and west China lay outside their authority. At the end of the T'ang dynasty the provinces furthest from the Court had already become virtually independent under hereditary governors paying a nominal allegiance to the shadow emperors in Ch'ang An. When Chu Wên, founder of the Later Liang, dethroned the last T'ang Emperor and exterminated the princes of the imperial family, these distant governors repudiated his authority and became rulers of

independent states, styling themselves kings or emperors in
accordance with their power and the extent of their territory.
The Chinese historical convention which recognises the ruler of
the largest territory as true Emperor is the only justification for
classing the five dynasties as legitimate lines, and ignoring the
claims of the southern kingdoms which, as a matter of fact, were
both better governed and far more stable.

It was in these states (Map 11), which for the most part refrained
from wars either among themselves or against the rulers of the

MAP 11. *China in the Five Dynasties Period.*

north, that the culture and literature of the T'ang period was preserved in this dangerous period of confusion. Shu, or Szechuan, was distinguished by its poets and scholars, fugitives from ruined Ch'ang An. Nan T'ang (Southern T'ang) which covered the modern provinces of Anhui, Kiangsu and Kiangsi—the lower Yangtze basin—was a refined state, well and pacifically ruled by sovereigns who were strong patrons of Buddhism. Hunan, the kingdom of Ch'u, remained tranquil throughout this distressed period. Canton was the capital of the rich kingdom of Southern Han (Nan Han) covering the two provinces of Kuangtung and Kuangsi. The eastern coast was divided between two states, Min in Fukien, and Wu Yüeh in Chekiang. A small region between the Han and Yangtze Rivers in Hupei formed the diminutive state of Nan P'ing, which by wise policy avoided all conflicts with its greater neighbours. In the north-western provinces of Shansi and Shensi less durable kingdoms rose and fell as the authority of the sovereigns of the Five Dynasties fluctuated.

The detailed history of this confused age is of no importance, but one or two events which were to decide the character of the period to follow, deserve mention. The first ruler of the Later Tsin dynasty (A.D. 936), a Turkish adventurer who owed his throne to the assistance of the nomad Kitans, ceded to that nation, as the price of their support, the north-eastern corner of the Chinese plain, the territory from Peking to the Great Wall, including the city of Peking itself (then called Yen), and the passes through the Yin Shan mountains which separate Mongolia from the Hopei plains. The nomads thus obtained a footing on the plain, a strategic starting point giving easy access to invasion of the south. Here was the first cause of the nomad conquests in China which paved the way for the Mongols.

The same first ruler of the Later Tsin moved the capital from Lo Yang to a new city, K'ai Fêng Fu, which had never hitherto been capital of the empire. K'ai Fêng had the advantage over Lo Yang and Ch'ang An in the ease of communications by river and canal, for it stands in the midst of the northern plain, some miles south of the Yellow River. The facility with which it could be provisioned was offset by the fact that it lacked any natural strategic strength, and was therefore exposed to the attacks of nomad cavalry. This fact was of importance in determining the policy of the Sung sovereigns who retained K'ai Fêng as capital.

The only important event in the history of literature during the Five Dynasties was the printing of the Classical Books, now undertaken for the first time. Printed books had begun to appear in the later years of the T'ang dynasty, but no printed edition of the classical collection had been attempted. The cutting of the blocks was begun in A.D. 932, but the printing was not finished until A.D. 953, no doubt delayed by the troubles of the times. The printing of the classics had an important influence on Chinese thought. For the first time the supply of books became cheap and abundant. Scholars multiplied and the knowledge of literature was spread more widely through the nation. The consequences of this expansion of the literate class was to be manifest under the Sung dynasty.

The Sung dynasty, under which the Chinese lands were reunited in the third centralised empire (A.D. 960) differs in many respects from its predecessors the Han and the T'ang. The manner of its foundation, the extent of its authority, its internal and external policy, and not the least the factors which in the end destroyed it, are peculiar to it. Unlike the Han and the T'ang, the Sung reunion of the empire was the work of policy rather than conquest, an almost peaceful submission of a nation weary of disunity and now fully conscious of its cultural identity. The Sung were chosen by consent, and they ruled by general acquiescence, hardly troubled by any formidable rebellion such as had shaken the thrones of the Han and T'ang emperors. The enemies of the new dynasty were not found in the empire, but among the powerful alien races who in turn dominated the northern steppes.

Chao Kuang-yin, founder of the Sung dynasty, was a northerner, scion of an official family from Cho Chou, a city forty miles south of Peking. His immediate forbears had been civil officials and governors under the T'ang Emperors and their successors of the Five Dynasties. The future Emperor himself was a general who had won distinction under the second Emperor of the Later Chou dynasty, who, dying in A.D. 959, made the mistake of transmitting his throne to a young child, under the regency of the Empress. Chao Kuang-yin was then sent north with the army to repel a threatened invasion of the Kitans. The officers and soldiers of his army were discontented at this order, for they believed that with an infant on the throne and power in the hands of an Empress and her Court, their services would be unrewarded and promotion denied to them.

When the army had moved a few days' march from the capital a mutiny occurred, inspired by the chief officers, though not by Chao Kuang-yin. At dawn their leaders entered his tent with drawn swords and forcibly robed the half awakened general in a yellow gown, the symbol of imperial authority. Chao Kuang-yin* was then unwillingly presented to the army as the new Emperor. Forced into rebellion, the general was under no illusions as to the motives of his supporters. Before marching on the capital he frankly told them that he realised that their actions were inspired not by admiration for him, but by self-interest, and he refused to accept the position thrust upon him unless they would take an oath to obey him in all matters. This given, he ordered that no harm should be done to any member of the imperial family, to the ministers and officials of the capital, or to the inhabitants.

He was obeyed, and the army occupied the capital without disorder, for the Empress Regent bowed to the inevitable. Such revolutions had been the commonplace of politics under the Five Dynasties, and there was nothing to suggest that the Sung dynasty would be more respected or permanent than its predecessors. Chao Kuang-yin, however, was not the man his soldiers had supposed him to be. Once on the throne he consolidated his position by a series of skilful political moves. He spared the fallen family of the Later Chou, conciliated the civil officials by restoring the dominant position of the civilian element in the government, and lastly his masterstroke was to get rid of the army which had raised him to the throne, and might so easily elect another candidate. The measures he took to achieve this reveal the character of the man, and explain why it was that in an age of

*This incident, so strongly reminiscent of the military revolutions of Imperial Rome, is unique in Chinese history, and far removed in time from the numerous similar events in Roman history.

strife and treachery he commanded the respect and confidence of all classes.

In the first year of his reign the new Emperor summoned all his military officers—the men responsible for the mutiny to which he owed his throne—to a banquet. When the company had drunk deeply and were in cheerful mood, the Emperor said:

"I do not sleep peacefully at night."

"For what reason?" inquired the generals.

"It is not hard to understand," replied the Emperor. "Which of you is there who does not covet my throne?"

The generals made a deep bow, and all protested:

"Why does Your Majesty speak thus? The Mandate of Heaven is now established; who still has treacherous aims?"

The Emperor replied:

"I do not doubt your loyalty, but if one day one of you is suddenly roused at dawn and forced to don a yellow robe, even if unwilling, how should he avoid rebellion?"

The officers all declared that not one of them was sufficiently renowned or beloved for such a thing to happen, and begged the Emperor to take such measures as he thought wise to guard against any such possibility. The Emperor, having brought them to this point, promptly made his proposals known:

"The life of man is short," he said. "Happiness is to have the wealth and means to enjoy life, and then to be able to leave the same prosperity to one's descendants. If you, my officers, will renounce your military authority, retire to the provinces, and choose there the best lands and most delightful dwelling-places, there to pass the rest of your lives in pleasure and peace until you die of old age, would this not be better than to live a life of peril and uncertainty? So that no shadow of suspicion shall remain between prince and ministers, we will ally our families with marriages, thus, ruler and subject linked in friendship and amity, we will enjoy tranquillity."

The officers and generals immediately vowed to follow the Emperor's wishes, and the next day, pretending imaginary maladies, all offered their resignations. The Emperor accepted their offer, and carried out his part of this strange bargain. All were given titles of honour and richly endowed with wealth and land. In this way the founder of the Sung broke the vicious circle of suspicion and mutiny which had kept the government in a state of turmoil under the Five Dynasties. That such a plan was possible, is perhaps the highest tribute to the character of the new Emperor, and proves him to have been a man in whose word everyone reposed a perfect confidence.

There can be little doubt that the general respect felt for the integrity of the new ruler of the Sung was an important contributing factor in the rapid and almost bloodless reunion of the independent parts of the empire. Some of these states, such as Nan P'ing (Hupei) and Shu (Szechuan) submitted without any resistance, and as in the case of the deposed Emperor of the Later Chou, their rulers were not only spared, but allowed to live in honourable freedom at the Sung capital. The two largest southern principalities, Nan Han (Canton) and Nan T'ang (the lower Yangtze provinces) offered a half-hearted resistance which was speedily overcome. They capitulated in A.D. 971 and 975 respectively. Their rulers were brought to K'ai Fêng, where they were permitted to reside at the Court.

The submission of the last independent states, Wu Yüeh (Chekiang) and the Northern Han (Shansi), was not received until A.D. 978-79, three years after the first Emperor of the Sung had been succeeded by his brother, the Emperor T'ai Tsung. The choice of this Prince as successor was due to the wise advice of the Empress mother, an old lady of shrewd intelligence. When she lay dying she insisted that the succession be settled in this way, and when asked her reasons, said to her son: "Why do you suppose that you have obtained the empire?" The Emperor replied in the conventional terms that he owed his throne to the wisdom and virtue of his ancestors, and of his mother herself in particular. The Empress would not hear of this explanation.

"Neither I, nor your ancestors have anything to do with it," she answered. "The only reason that you are on the throne to-day is because the late Emperor of the Later Chou was so foolish as to nominate a young child as his successor. If you are succeeded by a child, our dynasty will suffer the fate that we meted out to them."

She might have added that another and potent reason for the rapid success of the Sung dynasty was the universal desire for peace and unity. The Chinese people were now fully conscious of their common culture and racial affinity. The revived feudalism of the Five Dynasties was decried by all as a senseless retrogression; the united empire was accepted as the only reasonable and proper form of government. This sentiment is well illustrated by the reply which Chao Kuang-yin made to the King of Nan T'ang, who, when threatened with war unless he submitted, offered to hold his state as a feudal domain under the Sung Empire. "What crime has the land south of the River committed that it should be separated from the empire?" was the Emperor's only comment on this proposal.

If the Chinese states and provinces welcomed the Sung Empire with relief and joy, the nomad races to the north were not disposed to yield up their conquests without a struggle. When the second Emperor of the Sung endeavoured to regain the lost territory between Peking and the Great Wall, he was met by the Kitan army and disastrously defeated near Ch'ang P'ing, north of Peking. Subsequent Chinese successes prevented the Kitans profiting by this victory, but it set a limit to the Sung Empire which was never exceeded. The war dragged on for some years until the third Sung Emperor, Chên Tsung, made a firm peace with the enemy, yielding up his claim to the lost territory, and also paying the Kitans a large annual subsidy, which they might well regard as tribute (A.D. 1004).

The acceptance of what the T'ang or Han Emperors would have regarded as a shameful peace was characteristic of the Sung, for whom pacifism was the guiding rule of foreign policy. The Sung period indeed marks a definite change in the character of the Chinese government. Just as the internal troubles of the empire had been settled by a policy of conciliation and clemency unheard of in the past, so the empire from the first renounced the imperialism which had been so prominent a part of the Han and T'ang policy. The founders of those dynasties had ruthlessly exterminated their internal rivals, and then actively pursued a policy of conquest in the north and west. The Sung not only spared the rival princes of the southern kingdoms in China, but never made any attempt to extend their empire beyond the Great Wall.

The empire they founded was therefore more restricted in area than its predecessors. Not only was the north-east left to the Kitans, who also ruled over Manchuria and the part of modern Shansi lying north of the Great Wall; but the north-west, the "arm" of Kansu province which commands the route to Central Asia, together with the territory north of the great bend of the Yellow River (now Ning Hsia province in the former Inner Mongolia), was outside the Sung domain. This region came under the rule of the Tibetan-Tangut kingdom of Hsia, which endured until the Mongol conquest. The Sung were thus cut off from the traditional land route across Turkestan to western Asia and Europe. (Map 12.)

The Empire of the Sung, although thus confined to strictly Chinese territories, soon became more populous than the T'ang Empire had been at the height of its power. This rapid increase in the population was partly caused by the growing importance of the southern provinces, and fostered by the peaceful policy of the Sung sovereigns. The Sung were never threatened by internal rebellions of any importance. No An Lu-shan or Huang Tsao arose to devastate the empire, and the fact is good proof of the efficiency and humanity of their rule, a truth attested by other evidence. The ministers of the Sung Court who fell from power, or who were disgraced, were not put to death, a fate which had almost invariably attended their predecessors under the Han and T'ang. The fallen ministers of the Sung were sent to govern some minor city in a remote province, and this new clemency was one reason why the internal politics of the Sung period were more constitutional than had ever been the case in previous ages. There arose two parties in the state, Conservatives and Innovators, who strove to enforce opposite policies, but who carried on their warfare with pens rather than with death sentences.

The internal administration was patterned upon the T'ang centralised government, but the civil service under the Sung was even more thoroughly organised and better controlled than before.

MAP 12. *The Sung and Kin Empires.*

The examination system was now well established. To enter the civil service the candidate had to submit to a carefully supervised public examination in various subjects—subjects which formed one of the principal points at issue between the two parties who disputed the policy of the empire. This development tended to raise the prestige and confirm the power of the civil officials, who throughout the Sung period were dominant, relegating the generals and military officers to the inferior status which was henceforward their lot in Chinese society. It was a change very much in accordance with the prevailing pacifist feeling, characteristic of Sung policy.

The empire itself was divided into new provinces, more numerous than the ten T'ang *tao*. The number varied during the course of the dynasty, and the increase no doubt reflects the rising population of the empire. The Sung provinces, called *lu*—circuits or routes—were at first fifteen in number, but were finally increased to twenty-five, the large areas which T'ang T'ai Tsung had included in one province, especially in the south, being now split up into two or more separate provinces by the Sung. The number of prefectures (*chou*) was 321; of sub-prefectures (*hsien*) 1162. If these figures are compared with the T'ang census of A.D. 754 (p. 312) it will be seen that while the number of prefectures was the same, the Sung *hsien* were considerably fewer. The decrease is partly explained by the smaller area of the Sung Empire, but also to changed administrative boundaries.

On the other hand the empire, though smaller, was far more populous. In 1083 a census gave the number of families, both Chinese and foreign, resident in the empire as 17,211,713, approximately ninety million souls. In A.D. 1124, after more than a century of internal peace, when the Sung Empire was on the eve of the Kin Tartar invasions, a census gave the population of the twenty-six provinces as:

Prefectures (*chou*)	254
Sub-prefectures (*hsien*)	1,234
Families	20,882,258

or approximately more than one hundred million souls. It will be noticed that the number of prefectures had been reduced and the sub-prefectures increased, probably an administrative change, as the empire had not then lost any territory.

The peace of A.D. 1004, which settled the common limits of the Sung Empire and the Kitan kingdom of Liao, remained unbroken except for minor border troubles in the north-west for more than a hundred years. This century, which almost exactly coincided with the 11th century of the Christian era, was an age of culture and refinement, famous for its intellectual activity and artistic development. In the opinion of many, the Chinese civilisation reached its apogee in these years, and in later centuries never recovered the level to which the Sung had attained. This view is necessarily one of personal taste, and is perhaps too much coloured by a high regard for Confucian philosophy as re-shaped by the Sung scholars, and an unjustifiable disregard of the literary forms in which the genius of later ages found its expression. Nevertheless the Sung was one of the greatest ages of Chinese culture, and the credit for the peace and order in which this civilisation flourished is due in large measure to the five able and original personalities who ruled over the empire. These five emperors have been much maligned both by Confucian historians and by European writers who have either adopted the prejudices of their Chinese authorities, or imported their own.*

Chên Tsung (A.D. 998-1022), the third Emperor of the Sung and nephew of the founder, was responsible for the peace with the Kitans, and has been abused by those historians who consider that the risks of a desperate war against a barbarian enemy were to be preferred to an unfavourable treaty, which none the less secured the integrity and prosperity of a great empire. They disliked his religious policy, and his deliberate encouragement and invention of new cults, designed to fuse the rival Buddhist and Taoist religions. He is accused of having deceived the empire by claiming divine revelations which were in fact entirely fictitious. The attitude which treats Chên Tsung's "revelations" as a practical joke in poor taste, is quite uncritical, and ignores the problem which the Emperor was endeavouring to solve.

Chên Tsung deserves the credit of realising that his throne needed a stronger moral title than that of election by a mutinous army. The new dynasty needed some quality which should distinguish it from the dreary sequence of military despotisms known as the Five Dynasties. An Emperor to command the respect of his subjects must be either general or priest. The Sung were pacifists, and as the war with the Kitans had proved, Chên Tsung stood little chance of acquiring the reputation of a military hero. He therefore decided to appear in the eyes of the common people as the divinely accepted ruler, whose authority had been confirmed by the special revelation of Heaven. The Confucianists

*The Confucian historians, who all belong to the finally dominant school of the Conservatives, followers of Ssŭ-ma Kuang and Chu Hsi, have no word of understanding or sympathy for the emperors who did not happen to favour their patrons. P. Wieger, *Textes Historiques*, has scant sympathy with the artistic temperament and exhibits the marked religious bias of a Catholic missionary.

complain that no man of education was deceived by his missives which fell from Heaven, the divine messengers which appeared to him in the night, and other devices. The Emperor probably never supposed that scholars would be deceived, nor cared whether they were. His object was to impress upon the common people that his family were the chosen of Heaven, not to be confounded with the common run of usurpers of which the empire was so weary. That he succeeded is evidenced by the unbroken internal peace which prevailed under his line.

Jên Tsung (A.D. 1023-1063) has been better treated by the historians because he was a more orthodox Confucian and patronised the celebrated scholars, Ssŭ-ma Kuang and Ou-yang Hsiu, who were the leaders of the Conservative party. In consequence Jên Tsung has been highly praised by the followers of this party, who wrote the history of his times. It was during his long reign that the two opposing political and philosophic parties developed into clearly distinguished factions, which, during the rest of the Sung dynasty, disputed with equal fervour for their own particular interpretations of the classical books, and for the actual political control of the empire. This alliance of scholarship and politics is characteristically Chinese, and characteristically Sung. It had far-reaching results, for the aftermath of this long struggle has coloured the history of the past, which has until modern times been interpreted in accordance with the ideas of the Conservative school, who ultimately triumphed. It led also to that rigid orthodoxy which excluded from polite literature any mention of the opposing schools of thought, relegated religion to the common people as "superstition" and shut its mind against any innovation or adaptation of alien ideas. These consequences of Sung Conservative scholarship did not appear in the Sung period itself, but their origin lies in the doctrines taught by this school.

The successor of Jên Tsung was Ying Tsung, who reigned only three years, and was followed by Shên Tsung (A.D. 1068-1085) under whom the Conservatives were dismissed from office, and the ministry conferred upon their arch-enemy, the innovator Wang An-shih, one of the most original minds in Chinese history, whose economic and social theories, so close to ideas now current, must be made the subject of another chapter. Throughout the reigns of Shên Tsung and his two successors, Chê Tsung (A.D. 1086-1100) and Hui Tsung (A.D. 1100-1125), who was an artist of great merit, the Innovators were more or less consistently dominant in the empire, and in consequence the memory of these sovereigns has been blackened by historians of the opposite party.

These emperors, tolerant, humane, artistic and intellectual, free from the vices which have so often disgraced Oriental monarchs, were the most enlightened sovereigns who ever ruled in China. There was then no aura of orthodoxy about the doctrines of the Conservative scholars, doctrines which were in fact not truly Conservative at all, but merely one of two or more interpretations of the ancient literature then current. The Sung Emperors favoured sometimes one school and then another, not so much on account of their philosophic teaching as by reason of their ability in actual administration. That they chose their ministers— whether Innovators or Conservatives—wisely, is proved by the admitted prosperity of the empire, the absence of popular rebellions, and the rapid rise in the population.

Unfortunately, the Sung were too civilised for the world of the 11th century. While they debated matters of literature, economic theories and political philosophy, rude nomads of the Mongolian steppe were coalescing into formidable states, organised for war. The Kitans who had founded the Liao state, lying north of the Sung Empire in Manchuria, Jehol and Inner Mongolia, had quickly adopted the civilisation of their great neighbours. They borrowed Chinese customs, gave up their nomad life for the comforts of cities and fixed dwellings, learned the language and studied the literature of China. They lost, in consequence, perhaps, their fighting spirit and virility. The Chinese culture has ever proved fatal to the northern nomads.

The Kitans therefore soon lost their prestige among the untamed tribes of the north. In A.D. 1114, one of their vassal tribes, the Nüchên or Kin (*chin*, i.e. golden), who were of kindred stock, dwelling in the valley of the Sungari River, now Kirin province in Manchuria, repudiated the authority of the Liao sovereign, and started a war of extermination against their former overlords. The Liao Kitans were unable to resist the attacks of their hardier opponents. In A.D. 1124 the Kin completed the conquest of the whole Liao Empire, and drove the remnant of the Kitan people to seek refuge in western Turkestan. There the Kitans established themselves in the Ili Valley, where they became known to the peoples of Western Asia and Eastern Europe as the Keraites, Kara-kitan, Kitay, and lastly, Cathayans, from which name that of Cathay for China, is derived. The western Kitan were converted to Nestorian Christianity in their new country, and this change of religion is the origin of the picturesque legends of the "kingdom of Prester John" which were later current in Europe. Their kingdom endured until the Mongol conquest.

The Sung Emperor Hui Tsung did not realise the danger to his empire which the arrival of the warlike Kin portended. He welcomed the change which rid the empire of the Liao, and terminated the subsidy which the Sung had paid to them. He also regarded events in the north as a good opportunity to recover those lost territories in north-eastern Hopei province, within the Wall, which gave the enemy a footing on the great plain. Had the Sung Empire possessed the military strength to sustain a campaign against the Kin, this policy might have been successful, but the empire had been at peace for more than a century, the army was untrained, had no experience of war, and lacked capable commanders. Under these circumstances the policy of expansion unwisely undertaken by Hui Tsung was necessarily disastrous.

When the Liao fell, the governor of P'ing Chou (the modern district of Yung P'ing, the territory bordering the Great Wall near Shan Hai Kuan) refused to submit to the Kin, and offered allegiance to the Sung. Hui Tsung accepted this submission, and despatched an army to take possession of the territory. This intervention in what they regarded as a domestic rebellion infuriated the Kin. Turning their arms upon the empire, the nomad cavalry poured over the frontier, and swept down to K'ai Fêng itself. Hui Tsung abdicated in favour of his son, and a treaty was hastily concluded with the Kin, by which a huge ransom was paid to deliver the empire of the invaders. This peace was concluded by the Innovator minister Ts'ai Ching, who was forced to resign and go into exile immediately afterwards, as he was held responsible for the disaster. The Conservative ministers who succeeded Ts'ai Ching, with wanton irresponsibility, persuaded the Emperor to break the pact and send an army in pursuit of the retiring Kin.

This folly ruined the Sung Empire. The Kin returned, defeated the Chinese army, besieged and captured K'ai Fêng with the two emperors and the entire Court (A.D. 1126) carrying off more than 3,000 prisoners of rank. Pursuing their conquests in a country now open to invasion on all sides, the Kin cavalry crossed the Yangtze in 1129 and pushed south as far as Hang Chou and Ningpo, in the modern province of Chekiang, which cities were captured and sacked. It was not until 1131, that the Sung, who had now found in Yo Fei a general capable of defeating the Kin, began to recover the territory south of the Yangtze and Huai Rivers.

The wet rice-growing valleys of southern and central China were unsuitable country for the nomad cavalry, moreover, dynastic troubles wasted the strength of the invaders in civil war. Had the Sung Emperor, Kao Tsu (A.D. 1127-1162), who had set up his capital at Hang Chou, permitted Yo Fei to press the campaign it is possible that the Sung might have recovered North China. The Court of Kao Tsu was pacifist, and the chief minister, Ch'in Kuei, was convinced that any attempt to continue the campaign in the north would end in disaster. In 1141 he had Yo Fei put to death in a secret and discreditable manner, and concluded a firm peace with the Kin, by which China was divided between the two empires.

The southern Sung, as the emperors who reigned at Hang Chou are called, had lost seven provinces, everything north of the Huai River, the mountains of southern Honan and the range which forms the watershed of the Han and Yellow River basins in southern Shensi. They retained the Yangtze Valley and everything to the south of it. The Kin, established in these lost provinces, also ruled over the Mongolian and Manchurian plains which had formerly been part of the Liao state. This second partition of China (see Map 12) between nomad conquerors and a native dynasty lasted for 153 years, until both Kin and Sung Empires were reunited by a common conqueror, the Mongols. It is to this period, though the fact is not attested in historical records, that the southward migration of the people known as the Hakka of Canton is generally attributed. The Hakka (mandarin *K'o Chia*, guest families) are certainly the descendants of northern Chinese, for their dialect still retains many northern words almost unaltered. They settled in the provinces of Kuangtung and Kuangsi, and have never mingled with the natives of the soil, probably on account of the wide differences between the two dialects.

As soon as peace with the Kin had settled the frontiers of their diminished empire, the Sung devoted themselves to the arts of peace and the prosecution of the great philosophic controversies of the day with as much energy and enthusiasm as before. The menace of nomad attacks was apparently speedily forgotten, and the evident fact that pacifism was no safeguard against the attacks of barbarians, was disregarded. Although a new Kin invasion was successfully repulsed at the Yangtze in A.D. 1161, the Sung made no attempt to regain the north. They remained, as before, a peaceful and peace-loving state, untroubled by internal rebellions. In spite of the abuse which Confucian historians have showered upon the Southern Sung Emperors for abandoning the north and for failing to appreciate or patronise the philosopher Chu Hsi, the empire was prosperous and well contented under their rule. The Sung Empire enjoyed a further seventy years of unbroken peace, until the unwise policy of the Emperor Li Tsung brought the calamity of the Mongol invasion upon his empire.

The Sung had at first ignored the appeals of the Kin, who were on the point of succumbing to the Mongol invaders. On the contrary Li Tsung assisted the Mongols by sending infantry which the invaders lacked, to help in the siege of the last Kin stronghold, Ts'ai Chou in Honan. When, after the fall of Ts'ai Chou, the Mongol army retired northward to remount its cavalry, the Sung Emperor committed the extreme folly of endeavouring to seize the northern part of China for the profit of his own empire. The Mongols, hearing of the Sung advance, immediately returned and invaded the Sung Empire, which was incapable of resisting them. Although the war lasted many years, the end was certain, and the delay was only due to the pre-occupation of the Mongols with other campaigns. In 1276 Hang Chou surrendered and the

Emperor was carried off captive to the north. In 1279 the last Sung pretender, a young boy, was trapped with his fleet in a bay on the coast of Kuangtung, and threw himself into the sea, together with his ministers and family, in order to escape capture. The Sung dynasty perished with him.

Chapter XIX

THE ECONOMIC EXPERIMENTS OF WANG AN-SHIH

THE reign of Shên Tsung (A.D. 1068-1085), sixth Emperor of the Sung dynasty, is chiefly memorable for the ministry of Wang An-shih, and the revolutionary economic policy which he initiated. The same period was also that in which the famous historian, Ssǔ-ma Kuang, lived and worked, and as he was the lifelong opponent of Wang An-shih and his policy, Shên Tsung and Wang An-shih have been covered with obloquy by the orthodox historians of China, followers of Ssǔ-ma Kuang and his equally famous continuer, the philosopher Chu Hsi. More recently it has become the fashion to describe Wang An-shih as a "socialist" and the alleged failure of his policy has been held to provide a useful illustration of the fallacies of socialist economic theory. So long does the dust of an 11th century dispute continue to obscure the historical scene.

No true appreciation of Wang An-shih's aim, or of the results of his policy, can be obtained by blindly accepting the hostile judgments of his opponents and interpreting the problems and policies of 11th century China in terms of modern movements with which they had little in common. Wang An-shih was an "Innovator," the leader of a political party which continued to dispute power with its Conservative opponents throughout the Sung dynasty. Ultimately the Conservative elements triumphed, their enemies were branded as trouble-makers and unorthodox Confucians—for politics and philosophy went hand in hand—and their memory has been reviled by the historians of the victorious side. Although the historians have recorded every fact or opinion which can discredit the policy of Wang An-shih, they have not been able to conceal certain evidence which is in its favour.*

The "New Laws" as they were called, were in force for nearly twenty years, throughout the reign of Shên Tsung, while some of them were revived for shorter periods by his successors when the Innovators were once more in power. During this time the empire

*The reforms of Wang An-shih are described in the *Sung Shih Chi*, Ch'uan. 37

remained internally tranquil, in spite of dire prophecies by the Conservatives, who repeatedly declared that the new policy would produce a great popular upheaval similar to the rebellions of An Lu-shan or Huang Tsao in the T'ang period. Nothing of the kind occurred, nor is positive evidence lacking that the reforms were at least partly successful. The census of A.D. 1083 was taken after the reforms had been in force for several years, and showed a considerable increase in the population. That of A.D. 1124, thirty-nine years later, shows a still more striking advance.

A.D. 1083. 17,211,713. Families = 90,000,000 persons.

A.D. 1124. 20,882,258. Families = 100,000,000 persons.

If the peasantry, who formed nine-tenths of the population, had really suffered the miseries and oppression which the critics of Wang An-shih delighted in describing, it seems strange that their numbers should have increased so greatly, and that there were no revolts. The Chinese masses have never been slow to rebel against misgovernment. It is very probable that some of the new laws failed to produce all the good effects which their author expected of them, for the official class as a whole was not in sympathy with the new policy and did not willingly co-operate in administering it. When the criticisms of the Conservatives are analysed they are in the main not directed to the results of the new laws, but to the spirit in which they were conceived.

The Conservatives criticised the new laws not because they were bad, but because they were new. The methods of the past, the way of the ancestors, were right simply because they were traditional. New policies must be wrong because they did not conform to these ancient patterns. That is the burden of Ssŭ-ma Kuang's frequent memorials of complaint. When he was asked whether, in fact, one of the New Laws was not operating well in Shensi province, he replied that although he was himself a native of that province he did not know how the laws worked, but that as the old laws had meant much hardship for the people, it was evident that the new ones must be still more oppressive. This was the mentality with which Wang An-shih had to contend.

Wang An-shih's new policy was intended to raise the condition of the farmer, benefit agriculture, and curb usury. These are the reasons why he is often described as a Socialist. Such a description is misleading. Wang An-shih, though an original mind, was a man of his time and country. He never questioned the accepted form of government, autocratic monarchy. He did not entertain such ideas as class equality, and the source of his reforms was not a belief in the rights of man, but a return to authoritarian concepts held by the Chinese in the Ch'in and Han dynasties. Agriculture, he regarded as the fundamental occupation, the peasantry as the foundation of the state. The Ch'in Legists and Mencius held the same views. Wang An-shih differed from his opponents on the question of administration. He believed that the existing system was inefficient, wasteful and unnecessarily oppressive. The Conservatives, true to Confucian doctrine, taught that if the Emperor were truly virtuous and the officials loyal and sincere the state organisation could be left to take care of itself. Wang An-shih, also a Confucian, did not deny the principle of moral authority, but he thought that better organisation was also desirable, and he held that natural catastrophes such as floods and famines, were produced by natural causes, not as divine punishment for the misdeeds of the Emperor. He also believed that Confucian virtues in the ruler and officials were not in themselves sufficient to ward off foreign invasion.

The Conservatives were never tired of warning the Emperor that Wang An-shih's new policy would lead to a great popular rebellion such as those that had devastated the empire in the T'ang dynasty. They ignored the fact that these rebellions had been largely due to the oppressive tribute system, by which the whole empire forwarded vast quantities of grain and produce to the capital. This system Wang An-shih changed, and was attacked for endangering the peace of the state. Although the capital was now at K'ai Fêng Fu, in the central plain, not far from the Yellow River, the transport of grain and tribute produce was still most burdensome to the provinces. The western provinces might find the transport down stream more convenient than when the capital was at Ch'ang An, but the cost of forwarding produce from the southern provinces was almost as great as before. It was inevitable that when the power of the throne diminished, or a weak ruler relaxed the efficiency of the administration, the distant provinces would attempt to shake off the incubus of Court rule and the tribute system. Wang An-shih attempted to prevent this danger by reforming the tribute system and making it less burdensome to the remoter provinces.

The first of the new laws, called the "Equalisation of Loss," was directed to this end. It was indeed not so much a new plan as a return to the system which Sang Hung-yang had invented under the Emperor Wu of the Han dynasty. This in itself was offensive to the Conservatives, for Sang Hung-yang had been one of the Emperor Wu's "new men," not a scholar, but a merchant. Under Wang An-shih's law tribute grain was no longer forwarded to the capital, there to be stored in state granaries, and sold at a low price, for under the old system there was always a glut at the capital and often a scarcity in the provinces, the cause of provincial discontent and rebellion.

Wang An-shih arranged that the produce of one province should be exchanged against the tribute of some distant region. Tribute grain and silk could now be sold locally for the profit of the treasury rather than transported to the capital where it would fetch only a very low price. Prices were kept even, gluts and famines avoided, and the peasantry assured of a steady and equal demand for their crops. Such at least was the ideal which Wang believed his law would bring about, nor is it possible to discover how far short of it the practice fell, for his critics are so occupied with denouncing the novelty of his methods that they have little time to describe its working.

One of the criticisms urged against the new laws was that their working involved the creation of a large number of new officials, or else threw upon the existing officers duties which they were not trained to perform. It was said that when the officials took charge of matters of commerce of which they had no experience, prices were raised above those the merchants had been accustomed to charge, even though the object of the new laws was to make things easier for the poor. It is indeed quite clear that Wang An-shih had no consideration for commercial or financial interests, for some of the new laws were expressly directed against the merchants and moneylenders.

The Emperor and his minister soon found that a more even and scientific system of tribute gathering was not sufficient to raise the condition of the peasantry. Then as now the chief obstacle to improved agriculture and a raised standard of living was the utter penury of the farming population, who had no capital resources at all, and were year by year driven to the moneylenders to raise cash for seed grain and necessary implements. Very often land was left uncultivated because there were no farmers able to buy the seed to sow it. The boldest and most original of the new laws was designed to bring a remedy to this state of affairs. This was the law called "Young Shoots," a system of state loans to the farmers on the security of growing crops.

Under the new plan, the state made a loan to the farmer in the spring, in proportion to the amount of land sown, and the loan was to be repaid with a light interest at the harvest. Wang An-shih hoped that this system would lead to largely increased cultivation, and at the same time free the peasant from his dependence on the village moneylender and his extortionate rate of interest. The state, meanwhile, would have a safe yield on the money both from the interest on the spring loans, and also in taxation on the increased cultivated area. The "Young Shoots" law was thus an early forerunner of the land and credit banks which at the present time are being started in China as the only way to help the peasantry to better their conditions.

It was, of course, bitterly denounced by Wang An-shih's enemies, who alleged that it failed in its purpose. Ssǔ-ma Kuang declared that while the peasants were willing enough to borrow government money in the spring, they could only be induced to repay the loans at harvest by the use of stern police measures, and, in consequence, the working of the new system was more oppressive than the old one had been. This criticism, whether founded or not—and Ssǔ-ma Kuang's admitted ignorance of how the law worked in his native Shensi weakens his case— ignored the fact that before the reform the peasant equally borrowed money, but from a local moneylender at a high rate of interest, and that when he failed to repay the loan, the usurer, usually a local magnate of influence, ruthlessly invoked the assistance of the officials to recover his money.

Wang An-shih's interest rates were lighter, and the state,

having at heart the promotion of agriculture rather than a profit on the money, was a better creditor. Although the conservatives denounced the new law as an unmitigated evil, nothing is heard from the peasants' point of view, except the negative proof afforded by the fact that there was no revolt or popular uprising, the only and traditional peasant protest against injustice. If the "Young Shoots" law was as unpopular as Wang An-shih's enemies make out, it is curious that the peasants put up with it for twenty years without an insurrection.

The law called "Remission of Services" was designed to place the forced labour system on a more efficient basis, and as such it marked a great advance in Chinese administrative practice, for it was intended to substitute taxation for forced labour on state works. Wang An-shih considered that the old methods by which the people were liable for periods of state forced labour was uneconomic and inefficient. It was an inflexible plan under which it sometimes happened that the call would be made at a time when every man was needed for the harvest or the sowing season. At other times there would be no reason for forced labour at one place, but an urgent need for many workers elsewhere to repair a dyke or the defences of a city. He therefore substituted a graded tax for the obligation to serve.

Under his system five grades of wealth were distinguished, and taxed proportionately. With the proceeds of this tax labourers were hired as required for public works. This plan was obviously more flexible. The surplus of the new tax from one district could if necessary be applied in another where works of urgency required a large enrolment of coolies. If no public works of great importance were needed, the treasury collected a surplus which could be used for other purposes, or in relief works during years of famine and flood. Nevertheless, it did not escape the opposition which all the new laws aroused in the ranks of the conservative Confucians. It was alleged that the tax was at once oppressive to the poor, who could spare their labour more easily than their money, and insufficient for the purpose it was designed to serve.

The difficulty would seem to have been, with this as with the other new laws, that Wang An-shih had no civil service trained to carry out his advanced ideas. The existing officials were accustomed to the minimum activities of the traditional system, tax collecting and maintenance of the peace. They were neither able nor willing to supervise the detailed and elaborate plans which Wang An-shih thrust upon them. When he enlisted large numbers of new officials more suited to this kind of work, their presence was resented by the old hierarchy, and too often they made a corrupt use of their opportunities.

Wang An-shih, however, enjoyed the confidence of the Emperor, in spite of unceasing attempts to undermine his position. Shên Tsung deserves credit for his impartiality. He listened, almost daily, it would seem, to bitter denunciations and diatribes against his minister and the policy which he himself had authorised. He sometimes had his doubts, where Wang An-shih, a most self-opiniated man, had none, but the Emperor was sincerely interested in the questions involved. He was not an idler who left the government to his forceful minister. Shên Tsung was himself a very frugal liver, he banished luxury from his Court, paid close attention to business, and seems to have indulged in few of the pleasures traditional to one of his station. Even the critics, who can never forgive him for preferring the counsels of Wang An-shih to those of Ssŭ-ma Kuang, can find no other fault to record against him.

One of the most ambitious of the new laws was a system of official price fixing and limitation of profits. The officers of every sub-prefecture (*hsien*) were charged with the duty of determining the value of all property in their district, and the price at which it might be sold. No profit was allowed in excess of one-fifth of the total value of the property sold. Household implements, food, and grain were not included in this scheme. Every owner was ordered to make a true return of his property not concealing or diminishing the value of anything. A register was compiled from these returns, and property divided into five categories of wealth, probably on the same scale as that adopted in assessing the Remission of Services Tax. If any sub-prefecture was found to be far more wealthy than the average, its taxes were assessed in common with a poor neighbour so that wealthy districts should assist the needy areas.

This law, and that known as "Plane Mensuration" (Fang T'ien) was designed to equalise the land tax. The second law was concerned with a remeasurement of land and a new scale of taxation upon it. Although the reason for this reform is not very plain, it was probably due to the fact that land tenures had not been revised for many years, perhaps since the T'ang dynasty. Under the new plan land was divided into squares of 1,000 paces in length and breadth, or where the nature of the country made this impossible, into blocks of other shapes equal in area to the standard "*fang*" or square. The land was graded for taxation purposes into five classes, according to its fertility and the nature of the crops raised. Barren, salt, and desert lands, mountains, forests, dykes, ditches, roads and cemeteries were not included in this scheme and were untaxed. Timber growing on waste and mountain land was inspected and taxed in accordance with its value. Every farm, village or hamlet was registered, and the gross assessment of taxes for each sub-prefecture compiled and fixed as a limit not to be exceeded.

It was hoped that in this way the old methods by which false returns and short measures were accepted by corrupt officials would be prevented. In practice it seems very probable that all this close inspection and meticulous administration gave very many opportunities of oppression and corruption to the hordes of minor officials who were employed as surveyors and assessors, while the old scholar officials, mostly out of sympathy with the new policy, made little attempt to work it in a willing spirit. Their criticisms were reinforced by those of the moneylenders and richer landowners, who found their traditional sources of wealth invaded by the state. It was no doubt in these classes that the keenest opposition was felt to another of the new laws which would otherwise seem to have been a wise reform, the establishment of government pawnshops, and markets for bartering.

The pawnshop is in China the poor man's bank, where in spring the peasant pawns his thick winter clothes until he can redeem them at harvest time. The pawnshop is the only alternative to the moneylender, and often the proprietor of the former is none other than the latter. Pawnshops were a favourite investment for wealthy men until the rise of modern banking and commercial enterprises. Wang An-shih, by establishing state pawnshops, giving easier terms than the private concerns, was striking a blow at a most powerful vested interest, and one which was closely bound up with the richer landowning class, from which his conservative scholar opponents came. His object was, however, not any animus against the wealthy classes, but an endeavour to ease the lot of the peasants. This, it must be emphasised, was a policy inspired more by the desire to raise the revenue of the treasury than by humanitarian ideas.

The source of almost all Wang An-shih's economic policy is not in modern ideas of class equality, of which he naturally knew nothing, but in the ancient Chinese economic theories first propounded in the kingdom of Ch'in, and later developed under the Emperor Wu of the Han dynasty. This, indeed, was clearly recognised by his enemies, who used the argument against him, urging that the policies of Ch'in, which had culminated in the burning of the books and the persecution of the scholars, were necessarily bad, and contrary to the Confucian principles of government. Both Wang An-shih and his opponents, typical of their age, the archaistic Sung, turned back to the remote past of their country for inspiration and justification.

The second part of Wang An-shih's new policy was intended to guard against internal revolts and banditry, and also to provide against invasion by foreign enemies. Almost alone of the prominent statesmen of the early or northern Sung, Wang seems to have realised the serious danger to which the empire was exposed by the development of powerful enemy states on the northern frontier, and their possession of the passes leading down into the north China plain. Unlike his opponent Ssŭ-ma Kuang, he did not believe that Confucian virtues would in themselves suffice to keep the nomads out of China.

The Tithing System (*pao chia*) was designed to cope with banditry and crime, and also to provide a regular trained army for the defence of the state. For this purpose every ten families were combined to form a tithing (*chia*) with a headman, every fifty families formed a "great tithing" and ten of the latter made a "head tithing," each division having its responsible head. Every member of these groups was responsible for the crimes and misdemeanours of every other member, and if a crime was concealed, or abetted, the whole tithing was held responsible equally with the criminal himself. The headman had to keep a register of every member of his tithing, and he was also charged with the duty of investigating and reporting crimes. The tithing was furthermore responsible for the behaviour of strangers and guests who came amongst them.

The tithing system was also used for military purposes. Every family having more than two adult males had to provide one soldier, armed with bow and spear, and trained in the use of these weapons. The tithing was responsible for the training of these levies. By this double function of the tithing Wang An-shih hoped to check and reduce crime, eliminate brigandage and provide the state with a steady supply of trained men ready to be called up for service in time of war. The general tranquillity of the Sung dynasty in respect of internal disorders suggests that the system certainly did work well as a cure for banditry and local revolts. It is noteworthy that this reform, almost alone of the new laws, has been revived by later rulers of China. The tithing system was re-established by the Manchu dynasty, and in very modern times Chiang Kai-shek has instituted it in districts adjoining the Communist areas, as the best method of checking subversive influences.

The military provisions of the system seem to have been less successful. The critics of Wang An-shih declared that the greater part of the peasantry were too poor to buy the weapons and equipment needed for the tithing levies, and that this expense was an unjustifiable burden upon them. Nevertheless the Sung dynasty might have been better able to withstand the Kin invasions if Ssŭ-ma Kuang and his colleagues had not abolished the system when Wang An-shih's reforms were repealed.

The chief arm of the nomad invaders was cavalry, and, as the experience of the Han and T'ang empires proved, Chinese armies could not hope to oppose these enemies successfully unless they too were well provided with mounted troops. Horses, however, are not widely bred in China, being mainly imported from the Mongolian plateau. Wang An-shih saw that this dependence on enemy controlled areas for the supply of cavalry remounts would be a fatal handicap in war. The empire did not now possess any tributary horse-breeding area, such as the Han and T'ang Emperors had at their disposal. He therefore decided to institute a national horse-breeding scheme, which would render the Chinese army independent of Mongolian bred horses.

The Horse-breeding Law (*pao chia yang ma*) made it obligatory upon every family in the northern and north-western provinces (where there is suitable pasture) to keep one horse, which was supplied by the government, together with fodder for its keep in the winter months. Families of greater means were obliged to keep two horses, and inspectors were appointed to see that the law was carried out, and that the animals were properly cared for. The plan seems to have been successful, for the province of the Court, Honan, raised 3,000 horses, and each of the five provinces of the north-west raised 5,000, so that the government could rely upon nearly 30,000 remounts for the cavalry. Had this law remained in force for a few years more the Chinese armies would have been well mounted when the Kin hordes broke into the empire, and might have succeeded in stemming the invasion.

The New Laws, the reform policy of the Emperor Shên Tsung and Wang An-shih, remained in force for nearly twenty years, from the appointment of the minister in 1068, until they were repealed in A.D. 1086, under the regency governing in the name of Shên Tsung's young son, Chê Tsung. Wang An-shih himself, however, had resigned in A.D. 1076, having lost the Emperor's favour, although Shên Tsung did not change the policy which Wang had initiated. The minister retired to Nanking, where he died in 1086, the year in which his chief opponent, Ssŭ-ma Kuang, recalled to power by the Empress regent, swept away the whole system of the New Laws, and returned to the traditional forms of government.

It is difficult to discover the real effects of the New Laws. The Conservatives condemn them root and branch, using criticisms of unequal value, ranging from mere praise of traditional ways as in themselves better than any possible alteration, to allegations that the New Laws failed of their purpose and actually inflicted greater hardship on the class they were intended to relieve. It is difficult to believe that the peasants would have peacefully accepted such revolutionary changes if they did not find them to their advantage. The negative evidence of continuing peace and absence of disorder argues in favour of the New Laws and carries more weight than the diatribes of political opponents.

It would seem indeed that much of the resentment which the new policy called forth was directed against Wang An-shih himself rather than against his measures. There can be no doubt that the great Innovator had a repellent personality. All writers insist on his obstinacy and self-conceit, while the poet Su Tung-p'o declares that he was uncleanly in his personal habits. The scholars, moreover, resented his heterodox views on points of Contucian scholarship and interpretation, and since in Sung China politics and philosophy could not be separated, the heretic in Confucian doctrine was inevitably regarded as a dangerous man to govern the empire, a trouble maker who should be kept out of the administration. Detesting the man, the Conservatives therefore condemned his work, but history in passing judgment on the New Laws, cannot pay attention to these personal considerations.

The death of Shên Tsung and Wang An-shih did not put an end to the reform policy of the New Laws. For the moment, indeed, the triumph of the Conservatives was complete. Under the regency of the Dowager Empress Kao, who had always been an opponent of Wang An-shih, Ssǔ-ma Kuang was recalled and immediately annihilated the work of his opponent. After his death, however, in 1086, and that of the Empress Dowager herself in A.D. 1093, the young Emperor Chê Tsung took charge of the government himself and recalled the Innovators. The change was partly due to the quarrels which had broken out among the Conservatives themselves, who were divided on matters of Confucian doctrine, and partly occasioned by the Emperor's dislike for his consort, a lady chosen for him by the late Empress Dowager (who was not Chê Tsung's own mother), as a political support in the palace for the Conservative party.

In A.D. 1094 the Emperor conferred the ministry upon Ts'ai Ching, an ardent disciple of Wang An-shih. Immediately the New Laws were put into force once more, the Conservative ministers and officials degraded and exiled, and the memory of Ssǔ-ma Kuang and his associates publicly scorned by a decree of posthumous degradation. In spite of the death of Chê Tsung in A.D. 1100, the Innovators continued to dominate the Court under his successor, Hui Tsung, the artistic last Emperor of the northern Sung. The struggle centred about the personality of Ts'ai Ching, who, though several times dismissed, always obtained his reinstatement after a brief disgrace, and was still in power when the Kin invasions overwhelmed the empire and the two political factions in a common ruin.

Under Ts'ai Ching and Hui Tsung the Innovators became more and more identified with the Taoists, upon whom they relied for support, for, although the educated classes were predominantly Confucian, the Taoists and Buddhists were numerous and influential among the mass of the people. Hui Tsung, who favoured Taoism, was responsible for this new departure, for since the position of the minister depended on the continued favour of the Emperor, Ts'ai Ching found it necessary to conform to his predilections. The changed attitude of the Innovators tended to embitter the conflict even more, for Wang An-shih was a Confucian, even though he did not see eye to eye with other scholars on points of doctrine.

Whatever value the New Laws may have had it is certain that this political struggle, marked by sudden reversals of policy and violent changes in the economic system, as Innovators or Conservatives obtained power, was an evil which weakened the empire. The administration was rent by hatreds and political feuds, and disorganised by wholesale changes of personnel and lack of continuity in policy. Moreover, the quarrel in which the governing class was absorbed blinded them to urgent dangers arising beyond the frontiers. While Ts'ai Ching and his enemies contended for power, the Kin Tartars were rapidly conquering the Kitan kingdom of Liao, the northern neighbour of the Sung Empire; but the Sung statesmen engrossed in their own affairs, paid no attention to this momentous development and made no preparations against the new enemy from the steppes.

Chapter XX

CHU HSI AND THE NEW CONFUCIANISM

The Sung dynasty was an age of many-sided intellectual activity, in which the T'ang poetic tradition was carried on by men such as Ou-yang Hsiu and Su Tung-p'o, worthy to rank with the best of the T'ang poets, while history was enriched by the great works of Ssŭ-ma Kuang and other writers. It is, however, for its contribution to philosophy that the Sung period is most famous; the writers of the Sung school being second in importance only to the classical authors of the Feudal Age. As it is the philosophy of the Sung writers which has been accepted as the orthodox Confucianism of all subsequent ages, its importance as a cultural influence in the later centuries of Chinese civilisation cannot be over-estimated. Confucianism, as taught in the seven centuries following the Sung period, is the doctrine of the Sage as interpreted by Chu Hsi and his predecessors in the Sung school: in fact, this philosophy has often been called "Chu-Hsi-ism" by western writers, to emphasise the extent of the modifications introduced by the Sung philosopher.

The word is too clumsy to be accepted, and it is, moreover, important to realise that neither Chu Hsi himself, nor any orthodox Confucian would admit that the doctrines of the Sung school were innovations: on the contrary, they would argue vehemently that Chu Hsi had grasped the true meaning of the ancient texts, and that all other interpretations were erroneous. Chu Hsi himself made this claim, and his followers held that in so far as the traditional interpretation differed from the work of their master, it was incorrect, and that for fifteen centuries the world of Chinese scholarship had mistaken the meaning of the classical texts. It need not be doubted that Chu Hsi and all the Sung school really believed this astonishing proposition, but in the Sung period it would have been quite impossible to preach a new philosophy that did not claim to be founded on the classics. The disputes of the Sung philosophers were not between Confucians and the followers of other teachers, but between rival schools of Confucians, differing on the meaning and interpretation of the

Confucian books. The works of other classical schools did not enter into the discussion.

The characteristics of Sung thought were a retrospective return to purely Chinese sources, a conscious archaism and a kind of cultural introspection. The T'ang had paid little attention to classical studies. They accepted the traditional Confucianism, but the mind of that age was set on other things. The new Indian and western religions, things foreign and strange, were more attractive to the most cosmopolitan of all the Chinese dynasties. Under the Sung an intellectual reaction led to a real renaissance of classical literature, and branched off into the formulation of a new native system of philosophy, although it was never admitted to be an innovation. This concentration on purely national thought was the intellectual aspect of the Sung outlook, which was national, conservative, and pacifist. Just as the empire had accepted a restricted territory which cut off China from the old land route to the west, so, in thought the Sung confined themselves to the national literature, and ignored the alien systems which had intrigued the T'ang.

The conscious archaism of the Sung can scarcely be better illustrated than in the jade *p'i* shown in Fig. 55. On it are graved the animals of the four quarters, with just such slightly exaggerated energy as archaism is apt to produce.

Although it is impossible to assign to any one cause the sudden revival of classical learning under the Sung, the invention of printing, and the publication of cheaper printed editions of the classics, which made the ancient literature accessible to a larger public, was an important contributory factor; similar in its effects to the influence of the printed Bible among the Protestant nations at the Reformation. The progress of foreign religions under the T'ang also roused the Confucian scholars, who had always opposed these alien systems, to make a new study of their own philosophy, and endeavour to present it in a more systematised form. The influence of Buddhist theology and perhaps of theories from even further west is evident in the system of Chu Hsi.

Although the new Confucianism is attributed to Chu Hsi, and was, in fact, perfected and systematised by him, he was not the originator of its leading ideas, for he was the last of the six

FIG. 55. *Sung Jade pi with archaistic animal motifs.*

celebrated philosophers of the Sung dynasty. He is none the less the most famous, for he gathered up the work of his masters, and formulated the system which was to become, after his death, the orthodox school of Confucian doctrine. The distinctive feature of Chu Hsi's teaching, in common with that of all the Sung school, is its ethical character. The Confucian texts were interpreted from an ethical standpoint, the crudities of primitive rites explained, or, if this was inconvenient, explained away, and the ancient aristocratic code of the Feudal Age presented as a universal moral law equally applicable to all men. Confucianism, in a word, was modernised, stripped of its religious character, and left as an ethical system divorced from supernatural sanctions.

Any attempt to present a survey of the Sung philosophy and indicate the character and scope of the changes made in the traditional doctrine, is hindered by the fact that in the first place the Sung writers and their followers have never admitted that they made any changes at all, and also because they are themselves the accepted commentators and interpreters of the classical texts. It is first necessary to find out what Confucianism was before the Sung school re-shaped it. It is only in recent years that Chinese and foreign scholars have freed themselves from the Sung interpretations and to a considerable extent penetrated the original character of the classical texts. In Chapter IV the Confucian texts have been discussed in the light of this modern view. It has been shown that while on the one hand many of the texts upon which the Sung relied were certainly not written by Confucius or any member of his school, others, particularly the Odes and the *I Ching* or Book of Changes, had a character entirely different to that attributed to them by the Sung writers.

The Sung scholars ignored the historical development of the Confucian doctrine, and disregarded the varying social background which had moulded the original teaching and modified it in the Han period. In their own day both the feudal aristocratic society of Confucius and the post-revolutionary age of the Han were equally remote. The centralised empire was the accepted, the only legitimate form of government. Society was controlled by the large class of scholars who owed their position to education and not to birth. No caste barriers prevented the clever son of a peasant from rising to the highest rank. Consequently they were not concerned, as in different ways, both Confucius and the Han scholars had been concerned, to find a principle of moral authority for the government and for society. The Sung, realising the cosmic limitations of this traditional political Confucianism, endeavoured to find a moral authority for the whole universe, and gave an ethical interpretation to what had been originally a social doctrine. Since they could not discover any clear teaching on the Absolute in the better known Confucian texts such as the Analects, they turned to the *I Ching*—which had hardly been regarded as a philosophic book in the classical age—

and in the obscurities of this ancient text they found phrases to justify their own advanced thought.

Having formulated a new system on this slender authority, they interpreted all Confucian and classical literature in accordance with it, and forced them into its framework. The Chinese people have always demanded that all innovations should be founded upon some ancient authority, and as philosophers anxious to spread a new ethical system the Sung were quite justified in modernising and adapting Confucianism to suit their purpose, but a distinction must be made between Sung philosophy as an original doctrine based upon a forced interpretation of ancient texts, and Sung doctrine as historical criticism. The former is an important contribution to ethics and philosophy, the latter is a hindrance to a true conception of the ancient Chinese culture. It must be once more repeated that the Sung themselves were unaware of this distinction. They believed that they had grasped the true and original meaning of the ancient obscure texts, which had been lost for centuries.

The most important Sung innovation in Confucian doctrine was the work of Chou Tun-i (1017-1073) who was also the earliest of the Sung philosophers. Chou Tun-i found in the *I Ching* (Book of Changes) an obscure reference to T'ai Chi, the Supreme Ultimate. The phrase occurs nowhere else in classical literature, and is certainly not the work of Confucius. The passage in which it occurs deals with divination and the trigrams. Chou Tun-i, however, seized upon it and made T'ai Chi the central point of his doctrine, and of the Sung system. In this Supreme Ultimate he found the First Cause of the universe, the co-ordinating point from which the two principles *yin* and *yang* proceed. The *yin* and *yang* are to the Sung the negative and positive expressions of the Supreme Ultimate. By their alternation they produce the Five Agents—or elements—Earth, Fire, Wood, Metal and Water. These, by their interaction, produce the world of phenomena.

To Chou Tun-i and his successors the Five Agents are cosmic forces, not to be strictly identified with the substances from which they take their names. As in the earlier system the Five Agents are related to the Virtues and the Seasons, but the Sung school insisted that the Supreme Ultimate is the final cause which controls the alternating forces of *yin* and *yang*, and through them the operation of the Five Agents. The Supreme Ultimate "is all things and is in all things." Moreover, it is a moral force. To the Sung school there is no distinction between the law of nature and the moral law. They are one and the same. The world is controlled and inspired by the Supreme Ultimate which is Li (law), a moral law, identical with the ethical standard upon which human conduct should be modelled.

It is difficult to decide how far the Sung school considered the Supreme Ultimate, identified with law, as having personality—how far T'ai Chi, which Chu Hsi identified also with the ancient T'ien, Heaven, was God. By some the Sung school have been regarded as materialists who set up abstract law as the First Cause; while others, arguing that this First Cause was moral, contend that Chu Hsi, at least, held that T'ai Chi had personality. The difficulty arises from the fact that this aspect of the problem was the least stressed by the Sung themselves. They were, like the earlier Confucians, at bottom more interested in conduct and ethics than in the theological side of their doctrine, a characteristically Chinese standpoint.

Chu Hsi says indeed, that "there is not a man in Heaven judging sin," but when pressed by a questioner he also said: " It would be wrong to say that there is no ruler of the universe at all."

The Sung school combated the anthropomorphic ideas which were derived from Buddhist and Taoist sources, but stopped short of affirming that the T'ai Chi was pure law, like a law of nature such as gravity. The tendency of their teaching was certainly to whittle away the conception of a personal deity which underlay the ancient Shang Ti, a term which probably originally meant the Great Ancestor. Shang Ti occurred in too many ancient texts, and was invested in them with attributes incompatible with the idea of a pure, impersonal law, to be ignored by a school which claimed to be interpreting the classics, not preaching a new doctrine. So in the Sung system Shang Ti T'ai Chi and Li, the Law, are treated as equivalent terms illustrating different aspects of the First Cause.

They could not admit that the world had outgrown the primitive religious beliefs of which the texts showed such abundant traces, for to do so would destroy the essential Confucian tenet which regarded the age of Yao and Shun as the type of perfection to which the world must return. They preferred to concentrate attention upon the ethical quality of T'ai Chi, the First Cause, in its aspect as Li, the law, leaving the question of personality in some obscurity. In the event the rather half-hearted admission of Divine Personality made by Chu Hsi as quoted above was ignored by later Confucians, to whom moral law, impersonal and abstract, became the First Cause of the universe.

Li, or moral law, became for the Sung philosophers the supreme controlling force in the universe. "Heaven is Law," wrote Chu Hsi. This moral law which operating through the *yin* and *yang* and the Five Agents was the mainspring of the world of phenomena was also the ethical law by which man lived. It was expressed as the four chief virtues, Benevolence*, Righteousness, Reverence and Wisdom, to which Sincerity was added. According to the Sung theory, which drew no distinction between the moral and material, both being equally the work of Law (Li), the virtues were the moral expression of the five cosmic forces called the Five Agents, which in the material world produced the seasons. A table of these equivalents was expressed thus:

Benevolence (jên)	Wood	Spring
Righteousness (jên)	Metal	Summer
Reverence (chung)	Fire	Autumn
Wisdom (chih)	Water	Winter
Sincerity (hsin)	Earth	

The fifth virtue and its corresponding agent, having no season, were allotted eighteen days in each of the four seasons. Benevolence was the highest of the virtues, the supreme quality of Li (Law), and the other virtues were subordinate to it and in a sense regarded as aspects of Benevolence.

The Sung, therefore, having added T'ai Chi, the Supreme Ultimate, to the Confucian theory, and equated it with the

*Jên. This has sometimes been rendered as "Love," and is so translated by Prof. J. P. Bruce in his translation of Chu Hsi. *The Philosophy of Human Nature.* London. 1922. "Love," however, as a philosophic or theological term is so intimately associated with the Christian doctrine that it seems liable to cause confusion if used for the Confucian *Jên*, which is more abstract.

traditional Heaven, and Li, the moral law, held that it operated as Benevolence. It was necessary, of course, to account for evil, which would appear to have no place in the system outlined by the Sung school except in the nature of man. Even here a careful distinction was drawn. Mencius had said that the Nature of Man (*hsing*) was good, and Hsün Tzǔ, who taught the opposite, was regarded by the Sung as a heretic. Moreover, as man obtained his nature from Heaven, that is from the moral law, it was of necessity good. Chu Hsi was very severe on those who believed that the nature of man was neither good nor bad, but depended for its development wholly on its training. This was called the "whirling water" heresy, because Kao Tzǔ, an opponent of Mencius, had declared that the nature of man was like water whirling in a rocky gorge, and would flow out along the line of least resistance, whether that was bad or good. This doctrine was still held by certain scholars in the Sung period.

According to Chu Hsi the nature of man, the original nature which he obtained from Heaven, is both good and incorruptible. When exposed to the temptations of the world it may be obscured, and lost. Nevertheless, like a pearl in a bowl of dirty water, the original nature remains pure and unchanged, and can shine forth in all its brilliance if the impurity is removed. This simile, and that of a mirror covered with dust which if cleaned will be as bright as ever, are favourite illustrations of Chu Hsi's doctrine of the nature of man. Evil, therefore, was the result of neglect of this nature, by which it became obscured by the temptations of the world. The duty of man was to cultivate his nature and keep its original purity unsullied. Since man, alone of the animals and created beings, possessed the full and perfect nature, while all other creatures had only received a partial one, incapable of true perfection, he alone could attain the proper development, or the Mean (*Chung Yung*), a doctrine to which Chu Hsi attached great importance. It was derived from an ancient book, entitled *Chung Yung*, attributed to the grandson of Confucius, and was regarded as an orthodox exposition of the teaching of the Sage himself. The Sung school conferred a new importance and authority upon this book, which does not seem to have been classed as a classic of the first importance in earlier times.

The Sung school's insistence on the Mean applied to both excesses, failure to cultivate the *hsing* (nature), and also to asceticism. While the profligate obscured his nature by exposing it to worldly temptations, the Buddhist monk, who renounced his family and cut himself off from human relationships, erred equally against the Mean. He ignored those duties which bind parents and children, and living men with the ancestral spirits. These relationships, which form an essential part of the world order, must necessarily be good and right, for they proceed from the Law. Chu Hsi therefore roundly condemned the Buddhist doctrine which taught that the world of phenomena was an illusion, and the only reality the mind of Buddha.

In Chu Hsi's system man gets no assistance from supernatural agencies in his endeavour to keep the Mean. There is no redemption of sin through divine intervention, nor any judgment or future reward. The duty of man is his alone, and it is its own reward. Prayer, accordingly, plays no part in his system, for the moral law, to which Heaven is reduced, though benevolent, does not intervene in the individual problems of mankind. It is true that Chu Hsi retained the idea developed by Han scholars, that natural calamities were manifestations of Heaven's displeasure with the conduct of the rulers of mankind. Sung doctrine, however, regards these phenomena less as the wrath of a divinity than as disturbances in the harmony of the universe due to wilful opposition to the Law.

This was the only explanation given by the Sung school for the most difficult of all problems, that of evil for which the individual cannot be held responsible. Chu Hsi believed that man's material destiny (poverty or wealth, health or infirmity) was ordered by the Decree of Heaven, but that this Decree did not prevent the cultivation of the moral nature, which was the duty of man, however he might be circumstanced. He offered no answer to the problem why men were born with such varying fortunes, nor why some endured misery for which their conduct offered no justification, and others escaped the consequences of folly and sin. This omission left Buddhism with an unchallenged answer to the great problem. Man, said the Buddhists, suffers in this incarnation for the sins he committed in the last, or is rewarded by happiness now for his virtuous life in past ages. Perhaps for this reason Buddhism held its own against the New Confucianism, particularly among the mass of the people who suffered the inequalities of this world.

Although the teaching of Chu Hsi was finally accepted as orthodox, it was vigorously opposed during his own lifetime. The school of which he was the most famous teacher was not the only one to flourish in the Sung period, nor was Chu Hsi the first to preach its peculiar tenets. Chou Tun-i, as has been mentioned, originated the theory of T'ai Chi, and his teaching was transmitted by three of his pupils, counted among the six great philosophers of the Sung school. These were Ch'êng Hao (1032-1085) and his brother Ch'êng I (1033-1107), their uncle Chang Tsai (1020-1076), and Shao Yung (1011-1077), who first turned the attention of scholars to the *I Ching* and raised the question of the nature of man. Chu Hsi himself came after all these scholars, for he lived in the southern Sung period, after the Kin invasions (1130-1200). The Hu and Su schools, though Confucians, were the most important of the opponents of Chu Hsi. These schools were called after their respective founders, Hu An-kuo (1074), and the Su family, Su Hsin and his sons, one of whom was the famous poet, Su Tung-p'o. The points in which they differed from Chu Hsi were mainly matters of definition and the interpretation of terms. The Hu school, for instance, contended that it was not possible to describe the nature of man as "good" without implying that it must also be capable of evil, because "good" is a relative term which suggests the existence of evil as its contrary. Mencius therefore when he said: "The *hsing* (nature) is good," was merely making an exclamation of admiration. They also argued, rather in the Taoist manner, that the original *hsing* could not be described in such terms as good, for it was sublime and transcended all contraries. Finally, they argued that the nature of man as it exists in the living man (as opposed to the pure nature which he obtains at birth) can be defined as the faculty of liking and disliking. The enlightened man is guided in his likes and dislikes by the moral law, the base man merely by his selfish desires.

The Su school held that the nature of man (*hsing*) did not necessarily consist of the four virtues, but that before it assumed this moral quality it was necessary for man to adopt them by an act of voluntary acceptance. The *hsing* existed eternally, before the birth of the individual, but until man cultivated it by implanting the four virtues, it could not be considered to be moral. They were thus opposed to Chu Hsi's doctrine that the nature of man is the sum of the four virtues, and not an entity separated from them.

The doctrines preached by the Sung school, perfected by Chu Hsi, were not accepted as orthodox until nearly the end of the Sung period. During the lifetime of the philosopher himself the great majority of scholars were strongly opposed to Chu Hsi and his teaching. The fact is important for it proves that the philosophy of the Sung school was regarded as heretical by contemporaries and not as a return to the real meaning of the Confucian classics. It would, indeed, have been remarkable if such striking innovations has been allowed to pass without arousing opposition among those who held to the traditional interpretation of the ancient literature.

Politics, however, were mixed up with philosophy in this opposition. Chu Hsi was born in 1129, a few years after the Kin conquest of the northern provinces of the Sung Empire. He died in 1200 at the age of 71, and his life thus covered the major part of the southern Sung period. After the fall of K'ai Fêng to the Kin the quarrel between the Innovators and Conservatives which had centred round the personalities and policies of Wang An-shih and Ssǔ-ma Kuang respectively, was extinguished with the disappearance of the former party. In the southern empire a new alignment of parties perpetuated the strife of the scholars. Their disputes arose from a split in the ranks of the triumphant Conservatives.

Chu Hsi, and those who shared his views, were in favour of a war of revenge, to chase the Kin out of China, and recover the lost provinces. They based this policy on the Confucian doctrine that a filial son must avenge the death of his father. The southern Sung Emperors were the sons and descendants of the unfortunate Hui Tsung, who had died in captivity after the surrender of K'ai Fêng to the Kin. Therefore, contended Chu Hsi, the first duty of the Sung Emperor was to avenge his death.

The party in power, headed by the minister, Ch'in Kuei, were on the contrary in favour of peace. They doubted, probably rightly, whether the empire had the military strength to overthrow the Kin, and feared that if an aggressive policy was adopted the only result would be a fresh invasion which would finally destroy the Sung Empire. They accepted the loss of the north as irretrievable, and strove to consolidate the remaining provinces into an empire bounded to the north by the watershed of the Yangtze and Yellow River basins.

The opposition between these pacifists and the war party was aggravated by doctrinal differences. The views of Chou Tun-i, the two Ch'êngs, and Chu Hsi were by no means generally approved. In 1178 both Ch'êng I and Wang An-shih, opponents in matters of philosophy, were excluded from the list of sages honoured in the Confucian temples, on the advice of a minister. It was urged that these vain discussions and involved interpretations only encouraged the formation of factions and acrimonious disputes. These writings should be discouraged, and scholars adjured to abide by the plain text of the classics and the traditional interpretation. Chu Hsi replied by forming his followers into an association known as the "School of the Way," i.e. "the Truth," and stigmatising his opponents as "*hsiao jên*," the classical term which he interpreted not as " little men" in the sense of social inferiors, but as persons of mean moral stature.

Although Chu Hsi was several times recommended for office by his friends, and was employed in different capacities for short periods, the hostility of the dominant party prevented him from exercising any real influence upon governmental affairs, and he spent the major part of his long life as a "sleeping dragon" an official in retirement in the provinces. In 1193, indeed, he obtained a brief promotion. The ambassador at the Kin Court reported to the Emperor that the Kin ruler had enquired what post the " great Chu Hsi" occupied at Hang Chou, the Sung capital. The Emperor, perhaps fearing that if the School of the Way heard how much they were appreciated in the northern empire, they might become pro-Kin, hastily appointed Chu Hsi prefect of Ch'ang Sha in Hunan, an important post, but far removed from the Court.

Two years later the minister Han T'ou-chou, a vehement opponent of the School of the Way, came to power, and at once initiated a proscription of his enemies. A register of members of the School of the Way was compiled and they were debarred from holding any official post. Candidates for office were required to abjure the doctrine of Chu Hsi before obtaining a position. The leading members of the school were put under police observation, and the name of the school prohibited. In future the followers of Chu Hsi were officially described as "the School of Lies," and later "the Rebel Faction." Apart from opprobrious labels and exclusion from office, the government, true to the civilised practice of the Sung, did not proceed to acts of violence against the proscribed party.

Chu Hsi himself did not long survive the reverse of his fortunes. He died in 1200, surrounded by faithful disciples, but also by police observers. Like Confucius himself, the Sung philosopher was rejected and persecuted during his lifetime, but honoured after his death. In 1227 the Emperor Li Tsung, who reigned over an empire fast dwindling before the Mongol invasions, rehabilitated Chu Hsi, and ardently espoused the teaching of the School of the Way. The offensive epithets were expunged, Chu Hsi was posthumously made a duke, and a few years later, in 1237, his commentaries and the historical works of Ssŭ-ma Kuang were officially recognised as texts for school instruction and the examinations for the civil service. In 1241 the Emperor, more occupied with philosophy than the defence of the state, issued an edict commending Chu Hsi and the Sung school.

The true doctrine of Confucius, it was declared, had been lost after the death of Mencius, some thirteen centuries previously. Chu Hsi and his masters had re-discovered the real interpretation, which henceforward should alone be admitted to be the orthodox doctrine. While the Sung were thus tardily recognising Chu Hsi as the re-founder, or rather, in the official view, re-discoverer of Confucianism, the new doctrines were spread in the northern provinces subject to the Mongols. A Chinese scholar who had accompanied the Mongol army which invaded Szechuan province, returned to the north in 1238 with a library of the Sung school's works, and after founding a college at Peking, made the new doctrines paramount in the north.

Thus the School of the Way triumphed in both north and south, just at the moment when the Chinese Empire was about to be extinguished by the Mongol conquerors. The Sung state succumbed to the nomad attacks, but the philosophic victory of the Sung School proved more lasting than the military successes of the Mongols.

Chapter XXI

THE NOMAD INVADERS

INTERCOURSE between China and foreign nations in the Sung period was of two kinds; peaceful trading relations with the Arabs who came by sea to the ports along the south-east coast, and devastating invasions by nomadic raiders from the Mongolian steppes. The contact with the Arabs not only brought great wealth to the southern Chinese provinces, but also increased geographical knowledge of the countries to the west of the Indian Ocean. The nomadic invasions largely ruined the north-west of China, and led to the rapid decline of the ancient caravan route to Central Asia and the Chinese cities which formed its eastern termini.

The Mongol invasion, the last and most destructive of these incursions, destroyed for ever the ancient importance of the "land within the passes"—Shensi and Kansu—which in Han and T'ang times had been the centre of Chinese civilisation. The diminished population was no longer able to keep the irrigation works in repair, and many of the cities on the northern frontier were in time overwhelmed by the drifting sands of the desert. The south, on the other hand, escaping the worst fury of the Mongols, became the real centre of Chinese culture, and it was from this region, a mere colonial territory in Han times, and still very little exploited in the T'ang dynasty, that the later Chinese dynasties took their origin and derived their support. The invasions of the north, and its separation from the south for more than a century, had another consequence. It is after the Sung dynasty that the rivalry and distinction between north and south first becomes a factor of importance in Chinese history. In earlier dynasties the south was not sufficiently important to claim equality with the older provinces north of the Yangtze, but after the Sung the pretensions of the southern provinces, and the hostility they aroused in the north, are a constant feature of Chinese politics, and even affected questions of literature and art.

Although the outlook of the Chinese in the Sung period was less cosmopolitan than it had been under the T'ang, geographical knowledge was considerably extended. It is characteristic of the Sung that exploration and oversea trade was left in the hands of foreigners, the Arabs, so that Chinese knowledge of the west was largely vicarious. Sea-borne trade, checked by the sack of Canton during Huang Tsao's rebellion in the closing years of the T'ang dynasty, swiftly recovered under the Sung. While Chinese ships seem to have visited Japan, the Philippines, Cochin China and the Malay Archipelago, the traffic across the Indian Ocean was entirely in Arab hands. This monopoly was probably enforced by the Arabs themselves, to judge from the hostile reception they accorded to the Portuguese when they first entered there seas.

Canton, Ch'üan Chou in Fukien, and Kanpu, the port of Hang Chou, were the chief centres of Arab trade in China, and in these places Arabs were permitted to reside and follow their own religion and customs, as had been the case under the T'ang. The Chinese Government, however, carefully controlled the trade, collecting a customs duty which was very remunerative. Inspectors of Foreign Trade were appointed to the chief ports, and it is in a book written by one of these officials, Chao Ju-kua, a scion of the imperial family who held the post in Fukien province in the early 12th century, that most of the geographical information derived from the Arabs is contained.*

Chao learned from his Arab informants not only new details about countries such as Persia and Mesopotamia, which were already familiar to the Chinese, but also information about parts of Africa and the countries of the Mediterranean, which had hitherto been entirely unknown to China. He gives an account of Egypt, which includes a description of the rising of the Nile, "a river whose source is not known," and also a reference to the Pharos at Alexandria, where "on the seashore there is a great tower"—but this was probably a tradition, and not contemporary evidence.

Zanzibar, where Sung porcelain has been found, is mentioned as "as an island in the sea, to the west of which is a great mountain," which may possibly be a reference to Kilimanjaro. The

*Chu fan chih. It has been translated into English, under the title, Chau Ju-kua, by Hirth & Rockhill. St. Petersburg Academy of Sciences. 1911.

giraffe and zebra of the Berbera coast are described, the latter as "a kind of mule with brown, white and black stripes around its body." Madagascar is

"An island in the sea on which there are many savages with bodies as black as lacquer and with frizzed hair. They are enticed by offers of food and then caught and carried off as slaves to the Ta Shih country (Arabia), where they fetch a high price. They are employed as gatekeepers, and it is said that they do not pine for their home land."

Chao Ju-kua also heard of Morocco and Spain, but his informants, who had probably never been there, could tell him nothing but the names of these distant lands, and that to the north of Spain, "if one travels by land for two hundred days, the days are only six hours long." This is the first reference in Chinese literature to the north-west of Europe. Other European countries were better known. Sicily (Ssŭ-chia-li-yeh) is fully described:

"The country of Ssŭ-chia-li-yeh is near the frontier of Lu-mei [Rum, i.e. the Byzantine Empire]. It is an island in the sea, a thousand *li* in breadth [300 miles]. The clothing, customs and language of the people are the same as those of Lu-mei. This country has a mountain in which there is a cavern of great depth. When seen from afar smoke issues from it in the morning, and fire at night. When seen from a short distance it is a madly roaring fire. When the people of the country carry up a big stone weighing 500 or 1,000 catties and throw it down into the cavern, after a little while there is an explosion, and the stone comes out in little pieces like pumice stone. Once in every five years fire and stones break out and flow down as far as the sea coast, and then go back again. The trees in the woods through which the fire passes are not burned, but the stones in its path are turned to ashes."

It would seem that this account of Etna had been somewhat distorted, either by the Arab traveller, or because Chao himself did not quite understand what his informant wished to say. There are no active volcanoes in any part of China, therefore the Chinese had no knowledge of eruptions.

The Sung History recounts further contacts with the Byzantine Empire, including a description of that Empire by the ambassador of a certain "King" Mieh Li I Ling Kai Sa, who has been identified as the Emperor Milissenus Nicephorus Caesar (A.D. 1080). The ambassador is called Mi Ssu Tu Ling Ssu Meng Pan in the Chinese history and it has been suggested that this represents "Maitre Simon de Montfort"—a member of that famous family in the service of Byzantium.* The object of this embassy and two others which followed in the decade between A.D. 1081 and 1091 was probably political. The Byzantine Empire had recently suffered the disaster of the battle of Manzikert, which cost the empire the loss of Anatolia. The Greeks hoped to enlist Chinese aid in their struggle against the Turks, whose domains stretched eastward to Central Asia. Had the Sung been willing to resume in these regions the policy of expansion which the Han and T'ang had followed, their intervention would have diverted Turkish pressure from the hard pressed Byzantine Empire. The pacifist Sung, however, contented themselves with making some fine presents to the ambassador, but offered no armed assistance.

The extent of the new geographical knowledge obtained by the Chinese at this time is interesting, as showing that the Chinese were fairly well informed before the Mongol conquest of Asia first opened that continent to European travellers. Marco Polo, and other Europeans in the service of the Great Khan, or on embassies to his Court, were the first to bring precise knowledge of China to the west. China, on the other hand, acquired no new knowledge of the west through the Mongol conquests. This fact is important. For Europe the chief result of the Mongol conquest was the temporary elimination of the hostile Moslem states which had barred the way to Asia, and in consequence there was a great extension of geographical knowledge. To the Chinese, however, the land routes to the west had been known for centuries before the Mongols, and the sea route was also already fully developed.

*"Two Studies in the History of Foreign Relations of the Chinese Empire." Yang Hsien-Yi. *Philobiblon*. Vol. II, No. 1. The National Library, Nanking. 1947.

Thus China suffered the destruction and appalling wastage of Mongol savagery without any compensating gain in knowledge, while Europe, escaping the worst of the onslaught, learned of new lands of incredible wealth and far higher civilisation. It was in quest of this new world that her adventurous seamen soon set out, to find, by accident, another new world, the American continent. The devastation of Asia by the Mongol conquest and the increased knowledge of geography which Europe acquired by the same agency, was the origin of the ascendancy which the western continent later obtained.

The Sung Empire never extended over the whole of the Chinese lands, and from 1124 it was confined to the provinces south of the Yellow River basin. From the first Sung China was hemmed in to the north and north-west by hostile and powerful states, which had borrowed Chinese forms of government, and were not merely tribal confederacies such as those which the Han and T'ang dynasties had successfully repulsed. The border kingdoms in the Sung period, although ruled by the conquering nomad people, included many Chinese among their subjects, and established their capitals in purely Chinese cities. For this reason they rapidly assimilated Chinese culture and became semi-Chinese states. The Sung dynasty never had an opportunity to re-establish the ancient Chinese domination in Central Asia, from which it was cut off by these border kingdoms. Having lost the defensive line of the Great Wall, it was always at a disadvantage and was forced to follow a policy of passive defence, and if possible, of peace.

In the later years of the T'ang dynasty a great change had occurred in the northern steppes. The Turkish tribes, Uighurs, and others, who had for some centuries been the dominant race, were displaced by newcomers from two directions. In the west the Tanguts, a people of Tibetan stock, descended the upper valley of the Yellow River and established themselves on the north-western frontier of China, in the long "arm" of Kansu stretching out towards Turkestan, and in the Alashan region to-day called Ning Hsia province. Here they founded the kingdom of Hsia, which endured until the Mongol conquest, and effectively barred the Chinese from the land route to the west. The Kings of Hsia, however, were to some extent influenced by Chinese culture. They bore a Chinese surname, Li, granted to their ancestor by the T'ang Emperor Hsi Tsung as a reward for their assistance against the rebel Huang Tsao*.

In 982 the ruler of the Tanguts, who had hitherto only used the title of Duke, granted him by Hsi Tsung of the T'ang, proclaimed himself King of Hsia, and refused to acknowledge the authority of the Sung Emperors. In 1028 the Hsia conquered the whole of the "arm" of Kansu province, and what is now Ning Hsia province. Their capital was fixed at Ning Hsia, a Chinese city, and they also held the important cities of Liang Chou, Kan Chou and Su Chou, on the caravan route to Central Asia. In spite of this considerable Chinese population the Hsia did not accept Chinese culture as a whole. They used their own system of writing, a character which has not yet been deciphered.

Although small in area compared to its neighbours, the Sung Empire, and the Kitan kingdom of Liao, Hsia was a warlike and powerful state which successfully repulsed every attempt to reduce it, whether made by the Chinese or nomads, until it succumbed before the appalling onslaught of the Mongols, who exterminated the Hsia people and left the country a wilderness. It is largely owing to this terrible end that so little is known of the Hsia state and its culture. Everything, and almost everybody in the kingdom, perished at the hands of Genghiz Khan.

While the far north-west of China had fallen into the hands of the Tanguts of Hsia, the eastern portion of the steppe lands was occupied, at about the same time, by a Tungus people, the Kitans, who had originally inhabited the Amur and Sungari Valleys in what is now North Manchuria. The Kitans are first mentioned by the Chinese history in 696. They were then divided into eight hordes, the khans of which elected a Great Khan, who held that office for three years, and then retired. This elective monarchy came to an end at the beginning of the 10th century when the Great Khan Apaoki refused to resign at the end of his three years, and, after overcoming the opposition which his

*Li was the surname of the T'ang imperial family. It was frequently granted as an honour to deserving families, both Chinese and barbarian, who were thus affiliated to the imperial clan. The custom, much practised by the T'ang Emperors, was maintained by the Sung, but more rarely used.

pretensions aroused, made himself hereditary King of the united Kitan nation. In 916, no doubt after learning of the deposition of the last T'ang Emperor, he himself took the title of Emperor, and started to raid the northern frontiers of China, which were left exposed in the chaos which followed the collapse of the T'ang.

Ten years later, in 926, in return for helping the founder of the Later Tsin "dynasty"—himself a Turkish adventurer—the Kitans obtained the cession of the north-east corner of Hopei province, the area, including the site of modern Peking, between the Great Wall and the sea as far south as a line drawn south of Tientsin tō the border of Shansi province, all purely Chinese territory. Rather later the Kitans took possession of the territory between the Inner and Outer Great Wall, in the modern provinces of Chahar and Suiyuan, including the city of Ta T'ung Fu, which became one of their capitals. They had already conquered South Manchuria, the Liao Tung peninsula, which had been a T'ang province, and which had been for many years a settled country with numerous cities and towns.

Thus, although the Kitans never conquered any large extent of China south of the Great Wall, they actually ruled over a wide extent of country inhabited by Chinese, and fixed their capital in a Chinese city. It is not possible to know the proportion which the Chinese bore to the Kitans themselves in the new Liao kingdom (Liao was the dynastic name chosen by the Kitans), but it seems very likely that the Chinese outnumbered their conquerors several times. When Apaoki swept down to the Great Wall, he was said to have had 300,000 fighting men, the whole strength of the Kitan nation. Accepting this figure as approximately accurate, the Kitan people, including women and non-combatant males would have hardly numbered more than two million souls. The Chinese of Liao Tung, Northern Hopei and the intra-mural territory must have been at least as numerous.

Established on the borders of the Sung Empire, and ruling over a large Chinese population, it was not long before the Kitans adopted Chinese civilisation and abandoned the customs of their nomadic ancestors. The bulk of the tribe settled in the border land, the modern provinces of Jehol and Chahar, while the original home of the Kitans became the cradle of another nomadic conquering race. After making peace with the Sung Empire in the year 1004—a peace by which they received a large annual subsidy, or tribute from China—the Kitans left the Sung Empire alone, and, except for some unsuccessful attempts to conquer the Hsia kingdom, remained at peace with all their neighbours. From this date until their destruction by the Nuchens, the Kitan Liao dynasty was to all intents a Chinese dynasty, and as such it certainly appeared to foreign peoples. The name Cathay, which the European peoples first applied to China, is derived from the word Kitan, and the Russians to this day use the variant Kitai as the name of the Chinese people. Cathay, however, originally meant north China, the part of the country reached by the land caravan route across Asia. To Marco Polo, south China was Manzi, a corruption of the Chinese word Man Tzŭ, which really means a non-Chinese aborigine of the southern provinces. It is a singular fact that the Chinese were first known to Europe by two names, neither of which correctly belonged to the Chinese people at all, but on the contrary, to their traditional enemies.

The Nuchen, like the Kitans, were a Tungus tribe who dwelt on both banks of the Amur River. During the heyday of the Kitan Liao dynasty the Nuchens were a tributary people, governed by their own chiefs. Early in the 12th century, under a leader of genius named Akuta, the Nuchens threw off the yoke of their Kitan rulers, and started a war which was not to end until the Liao dynasty and the Kitan nation had been utterly overthrown. In 1124, after conquering the whole Kitan kingbom, Akuta quarrelled with the Sung, and swiftly overran the whole of north China. Had his generals shown more persistence, and had he himself lived, the whole of China would have been conquered with as little resistance as was shown in the north. The Nuchens burned Hang Chou and captured Ningpo far down the south-east coast, but on account of the dissensions which broke out after Akuta's death, they relaxed their efforts to conquer the south and finally accepted the north watershed of the Yangtze Valley as their southern frontier.

In 1147 they were compelled to abandon their original

territory to a new conquering nomad people, the Mongols, who defeated the Nuchen and expelled them from their old home in the Kerulen Valley. The Nuchens then moved south into China, and fixed their new capital at Peking, then called Yen, which now for the first time became the capital of a large empire. The Nuchens also adopted the Chinese name of Chin for their dynasty (more commonly spelt Kin when applied to them). Spread thinly over the populous provinces of north China, which, to judge by the census figures of the Sung Empire taken the year before the invasion, must have contained nearly 50 million people, the Nuchens speedily lost their identity, and rapidly became absorbed in the Chinese population. In 1187 the Kin Emperor, alarmed by the extent to which this assimilation had already taken place, endeavoured to check it by forbidding his Nuchen subjects to take Chinese surnames or wear Chinese costume.

If these edicts enforced an outward distinction between the two peoples, in every other respect the Kin soon became a Chinese dynasty. Confucius was as much honoured in the Kin Empire as in the Sung. Chu Hsi, in fact, the great contemporary Sung philosopher, was better appreciated in the north than in his native state, during his own lifetime.

There is nothing surprising in this swift transformation of a race of nomad warriors. The Chinese Empire was then more populous and civilised than it had ever been before. K'ai Fêng Fu, which surrendered to the Kin, was the centre of this civilisation, a city inhabited by thousands of skilled artisans, and hundreds of refined scholars. The Kin had been an uncivilised tribe of nomads when they conquered the northern provinces. They had nothing to contribute to this civilisation, except their fighting spirit, which, on the contrary, they soon lost. Therefore, although the Sung political control of the north was lost in 1124, the cultural unity of the empire continued, unchanged by the nomadic conquest.

If the Liao and Kin conquests had been the last of the nomad invasions suffered by China, the empire and its civilisation would not have sustained much lasting damage, but the Kin were to be followed by the Mongols, the most savage and pitiless race known to history. In 1206, little more than eighty years after the Kin conquest of north China, Temujin became Great Khan of the

Mongols, under the title Genghiz Khan. Four years later he attacked the Kin Empire, and began a war which only ended with the ruin of that state.

No nomad people has ever attained a fame equal to that of the Mongols, and Genghiz Khan and his sons ruled over a wider land empire than has ever been formed before or since. This achievement, truly astonishing for the obscure chief of an obscure tribe, has provoked the admiration of soldiers and military historians, who acclaim Genghiz as one of the greatest soldiers of history. It is, however, the only title to greatness which he or his people can claim. The Mongol conquests were in every respect an unmitigated curse. They destroyed everything worth preserving in the civilisations of western Asia and north-western China, and saved only the elements in those civilisations which the world could well spare, cruelty, brutality and poverty.

They contributed nothing, except a new standard of ferocity and a rule of warfare which practised cold-blooded massacre on the grandest scale. Genghiz Khan laid down the rule, which his successors maintained, that any city or town which loosed a single arrow or stone in its defence should be refused any composition, and even if it surrendered, the inhabitants, combatants and non-combatants alike, should be exterminated to the last man, woman and child. By these methods of massacre and terror the Mongols conquered the whole of west Asia, Russia and eastern Europe. Only the death of the Great Khan Ogotai, Genghiz's son and successor, prevented the invasion of western Europe. The news reached the Mongol generals after Hungary had been laid waste, just as they were preparing to attack the Holy Roman Empire. But for this accident, which recalled the Mongol leaders for the election of another Great Khan, Europe as a whole would have certainly experienced the destruction and ruin which had already overwhelmed Asia.

Although the Mongol throne was transmitted in the family of Genghiz Khan, it was in theory at least, elective, and each new Great Khan had to have his authority confirmed by a Kuriltai, or diet of the nation. In other respects the Mongols conserved the barbarous customs of their nomad ancestors longer than other steppe people who had come in contact with civilisation. They practised unlimited polygamy, or rather the only limit set to the number of a Mongol's wives was his capacity to support them. Genghiz himself had more than five hundred. As had been the custom of the Turks in the T'ang period, every Mongol married all his father's widows except his own mother, and also all the wives of his deceased brothers.

With such an ample provision for legitimate marriage it was quite natural that the Mongols regarded adultery as a serious crime, which was punished with death. Every Mongol male was a soldier, and, apart from hunting, he was not allowed to engage in any other occupation. Even domestic service was forbidden to the Mongols, and all such duties were performed by captive slaves. In consequence of this law they employed great numbers of foreign captives and adventurers in the administration of the kingdoms they conquered. The army alone was Mongol, the civil service was recruited from all the nations of Asia and Europe with which they came into contact. Marco Polo, who served Kublai for seventeen years, was a typical example and his colleagues were Muhammadans from Persia and Iraq, Georgians, Armenians, Indians, as well as Chinese and Koreans.

The Mongols were an uncleanly people. They were in fact expressly forbidden ever to wash or bathe from the cradle to the grave, and also forbidden to wash anything in running water. They were extremely addicted to alcohol, and drank to excess. This vice is still a characteristic of their descendants, the Mongol tribes of to-day, who are rapidly diminishing partly in consequence of their partiality for vodka and imported brandy. The outstanding characteristic of the Mongols was their inhuman cruelty, or rather their total lack of any human feeling of pity. Genghiz himself expressed the Mongol idea of happiness: "The greatest joy is to conquer one's enemies, to pursue them, to seize their property, to see their families in tears, to ride their horses, and to possess their daughters and wives."

The Mongol invasion of the Kin Empire began in 1210, but, although Peking was taken, the inhabitants butchered, and the city burnt, three years later Genghiz himself left his generals to complete the task, and set out to conquer western Asia. Returning from these campaigns in 1224, he fell upon the kingdom of Hsia, which was utterly destroyed. According to the Chinese history not more than one hundredth part of the population survived, the countryside was covered with human bones, the cities left desolate. The north-west has never recovered from this disaster. Many of the border cities were never re-occupied, and have been invaded by the drifting sands of the desert. The irrigation works fell into decay from lack of attention, and the country reverted to steppe. A region which in T'ang times had been wealthy and cultured, as the Buddhist sculptures and cave monasteries prove, became a semi-desert, the poorest and most backward part of the Chinese Empire.

Genghiz Khan died in 1227, but his successors continued his policy of conquest by terror and massacre. Indeed, but for the intervention of a man who deserves a wider fame, the extermination of Hsia would have been followed by that of all the provinces of China. When Genghiz returned from the west and invaded China, the Mongols were disgusted to see the whole country cultivated, and no pasture available for their horses. "Although we have conquered the Chinese," they said, "they are of no use to us. It would be better to exterminate them entirely, and let the grass grow so that we can have grazing land for our horses."

Genghiz was about to put this plan into operation when he was dissuaded by Yelu Ch'u-ts'ai, a descendant of the former royal house of the Kitans, who had been taken prisoner by the Mongols at Peking, and entered their service. This remarkable man, who although of Kitan descent was a fervent admirer of Chinese culture and Confucian doctrine, was the only counsellor who ever succeeded in dissuading Genghiz Khan from committing a massacre. He had already induced the conqueror to leave India, by playing upon the Mongol's superstitions. He now saved China by pointing out that if the Chinese were allowed to exist the Great Khan could draw a vast revenue from the conquered country, which would suffice to supply the Mongols with all the comforts and luxuries which they could never obtain in the steppe.

Genghiz followed this advice. The Chinese were taxed instead of being butchered, and the Mongols soon made their tents of the richest silks, and decorated their weapons with gold and jade.

Ogotai, Genghiz's successor, also listened to Yelu Ch'u-ts'ai. In 1233, after a heroic defence, K'ai Fêng Fu, the Kin capital, formerly that of the Sung, was forced to capitulate. The city, in which everyone who could flee had taken refuge, was packed with more than a million refugees, almost the entire population of the surrounding provinces, if the Chinese history is to be credited. As it had defended itself desperately, all these lives were forfeit according to the Mongol rule of war. Subutai, the general who had conducted the siege, sent word to Ogotai demanding permission to butcher the inhabitants in the usual way. Yelu Ch'u-ts'ai saved K'ai Fêng by pointing out to Ogotai that all the skilful artisans and workmen of north China had fled to K'ai Fêng Fu, and a waste city was no use to an Emperor. If they were exterminated the Mongols would lose the value of their services. The second argument did not move the Great Khan, but the first persuaded him to spare K'ai Fêng. It was the first time the Mongols had shown such clemency, and the credit for it must go to Yelu Ch'u-ts'ai, who realised that it was waste of time to appeal to Mongol humanity, since they had none, but that an appeal to their cupidity might have good effects. If, as Gibbon remarks, "Mankind were accustomed to bestow upon their preservers the fame which they lavish on their destroyers," the name of Yelu Ch'u-ts'ai would be infinitely more honoured than that of the savage he served.

Thanks in part to the counsels of Yelu Ch'u-ts'ai, the centre and south of China escaped the worst horrors of the Mongol conquest. The Sung Empire, indeed, remained untouched until many years after the death of Genghiz, for it was screened to the north by the Kin and the Hsia kingdom. Once this barrier was removed, the fate of the Sung was merely a question of time. As the last Kin Emperor warned them, when he appealed in vain for an alliance: "We are to you as the lips are to the teeth; when the lips are gone the teeth will feel the cold"—a saying which has become proverbial.

Nevertheless the conquest of the Sung was more gradual and marked by fewer massacres than the invasion of the north. Ch'ang Chou, in Kiangsu, not far from Nanking, was the worst sufferer. The city, having dared to resist, Bayan, the Mongol general carried it by storm and exterminated the inhabitants to the number of over a million. No doubt here, as at K'ai Fêng, the people from miles around had flocked into the walled city for safety. Hang Chou, capital of the southern Sung, capitulated and was spared. Marco Polo, who calls the city Quinsay, has left a famous description of its glories, as seen a few years later.*

The invasion of the Sung Empire began in 1235, but the last Sung pretender was not destroyed until 1279, the date from which the reign of the Mongol Yüan dynasty is reckoned. In actual fact the establishment of a separate Mongol Empire over China coincides with the accession of Kublai Khan and the foundation of a new capital at Peking in 1263. Karakorum, in outer Mongolia, where the earlier Great Khans had held their Court, was now abandoned, and the cohesion of the vast Mongol Empire was relaxed. The conversion of the western Mongol khans to Islam in 1295 definitely marked the end of the Mongol world Empire, of which Kublai was the last nominal sovereign. (Map 13.) The Moslem khans refused to recognise his successor as suzerain, since he was a Buddhist, and thus an infidel.

Although the western khans were practically independent throughout Kublai's reign, the Mongol Empire appeared outwardly to be stronger and more formidable than ever. This Great Khan followed up the conquest of South China by invading Burma and Cochin China. In the latter country, however, the Mongols met disaster. Invincible in the field, they could not support the moist heat of the tropical jungles. The people of Champa, the modern Cambodia, though unable to meet the Mongols in battle, harried them with guerrilla warfare in the jungle, until the Mongol army, riddled with fever, was forced to abandon the campaign. The attempt to invade Japan was also a total failure. Kublai's vast fleet, manned by Chinese seamen and

---

*The origin of Marco Polo's name for Hang Chou is uncertain. The Chinese name, Hang Chou, is certainly not to be distorted into "Quinsay." One suggestion is that the name in common use was *Ching Shih*, meaning "the capital," which the Venetian distorted into Quinsay. It has also been suggested that this name represents *Hsing tsai*, "the travelling palace," or "temporary capital," a term used to denote the place where the Emperor resides when away from the capital. The Sung did not recognise the loss of the north as final, and therefore termed Hang Chou, "Temporary Capital," Hsing tsai.

MAP 13. *The Mongol Empire under Kublai Khan.*

Mongol soldiers, was destroyed by a storm, and the survivors who landed on Tsu Shima were exterminated by the Japanese samurai.

Marco Polo was deeply impressed by the magnificence of the Great Khan, the cosmopolitan nature of his empire, and the wealth and civilisation of China. Thanks to the intrepid Venetian the glory of Kublai has become a European legend, and he is perhaps the only Emperor of China whose name is commonly known in the west. From the Chinese point of view, the picture is rather different. The empire over which Kublai reigned was largely ruined. The figures of his census speak for themselves. Under the Sung the population of China had reached one hundred million; under Kublai, who ruled a far wider empire, it did not number more than 58,834,711. These figures, as in other examples of a Chinese census, refer only to taxpayers. The vast decrease therefore reflects the impoverishment of the empire rather than a reduction in the actual number of the inhabitants. These figures were compiled in 1290, when most parts of China had been pacified for nearly a generation. A census taken twenty years before would have yielded a much smaller total.

European readers of Marco Polo admired the tolerance of the Great Khan, who employed Christians, and Moslems, Buddhists and Taoists, and men of all nations according to their capacity, regardless of race and creed. To the people of Moslem Asia and Christian Europe of the Middle Ages this attitude was indeed novel and enlightened, but in China tolerance was no new thing, and the policy of the Mongol conquerors was the policy which every Chinese dynasty since the Han had consistently employed. There was, however, this difference, that whereas the Chinese Emperors tolerated foreign religions out of indifference, and employed foreigners for their skill in strange arts and crafts, the Mongols used aliens out of policy, fearing to give authority to the natives of the land.

In consequence the Mongol administration was unsympathetic to the people, the officials corrupt and ruthless. Ahmet, Kublai's Muhammadan finance minister, provoked such hatred by his peculation and extortion that he was assassinated by a Chinese patriot in the palace itself. The favour shown to the Buddhists, and in particular to the alien Tibetan Lamas passed all bounds. Priests who murdered and robbed were not brought to justice. Palaces and lands were conferred upon Buddhist temples, and they were exempted from taxation. The corruption of the civil service was so great that under Kublai's successor more than 18,000 officials had to be degraded for venality. The Mongol Empire, established by terror, remained peaceful only as long as the conquerors themselves remained formidable. After the death of Kublai (1294) the decline was rapid.

His successors were both weak and short-lived. In less than forty years, 1295 to 1333, seven emperors succeeded each other on the throne, many dying by violence as the result of palace plots. The tale of the dynasty was completed by the long reign of Togan Timur, 1333-1368, a voluptuary who reigned in Peking over an empire rapidly dissolving into chaos under the waves of revolt which heralded the Chinese reaction. Bayan, the last Emperor's minister, contributed not a little to the rising unrest. A Mongol, he was a violent hater of the Chinese. At his instigation many vexatious laws debarring the Chinese from wearing certain colours in their clothes, using certain characters, such as those for long life and happiness, and from learning or speaking the Mongol language, were passed. Finally, he proposed to revive the project of mass massacre. He suggested that all Chinese of the surnames Chang, Wang, Liu, Li and Chao, should be exterminated. These are the most common names in China, and would have accounted for nine-tenths of the population.

The Emperor did not feel strong enough to employ this typically Mongol solution of his difficulties.

In 1348 the rising unrest broke out in open rebellions which did not cease thereafter until the Mongols had been driven out of China by the victorious founder of the Chinese Ming dynasty. The Mongol resistance was feeble. At the end (1368) the last Great Khan fled from Peking without a fight and took refuge in his ancestral steppes, hunted northward by the generals of the Ming Emperor. The Mongol dynasty, founded on terror and butchery, passed away after only eighty-nine years, leaving behind it no lasting or valuable contribution to Chinese civilisation, but having destroyed much that was irreplaceable.

Chapter XXII

SUNG PAINTING

In postponing any discussion of Chinese painting to a chapter included in the Sung section of this book it was not intended to imply that the art did not flourish before the 10th century A.D. Merely as a matter of convenience each branch of Chinese art has been treated in a separate chapter under the period in which this particular art attained its apogee. Moreover, although there is evidence to show that painting in the T'ang, and even pre-T'ang periods equalled the finest work of the Sung masters, only a very few genuine works of these early dynasties have survived. Sung originals are more numerous, though all too scarce. Later paintings are more plentiful: there are many fine works of the Ming period extant, but by that age the art was tending to become imitative. Painting in the Sung dynasty touched perfection and has never been surpassed or even equalled in later times. It was, moreover, the chosen mode of artistic expression in that age, revealing better than any work of literature, the spirit of Chinese civilisation, mature and refined, before the Mongol cataclysm laid waste the eastern world.

Painting, however, had a long history before the Sung dynasty. Chinese literature abounds in references to artists of great merit in the earliest, indeed, in legendary times. These stories can be safely ignored, not only because no work of such antiquity exists to confirm them, but also because there is very strong ground for assuming that painting, as opposed to decorative design, cannot have been practised before the Han dynasty. This dogmatism is possible because it is known that the invention of the writing brush, which replaced the stylus, can be dated to the Ch'in dynasty, the reign of Shih Huang Ti, the First Emperor (221-210 B.C.). The story which attributes this far-reaching change to the initiative of the general Mêng T'ien need not be taken literally. Possibly Mêng T'ien accorded his patronage to the invention of someone less eminent. It can be accepted as a fact that one of the many revolutionary changes introduced by the First Emperor and his counsellors was the use of a new instrument for writing, with

all the important consequences to calligraphy and the arts which
followed.

This question of the use of the brush for writing has a closer
relation to the history of Chinese painting than may appear at
first sight. It is the cause of the chief technical difference between
Western and Far Eastern art. In Europe the divorce between
calligraphy and painting is complete, and has been so ever since
the quill pen became the instrument of writing. In China, on the
contrary, the use of an identical instrument for writing and
painting, the brush, linked the two arts with an indissoluble bond,
the ultimate consequences of which were not altogether happy.
Calligraphy became an art, but art, in the decadent period, sank
to something not far above mere calligraphy.

The adoption of the brush as the instrument of writing thus
exercised a very profound influence on Chinese culture. It completely altered the manner of writing characters, and the style
of the script. The bone inscriptions and the bronze inscriptions
of the Shang and Chou period are written in a scratchy angular
style, which could never have made a great appeal to the artistic
feelings of the beholder. With the brush all this was changed.
Graceful curves, thick and thin lines, a flowing continuity transformed the written character into a work of art, and give calligraphy a place in the Chinese culture which has no parallel
elsewhere, even in the illuminated manuscripts of Mediæval
Europe. Fig. 56 shows a few examples of ancient seal characters
and their modern equivalents.

'horse'	馬	馬
'bird'	隹	隹
'anxious'	恖	恖
'seize'	取	取
'door'	門	門

FIG. 56. *Ancient and modern types of script.*

It is pointless to ignore, or deride, the value of the calligraphic
art in Chinese eyes. No European, perhaps, will ever be moved
by a scroll of characters from the greatest master as he may be

moved by a somewhat mediocre painting from the same hand. To deny the existence of the Chinese art of calligraphy or to assert that its influence upon painting has been wholly bad, and a symptom of the later decadence, as some western critics have done, is to repudiate all belief in the Chinese æsthetic tradition as known to the Chinese themselves, and to pronounce an uninstructed judgment in the traditional phrase of the Philistine: "I know what I like." Had the quill pen become the instrument of writing in China, as it might well have done, the subsequent history of Chinese calligraphy and painting would have been entirely different. This possibility is, however, irrelevant. As a matter of historical fact, calligraphy and painting were closely associated and reacted upon each other throughout the course of Chinese history and not merely in the decadent period.

Painting, indeed, was probably an outcome of the use of the brush for writing. From the first, and in all subsequent times it was an art practised by the educated class, the class who from childhood were taught and trained in a masterly dexterity with the brush. For this reason painting as a scholar's art has received the minute attention of historians and men of letters. The lives and even the detail of the works of painters long dead, and now unrepresented, are recorded. These accounts make plain how very few Chinese artists were men without education, or of humble origin, not because talent did not exist among the poor, but because the common use of the brush for writing and painting gave the man educated in brush work for writing characters an immense advantage and a long and arduous training.

A more remote consequence of this link between writing and painting appears in the choice of subjects favoured by Chinese artists. The literary subject, far from being contemned was very frequently employed, although the fact is not necessarily apparent to observers unfamiliar with the vast storehouse of Chinese literature. Landscape, for example, is a literary subject to the Chinese artist, on account of the strong and old tradition associating wild scenery with the hermit scholar, and the symbolism connected with pines, rocks and running water. The Chinese genius in the great periods was not fettered by these associations. The artists of the T'ang and Sung painted not only landscapes, but

every variety of subject. When inspiration began to fail under the
Ming dynasty the literary side of the partnership between calligraphy and painting gradually became dominant. Brush technique, of the first importance in calligraphy, came to be the
crucial test in judging painting, to the detriment of subject,
inspiration and feeling. In the calligraphic art the meaning
of the characters chosen—a classic text or a poem—was less
important than the manner of execution, for the subject was
never original, only the treatment was proper to the artist. The
transference of these standards to painting was the fatal perversion
which befell Chinese art in the decadence. In this latter art,
known as *wên jên hua*, "scholar's painting," an all-too apt designation, it is the number of brush strokes and the manner in which
they are applied that supply the criteria for judgment. Subjects
are of little or no importance, the picture, whether landscape,
flower painting, or a human subject is made to a formula in
which brush technique alone counts. This over-refined art is often
extremely decorative and graceful, but it has not the strength and
freedom found in the works of the Sung masters.

No Han painting on silk has survived, but among the finds
made at Lak Lang in Korea there is a painting on lacquer, done
upon the lid of a tortoise-shell box. The execution is fine and
mannered, showing little trace of primitive awkwardness. It has
great interest as a concrete proof that the Han painting mentioned in literary sources had a real existence, and had passed
beyond the rather simple conventions of the contemporary
bas-reliefs. The phœnix shown in Fig. 57, a polychrome painting in tempera on the lid of a cosmetic box (*lien*), is also Han work
and illustrates the high level of draughtmanship in that period.

A picture attributed to a great master who lived only 150 years
after the fall of the Han Empire would, if an original, confirm
the supposition that the art of painting flourished in the Han
dynasty. Ku K'ai-chih (*circa* A.D. 364) lived under the Tsin
dynasty which succeeded the Han, and, in the opinion of all
critics in the T'ang and Sung periods he was the first and greatest
of the early painters known to them. In the 12th century, when
the *Hsüan Ho hua p'u*, the catalogue of the imperial collection
in the Sung palace was compiled, nine pictures attributed to

FIG. 57. *Han painting of a phœnix on the lid of a lien (box).*

Ku K'ai-chih still existed. A picture which has been claimed to be one of these: "Admonitions of the Imperial Preceptress," which bears the seals of the artist Emperor Hui Tsung of the Sung and of Ch'ien Lung of the Manchu dynasty, is now in the British Museum.

Binyon writes of this picture:

"The basic character of design agrees with what few relics of pictorial art, previous to the T'ang era and subsequent to the Han era, remain for comparison. The basic character of design is the same as in the 6th century Tun-huang frescoes, though the frescoes are in rather provincial style. . . . When we add that the types, the costumes, and the style of painting are unlike any later Chinese work known to us, there can be no reasonable doubt that the picture represents the art of the 4th century. Most scholars have presumed it to be an ancient copy. . . . But that it is a copy is hard to believe."*

Painting in the Far East. 4th Edition. 1934. pp. 46-7. M. Pelliot, on the other hand, regards it as being of the 6th century.

The importance of this picture, apart from the astonishing fact of its survival for so many centuries, is that at this period, the Tsin dynasty, Buddhism was only beginning to permeate Chinese culture. As yet the new religion, though rapidly spreading, had not had time to exercise a deep influence on the artistic tradition inherited from the Han period, to which the Tsin dynasty is really a kind of postscript. If, as was once supposed, painting was introduced to China with Buddhism, it would be natural to expect to find a strong alien touch in the earlier works, and exclusively religious subjects. If this picture is a 4th century work it proves that this was not the case. The style is wholly Chinese, and the subject secular. "The Admonitions of the Imperial Preceptress" illustrates a literary subject; the advice given to the consort of the first Emperor of the Tsin dynasty, Wu Ti (A.D. 265-290).

The period of the Six Dynasties, the partition of China between the Chinese dynasties ruling at Nanking and the Tungus dynasties at Lo Yang and elsewhere in the north, does not seem to have been unfavourable to art. Buddhism, strong and vigorous as a new religion, was patronised at both Courts. Artists were encouraged by the cultivated rulers at Nanking and their services were constantly required to paint pictures of the Buddha and the Bodhisattvas. Ku K'ai-chih is known to have painted many religious pictures, which probably all perished with the temples in which they were displayed. The religious influence in painting was strong and continuous, lasting through the T'ang dynasty to the Sung, but it was never dominant. The Chinese painter was not, like his early Italian successor, forced to fit his talent to a dictated subject, or a narrow range of sacred themes from which he must not stray. Artists in China were also men of education and scholarship, not infrequently high officials at Court. They painted as they pleased, and if they often painted religious pictures it is a proof, among many, that Confucian scholarship and Buddhist piety were not so utterly incompatible as later Confucian purists have tried to maintain.

Literary notices by later critics are all that now remain to prove the value of the Six Dynasty painters' art. One of these artists, Hsieh Ho, who lived towards the end of the 5th century under the short Ch'i dynasty of south China, has left the first treatise on painting, including his "six canons," which have always been accepted as the standard of criticism in China. These canons he expressed in four word sentences, which are not easily translated into the terminology of western criticism. As is often the case with Chinese prose, as well as with poetry, "the words stop but the sense goes on." The translations of the Six Canons of Hsieh Ho given here are those made by Professor Giles*:

THE SIX CANONS OF HSIEH HO (*circa* A.D. 475).

1. Rhythmic vitality.
2. Anatomical structure.
3. Conformity with nature.
4. Suitability of colouring.
5. Artistic composition.
6. Finish.

These were the qualities which a painting should possess if it was to be ranked in the highest class. It is perhaps unfortunate that Hsieh Ho did not express himself more clearly, for if he had listed the faults of painting as well as the qualities, the lesser artists of the Ming and Manchu periods might have avoided the error of concentrating upon his second and sixth canon to the exclusion of some of the others, particularly the first.

The T'ang dynasty was the golden age of the arts in China, more catholic in its taste and more direct and vigorous than the refined Sung. Painting, as can be proved by the few surviving T'ang originals, and by the unanimous testimony of Sung critics who had the works of T'ang masters before them, had reached as high a level as poetry. T'ang poetry has come down to posterity almost complete, but only a haphazard selection of T'ang pictures, preserved by chance rather than by choice has survived the numerous calamities of 1,000 years. The greatest work of the T'ang painters was done at the capital, and much of it for the imperial collection. For this very reason it has perished. In the closing years of the dynasty Ch'ang An was repeatedly sacked, and finally utterly ruined. The assiduity with which the Sung

*An Introduction to the History of Chinese Pictorial Art. London. 1918. p. 28.

imperial connoisseurs collected T'ang masters shows that these were uncommon even in the 11th and 12th centuries. An art treatise of the 12th century, the *Hua P'in* by Li Chih, says that works by Wu Tao-tzŭ, the most famous of T'ang painters, could not be found. This may be a slight exaggeration. There are pictures attributed to Wu Tao-tzŭ in existence to-day, and it is recorded that the Sung imperial collection had specimens of his work. Li Chih probably meant that they were so rare as to be unobtainable by private individuals.

A certain number of T'ang masters seems to have been preserved in Japan as well as China, for it was during the T'ang period that Japan was eagerly adopting the customs and culture of Ch'ang An. Religious paintings by great Chinese artists were taken to the newly founded Buddhist monasteries in Japan, and there in the fortunate seclusion of famous temples, some of them perhaps survived to the present day. It is true that experts are often in doubt whether these famous pictures are true originals or early copies. The point is naturally of great importance to collectors, but perhaps not quite so important for the history of Chinese and Japanese art. These copies may be weaker than the originals, but they preserve the style and the design of the painter and provide evidence for judging other works attributed to the T'ang period.

The records of the T'ang dynasty have preserved long lists of artists and the titles of their works, notes on their style, descriptions of the pictures themselves, and the circumstances in which they were painted. A whole literature of art, the paintings themselves being all that is lacking. There are a few artists, however, still represented either by originals or early copies, and others whose influence on later work is attested by Sung critics. These famous names cannot be passed over without a mention.

Yen Li-pên lived in the early years of the dynasty, the first half of the 7th century, and was a high official at Court. He was a prolific painter, and some of his works were still extant in the 12th century. The designs from which the bas-reliefs of T'ai Tsung's chargers were carved are attributed to this artist.

Han Kan was also a painter of horses famous in the T'ang period. He is one of the few Chinese artists of humble origin. He was as a youth employed as a pot-boy in an inn near the capital.

Wang Wei, a renowned artist to be mentioned presently, frequented the inn, and discovered the boy's talent. With the generosity of the true artist he took Han Kan under his patronage and paid for his education. In later life he became famous and was employed by the art loving Emperor Ming Huang. Although he painted religious pictures, as did all the artists of his time, it is for his horses and hunting pictures that he has remained famous. Fifty-two of his pictures were in the imperial collection of the Sung dynasty at the end of the 12th century. Han Kan's work exercised a deep influence on the early Japanese painters, and as the poet Tu Fu testifies, he was highly esteemed by the most refined spirits at Ming Huang's capital.

Another contemporary of the Emperor Ming Huang was Wu Tao-tzǔ, who, in the opinion of Chinese and Japanese critics is the greatest master of painting in the history of the Far East. In the Sung period over ninety of his pictures were listed as belonging to the imperial collection, but it is doubted whether at the present time any original works survive. One, which was long accepted as genuine, though now suspected as an early copy, is, like many other early Chinese pictures, preserved in a temple in Japan. (Plate XII.)

Whether an original or early copy this wild fantastic landscape, inspired probably by the rugged scenery of northern Szechuan, is characteristic of what is known of T'ang landscape painting, in which the splendour and romantic side of nature was emphasised, and even exaggerated. The towering rocks and rushing stream dominate the composition, while the only human figure, the fisherman with his basket, is dwarfed by his awe-inspiring surroundings. Man was not the centre of this artist's world, his place in the cosmos was insignificant.

Li Ssǔ-hsun, a great grandson of the first T'ang Emperor, was regarded as the greatest master of landscape painting before the Sung period. Ou-yang Hsiu, the scholar, poet and historian, writing in the 11th century, declared that Li had no equal in landscape painting, either in his own period or subsequently. This opinion, of course, was written before the greatest Sung landscape painters had been born. Li Ssǔ-hsun and Wang Wei (who was equally celebrated as a poet) are regarded as the founders of the Northern and Southern Schools of landscape painting respectively. They were contemporaries, Wang Wei, born in A.D. 699, being the younger man.

The terms Northern and Southern in landscape painting have led to a deal of misunderstanding. They are not used in a geographical sense to imply that the followers of one school were men from the north of China, or *vice versa*, nor yet that their style was inspired by the scenery of the north or south. The Chinese have a habit of classifying everything either by a number, as the "eight virtues" and the "hundred names," or by a geographical term. This does not mean that they consider the virtues limited to eight in number, or that there are only one hundred surnames in use, it is an idiom of the language. Similarly geographical terms carrying no territorial connotation are used to distinguish between categories of ideas. The real difference between the two schools of landscape painting was technical, a question of brush work. The "Northern school" used strong vigorous strokes, the "Southern" a more delicate, intimate touch.

Those who followed the style of Li Ssŭ-hsun called themselves the Northern school, or more properly, called his manner of painting the "Northern" manner, for artists did not adhere rigidly to one style, but sometimes painted in both. The question of the "Northern" and "Southern" schools, or styles, would not be very important if it did not lend itself to an easy confusion between the painters of the northern Sung dynasty with its capital at K'ai Fêng Fu, and the later painters of the Southern Sung, who worked at Hang Chou. The geographical position or origin of the artists has nothing whatever to do with the "Northern" and "Southern" schools. As a matter of fact Wang Wei, regarded as the founder of the Southern style, was born in Shansi in north China, and did most of his work in retirement at his native place.

In spite of the ruin of Ch'ang An at the close of the T'ang dynasty, many T'ang pictures escaped destruction and were still to be found in the Sung period. The troubled age of the Five Dynasties, the first half of the 10th century, which intervened, did not interrupt the artistic tradition established by the T'ang masters. During this half-century the southern provinces were divided among several small independent kingdoms which were on the whole free from the incessant wars and revolutions which disturbed north China under the Five Dynasties proper. It was to these southern Courts, asylums of culture in a troubled world, that the surviving artists and poets of the T'ang retired. At the Court of Shu, a state comprising Szechuan province, poets such as Wei Chuang maintained the literary traditions of the fallen empire, and a few years later an artist of the first rank, Huang Ch'uan, worked in the same state. Huang Ch'uan was especially noted for his painting of flowers and birds, subjects for which he no doubt found endless inspiration in the garden province of China, the really "flowery land" of Szechuan. A painting attributed to him, "Fowls and Peonies," is in the British Museum.

When peace and unity were restored under the Sung dynasty the artists who assembled at the new capital, K'ai Fêng Fu, had a living tradition to work upon. Painting was not the monopoly of the Sung period. If we had more T'ang pictures to compare with the Sung masters it is possible that the earlier art would prove superior to the Sung, at least in certain qualities of strength and vigour. The Sung inherited a great tradition but they did not merely imitate earlier work. In the absence of sufficient T'ang pictures to form a judgment it is perhaps untrue to say that Sung landscapes had never been equalled by the T'ang painters. Ou-yang Hsiu, as has been pointed out, held Li Ssŭ-hsun superior to the early Sung masters. Nevertheless it is certain that Sung work is of unsurpassed excellence, and reflects the changed spirit of the new age. The painters of this dynasty were very numerous and the range of subjects very wide. If more emphasis is given to the Sung landscapes than to the religious and other pictures of this period it is because Sung landscapes are in a class apart, unrivalled in their own Far Eastern art and unequalled in the painting of any other land.

More clearly than any other pictures, or any other branch of art these landscapes reveal the wide difference between the Western and Chinese artistic traditions in the past, and at the same time they appeal to the modern European more than any other Chinese work of art. This paradox is easily resolved. Until the 19th century, the West had no feeling for wild nature other than one of marked aversion. No one admired the English Lake scenery before Wordsworth. In the 17th century the West Highlands, the Alps and the Pyrennees were shunned by men of taste. Mountains were "horrid rocks," moors, "blasted heaths." This aversion to untamed scenery has been explained by the insecurity of the times, mountains and wastelands were associated with brigands and highwaymen. It has been suggested that an efficient police force is the foundation of a delight in wild nature.

This explanation is refuted by the fact that in China, where mountains have always been the haunt of bandits, and the dangers of travel at least as great as in renaissance Europe, poets, painters and scholars of the highest intellectual status have for centuries delighted in the wild beauty of the high hills and frequently retired from the comforts of civilisation to some remote mountain solitude. Perhaps an appreciation of natural scenery uncontrolled by the work of man is a product of long and continuous civilisation, of sophistication in fact, which is only achieved after many generations of culture. In China that point had been reached by the educated class in the T'ang period, and was a universal attitude in the Sung dynasty. In Europe, where the cultural tradition was set back by the Dark Ages after the fall of the Roman Empire, it was not attained until the end of the 18th century.

To the European of to-day the Sung landscapes seem "modern" because, in spite of a different artistic tradition they are products of a people on the same level of artistic culture as ourselves. The 17th century would not have appreciated them. Indeed the early European travellers to the Far East never thought of bringing home pictures, although they admired and imitated other Chinese works of art. It was not only because Chinese art followed a different convention to that of the West, but because the spirit which informed the landscape painters of China was then alien to European taste. To the modern the Sung landscapes are a revelation. Better than any detailed history or work of literature one Sung landscape will illuminate the gracious spirit of that refined and sophisticated age, soon to be overwhelmed in the Mongol invasion from which, in art, there has been no recovery.

Li Ch'êng (circa 970), who claimed descent from the imperial clan of the T'ang dynasty, was one of the first great landscape painters of the Sung period. One of his pictures now preserved in the Palace Museum at Peking is reproduced in Plate XIII. The subject, "Woods in Winter," is a fine example of the Sung style, intimate and restrained, in contrast with the Wu Tao-tzǔ illustrated in Plate XII; Li Ch'êng's picture shows nature in less fantastic guise. The distant hills form the background, and the real subject is the group of pine trees overlooking the valley. In Chinese painting the pine has a symbolical meaning which made it a favourite subject with the artists of the Sung age. The straight stemmed pine with its gnarled and twisted branches, standing isolated upon the edge of a ravine, typified the scholar-official, who, though he might be shaken by the wind of calumny and misfortune, remained erect and steadfast, his character rooted in the unchanging principles of Confucian virtue.

The 11th century, which in Europe was almost the nadir of culture, was one of the greatest periods in the history of Chinese art, and the crown and glory of the age was the reign of the artist Emperor Hui Tsung (1100-1126). Although neither a wise nor successful ruler, the Emperor was both a devoted patron of all the arts and a painter of high rank himself. He lavished upon pictures and ceramics the care and attention which he denied to affairs of state, and, while his name is remembered in history as that of the last northern Sung ruler who ended his life in captivity among the Nuchen Tartars, in art he holds rank with his equally unfortunate predecessor, Ming Huang of the T'ang dynasty.

Hui Tsung founded the first academy of painting in China and organised it on the model of the Confucian college. Degrees were awarded at the T'u Hua Yüan, and the Emperor himself instructed his pupils, adjudged their works, and set the subjects for competition. Many of the academicians are well known painters of the period, and a significant indication of the fame of this institution is the far off places from which they came. Li Ti, who was painting there in 1119, was a native of Yunnan, then an uncivilised border region mainly inhabited by aboriginal tribesmen.

The Hsüan Ho Hua Yüan, the Imperial Gallery which Hui Tsung enriched and enlarged, contained at that time the finest collection of paintings which has ever been assembled in the Far East. A catalogue of its contents was published in the last years of the northern Sung, and this work mentions the titles of no less than 6,192 pictures* which were kept there. Many of these pictures must have been by contemporary or recent artists, as it is known that T'ang paintings were becoming rare. In this gallery, no doubt, the Emperor's own pictures, some of which still survive, were shown. Plate XIV reproduces a bird study by Hui Tsung, now in Japan. This "Pigeon on a Peach Branch" is typical of the Chinese treatment of animal subjects. There is close observation and real understanding of nature, and yet no attempt to introduce human feeling and emotion. An artist who had such intimate sympathy with wild life cannot have found his exile in the Manchurian wilderness wholly insupportable.

Li Kung-lin, who is usually known by his pen name, Li Lung-mien, was born about 1070, and died in 1106, shortly before the Kin invasion. He was one of the greatest Sung painters, and also a brilliant scholar and high official. The last years of his life were spent in retirement at a country estate opposite the Dragon's Face hill (Lung Mien Shan), from which he took his pen name. A certain number of his pictures survive, one of which, a "Khotani Groom and Horse," is reproduced in Plate XV. In this picture the foreign type, which is so often emphasised by Chinese artists, is drawn with sympathy and the prominent features are not exaggerated.

The disaster which befell the Sung Empire in 1125 did not extinguish the artistic inspiration. When the Court was re-established at Hang Chou, the artists and scholars who had fled from K'ai Fêng maintained the tradition which had been the glory of the northern Sung, and, indeed, excelled their predecessors. Two of the greatest landscape painters, Ma Yüan (1190-1224) and Hsia Kuei, who was his contemporary, belong to this period. The new capital, Hang Chou, stands upon the shores of the West Lake, in the lovely country of Chekiang. The immediate vicinity of the city is one of the most celebrated beauty spots in China, scenery so often painted that it has become immortalised—and vulgarised—in the all too familiar "willow

*Hsüan Ho hua p'u; author unknown.

pattern." Living in these surroundings the artists of the southern Sung could not fail to find inspiration for their unsurpassed landscapes.

The panoramic roll, which depicts a wide stretch of varied country, was a favourite form with these artists. Such rolls, which may be many feet in length, are intended to be kept in a box and unrolled slowly, so that the beholder seems to follow the artist in a journey across mountains and rivers. Hsia Kuei's roll of the Yangtze is one of the most precious treasures of the Peking Palace Museum. It covers the whole upper course of the Great River, from the wild mountains of the Tibetan border where rocks and cliffs pen the river in a narrow gorge, down to the wide and tranquil valley of the middle reaches. Beginning among the rapids and defiles of the upper course every type of scenery and all the life of the great river is shown; famous cities and temples built high up on projecting bluffs, ships rushing down stream among the "boiling water" of the dreaded rapids, or toiling painfully up against the current. Fishermen in little boats ply their trade in the sheltered creeks, and wayfarers mounted or afoot follow the rock-hewn road which winds along the face of the gorges.

Another famous panoramic roll, "The Ch'ing Ming Festival at the River," by Chang Tse-tuang, dated A.D. 1101, is one of the clearest pieces of evidence for an important social change which occurred in the period of the Five Dynasties and the Northern Sung; the practice of sitting on chairs instead of on floor mats. The introduction or development of the chair in China, possibly influenced from a foreign source, had begun many centuries earlier in the period of division following the fall of the Han empire. Chairs or stools were at first exclusively confined to the camp, and never used in the house. Later, in the T'ang period they became popular for use in the garden. It is not until A.D. 960 that an extant picture from the very end of the Five Dynasty epoch shows a fashionable evening party held in the home of a Court grandee, in which the room is fully furnished with chairs, couches and tables.

The panoramic roll of Chang Tse-tuan shows that rather more than a century later this new habit had become general. The roll shows the people of the capital, K'ai Fêng, streaming out of the city to enjoy the spring festival upon the banks and waters of the Pien river. In open-air restaurants, as in the houses of the citizens, chairs and tables are shown in general use, the styles of such furniture differing hardly at all from their modern successors. The custom of sitting on floor mats, still followed in Japan, seems to have died out in China in this period.

The Mongol conquest, which imposed cruder values than the æsthetic ideals of the Sung scholars, brought the great age of painting to an end. In the Yüan dynasty founded by the conquerors, there were indeed, some famous artists. Chao Mêng-fu (b. 1254), himself a descendant of the Sung imperial family, was really the "last of the Sung" although the greater part of his life was passed under the alien dynasty. His great fame rests upon his pictures of horses, a subject inspired by the nomad rulers of his time, but he also painted landscapes and nature studies. With the passing of the generation which had directly inherited the Sung tradition, painting began to decline. The later artists paying ever more attention to brush technique and becoming increasingly imitative in their choice of subject. Late art, though often delightful and decorative, rarely recovers the master touch of the Sung genius.

PART SIX—THE MING DYNASTY

Chapter XXIII

THE CHINESE RECOVERY

WHEN the authority of the Mongol Emperors collapsed in the middle of the 14th century, China was overrun by rebel armies who not only stormed the fortresses held by the Mongols, but also pursued an internecine struggle among themselves. The incoherence of the Chinese revolt extended the term of the Mongol dynasty's power, but when the Chinese found an acknowledged leader of ability, the doom of the alien dynasty was certain. Several years of anarchy passed before the emergence of this leader, who won his way to the throne from the lowliest circumstances.

Chu Yüan-chang, who became the founder of the Ming dynasty, was born in 1328, the son of poor peasants in the Huai Valley, the country between the Huai and Yangtze Rivers. When still a boy his parents and almost all his relations died in a famine, and the orphan became in turn a shepherd boy, and then a Buddhist monk. The cloister, however, did not satisfy his ambitions; he abandoned his monastery and became a beggar, turning, by natural transition, into a bandit. In the ranks of the insurgents who were then multiplying on all sides, Chu Yüan-chang found his true vocation. He rose rapidly until he became commander of a large band, and then breaking with his nominal superior, set himself up as a partisan chief with independent ambitions.

Such a career is familiar enough from the history of all disturbed periods in China, not excluding the present day. Chu Yüan-chang only differed from many rivals in his ability to profit by his victories and consolidate the country he overran into a compact and orderly kingdom. While the other bandit chiefs swept the country, sacking cities and seeking only to amass booty, Chu concentrated on capturing certain places, of real strategic importance, and using them as bases for a systematic extension of his rule. In 1356 he gained a decisive advantage by capturing Nanking, which became his capital and that of all China under the Ming dynasty.

In these early years Chu left the Mongol strongholds almost unmolested, turning his arms instead on the rival rebel leaders who had occupied most of the south-eastern part of China. After

ten years of campaigning Chu destroyed the last of his competitors, and became sole pretender to the throne and acknowledged leader of the Chinese insurrection. Thenceforward his
progress was rapid. Two years later, in 1368, after conquering
the whole of eastern China from Canton to Shantung, his general
Hsu Ta advanced on Peking with an army said to have amounted
to nearly a quarter of a million men. The Mongol Emperor did
not wait to be besieged. Before the city was invested he fled
quietly to the north, abandoning China to the triumphant
founder of the Ming dynasty. Peking capitulated.

Several years of warfare in the western and south-western
provinces followed before the Ming dynasty was acknowledged in
every part of the empire. The Mongol tribes, driven from China,
still disputed the Ming conquest, and endeavoured to recover
their lost empire, but the military ascendancy had now passed
to the Chinese. In 1372 General Hsu Ta* crossed the Gobi,
burned Karakorum, the old capital of Genghiz Khan, and
advanced to the northern side of the Yablonoi Mountains, in the
modern Siberian province of Trans Baikalia. No Chinese army
had ever before penetrated so far north. In 1381 the Mongols
were driven from Yunnan where they had remained in isolation
since the fall of their dynasty. Ten years later the Ming armies
occupied Hami in Central Asia and so completed the reconquest
of the empire.

The Chinese reaction had thus carried the limits of the empire
further to the north than at any period since the fall of the T'ang
dynasty. Indeed, the Ming Empire was more extensive than any
previous Chinese Empire. Liao Tung, or south Manchuria, was
incorporated as an integral part of the province of Shantung.
Yunnan and Kueichou, regions of the south-west, which had only
been partially and fitfully occupied by the Han and T'ang rulers,
became settled countries under the regular provincial administration. Although a large aboriginal population remained in a
state of quasi-autonomy in these provinces the cities and valleys
became centres of Chinese colonisation.

*Hsu Ta's tomb can still be seen outside the T'ai P'ing gate at Nanking. His
official residence still exists in that city, where it is now used as the Ministry
of the Interior.

The Ming armies had acquired a marked superiority over the Mongols and other nomad peoples, but the emperors of this dynasty never attempted to establish direct Chinese rule over Central Asia, or Chinese Turkestan. They were content to hold Hami, the first city on the caravan route guarding the approach to the Chinese province of Kansu. The decline in the importance of this trade route was the reason why the Ming never followed the example of the T'ang and Han Emperors, who had spent their efforts for centuries in the conquest of Central Asia. The rising importance of the sea route from the west and the devastation of the north-west by the Mongols, the effects of which remain evident to-day, made Turkestan of less value to China.

Chu Yüan-chang did not adopt the foreign policy of the T'ang Emperors, but in other respects he openly proclaimed that dynasty as his model. The government was organised on T'ang models, even the provinces were re-arranged to conform with the ten *tao* instituted by T'ang Tai Tsung, in so far as changes of population and territory permitted. It is in the Ming period that the present arrangement and names of the provinces took their origin, but, under the Ming, there were fifteen provinces instead of the eighteen established by the Manchus (Map 14). In view of the pre-war Japanese propaganda which treated the Manchurian region, renamed "Manchukuo" as a territory distinct from, and never having formed any part of, China, it is worth recording that the Ming province of Shantung included not only the peninsula of that name, but also the whole of the Manchurian region on the north side of the Gulf of Chihli, from the Great Wall up to Mukden, and as far east as the Korean border, then as now, defined by the Yalu River. This territory was already fully occupied by settlers of Chinese stock. The Ming province of Ching Shih, the modern Hopei, extended beyond the Wall as far north as Jehol City and the banks of the Liao River. Except that certain of the modern provinces were combined to form one Ming province, the names and areas of the existing divisions are those determined by the Ming government.*

The practical spirit shown in these administrative changes was

*Shensi in Ming times included Kansu. Kiangsu and Anhui were combined as the province of Nanking, Hunan and Hupei as Hu Kuang.

MAP 14. *The Ming Empire.*

also manifested in less important matters. Previous dynasties had been called after the classical names of the founder's native provinces, or the fiefs which they had held before obtaining the throne. Thus, Liu Pang had named his dynasty Han because he had been King of the ephemeral state of Han during the interregnum following the fall of the Ch'in dynasty (Chapter

VI), and the first Emperor of the T'ang had been Duke of T'ang, a part of Shansi, under the Sui dynasty. The Sung derived their name from a similar association with the eastern part of Honan, the ancient state of Sung, and the less famous dynasties had all followed the same practice. The founder of the Ming, however, who had been a leader of bandits before he became Emperor, had enjoyed no such distinction, therefore in choosing a name for his dynasty he broke with the time-honoured territorial tradition and called it Ming, the brilliant dynasty.

He made another sensible innovation in the use of reign titles, the official style by which the reign of an Emperor was known and dated. He abandoned the old custom of changing this style every few years; every Ming Emperor retained the same reign title for the full duration of his reign, and, in consequence, the Yung Lo period, for example, exactly corresponds to the reign of the Emperor Ch'êng Tsu. This had not been the case in earlier dynasties ever since the Han Emperor, Wu, introduced the use of reign titles. The Ming sovereigns were therefore returning to the ancient practice of the Chou Kings and Ch'in Shih Huang Ti, who had dated their reigns consecutively under one style. There were obvious advantages in this change, for under the old practice one Emperor sometimes used as many as five or six reign titles in succession, each separately dated, making it impossible to know how long this sovereign had occupied the throne without a mathematical calculation. The Manchus followed the Ming custom and in consequence the habit has grown up of referring to the emperors of these two dynasties by their reign titles, which are really only the name of a period of years, and not of an individual. Such reign titles as Wan Li and Ch'ien Lung are now universally used in this technically incorrect way, and few Chinese would recognise Shên Tsung as Wan Li or know who was meant if the Manchu Emperor Kao Tsung Shun was called by his correct title instead of by his reign title of Ch'ien Lung. As the reign titles of these emperors are familiar to Europeans from the date marks on porcelain, it would be tiresome and confusing to use the correct titles, and these sovereigns will therefore be referred to in the customary, though incorrect manner.

The capital of the Ming dynasty was at first situated at Nanking, and the city, apart from recent improvements, stands to-day as Chu Yüan-chang rebuilt it.* Although the palace itself was later destroyed, leaving only a ruined gateway to mark the site, the magnificent wall over twenty miles in length and more than 60 feet high, remains the longest city wall in the world. In choosing Nanking as capital the founder of the Ming was probably moved by the desire to fix the seat of government in the part of China with which he was most familiar, and from which he himself had sprung. In fact, it was a wise choice which would have established the dynasty most securely had his successors maintained it.

Since the fall of the northern Sung dynasty, when many thousands of the most influential and cultivated inhabitants of the northern provinces fled south of the Yangtze, the north had lost both its cultural and commercial importance. Nanking, on the Yangtze, easily accessible for tribute boats and merchant craft, was ideally situated to govern the most wealthy and populous part of the empire, and was at the same time protected by its situation against sudden raids from the northern frontier, while sufficiently central to keep in touch with the northern provinces. These are the considerations which have led the founders of the Chinese republic to move the capital back to the city chosen by Chu Yüan-chang.

Unfortunately they were ignored by the third Emperor of the Ming dynasty, Yung Lo, who, following his usurpation of the throne, moved the capital to Peking. This change emphasised and exaggerated the principal internal weakness from which the new dynasty suffered, the increasing divergence between the north and south, and the consequent mutual hostility of the officials from these different parts of the empire. The division between the two halves of the empire was now more marked than at any previous period. Until the south was colonised under the T'ang dynasty, and, subsequently enriched and civilised by the Southern Sung, there had been no significant rivalry between north and south, since allculture, power, and population had been

*There are large areas unbuilt upon inside Nanking's wall, but it is unlikely that all this ground was occupied by houses even in the Ming period. The wall was built to include hills of strategic importance as well as the actual city.

concentrated in the northern provinces of the Yellow River Valley. After the Kin and Mongol invasions the balance between the two regions was radically altered, the north was devastated, and the south became rich and populous.

Furthermore, a great emigration of the most cultured families occurred. Not only the Hakka or "guest families" of Canton took refuge in the far south, but also the famous scholar clans which had for centuries ruled the empire. Up to the end of the northern Sung period the old double surnames, such as Ssŭ-ma, Ssŭ-tu, Shang-kuan and Ou-yang, names which as their meaning prove, originated in offices in the feudal period, were still common in the north, and prominent in public life. To-day they are only found in Canton. Since these clans mostly originated in Shensi and the Yellow River valley it is clear that the ancestors of their modern representatives were refugees from the north. There is hardly a notable family in Canton which does not trace its descent to an ancestor who "crossed the Mei Ling," the great range dividing the Yangtze and West River basins. These migrations are almost always referred to the period of the Kin and Mongol invasions.

By the Ming period this great change in the character of the two halves of the empire was only too evident. It was found that the southern candidates secured a great majority of the higher places in the examinations for the civil service, while northerners were not even represented in proportion to the population of the north. The bitterness and discontent caused by these facts forced the emperors to allot one-third of the places to northerners irrespective of their success over their southern competitors, but the proportion which was deemed a fair division is itself very significant.

The move to Peking was a dangerous incentive to this rivalry. Yung Lo established the capital in the north because Peking had been his headquarters before he came to the throne, and it was from this region that he drew his support. Judged by more enduring motives, Peking was a bad site for the capital. It is situated in a sandy and rather arid plain, without good waterways communicating with the wealth producing provinces. It is, moreover, only 40 miles from the passes through the Great Wall, by which nomad invaders have at all times swept down into China. Lastly, it is tucked away in the extreme north-east corner of the empire, remote from the main centres of industry and population. This frontier site was a natural capital for invading conquerors such as the Kin and Mongols to choose. They remained in close touch with their homelands, inside the frontiers of the conquered empire, but not engulfed in the centre of a hostile population. These advantages meant nothing to a Chinese dynasty, and proved, on the contrary, a serious danger.

The moment the military strength of the government declined, the capital itself was exposed to the danger of enemy attack. It was not necessary for the nomads to undertake a formidable invasion of the heart of China, a sudden frontier raid was sufficient to menace the Court and disorganise the government. In consequence the Ming Court was constantly preoccupied with frontier affairs, to the neglect of the true interests of the empire. Money and armies were needed to guard the exposed capital, which should have been better employed policing the interior provinces. The Court, isolated in the far north-east, lost touch with the sentiment and needs of the south and west, which, as time passed, became more and more indifferent to the Ming dynasty. The position of the capital was one of the principal weaknesses of the dynasty, and the chief cause of its extinction.

Chu Yüan-chang, the founder of the Ming dynasty, known in history as Hung Wu, died in 1398, after a reign of thirty years, a period of stability at home and successful conquest abroad which should have inaugurated a long peace. Unfortunately his eldest son, the heir of the empire, died before coming to the throne, and the founder of the Ming was succeeded by his grandson, Hui Ti, a youth 16 years old. The authority of the young Emperor was almost immediately challenged by the most influential of his uncles, the Prince of Yen, who was in command of the northern frontier and resided at Peking. The new empire was thus ravaged by a long and destructive civil war within a generation of its foundation. After a varying struggle in which the Prince of Yen was not uniformly successful, the Emperor's supporters dispersed and Nanking fell into the hands of the rebels (1402).

At the time it was generally believed that the young Emperor had lost his life in the burning palace, but it later became known that Hui Ti, disguised as a Buddhist monk, and attended by only a handful of followers, had escaped from the city. In spite of the efforts which the Prince of Yen, now Emperor,* made to capture the fugitive, Hui Ti managed to avoid detection and lived the life of a mendicant monk, travelling all over China. It was not until many years later, in 1441, that he was recognised, arrested and sent to Peking. By that time the reigning Emperor was Chêng T'ung, great grandson of Yung Lo. The aged monk was identified by an old eunuch, but the government, in order to keep the embarrassing discovery quiet, allowed Hui Ti to pass the last year of his life in peaceful obscurity at Peking.

The disadvantages of Peking as a capital were not apparent in the reign of Yung Lo. The Emperor was an experienced and capable soldier who had served for many years in the war against the Mongols. He was always ready to take command himself when any nomad chief threatened to make trouble, and he led many expeditions into outer Mongolia, and even into territory now part of Siberia. During his reign there was no question of any nomad invasion of China. On the contrary, the Chinese military supremacy remained unchallenged. In this connection it is interesting to note that the Ming Empire narrowly escaped a danger which would have put the military ability of Yung Lo to a high test. Tamerlane, the great Central Asiatic conqueror, who had overrun Persia and taken the Ottoman Sultan a prisoner, set out to invade China in the year 1404. No state or city had yet successfully withstood this terrible conqueror. His armies were the terror of western Asia, and their reputation long survived even in Europe. What would have happened if the armies of Yung Lo had met the mighty Tamerlane,

"Threatening the world with high astounding terms and scourging kingdoms with his conquering sword"

must remain an unanswered problem, for Tamerlane died when already on the march. The event is not mentioned by the Chinese, who perhaps remained blissfully ignorant of the menace which had come so close to them.

*The Prince of Yen reigned as third Emperor of the Ming; it was he who built the present city of Peking, and the Forbidden City palace. His tomb is the principal of the Ming Tombs near Peking. His dynastic title was Ch'ang Tsu, and the reign title Yung Lo.

The government of the Ming dynasty continued to be modelled upon the T'ang pattern after the move to Peking, but in some respects it cannot be said to have come up to that standard. It was characteristic of the Ming period that men turned back to the T'ang rather than to the last great Chinese dynasty, the Sung. The Sung had been pacific, and their unwarlike policy had paved the way for nomad conquests. The T'ang, on the other hand, had been a great conquering dynasty, exercising authority far beyond the limits of China itself. The early Ming Emperors, warriors themselves, felt little sympathy for the cultivated pacifists who had ruled the Sung Empire, and had been content to leave integral parts of China in alien hands. Unfortunately, the Ming rulers discarded not only the pacifism of the Sung, but also the civilised restraint which had marked the internal administration of that dynasty.

Mongol methods had left a more barbaric standard of war and politics as a legacy. Under the Ming the treatment of rebels, conspirators, and enemy peoples, was more severe, a return to the ruthless methods of an earlier age. Sung pacifism had been discredited by the nomad invasions, and Sung humanity was equally forgotten. Nevertheless, the fact that the Ming administration was often needlessly harsh, and the government consciously modelled on ancient lines, does not justify the charge of reaction and stagnation, which has sometimes been laid against it.

It is certain that under this dynasty the Chinese civilisation for the first time began to lag behind the progress made in other countries, particularly in Europe, but this was more on account of the rapid progress in the west than because the Ming period in China was static. When Marco Polo returned from China, a few years after the extinction of the Sung dynasty, the civilisation which he made known to Europe was far superior in every respect to that of his native land. When the Ming dynasty fell in A.D. 1644, Europe had made immense advances, especially in navigation, science, and knowledge of the other parts of the world. China, on the other hand, had remained self-contained, and rather more isolated than it had been in the T'ang period. In spite of this the two civilisations were still at the same stage of development, and in China the Ming had made valuable contributions to the national culture.

Partly because these expressions of the Ming genius were not obvious to foreign investigators, and partly because the dominant Confuciansim itself ignored popular art and literature, the Ming period has had to wait for recognition. In the well-cultivated fields of poetry, philosophy and painting, arts at which preceding dynasties had excelled, the Ming were mainly imitative. These traditional arts had become standardised and formalised, but since they were the recognised and orthodox artistic and intellectual activities, they alone met with the approbation of scholars. The real Ming genius appeared in the unorthodox arts such as the drama, and particularly in the creation of an entirely new literary form, the prose novel. In art the Ming developed ceramics and originated a noble school of architecture. Chinese culture did indeed become static, as compared with the rapid advance of the west, but only in the last two centuries of the Manchu dynasty.

In spite of frontier wars, in which the Emperor himself commanded in person, the reign of Yung Lo was a period of internal peace, marked by great activity in the rebuilding of city walls and fortifications. Throughout north China the immense and solid walls of the early Ming period are a feature of every city, even those of small administrative importance. The Great Wall itself, at least in its eastern stretches, is really largely Ming work, for the pre-existing wall had fallen into disrepair during the long centuries of nomad rule, when naturally, this defence was neglected. Yung Lo has also left the city and palaces of Peking as the most eloquent testimony of his power and the civilisation of his period. Peking as it stands to-day is almost entirely the city he built, for the Mongol capital was so extensively altered and rebuilt that only a small part of the former walls and the Bell Tower remain in the present city.*

*The Ming city as built by Yung Lo is the misnamed Tartar City, called by the Chinese the North City. The commercial quarter to the south, now often called the Chinese City, was really only a suburb which was later enclosed by a subsidiary wall. The Forbidden City, apart from minor alterations and reconstructions, is the palace of the Ming Emperor, and was completed in A.D. 1422.

The founder of Peking died in 1425, on the way back from his last expedition into Outer Mongolia. His son and successor, Hung Hsi, was already a sick man, and died the same year, after a reign of ten months. The throne then passed to Yung Lo's grandson, Hsüan Tê, who only reigned for eleven years. Thus in less than twelve years after Yung Lo's death, the throne was occupied by his great-grandson, a boy of eight, the Emperor Chêng T'ung. The accident of these rapid changes of ruler was a great misfortune for the Ming dynasty and for China. Frequent short reigns are always a source of weakness in an autocratic government, since they prevent continuity of policy, but this disadvantage is greatly enhanced when the government is a regency acting for a child Emperor. Under Chêng T'ung, the regency was exercised by the Empress Dowager, and before long the misfortune of eunuch influence made its appearance.

Cheng T'ung was brought up in the palace surrounded by the exclusive and elaborate etiquette which isolated the Emperor from ordinary human contacts. Inevitably he fell under the influence of his only intimate companions and servants, the eunuchs. When the Emperor came of age, in 1443, he gave his entire confidence to one of these favourites, Wang Chin, whose authority became almost unlimited. Seven years later (1450) the eunuch, wishing to do honour to his family and display his power in his native country, persuaded the Emperor to lead an expedition to the border lands of Mongolia, where a Mongol chief had been raiding, and to pass by the city of Huai Lai, which was Wang Chin's native place, where he intended to entertain the Emperor in his own home.

Cheng T'ung not only consented to undertake this wholly unnecessary expedition, but also made Wang Chin commander-in-chief of the army. The eunuch had no experience whatever of war or the command of troops, and his promotion was in the highest degree offensive to the old and experienced generals who had fought under Yung Lo. The campaign was grossly mismanaged and bungled from the first. Ignoring the advice of the regular officers who had long experience of the frontier, Wang Chin exposed the army to attack in a situation where it had neither water nor provisions. Finally, refusing to renounce his

plan of entertaining the Emperor in his native village, he post-
poned the retreat for this purpose, and the entire Chinese army
was surrounded and cut to pieces near Huai Lai, a city about
50 miles north-west of Peking, beyond the Nan K'ou Pass in the
inner Great Wall.

The disaster of Huai Lai was the end of Ming superiority over
the Mongol tribes. Chêng T'ung himself was taken prisoner, the
eunuch Wang Chin, and all the experienced generals in the
Emperor's service, slain. The Emperor himself at least displayed
a suitable courage in this desperate situation. The Mongol chief
found him seated, perfectly serene, and with no trace of emotion
on his face, on a carpet, in the midst of his slaughtered bodyguards. He was carried away to Mongolia a prisoner, but well
treated, and later released. Indeed, the nomad victory was a
chance success against an army which had been led by folly
into disaster. The Mongols were not strong enough to take full
advantage of their victory. Although they raided down to the
gates of Peking, they were quickly driven back when Chinese
reinforcements arrived from the neighbouring provinces. Some
years later, finding that another prince had taken possession of
the throne, the Mongols released Chêng T'ung, who had ceased
to be a valuable hostage. The captive Emperor, indeed, enjoyed a
fortune which he did not deserve, for when the Emperor Ching Ti,
who had taken his place, fell ill, Chêng T'ung was restored to the
throne by a cabal of ministers and generals. He seems to have had
a winning personality, for he made lasting and intimate friends
among his Mongol captors. His second reign, under the style
T'ien Shun, lasted until his death in 1465.*

Although the immediate consequences of the disaster at Huai
Lai were less calamitous than might have been anticipated, the
event was a landmark in the Ming period. The era of Chinese
military supremacy had ended, and henceforth the empire was
on the defensive on the northern frontier, a defensive which

---

*The unfortunate Ching Ti, Chêng T'ung's younger brother, who was
forced to take the throne during his elder's captivity, was shabbily treated
after his death. Deposed, when already dying, he was refused burial as an
Emperor, and is interred in an isolated tomb, situated behind the Jade
Fountain Park, some miles west of Peking, in a spot remote from the tombs of
the other Ming Emperors.

increasingly failed to withstand the nomad onslaughts. During the last third of the 15th century, the reigns of Ch'êng Hua and Hung Chih, the empire was tranquil, and still strong enough to guard the frontiers effectively, but early in the 16th century it became clear that the Court at Peking was losing prestige and authority.

It was under the Emperor Chêng Tê (A.D. 1505-1520), who succeeded at the age of 15, that the eunuchs, whose influence had been checked by the defeat at Huai Lai, obtained inordinate power. As in the Han dynasty, the consequence of eunuch control was unrest and revolt in the provinces. The eunuchs were for the most part northerners, and as such had neither sympathy nor consideration for the southern provinces, which, remote from the Court, could not make their grievances easily known. Once the eunuchs had acquired control of the government they employed their power, like their predecessors in the Han period, thirteen centuries before, entirely for the pursuit of wealth. Offices were sold to the highest bidder, and could only be retained by paying the eunuchs a yearly tribute. In consequence the officials were forced to levy excessive taxation and exploit the provincials in order to satisfy the rapacity of the eunuchs. The provinces which were furthest from the Court suffered the most under this system.

The Emperor Chêng Tê, an eccentric youth who delighted in going about in disguise, and was not easily persuaded to fulfil the imperial functions in a dignified manner, was not an incapable or lethargic ruler. Had it been possible for him to realise what were the effects of eunuch corruption he might have checked the evil. As it was, cut off from other sources of information, he suspected those who accused the eunuchs of malversations to be intriguers themselves. Nevertheless, when the proofs were convincing enough, he was willing to act. The fall of the eunuch Liu Chin in 1510 revealed the extent of the corruption which was undermining the empire.

The property of this man was seized by the state and confiscated for the benefit of the treasury. Expressed in terms of the current unit, a tael, or ounce of silver, Liu Chin was found possessed of gold and silver, coined and unminted to the value of

251,583,600 taels. He also had 24 lbs. of unmounted precious stones, two suits of armour in solid gold, 500 gold plates, 3,000 gold rings and brooches, and 4,062 belts adorned with gems. This inventory did not include his mansion in Peking which was described as more magnificent than the Emperor's palace, which is no doubt an exaggeration. Liu Chin, like all eunuchs, came of a poor and obscure family. Consequently this vast wealth had been acquired during his service in the palace, and at the public expense.

Two long reigns, those of Chia Ching, 1520-1566, and Wan Li, 1572-1620, gave a certain stability to the last century of the Ming dynasty, largely due to the capable ministers, Yang Ting-ho and Chang Ku-ching. Although the internal rebellions in the west which had troubled the country under Chêng Tê were suppressed, the empire was throughout this century harassed on its frontiers and coasts by foreign enemies. Nomad raiders constantly harried the northern frontier, and even appeared before the walls of Peking (1550), and Japanese pirates made innumerable descents on the south-eastern coast, where they sacked cities and carried off hostages for ransom. These expeditions were a regular industry in which the leading Japanese nobles of southern Japan invested sums of money, and from which they drew large profits.

Hostilities with Japan on a more regular footing broke out in Korea, which was invaded by the Shogun Hideyoshi in 1592. Korea appealed to China, as suzerain, and the Ming Court despatched an army to drive out the invaders. A six years' war followed, in which the Chinese after some early progress were uniformly unsuccessful. The armies despatched to Korea were large and costly. Reinforcements from the most distant provinces were poured into the peninsula, and the resources of the empire wasted in a struggle from which China derived no benefit whatever. When at last the death of Hideyoshi caused the Japanese to evacuate Korea, the Ming Court could congratulate itself upon a barren victory which had exhausted the strength of the empire, and left it an easy prey to rebels and enemies beyond the Great Wall.

In 1618 the Manchu tribes, organised under a leader who

became the founder of their power, established a kingdom in the modern province of Kirin, and in the same year began to invade the Chinese province of Liao Tung. During the remaining years of the Ming dynasty this war with the Manchus was a perpetual source of weakness and expense, which distracted the attention of the Court from the more urgent menace of internal rebellion. It is improbable that the Manchus would have succeeded in conquering any large part of China if the Ming dynasty had not been destroyed by internal troubles, which, in turn, were largely a consequence of the remote situation of their capital.

Although the Manchus had conquered the whole of Liao Tung, in south Manchuria, by 1629, their further progress was held up by the defences of the Great Wall. The Ming dynasty fell as the result of an internal rebellion, the consequence of eunuch extortion and the resulting oppression of the provincials. Li Tzŭ-ch'êng, a native of Shensi, became the leader of this movement, and, after some years of varying fortune, conquered Honan in 1640, and then sweeping rapidly over Shensi and Shansi, fell upon Peking from the north-west. In 1644 he appeared before the walls of the capital. The defence of the city, foolishly entrusted to eunuchs, was betrayed, and the last Ming Emperor, Ch'ung Chêng, committed suicide on Coal Hill in the grounds of his palace. The pavilion which was the scene of this tragedy still stands.

The Manchu conquest of China did not occur till after the fall of Peking. The Chinese general, Wu San-kuei, who was guarding the frontier defences, refused to recognise the rebel Li Tzŭ-ch'êng as emperor, and invited the Manchus to assist him to recover Peking. Profiting by this opening the Manchus installed themselves in north China, while Wu San-kuei pursued the beaten rebels into the western provinces, from which they had come.

Chapter XXIV

THE BEGINNINGS OF EUROPEAN TRADE

EARLY in the Ming dynasty, under Yung Lo and his immediate successors, between A.D. 1405–1433, the Chinese Court sponsored a number of powerful naval expeditions to the Indian Ocean and neighbouring seas. This sudden and unprecedented interest in navigation, discovery and sea power has many features which sharply distinguish it from the European ventures into the eastern seas which were to follow before the 15th century was over. The Chinese expeditions were large and powerful; more than 70,000 men were embarked in fleets of specially built great ships. They were commanded by a Court eunuch, the celebrated Cheng Ho, who was nonetheless undoubtedly an able and adventurous navigator, a resolute commander, skilful diplomat and influential courtier; a combination of qualities rarely matched. Cheng Ho was the main inspiration for these expeditions which lasted as long as he remained active, but ceased with his death.

The purpose of these expensive activities was neither trade nor conquest: the Chinese did indeed intervene in the political affairs of many of the kingdoms in the Indonesian islands, the Malay peninsula and in Ceylon, but this action was incidental to the main purpose which was to display the power of the Ming empire and win nominal suzerainty of China in these regions. Kings who acknowledged the overlordship of the Ming Emperor were helped against their rivals who refused such homage. The Chinese at no time seem to have established permanent bases under their own sovereignty; they were content to use the ports of friendly states.

On the later voyages, ranging ever further over the ocean, it would seem that this primary motive of diplomatic prestige was overlaid by a new and growing interest in discovery and navigation for its own sake, and for the curious and rare products of distant lands which the fleets brought back for the delectation of the Court. Cheng Ho sailed his fleet up the Persian Gulf and the Red Sea; cruised down the east coast of Africa, and brought back from that country a live giraffe, which was duly presented to the Emperor in Peking. Courtiers suggested to Yung Lo that this must be indeed the Chi Lin, a fabulous beast which only appeared on earth during the reign of a perfect sage. The Emperor told them not to be so silly. Southwards the Chinese fleets touched upon Timor, recording the name of that island, so close to the Australian mainland, in ideographs which only give the sound 'Timor' when pronounced in the dialect of Foochow (from whence the fleets sailed). This rendering of the name remains in use to-day, although almost every other place in the south seas is named in Chinese in accordance with the pronunciation used by Amoy dialect speakers, who predominate in the region.

The voyages of Cheng Ho, popular with the Court, were not so with the civil service. The old rivalry between Court eunuchs and bureaucrats was soon to distract the Ming dynasty, and the expense of these expeditions, the fact that they were controlled and commanded by Court eunuchs, not by civil servants, sustained a constant opposition which, after the death of Cheng Ho, prevailed. When a further expedition was planned the bureaucracy intervened effectively by "losing" the essential documents dealing with navigation and sailing directions. The expedition was abandoned, and no more were launched.

Only sixty-four years after the last great voyage of Cheng Ho in A.D. 1433 Vasco da Gama and his fellow countrymen who followed him entered the Indian Ocean to begin the era of European domination of the eastern seas. Had the Chinese sustained the work so well begun by Cheng Ho, established permanent bases, maintained their sea power and founded an overseas empire, it is at least possible that the course of history would have been profoundly different. But the Ming Court lost interest in the question: sea power fell into a complete decline; after half a century the Portuguese were able to gather up what China had let slip, and achieve the empire of the seas with resources far inferior to those at the disposal of Cheng Ho. China in later centuries was to pay dearly for missing this opportunity.*

The period of Chinese history covered by the three centuries of direct contact with Europe is naturally the best known to western readers, but the history of this intercourse has almost always been presented from an exclusively western point of view,

*China's Discovery of Africa. J. J. Duyvendak. London: Probsthain, 1949.

and the facts emphasised are not always those which really determined the course of events. It is customary to pass over the first century of Sino-European relations very briefly and concentrate attention on the difficulties which arose between the foreign traders and Chinese officials at Canton in the 18th and early 19th centuries; difficulties which culminated in the Opium War and the foundation of the concession and extraterritorial systems. This is the more intelligible as in the problems of those centuries the foreign nations were, generally speaking, in the right, and the policy of the Manchu government unwise. The underlying causes of these problems, and the reason why the attitude of the Chinese authorities was stiff and hostile, are to be found in the history of the early contacts between Chinese and foreigners in the 16th and 17th centuries. The behaviour of the Europeans at that time cannot be easily justified, consequently western historians have devoted little space to this period.

The history of European trade with China by the sea route falls naturally into three main divisions. The early part in the 16th and 17th centuries, when the trade was practically a Portuguese monopoly, broken only by the Dutch and English at the end of the 17th century, is the sole period which falls within the Ming dynasty. The second epoch, of "company trade," when the East Indian Companies of all the seafaring nations competed vigorously for the trade at Canton, ended in 1840 when the Opium War opened a new era, which has only ended in our own time, that of the concessions and extraterritorial system, or more simply, that of capitalist imperialism. It is with the first period, the 16th and 17th centuries, that this chapter will deal, for it was then that the attitude of the Chinese towards western foreigners took shape and the character of the relationship between westerners and the Chinese was defined.

In studying the history of the intercourse between the Chinese and other peoples one cannot fail to be struck by the great difference between the treatment accorded to the Arab and Persian merchants in the T'ang and Sung dynasties, and that meted out to the western peoples by the Ming and Manchu governments. In the earlier dynasties the empire was freely opened to foreigners, who traded and resided not only in the ports, but in the principal cities of the interior, and particularly in the capital. Under the Ming and Manchu Emperors the Europeans were carefully restricted to one single city and its immediate environs, and were positively prohibited to travel or reside in any other part of the empire. This contrast must have an explanation, and it is only too plain from the records, both Chinese and European, that the unfavourable treatment received by the Europeans was the consequence of their own violent and barbarous behaviour.

When the first Portuguese navigators arrived in China they were accorded exactly the same liberties and welcome as the Arabs and Malays had long enjoyed. It was the fault of the Portuguese themselves that they afterwards suffered under a vexatious system of restrictions. It was a great misfortune for Europeans in general that the Portuguese were the first to open up the sea route to the east. The Iberian nations had developed a peculiar outlook on questions of trade and exploration, which was the outcome of their age-old struggle against the Spanish Moors and the Barbary corsairs. Schooled in this atmosphere of religious hatred and constant warfare the Portuguese and Spaniards had learned to think of every non-Christian people as *ipso facto* enemies, and every pagan ship that sailed the seas as a legitimate prize. They had, as so often happens, adopted the vices of those against whom they had fought for so long. In religious matters the Iberian peoples imported an Islamic fervour alien to other parts of Christendom. Conversion or the sword became with them a Christian doctrine, which in the east and in America was ruthlessly enforced.

The Portuguese, bringing these Mediterranean traditions into the eastern oceans, applied them on the coasts of India and China —pagan lands—which to the navigators were to be treated in the manner familiar on the Barbary coast. Trade was only the weaker alternative to a plundering foray. When the enemy was weak or unprepared the Portuguese plundered his ships and cities, massacred the "heathen" and seized the harbours as bases. When he was strong or ready for battle they traded—always ready to assume the more congenial rôle of marauders if opportunity presented itself.

These ideas were foreign to the Chinese of that date. They had been accustomed for many centuries to the visits of Arab and other Asiatic traders. They were well aware that these nations had their own religions, which in their own countries were universal and almost obligatory. In China this had never been the case. Foreigners might practise what faith they pleased, provided it was not one subversive of public order. The idea that because a man had a peculiar religion he was at liberty to plunder and massacre all those who held a different faith was unknown in China. On the other hand, it was axiomatic to the average Portuguese of the 16th century.

The Portuguese cannot be blamed for acting in accordance with ideas which were the result of their own history and the common practice on the Mediterranean coasts in their time, but the Chinese, equally, cannot be blamed if they regarded the new-comers as a brand of pirate in every way similar to the Japanese corsairs who had troubled the coasts and shipping of the empire during the Ming period. They had adopted measures to deal with Japanese raiders, and these measures they not unnaturally applied to the Portuguese who behaved in a similar way.

Perestrello, who had only one ship, offered no violence, and was well received—just as if he had been an Arab or a Malay. The next year, however, four Portuguese ships arrived commanded by Fernando d'Andrada with an ambassador from the Viceroy of Goa to the Chinese Court. The Portuguese were received on exactly the same traditional footing as other emissaries from far distant countries. Their embassy was sent up to Peking, where no doubt, its gifts would be received as "tribute," and presents accorded in return ; but while the embassy was yet in the capital the Court heard news which threw a different light upon the newcomers.

The Chinese were informed—perhaps by Arabs or by Chinese who had visited the East Indies—that the Portuguese were accustomed to appear first as peaceful traders, but, when they had once gained a footing, to pillage and seize cities, overthrow the government, and establish their own authority. Such had been their procedure in India, on the Persian coast, and in the East Indian Islands (Map 15). These unfavourable reports were

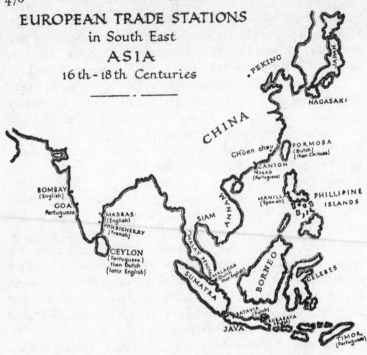

MAP 15. *European Trade Stations in South East Asia.*

speedily confirmed by news of the activities of Simon d'Andrada—brother of the commander—at Canton. The Portuguese had committed acts of piracy in the Pearl River and their increasing violence and aggressive conduct led to open hostilities. The Viceroy of Canton, alarmed for his city, resorted to military measures, and drove the Portuguese ships out of the river by force. Nothing is known of the fate of the ambassadors in Peking, but it seems likely that they were treated as pirates.

The Chinese considered that they now had ample proof that the Portuguese were really pirates masquerading as peaceful merchants. They were forbidden to touch at Chinese ports in the future. When in 1522 Alphonso de Mello appeared off Canton he was promptly attacked by a Chinese naval force and defeated after a stiff action. One Portuguese ship was captured and the surviving members of the crew executed as pirates.

Nothing more is heard of the Portuguese in China until 1542, when, unable to re-appear at Canton, they came to Ningpo. Here they were at first permitted to trade, partly perhaps because their behaviour twenty years before had been forgotten, and partly because the Ningpo officials, exercising the wide power of local autonomy common in the provinces of China, considered that a prohibition at Canton in Kuangtung province did not necessarily apply to Ningpo in Chekiang.

They were not long in discovering that the Portuguese were no more to be trusted in Ningpo than in Canton. The Ningpo establishment prospered mightily for two years. It is stated that some 3,000 Portuguese were resident in the city and a great volume of trade was transacted. No sooner did the Portuguese find themselves numerous and powerful than they began to put their usual plan into practice. Assaults and murders of Chinese in and around the city became common. Then the Portuguese, perhaps alarmed at the hostility which their arrogant behaviour was arousing, began to construct a fort. This open exhibition of their designs roused the Chinese officials, who had hitherto condoned the Portuguese aggressions for the sake of the large personal profits they made from the trade. They raised the populace, brought in troops, attacked the Portuguese fort and exterminated all who could not escape to the ships. The establishment at Ningpo came to an abrupt and violent end.

The experience of Ningpo was repeated in 1549 at Ch'üan Chou, in Fukien, a city which under the name of Zaytun, is mentioned in many Arab works as one of the principal centres of foreign trade in the Sung period. Here too, the Portuguese, at first received on the same footing as the long established Arabs, soon proved intolerably aggressive, and were expelled by force. It was at this time that the westerners earned the nickname of *yang kuei tzǔ*, "Ocean Devils," which has continued in popular usage to the present day. Foreigners who find it offensive should remember its origin.

The treatment which the Portuguese received at Ch'üan Chou is significant, for this city, an ancient trading centre, was well accustomed to the visits of foreign merchants. If the people of Ch'üan Chou found it necessary to drive out the Portuguese, when for centuries they had welcomed the Arabs and Malays, it was certainly due to the conduct of the Portuguese themselves. There is, in fact, no doubt about the matter for the accounts of the Portuguese behaviour and the reasons for their expulsion are given not by Chinese, but by contemporary European writers.*

In spite of these bad beginnings the Chinese were anxious to trade with the westerners, if trade could be conducted on reasonable terms, without violence and treachery. The profits obtained by both sides were great, and the officials took a large share of them. In 1557 a compromise was reached, the Portuguese were allowed to trade at Macao, a peninsula in the Canton estuary, sufficiently remote from any city of importance to make serious aggressions difficult. The peninsula was, however, walled off on the landward side, and the fortification carefully guarded by a strong Chinese force. Moreover, the Portuguese were subject to a number of restrictions and prohibitions which their early violence at Ningpo and elsewhere made quite justifiable.

The Portuguese pioneers had given the European nations a bad name in China, and it was very many years before the Chinese thought of them as anything but a piratical and barbarous people who could not safely be permitted to live in the civilised celestial empire. It may seem absurd that representatives of the nations of 16th century Europe should be treated as barbarians, but it must be remembered that the Chinese had had little or no opportunity of discovering that these buccaneers were the compatriots and co-religionists of the cultured peoples of Italy and western Europe. Unfortunately, the kind of man who was prepared to go adventuring to the farthest confines of the earth in a small and scarcely seaworthy vessel was not the type who could give the Chinese a fair idea of European civilisation. The missionaries, who did represent the culture as well as the religion of Europe, did not appear in China until the marauding trader-pirates had already created an indelible evil impression.

St. Francis Xavier was the first Catholic missionary to China, but he never set foot in the empire itself. After spending many years in the East Indies and in Japan, he died on a small island

---

*The Chinese and Portuguese sources are collected and compared by T'ien-Tse Chang. *Sino-Portuguese Trade*, Leyden, 1934.

near Macao in 1552. It was not until 1575 that Catholic missionaries reached Canton, in the same year that the Chinese, having now taken the measure of Portuguese power, permitted the merchants of Macao to come up to Canton on certain fixed days for trade. At the very end of the century, in 1598, Father Ricci was permitted to travel to Peking and present his doctrine to the Throne. In 1601, after a delay of two years, his gifts were offered to the Emperor, and the incident is thus recorded by the Chinese historians:

"In the second month [of 1601] the eunuch Ma Tang of T'ien Ts'in brought to the Court Li Ma-tou,* a man from the western ocean, who had some rare gifts for the Emperor. The Emperor sent the eunuch's memorial to the Board of Rites who replied:

" 'The western ocean countries have had no relations with us, and do not accept our laws. The images and paintings of the Lord of Heaven and of a virgin which Li Ma-tou offers as tribute are not of great value. He offers a purse in which he says there are the bones of immortals, as if the immortals, when they ascend to heaven did not take their bones with them. On a similar occasion Han Yü† said that one should not allow such novelties to be introduced into the palace for fear of bringing misfortune. We advise, therefore, that his presents should not be received, and he should not be permitted to remain in the capital. He should be sent back to his own country.'

"In spite of this decision, the Emperor received the presents and permitted Li Ma-tou to live at the capital."

This entry is typical and illuminating. The Confucian Board of Rites took up a strictly traditional opposition to all foreign novelties, while the Court tolerated the foreigner in just the same way as the T'ang Emperors had tolerated the foreign religious wanderers of the 8th and 9th centuries. No doubt Father Ricci, with his relics and images of the saints, seemed to the Chinese

---

*The Chinese rendering of Mathew Ricci.

†The great T'ang scholar and anti-Buddhist. The occasion referred to is no doubt the offering of a reputed finger of Buddha to the Emperor mentioned in Chapter XVI.

indistinguishable from the innumerable very similarly equipped Buddhist monks who had from time to time sought Court protection for their particular deities. Ricci remained in Peking, where he died in 1610.

While the Catholic missionaries headed by Ricci were rather tardily endeavouring to present a more favourable aspect of European culture to the Chinese, their Catholic co-religionists the Portuguese were finding their monopoly of the eastern trade menaced by Protestant competitors, who brought all the hatreds of the wars of religion to stimulate a commercial rivalry which was in any case sufficiently acute. In 1596 Sir Robert Dudley was despatched by the English Court to endeavour to open up the eastern trade. Nothing was ever heard of this expedition after it sailed, and so it must be presumed to have met with shipwreck somewhere on the way to China. The disappearance of Dudley checked English enterprise for the time being, and it was the Dutch who first challenged the Portuguese in the China seas.

In 1622 they attacked Macao, but were beaten off by the Portuguese, and established themselves in Formosa, which was not then a part of the Ming Empire. There they built themselves a fort, called Zelandia, as a base. Already some years previously the Dutch had become known to the Chinese in a manner very reminiscent of the first appearance of the Portuguese. In 1607:

> "In the eleventh month Hsu Hsiu-tsu, viceroy of Fukien, reported to the Court that the 'Hung Mao' ['redheads,' Dutch, later also English] had slain some Chinese merchants and pillaged their vessels, and that thereafter they had landed as if they proposed to establish themselves on the mainland."

The historians do not relate what became of these "Redheads," but, as no more is said, it would seem that after plundering their fill they once more put to sea. At least it is fairly clear that the Dutch, on arriving in the China seas, adopted the same standard of piracy that the Portuguese had set up a century before. The short note in the Chinese history is the first mention of northern Europeans in China; an unfortunate introduction.*

*The existence of red hair was a source of popular prejudice in itself. The Chinese are uniformly black haired, and had been accustomed to depict the demons of the Buddhist Hell with red, or blue hair; hence "foreign devils."

The Portuguese had very little difficulty in persuading the Chinese that these newcomers, whether Dutch or English, were not suitable people to be allowed to trade in Chinese ports. Naturally, after their experience with the Portuguese themselves, the Chinese were suspicious of all western ships, and, when the first thing the Dutch did was to plunder the coast, their suspicions received a sufficient confirmation. The English, when they arrived, behaved in the same way. In 1637 John Weddel arrived at Canton with three ships. The story of d'Andrada was now repeated. The English, unable to communicate with the Chinese except through Portuguese interpreters, completely misunderstood the cautious attitude adopted by the Chinese, who for their part were no doubt warned by the Portuguese to beware of the English. The merchants of Macao wanted no Protestant competitors for the Chinese trade.

Weddel found the restrictions and delays to which he was subjected irritating and inexplicable. He probably realised nothing of the background in the minds of the Chinese officials, who may very likely have believed him to be a compatriot of the "Redheads," who had pillaged in Fukien a few years before. When, losing patience, the English captain sent his boats to take soundings with the intention of moving his ships up to the city, the Chinese promptly opened fire on the boats.

Hostilities followed. Weddel bombarded a fort, landed and captured it. Whereupon he:

> "Tooke downe the China Flagge, hung it over the wall, and thereon advanced our King's coullours."*

There was more fighting, but Weddel had allowed some of his companions to go up to Canton to negotiate; fearing for the lives of these hostages, he was forced to agree upon a composition. The Chinese, willing, as is their practice, to negotiate with a leader of bandits if such conduct offers the best chance of being rid of the nuisance, released the hostages on condition that Weddel left Chinese waters at once and never returned. These terms were agreed upon.

Here was a typical instance of the mistrust and mutual suspicion

*H. B. Morse. *The East India Company Trading to China.* Oxford: 1926. Vol. I. p. 19.

which had arisen between the Chinese and western seamen as a result of the Portuguese aggressions in the early years. The only result of Weddel's voyage was that the English were placed in the same category as the Dutch—untamed barbarians who could not safely be allowed near the coasts of China.

Weddel's conduct at Canton was not the only reason that the Chinese had to fear that the English were no more to be trusted than the Dutch or the Portuguese. Reports which reached China told of the piracies which all the western nations constantly practised upon Chinese shipping in the South China Sea. These reports were indeed true enough for they are also given in the English accounts of early trading ventures to the Far East. In 1619—several years before Weddel came to Canton—the English and Dutch combined to plunder the Chinese merchant junks trading to the Philippines. At the same time it was reported that the Dutch had plundered and massacred all the junks and their crews going to Bantam in the East Indies. The trade with Java was almost entirely stopped by Dutch piracies and massacres. Throughout the Eastern seas all nations had adopted the old Portuguese practice of treating every pagan ship as a legitimate prize.

When it is realised that these junks came from the very ports where the European pirates were fain to appear in the guise of peaceful traders, the cold reception they received from the Chinese authorities is most intelligible. Moreover, these conditions continued for many years after the trade at Canton had been regulated and was open to all nations. In the 18th century the Dutch perpetrated a large-scale massacre of Chinese in Java, and the Spanish exterminated the much larger Chinese colony in the Philippines in cold blood. It seems that the Chinese would not accept Catholicism.

There is no doubt that had the European trade not been highly profitable to the Chinese officials of Canton, all access would have been forbidden, as it was to Japan, and, for the same reason. It is indeed, very likely that had the Ming dynasty continued to reign the Court would have prohibited dealings with such dangerous customers. Shortly after the entry of the English and Dutch, however, the Ming dynasty was overthrown, and in its final struggle against the Manchus, the Ming Court was forced to seek assistance on all sides.

The coast region was the stronghold of the last Ming pretenders and partisans, and thus the Chinese were brought into closer contact with the foreigners. Already Catholic missionaries, divorced from the piracies of their seafaring compatriots, had created a favourable impression on the Court, and had even made numerous converts, some of whom were men of great influence and high position. Through the agency of these powerful protectors the missionaries were able to smooth away some of the misunderstandings which had arisen in the ports, and even afford the Chinese Court valuable assistance in the war against the Manchus.

In 1581 Michel Roger, a Jesuit, the first of his order, reached China, and his successors acquired a considerable influence at Court. The Jesuits were ready to serve in other than purely missionary capacities, and their knowledge of mathematics, astronomy and artillery won them a position which had not been accorded to missionaries with fewer intellectual attainments. In 1613 Li Chi-tsao, President of the Board of Rites at Nanking, the Ming southern capital, introduced Jesuits into his department to correct errors in the astronomy and calendar. Li was himself a convert to Christianity. A few years later, an even more important convert and patron of the Jesuits, Hsu Kuang-chi,* a minister, used his Jesuit teachers not only in the mathematical bureau of the Board of Rites, but also as artillery instructors in the war against the Manchus and the rebels. It was through his influence that the Ming government turned to the Portuguese for assistance, and enlisted the first European force which ever served in China.

In 1630 Gonsalvo Texeira and 400 Portuguese were enlisted at Macao, at the expense of the Ming Court, and started to travel north across China to assist in the war against the Manchus along the Great Wall. Much was hoped of this force, which, though so small, was equipped with firearms and artillery of a quality far superior to any so far used in China. Although Texeira and some of his officers reached Peking, and were engaged as advisers in the defence of certain northern cities, the main force was halted at

*He came of a family resident near Shanghai, where he owned property which he later bestowed on the mission. This is the famous Ziccawei Observatory, the Greenwich of China. Ziccawei is a Shanghai dialect form of the mandarin Hsu Chia Wei, "farm of the Hsu family."

Nan Ch'ang, in Kiangsi province, through the opposition and intrigues of the Cantonese merchants and officials.

As was so often to be the case in the later relations between the foreigners and the Court, the interests of Peking and Canton were at variance. The Cantonese, having now come to a working arrangement with the Portuguese at Macao, were reaping huge profits from the concentrated trade which passed through their port, and through no other. They feared that if Texeira's army performed conspicuous service in the north, the Emperor would grant the Portuguese the privilege of trading in other places, and also in the interior of the empire. Canton's valuable monopoly would be broken.

They therefore spared neither money nor persuasions to change the views of the Court, and when they had corrupted a sufficient number of important ministers, they obtained a decree halting the army at Nan Ch'ang. The Portuguese, after marching half across China, were then turned back, and disbanded at Macao after receiving good pay and a free excursion through south China, but never having fired a shot against the enemy. Texeira remained in the north, as an artillery expert, and was killed in the defence of an unidentified city a year later.

After the fall of Peking (1644) the Ming pretenders who held the south coast turned again to the Portuguese for help. The fugitive Court was strongly influenced by missionaries and converts. One of these Chiu Shê-ssŭ, was chief minister and grand general of the last Ming pretender in Kuangsi and Yunnan, and he used Portuguese gunners with some success. Indeed, his superior artillery was the main cause of the prolonged, and for the time successful, resistance of the Ming army in the south-west. The last Ming Empress in this fugitive Court was also a Christian, and her son, born in 1648, was baptised under the name of Constantine, traditional for royal converts. The Christian heir of the Mings never lived to found a Christian Empire. After his father's defeat and flight into Burma, the little Constantine fell into Manchu hands, and "died" in captivity.

The close association of the Catholic missionaries and Portuguese with the Ming pretenders was not calculated to win them the favour of the ultimate conquerors, the Manchus. Unfortunately, the English had also approached the Chinese partisan

Chêng Chêng Kung, known to the foreigners as Coxinga,* who dominated the China Sea, and had expelled the Dutch from Formosa, where he reigned as King. Coxinga at times seized parts of the mainland coast of Fukien and Chekiang, and the English, from whom he was anxious to buy cannon and powder, were permitted to trade at the ports he held. When in 1683 his son surrendered to the Manchus, the English remained under the suspicion of the conquerors as having been allies of the rebels.

The behaviour of the Dutch, after their expulsion from Formosa, was not such as to prejudice the new rulers of China in their favour. In 1661 a fleet of Dutch ships arrived off P'u To Shan, the famous Buddhist shrine and sanctuary in the Chusan Islands off the Chekiang coast. They landed, pillaged the temples, burnt and sacked the shrines, and maltreated the monks in barbarous fashion. Since P'u To Shan was a sacred island undefended by any garrison, and uninhabited except by monks, there can have been no possible excuse for these wanton aggressions. The Manchu government, when it had reduced the coast to obedience, therefore once more put into effect the prohibition of all foreign trade except at Canton, and, though attempts were made by English ships to call at Ningpo and Amoy, they found the attitude of the new rulers so obstructive that nothing could be done.

The Manchus had a further reason for treating the foreign trader with suspicion. The Cantonese had been among the last to submit to Manchu rule, and it was here in the extreme south that the conquerors had met with the stiffest opposition. They knew that the natives of south China detested their new rulers, and would seize any opportunity to rebel. Already the secret societies, born in Canton, were preparing the way for future revolts. Under these circumstances the Manchus feared that any free intercourse with foreigners would lead to the secret stimulation of these rebellious schemes. The Chinese rebels would perhaps offer the foreigners free trade in return for assistance against the enemy. It was a justifiable fear, for in fact, this was precisely the offer which the T'ai P'ing rebels made to the European nations in 1860.

*Coxinga is a corruption of Chêng's title "Kuo Hsing Yeh," "Lord of the Imperial Name," i.e. the Ming surname, which had been granted to him by the Ming pretender. In the southern dialects *kuo* becomes *kuok* or *kok*.

Then, however, the foreigners had just exacted large concessions and wide privileges from the Manchu Court, and so, mistakenly, refused the Chinese offer, and assisted the imperial armies.

The suspicions and fears of the Manchus, and the ready violence of the early western traders combined to perpetuate the misunderstandings and enmities of the early years of Sino-foreign trade. The better understanding which had grown up through Catholic influence in the later Ming Court, and with the Chinese partisans in the south, was checked, and the history of trade at Canton in the 18th century was one of increasing friction leading to open hostilities in the next century.

An important factor in this growing friction was the change in the character of the trade. In the first three centuries of the China trade, the balance was wholly in China's favour. The foreign ships came to Canton with a "stock" of silver, and bought silk and tea for cash. Even in the 18th century the Company ships were unable to dispose of their English cloth except at a loss, and in very small quantities. There was no demand for European manu-factures in China. After the growth of the opium habit, this position changed. The foreign traders found in opium, which came from India, a commodity which could be sold at a high profit in China. Thus the necessity for importing silver to pay for silk and tea decreased. The Chinese government was not pleased to discover that this change was depleting the hitherto enormous profits made on the foreign trade. The economic motive was the spur which roused the Court to make the smoking and importation of opium illegal. This decree, which cut at the root of the foreign traders' profit, led directly to the outbreak of war.

One of the consequences of the Opium War (1840) was the opening of Shanghai to foreign trade, and the gradual growth of its importance to the detriment of Canton, Amoy and Ningpo, the older trading ports. These southern cities had grown rich on their long monopoly, which set the seal on the slow process of development which had completely transformed the economic map of China. By the Manchu period the south coast was already the richest region in the empire. It was only in the last century of Manchu rule that the Yangtze estuary, with its chief city, Shanghai, became the centre of trade and modern industry.

Chapter XXV

THE DRAMA AND THE NOVEL

(A) THE DRAMA

DRAMATIC art developed late in China. In the west some of the earliest and greatest literature has been written for the stage, and the drama ranks high among the arts. In China, on the contrary, plays were not considered to be literature at all, the theatre was a place for frivolous amusement, and the drama, instead of developing in early times, lagged far behind poetry, history, or philosophy. It was not until the 13th century A.D., in the Mongol Yüan dynasty, that the Chinese drama really began to take shape as a separate branch of the arts. Although so late in developing, and, in spite of the neglect and derision of the scholar class, the drama, like the novel, with which in China it is closely linked, attained a universal popularity, and became one of the most vital elements in the popular culture.

The rise of the drama properly belongs to the Yüan and early Ming period, the 13th and 14th centuries, but it had existed in rudimentary form for many centuries before this development occurred. Under the republic Chinese scholars have done much to rescue the history of the theatre from the oblivion and neglect which was the portion of mere "popular" arts under the empire. It has been shown* that the art of the stage had its beginnings in the exorcist dances of the *wu*, the magicians, or medicine men, of the early Feudal Age. These performances, originally purely religious, came in time to serve as spectacles at banquets and festive occasions, when the assembled guests were more entertained than impressed by the dancers and the accompanying music.

Unlike the religious dances performed at Greek temples the *wu* dancing did not develop into true drama. Indeed, there does not appear to be much direct connection between these performances and the stage plays which became so popular nearly two thousand years later. An element of the older culture which

*The best modern work on the subject is in Chinese. *The History of the Drama under the Sung and Yüan Dynasties*, by the late Wang Kuo-wei.

made a more direct contribution to the theatre was the rite performed in honour of the deceased ancestor of a family or clan. It was customary for some member of the family, usually, if not always, a young boy, to impersonate the deceased and receive the sacrificial offerings on his behalf. The custom arose of celebrating the famous acts of the dead man at the same time, and short dramatic scenes were performed on these occasions.

At a later period, under the Han and subsequent dynasties down to the T'ang, military victories were celebrated by dances, accompanied by music and songs forming a kind of ballet, which may be regarded as the direct ancestor of the popular *wu* or military plays, in which such dancing fulfils a very important part. In the early years of the T'ang dynasty these ballets were a favourite Court entertainment and some particulars of the most famous have been preserved in history.

The P'o Chên, "Breaking the Battle Line," was a ballet written by a Court musician named Lu Ts'ai to commemorate the victories gained by Li Shih-min (the Emperor T'ai Tsung) over the various pretenders who disputed the throne at the fall of the Sui dynasty (A.D. 618). It was a dance, in which 128 boys performed wearing silver armour and carrying lances. The piece derived its name from a song which was said to have been the marching song of the T'ang army during the campaign against the pretenders. It is certain that this ballet was in some respects a true drama for it was proposed to add scenes showing the fallen pretenders led captive to execution. This addition was banned by the Emperor, who did not want to hurt the feelings of the numerous ministers and officers in his service who had formerly served under his enemies.

Other references show that in the first years of the T'ang dynasty Court theatricals were a popular and frequent entertainment. The Emperor T'ai Tsung's son, the Crown Prince, who was an eccentric character, used to take part in private theatricals in his own palace, and composed the play himself. The T'ang dynasty, so famous for other arts, was in fact the period in which dramatic art first began to emerge. The Emperor Ming Huang (A.D. 712-756) is still honoured as the patron of actors, for he is credited with having set up the first dramatic school. This establishment, known as the Pear Garden, from the place in the palace reserved for it, was really more a training centre for the singers and musicians destined for the Court entertainments. Ming Huang was himself a gifted musician and took a personal interest in the Pear Garden and its pupils. To this day actors are known as "sons of the Pear Garden."

The T'ang drama, however, apart from the ballets of the *P'o Chên* type, was limited to short scenes in which only two actors performed at a time. The characters were confined to a few stock parts, reminiscent of the pantaloon and punchinello of early Italian plays. Moreover, it was purely a Court art, an imperial pastime, not a popular amusement. Outside the palace it is probable that certain quasi religious dances and pantomimes were given at temples and religious fairs, but as yet there was no public drama. The Sung period saw a continuation of the Court drama, but very little development. The plays were short, and as under the T'ang only two actors performed in each play.

The Mongol conquest, carried out by massacre and destruction, was a set-back to civilisation in the Far East. It seems curious, therefore that the Mongol dynasty should be the age in which a new art began to flourish. The fact has led to the suggestion that the Chinese drama, suddenly developing under this short dynasty, owed much to importations from foreign sources. The Mongols employed large numbers of foreigners from all parts of Asia, and even from Europe. It does not seem impossible that some of these aliens should have introduced an art hitherto hardly known in China. There is however, no evidence that this was the case, and the internal and indirect evidence from the Yüan plays themselves shows no trace of foreign influence.

On the other hand the large number of T'ang grave figures representing dancers and actors, who are obviously foreigners, strongly suggests that the early drama of that age, four hundred years before the Mongol conquest, was potently influenced by contact with alien lands. It is possible that the Court drama which Ming Huang encouraged and patronised was directly inspired by west Asiatic models, for, as has been shown, the T'ang Court was cosmopolitan and not averse to foreign arts and fashions.

With only one exception, all the ninety or more known playwrights of the Yüan dynasty were Chinese. Only one was a Mongol, none were west Asiatics. The foreigners in Mongol service were for the most part (like Marco Polo) ignorant of the Chinese language, certainly of the written characters. They used Mongol as the language of government. Consequently, their contacts with the native culture were slight, as is clearly shown by Marco Polo's references to Chinese religion and customs. The subjects of the Yüan plays are in all cases taken from Chinese life or history, none show any evidence of foreign customs or legends connected with western sources. Had the Chinese drama been inspired by some western model it is hardly possible that the earliest plays would not have borne clear evidence of their origin.

The Mongols and the foreigners they brought to China were clearly not responsible for the expansion of the Chinese drama. The Mongol conquest was nevertheless a contributory cause. Under the rule of this foreign dynasty the Chinese scholars were relegated to subordinate positions, often not employed at all. The classical examinations for the civil service were discontinued, for this system would have put the administration entirely in Chinese hands. The educated Chinese were thus perforce freed from their pre-occupation with classical literature and the examinations based upon it, and the new rulers did not frown upon or forbid non-classical studies as had too often been the practice of native governments.

Scholars began to turn to new forms of literature for distraction. The earliest novels developed from tales which were written down in the Mongol period, but the most important intellectual activity of the time was the writing of stage plays. This was the first of the new popular arts which arose under the three last dynasties, Mongol, Ming and Manchu. The destruction of the Sung dynasty meant far more than the dethronement of a Chinese imperial family and the substitution of an alien house. It ruined and dispersed the cultured Court society which had been the centre of Chinese civilisation under the T'ang and Sung, for the Court at K'ai Fêng had continued the tradition of Ch'ang An, reuniting the scholars and artists who had taken refuge in the southern provinces during the chaotic interlude of the Five Dynasties.

After the Sung there is a marked decline of all the arts which had flourished at Ch'ang An, K'ai Fêng and Hang Chou. Poetry, painting and philosophy, the culture which had been centred in the vast and splendid capitals of T'ang and Sung, which drew together all the talent as well as most of the wealth of the empire, decayed under the barbarian Mongols. Perhaps for that very reason less sophisticated and more widespread arts prospered. The new rulers of the empire ignored the native culture, which was indeed far above their heads. The concentration of art and talent at the capital ceased, and the educated natives of China, deprived of imperial patronage put their talents at the service of a wider, less cultivated public. Art and literature were popularised, first on the stage, and then, thanks to the printing press, by means of the novel. The Ming dynasty, though it restored a Chinese family to the throne, did not succeed in reversing the new tendency. The founder of that dynasty and his supporters were themselves men of very humble origin. Peasants, ex-bandits and soothsayers were found among the grandees of the new Court at Nanking. The cultivated aristocracy of the Sung Court could not be re-created at once, and the arts at which they had excelled suffered from their disappearance.

Under the last three imperial dynasties (Mongol, Ming and Manchu) a line of cleavage appeared in the Chinese culture. The scholars of the Court, bred in the Confucian classics, perpetuated an ever more formalised literary tradition and an ever more imitative art, dimly reflecting the vanished glories of Ch'ang An and K'ai Fêng Fu. Ignored by them, and therefore neglected by history, the vital artistic and literary impulses of this age found new forms of expression, the stage, the novel, and the potter's art. The later dynasties are often regarded as a period of cultural and artistic decline, but this is only true of the "Court arts." The living culture of the Ming and Manchu period was popular, not scholastic.

Nevertheless the new arts, however flourishing, were not admitted to the same consideration as the old. The "One Hundred Plays of the Yüan Dynasty" are so well known to a Chinese audience that every spectator is familiar not only with the plot, but almost with every line that is said or sung. Yet almost nothing is known of the authors of these famous plays. As with the Ming novelists, the Yüan playwrights did not advertise their authorship, for drama was not "literature," and the writing of plays was not becoming to a scholar. The names of the Yüan dramatists are known, and of them Kuan Han-ching is considered to be the best, but it is vain to enquire what manner of men they were, or look for details of their lives. Their plays are famous; they themselves are almost forgotten.

The new plays were no longer composed of short scenes like the old Court drama of the T'ang and Sung. There were usually four acts, but some pieces were even longer. A still more significant change occurred in the character of the language in which they were written. The ancient drama was a Court art, acted in a polished language akin to the classical *wên hua*, and the characters were limited in number and conventionalised. The Yüan plays were written and acted in an idiom hardly more classical than the speech of educated people, and more characters were introduced. The subjects of the plays were more varied, freely drawing upon historical material and the life of the people. From a limited Court entertainment the drama swiftly developed into a truly national art becoming and remaining, the chief recreation of the common people of China.

The Yüan dramatists are divided into two schools, northern and southern, and unlike the two schools of painting, the terms are here used in their geographical sense. The northern was both the earliest and the most prolific. Centred at Peking, the new capital of the empire, it flourished from 1235 to 1280 and the dramatists who wrote for it were all natives of the three provinces of Shansi, Shantung and Hopei. The southern school, at Hang Chou, the former Sung capital, only became important after the northern was losing ground; it was chiefly active between 1280 and 1335.

Very little is known about either school, for the drama, although it is now regarded as the most important contribution made to culture under the Yüan dynasty, was consistently ignored by critics and historians, who lavished their labours on endless commentaries on the classical books. The fact that the stage made use of the spoken language, instead of the classical, which is unintelligible if spoken,* was in itself sufficient to condemn the drama to an inferior rank in the minds of scholars. Literature must, by its very essence, be written in the classical language. This was the canon of criticism until the contemporary "renaissance movement" dethroned the Confucian classics a few years after the republicans had, in 1911, dethroned the Emperor.

The Chinese stage both suffered and profited by this neglect. It suffered in that plays were written by men of inferior education and taste or as pastimes by scholars whose serious work was devoted to classical commentaries. In consequence the plays reflect the limitations, or the negligence of their authors. No Shakespeare, Congreve or Sheridan wrote for the Chinese stage. On the other hand, though the plays were not great literature, the standard of acting became very high, and the art of the stage escaped the paralysing influence of antiquarian classicism. Up to the very end of the empire, and still to-day under the republic, the Chinese drama has remained vigorous and alive, showing no sign of the petrifaction which attacked the older arts. It has successfully resisted the influence of alien European dramatic traditions.

A native growth, the Chinese drama has naturally developed conventions very different from those of the western stage. The divisions of comedy and tragedy as such are unknown to the Chinese theatre. A Chinese play would be more properly described as an opera, for the script is in verse, the parts are sung, and the orchestra is as important as the actors. In the Yüan plays, which were usually divided into four acts, there were four principal characters, each having a singing part in a separate act, but never singing in the same act as another actor. This convention was abandoned in the Ming period, when more characters were introduced, and the singing parts multiplied. The Ming plays were

*The classical language, perhaps the literary form of the spoken language of the Feudal Age (1000-200 B.C.), is so different from everyday speech that a scholar could not understand a passage spoken aloud, if he was unfamiliar with the text. The fact that in modern Chinese only a small number of vocables (less than 350) are in use, and that the original pronunciation of classical words is now forgotten (owing to the ideographic script which gives the sense but not the sound of a word), makes a classical text spoken aloud nothing but a string of homophones.

also much longer, abandoning the limitation to four acts which had been customary, though not invariable on the Yüan stage.

In the Yüan drama the four principal rôles, or character types, which were to be found in every play, were the *chêng shêng*, "elderly man," who played the parts of emperors, generals, and old retainers. The *wu shêng* is the military hero, the principal part in *wu* or military plays. These plays, in which very skilled acrobatic dancing is a prominent feature, need a highly trained athlete for the leading rôle, and as the actor must also have a good singing voice, a good *wu shêng* must be something of a prodigy. The *ching i* and *hua tan* are two types of heroine, the first a "leading lady," either a high-born maiden or a simple country girl, the second a courtesan or a slave girl, usually the focus of the intrigue. Other parts, such as the *hsiao shêng*, the "juvenile lead" of the western stage, are in China of less importance.

On the Chinese stage all female parts are taken by male actors, usually youths. The female impersonators are the most skilled actors in the company and play their rôles with such perfection that it is almost impossible for a stranger to believe that they are in fact male actors. The custom, as on the Elizabethan stage, arose from reasons of propriety, but to-day, although women are no longer forbidden the stage, the female impersonators have achieved such perfect technique that the Chinese audience would deplore their disappearance as a catastrophic loss to the stage. Apart from the skill of the acting in itself the audience derives the added pleasure of admiring the perfection of the illusion.

A very high standard of ability is required of Chinese actors, for they perform on a bare stage, without the assistance of any scenery at all. There is not even a curtain, and the stage, without proscenium arch, is open on three sides. Changes of scene, or the end of an act are marked only by a "flourish" from the orchestra. In contrast to the bare stage the costumes of the actors are elaborate, gorgeous and costly. They are designed in accordance with recognised stage conventions, which assist the audience to follow the play. Thus, a Chinese playgoer immediately recognises a general by the long sweeping pheasant feathers of his head-dress, while a young scholar always carries a fan. Most of the costumes worn on the stage are an elaboration of the actual styles in fashion during the Ming dynasty. It is only in plays that specifically deal with historical episodes of the Manchu period that later styles are worn. For all plays dealing with ancient times, whether Ming or pre-Ming, the Ming costume is used. Fig. 58, depicting a scene from one of the historical plays dealing with the Three Kingdoms Period, shows Chou Yü, a general of Wu, ordering one of his officers, Huang Kai, to be flogged, so that, thereafter deserting to the enemy, he may be received without suspicion and obtain their confidence in order to betray them. Chu-ko Liang and other famous figures of the period are seated on either side.

The absence of any scenery makes it necessary for the Chinese stage to employ many conventions, some of which are strange to western dramatic tradition. The make-up worn by actors is very heavy, and is intended to convey an indication of the character he represents. A villain, treacherous general, or oppressive official (a common character on the stage) has his face painted a blank white. Generals and warriors have faces painted with a terrifying effect of heavy red and yellow, a custom which is said to have a historical basis, in that a Sung general adopted this fashion to disguise his naturally timid and unwarlike appearance. Other conventions replace the absence of properties. An actor carrying a horse whip indicates that he is mounted. When he lifts one leg he is dismounting. A hill, or a city wall is indicated by a table, or a chair. Persons dressed in black are invisible, characters carrying a horse hair switch are supernatural beings. These numerous conventions, which are for the most part founded on some legend or old custom, are perfectly familiar to the audience, who take them for granted.

No Chinese play is without music. Indeed, the orchestra plays an important part in the production. In military plays the complicated and extremely rapid acrobatic dances, a highly conventionalised form of stage fighting, are regulated in exact accordance with the time given by the orchestra. Any mistake by the musicians might be disastrous, for the actors, whirling long spears and performing somersaults and astonishing leaps at very close quarters, would be thrown into confusion. The musical accompaniment in other plays is intended to symbolise and express

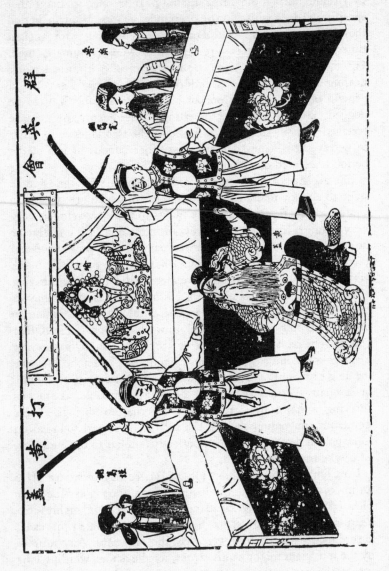

FIG. 58. *Actors in an historical play.*

the emotions which the actors are representing, violent and clamorous to portray anger or passion, soft for grief, or love.

Chinese music, using a different scale from occidental, is not easily appreciated or understood by Europeans. In the theatre two styles are in common use, the old Yüan and Ming Chinese music, called *kuan ch'ü*, which is now being revived, and the *pan tzŭ*, a much more noisy and, in the opinion of the Chinese, vulgar, music, which came into popularity in the Manchu dynasty, especially under the Empress Dowager Tzŭ Hsi. The *pan tzŭ* music, which is Mongolian in origin, was intended for open air performance, and, consequently, when played in a closed theatre, it is quite deafening.

One factor which has hitherto prevented the drama being regarded as an "art" on the same level as poetry or painting is the low social position of actors. As an inevitable consequence of the custom of having female rôles played by youths, actors in general had, and still have, a very poor moral reputation, perversion being openly recognised in theatrical society. The sons of actors were forbidden to sit for the examinations for the public service, and respectable families would not intermarry with stage folk.

In many respects the Chinese theatre of the Yüan and Ming period resembled the early European stage. There was in both an absence of scenery, a prohibition of female acting, an open three-sided stage, and a reliance upon gorgeous costumes to give colour and life to the production. In China the quality of the plays was not improved rapidly as time passed, the theatre remained broadly a popular entertainment, and was not encouraged by the collaboration of writers of genius. Consequently no great progress in production or staging was made. The standard of acting became very high, but the quality of the plays remained second rate, and the production rather primitive. Quite recently there has been a change in these respects. New plays, drawing upon the rich material to be found in some of the best known novels, have been produced and some attempt has been made to improve the production.

These changes can only be made gradually, for the theatre public in China is conservative, and slow to approve of novelties. Even now the orchestra is still accommodated on a corner of the stage itself, unwilling to be banished to a less prominent position. This, indeed, is not the only obstruction to improved production which the Chinese actor or manager encounters. The manners of the audience are very different from those to which the European actor is accustomed. No attempt is made to keep silence during the performance, vendors of sweetmeats, peanuts and melon seeds, cry their wares among the audience, and attendants distribute the steaming towels with which the Chinese playgoer is wont to refresh his face and hands. Since the audience already knows the play, and probably every line in it, this does not cause anyone much inconvenience.

One reason for this inattentive attitude is the length of the performance. Although individual plays are as a rule shorter than western pieces, several plays are put on in succession, and the ardent theatregoer who arrives at four or five in the afternoon need not leave till well after midnight. He would be ill-advised to do so for the best plays and the most celebrated actors only appear at the end of the programme, when the wealthy patrons, having dined leisurely, arrive at the theatre for the concluding plays in which their favourites will perform.

(B) THE NOVEL

The appearance of the prose novel was the most important development in Chinese literature during the Ming period, a development of which the true significance only became apparent in modern times. The Ming novels were the first literature to be written in the *pai hua* or spoken language, the speech of daily use, as opposed to the *wên li* or classical style, which by the Ming period had already long been a dead language. The modern Chinese renaissance movement, which is the most important intellectual manifestation of the Chinese revolution, has adopted the living language of to-day as the medium for all literature, as an essential factor in the spread of education through the mass of the nation. This change would have been very difficult and perhaps far longer delayed if there had not already existed a literature in *pai hua*, which enjoyed an established popularity, particularly among the common people. This old *pai hua* literature consisted almost exclusively of novels, of which the most famous

—with one important exception—were written in the Ming dynasty.

Although the most celebrated works of fiction in Chinese were written centuries ago, it is only in recent times, since the Revolution, that this class of writing has been recognised as literature at all. Under the empire the scholars of Confucian tradition frowned upon all fiction as frivolous, licentious, and subversive. Partly on account of the popular style in which novels were written, and partly by reason of their fictitious character, the official world of learning treated the new literary form with the greatest contempt. It was shameful to admit a liking for novels. No scholar would confess to reading or writing such books except as a trifling amusement, much as an eminent modern statesman might read detective stories. It was the nadir of bad taste to quote a phrase from a novel or make any mention of this vulgar literature in a serious composition. Children, in many homes, were strictly forbidden to read novels, and many men now living can recall being soundly thrashed by parents or tutors when caught reading novels in their boyhood.

In spite of this official contempt the novels of the Ming and Manchu periods were immensely and deservedly popular, were universally read by educated people, and not least by scholars themselves. The petrified tradition of classical scholarship was unable to destroy or resist the charm and freshness of a new and vital form of literature. In one respect, however, the official attitude to novels was truly detrimental. Owing to the contempt and disregard meted out to fiction it is very rarely that anything is known of the authors of the most famous Chinese novels, for, though they were scholars and great artists, they usually wrote under a pseudonym, or even published their works anonymously. Under the empire, novels being regarded as outside the literary pale, no criticism or research could be devoted to them, and the writers of the republic found an almost virgin field before them, when at long last the novel was recognised for what it is, the most vital and original development in Chinese literature of the last 600 years.

The long neglect has now in great measure been repaired, and it is possible to trace the origin and growth of the novel as well as its great influence upon the national culture. Although true novels, written in the living language, and running to some eighty or a hundred chapters, did not appear until the Ming period, there had been earlier fiction, both literary and popular, precursors of the real novels. Under the T'ang dynasty there existed a class of fiction known as Ch'uan Chi, or short stories, written by scholars in the most cultivated classical style, dealing mainly with legendary subjects or single episodes of a romantic or adventurous character. This literature was confined to polite society, and the tales were short, without a sustained plot, or characterisation. Though Ch'uan Chi continued to be written under the Sung, they did not develop, and were often inferior to their T'ang models. Another, ruder and more vital element was needed to give birth to the true novel.

The storyteller, seated at the street corner with his audience of children and idlers, is probably one of the oldest figures in the everyday life of an eastern country. In China he has no doubt exercised his calling for millennia. In the Sung dynasty it seems that the common people, either because they were naturally more frivolous than their ancestors, or perhaps because they were more prosperous and therefore had more time to spare for entertainment, developed a much keener appetite for stories and romantic tales. The storytellers of the Sung period multiplied and made a comfortable living. As the public appetite for its favourite tales was insatiable, the leading points of these stories were written down in everyday language as a professional "libretto" for storytellers who had not yet mastered all the intricacies of a long plot. These précis or guidebooks, were known as *hua pên*, "story roots," and were the real ancestors of the Ming novels.

In the Yüan dynasty many of these *hua pên* were turned into plays, which added precision to their contents, and popularity to the stories themselves. Early in the Ming dynasty scholars began to take the *hua pên* and incorporating the added material evolved in the theatre, re-wrote them in a semi-popular style, more literary than the *hua pên*, but far from the classical style of recognised literature. This was the genesis of the Ming novel.

From their first appearance, in the 15th century, the novels had an immense success. This was no doubt partly due to the ease with which books in the living language could be read by people of little education, but the appeal of the novels went deeper than questions of style. Hitherto all literature, history, and philosophy, had not only been buried in the difficulties of archaic language, but also was presented in coldly restrained terms which excluded all warmth and life. Chinese history might be meticulously accurate, but save in rare passages it was frigidly objective and, moreover, entirely ignored popular customs and common everyday life.

In the new novels the Chinese reader for the first time found a story which was not only easy to read, but also vivid with characteristic touches of real life, warm with passion, and salted with wit and humour. Not only were the novels a new and lively presentation of the dry facts of history—for the early novels were all historical—but under cover of their semi-historical garb they directed telling criticisms against the government of the day and the corruptions of the official world. If this subversive character made them displeasing to authority, it greatly increased their popularity with the governed.

The qualities which made the novels popular with contemporaries are equally those which have made these books valuable to later generations. What history has too often left out, the novels supply. In them we can see something of the real life of the 15th century common people of China, hear them talk, and watch them at their daily work and recreations. It is true that in the novel the characters are supposed to belong to long past ages, the 4th century A.D., or the Sung dynasty, but in actual fact it is the manners and language of contemporary China that the authors described, life as they saw it and as their readers lived it.

In contrast to the wide, indeed, almost universal popularity of the most famous novels, next to nothing is known of their authors, and if some facts have been established, it is only by the exact and painstaking researches of the modern scholars of the republican period, who have completely reversed the old contemptuous attitude of the academic world towards the novels. It would not be possible or desirable to expand this chapter into a treatise on the Chinese novel, or enter into the still vexed problems of authorship and origin. A brief review of four of the most famous and characteristic novels will be given, with an attempt to indicate the nature of the influence they have exerted on Chinese thought and culture.

Although Chinese novels have been classified into some seven or eight types, the broad division is between those which embroider and romanticise facts of recorded history, and works of pure imagination which deal with domestic life or love stories. The first type was the earliest, and the outstanding example, still the most popular book in the Chinese language, is the first novel ever written in China, the *San Kuo Chih Yen I*, or *Popular History of the Three Kingdoms*,* written by Lo Kuan-chung in the early years of the Ming dynasty. Lo himself is also credited with other novels, but if these were really by him, they do not compare favourably with the *San Kuo*.†

The *San Kuo* is a very long book, running to 120 chapters, and covering a period of nearly 100 years, from A.D. 168, when the massacre of the eunuchs heralded the downfall of the Han dynasty, to A.D. 265, when the empire was reunited by the founder of the Tsin dynasty. This troubled and confused period, known as the Three Kingdoms, from the division of the empire which followed the fall of the Han, was in reality an age of treachery, strife and misery (see Chapter XI); but Lo Kuan-chung has transmuted it into a romantic age of chivalry and noble deeds of arms, a colourful pageant which has successfully supplanted the real Three Kingdoms era in the imagination of the people of China.

The heroes of the book, Liu Pei, who founded the Shu Han dynasty in Szechuan, Kuan Chung, who is now the deified Kuan Ti, God of War, and Chang Fei, were, like the chief villain, Ts'ao Ts'ao (who was the father of the first Emperor of the Wei, the northern kingdom), all historical personages.

---

*Translated into English by C. H. Brewitt-Taylor under the title *San Kuo, or Romance of the Three Kingdoms*. 2 Vols. Shanghai. 1925. A complete translation which is never likely to be bettered.

†It was for long believed that Lo Kuan-chung lived and wrote in the Yüan dynasty. Prof. Hu Shih has shown reason to believe that, though Lo was probably born when the Mongols were still on the throne of China, his book was written in the reign of the first Ming Emperor.

In fact, few of the characters, and none of any importance, are creations of Lo Kuan-chung. While the chief characters and the main lines of the story follow authentic history, the author has enlivened the tale by introducing romantic and dramatic adventures which have no such foundation, and has arbitrarily divided his characters into sheep and goats. Ts'ao Ts'ao, who was no more and no less an usurper than Liu Pei, is a double-dyed villain, the arch type of ruthless and unscrupulous schemer, while Liu Pei and his two friends, with their later colleague Chu-k'o Liang, are models of fidelity, courage and honour.

Early in the story a characteristic adventure puts the reader on his guard and stamps Ts'ao Ts'ao for the villain of the piece. Ts'ao Ts'ao is still an unknown adventurer and is in ill favour with the party in power at Court. He is travelling in disguise through the country with a single chance companion, when he lodges for the night at the farm of an old friend and sworn blood brother of his father. His host knows that Ts'ao Ts'ao is a wanted man, but receives the fugitives and goes into the inner part of the house to prepare a meal.

"When he came out, he said: 'There is no good wine in the house, I am going over to the village to get some for you.' And he hastily mounted a donkey and rode away.

"The two travellers sat for a long time. Suddenly they heard at the back of the house the sound of a knife being sharpened. Ts'ao Ts'ao said: 'He is not my real uncle; I am beginning to doubt the meaning of his going off. Let us listen.' So they silently stepped out into the straw hut at the back. Presently someone said:

" 'Bind before killing eh?'

" 'As I thought,' said Ts'ao Ts'ao. 'Now unless we strike first we shall be taken.'

"Immediately they dashed in and slew the whole household, male and female; in all eight persons. After this they searched the house; in the kitchen they found a pig bound ready to kill.

" 'You have made a huge mistake,' said Ch'ên Kung, 'and we have slain honest folk.'

"They at once mounted their horses and rode away. Soon they met their host coming back and over the saddle in front of him two vessels of wine. In his hands he carried fruit and vegetables.

" 'Why are you going sirs?' he called to them.

" 'Accused people dare not linger,' said Ts'ao Ts'ao.

" 'But I have bidden them kill a pig. Why do you refuse my poor hospitality? I pray you ride back with me.'

"Ts'ao Ts'ao paid no heed. Urging his horse forward he suddenly drew his sword and rode after Lu [his would-be host].

"Lu turned and looked back, and at the same instant Ts'ao Ts'ao cut him down. His companion was frightened."

He then upbraids Ts'ao Ts'ao for his treachery, and the argument terminates by Ts'ao Ts'ao's famous epigram:

" 'I would rather betray the whole world than let the world betray me.' "*

The San Kuo is thus an historical romance, "seven parts truth and three parts fiction," as one critic described it, but the author had also a serious purpose. Throughout the long book, the "legitimate monarchy" party, which, in Lo Kuan-chung's opinion, was that of Liu Pei and his friends, is held up to admiration, while the "usurpers," such as Ts'ao Ts'ao, are painted as rogues. The opening phrase of the book, now almost a proverbial saying, sums up the theme of the story, and also aptly epitomises an abiding truth of Chinese history:

"The empire when united, tends to disruption, and when partitioned, strives once more for unity."

Lo Kuan-chung had seen in his own lifetime a period not unlike that of the San Kuo, the confused anarchy of the last years of Mongol rule. He had seen, too, a hero not unlike Liu Pei, who was born in poverty, bring order out of chaos and found the Ming dynasty. Writing in the first peaceful years of that dynasty, when the Emperor was powerful and the administration vigorous, it was natural that Lo exalted the government and reviled the rebels and bandits—even though the government and rebels he described were those of a long past age. His book therefore represents the feelings of educated people in the early Ming

*C. H. Brewitt-Taylor. *op. cit.* pp. 41, 42.

period, relief at the ending of civil wars, and a firm belief in a strong centralised government.

Very different was the attitude of the second great Ming novel, the *Shui Hu*, a title which is not easily translated, but which means the "The Story of the Fringes of the Marsh."* This book in its earliest form was also attributed to Lo Kuan-chung, but it was re-shaped in the early 16th century by a certain "Shih Nai-an," a pseudonym, which conceals the identity of some scholar of that age.† This is the edition, in seventy chapters, which is now generally accepted as the best of the many versions which have appeared at different periods. If the *San Kuo* can be compared to the Morte d'Arthur of Malory (with the difference that the personages in the Chinese novel had a real recorded historical existence) the *Shui Hu* is a saga similar to the cycle of Robin Hood tales, worked up into a novel centring round the personality of Sung Chiang, a bandit leader who lived in Shantung in the last years of the Sung dynasty, immediately before the Kin invasions (*circa* 1000.).

Sung Chiang is an historical character, but, apart from a brief mention of his ravages in the provinces of Honan and Shantung, and his thirty-six companions, nothing else is known of his life, or his end. It is certain that long before the Ming dynasty a cycle of tales dealing with this band had been current among the people, and had found its way into stage plays during the Yüan dynasty. It was not until the Ming dynasty that the saga took shape as a novel. It is in many ways a more important book than the *San Kuo* and enjoys a popularity hardly second to the earlier novel. The *Shui Hu* is written in pure *pai hua*, that is to say in the actual everyday speech of the 15th century; and as the style of the *San Kuo* still retains many classicisms, the importance of the *Shui Hu* as evidence of the development of the language, and its influence on subsequent *pai hua* literature cannot be over-estimated.

*Recently translated into English by Pearl S. Buck, under the title, *All Men are Brothers*. 1933.

†Such is the opinion of Prof. Hu Shih, who has devoted a long study to the problem of the authorship and development of the various versions of the Shui Hu, and printed his conclusions in a preface to the new edition published by the Ya Tung T'u Shu Kuan, at Shanghai 1923. It was formerly believed that Shih Nai-an was a scholar of the Yüan period, but this opinion is no longer tenable.

The merits and interest of the *Shui Hu* are not, however, merely matters of style and language. The story relates the adventures and exploits of the 108 companions of Sung Chiang, and the plot, unwinding from chapter to chapter, tells how each of these men came to "hide in the grass" (become an outlaw) and join the band on the mountain fastness of Liang Shan Po. Throughout the book it is the bandits who are the heroes; courageous, loyal, and honourable men, while the officials, ministers, and princes of the Sung dynasty are uniformly represented as vile oppressors, sordid scoundrels, and degenerate cowards.

The *Shui Hu* is thus a frankly revolutionary book, and it is not surprising that the government of the Ming, and later Manchu, dynasties, frowned upon it. One and all the bandit heroes are driven to outlawry by the gross injustice of the officials and the cupidity of the Court; they are honest men, with no thought of crime in their heads until they suffer unbearable wrongs. Then, indeed, once outlaws, they avenge their miseries upon the officials, over whom, and the cowardly soldiers of the government, they score easy triumphs. Professor Hu Shih has justly remarked that such a book could only have been produced, and won universal popularity, in an age when the government was bad and weak, for its pungent criticisms are really directed not against the "Sung" dynasty, which had long since disappeared, but against the actual Ming government of the later 15th and early 16th centuries.

To the European reader, the *Shui Hu* has perhaps its tedious passages. The frequent descriptions of single combats and ambuscades are rather unsophisticated. In compensation there are innumerable pieces of lifelike description of everyday scenes on the great roads and in the wayside inns of the empire. The reader who knows interior China, even to-day, will find himself at home in the *Shui Hu*, and, when travelling in China, would hardly be surprised to meet Sung Chiang on some lonely mountain pass.

The characterisation of the 108 bandits and their enemies, the officials, as well as of a host of minor characters, is never conventional or stereotyped. Each and every man has his quality clearly defined, and his acts and speech are appropriate to him and to him alone. Moreover, the *Shui Hu* affords a more intimate picture of life than that given in the *San Kuo*. In the earlier novel the personages are princes and generals of great power and authority, and the author kept closely to the historical facts known about them. The author of the *Shui Hu*, on the other hand, had no such limitations. Sung Chiang, though historical, was a shadowy figure, and could be endowed with a character to suit the author's fancy. His followers are men of the people, some gross country louts, others ex-soldiers, petty officials, or small landowners.

One of the bandits, Wu Sung, has become a Buddhist priest to escape detection, and is wandering through the country in this disguise. As he was formerly a military officer, Wu Sung finds the Buddhist rule forbidding a priest to eat meat or drink wine very irksome. At a wayside inn he has been refused meat, and served only with the regulation vegetable dish, although a guest who arrives later, obtains both meat and wine. Wu Sung watches him eating a hearty meal and cannot restrain his envy.

"Then he saw the keeper of the shop go again into the kitchen, and he saw the man bring out upon the palm of one hand a tray whereon were a pair of cooked chickens and a great plate of lean meat, and these he put before that fellow. On the table he placed other vegetables also, and he took a dipper and went several times to dip up wine and heated it. Now Wu the priest looked and he saw before him only this small saucer of vegetable food and, in spite of himself, he could not keep down his anger; although his eyes feasted his belly starved, and the heat of the wine came up in him, and he longed to break the table apart with one blow of his fist. He shouted out in a mighty voice: 'Keeper, come here. How can you deceive a guest like this?' Then the keeper came in great haste and he asked: 'Master, do not make trouble here, if you want wine, then say so.' But Wu the priest stretched wide his two eyes and shouted out: 'You thing that knows no reason! Why should you not sell me this green flowered jar of wine and these fowls and the like? I would pay you with silver also.' The keeper of the shop replied: 'The green flowered jar of wine and the fowls and meat were all sent from the home of that young lord, and he only sits in my shop and feasts on his own food.' Now, Wu the priest longed much in his heart to eat, and so how could he be willing to listen to this explanation? He bellowed forth: 'Pass your wind, pass your wind' [a vulgar expression for 'don't talk nonsense']. The keeper of the shop said: 'I have never seen such a priest as you and so savage as this.' Then Wu shouted out: 'And how is this lord savage; have I eaten your wares and paid you nothing?' The keeper of the shop muttered: 'I have never heard of a priest calling himself a lord.'"

Wu Sung then knocks the shop-keeper down and the other guest intervenes in the quarrel:

" 'You accursed old priest; how little do you fulfil your duty. How is it that you put out your hand and foot to fight? Do you not know priests may not give way to anger?' Wu, the priest, answered: 'I did but beat him and what has that got to do with you?' That big fellow spoke in wrath and cried: 'I exhorted you out of good purpose and you accursed priest dare to come and offend me with your speech.' When Wu heard this he was very wroth and pushed over the table, came out and shouted: 'Of whom do you speak you thing?' That big fellow laughed and said: 'Accursed priest that you are, you seek a quarrel with me—you are stirring the earth over the earth god's head, you thievish priest come out, and I will talk with you.' "*

The point of this passage is the very unpriestly conduct of Wu Sung, for anyone acquainted with China will recognise the normal behaviour of an undisciplined soldier in an inn.

Both the *San Kuo* and the *Shui Hu* enjoy an immense popularity with the Chinese people, and it is from these two books, and the many plays based upon them, that the common people have derived most of their ideas of past history. There is hardly any man in China who has not heard these stories, even if he cannot read them himself. In Szechuan, where much of the plot of the *San Kuo* is laid, it would be true to say that the characters of that

*Pearl S. Buck. *op. cit.*

novel are more real to the people than their present rulers, and the events of 1500 years ago more vivid than recent history. Ignored by the scholars, whose classical literature was far above the heads of the masses, the Ming novels created a popular literature which has had a far-reaching influence on the Chinese people in the last 500 years.

The popularity of the *Shui Hu* led to the publication of many "continuations," most of which are far from having the value of the original. One novel which grew out of the *Shui Hu* cycle marks an important advance, and is the first example of a new type of story. The *Chin P'ing Mei*, a title which, being a compound of the names of the three heroines, is quite untranslatable,* was written in the first years of the 17th century by an unknown scholar, though it is believed that it was the anonymous work of Wang Shih-chên, a celebrated writer of that period who lived between 1526-1593, and rose to be President of the Board of Punishments, or Minister of Justice.

The book is an expansion of Chapters 23, 24 and 25 of the *Shui Hu*, which relate the story of how Wu Sung, one of the heroes of the *Shui Hu*, mentioned above, came to be a bandit. In the original book, Wu Sung, a petty officer of the city guard, discovers that his sister-in-law has committed adultery with a rich man of the town, and poisoned her husband to escape detection. Through the assistance of a little boy, who sells pears on the streets, Wu Sung lays a trap for the lovers, and, having obtained convincing proof of the woman's crimes, wreaks a terrible vengeance upon her and her paramour. After this, to escape the consequences of his act, he takes to the hills.

The *Ching P'ing Mei* takes up the story at the point where Golden Lotus, the adulteress, makes the acquaintance of Hsi-mên Ch'ing, the rich young wastrel. Following the original plot, it recounts the murder of Wu the Elder, Golden Lotus's husband, but when Wu Sung returns to the town and hears the truth, the story is changed. Golden Lotus has become the concubine of Hsi-mên Ch'ing, and Wu Sung fails in his first plan to exact

---

*There exists a partial translation of this work in French, under the title *Lotus d'or*, by G. Soulié. A complete translation has been made into English by F. C. C. Egerton (Routledge).

vengeance, and is exiled for the attempted murder of Hsi-mên Ch'ing. Then the *Chin P'ing Mei* takes the story into the home of Hsi-mên Ch'ing, where Golden Lotus is now established as his concubine.

From this point the *Chin P'ing Mei* is entirely original, and develops into a story wholly unlike the historical romances which had preceded it. In those novels the few feminine characters are stiff and conventional figures, playing only a minor rôle. In the *Chin P'ing Mei* on the contrary, it is Golden Lotus, and her two rivals in the harem, the principal wife of Hsi-mên Ch'ing and another concubine, who are the chief characters. The story is one of domestic life in a middle-class family in some small provincial town. Hsi-mên Ch'ing, though well to do, is a medicine merchant by profession, and scholarly ambitions and official life do not play any part in this novel.

The plot is concerned with the intrigues of the three women for the favour of their husband, their mutual jealousies, and the daily incidents of life in this class of society. It is only at the very end of the book, when Hsi-mên Ch'ing himself is dead, that the story returns to the original plot of the *Shui Hu*, and relates the return of Wu Sung from exile and the vengeance which he exacts on his brother's murderess. Until recent times western writers who had noticed the book, loudly condemned the *Chin P'ing Mei* as a licentious, almost pornographic novel. It is true that there are some passages which could not be rendered into a European language without incurring the charge of obscenity, but the undue emphasis paid to this aspect of the *Chin P'ing Mei*, especially by missionary writers, does an injustice to the real merits of the *Chin P'ing Mei* and its importance in the development of the Chinese novel. If this book is indecent in parts, it is only because, telling a story of domestic life, it leaves out nothing. In those passages where 19th century writers were wont to pause and insert three stars, the *Chin P'ing Mei* proceeds with the narrative undismayed, nor is the erotic side of the book emphasised at the expense of the story as a whole. In the *Chin P'ing Mei* the plot is not twisted to present as many erotic scenes as possible, it merely presents a balanced, if exceedingly frank, picture of human relationships.

As a step in the progress of the Chinese novel its significance is great. For the first time feminine characters are given a rôle of equal importance to the men and drawn with skill and sympathy. Moreover in place of the somewhat wearisome recurrence of combats and warlike exploits which occupy a large place in the *San Kuo* and *Shui Hu*, the *Chin P'ing Mei* is uniquely concerned with the peaceful and obscure lives of a middle-class family, and it is the clash of temperaments and characters which provides the material for the plot.

The *Chin P'ing Mei* had to wait many years for a rival in the new field of domestic stories. In the Ming dynasty several novels of this type were indeed produced, and they mark a certain advance in other respects, introducing characters of more refinement than are found in the *Chin P'ing Mei*, but on the other hand losing much of the truth and realism which characterised the earlier novel. Such books as the *Yu Chiao Li* and the *Hao Ch'iu Chuan** have their good points, but the characterisation, particularly of the hero and heroine, is too conventional and formal to be convincing. The young scholar, to whom no feat of arms or of poetic composition presents any difficulty, and who is invariably first on the list at the examinations, is in the end, after many vicissitudes and adventures, happily married to the radiant heroine, for whom, equally, no art or poetry has any difficulties. The chief merit of these stories is that when not dealing with the hero or heroine they do present a lively and agreeable picture of the intrigues and machinations of official life in and about the Court.

These stories may be said to have prepared the public taste for the greatest of all Chinese novels, which though not written in the Ming dynasty, sums up and surpasses the achievement of the preceding two centuries. The *Hung Lou Mêng*, usually rendered as *The Dream in the Red Chamber*, was written in the middle of the 18th century, and therefore belongs to the Manchu period, with which, in fact, it deals. Like the *Chin P'ing Mei* it is entirely concerned with the affairs of one family, and among the chief characters women are prominent.

*The first has been translated into French under the title *Les Deux Cousines*, by S. Julien; and the second into English as *The Fortunate Union*, by J. F. Davis. 1829. This translation is incomplete.

For many years the authorship of this novel was a mystery, and even in modern times several theories have held the field, both as to the identity of the author and the purpose and "hidden meaning" of the book. It was widely believed to be a satire on the youth of some great personage, one of the most popular theories being that it was an unfriendly account of the boyhood of the Emperor K'ang Hsi. These theories, however attractive to lovers of scandal, must now be discarded. Professor Hu Shih has shown overwhelming proof of his conclusion that the first eighty chapters are the work of Ts'ao Hsueh-ch'in and the last forty that of Kao Ou. The first author, who may be regarded as the real designer of the book, was the impoverished scion of a great family, Chinese by race, but enrolled in one of the two Chinese Banners of the Manchu military organisation.*

The Ts'ao family had enjoyed honours and wealth at the beginning of the Manchu dynasty, they had even entertained the Emperor K'ang Hsi himself when he was making a progress in Chekiang province. By the time, however, that Ts'ao Hsueh-ch'in wrote his masterpiece, this wealth had been dissipated. He himself lived almost in squalor in a back street of Peking, and his book was written in these circumstances to commemorate his own youth and the fallen fortunes of his family.

The *Hung Lou Mêng* is autobiographical. Precious Jade, the boy hero of the story, is, in fact, Ts'ao Hsueh-ch'in himself as he remembered his boyhood, or perhaps as he would like to have pictured himself; and the great family of Chia in which the story passes is the Ts'ao family on the eve of its decadence. The *Hung Lou Mêng* is in every way a unique book. No Chinese novel can compare with it, either for the grace and refinement of the language—which is none the less *pai hua*, the spoken Mandarin of Peking—or for the subtle characterisation and artistic integrity of the plot. It is true that these qualities are somewhat diminished in the concluding chapters, Kao Ou's continuation, which however, though not up to the level of the first part of

*The Eight Banners were instituted before the conquest of China. Six were reserved for the Manchus, and the two Chinese Banners were enrolled from those Chinese who submitted to, or voluntarily joined the Manchus before the fall of the Ming dynasty. The Ts'ao family therefore belonged to this class.

the book, are a meritorious piece of work, following, there is some reason to believe, the lines of the plot indicated by the original author.

The hero of the *Hung Lou Mêng* is Pao Yü, Precious Jade, the second son of a great official and hereditary duke, who is drawn as a correct but somewhat limited Confucian scholar, a true type of the high official class. Pao Yü, however, is anything but the model of filial piety and scholarly industry which a Chinese boy of that class and age was supposed to be. On the contrary, though handsome and intelligent in his own way, he is idle and indifferent to classical studies, at which he makes poor progress. He is also frequently in trouble for his rather precocious interest in frivolous entertainments and his preference for the company of his girl cousins, and indeed for female society in general. Pao Yü, in fact, has the artistic temperament, and a natural gift for poetry which is not exaggerated into a divine inspiration as in earlier novels.

The plot of the story, as developed in the first eighty chapters and continued by Kao Ou, is the love of Pao Yü for his cousin Lin Tai Yü (Black Jade), who, left an orphan in childhood, comes to live in the Chia family under the care of her grandmother, the old Lady Chia, benevolent but autocratic ruler of the household. The old lady is indeed one of the most successful and delightful creations in the book. She is the very type of the old ladies who rule Chinese households with an iron rod of convention, yet fondly indulge the weaknesses of their favourite grandchildren.

The girls, Black Jade, and another cousin, Pao Ch'ai, who also comes to live in the great mansion of the Chia family, are drawn with skill and real understanding. Though beautiful, elegant and well educated, they are no prodigies, and the tragedy of their fate—marriage to an unknown man, of a strange family, without their consent or foreknowledge—is feelingly revealed. In this respect the *Hung Lou Mêng* is epoch making. It is the first open revolt against the tyranny of the old marriage customs. The author is too much an artist to rail. He shows the parents of Pao Yü, and guardians of Black Jade as essentially human, well meaning, conventional people, anxious to arrange marriages for their children which will secure the prosperity of the family, without sacrificing the happiness of the parties by some ill-assorted match. Black Jade is too delicate—she is threatened with consumption—and Pao Yü is married, against his will, to Pao Ch'ai, the other cousin. Black Jade, believing herself deliberately forsaken by her lover, dies almost unattended on his wedding night.

The tragic element provided by the frustrated love of Pao Yü and Black Jade is only one aspect, and perhaps not the most important, of this book. The real plot is the conflict of the artistic temperament, personified in the wayward and morally weak Pao Yü, and the stern, matter of fact world of reality and convention. It is a remarkable fact that, considering the period in which it was written, a period when children were rarely seen and never heard, Ts'ao Hsueh-ch'in makes his hero a boy only twelve years old at the beginning of the story, and not yet adult at the end. The heroines, Black Jade and Pao Ch'ai, are about the same age.

Although the *Hung Lou Mêng* is partly autobiographical, re-calling scenes and persons known to the author in his boyhood, the real aim of the book is a criticism of the rite-bound society of 18th century China and the Confucian philosophy which dominated it. It is subtle criticism, for the author never openly takes the side of art and liberty against convention and industry, but exposes his idea by implication, enlisting the reader's sym-pathy for Pao Yü, while apparently condemning his faults and misbehaviour. Ts'ao Hsueh-ch'in's outlook is more clearly ex-pressed in the passages dealing with the Buddhist priests who make an occasional, but always highly significant, appearance in the story. The sharp contrast between the worldly atmosphere of the great Chia mansion and these wandering mendicants, who have renounced all possessions and every human contact, is always in favour of the latter. There is therefore good reason to suppose that the conclusion of the novel—in which Pao Yü abandons his family to enter the "gate of emptiness"—the Buddhist church—was really in accordance with the intention of the author.

The *Hung Lou Mêng* is considered to be a masterpiece of style, although the many passages of dialogue are written in the colloquial speech of north China, and the phraseology is natural and appropriate to the speakers. The following extract, from the twentieth chapter, is typical. Although they are still children, Black Jade is becoming jealous of Pao Ch'ai, and is secretly annoyed when Pao Yü pays any attention to the rival. During the New Year holiday (a festive time corresponding in China to the western Christmas), Pao Yü has been visiting Pao Ch'ai in the apartments where she and her mother lodge in the great Chia mansion. They are called away to meet a visitor who has come to see the old Lady Chia, Pao Yü's grandmother and head of the whole household. Black Jade is already there when they arrive, and guesses that Pao Yü has been with Pao Ch'ai:

"Just then Black Jade, who was standing close by, asked where Pao Yü had been. Pao Yü himself replied: 'I have come from Pao Ch'ai's rooms.' Black Jade smiled coldly, and said: 'I should say so. When you are not actually tangled up there, then you have just flown away for a moment.'

"Pao Yü said: 'So I am only allowed to play with you, and amuse you when you are sad? If by chance I go over to her for once, then you talk like this.'

"Black Jade said: 'What utter nonsense. Why should I care whether you go or not?—and I never asked you to come and cheer me up when I was sad. After this please leave me alone.'

"So saying she swallowed her anger and went back to her own rooms.

"Pao Yü hurried after her, pleading: 'Dearest, angry again? It's just because I was rude; surely you will come back and join the fun with the others for a bit? Or are you yourself unhappy?'

"Black Jade replied: 'Are you giving me orders?'

"Pao Yü laughed, saying: 'Certainly I would never dare to give you orders; only you are trampling upon your own body.'

"Black Jade said: 'Trampling on my own body! If I kill myself what business is it of yours?'

"Pao Yü said: 'What's the use? In the First Month, even the dead live.'

"Black Jade retorted: 'I *shall* talk of death. This time I really will die. If you fear death, how will you live to be a hundred?'

"Pao Yü said, laughing, 'If there is going to be nothing but quarrels like this, am I likely still to fear death? Stone dead would be far better.'

" Black Jade answered quickly: 'Just so. If this sort of quarrelling goes on, better be stone dead.'

"Pao Yü said: 'I spoke of my being stone dead; I did not mean anyone else.' "

It will be seen that Tsao Hsueh-ch'in has skilfully portrayed the illogical and inconsequent character of an argument between two children.

Chapter XXVI

ARCHITECTURE

ARCHITECTURE in China is associated with the Ming period, not only because the art was greatly developed under that dynasty, but because very few existing buildings or monuments are of earlier date. The Ming Emperors were great builders, reconstructing and embellishing cities and temples; their work survives, while that of their predecessors, which was possibly just as magnificent, has disappeared.

Unlike the ancient civilisations of the Near East, China has no architectural monuments of the remote past. The early Chinese built in wood and mud bricks, materials which have not survived the ravages of time. With the exception of the tomb chambers buried in huge tumuli there are no surviving edifices of the Feudal Age, nor even of the Han dynasty. The Great Wall, though built by the Ch'in Emperor, Shih Huang Ti, has so often been repaired that the existing structure owes its outward form to later builders. Only shapeless earthen mounds mark the site of the T'ang palaces at Ch'ang An and Lo Yang. The earliest Buddhist foundations, such as the White Horse Monastery at Lo Yang and the Ta Yen monastery outside Ch'ang An, though still occupying the original sites, have frequently been rebuilt, and with the exception of a few pagodas of T'ang date, the existing structures are Ming work.

Any study of the history and development of Chinese architecture is therefore seriously hampered by a lack of materials. Fortunately, literary sources and archæological finds have in some measure filled the gap, particularly the discovery of Han clay model dwellings and bas-reliefs depicting buildings. These finds supply a clear idea of the design and style of Han domestic architecture, for the models were tomb furniture intended to supply the spirit of the deceased with a habitation in the next world similar in all respects to the one in which he had lived on earth. A simple form of spirit-house is represented by the green glazed model of Han date reproduced in Fig. 59. The bas-reliefs show typical buildings of the day, with domestic scenes

FIG. 59. *Han clay model of a house.*

in the kitchen, the women's apartments, and the banqueting hall.

The clay models prove that, with some minor exceptions, the Chinese domestic architecture of the Han period was almost identical with that of the present day, both in plan and style. The Han house, like its modern successor, was arranged in a series of courtyards flanked and faced by detached halls, which are sub-divided into smaller rooms. The high-pitched roof supported on columns and roofed with tiles is similar to that of the modern house, although the concave curve of the roof appears to be less marked in the models than in existing buildings. Here, perhaps, there has been a change, but the evidence of clay models is not absolutely conclusive.

In minor features and details of ornamentation the clay model houses from Han tombs closely resemble existing styles. The main entrance is defended on the inside by a spirit screen, a wall built opposite the opening in such a way as to block out any view of the inside courtyard. The purpose of the spirit screen is to prevent evil spirits from entering the house. According to Chinese demonology, devils can only move in straight lines, therefore this device is a perfect safeguard against their intrusion into the house. The Han models prove that this belief and the custom of building spirit screens are at least as old as the first century of the Christian era.

This type of house has no doubt continued unchanged because it was perfectly adapted to the social conditions of Chinese life. A Chinese home was intended to be the common dwelling-place of a very large family, and the several collateral branches of the family each inhabited a separate courtyard, a system which combined a necessary separation of possibly incompatible relations with the ruling ideal of unity under the paternal sway of the head of the family. Consequently all Chinese houses, small and great, were planned in the same way. From the small country farm or humble town dwelling of the people, with only one court-yard, to the vast and spacious palaces well called "palace cities," the plan was always the same, the courtyard unit multiplied and enlarged until it reached imperial dimensions. A good example is afforded by the Confucian temple at Chu Fou, the birthplace of the Sage, of which a plan as popularly sold, is shown in Fig. 60.

Clay models and the bas-reliefs afford some idea of the plan and style of the better class of houses in Han times, but only a literary description remains to attest the magnificence of the imperial palaces of the early empire. The site of Ch'in Shih Huang Ti's palace at Hsien Yang in Shensi has been identified, but as yet no scientific excavation has been attempted. Ssŭ-ma Ch'ien gives a description of this palace in his history, which, though written a century after the fall of the Ch'in Empire and the destruction of Hsien Yang, no doubt embodies the traditional account of its glory.

"Shih Huang, considering that the population of Hsien Yang, was large and that the palace of the kings his predecessors was small . . . began the construction of a palace for audiences, to the south of the Wei River in the midst of the Shang Lin Park. He first built the main hall. It measured from east to west [length], 500 paces, and from north to south 100 paces. Ten thousand men could find room in it and standards 50 feet high could be raised up. There was a circular riding road on a raised way [round the courtyard]. From the front of the hall a road led in a straight line to the Nan Shan Mountain, and on

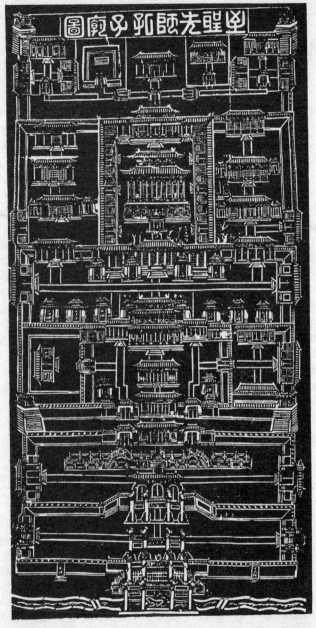

FIG. 60. *Pictorial plan of the Confucian Temple at Chu Fou, Shantung.*

the crest of the mountain a ceremonial arch was erected as a gateway. A covered way led from the palace across the Wei River to Hsien Yang city. It symbolised the bridge T'ien Chi which crosses the Milky Way to the constellation Ying Chê."

Ssǔ-ma Ch'ien also says that Shih Huang Ti had erected, along the banks of the Wei river, copies of the palaces of all the kings whom he had conquered and despoiled. In these palaces the harems of the conquered monarchs and all the treasures and furniture of the originals were kept ready for a visit from the Emperor. Not content with these sumptuous buildings, Shih Huang Ti constructed several summer palaces and hunting lodges in the vicinity of Hsien Yang, and linked them together with covered ways and roads bordered with walls, so that he could pass from one to the other without his movements being known.

The traditional account of Shih Huang Ti's palace may be somewhat exaggerated, but it is clear that under the new empire architecture received a strong impulse and buildings were conceived on a scale hitherto unknown. It was because Shih Huang Ti found the palace of his ancestors small that he built one more in consonance with his power and ambitions. The palaces of the conquered kings which were copied upon the banks of the Wei, were no doubt also on a modest scale. An anecdote recounted by Chuang Tzǔ, some two hundred years before Shih Huang Ti's time, tends to show that the palaces of the feudal princes were quite modest dwellings. This is the story of Prince Wên Hui's cook, who applied Taoist principles to the domestic duty of cutting up a bullock. The Prince, delighted with his skill, was watching the operation from the hall of his palace. It is plain therefore that the cook was preparing the meat in the main courtyard in front of the Hall of Audience, which suggests that the palace of the Prince must have closely resembled the homely arrangements of a prosperous modern Chinese farm house. Even if Chuang Tzǔ invented the story to point a moral, it is none the less clear that the possibility of a Prince being able to observe the domestic activities of his cook from the audience chamber did not appear incongruous to men of the Feudal Age.

Fortunately we have other evidence of the building activities of the Ch'in period. The Great Wall, though often repaired and refaced, was planned and linked together by Shih Huang Ti; although probably only the core of the modern wall is Ch'in work, the design and the trace of the wall were planned by the great Emperor, and subsequent generations have only restored or maintained his monument. Anyone who has seen this stupendous fortification following the crests of precipitous mountains, scaling the steepest slopes, curving and winding among the barren hills of North China for hundreds of miles, will not find it difficult to believe in the splendours of the Hsien Yang palaces.

Apart from the remains of the earthen mounds which formed the terraces, nothing survives of the Han, Sui and T'ang palaces at Ch'ang An and Lo Yang. There exist, however, literary sources giving the plans and dimensions of the two capitals of the T'ang dynasty, Ch'ang An and Lo Yang. From these sources it is possible to obtain a clear idea of the design of the great buildings of the capital, and the plan of the city itself. In the T'ang period Ch'ang An was a very large city, covering an area several times as great as the modern town of Sianfu, which is built on the site of the Imperial City of T'ang times, and incorporates the south and west wall of the 7th century capital.

The general design is reminiscent of the plan of Peking, proving that the Ming Emperors were using a city plan which was already of great antiquity. (Map 16). As in Peking, the plan of Ch'ang An (see Map 9) was rectangular, the city itself enclosing a smaller walled area, called the Imperial City, in which the officials and members of the Imperial clan had their residences. The Palace City, corresponding to the Forbidden City of Peking, was situated inside the Imperial City, but unlike Peking, at Ch'ang An the Palace City was not in the centre of the Imperial City, but occupied its northern half, sharing a common north wall with the two larger cities surrounding it. Beyond this north wall was a vast Imperial Park, the Chin Yüan, or Forbidden Garden, in which, at a later date, the Emperor T'ai Tsung built another Palace City, called the Ta Ming Kung, detached from the general design. The plan of these buildings exactly corresponds to their

successors at Peking, and is in fact the original Chinese courtyard house on a very large scale.*

The descriptions and plans of Ch'ang An as it was under the
Sui and T'ang dynasties prove that in Peking the Ming Emperor
Yung Lo, who built the city as it now stands (Map 16), was
copying, with slight modifications, an ancient city plan, probably
dating back far earlier than the T'ang period. If the Ming builders
showed no originality in design their work was none the less a
masterpiece. An important innovation, the coloured porcelain
tiles which are such a distinctive and beautiful feature of the
palace roofs at Peking, is found in Ming buildings intended for
imperial use, and on some temples. This feature was a consequence
of the improved technique in glazing and porcelain manufacture.
In the grace and strength of their lines and the harmonious
grouping of the buildings themselves the Ming architects cannot
easily have been surpassed in any previous age.

The Forbidden City—Tzŭ Chin Ch'êng, the Purple Forbidden
City, is the full name—is a rectangular enclosure, defended by a
crenellated wall and wide moat, standing almost exactly in the
centre of the city of Peking itself. There are four gates, three
of which, in the south, east and west walls open into the grand
courtyards flanked by the halls of audience and official buildings
which occupy the southern half of the enclosure. This part of
the palace was accessible to ministers and officials for audience
with the Emperor and for official ceremonies and functions. The
northern gate opens directly into the private part of the palace,
occupied by the Imperial family and concubines, to which no
one except the eunuchs had access.

The southern half is arranged in a series of spacious courtyards
faced by magnificent halls and gateways, a perfectly symmetrical
and harmonious grouping designed for ceremonial occasions,
and well calculated to impress the visitors with a sense of the
power and splendour of the Son of Heaven. The northern half
of the palace, divided from the ceremonial courts by a continuous
wall, is arranged on a more intimate plan. These residential
quarters are cut up into a maze of courtyards, gardens and alley-

*Map 9 reproduced from the two Chinese books dealing with the T'ang
capitals, the *Ch'ang An chih* and *T'ang liang ching Ch'eng fang K'ao*

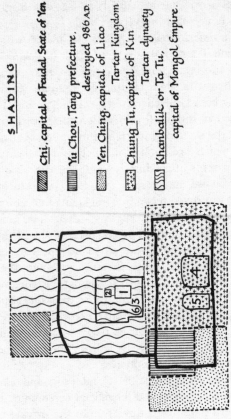

MAP 16. *Peking, and Cities formerly upon the same Site.*

PEKING
and cities formerly on the
same site.

SHADING

▨ Chi, capital of Feudal State of Yen.

▥ Yu Chou, Tang prefecture.
destroyed 986 A.D.

▢ Yen Ching, capital of Liao
Tartar Kingdom

▦ Chung Tu, capital of Kin
Tartar dynasty

▧ Khambalik or Ta Tu,
capital of Mongol Empire.

LEGEND

Heavy Black line = Walls of Peking
(Ming, Manchu
and present day)

1 - Forbidden City
2 - Coal Hill.
3 - Imperial City.
4 - Temple of Heaven.
5 - Temple of Agriculture.
6 - Lakes.

ways, a complexity of buildings in which the imperial family and the concubines each had their own separate apartments. Here symmetry and grandeur give place to domestic convenience.

The emperors of the Ming and Manchu dynasties, who successively lived in this palace for over 500 years, did not all occupy the same apartments. As fancy pleased them, or in the belief that one part of the palace had become "unlucky," they moved to different courts, and sometimes sealed up and abandoned the quarters of their predecessors. Princess Der Ling, who was a maid of honour to the Empress Dowager Tzŭ Hsi, records how on one occcasion the Empress making a tour of inspection, found a range of buildings which had been sealed and disused for so long that weeds and bushes almost choked the approaches. On enquiry it was found that no one knew the reason why this palace had been closed up, though it was conjectured that some member of the imperial family had died there of an infectious disease. No one then in the palace had ever been inside the deserted court.*

In spite of the variety and extent of the residential quarters in the Forbidden City itself, the emperors found the close air of the city in the summer months unhealthy. From very early times the custom of moving the Court out to a summer palace in the vicinity of the capital had been followed, and the construction of these less formal residences called into existence a rather different architectural style. Ch'in Shih Huang Ti, as has been mentioned, built many summer palaces, which were at the same time hunting lodges, in the vast parks which he maintained round his capital. The Han and T'ang Emperors, and in particular the extravagant builder Sui Yang Ti, followed his example, and though no traces of these buildings and gardens remain, the description of them which historians have preserved show that they must have been planned on the same lines as Ch'ien Lung's Yüan Ming Yüan, about ten miles from Peking, a vast park containing many palaces and pavilions which was destroyed by the British and French armies in 1860. The existing Summer Palace, a partial restoration of the Yüan Ming Yüan, made by

*Two Years in the Forbidden City. Princess Der Ling. London. 1912. p. 318.

the Empress Dowager in the 'nineties gives but a faint and imperfect idea of the original.

Just as grandeur and formality combined into a symmetrical harmony was the keynote of the formal Palace Cities of which the Forbidden City in Peking is the last representative, in the summer palaces the architects sought informality, charm, and an artificially enhanced ruralty. Where lakes or hills were lacking, they were constructed at immense cost and labour to provide every form of natural scenery and variety. Trees were planted, or transplanted, as by Sui Yang Ti who caused well grown forest trees to be brought on specially constructed carts from distant forests. A delicious landscape was fashioned which excelled in charm and unexpected beauty anything which unaided nature could provide, and imitated the scenery of the landscape painters. Among the woods and streams, on the edges of lakes, and the slopes of the hills pavilions designed to harmonise with their surroundings were scattered in apparently haphazard, but really carefully planned design—each was self-contained, so that the imperial owner could move from one to another as caprice moved him, and find everything prepared for his reception.

The splendours of these imperial pleasaunces were reproduced, on a more restricted scale in the gardens of the wealthy families, both in the city and in the neighbourhood. No people—except the English—have been more successful in the art of creating gardens and country residences than the Chinese, and the success of the two peoples at this art is due to like cause. The Chinese, in spite of their large and populous cities, have always been closely in touch with rural life, always in love with natural beauty. From an early date the belief in the purifying moral effect of living in lonely and remote mountain country was strong in China. Taoist sages withdrew to the forest-clad slopes of the higher mountains and refused to descend even to share the highest honours offered by the emperors. Many of the best known scholars and poets lived for years in the depths of the country, rarely visiting the cities. The horror of wild scenery, which was so characteristic of Europeans in the 17th and 18th centuries, was never shared by the Chinese.

The introduction of Buddhism does not seem to have effected

any major change in the design of Chinese temples. Taoist and Buddhist temples are built upon the same plan, which is precisely that of the Chinese house, modified for religious purposes. The courtyard arrangement, with flanking halls is the same as in the residential houses, the main halls in the front courts being assigned to the worship of the gods, or the Buddha, while the domestic quarters at the rear of the temple are the residential apartments of the monks. In the decoration and ornamentation of the principal halls some motifs have been introduced which are of Buddhist origin and show the influence of Greco-Indian art, particularly the caryatides supporting the roofs in the K'ai Yüan Ssŭ temple in Ch'üan Chou, Fukien.*

Although the existing buildings of the K'ai Yüan Ssŭ are Ming (A.D. 1389) the temple was founded in the T'ang dynasty. It is therefore very probable that the caryatides now existing were copied from the earlier T'ang structure, a period in which foreign influences were strong.

The pagoda, usually regarded as the most characteristic Chinese type of structure, has been conjectured to be of Indian origin. There is, however, very little resemblance between the Indian stupa monument on its low base and the lofty Chinese pagoda. Although the latter is now only found at Buddhist temples its true origin would seem to be the pre-Buddhistic Chinese storied tower, shown in Han bas-reliefs as flanking the main hall of important buildings, of which a sketch is reproduced in Fig. 61.

These Han towers usually have two stories with projecting roofs, similar to those of the modern pagoda. On the other hand the Han tower seems to have been very slender, indeed it would appear doubtful whether in some cases it was more than a solid

*Bulletin No. 7 of the Catholic University of Peking. Atlantes and Caryatides in Chinese Architecture, by Dr. Gustav Ecke. Dr. Ecke, who is an expert on Chinese architecture, states that he knows of no other Chinese temple which has true caryatides. If the K'ai Yüan Ssŭ is in fact unique in this respect, this feature can hardly be regarded as a characteristic of Buddhist architecture in China. It is of course possible that caryatides were more common in temples of the earlier dynasties, when Greco-Indian influence was stronger, and that this feature was not maintained when the buildings were restored in Ming or Manchu times. Very few Chinese temple buildings can be assigned to a date earlier than the last two dynasties.

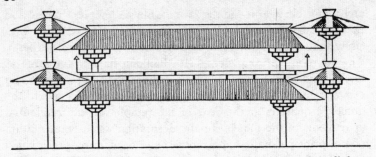

FIG. 61. *Han mansion with flanking towers. Sketch from a bas-relief.*

pillar of masonry. While the relative size of buildings cannot always be inferred from the scale shown on the bas-reliefs (for the artist emphasised the size of the subjects he considered to be the most important) it seems that these towers, usually placed on either side of a large hall, were very little higher than the roof ridge of the hall itself. The pagoda thus seems to have gained both solidity and height in later centuries (Plate XVI).

It is particularly in religious buildings, pagodas and temples, that the existence of two distinct styles in Chinese architecture is apparent. These two styles are usually called the northern and southern, though their distribution does not always follow strictly geographical lines. In Yunnan, one of the most southerly provinces in China, the northern style is dominant, and in south Manchuria there are some examples of the southern style. These exceptions are due to historical causes. Yunnan received strong northern influences in the Ming and early Manchu periods, while southern Manchuria was influenced from the south by the sea route.

The chief differences between the two styles are the degree of curvature in the slope of the roof and in the amount of ornamentation with which the roof ridges and eaves are decorated. In the southern style the roofs are sharply recurved until the projecting eaves at the corners turn upwards like a horn (Fig. 62). The roof ridges are often heavily encumbered by rows of small figures representing Taoist deities and mythological animals, in such profusion that the lines of the roof itself are almost obscured. Eaves and

FIG. 62. *Southern style pavilion. After Sirén, Chinese Architecture.*

pillars are carved and decorated in a similar way, leaving very little of the surface smooth and unornamented. The extreme examples of this taste for over-decoration—the buildings which inspired the *chinoiserie* of the European 18th century—are found in Canton and the provinces of the southern littoral. From the artistic point of view they are not easy to admire, for while the ingenuity of the carving and decorations is sometimes pleasing in itself, the lines of the building as a whole are lost and the general effect is tortuous and overburdened. Chinese taste is turning away from this style, and even in Canton itself recent public buildings such as the Kuomintang Memorial Hall have been built in the northern style.

The northern style is often called the Palace style because the best examples of this architecture are the magnificent buildings of the Forbidden City and the imperial tombs of the Ming and Manchu dynasties. In the Palace style the curve of the roof is gentle and restrained, and has been compared to the slope of the roof of a tent, although the belief that this style was inspired by memories of the great tents of the nomad Mongol Emperors has no foundation in fact.* Ornamentation is also less florid and more limited. Roof figures are confined to the corner ridges, and are smaller and more stylised than the elaborate groups represented on southern buildings. In Shansi a happy compromise between the over-elaboration of this feature in the southern style and the stylisation of the Peking palaces occurs. Here the roof ridges are decorated with graceful and vigorous little figures of men mounted on galloping horses.

The origin of the two styles is obscure. In the Han models and bas-reliefs, the earliest representation of Chinese buildings so far known, the curvature of the roofs is very slight; indeed, in some instances there does not appear to be any at all, though whether this is due to the technical limitations of the potter or sculptor, or whether it really represents an earlier design is doubtful. In T'ang reliefs and Sung paintings the curvature is present, but never approaches the degree seen in existing buildings in the southern provinces. On the other hand the extreme emphasis of this feature is particularly noticeable in Burmese and Indo-Chinese architecture which suggests that the style may have come from contact with these southern neighbours. In Japan, which received its architect   dition largely from T'ang China, the curve is slight, conforming to the northern Chinese style.

With the exception of a temple in the Shansi mountains discovered by Dr. Liang Ssu-Ch'eng in 1937, the only wood and brick building of T'ang date which still survives, is in Japan, and not in China. The Kondo or Golden Hall of the Horyuji monastery, built in A.D. 607 and probably rebuilt after a fire a century later, is a beautiful example of the style of architecture practised by the T'ang (Fig. 63), a style often represented in Sung paintings, and consequently sometimes known in China as the Sung style. It differs from the Ming style in one important respect. In the Kondo only the front and rear faces of the roof are continued uninterruptedly to the eaves, and on the east and west faces the upper part is gable-ended. In the Ming style the four faces of

*This theory has received wide publicity, though based on no evidence and actually contradicted by representations of buildings in Sung paintings, T'ang and Wei reliefs and the existing temples at Nara in Japan, which were built in imitation of T'ang models. Moreover the form of the nomad tent is round, in no way resembling the western marquee.

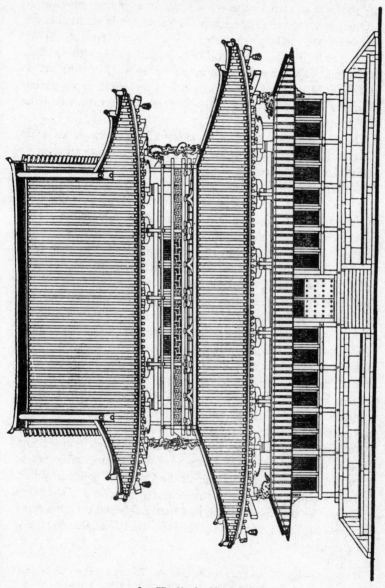

FIG. 63. *The Kondo, Nara, Japan.*

the roof are treated in the same way, all sweeping down in an uninterrupted curve to the eaves. This is the style adopted in the Wu Men, the main south gate of the Forbidden City (Plate XVII), as well as in several other halls and gates in the palaces at Peking. The Sung style continued to be used in conjunction with the Ming, and the Forbidden City contains numerous examples of pavilions and halls in which this treatment of the roof accurs.

The characteristic feature of every Chinese city is its wall. No city is without a fortified wall, and this fortification is so essential to the Chinese idea of a city that the words for "city" and "wall" are identical; *ch'êng* means both a city and the wall of a city. It is only in modern times that some cities have been deprived of their fortifications, and only as a result of foreign commerce on the coasts and rivers that certain market towns have grown to the status of cities without being girdled with a wall. This feature which gave a city its status, which was in fact the essential attribute of cityhood, naturally received the greatest care and the most thorough workmanship. Therefore the Chinese city walls are in a class apart, by far the most solid and impressive in the world.

It was particularly in the northern provinces, which were more often exposed to nomad incursions, that the art of wall building attained its highest development. The walls of the so-called Tartar City of Peking, in reality Ming work of the early 15th century, are well known, and justly famous.* Walls as solid and as high are commonly found in all the cities of the north-west provinces, and particularly in Shansi where every *hsien* or sub-prefecture has walls as imposing as those of the capital, although not as long. As they exist to-day most of these city walls are Ming work. After the expulsion of the Mongols the Chinese Emperors of that dynasty found it necessary to restore the fortifications of the cities in the border provinces, which had been neglected by the nomad peoples who had ruled the north since the fall of the Northern Sung dynasty.

---

*The expression Tartar City is not Chinese. To the Chinese the original city is known as the North City, and the southern extension, called the Chinese city by foreigners, is the South City. Both are the work of Ming Emperors, owing nothing to the Manchu conquerors.

In town planning and fortification there are two styles in China, which like the two styles of architecture belong to the north and south respectively. In the north, where the builders had plenty of space, and a choice of level unencumbered sites, the plan of the cities is always rectangular, and the city is divided into four quarters by two straight streets meeting in the centre of the town. Except in the largest cities there are only four gates, each in the centre of one of the side walls. The junction of the two principal streets is defended by the drum tower, a large fortified four-way gateway which is built over the cross-roads so that in times of riot or disorder each street can be isolated from the others. In the three-story pagoda-like tower which crowns this gateway troops were stationed, and here was sounded the great drum which acted as a public timepiece marking the hours of the day.

Regularity and symmetry mark the arrangement of the gates and two main streets, similar to the Roman *decumanus* and *via principalis*, but the residential lanes which cut up the four quarters of the city are usually arranged on no fixed plan, but meander and twist as the size and shape of the houses dictate. It is rare to find Chinese cities divided into a rich and poor quarter. The large houses of the well-to-do, with their many courtyards and gardens, jostle the small single courtyard houses of the poor in the same lane. If one part of the city is more liable to be flooded by the summer rains than another, the low-lying part is not favoured by the wealthy, but even here large houses will be found as well as the cramped quarters of the poorest class.*

The city walls in the north are built to resist the danger of floods as well as attack by the enemy. The core of the wall is a solid mound of hard clay which is faced both on the outside and the inside with very large bricks measuring 2 feet by 6 inches, and some 4 to 5 inches thick. The top of the wall is also paved with these bricks. The wall is tapered, so that though 40 feet thick at the base, it is not more than 20 to 25 feet thick at the top. The

*In Peking the eastern half of the city, and particularly the south-east corner, was regarded as damper than the west. For that reason it was this eastern corner which was allotted to foreigners when they established legations in Peking. Even to-day, when the drainage of the whole city has been modernised, Chinese of means prefer the western part of the city.

height varies, but in the Shansi cities, Peking, and at Sianfu (the ancient Ch'ang An) it is not less than 60 feet. At intervals of some 50 to 100 yards large bastions are built out from the curtain wall, being about 40 feet square at the top. The moat runs at the foot of these bastions leaving a strip of unoccupied land between the moat, the curtain wall, and the bastions.

Towers are erected at the four corners of the wall and over the gates. The corner towers are fortified on the outer faces, which are built of brick and loopholed for cannon. The gate towers, designed like a three-story pagoda, only rectangular, are built largely of wood with tiled roofs. These towers, which are the most striking feature of the city's architecture, were intended to act as living quarters for the soldiers on duty at the gate, and as posts for archers or sharpshooters in time of war. The gate towers of Peking, which are the only part of the city visible from a distance, are 99 Chinese feet in height. One hundred feet from the ground, according to Chinese demonology, is the zone in which evil spirits commonly fly, so the towers were deliberately designed to reach the maximum height free from these malign influences. The city wall and corner tower of T'ai Ku Hsien in Shansi is a fine example of Chinese military architecture (Plate XVIII).

The gates of important cities are usually defended by a semi-circular outwork, in which there is an outer gate, placed at right angles to the opening of the main gate so that if this outer gate was blown in there would be no free field of fire upon the main gateway. Occasionally a suburb beyond this outer gate would be roughly fortified with a clay wall unfaced with bricks, more to prevent it being plundered by bandits than to assist in the defence of the city itself. Before the introduction of modern artillery the city walls were almost indestructible. Their solidity made any attempt to breach them by mining or bombardment a hopeless task. Their height made an escalade very difficult and hazardous. A city resolutely defended could withstand the attack of the largest army, and Chinese history has many tales of famous sieges and heroic defences. Famine and blockade was the only certain way of reducing a city so defended, and the large population of most Chinese cities, and their dependance on the daily marketing of the country produce, made this the more certain method.*

The city walls of north and north-west China are in every respect superior to the defences of the southern cities. In the south, on account of the high value of rice lands and the irregularity of the terrain, few cities can be planned on the spacious scale and symmetrical design used in the plains of the north. Streets are narrow and winding, the walls lower, though often built of stone, and the gates narrow. Wheeled traffic was almost unknown in the south until modern times. The sedan chair, the pack mule, porters and wheelbarrows made up the traffic of the streets which therefore did not need to be wide. In Canton many of them were little more than alleys only wide enough for two men to walk abreast. In the south the principal means of travel was by boat, and nothing but local traffic coming to and from market entered the city by land. On the other hand the southern cities were not often exposed to attack by invaders, therefore less care was paid to the fortifications.

*Even field artillery is useless against a really strong city wall. In 1926, Sianfu (Ch'ang An) was besieged for over five months by an army equipped with field guns, but no heavy artillery. The city was successfully held for this long period against every attack. The damage done to the walls by the bombardment is insignificant. Only the parapet of brick has suffered severely. On the other hand the blockade inflicted the most horrible sufferings on the inhabitants, of whom several thousands died of starvation and disease.

PART SEVEN—CHINA UNDER THE MANCHUS

Chapter XXVII

THE MANCHU CONQUEST

Two sovereigns had already ruled over the united Manchu nation before the empire of the Ming dynasty fell into their hands. Nurhachu, the civiliser of his people, founded the kingdom in 1618 on the banks of the Sungari river, in what is now Kirin province, Manchuria.* His son, succeeding to the throne in 1625, established the capital at Mukden and conquered the Ming province of Liao Tung, corresponding to the modern south Manchuria. These additions to the Manchu kingdom still left the Chinese in possession of the line of the Great Wall and all the country to the south of it. In spite of raids and forays the Manchu armies had failed to dislodge the Ming hold on this strong defensive line, which effectively barred their way to any permanent conquest of Chinese territory. Had the Ming Empire not succumbed to internal rebellions it is probable that the Manchu kingdom would never have exceeded these limits.

The Manchu conquest of China proper was in fact due to a combination of circumstances, largely accidental. Consequently there was a fundamental difference between the character of the conquest in the northern and southern provinces of China respectively. The Manchus occupied northern China by consent, unopposed: they conquered the south by force after a long and bitter struggle. This fact dominated the later history of the dynasty, and still to-day explains the differing attitude of the northern and southern Chinese towards the Manchu dynasty and the imperial system.

In 1644 the Manchu Court was not prepared to undertake a

*The name, Manchuria, is unknown to the Chinese and Manchu languages. It is a foreign term coined by Europeans. The Chinese name for this region was anciently Liao Tung, the land "east of the Liao" (river). After the Manchu conquest the three provinces of Manchuria were collectively known as "the three eastern provinces." The Manchus designated their empire as "Ch'ing" (Pure) and in accordance with the Chinese custom the official name of the empire was that of the dynasty reigning. Manchukuo, the name given to Manchuria during the Japanese controlled puppet regime 1931-1945, was merely a translation into Chinese of the word "Manchuria." To the Chinese the country is commonly known as Tung Pei, the North East, and has been divided into nine provinces.

war of conquest. The second Manchu Emperor, T'ai Tsung, had died the year before, leaving his throne to his son, a boy of eleven. The government was administered by a regency composed of the late Emperor's brothers, and in such circumstances the regents would not have contemplated embarking on so vast and hazardous an enterprise as the conquest of China, if they had not been presented with an opportunity too good to be missed and never likely to recur. For the road was opened to them to enter China, by invitation, as allies.

Li Tzǔ-ch'êng, the Chinese rebel leader who had already over-run the western provinces and shattered the authority of the Ming dynasty in the north, captured Peking in 1644 and pro-claimed himself Emperor of a new dynasty, the Shun. The Ming Emperor had committed suicide, and the Chinese people, weary of the misrule of the eunuch-ridden Ming Court, would have accepted a new native dynasty with relief. Li Tzǔ-ch'êng, although a man of little or no education, was an able general, an adventurer of exactly the same type as the founder of the Ming dynasty itself. Under a vigorous imperial family, sprung from the people and backed by a war trained army, the new dynasty would have had little to fear from the Manchus.

Even during the distracted reign of the last Ming, a Chinese army, encamped at Shan Hai Kuan, where the Great Wall reaches the sea, had successfully prevented the Manchus from effecting a permanent conquest of any territory south of the Great Wall. This army, commanded by an able general, Wu San-kuei, was still intact. If Wu San-kuei had accepted the revolution at Peking, and submitted to the new Emperor, Li Tzǔ-ch'êng's Shun dynasty would have been established beyond dispute. There was no good reason why Wu should do otherwise, for as his subsequent conduct proved, he was not a fanatical adherent of the Ming dynasty.

The reasons why Wu decided to oppose rather than to accept the pretensions of Li Tzǔ-ch'êng remain something of an his-torical mystery, but it is nearly certain that it was no consideration of state policy or far-sighted ambition, but rather a personal quarrel. Li Tzǔ-ch'êng, after the fall of Peking, took into his own harem a singing girl of great charm and beauty who had been

Wu San-kuei's concubine. Moreover he refused to deliver this lady to her rightful husband, when Wu San-kuei demanded her. This personal quarrel wrecked the negotiations; Wu San-kuei refused to recognise the new dynasty, and with rather tardy and doubtful loyalty proclaimed himself the avenger of the Ming Emperor. Then he opened the fortress of Shan Hai Kuan and invited the Manchus to come to his assistance.

Whatever Wu San-kuei expected to be the final result of this step, it proved to be fatal to the ambitions of all the Chinese claimants for the throne. Li Tzŭ-ch'êng was defeated by the combined armies, and forced to abandon Peking. He retreated into the western provinces, relentlessly pursued by Wu San-kuei, who finally destroyed the Shun pretender and ruined his party. Meanwhile the Manchus, leaving Wu San-kuei to prosecute his vengeance, quietly occupied Peking and proclaimed their boy sovereign Emperor of China.

The Ming administration in the north had already collapsed. The Manchus were therefore able to occupy all the north of China, and much of the north-west also, without meeting the least opposition. In the south, on the contrary, a Ming Prince was recognised as Emperor at Nanking, and other princes organised resistance at Foochow and Canton. The Manchus left the conquest of these pretenders to Wu San-kuei and other Chinese generals who had submitted to them. Only small detachments of Manchu troops were employed against the Ming pretenders and the remnants of Li Tzŭ-ch'êng's army. This first conquest of the south was completed after eighteen years of continual fighting by the flight of the last Ming pretender into Burma. The southern provinces were then divided between three Chinese princes, Wu San-kuei in the south-west, and two less powerful ones on the east coast. Direct Manchu rule did not extend south of the Yangtze, and even in the north-west the hold of the conquerors was weak and menaced by serious rebellions.

During the first thirty years of the new dynasty the empire was thus only superficially obedient to the Manchu Court, which, under the rule of the Emperor Shun Chih (1644-1661) was lax and feeble. Shun Chih himself had fallen under the tutelage of the eunuchs whom he found in the Peking Forbidden City. He devoted most of his time to Buddhist religious exercises, gradually becoming a religious fanatic. At his death in 1661 the new dynasty was far from secure, while the succession passing to a boy of eight made another regency with its attendant dangers a further source of weakness. Few could foresee that the child Emperor who now succeeded was to be the saviour of the dynasty, the great K'ang Hsi.*

If Wu San-kuei, who was still ruling the south-west as a nominally subject prince, had chosen this moment to repudiate Manchu rule, he would almost certainly have driven the new dynasty from the throne. Instead, he waited ten years. It was not until 1673 that the great revolt of the south broke out. By then the young K'ang Hsi had dismissed his regents and taken over the government himself, and he proved from the first to be a ruler of character and decision. None the less the revolt of Wu San-kuei very nearly broke the Manchu power. All south China was immediately lost to them. Wu had an alliance with some Mongol tribes, and invaded the north-west to make contact with them.

The failure of this formidable combination was largely due to the defection of the Chinese princes of the coast provinces, who after supporting Wu, submitted to the Manchus, and were dethroned for their pains. The re-conquest of the coast, and the defeat of the Mongols, would not have saved the dynasty if Wu himself had not been too old for the fatigues of a long campaign After five years of successful resistance he died, still undefeated and still in possession of all south-west China. His sons did not inherit his ability or his authority, and they quarrelled among themselves. K'ang Hsi was able to suppress the great revolt and complete the real Manchu conquest of the south by the extermination of the Wu family when Yunnanfu, their capital, was captured in 1682. The effective reduction of the south to Manchu rule, therefore, did not begin until forty years after their peaceful occupation of Peking.

*According to a strong Peking tradition Shun Chih did not die in 1661, but secretly left his throne to become a Buddhist monk at a temple in the Western Hills, a few miles from Peking. The south-west gate of the Northern City is still commonly known as the Shun Chih Mên because it is said that it was by this gate that the fugitive Emperor fled from his capital.

The attitude of the Manchus towards their Chinese subjects in north and south respectively was determined by this fact. The north was loyal, and was trusted—up to a point. The south, embittered and rebellious, was feared, mistrusted, and oppressed. The Manchus made Peking their capital, a city close to their home country and to their Mongol allies. All the benefits of the new government were felt in the northern provinces and in the capital; most of the revenue came from the south. The conquerors were only a handful in comparison to the numbers of the subject race. At the end of the dynasty there were some ten million Manchus in the empire, and about 350,000,000 Chinese, to adopt the more conservative estimate. Three centuries earlier the population, reduced by the long wars, was certainly less, but the proportion of Manchus to Chinese was no greater.

It was obvious that the invaders could not hope to govern this huge empire without the co-operation of the Chinese themselves. It was equally obvious that if Chinese and Manchus were placed on an equality the Manchu minority would be completely swamped. To prevent this it was decided that one-half of the posts in the civil service should be reserved for Manchus, and one-half left to the Chinese. From the very nature of the Chinese Empire this meant an uneven distribution between the northern and southern provinces, which competed separately at Peking and Nanking respectively. The southern provinces accounted for the majority of the population, yet they were allotted only a quarter of the official posts.

This meant that the competition at the examinations was far keener for the southerners than for the northerners, while for the Manchus there was little or no competition. Consequently, the southerners who succeeded tended to be the most intelligent element in the civil service, while the Manchu officials, almost certain of their posts from childhood, had no need of exceptional talents to qualify for office. From this state of affairs two serious perils to the government developed. Firstly the element which merited the highest positions, and, the most rapid promotion, the southerners, were the least trusted by the government, which feared to find the administration dominated by men drawn from the ever hostile south. In consequence the southerners, and in particular the Cantonese, did not obtain the posts to which their ability entitled them, and such treatment did not encourage their loyalty.

Even more serious was the unrest among the educated southerners who were not officials. The keen competition which the limited number of posts made inevitable created a large class of unsuccessful candidates, men who were obviously better equipped for office than the Manchu officials, or than some of their northern countrymen, but for whom there was no opening under the Manchu government. This class has always provided the material for revolutionary movements, but owing to the reservation of half the posts to Manchus, the unemployed intellectuals were more numerous under this dynasty than ever before, and more dissatisfied. The southerners came to feel that the Manchu government was an empire run in the interests of the Court of Peking and its neighbouring provinces, but sustained by revenue derived mainly from the south.

There was much justice in this view. The revenues of the empire were spent in Peking. Superb palaces were added to the already extensive buildings left by the Ming Emperors. Temples and tombs were constructed at an immense cost, a cost met by taxing the rich provinces of the south, which derived no benefit whatever from these works. The entire Manchu nation, forbidden by law to engage in commerce or industry, was fed at the state expense on "tribute rice," which was levied from the south and transported to Peking and other Manchu garrisons.

Unlike the invaders of previous centuries, the Manchus never relaxed the barrier between conquerors and subjects. The whole Manchu nation, organised into eight corps (the eight banners), was distributed in military garrisons throughout the provinces, and at the capital. They were maintained by the state, forbidden to intermarry with the Chinese or to have any other occupations than the service, either military or civil, of the state. Under such a system of enforced idleness, the Manchus gradually degenerated. Little ability was needed for a Manchu to obtain a government post, and the garrisons, condemned to a drone-like inactivity, soon lost the fighting qualities of their invading forefathers.

The evils of this system, though finally ruinous to the dynasty, were not at first apparent. The long struggle in the south which marked the first period of Manchu rule prevented any rapid deterioration. After the pacification of the south internal peace was maintained for over a century, thanks to the ability and personal qualities of the three Emperors, K'ang Hsi, Yung Chêng and Ch'ien Lung. The outward splendour of their reigns concealed the inward decay of the Manchu power, but when, early in the 19th century, the empire was faced with internal revolts and foreign wars, it was found that the Manchu garrisons were utterly unable to stem the tide of rebellion or repulse the foreigners.

For a century the Manchu government struggled against their Chinese subjects within and the foreign powers without. In this losing battle they were compelled to rely on Chinese troops of doubtful loyalty, inadequately equipped. Rebellion at home and defeats at the hands of foreign enemies discredited the dynasty and finally involved the Chinese Empire in a comprehensive revolution, in which the disappearance of the Manchu dynasty was perhaps the least significant event.

Nothing is more striking in the recent history of China than a comparison between the state of the empire in the 18th and in the 19th centuries. Under K'ang Hsi and his two successors the Chinese Empire attained its maximum material prosperity both in the extent of the territory and the number of subjects governed by Peking, and in the renown and admiration of distant nations. The missionaries who first described China to the west regarded the empire as the equal, if not the superior (except in the matter of religious faith), of their native France. To them the empire of Ch'ien Lung was the most splendid, as it was certainly the most extensive in the world.

A complete change occurred in the next century. Internal rebellions and disastrous foreign wars followed each other—one might say engendered each other—in quick succession. The century which saw the coming of mechanical power and the rise of science in the west was for China a period of stagnation, bad government, weakness and decline. The empire which had been the admiration of the 18th century Jesuits was by the end of the 19th century treated as a decrepit and backward absolutism, destined to be carved up by the predatory imperialism of half a dozen foreign powers.

The cause of this swift decline was not political or economic mismanagement, but the psychology of the governing class themselves. Foreign rule is fatal to a native culture. If the foreign rulers are more civilised than their subjects they impose their own culture upon the natives, and the existing arts tend to sink to a despised position in which there can be no development. If, as was the case with the Manchus, the conquerors are barbarians who adopt the superior culture of the conquered race, the alien rulers instinctively favour all that is most conventional, recognised and orthodox in the native culture, and distrust all novelties for fear of being despised as uncivilised illiterates by the cultured native aristocracy.

Having no tradition of their own, they have no confidence in their power to judge art and literature. This was the attitude of the Manchu Court. Under K'ang Hsi, Yung Chêng, and Chi'en Lung, the Manchu princes and courtiers became more Chinese than the Chinese themselves. They adopted and protected the most rigid Confucian traditions. The literature they patronised was modelled upon the classics of the Feudal Age, the poetry imitated the T'ang masters, the art looked back to the Sung. Any art or any idea which did not conform to these models was ignored or despised. The Manchus were impelled to take up this attitude by policy as well as by a natural admiration for a great and ancient civilisation. They were a mere handful of warriors immersed in the vast number of their Chinese subjects. They realised that they could only govern the empire by enlisting the support of the Chinese scholars themselves, the traditional ruling class. Wholehearted patronage of the arts and literature which that class cultivated was the surest way to gain their esteem and secure their loyalty.

Consequently the Manchu Emperors devoted themselves to Chinese culture, but only to the orthodox Confucian tradition. Vast collections of classical literature were made at their command. The examinations became more conventional and classical, ever further removed from reality. Taoism, and with Taoism anything which seemed to smack of alchemy, was ignored. In this despised class of knowledge, not Confucian and therefore unimportant, the new sciences developed in Europe were included. The Manchu Emperors employed Jesuits to cast cannon or make astronomical calculations, but they treated the scientific knowledge of these foreigners as a mere technical skill, such as that of a carpenter or jade carver, and never troubled to enquire whether there was a valuable theory of knowledge behind it.

This extreme conservative outlook was shared by the whole official hierarchy, Chinese and Manchu alike. Trained in a classical tradition which excluded all consideration of non-Confucian philosophy, and chosen by a highly competitive examination based upon the most conventional interpretation of that philosophy, the type of mind that entered the civil service was a mind closed to all idea of progress, almost incapable of grasping the possibility, still less the need, for change. The men who rebelled against this training or found this tradition unsatisfying, did not succeed in these specialised examinations, or if they occasionally passed into the civil service, they found an atmosphere so uncongenial that they either resigned, or were relegated to unimportant posts where they exercised no influence. The system was self-perpetuating, seemingly immutable.

The real cause of the rapid decline of the Manchu Empire in the 19th century was intellectual stagnation brought about by the domination of a small alien ruling class, itself dominated by a petrified cultural tradition. To the end the Manchus clung to this tradition as their sheet anchor. The rising unrest, the progress of their foreign enemies—identified with change and the challenge of an opposing philosophy—only confirmed them in their belief that Confucianism was "for the Chinese what water is for fish"— a vital necessity. Every rebel movement was associated with some other doctrine. The White Lotus sect, which disturbed the closing years of Ch'ien Lung's reign, and the whole of that of his successor, Chia Ch'ing, was based on esoteric Buddhism. The T'ai P'ing rebellion, which shook the dynasty to its foundations in the middle of the 19th century, was inspired by Protestant Christianity.

All these movements, and the activities of the foreign powers, with their missionaries and their pretensions to an equality with the empire, struck at the root conception of the philosophy adopted by the Manchu rulers. A native dynasty might have boldly welcomed change and headed the party of the innovators, as happened in Japan, and as the T'ai P'ing leaders hoped to do, but the Manchus feared that if they abandoned the Confucian tradition they would lose the support of the Chinese scholar class, on which their dynasty depended since the degeneration of the Manchu bannermen. It was a fatal policy. If the Manchus succeeded for a time in conciliating the more reactionary scholars, it was at the price of alienating all the original and independent thinkers, ignoring the cause of popular unrest, and enfeebling the empire in the face of powerful enemies.

These consequences inevitably followed the attitude of rigid conservatism which K'ang Hsi, Yung Chêng and Ch'ien Lung adopted in the 18th century, the century of pregnant changes in European civilisation. At the time their empire appeared splendid and secure. For 120 years up till the end of the 18th century, there was unbroken internal peace. The conquest of Mongolia, Tibet and Turkestan incorporated territories lost since the T'ang dynasty or never previously part of the Chinese Empire. Burma, Korea and Annam were tributaries. Nepal suffered the only defeat and invasion the Ghurkas have sustained (1792). Map 17.

No doubt the exhaustion of the empire following the long wars which preceded and followed the fall of the Ming dynasty contributed to this long peace. The south, which was the least loyal, had suffered the most, and for many years was too weak to rebel. Szechuan in 1649 had been ruled by a homicidal lunatic, the terrible Chang Hsien-chung, who butchered the majority of the population of that province. Eighty years after the Manchu conquest of this province, Father de Mailla, writing from China, declared that, in spite of every care and privilege, Szechuan had not recovered from this catastrophe. To this day the people of that province mostly descend from immigrants from Hupei and Shensi.*

---

*Chang Hsien-chung was a madman. He exercised a terrible fascination over his unfortunate subjects. At his orders his soldiers massacred their own wives so that the army should not be incommodated by camp followers. He erected a stone tablet in Chêng Tu, his capital, on which was written the one word "sha"—"kill," which was his motto. After his death the tablet was turned round and walled up so that the word cannot be read. It is the belief of the people of Chêng Tu that if this tablet is exposed, Chang Hsien-chung will re-appear on earth and resume his bloodthirsty career.

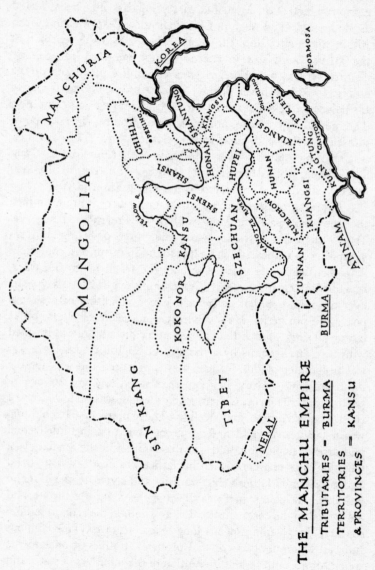

MAP 17. *The Manchu Empire.*

The long reign of Ch'ien Lung (1735-1795) was the most glorious period of the Manchu dynasty, and has often been treated as the most glorious reign in Chinese history. Peace was unbroken within the empire until the closing years, when the rebellion of the White Lotus sect in central China heralded the coming century of disorder. Foreign wars expanded the limits of the empire to regions never before conquered. Splendid additions to the palaces of Peking remain to attest Ch'ien Lung's magnificence. The population of the provinces rose rapidly. The Emperor himself, scholar and poet, in the classical and T'ang manner, was a strong and able ruler, who liked to be compared to T'ang T'ai Tsung, just as the Empress Dowager Tzŭ Hsi, in the next century, liked to be compared to the T'ang Empress Wu.

A flattering comparison, but if the grounds of it are examined the true weakness of the Manchu dynasty is revealed. T'ang T'ai Tsung reigned for twenty-two years, after pacifying and re-organising an empire which he had found in the utmost confusion. After his death 150 years of peace, the result of his life work, remained as his monument. Ch'ien Lung reigned for sixty years over an empire which he inherited in a condition of profound peace and prosperity. He was hardly dead before rebellions broke out on all sides, and within half a century the empire was invaded with ease at all points by a handful of English troops.

The founder of the T'ang dynasty prepared the way for the most brilliant century in Chinese history, the golden age of poetry and the arts. Ch'ien Lung's reign was followed by a century of confusion and decline. The empire of Ch'ien Lung was a facade, splendid and imposing, but masking intellectual and artistic stagnation, and gross corruption in the official class. Chia Ch'ing's first act—when his father was dead—was to arrest and imprison his father's chief minister and favourite, the Manchu Ho Shên. His confiscated wealth was escheated to the throne, and amounted to the enormous total of 223 million taels, or 70 million sterling, the gleanings of his long years of power. This fabulous sum, all in specie, gems or real property, testifies at once to the wealth of the empire, the corruption of the ministers of state, and the blindness of Ch'ien Lung to the realities of his reign.

The history of China during the 19th century is comparatively

well known, and has been very fully dealt with by many foreign
writers. For the Manchu dynasty it was a period of constant
decline and catastrophe. The Opium War with England (1840)
was followed ten years later by the great T'ai P'ing rebellion,
which starting in the far south, swept across China to within 100
miles of Peking, and came within an ace of substituting a Chinese
dynasty for the ruling house. For nearly nine years the T'ai
P'ing, "Heavenly King," Hung Hsiu-ch'uan, ruled half China
from his capital at Nanking. When at last the rebellion was
suppressed, it was due not to the state-maintained Manchu
bannermen, who were useless as fighting troops, but to Chinese
armies led by the Englishman, General Gordon, and by Tsêng
Kuo-fan, a Chinese.

Thus, a movement which would, there is good reason to
suppose, have done for China what the almost contemporary
Meiji restoration movement did for Japan, was crushed by the
alliance of capitalist imperialism and Manchu despotism. China
was doomed instead to another fifty years of incompetent and
obscurantist reaction under a Court ruled by the Empress
Dowager Tzǔ Hsi and her eunuchs. When this forceful woman
died the dynasty swiftly collapsed in the face of an incoherent
national rising led by idealistic republicans, but backed by self-
seeking generals.

This miserable half century was the close of the old era. The
compact, integral, Chinese civilisation was now in contact with
world forces which could not be shut out and which were certain
to exercise a profound influence. A study of the impact of these
new ideas and inventions, which have combined to involve
China in the most far-reaching revolution of her long history,
must go back to the middle of the 19th century for a starting
point. It is impossible to deal adequately with this vast transformation in one or two chapters at the end of a book. The
history of modern China is a subject in itself.

Chapter XXVIII

THE ECONOMIC CONSEQUENCES OF SEA-BORNE TRADE

By the middle of the 18th century the foreign trade of China had become concentrated at Canton, the only port at which European ships were permitted to call. The jealous suspicion which characterised the attitude of the Manchu government towards the southern provinces had led to the exclusion of the old marts at Ch'üan Chou, Amoy and Ningpo from any share in this commerce, in spite of repeated efforts to effect an opening made by the English, Dutch and other maritime nations. The Canton monopoly was not imposed through any consideration of favour for the inhabitants of that city, it was due rather to the determination of the Court to limit trade to one port, and that the furthest from the heart of the empire and the seat of government.

The Manchu government remained to the end incurably suspicious of the results of contact between its Chinese subjects and foreign nations. The Yangtze valley was the most disaffected area in the empire, the region in which the White Lotus and other rebellions took their rise. Consequently these provinces could on no account be permitted to have direct intercourse with the foreign traders, from whom the rebels might obtain assistance. The Court had some reason for these fears. Contact with foreign peoples did indeed stimulate the latent antagonism to Manchu rule which was felt throughout the south. Every rebellion against the dynasty soughtthe sympathy of the foreigners, and Canton itself, precisely because it was the centre of foreign trade, became in the end the focus of the anti-Manchu movement.

The Canton monopoly was of course none the less a very valuable privilege for the southern city, and one which it strove hard to keep. In this respect the merchants of Canton itself found themselves in accord with the Court, and with the officials ruling Canton, who were of course either Manchus or natives of other provinces, for the Manchus never permitted any Chinese official to serve in his native province. The merchants were anxious to retain a valuable commercial monopoly, the Court wished to keep the foreigners to one port, and the officials of Canton were determined to maintain their monopoly of the enormous corrupt extortions which they exacted from the trade. Against this alliance of vested interests, disunited though they were on other matters, the foreign traders and ambassadors of the 18th century strove in vain. Nothing short of armed attack could break the Canton monopoly.

Yet the economic objections to Canton as the sole port for the Chinese Empire were serious. Tea and silk were the only exports of any importance, and both these commodities were produced in provinces far to the north, in the Yangtze valley. For this area the true outlet was some port in the Yangtze delta, such as Hang Chou had been in the Sung dynasty, and Shanghai was to become in the 19th century. Canton was most awkwardly situated for this trade. Every bale of silk and chest of tea had to be transported by a tedious land journey through Kiangsi province, over the Mei Ling pass, and down the East River to Canton, a distance of at least 500 miles. Even the coastwise transport of goods to Canton was prohibited. Not only was the risk of piracy very great, but the government fearing that once goods were on the sea they would be beyond the reach of its tax gatherers, absolutely forbade the coasting trade.

Under the Manchu dynasty China suffered from two dangerous anomalies, economic and political. The capital was tucked away in the furthest north-east corner of the empire, and the chief centre of trade was situated near the equally inaccessible southern border. Both were remote from the main centres of population and production, and their distance from each other, more than two thousand miles, contributed potently to the total lack of economic common sense which distinguished the Manchu administration. These geographical considerations greatly in-fluenced the economic development of China under the Manchu dynasty, and in turn, determined the political fate of the empire.

The Manchu government was carried on by two classes of men, neither of which had the least training in or understanding of matters of trade. The Manchu nobility had been a warrior caste, forbidden by law to engage in commerce. From the reign of Ch'ien Lung onward they became a degenerate and spendthrift aristocracy, solely concerned to extort the money which their extravagances so rapidly dissipated. The other class, the Chinese scholars, owed their rank and position to proficiency in a pedantic knowledge of the ancient classics, and were neither expected nor encouraged to study practical sciences or economic problems. The officials who controlled the trade of Canton were drawn from these two classes, and the officer actually most concerned, the Hoppo, was always a Manchu of low rank, who owed his position to the patronage of a Court noble, a patronage which needed to be nourished by a constant stream of silver.*

The Hoppo was, of course, theoretically a subordinate official, ranking well below the Kuang Chou Fu, or Governor of Canton City, and the Viceroy of the two Kuang provinces (Kuangtung and Kuangsi), who was one of the highest officials in the imperial service. These provincial officials, who were more often Chinese than Manchus, were concerned with many matters besides the foreign trade of Canton, and in spite of their high rank, often lacked the occult Court influence from which the Hoppo drew his strength. In the eyes of his masters, and of himself, the functions of the Hoppo were indeed little more than undisguised extortion of the maximum sums the trade could afford to pay. Appointed for three years, the Hoppo had to satisfy his patrons, his rivals for their favour, buy off his enemies at Court, make his own fortune and that of his family, and satisfy the horde of retainers who had accompanied him to Canton. Under these circumstances economic problems and plans to improve the conditions of trade were not uppermost in the mind of this official.

It is illuminating to compare the Manchu attitude to foreign trade and intercourse, as exemplified by the nature of the Hoppo's functions and character, with the attitude of the Sung dynasty. In the early 12th century the precisely equivalent office had been filled by such scholars as Chao Ju-kua, a scion of the ruling imperial family, who had devoted his spare time to compiling a book on the geography of the outside world and the customs of foreign nations (p. 423).

*The "Hoppo" was the foreign name for this official, a corruption of the Cantonese abbreviation *Hoi Po*, of the Mandarin title of this official, *Yüeh Hai Kuan Pu*—Superintendent of the South Sea Customs.

The nature of the Canton trade facilitated the extortionate methods of the Hoppo and his employers. The balance of trade was entirely in favour of China. Tea and silk were exported in ever-increasing quantities, for China then supplied the needs of all Europe as well as of America, and these commodities were paid for in silver. Constant attempts were made to find some product of Europe which would find a sale in the Chinese Empire, but for very many years they met with no success. The English East India Company, forced by the terms of its charter to export a certain proportion of English woollens and cloth, found that in China these goods never fetched a price high enough to cover the cost of freight and production. It was not until 1827 that Manchester goods were for the first time sold in China at a profit. Towards the end of the 18th century the foreigners found a market for furs and sandal wood, the first brought from Canada, and the second from the South Sea Islands, but these minor imports were very far from balancing the export staples of the trade, tea and silk.

The Manchu Court regarded the economic self-sufficiency of their empire with complacency. The "outer barbarians" were supplied with tea and silk, and paid a steady stream of silver into the Empire in return. This made taxation, extortion, and corruption easy and profitable. On the other hand, as long as this continued to be the case, the Hoppo, though vexatious to the merchants, never became wholly intolerable. A threat to stop the trade altogether would always lead to a compromise. It was only when the foreign importers discovered an article in keen demand in China, opium, that the officials, finding their source of revenue drying up, adopted measures which precipitated an open conflict. This, however, did not occur until nearly half way through the 19th century. In the 18th century the Chinese needed nothing which the European could import. The Emperor Ch'ien Lung was stating facts when, in reply to the embassy of Lord Macartney, he said,

"The Celestial Empire possesses all things in prolific abundance and lacks no product within its borders. There is therefore no need to import the manufactures of outside barbarians in exchange for our own products."*

This was true enough as far as it went, but Ch'ien Lung ignored a vital consideration. Neither the Emperor nor any other influential Manchu or Chinese knew or cared to know anything about these distant European nations "dwelling at the ends of the sea." They disregarded the science and culture of the western world as unworthy of a scholar's attention. Clocks and watches imported from France did indeed make welcome presents to high officials and princes, but no one troubled to inquire why it was that the barbarians made such ingenious toys, nor why they could make them better than Chinese craftsmen. Not even the palpable fact that the size and seaworthiness of the foreign ships had immeasurably improved since the Portuguese first came to Canton seems to have impressed the official world with any realisation of the fact that China was falling behind. Completely dominated by Confucian pedantry the official world of the Manchu Empire closed its mind to all other knowledge and refused to believe anything valuable could possibly be learnt from foreigners.

In the T'ang dynasty Ch'ien Lung's attitude would have been irreproachable, for then China had indeed nothing to learn from any other people. Yet an attitude of lofty aloofness had not characterised the T'ang rulers. They had been keenly interested in foreign peoples and their products. The Manchus, on the other hand, not only despised and ignored the civilisation of the west, but forced their subjects to remain in a like ignorance. The trade at Canton was hemmed about with innumerable restrictions designed to reduce the contact of foreigners and Chinese to the minimum, and to confine it strictly to the business of buying and selling.

The origin of much of this suspicion and of many of these restrictions was no doubt the violence and aggressive behaviour of the early Portuguese navigators and their imitators of other

*Mandate of Ch'ien Lung to George III on the occasion of Lord Macartney's embassy. Translated in full in *Annals and Memoirs of the Court of Peking.* Backhouse & Bland. 1914.

nationalities; but the Manchu government proved quite unable, or unwilling, to recognise that the character of the foreign merchants had changed. The semi-piratical adventurers of the 16th century were now replaced by the cultivated representatives of the great European monopolistic companies, men who were often connected with the ruling classes in their own country. Nevertheless the Manchu government continued to treat them as buccaneers who had to be kept under the closest surveillance.

Restrictions of a kind were necessary, and freely admitted by the foreign traders. For if the supercargoes and captains who conducted the trade were men of education and refinement, the sailors who manned the foreign ships were on the contrary a turbulent and quarrelsome type drawn from the waterfront of many European ports. After a long voyage, sometimes six months at sea, the seamen were hard to restrain in port. Homicides, drunken affrays, riots and quarrels disturbed the peace of Canton, and afforded a constant source of anxiety to the supercargoes and to the Chinese merchants, upon whom the official world visited its displeasure on these occasions.

It was to the interest of both parties that the lawless sailors and ignorant mob of Canton be kept apart, but the sailors who wanted distraction, and the hawkers who sold them strong drink and procured them other diversions, had just as strong an interest in the opposite sense. The fact that the European nations were not infrequently at war with one another, and that the neutrality of the port of Canton was not always strictly respected by zealous sea captains, did not make the difficulties of the merchants of both races any the less. Whether a sailor had killed a coolie in a drunken fury, or the rival seamen of England and France had come to blows, the Chinese merchants had to foot the bill, and the officials of Canton saw that it was paid in full.

The European supercargoes suffered in other ways. The riotous conduct of the seamen gave the officials an excuse to enforce irksome restrictions on all foreigners, no matter what their status. Foreign merchants were confined to their factories on the Canton waterfront, and were not allowed to enter the city, or even to take exercise in the country adjacent except under strict limitations. At the end of the summer, when the ships sailed, the traders were forced to leave Canton and spend the winter at Macao. No foreign women were allowed to come to Canton, and foreigners were even refused permission to ride in sedan chairs. A prohibition against employing Chinese servants also existed, and, though ignored in practice, was occasionally revived when the official world desired to put pressure on the foreigners. It was strictly forbidden to learn the Chinese language, and Chinese who taught it were liable to very severe penalties. Nevertheless, some foreigners did succeed in becoming proficient scholars, and this prohibition tended to become a dead letter in later years.

The natives of Canton suffered almost as many disabilities in their relations with the foreigners. All trade was confined to a handful of merchants, known as the Hong Merchants, who rarely numbered more than ten firms, and sometimes were as few as five or six. For their privilege they paid great sums, were not allowed to retire from the trade without paying a huge ransom, were forced to hold themselves responsible for the acts of the foreigners, and were mulcted at every turn by the Hoppo and other officials. Many of these merchants were forced into bankruptcy by excessive extortion, and when this happened they were stripped of their last copper and exiled to Central Asia. In time the terrible privilege of being a Hong Merchant was shunned by all, and new recruits had to be forced to assume the unwelcome honour.

Every endeavour of the government was directed to preventing their subjects from acquiring any knowledge of the foreigners' culture or civilisation. Conversion to Christianity was forbidden. Emigration, or even travel on foreign ships was a crime. As foreigners were forbidden to learn Cantonese (which of course was a dialect unintelligible to Manchus and Chinese officials from other provinces) the trade had to be carried on in Pidgin English, that curious language, composed of English and Portuguese words, often used in a sense unknown to their native lands, and strung together according to Cantonese grammatical forms. The true Pidgin English, now an extinct language, was equally unintelligible to a native of Canton or to a foreigner who had not studied its peculiar vocabulary.

With all these difficulties to contend with, both the Hong

Merchants and the foreigners made huge profits out of the trade. Year by year the volume of trade and the number of ships engaged in it increased. In spite of the enormous drain of bribery, extortion and legitimate taxation Canton grew rich, and the producing provinces shared in its prosperity. The incubus of the Manchu government battened on the trade, but could not kill it, and the extortions to which they were exposed brought home to the Cantonese a full realisation of the wasteful burden of the imperial system which they supported without getting any return for their money.

During the 18th century the foreign trade with China was conducted exclusively by the monopolist East India Companies organised by the various maritime nations. The English Company, on account of its sovereign position in India and the naval supremacy of the English in the eastern seas, soon became the dominant partner in the China trade. The rival companies, French, Dutch, Danish and Swedish, declined in importance until the Napoleonic wars, which swept the shipping of these nations off the seas, destroyed their trade with the east, and left the English almost the only nation trading with China. Their monopoly would have been complete had not the newly established United States entered into competition. The Americans did not form an East India Company, but opened the trade of China to all who cared to undertake the business.

The difference in the status of the English and American traders, the first the representatives of a great monopolist Company, the second free lance traders acting for their own account, was reflected in a marked difference of attitude on the part of the two nations towards the Manchu government and its pretensions. The Americans in Canton were not under the control of any authorised body of their fellow-citizens, such as the Select Committee of Supercargoes which had a statutory authority over all English subjects in Canton, and was empowered to deport persons who came to China without the licence of the East India Company. The Americans appointed a consul, but his authority was not effective over his own countrymen nor respected by the Chinese officials. The English supercargoes had for many years resisted the Chinese claim to try to punish English sailors for homicide. They had successfully established a custom—unsanctioned by Chinese recognition—but permitted in practice, of having such cases investigated in the English factory in the presence of the supercargoes as well as the Chinese officials, and of deporting the culprit to England if found guilty. Such incidents indeed invariably led to a tiresome dispute with the Chinese officials, and were only settled by liberal bribes paid by the Hong Merchant who "secured" (guaranteed) the English ship to which the guilty party belonged. Nevertheless the English had established as a general practice the immunity of their countrymen from the drastic and cruel punishments of the Chinese penal code.

The Americans, being a disunited body of independent traders, had no governing authority to defend their common interests. Each ship, if involved in a dispute of this nature, escaped from its difficulties by a compromise which often ended in a victory for the officials of Canton. American sailors who committed homicide, though the case might amount to no more than manslaughter, were seized by the Chinese authorities and executed on the public execution ground outside the city walls. The English greatly resented this compliance, which they feared would weaken their own position.

The attitude of the two nations was quite at variance and has remained so to this day. To the Americans, the troubles and adventures which befell a citizen who went trading to strange lands were his business, and were not considered to be the concern of the nation as a whole or of the government. The "frontier" point of view, which expected every pioneer, whether on land or sea, to conduct his business with a sturdy independence of official aid, prevailed. Moreover, the American traders in China were isolated individuals representing no great vested interest, and having no powerful influence in Congress.

The English, on the other hand, saw these matters from a wholly different angle. To them the English Company in China was the representative of the English King and nation, and should be treated as such. By the end of the 18th century the East India Company was exercising sovereign power over a very great part of India, it was administered by men of great political and

social influence in the English government, and the supercargoes
in Canton were usually close relatives of this new Anglo-Indian
aristocracy. Men whose brothers and cousins wielded the power
of princes in India were treated in Canton as if they were dangerous pirates temporarily posing as honest traders. They suffered
under degrading restrictions and experienced humiliating treatment at the hands of a government which was obviously as weak
as the Indian kingdoms which had succumbed to the East India
Company. This "Indian" outlook which pervaded the English in
Canton was a psychological factor of importance in the Canton
situation, and one which helped to make an armed conflict
inevitable.

The changed circumstances of the English traders in China,
who had been unsupported adventurers from a distant island,
and were now the representatives of a conquering imperialist
power, made no difference to the Chinese attitude towards them.
The Manchu government was apparently unaware, or indifferent,
to the development of English power in the east. India was not
far away, but China learnt nothing from the fate of Bengal.
The obvious fact that English sea power had driven the French
and the Dutch off the ocean made no impression. The Manchu
government did not either build a fleet of seagoing warships, or
even make any serious attempt to suppress the pirate fleets
which sheltered in every bay of the deeply indented south China
coast. When the pirates grew so strong that they menaced the
city of Canton itself, negotiations were opened, and the pirate
admiral was finally pardoned and invested with a commission
in the imperial service. The English were well aware of the
growing weakness of the Manchu government, and if they refrained in China from adopting the forceful methods which had
won them an empire in India, it was more on account of the
Napoleonic wars, than from any doubt as to the outcome of a
conflict.

Opium was the ostensible cause of the rupture when it came,
in 1841, but though there were Chinese and Manchu officials
who really deplored and feared the spread of the opium habit,
it was not solely on this account that the Manchu government
finally took violent action against the opium importers, and so

precipitated the long delayed war. It was a recognised fact that the importation of opium into the empire had been prohibited for many years. Decrees reiterating the prohibition had often been published. The English East India Company had always forbidden the import of opium in their ships, and had carefully enforced this order. Yet opium had been freely imported first at Macao, later at Lintin, a point in the Canton estuary (Pearl River) (Map 18) for more than half a century. It was grown in India,

THE CANTON ESTUARY

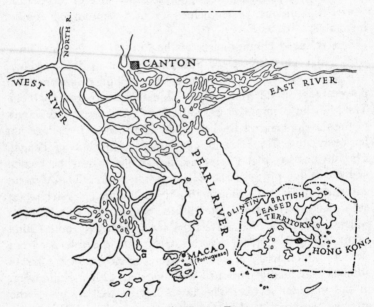

MAP 18. *The Canton Estuary.*

largely for the Chinese market, and shipped at first on Portuguese or Parsee vessels, later in English ships registered in Indian ports, which by a legal fiction were not regarded as "Company ships" though all Indian commerce was under the authority of the Company, the sovereign power. The trade was important to the Company and served to finance the China investment.

The Chinese officials at Canton, for their part, connived at the trade as openly as the government of India. The decrees from

Peking were a dead letter in Canton. Every official drew his regular revenue of bribes from the opium dealers, and none profited so handsomely as the preventive forces charged with the suppression of the traffic. From 1782 onwards the trade steadily increased. By 1823, 6000 chests were annually landed at Lintin. Two years later it is stated that the trade had doubled in ten years; and by 1832 20,000 chests were imported each year. The opium traffic on the coasts had attained the same proportions as the traffic in the west of China at the present time, and was just as difficult to suppress.*

Modern students of this problem are not likely to endorse the intemperate language in which 19th century writers condemned the opium trade and the corrupt connivance of the Chinese administration. The Prohibition experiment in the U.S.A. has shown how impossible it is for a government, however strong, to suppress a social habit which has become generally accepted, and which is not condemned by the opinion of the majority. The evil effects of opium smoking in excess are no doubt as profound as the prohibitionists claim; but not one in a thousand smokers experiences them, for opium sots in China are as rare as dipsomaniacs among ourselves. Public opinion refused to condemn a habit which appeared to the ordinary observer to be socially harmless.

Consequently the contraband trade expanded rapidly. The Chinese officials, dealers, and retailers of the drug made large profits, while the foreign traders had at last discovered a foreign product for which there was a keen demand in the Chinese Empire. It was this fact, rather than the moral objections to opium, which were only felt by a minority, that roused the Manchu government. As the opium imports grew, the flow of foreign silver into China diminished. Moreover, opium was contraband. It was not passed through the customs and paid no taxes. The fact that the trade supported an immense burden of illegal extortions, did not benefit the imperial treasury. The officials at Canton therefore found their opportunities for personal enrichment decreasing, while at the same time it became more difficult to satisfy the rapacious demands of the Court. The decline in

*The East India Company Trading To China. H. B. Morse. Oxford. 1926. Vol. iv.

revenue was regarded as a crime for which the Canton officials were in some way responsible.

The demands of the Court, the perplexities of the officials at Canton, and the growing impatience of the English traders made a situation which needed little aggravation to become insoluble by peaceful means. The attempts to suppress the opium traffic upset the precarious peace at Canton. Force was met by force, and the two nations drifted into a war which brought the Canton monopoly to an end and inaugurated a new economic era, that of the Treaty Ports and the system of extra-territorial jurisdiction.

For rather over two centuries the sea-borne trade of China had been conducted through the single port of Canton, yet, in spite of this restriction, and the hampering limitations which were imposed on the merchants both Chinese and foreign, the Canton trade had effected far-reaching changes in the economic life of the empire. Enormous wealth—for that age—came to Canton, and was distributed throughout the producing provinces of the south, and at the capital. In 1805 the value of the trade as computed by the East India Company was over six and a half million sterling, and the quantity of silver imported to Canton exceeded four and a half million dollars, but the revenue of the Chinese government (apart from official peculations and extortions) did not amount to more than 1,300,000 taels, or somewhat over £400,000. Individual Hong Merchants accumulated vast fortunes, even though they had to make constant heavy payments to the officials and to the Court. The merchant known to the English as Howqua, but whose correct name in Chinese was Wu Tun-yüan, was probably one of the richest men in the world at that time. In 1834 he himself estimated his fortune as over £6,000,000.

The sea-borne trade with Europe thus completed an economic change which had been in progress since the T'ang dynasty— the rise of the south and the decay of the north-west. From the reign of Ch'ien Lung onwards the south, and in particular the Yangtze delta and the tea-producing districts along the coast, became by far the wealthiest and most populous part of the empire, the centre of trade and industry, the focus of economic life. The fatal consequences to the dynasty itself of this concentration of wealth and population in the region most antagonistic to Manchu rule have already been indicated. Another consequence was longer in becoming apparent. The areas which became enriched by foreign trade were also those in which foreign ideas made the most rapid progress. The economic revolution in the south preceded and was the major cause of the great complex movement which is still in progress: the Chinese revolution and the cultural changes associated with it.

Chapter XXIX

T'AI P'ING CHRISTIANITY

"THREE ways to one goal" was a phrase commonly used in China to explain the fact, disconcerting to the European, that most Chinese practised the rites and revered the divinities of Buddhism, Taoism and Confucianism, without being disturbed by the knowledge that these theologies are often mutually contradictory. The average westerner, conditioned by a culture which admits only one true religion, finds such an attitude almost unintelligible. It seems to him, either that the Chinese are hypocrites who believe in nothing, or else that they must be entirely lacking in that essential quality of "faith" which to the western mind absolutely excludes the possibility of holding two religions to be equally valid.

It can hardly be denied that the Chinese Confucian scholar who condemned Buddhism and Taoism as "superstition" in his writings, but invoked Buddhist priests for the celebration of marriages, the conduct of funerals, and in times of sickness, was guilty of inconsistency, or at least of yielding to the prejudices of the unlearned and the conventions of ordinary society. But it must be remembered that in China there had never been a jealous God, who denied the existence of his rivals. The Buddhists admitted the godhead of the Hindu deities, though they treated them as inferior to the Buddha, and even to the great Bodhisattvas. The Taoists, equally, were always ready to acknowledge any deity who commanded a popular following, and to accord him a place in their pantheon. Confucius had never pronounced himself in favour of, or in opposition to, any deity, largely because in his age there was no religious conflict and the traditional rites were unquestioned. Therefore, "three ways to one goal"—the goal being a righteous life—seemed a very reasonable outlook to the Chinese. The scholar followed Confucius, the contemplative recluse sought Buddha in the mountain monasteries, the simple and ignorant populace worshipped the Taoist Queen of Heaven, and a multitude of other divinities, to avert calamity. A contemporary Chinese scholar has summed up this situation: "In China the educated classes believe in nothing, the uneducated class in everything."

By the 19th century the educated class had indeed lost all faith in Buddhism and Taoism. The priests of both religions were despised as mountebanks, and were the butt of stage plays and novels. Yet the government, with an eye to popular feeling, felt it necessary to protect and even patronise these decaying faiths. Buddhist and Taoist temples were repaired and enriched by the essentially Confucian Manchu Emperors. The Manchus, conservative in everything, were not willing to break with religions which might command popular support. They were also well aware that Confucianism, never a true religion, was limited in its appeal. The mass of the people, being illiterate, had never been able to read the classics, or to understand the ancient language in which they were written. For them the rites of Confucianism were matters for officials and scholars, the province of the government, to be respected, but not shared, by the populace.

Yet the two popular religions, Buddhism and Taoism, were rapidly losing their hold on the people themselves. Buddhism by the 19th century meant Amidism, the worship of Amidabha Buddha and the hope of entry into his Western Paradise at death. To achieve this end it was only necessary to believe in Amida (the shortened name of Amidabha) and call upon his name. The invocation of the sacred name was in itself sufficient to ensure rebirth in paradise, and the more often the invocation was made, the more certain was salvation. One consequence of this simplification was the decay of the essentially Buddhist virtues. The average "Buddhist" Chinese ate meat, drank wine, slaughtered animals, and on occasion, as a soldier, or in a village clan fight, took human life, but did not fear that these radical violations of the original Buddhist commandments would endanger his chances of paradise. It may be that the prevailing contempt for the military profession, and the low social position of butchers were consequences of Buddhist teaching, but apart from this the "eightfold path" had ceased to exercise any detectable influence on morals and customs.

True Buddhists did indeed still exist. In the great mountain monasteries, far from the corruption of daily life and city manners, at Chiu Hua Shan in southern Anhui, P'u To Shan in the Chusan Islands, and at other famous Buddhist shrines in different parts of the empire, the old rules and the pure theology still held fast. The very remoteness of these strongholds of the faith, the contemplative temperament of the monks who dwelt in them, and their detachment from the life of the people in general, contributed to the decay of the faith in the thousands of villages and small cities in which 90 per cent of the population of China live. Buddhism had failed to dethrone Confucius in the schools and the examination hall, and so played little part in the lives of the rulers of the empire. It had also failed to drive Taoism and its myriad gods out of the peasant villages, and so could not claim to be the sole source of moral guidance for the mass of the people. It remained the refuge of the world-weary and the contemplative natures who found the pressure of family life in the Chinese social system intolerable.

Taoism, although it was still one of the "three ways," had lost sight of the goal. Among all classes the Taoist priest was despised and disliked, but by the peasantry he was still feared. Derided by the educated as a gross superstition, fit only for the "stupid people," Taoism still flourished as a system of magic, and Taoist priests still found a ready market for their spells and charms, designed to bring rain, or avert disease. The close association between Taoism and the false sciences of astrology, quack medicine, fortune telling and alchemy was one potent cause of the contempt felt by Chinese scholars for all branches of learning not orthodox and literary. Chemistry, physics and all sciences dealing with the material world were suspect. These were the fields in which the Taoist priest, ignorant and dishonest as he usually was, flourished. For a scholar to take an interest in such matters was a serious breach of "good form." The fact that numerous popular movements hostile to authority took their origin from some Taoist sect which by mystic rites promised immunity in battle to its devotees contributed not a little to this attitude of distrust and neglect with which medicine and chemical experiment was generally regarded.*

The three religions of China, as they are often called, were in decay, but these three religions were in fact growths which existed independently of the fundamental religion of the Chinese people, which had long preceded them, and which will no doubt long survive their disappearance; ancestor worship, the cult of the dead, remained the one creed to which all Chinese paid reverence, which was so firmly established that it was accepted without question by all classes, and in consequence had no need of state-maintained temples or priests.

The fact that Buddhist theology ignores, and by implication opposes, the cult of the dead, and that this cult is and has always been the moral foundation of Chinese society, is striking testimony both to the failure of the Indian religion in its effort to convert the Chinese, and of the unshakeable hold that the most ancient of all religions has obtained on the Chinese mind. Confucius has been deposed by the republicans—his close association with the Manchu dynasty and the imperial system made this inevitable—Taoism is in process of dissolution, Buddhism either stationary or declining. The Cult of the Dead survives, if not openly acknowledged, yet implicitly recognised. The first act of the revolutionary party when they regained power and formed a government in Nanking in 1927 was to spend six million sterling on the mausoleum of their dead leader, Sun Yat-sen. Ceremonies to his memory are now the only religious rites obligatory upon officials and compulsory in schools.

Although the details of the ceremonies connected with ancestor worship have been modified by time and the influence of other ideas, the continuity of the cult in its principal features has been unbroken. The rites performed in the clan ancestral temple, the

*The Boxers, who after initiation believed themselves to be invulnerable, are the best known of these sects. But the Society of the Harmonious Fist, as they were correctly styled, had an ancient descent, and have had successors in recent years. In Shantung, where the Boxers arose, and where their successors, the Red Spears, Heavenly Gates and Big Swords, have flourished, the connection between these sects and Taoism is generally admitted. Indeed, it is claimed that all these sects descend from the Yellow Turbans of the Han dynasty, who were founded by an itinerant priest doctor in a time of pestilence (chapter XI).

care of graves, the duty of furnishing the ancestors with male posterity capable of carrying on the rites, with its corollary, the subordination of the individual to the control of the family group, these essentials were as universally accepted in the 19th century as they had been in the first millenium before Christ. The ancient fertility cult of the grain and the soil with its imperial offshoot, the worship of Heaven by the Emperor—the Son of Heaven—continued unchanged. In its official aspects this cult had become identified with Confucianism, for the Sage had enjoined the maintenance of these ancient rites, but among the people the worship of the T'u Ti, the local god of the soil, had nothing to do with Confucius or the official cult. It was the traditional and natural religion of peasant farmers wholly dependent on the yield of their small farms and the clemency of the elements. With the fall of the Manchu dynasty the official worship at the temples of the grain god and at the temple of Heaven in Peking came to an end, and the grounds of these shrines of the ancient cult became public parks; but in every field of the myriad farms of China the T'u Ti has his mud shrine, and still receives the traditional offerings of the cultivators.

The decay of the organised religions, Buddhism and Taoism, and the close identification of the official Confucian cult with the alien Manchu dynasty opened the way for a true religious revolution which at one moment promised to sweep the Chinese Empire and replace the older faiths. The T'ai P'ing movement, usually ignored in its religious aspects, was primarily a religious revival, and only secondarily a revolt against the Manchus. It is a curious fact that this movement, a product of the new contact with European civilisation, and the most positive consequence of Christian missionary enterprise, has been ignored by the missionaries themselves, and was finally destroyed by the armed intervention of the Christian Powers. In European histories of China the political character of the T'ai P'ing rebellion is emphasised, and the religious side is either misrepresented or derided. Yet to the T'ai P'ing leaders themselves it was their faith which mattered even more than victory over the Manchus. Had they abandoned their religious convictions and directed their efforts to raising a national revolt their success would have been assured.

The T'ai P'ing rebellion was the most formidable which the Manchu dynasty ever encountered, for the triumph of the republican movement in 1911 was due more to the internal collapse of the dynasty than to the armed forces of the rebels; the dynasty fell because no one could be found to fight in its defence. The T'ai P'ing movement, on the other hand, involved the whole Chinese Empire in a thirteen-year war which devastated the central provinces and exhausted the power of the Manchu dynasty. Its defeat was largely due to foreign intervention on behalf of the Manchus, intervention decided upon in the interests of European traders and with a view to an imperialist programme of partition and spheres of influence. The Manchus were preserved because they were weak and defenceless, the T'ai P'ings opposed because their victory would have made China strong and independent.

The T'ai P'ing movement was founded by Hung Hsiu-ch'uan, a Cantonese of the educated class who had failed to pass the civil service examinations. He certainly believed, probably with justice, that this failure was the result of prejudice on account of his southern origin and the fact that his clan had played a rather conspicuous part in the resistance to the Manchu conquest one hundred and fifty years before. Hung was thus typical of a large class of discontented scholars who laboured under a sense of injustice and harboured resentment against the Manchu government. In 1837 Hung Hsiu-ch'uan had a serious illness, during which he experienced visions—or as his enemies said, hallucinations—which he later believed constituted a divine revelation. Some years after he found a short tract which contained a part of the Christian Gospel translated into Chinese, the work of the recently established Protestant missionaries at Canton. On reading this Hung was convinced that the doctrine expounded in it corresponded to the revelation which he had received during his illness, the meaning of which had so far eluded him. He immediately adopted the doctrine found in the tract, which he believed to be confirmed by his visions, and he henceforward devoted his life to the propagation of this new religion.

This religion can only be described as a form of Christianity, though owing to the incomplete nature of the Christian tract which inspired Hung Hsiu-ch'uan, certain important doctrines of Protestant theology were misunderstood or unknown to the T'ai P'ing creed. The very fact that the prophet of the new religion was a Chinese * though his faith was largely of foreign origin, made for the success of the movement among his own countrymen, and called down the condemnation of and eventually aroused the fierce hostility of the majority of Christian missionaries. The success of the T'ai P'ing leader was extraordinary. After some years of missionary work among his own clan and the Hakka people to which it belonged, Hung's movement came under the hostile attention of the officials of the province. Orders were given for the arrest of the leader and the suppression of the Society of God Worshippers, as the T'ai P'ings were then called. Up to this point the movement had been purely religious, but as it condemned the practise of all existing religions, and denounced Buddhism as idolatry, the Manchu government regarded it as a subversive agitation, tending to cause disorder.

The followers of Hung Hsiu-ch'uan resisted the government proscription and took up arms. They were at once victorious over the provincial troops, capturing the small city of Yung An in Kuangsi province, which had now become the centre of their movement. Here, in 1851, Hung Hsiu-ch'uan proclaimed the T'ai P'ing T'ien Kuo, or Great Peaceful Heavenly Dynasty, and himself took the title T'ien Wang, or Heavenly King. He deliberately avoided the title of Emperor, Huang Ti, because the word *ti*, usually translated as Emperor, formed part of the expression Shang Ti, Emperor on High, which the T'ai P'ings in common with all Chinese Christians have used to translate the term God. It is noteworthy that in this point Hung was returning to a very ancient Chinese usage, for the term *ti* had been an appellation of divinity until Ch'in Shih Huang Ti for the first time used this divine title to express his own supreme royalty (Chapter VI).

*Hung Hsiu-ch'uan was himself a Hakka. The fact may well have been one cause of the eventual failure of his movement. In Kuangtung considerable hostility exists between the two sections of the population, and political movements associated with one or other rarely receive the support of the rival group. The T'ai P'ing movement was not supported by the rest of the population, nor by the great secret societies of Canton.

Following the capture of Yung An the T'ai P'ing army, swollen by recruits, marched northward across Hunan to the Yangtze, capturing every city in its path except Chang Sha, which successfully withstood them. Reaching the river at Yo Chou, which he captured, Hung Hsiu-ch'uan marched east, and following the course of the Yangtze captured Nanking, the southern capital of the empire, on 8th March, 1853, after taking all the cities along the Yangtze valley which he passed. Against this formidable rebellion the provincial troops of the Manchu government proved worthless. If Hung Hsiu-ch'uan had continued his march northward after the fall of Nanking it is almost certain that he would have driven the Manchus out of China in less than a year. Unfortunately for China he did not follow this plan. Settling down in Nanking, which he renamed T'ien Ching, the Heavenly Capital, he set about organising his theocracy, merely despatching small armies to spread the faith and expel the Manchus. One of these forces, only 7,000 strong, marched across North China from Nanking to the border of Shensi, and then eastward to Ching Hai 20 miles south of Tientsin. There, lacking reinforcements the commander, Li Hsin-chêng, styled the Chung Wang (Prince Faithful), the ablest and most forceful personality in the T'ai P'ing ranks, halted, and was later compelled to fall back to the Yangtze valley. This force, if properly supported, would have had no difficulty in capturing Peking itself, where panic had paralysed the Manchu Court.

Hung Hsiu-ch'uan had expected a general rising in the north, or at best a great increase in his following, but he was disappointed. The northern expedition received no recruits on its march. The reasons for this apathy were ignored by the T'ai P'ing King. His army was composed of southerners, very largely Kuangsi Hakkas, whose dialect was unknown to the northerners. The T'ai P'ing army, small and almost foreign, did not arouse confidence in the northern Chinese, who were in any case closer to the seat of government, and more in awe of its power. A great invasion would have shown promise of driving the Manchus out of China, but a raid by seven thousand Kuangsi Hakkas seemed a desperate gamble to the anti-Manchu elements in North China. Secondly, the T'ai P'ing religion, Christianity in fact, was strange and not very welcome to the mass of the nation. The destruction of Buddhist and Taoist temples, which the T'ai P'ings made their first duty on taking a town or village, roused hostility. The substitution of unknown Christian gospels for the time-honoured Confucian classics at once alienated many of the educated class. The north was not at first hostile, but it was neutral, almost indifferent, exactly as, sixty years later, the northern provinces failed to respond to the republican revolution which began in the Yangtze valley.

In a short chapter it is impossible to enter into a detailed account of the T'ai P'ing war in the years that followed the failure of the Chung Wang's expedition to the north. The Manchus, rallying in the north, made many unsuccessful attempts to drive the T'ai P'ings out of the Yangtze valley, the area which they had most thoroughly conquered, but until the foreign Powers came to the assistance of the Manchus these campaigns were fruitless. Indeed during these years the T'ai P'ing armies extended their authority over the whole of the Lower Yangtze provinces, and also penetrated into Szechuan, Hupei, Hunan and Honan. The T'ai P'ing dynasty had every prospect of ultimate victory, and seemed firmly established in the south until foreign intervention on their coasts opened the way for a Manchu re-conquest.

The alliance between the British and French Governments and the Manchus against the T'ai P'ing rebellion is one of the most remarkable, and certainly the most discreditable, episode in the history of Sino-European relations. Every consideration of sentiment and even of self-interest, if a long view were taken, pointed to an opposite policy. The T'ai P'ings were not only Christians, if unorthodox ones, but were most friendly to foreigners and very anxious to obtain their friendship in return. The evidence of every foreigner who visited Nanking or other T'ai P'ing possessions, confirms the fact that the T'ai P'ings regarded foreigners as co-religionists, and also as allies, for the foreign Powers had made war on the Manchus in 1841, and did so again in 1859-60 —during the T'ai P'ing rebellion itself. Not only were the T'ai P'ing leaders anxious to spread Christianity, and to assist the missionaries in this task, but they proposed to open the whole

Chinese Empire to the trade of foreigners, who might travel and reside where they pleased. Under the treaty wrung by force from the Manchu Government, foreign trade was restricted to a few ports, and the residence of foreigners confined to these places, while rights of travel and missionary work were constantly hampered by every sort of official interference.

Whatever may be thought of the T'ai Ping form of Christianity, and the destruction of temples and persecution of Buddhists which accompanied their progress, the evidence of those foreign observers who lived among or visited the T'ai P'ings shows that the movement had effected a great revival of the national character and self-respect. "The T'ai P'ings are practically a different race to the imperialist Chinese" is an expression constantly used, not only by missionaries sympathetic to their cause but by naval officers and merchants. It was remarked that the T'ai P'ing soldiers neither pillaged nor pilfered. The devastation in the war area was due to the atrocious reprisals inflicted by the imperial troops on rebel districts. The social reforms which the T'ai P'ings inaugurated are remarkable. Foot binding and opium were forbidden, the position of women was greatly improved, and some were even employed in an official capacity. Taxation in the T'ai P'ing kingdom was very much lighter than in the Manchu Empire, and more equitably adjusted.

During the early years of the T'ai P'ing movement the opinion of foreigners in China was entirely favourable to the rebels. The Anglican Bishop of Victoria (Hong Kong) frequently asserted his entire conviction that the T'ai P'ing movement was a Christian crusade, if perhaps unorthodox and ill-instructed in certain doctrines. This attitude altered in 1860 when the British and French Governments concluded a treaty with the Manchu Emperor which they deemed highly advantageous to themselves.

Although certain missionaries and a large number of lay foreigners in China deplored the policy of their government, their opinions were not heeded, and are now only recorded in long forgotten books and newspaper articles. It became customary to misrepresent the T'ai P'ing creed as a gross superstition composed of blasphemous distortions of Christian doctrine. In this way the embarrassing fact that armed forces of the British

Crown were engaged in suppressing a national and Christian rising for the benefit of the admittedly pagan, corrupt and untrustworthy Manchus could be condoned by missionaries and statesmen. China was very far away in the 'sixties, and such propaganda had an easy victory.

In essentials the T'ai P'ing creed was Protestant Christianity. The T'ai P'ings possessed the complete Bible, as translated into Chinese by Dr. Gutzlaff, an early Protestant missionary. This Bible they printed extensively in Nanking, and distributed free to their supporters and converts. In matters of dogma, though not quite orthodox in some particulars, they held the main tenets of Christian theology. They acknowledged only one deity, Shang Ti, God Almighty. Jesus occupied in T'ai P'ing theology a position almost identical with that upheld by European Protestants, but the doctrine of the Trinity was not clearly understood by the T'ai P'ings owing to the imperfections of their translations. The Holy Spirit was acknowledged, but it was believed by them that at certain times the Holy Spirit had descended and possessed one of their leaders, the Tung Wang, Yang Sui-ch'uan.

The Ten Commandments were the foundation of their creed and were the first thing every convert, and every child, was taught. The T'ai P'ings had also acquired that distinctive characteristic of Christianity, and other Judaic religions, intolerance. They admitted no other deity but the Christian God. Buddhism and Taoism were accursed superstitions to be rooted up, their temples destroyed, and their monks secularised. Had the T'ai P'ing movement triumphed, whatever else it might have accomplished for China, it is certain that it would have destroyed these ancient faiths as completely as Islam destroyed the Buddhism of north-western India, and of the East Indies. This would have been something of a calamity for the arts and architecture of the past, but hardly one which would have troubled the consciences of the foreign missionaries in China at that time. The destruction in 1860 of the Summer Palace (Yüan Ming Yüan), near Peking, with its priceless art treasures, was considered to be a reasonable and moderate reprisal for the ill-treatment of British envoys by the Manchu Court. Chinese art and culture was a sealed book to the European nations.

The real ground for missionary opposition to the T'ai P'ing movement was the position and authority of the leader, the Heavenly King, Hung Hsiu-ch'uan himself. The T'ai P'ing Christian movement was the outcome of this man's inspiration and leadership. It was only indirectly the product of missionary endeavour. Hung himself had never received instruction or baptism at the hands of a missionary. His theology was defective in some points, from the Protestant point of view, but to his followers he was not merely a King, but much more a prophet, a man directly inspired by God Himself, who had manifested the truth to Hung Hsiu-ch'uan in a vision. This doctrine was the core and heart of the T'ai P'ing movement. They regarded Hung Hsiu-ch'uan, not indeed as divine, but as inspired. Where his doctrine differed from that of the missionaries, the prophet, directly in touch with the Deity by revelation, was obviously right. Hung himself was unquestionably a sincere religious devotee who fully believed in his mission. He had been astonishingly successful, and without receiving the slightest assistance from missionaries. To pretend that this prophet and King should seek instruction from foreign missionaries seemed to the T'ai P'ings unreasonable presumption.

Much play was made by anti-T'ai P'ing writers with the title, "Younger Brother of Jesus," which Hung Hsiu-ch'uan assumed. It was invariably represented by these critics as a claim to divinity. It is possible that some of the missionaries who found this title so offensive were genuinely ignorant of the sense in which the Chinese words *hsiung ti*, "younger brother," were used by the T'ai P'ings. Others certainly deliberately distorted the meaning for propaganda purposes. The T'ai P'ings used this term for a co-religionist. Foreign Christians were called *wai hsiung ti*, " foreign brothers"— a fraternal greeting which should not have seemed strange to Protestant evangelists who were then coining the phrase, "black brothers" for Christian negroes. Hung Hsiu-ch'uan's title, "Younger Brother of Jesus," to his followers meant no more than the Manchu Emperor's title, "Son of Heaven," meant to other Chinese. In neither case was it understood as a literal assertion of divine relationship. T'ai P'ing leaders in conversation explicitly denied that the T'ien Wang was divine. "A man like other men, but a much greater one" was the phrase used. The fact that this title was merely an example of Oriental grandiloquence without literal religious meaning is proved by the account of a visit to Nanking by an anonymous foreigner, who published his impressions in a Shanghai newspaper over the signature XYZ.:

"Whatever Hung Hsiu-ch'uan may mean by calling himself the Brother of Jesus, it is but justice to say that no evidence was found of its being insisted on as an essential article of faith among the mass of his followers. Several officers who subsequently visited the steamer, when asked what was meant by it professed themselves unable to give any information upon the subject. They were so evidently puzzled that it was plain that their attention had never been called to the matter before."*

In this connection it may be observed that in the picture of the Heavenly King circulated among his followers he is described only as Tien Tê—his reign title, "Celestial Virtue"—not as "Brother of Jesus."† He is shown wearing the five-clawed imperial dragon robe (Fig. 64).

The character of the T'ai P'ing creed, and the points in which it accorded with orthodox Christianity, as well as the claims made on behalf of the Heavenly King, is clearly revealed in a long composition which was called the "Trimetrical Classic," as it was written in sentences of three characters each. This was the creed which the T'ai P'ings taught to their converts and children, and it was arranged in this way to make memorising easy. The document is too long to quote in full, but some extracts will suffice to indicate its character. It begins with an account of the Old Testament creation story:

"The Great God
Made Heaven and Earth
Both land and sea
And all things therein
In six days.
He made the whole."

*Lindley. *Ti-Ping Tien Kwoh, the History of the Ti-Ping Revolution.* London. 1866. Vol. I. p. 216.

†The text figure is taken from Gallery & Yvan. *Insurrection in China.* 1853.

德天

FIG. 64. *Hung Hsiu-ch'uan, the T'ai P'ing Heavenly King.*

The captivity of the Jews in Egypt and their deliverance is then described, with an account of the plagues of Egypt, and the delivery of the Ten Commandments to Moses at Mt. Sinai. Owing to the failure of later generations to keep this law:

> "The Great God
> Out of pity to mankind
> Sent His firstborn son
> To come down into the world
> His name is Jesus
> The lord and saviour of men
> Who redeems them from sin
> By the endurance of extreme misery.
> Upon the Cross
> They nailed His body
> Where He shed His precious blood
> To save all mankind."

An account of the Resurrection follows, and then the history of China is traced down to the revelation received by Hung Hsiuch'uan himself. In this review the sage kings praised by the Confucians are described as "honouring God," and the decline of true religion is attributed to Ch'in Shih Huang Ti, the Emperor Wu of the Han dynasty, the Emperor Ming of the same dynasty, who introduced Buddhism, and finally, the Sung Emperor Hui Tsung, who patronised Taoism. Although this view betrays a Confucian outlook on Chinese history, it is not inconsistent with the Christian approach to the same facts. The Confucian Heaven, or Shang Ti, could easily be identified with God, but the Buddhist and Taoist deities were manifestly opposed to Christian theology. It must be remembered that Hung Hsiu-ch'uan had studied the classics as every educated Chinese was bound to do at that time. His revelation is thus described:

> "In the Ting Yu year (1837)
> He was received up into Heaven
> Where the affairs of Heaven
> Were clearly pointed out to him
> The Great God
> Personally instructed him
> Gave him codes and documents
> And communicated to him the true doctrine."

Further revelations are recorded and the creed ends with a series of injunctions to observe the Ten Commandments and worship the true God.

This document and other T'ai P'ing literature was received by Sir George Bonham when he visited Nanking in 1853, and translated by Dr. Medhurst.*

To the missionaries, more concerned with sectarian rectitude than with the broad issue of paganism versus Christianity in some form, this claim was absolutely inadmissible. Christian theology was fixed and determined. There was no room for a new prophet, especially when the prophet turned out

*The T'ai P'ing creed is translated in full in *The Insurrection in China* by Callery and Yvan. London. 1853. Supplementary Chapter by J. Oxenford.

to be an unbaptised Chinese. If the Heavenly King had renounced his claim to revelation and inspiration and humbly
sought baptism and instruction from some English missionary, the western Christian world would have approved, but
the T'ai P'ing movement would have been robbed of its
motive and meaning. It might have been supposed that so vast
an upheaval, which promised, if successful, to result in the complete conversion of the whole Chinese people to T'ai P'ing
Christianity, entitled the leader to be considered a prophet,
indeed, to be the most outstanding Christian prophet known to
history. The English missionaries, however, would have none of
him. Christianity, if it came to China, must come through their
direct teaching. Direct inspiration to a Chinese was unthinkable,
God only acted in Asia through the medium of Europeans.

The opposition of the British and French Governments was not
inspired by disapproval of the claims made on behalf of the T'ai
P'ing Heavenly King, but on grounds of expediency and trade.
In 1859-60 these Powers had made war upon the Manchu
Government, moved thereto by the continued obstruction to
trade and interference with European merchants, an inevitable
consequence of the rooted fear and dislike of foreigners which
inspired the rulers of the empire. The war ended in a complete
victory for the western Powers. Peking was taken, the Emperor
fled to Jehol, and the treaty which terminated hostilities accorded
the invaders all their demands. Not only were more ports, including those of the Yangtze, opened to trade, and the navigation of the
great inland waterway granted to foreigners, but an indemnity
was imposed by which the Manchu Government was made to pay
the cost of its own defeat. This indemnity was secured upon the
customs revenues, the control of which was vested in foreign
officers, while the rate at which duties were to be levied was also
subject to a limitation determined by the foreign Powers in the
interest of their traders. The Manchu Empire had sunk to a
position in which its continued existence was dependent on the
goodwill of the western maritime nations.

Having obtained by this treaty all the advantages which could
be had without actually annexing the provinces of the empire,
the foreign Powers believed that they had assured the future of

their trade with China and established a position in which any further extension of control which might become necessary could be effected without difficulty. They therefore treated the offers of the T'ai P'ing ruler with contempt. They did not wish to trade freely in any part of the empire if they could monopolise the ports and collect the customs dues. They opposed by force the T'ai P'ing advance on the port of Shanghai, for, unless the Manchu authority was nominally maintained there, the customs revenue could not be applied to the payment of the indemnity. They sold arms, ships, and munitions to the Manchus, but refused like facilities to the T'ai P'ings. Finally, from the port of Shanghai which they had preserved for the Manchus, they launched an army to harry the T'ai P'ing flank, and lent the Manchu government officers—General Gordon among them—to organise the imperial troops and command them in battle.

With this assistance the Manchus, after several years of devastating warfare, finally recaptured Nanking and destroyed the T'ai P'ing movement. With it perished for half a century all hope of reform or modernisation in China. The Manchus, as corrupt and more degenerate than before, were re-established; and, although they owed their preservation to foreign intervention, remained as distrustful, hostile and reactionary in their outlook upon the western world as they had been in the 18th century. The T'ai P'ing faith, Chinese Christianity, perished with its founder and prophet when Nanking fell. It left no trace, and has never been revived. When the Chinese, some fifty years later, borrowed revolutionary ideas from the west it was not the religious creed but the political faith of Europe which they sought. The influence of western ideas is strong in the republic, but the influence of Christianity is negligible. The missionaries, having rejected the millions of Hung Hsiu-ch'uan's followers, have had to be content with the few thousands of their own converts, and are unlikely to find a second opportunity. The Chinese masses, to-day, if they accept a western ideology, are more inclined to turn to the doctrines of Marx and Lenin than to those of Luther.

The failure of the T'ai P'ing movement was a turning point in the cultural history of China. The success of a great national and religious revolution would have replaced the effete Manchus by a new dynasty, and a new cultural outlook, ready to accept the ideas of the west as a corollary of the new creed. It is very probable that the substitution of T'ai P'ing Christianity for Buddhism and Taoism would have given an impulsion to art and literature which the old faiths were no longer capable of performing. Under a political system to which they were accustomed, and to which they were alone suited, the Chinese would have been prepared, in the later 19th century, for the great changes which modern industry has forced upon the world. As it was, they remained sunk under a decaying despotism, until, at its fall, they were involved simultaneously in a political, cultural and economic revolution complicated by foreign aggression. For this tragic outcome the cynical policy of western imperialism in 1860 was mainly responsible.

Chapter XXX

LATE ART

WITH one important exception later Chinese art is derivative and increasingly stereotyped. Technical skill remained at the same high level achieved in the T'ang and Sung periods, but inspiration and originality declined steadily. In bronze the best Ming workmanship is almost flawless, but it consists of the mechanical reproductions of ancient pieces decorated with the classical motifs, and there is a complete lack of invention. When ancient models were forsaken the productions of the late bronzesmiths are insipid and the decoration trivial. The jade and ivory carving of the Manchu period shows extreme manual skill and delicacy which maintained these ancient arts on a very high technical level down to modern times. Ivory has perhaps never been wrought into so many intricate forms as by the Cantonese craftsmen, who are able to carve out of one tusk as many as three spheres one within the other, all pierced with delicate filigree patterns.

The quality of this skill, particularly in the fine workmanship of gold and jewellery, has been strikingly revealed by the excavation in 1958 of the tomb of the Ming Emperor Wan Li, who reigned from A.D. 1573 to 1620. An immense treasure of jades, porcelain, silks and precious metals was found intact in his tomb ranged round the imperial coffin. No similar collection of Chinese goldsmiths' work and jewellery had been previously known, since tomb robbers hardly dared to sell such finds in their original form for fear of detection. Now pieces such as the gold filigree helmet worn by the Emperor, the jewelled head-dresses of his two empresses, and a wealth of golden ornaments, vessels and utensils reveal the supreme skill and taste of the late Ming artist in this field. Great quantities of the finest porcelain of the period, interred with the Emperor, serve to establish a perfect criterion for judging Ming Wares. The remains of magnificent silks, *k'o ssu*, and embroideries, partly preserved by folding, confirm the belief that Ming textiles were of unsurpassed quality. All these remarkable finds, filling a large hall, are now exhibited in the Palace Museum at Peking.

Yet in all these crafts, in spite of the fine workmanship of their products there is a certain self-consciousness, an absence of real purpose which reflects the character of the age in which they were made. These things, upon which so much skill and patience were expended, were only intended to please. They had no ritual significance, no living inspiration derived from some ardent belief or high ideal. They were made for the wealthy as ornaments, to be admired for their technical perfection or ingenious workmanship, not to be venerated as symbols of a cult or as the expression of the artist's perception of truth. Ancient conventions lay heavily upon all the arts, as upon the mind of the educated class that patronised them.

This archaistic atmosphere was in itself a handicap to the creative spirit. Just as the Confucian was taught to look back to a remote classical age for his criteria of literary style, so the artist took his standards from the same distant past. The jade carver or bronzesmith was certain to please if he made an exact reproduction of an ancient piece, but if he struck out a new design his efforts would be ranked far below the copy of a classical model. This contempt for all that was not old created a sense of inferiority in the artist who tried new forms. It was accepted as a matter of course that any ancient work was necessarily superior to anything which could be produced in modern times, and the artists, succumbing to this psychological pressure, either copied the past or produced self-consciously trivial work which made no claim to challenge comparison with antiquity.

There was one art which escaped this paralysis, precisely because it had not existed in ancient times, and was therefore unfettered by an archaistic tradition. Porcelain, for which China is most famous, was really the last of the arts to flourish in the Far East, attaining its most perfect expression in the Manchu period, when all the others were in decline. For this reason porcelain was for long the only Chinese achievement about which anything was known in the western world, where it had become so identified with its land of origin that "China" came to mean both the country and the ware. Nevertheless the early porcelain of the Sung period, which was the most valued by the Chinese themselves, was hardly known to western connoisseurs until the late

19th century, and not seen in European collections until after the fall of the Manchu dynasty.

The early fame of Chinese porcelains was, in fact, built upon wares which were admittedly inferior, the export porcelain of the late Ming and early Manchu reigns, made for the foreign market, which lacked the finish of the products of the imperial factory. As intercourse between China and the west grew closer opportunities for acquiring the finest Ming and Manchu porcelain became more frequent and magnificent collections were assembled in the chief cities of Europe and America. The rich choice of examples to be seen in the west has formed a large and appreciative public who remain almost unaware of the character of the older arts of China; porcelain alone has become an integral part of the western cultural inheritance, and thus relatively early has been made the subject of a vast and detailed study.

The great collections in museums and private hands are as representative of all types of Chinese porcelain as anything still to be seen in China itself, and since the fall of the empire and the dispersion of part of the imperial treasures the rare wares of the Sung period, so highly prized in China, have enriched the collections of European connoisseurs. It would be redundant to attempt in a few pages to describe the porcelain to which experts have devoted so many beautifully illustrated volumes, but it may not be out of place to give a short account of the rise of the ceramic art and its relation to the cultural background of later Chinese history.

True porcelain was certainly made in the T'ang period; there are many specimens in collections which in paste and glaze are identical with fragments found at Samarra in Mesopotamia. The Chinese porcelain found at this site can only be T'ang, since the city was abandoned in the 9th century A.D. and never re-occupied.

In the Sung dynasty fine wares were produced for the first time, under the patronage of the Court, and in particular the artist Emperor Hui Tsung. At that time the industry was largely concentrated in the northern provinces, at sites in Honan and Hopei, which in later times have not produced porcelain of good quality. Ting Chou and Tz'ŭ Chou in Hopei, Ju Chou and Chün

Chou in Honan, were the first famous potteries. As regards the porcelain made at Ju Chou, it is only within the last few years that authentic pieces have been known to Europeans. One of the finest specimens in the David collection is a shallow saucer, thinly potted, with three spur marks on the base:

"The glaze is pale lavender netted over with a fine crackle stained reddish brown."*

One of the finest of the Sung monochrome wares was the porcelain made for the imperial Court, known as *kuan*, "official." The kilns were established by Hui Tsung at some time between the years A. D. 1107 and A.D. 1117 in the precincts of the imperial palace at K'ai Fêng Fu. This porcelain varied in colour, often of a pale bluish green, and it was undecorated. The great value which the Chinese at a very early date attached to *kuan* ware was not solely due to its beauty and noble simplicity, but also on account of its rarity. In A.D. 1125 K'ai Fêng Fu was captured by the Nu Chen invaders and the short lived *kuan* kilns were abandoned. Although the Southern Sung set up a new factory in their capital at Hang Chou, which endeavoured to perpetuate the K'ai Fêng *kuan*, the clay was naturally drawn from a different source and consequently the ware was not of the same quality. Nevertheless, it is very probable that the great majority of the existing *kuan* ware does in fact belong to the southern pottery, as it had a much longer life. Although the materials used at the two kilns cannot have been identical, the process and even the potters themselves were the same, for, like many of the skilled artisans of K'ai Fêng Fu and other northern cities, the imperial potters followed the Court to the south.

The rise of other potteries in the southern provinces is probably also due to the large scale migration of the art-loving inhabitants of the north. In Chekiang the kilns at Lung Ch'uan near Ch'u Chou became a great centre of the industry. In this district the *kô* ware, equally famous with the *kuan*, was made. This porcelain takes its name from the elder of two brothers Chang (*kô* = elder brother), who are reputed to have lived in the Southern Sung period, and who were masters of the ceramic art

*R. L. Hobson, *A Catalogue of Chinese Pottery and Porcelain in the Collection of Sir Percival David*, 1934, p. 4.

in Lung Ch'uan. The elder of the two is credited with the invention of the crackle in the glaze, which distinguishes *kô* ware. The story of the Chang brothers, which is lacking in precision, may well be a legend, but there were certainly two kinds of porcelain made at Lung Ch'uan, of which the *kô* was the finest and has always been the most valuable.

Lung Ch'uan also made a magnificent celadon ware, of which the coarser makes were largely exported. Specimens have been found in many parts of Asia, and Egypt, some even in Zanzibar. Some pieces later found their way to Europe, among them the Wareham bowl, which was bequeathed to New College by Archbishop Wareham in 1530.* The Lung Ch'uan kilns continued into the early years of the Ming dynasty, when the pottery seems to have been abandoned, possibly owing to the competition of the great ceramic centre in Kiangsi, Ching Tê Chen.

Ting Chou, in Hopei, was the home of the famous white Sung porcelain, and there is some literary evidence to suggest that this ware had been made at Ting Chou in the T'ang dynasty. The pottery received imperial patronage under the Sung, which is the period to which the expression "Ting ware" is always taken to refer. This pure white porcelain of a slightly ivory tinge was sometimes left undecorated, but more commonly bore incised patterns, especially the finest pieces, while the inferior quality was moulded or stamped. The best period of the Ting Chou pottery was that of Hui Tsung, and the making of fine wares came to an end with the catastrophe which ended that Emperor's artistic, but politically disastrous, reign. The skilled potters of Ting Chou fled to the south, where they settled at Ching Tê Chên, and carried on the Ting Chou tradition in their new home. "Southern Ting," as this porcelain is called, was one of the regular wares of the Ching Tê Chên factories in subsequent periods, but it is not ranked on the same footing as the genuine Ting of the old city in the north. There the industry still survives, but its products are intended only for common use and are not classed among the fine porcelains.

Tz'ŭ Chou, a city now in Hopei, but formerly included in

*R. L. Hobson. *Chinese Pottery and Porcelain*. 1915.

Honan province, is as the name, "Pottery Town," implies, an ancient centre of the industry. It first received this name in the Sui dynasty, a fact which suggests that it may have been one of the first places where porcelain was made. In the Sung dynasty Tz'ŭ Chou porcelain had a great reputation, and the surviving pieces of that date are now valuable. Two kinds of ware were made, white, which is very similar to the Ting, and a painted porcelain decorated with floral designs in brown and black. The same ware, with very much the same decorative motifs, is still made at Tz'ŭ Chou, though after the Sung period the quality is inferior. Although no longer prized by collectors the wares of Tz'ŭ Chou are widely used to-day for ordinary purposes in North China, as they have been for over thirteen centuries.

Chün Chou, the modern Yü Chou in Honan, made a lavender or purple porcelain in the Sung period, which, though not patronised by the Court at that time, is now treasured as one of the most beautiful of the early wares of China. The surviving pieces are mostly flower pots and their saucers, which were also used as bowls for bulbs. No doubt the fact that pieces intended for this purpose were more strongly made has saved them from the fate which has befallen the more delicate products of the Chün kilns. Like the celadons, the Chün ware was undecorated, trusting to the glorious colour of the glaze for adornment. Although the Chün potteries seem to have suffered a complete eclipse after the nomad invasions, Chün ware was very successfully imitated at Ching Tê Chên in later centuries, and less successfully at Yü Chou itself when the industry was revived there in the 19th century.

The products of another Sung pottery, at Chien Ning Fu in Fukien, have been more appreciated in Japan than in China itself. The porcelain called by the Chinese *chien* ware is the *temmoko* of the Japanese, and the speciality of this pottery was teacups of a rather rough appearance and a dark purple or blackish brown colour, which were used in tea tasting contests in the Sung period. The Japanese tea ceremony seems to have developed from this custom and the traditional *chien* ware cups were regarded as an essential feature of the ceremony. Genuine specimens of this Sung pottery command very high prices in

Japan, although the ware has been successfully copied by Japanese potters for many centuries.

The fall of the Southern Sung Empire and the short Mongol Yüan dynasty which succeeded it led to a temporary degeneration in the porcelain industry. The new masters of the empire were barbarians who had little appreciation for the fine arts and less sympathy with the cultivated taste of the Sung æsthetes. They treated the potteries as a source of revenue, and for this reason encouraged the production of the coarser export wares which could be shipped over sea or transported by caravan to distant countries. Nevertheless, it would seem that important developments took place in the technical side of the art. Blue and white, which has generally been regarded as a Ming innovation, was made in the Yüan period—if not in the Sung—as an inscribed piece proves. The inscription has the valuable evidence of a date, corresponding to A.D. 1352.

"Chêng Wên-chin, the adherent to the teachings of the Sages, of the ... circuit of Hsin Chou, joyfully offers an incense burner and a pair of flower vases as a prayer gage that his house and family may be prosperous and his children (male and female) at peace. Respectfully written on a lucky day in the fourth month of the eleventh year of Chih Chêng. Offered up to the Generalissimo Hu Ching-i of the Ancestral Hall of the Starry Desire."*

The establishment of the Ming dynasty and the pacification of the empire in A.D. 1360 speedily led to a great revival in the porcelain industry. No great development had been possible in an art so closely linked to industry when the empire was over-run by warring bands and the trade routes closed by predatory armies. Poetry, painting and calligraphy have sometimes flourished in disturbed times, since the individual artist could always find some quiet retreat, but porcelain needed peace and prosperity to develop. Raw materials had often to be brought from a distance, and the manufacture of fine wares was a costly

*R. L. Hobson. "The Charles Russell Collection." *Chinese Ceramics in Private Collections.* 1931. p. 161.

process, requiring the encouragement of an established government, and access to a wide market to enable it to flourish. Consequently the best periods of porcelain were always the peaceful ages, and when the empire was disturbed the industry swiftly declined. The end of the Ming dynasty, and the last years of Manchu rule are both negligible as regards porcelain, and the troubles of the republic have so far prevented any revival in modern times.

Under the Ming and Manchu Emperors the Court itself set the standard for the industry and directly controlled the most important pottery, which was at Ching Tê Chên in Kiangsi province. The northern kilns never recovered their importance after the fall of the Sung dynasty, and the potteries in Chekiang and Fukien which had been so famous in the Southern Sung sank to a second place. Ching Tê Chên became the sole centre of real importance, and it is there that all the imperial porcelain of the Ming and Manchu reigns was made. The imperial factory was under the direct supervision of an officer sent from the palace, at first one of the eunuchs in attendance on the Emperor, and in later years a sub-prefect of the regular civil service specially delegated for this purpose.

We have seen that Ching Tê Chên had already become a place of importance in the porcelain industry before the Ming dynasty. The town received its name from the reign title "Ching Tê" of the Sung Emperor Chên Tsung in the years A.D. 1004 to 1007, and at the same time orders were given that in future all pieces made for imperial use must be marked with the title and date of the reigning Emperor. The Ming Emperors took the same interest in porcelain as their Sung predecessors, and even sent down the designs for the decoration of the imperial wares.

This goes far to explain how the ceramic industry at Ching Tê Chên was a Court art, for the large palace orders and the constant demand for novelties, new designs, shapes, and glazes set a standard which commercial demand could never have sustained unaided by state support.

As opposed to the best Sung wares, mainly monochrome, the Ming period is distinguished by its use of colours and enamels, both put to pictorial use:

"The turquoise, green, violet blue, yellow and aubergine glazes of the *demi-grand feu* are used in the Ming 'three-colour' ware to fill in designs outlined in threads of clay, carved in open-work or incised with a point; and pictures were painted on the white glaze in a series of coloured enamels which are fired in the relatively low heat of the muffle kiln. These include red, green, turquoise, yellow, aubergine and brown, and they are sometimes supported by underglaze blue. Gilding was added either in leaf form or applied with a brush."*

Not that monochromes were neglected. Yung Lo eggshell porcelain has always been celebrated, as has the Hsüan Tê period, for a wonderful under glaze copper red. At the same time there was an enormous development of blue and white wares, which were exported in great quantities.

The reigns Hsüan Tê (1426-1435) and Ch'êng Hua (1465-1487) are two of the most famous periods in the ceramic industry, although comparatively little genuine porcelain of this period still survives. It was extensively copied even in the later years of the Ming dynasty itself, and the tiresome custom of marking these copies with the reign title and date of the original period has rendered any identification by this simple means entirely untrustworthy. This too faithful reproduction of the originals was carried on in later times, so that the marks on porcelain are in themselves of little assistance when determining the question of date. Most pieces marked with the early reign titles of the Ming dynasty were made in the K'ang Hsi reign of the Manchu dynasty, and by way of making the matter still more confusing most of the large quantities of porcelain marked with a K'ang Hsi date are in fact 19th century copies.

Ming writers on porcelain say that the blue and white of Hsüan Tê was superior to that of Ch'êng Hua, but the polychrome porcelain of the latter reign surpassed that of the Hsüan Tê period. One reason for this is said to be the fact that the supply of clay used in Hsüan Tê ware was running low by the middle of the century and gave out entirely in the Chia Ching period

*R. L. Hobson, *A Catalogue of Chinese Pottery and Porcelain in the Collection of Sir Percival David*, 1934, p. xxxiv.

(1522-1566). A satisfactory substitute was found in later times, but until this had been discovered it was not possible to get the excellent effects of Hsüan Tê blue and white. One of the chief ingredients, which was brought from Central Asia, was the cobalt ore called by the Chinese Muhammadan Blue, since it was imported from Moslem countries. Supplies from this source were intermittent and liable to be interrupted by wars, and the Chinese sources produced only an inferior quality which did not give the same results.

In the middle of the Ming period the contact with European nations along the coast opened up a new export market for porcelain which in later times attained enormous proportions. The Portuguese were of course the first to bring porcelain to Europe, where it was regarded as a great rarity. The owners of these early pieces mounted them on elaborate gold and silver stands, and their value in the 16th century was very high. Some of the earliest Ming porcelain to reach England was a gift made by the King of Castile to Sir Thomas Trenchard in 1506, consisting of blue and white bowls which bear the mark of Hung Chih (1488-1505), and were at that time, therefore, modern work.

While a few bowls were in Europe regarded as a suitable royal gift, in China the imperial annual demand ran into thousands of pieces. The list of porcelain supplied to the palace in 1546 has been preserved. There were:

> 300 fish bowls
> 1,000 covered jars
> 22,000 bowls
> 31,000 round dishes
> 18,400 cups.

Obviously the Court cannot have found a use for this quantity of porcelain, and much of it must have been presented to officials, temples, and courtiers. When it is remembered that this list only includes the ware made at the imperial factory for the palace, and not the productions of the private factories, it is obvious that the industry at Ching Tê Chên had greatly increased in importance.

In the later Ming dynasty the Wan Li period (1573-1619)

is a celebrated era in the history of porcelain. The long reign of this Emperor was indeed a time of increasing weakness and trouble for the empire as a whole, but neither Japanese raids on the coast nor rebellions in the western provinces seem to have affected the development of the ceramic art at Ching Tê Chên. The Ming Court attached so much importance to porcelain that whatever might happen elsewhere the imperial potteries were well protected. At this time a sub-prefect was permanently stationed at Ching Tê Chên to take charge of the factory, and the large demand from the palace was not reduced on account of the disturbances.

The work of the factory was minutely sub-divided between many hands, even the decoration itself was never the work of one artist. One worker specialised in some small part of the design, and passed the piece on to others, each adding a few details, until the calligraphists wrote the mark and date upon the completed vessel. It is a curious fact that these beautiful porcelains, the glory of the late art of China, were the products of a truly communal system, and not the work of any one inspired artist. The same system was continued under the Manchu dynasty, although at that time the director of the factory took an active part in the invention of new glazes and the improvement of technique.

Although Ching Tê Chên was the dominant centre of the ceramic industry under the last two dynasties, there were other potteries which made fine wares. Tê Hua in Fukien province made (and still makes) the ware known in Europe as *blanc de chine* specialising in statuettes and figurines, a favourite subject being Kuan Yin, the Bodhisattva often called the Buddhist Goddess of Mercy. In the Ming period Tê Hua potters occasionally made curious figures of Europeans, Dutch sailors or Portuguese merchants. They are represented in the characteristic pose of the Buddhist divinities, though one may suspect that this was a consequence of the potters' conservative habits of work rather than any belief in the divine character of the western visitors.

Yi Hsing near Ch'ang Chou in Kiangsu specialised in the red stoneware teapots which are still used in all parts of China. This factory was also at work in the Ming period, though it is not known exactly when it was started. As it was even then renowned for its teapots the European nations when they took up tea drinking copied the Yi Hsing ware. Late 17th century western porcelain is strongly influenced by Yi Hsing style, which in Europe became wrongly known as *buccaro*, a term properly belonging to a pottery made by the Indians of South America.

The troubles of the last Ming reigns and the uncertain position of the Manchu dynasty in its first years were reflected in the fortunes of Ching Tê Chên and its products. Between 1674 and 1678 the imperial factory was destroyed in the war against Wu San-kuei, although it was rebuilt two years later, when K'ang Hsi had pacified the empire. Authentic porcelains of the last Ming and first Manchu Emperor are therefore hardly to be found. Better days were soon to come, for the long reign of K'ang Hsi, 1662-1722, is the golden age of porcelain in China. The new Emperor took a keen personal interest in ceramics, as in all the civilisation of China, inspired by a desire to prove to his still restless Chinese subjects that the Manchu conquest did not mean a return to barbarism. The unfortunate effects of this excessive reverence for the past on other art and on literature have been noticed in another chapter; porcelain, which was still young, at first escaped the ill-effects of the conservatism of the Manchu Court.

In 1682 the Emperor appointed a resident director named Ts'ang Ying-hsüan, a man of refined taste and inventive genius who applied his skill to the improvement of technique and the discovery of new glazes. The polychrome ware in which green predominates, called *famille verte* in Europe, now began to rival the blue and white which had been one of the glories of the Ming reigns. The old types, however, were successfully continued, indeed, in technical skill, purity of form and tasteful decoration the K'ang Hsi wares were the equal of anything made in earlier times. It was only at the very end of the reign that the first signs of over-refinement and elaboration begin to appear.

In the K'ang Hsi period the European market for Chinese porcelain rapidly expanded, and to meet this demand the potters began to make ware in shapes suited to western requirements. Decoration was also modified to please the European taste. Designs, originally Chinese, which had been imitated by the

FIG. 65. *Porcelain plate decorated with a picture of a European ship, dated 1700.*

Dutch in Delft, were now re-adopted by the Chinese on export
porcelain. This cross exchange of patterns and motifs between
China and Europe is a feature of the Manchu trade which greatly
complicates the study of Chinese influence on early western
porcelain. During the 18th century some Chinese porcelain was
sent to Europe in the rough to be decorated there, some was
decorated in China to specified European designs, such as the
armorial china of noble families, and a third category was
decorated by the Chinese with patterns copied from European
pieces. In the last class there were vessels decorated with copies
of the Meissen flower patterns. As extreme examples of European
influence we may cite the Indiaman, and the pastoral scene
reproduced in Figs. 65 and 66.

FIG. 66. *Porcelain plate decorated with a European pastoral scene.*

For the Chinese market, and for the palace, the traditional native motifs were still preferred. Legends drawn from Buddhism and Taoism, historical events, and copies of famous pictures, were added to the patterns which the Ming had used, though all the old styles were perpetuated, and the old wares copied. A new monochrome, the beautiful powder-blue, was an invention of this reign and is ascribed to the fertile genius of the director, Ts'ang Ying-hsüan. One curious class of porcelain, which is to be attributed to the late Ming or very early K'ang Hsi period, is the so-called Jesuit china, vessels decorated with Christian motifs and made for the Catholic converts, who, as has been mentioned in Chapter XXIV, were numerous and influential at the end of the Ming dynasty. Some of these pieces have motifs taken from

Buddhism and Taoism as well as Christian scenes and symbols, either because the designers did not realise the incompatibility, or because, with Chinese tolerance, they ignored it.

The short reign of Yung Chêng (1723-1735) is the period in which the *famille rose*, in which a pale shade of rose pink is the dominant colour, begins to be preferred to the *famille verte*, which henceforward declines in importance. The new Emperor, like his father, was a keen amateur of porcelain, and in 1728 appointed an able and inventive director named T'ang Ying. T'ang Ying made a profound study of the technical side of ceramics and was able to find the secret of many new glazes, some of which had accidentally occurred on earlier pieces without the potters understanding how to produce them at will. Under T'ang Ying the imperial factory paid more attention to monochromes than had been the case since Sung times, and the fine new colours discovered by the director were much employed. The *famille rose* colours are known to the Chinese as *yang ts'ai*, or "foreign colours," and it is accepted that their use imitated foreign sources.

One of the specialities of the imperial factory under T'ang Ying, both in this reign and in that of Ch'ien Lung which followed, was the copying of ancient bronze vessels in porcelain. The antiquarian taste of the Court was responsible for this development, which in spite of the perfection of the workmanship and skill of the reproduction is something of a perversion of ceramic art, for the forms and decoration proper to bronze are not those most suited to porcelain. Under the long reign of Ch'ien Lung (1736-1795) the growing taste for such imitations was satisfied with masterly skill. There were porcelains perfectly imitating jades, ivories, glass and even wooden objects as well as bronze, but they are more apt to astonish by the perfection of the illusion than to provoke respect as works of art in themselves. The taste for the curious rather than for the beautiful is a sure sign of approaching decay. The brilliant colours and fine technique of Ch'ien Lung porcelain are qualities which compel admiration, but especially in the later years, when the influence of T'ang Ying was no longer present, the art, in common with all Chinese art of the late 18th century, lost strength and became increasingly self-conscious.

The verdict of an English scholar and connoisseur, R. L. Hobson,* has expressed the change in a lucid exposition:

"In the Ch'ien Lung period Chinese porcelain reaches the high-water mark of technical perfection. The mastery of the material is complete. But for all that the art is already in its decline. By the middle of the reign it is already overripe, and towards the end it shows sure signs of decay. At its best the decoration is more ingenious than original, and more pretty than artistic. At its worst it is cloying and tiresome. The ware itself is perfectly refined and pure, but colder than the K'ang Hsi porcelain. The *famille rose* painting is unequalled at its best for daintiness and finish, but the broken tints and miniature touches cannot compare in decorative value with the stronger and broader effects of the Ming and K'ang Hsi brushwork. The potting is almost perfect, but the forms are wanting in spontaneity; and the endless imitation of bronze shapes becomes wearisome, partly because the intricate forms of cast metal are not naturally suited to the ceramic material, and partly because the elaborate finish of the Ch'ien Lung wares makes the imitation of the antique unconvincing. In detail the wares are marvels of neatness and finish, but the general impression is of an artificial elegance from which the eye gladly turns to the vigorous beauty of the earlier and less sophisticated types."

These last words might well stand as the criticism for all the art of the Manchu period. In painting, also, there was artificial elegance, conscious archaism, and great technical skill with the brush. It is no longer the great art of the Sung masters, nor even of their imitators in the Yüan and early Ming dynasties, but it has its charm, and a certain æsthetic value. These qualities show to advantage in the decorative arts of lacquer work, of which the screen illustrated in Plate XIX, is a magnificent example. The composition is here perfectly adapted to the purpose of a screen, for each two panels contain in themselves a complete picture no matter which way the screen is folded.

In the first years of the Manchu dynasty, the reigns of Shun

*Chinese Pottery and Porcelain. R. L. Hobson. 1915. p. 247, vol. II.

Chih and K'ang Hsi, there was a celebrated school of painting in the south-eastern provinces, the region where the Southern Sung dynasty had reigned, and which had ever since been recognised as a centre of culture and art. Soochow and Hang Chou the two chief cities of the Yangtze delta* were famous not only for the beauty of the scenery, but also for the learning and civilisation of the inhabitants. Not for nothing the proverb runs:

"*Shang yu hsi T'ien
Hsia yu Su Hang.*"

"Heaven above, Soochow and Hang Chou on earth."

The most famous artists of the early Manchu period all came from the district of Soochow, and by an odd coincidence, all had the surname Wang. For this reason they are usually known as the "four Wangs." All four were born under the Ming dynasty, and the major part of the lives of the elder two were passed before the Manchu conquest. If these painters are classed as artists of the Manchu dynasty, it is in accordance with the custom which includes in the famous men of a dynasty all those who died under its sway, whether they were born long before it came to power or not. In reality all the four Wangs, who were landscape painters following the Sung style, had inherited and transmitted a cultural tradition which had never wholly disappeared in the civilised cities of the south-east. They belonged ·spiritually to the earlier dynasty, and were in no way indebted to the inspiration of the new régime.

It is therefore significant that these four artists, and their contemporary Yün Shou-p'ing (1633-1690), should be considered the greatest painters of the Manchu dynasty. It is an admission of the fact that art only flourished in the K'ang Hsi period, when the Ming traditions were still alive, and declined as the ultra conservative Manchu system became established. The "four Wangs" were, Wang Shih-min (1592-1680), Wang Chien (1598-1677), who was a grandson of Wang

*Before foreign trade brought about the rise of Shanghai, which is now not only far larger than the older cities of the province, but has become the largest city in the Far East.

Shih-chêng, Ming statesman and reputed author of the celebrated novel, the *Chin P'ing Mei* (see Chapter XXV)—Wang Hui (1632-1720) was a pupil of the second Wang, and was commissioned by K'ang Hsi to make the illustrations for the published description of the Emperor's southern tour, an event which marked the complete pacification of the provinces beyond the Yangtze. Wang Yüan-ch'i, the last of the four (1642-1715) was both an artist and a writer on art. He was one of the scholars ordered to prepare a history of painting for the Emperor K'ang Hsi.

All four were chiefly landscape painters, and much of their work was devoted to copying the famous Sung and Yüan pictures. They also painted original landscapes, in which they tried to perpetuate the Sung style. Yün Shou-p'ing, also a Soochow artist, was the son of a devoted Ming patriot who had followed the waning fortunes of his masters to Canton, and there became a Buddhist monk rather than submit to the Manchus and wear the queue, the style of coiffure used by the conquerors and imposed by them on their conquered Chinese subjects. The son of this hater of the Manchus became the recognised master of still life flower and bird studies under the new dynasty, and no subsequent artist of the Manchu period was considered his equal. The picture of pheasants and peonies (Plate XX) bears an early K'ang Hsi date, though the style of this picture is distinctly Ming. It is more mannered than the older school of painting, and the elaborate composition, tasteful as it is, has not the restrained simplicity of a Sung picture. A comparison between this fine example of the later painting and Hui Tsung's study of the pigeon (Plate XIV) eloquently reveals the changed quality of late art.

In the 18th century, distinguished for its taste for curosities, there was a style of painting which is attributed to a T'ang painter, but which does not seem to have met with serious consideration until the time of Ch'ien Lung. Discarding the brush, the artist used the long thumb nail as his instrument, and achieved broad impressionist effects quite unlike the delicate lines of brush painting. It may be that if artists had studied the possibilities of these new effects rather than the dexterity of thumb nail technique, Chinese art might have been revitalised by a new style. The atmosphere of that time, however, was too opposed to innovation for any such development to be possible. The thumb nail or finger painting, as it is sometimes called, remained a curiosity, and even in this limited range the acknowledged master was an artist named Kao Chi-p'ei who died as early as 1734.

The history of Chinese art after Ch'ien Lung is a record of decline. The porcelain of the early 19th century emperors, Chia Ching and Tao Kuang, is purely imitative. In the fifties the T'ai P'ing army destroyed Ching Tê Chên, and, although the industry was revived after the suppression of the rebellion, and recovered much of the technical skill of past days, its productions do not command respect as works of art. No movement of importance took place in painting during this century of weakness and decline. Art, like literature and the social system of the empire itself, was in need of a great revolutionary stimulus to shake off the burden of too powerful and conventionalised tradition. This stimulus, so far as politics and literature are concerned, was provided by the revolution of recent years, but art as yet has only made a tentative adjustment to the new influence.

This fallow period is to be expected under the first shock of a vast upheaval. The interests of a revolutionary age are concentrated upon practical issues, and the changes which are taking place. Literature, the medium of thought, is naturally quick to feel the mood of the time, and it is not surprising that in China to-day it is in this field that the renaissance movement has achieved its most striking effects. Art needs more time; when the character of the new age is definitely established and foreign influences have been harmonised with the national culture, art will revive, and the happy eclecticism of a new T'ang age may be once again the reward of contact with the west.

INDEX

MAP 19. China.